An Irish-Speaking Island

HISTORY *of* IRELAND
and the IRISH DIASPORA

James S. Donnelly, Jr.
Thomas Archdeacon
SERIES EDITORS

An Irish-Speaking Island

State, Religion, Community, and the Linguistic Landscape in Ireland, 1770–1870

Nicholas M. Wolf

THE UNIVERSITY OF WISCONSIN PRESS

Publication of this book has been made possible, in part, through support from the Humanities Initiative, New York University.

The University of Wisconsin Press
1930 Monroe Street, 3rd Floor
Madison, Wisconsin 53711-2059
uwpress.wisc.edu

3 Henrietta Street, Covent Garden
London WC2E 8LU, United Kingdom
eurospanbookstore.com

Copyright © 2014
The Board of Regents of the University of Wisconsin System
All rights reserved. Except in the case of brief quotations embedded in critical articles and reviews, no part of this publication may be reproduced, stored in a retrieval system, transmitted in any format or by any means—digital, electronic, mechanical, photocopying, recording, or otherwise—or conveyed via the Internet or a website without written permission of the University of Wisconsin Press. Rights inquiries should be directed to rights@uwpress.wisc.edu.

Printed in the United States of America

Library of Congress Cataloging-in-Publication Data

Wolf, Nicholas M., 1978–, author.
   An Irish-speaking island : state, religion, community, and the linguistic landscape in Ireland, 1770–1870 / Nicholas M. Wolf.
        pages   cm — (History of Ireland and the Irish diaspora)
  Includes bibliographical references and index.
   ISBN 978-0-299-30274-0 (pbk. : alk. paper) —
   ISBN 978-0-299-30273-3 (e-book)
    1. Irish language—History—18th century. 2. Irish language—History—19th century. 3. Irish language—Social aspects—Ireland. 4. Irish language—Political aspects—Ireland. I. Title. II. Series: History of Ireland and the Irish diaspora.
   PB1215.W65   2014
   491.6′209033—dc23
                                          2014007460

for
BEE

Contents

Acknowledgments ix
Notes on Names and Sources xiii

Introduction 3

PART I IDENTITIES

1 Language Bonds and the English-Speaking Other 23
2 Peasant Etymologies 63
3 Bilingualism and the Humor of Language Contact 83

PART II ENCOUNTERS

4 Education and Established Church 111
5 Courtroom and Polling Booth 149
6 Language and Catholic Devotional Reform 181
7 Priests, Pastoral Care, and Catholic Policy 223

Conclusion 268

Source Abbreviations 275
Notes 277
Bibliography 349
Index 419

Acknowledgments

This study was made possible by a National Endowment for the Humanities Summer Stipend, and through support for research in Irish publishing and linguistic history by a Newberry Library Short-Term Fellowship in Irish and Irish-American Studies and an O'Donnell Fellowship in Irish Studies at Newman College, University of Melbourne. Financial support for its publication was provided by Glucksman Ireland House, New York University, and by a grant-in-aid from the Humanities Initiative at NYU. Special thanks are due to the advisory board of Glucksman Ireland House and to its director, Joe Lee, for their generosity in providing this assistance, and to the Humanities Initiative, including faculty director Jane Tylus and director Gwynneth Malin, for their help in bringing this book to press. I have had the support of a number of archivists, librarians, and scholars who took the time to discuss my research and assist me in securing access to the records I needed. The staffs of the National Library, the National Archives, the Royal Irish Academy, Trinity College archives, University College Dublin archives, and the British Library and, here in the United States, the Library of Congress, the Newberry Library, and the interlibrary loan specialists at New York University worked tirelessly in responding to my inquires. Father Donat Lamothe at Assumption College, Damien Burke at the Jesuit Archives on Leeson Street, Alan Delozier of Seton Hall University Library, Ann Kenne of the archives and special collections at the University of St. Thomas in Saint Paul, MN, Denis Obermeyer of the Catholic University archives, Tom May of the Galway Diocesan Archives, and David Sheehy, formerly of the Dublin Diocesan Archives, all assisted greatly at various stages of the research and are owed many thanks for allowing me to consult the materials in their collections. I'll always be grateful for the kind hospitality shown during my visit to Cobh by the late Sister Cabrini Delahunty, archivist of the Cloyne Diocesan Archives. A special acknowledgment is due the staff of the Delargy Center at the National Folklore Archives, University College Dublin, Belfield, where the nature of the search required a huge number of requests across numerous volumes. At the archives of the National Folklore Collection, Críostóir Mac Cárthaigh, Jonny Dillon, and Emer Ní Cheallaigh devoted a considerable amount of time to helping me negotiate the catalog and assisting me with the project. Thanks are due to the National Folklore Collection for allowing me to quote from their collections.

Many, many individuals provided help and support during my time toiling at this project. My colleagues Ryan Smith, Antonio Espinoza, Brendan Kane, Sean Farrell, Michael de Nie, and Tim McMahon, having negotiated so successfully the many pitfalls of research and publishing, have served as excellent mentors. Pádraig Ó Macháin helped at key points during my most recent research trip to Dublin to help locate materials, as did William Murphy and David Dickson at the very beginning of this research many years ago. John Gibney has been a constant source of support and great discussant of all things historical, and Niall Ó Ciosáin deserves much credit for encouraging this work in every way. More recently, Brian Casey has been a huge help in procuring materials and Eugene Hynes in discussing Irish religion. Jim Rogers, as he has done with so many young scholars over the years, and my colleagues at Glucksman Ireland House, especially John Waters and Joe Lee, have opened many doors that have allowed this book to come to light.

Special mention should be made of the support and friendship of Nancy Stenson, Will Kenny, and the many folks in Minneapolis who gave me such a firm base in Irish: *an dream a thug Gaeilge dom*. Coilín Owens and Hilary Mhic Suibhne have also provided patient assistance in wading through Irish texts at various points. My time in Melbourne was a real turning point in focusing my thoughts about the research, and I am very grateful for the opportunity and hospitality shown by Elizabeth Malcolm, Dianne Hall, Kevin Molloy, and Angela Gehrig. Mary Doyle and Val Noone, who helped sort out so many conclusions while on a drive to Ballarat, are owed special thanks for extending so much good will and assistance that it will be impossible to repay. That the University of Wisconsin Press has been willing to take on the publication is much appreciated, and I thank Gwen Walker and the readers who provided feedback for their time. As for the genesis of this project, so much of its origins reside in the support and suggestions of Maria Luddy of the University of Warwick, who helped launch this work by advising me while on fellowship in Coventry back in 2005. My family—Marty, Cindy, Bonnie, Kayla, Paul, Debbie, and Stephen—have patiently awaited the finish.

An early version of chapter 3 and a portion of chapter 7 appeared in the *Journal of British Studies* 48, no. 1 (January 2009) and *New Hibernia Review* 12, no. 4 (Winter 2008), respectively. I am grateful for the permission to incorporate this material as part of this book.

Finally, two last acknowledgments are due. It is imperative to convey the importance of the training as a historian and teacher imparted to me by James Donnelly, Jr., at the University of Wisconsin–Madison. His mentorship, as my fellow Wisconsin graduates have noted many times before me, has made all the difference in being able to write, research, and contemplate history. Only my wife Elizabeth, however, has been there from the very beginning as an editor, critic, and supporter. The completion of this book is the result of her patience, understanding, and hard work. Thanks.

Notes on Names and Sources

Irish-speaking writers, scribes, and commentators of the period in question here often varied in the spelling of their names, presenting not only differences in Irish-language versions, but also signing their works using an anglicized version if their perceived audience was English speaking. This variety spilled over into the print world: anglicized spellings of names predominated, but Irish versions could also be found.

In the interest of preserving the identity of these individuals, whose first language was, in most cases, Irish, the Irish spellings of their names have been presented. The spelling of those names has been brought into line with conventions in Irish-language scholarship, whether in manuscript studies or, most especially, the versions provided in the *Beathaisnéis* series created by Máire Ní Mhurchú and Diarmuid Breathnach, and now widely available by way of Dublin City University and Cló Iar-Chonnacht's online edition of these biographies, *ainm.ie*. Thus, Seathrún Céitinn rather than Geoffrey Keating, and Aodh Mac Cruitín rather than Hugh MacCurtin. On the other hand, certain individuals who published widely under the English spellings of their name, such as John O'Donovan, Eugene O'Curry, and Edward O'Reilly, have been presented using English spelling. Major figures like Daniel O'Connell and various Catholic prelates who presented their names publicly using English spellings have been likewise introduced here under those versions.

In sources and footnotes, in the interest of enabling the locating of these sources, the author's name as given on the original document has been retained. If it was thought that this might lead to confusion, the alternate spelling used in the main body of the book has been offered in brackets next to the bibliographic name. The aim in all such cases was to present bibliographic entries in a way that minimized confusion and enabled sources to be identified properly.

An Irish-Speaking Island

Introduction

By the third decade of the nineteenth century, it is estimated that Ireland was home to between three and four million speakers of the Irish language, more than at any other time in the history of this language community. Despite declining as a proportion of the overall population of the island over the course of the last decades of the eighteenth century and first half of the nineteenth, falling to an estimated 25 or 30 percent of the overall Irish population in 1851, Irish speakers could nevertheless be found in every county of the island. The language was near-universal in its concentration in the western half of Ulster, in virtually all of Connacht, and in south and west Munster among the age cohorts born in the 1830s and 1840s and earlier. But Irish speaking in these earlier years was by no means confined to marginal uplands or western coastal regions; it is important to remember that the language was also widespread in comfortable farming regions of central and east Cork, the grazing and cattle lands of east Clare and southeast Galway, and in central lowlands and southern baronies of Kilkenny, where Irish speakers straddled the border parishes not only with heavily Irish-speaking Waterford but even portions of Wexford to the east. North Leinster and south-central Ulster, the border counties of Cavan and Monaghan, and, to an extent, Meath and Westmeath further south all had substantial pockets of Irish speakers, as did the countryside north of Dublin and the mountains of Wicklow. Northeast Ulster, particularly Down and Antrim, as well as south Armagh all had their Irish-speaking regions, and further west in mid-Tyrone at least one in five children still grew up speaking Irish in the prefamine years.[1]

Irish speaking in these years was not by any means a rural phenomenon confined to farmers and struggling agricultural laborers. All of Ireland's major cities had at least one neighborhood with significant pockets of Irish speakers throughout this period and, in fact, had gained new additions because of general migration from rural areas as well as intense waves during the Famine. In 1851, a year in which it is agreed that the overall census count of Irish speakers was underestimated, the returns for the cities of Cork, with over 10,000 speakers, Galway, with nearly 15,000, and Waterford and Limerick, each with over 4,000 speakers, all revealed significant urban Irish-speaking populations.[2] Irish could be heard on the streets of Dublin, certainly among the Liberties southwest of the city center and in pockets north of the Liffey, and in Belfast, where traces of Irish-speaking migrants from County Louth could be found in the Smithfield area of the city through the end of the nineteenth century.[3] Moreover, Irish speakers could be found among all social classes and religious persuasions, from bishops, MPs, judges, lawyers, and doctors to shopkeepers, printers, farmers, laborers, and the poorest beggars. There were Irish-speaking gentry: James McQuige (d. 1831), a Methodist preacher, recalled in 1818 being jostled on Grafton Street by a gentleman "of most noble appearance" who excused himself in Irish, and a Roman Catholic magistrate from Cork reported in 1843 that he regularly used Irish "in the habit of mixing and talking with the people."[4] Conversely, Protestant farmers and country shopkeepers spoke Irish as a means of conducting trade, while Protestant laborers spoke it habitually, according to the 1868 summary of an Anglican missionary who had done parochial work in Ulster.[5] These examples are just a few of many. In sum, the Irish-speaking community as it existed in the last decades of the eighteenth century and the first half of the nineteenth was sizeable, socially diverse, and geographically varied.

The existence of this speech community holds significance for historians and linguists on several levels. It matters to the history of the administration of the kingdoms united under British rule (and augmented by Ireland in 1800) and, more broadly, to the understanding of how a diverse global British empire operated amidst the jostling of speakers of hundreds of languages. Taking into account just Britain and Ireland, when the Irish-speaking community is considered alongside the estimated 4 or 4.5 million Welsh, Manx, and Scots Gaelic speakers of the early nineteenth century, a safe estimate would put the number of speakers of languages other than English at 20 percent of the combined population of England, Scotland, Wales, and Ireland as late as 1841.[6] Yet this linguistic diversity at such a late stage, if discussed at all, tends to be treated by historians as the last gasp of a passing phase of national difference soon to be effaced by integration (successful in the case of Britain, less so in the case of

Ireland). Imperial administration, in this telling, fills the vacuum left by the supposed retreat of these languages rather than having to contend with them head-on. Exacerbating this problem has been the lack of serious engagement with the sources of British and Irish history written in languages other than English, making the history of this region decidedly one-dimensional. As Vincent Morley has noted, echoing the observations of Nicholas Canny, the much-vaunted drive to incorporate Irish, Scottish, and Welsh history into the larger history of Britain has not brought a commitment to considering Irish-, Scots Gaelic-, or Welsh-language sources. Highly influential studies such as Linda Colley's *Britons* (1992, reprinted 2005) consequently portray the imagined concept of "Britain" in the eighteenth and nineteenth centuries as one that is exclusively (indeed, by definition) anglophone. The historical impact of non–English speakers becomes one of persistent existence prior to inevitable absence under a modern state portrayed as running comfortably on an all-English basis.[7] The availability of extended and detailed studies into, for example, the social history of the Welsh language—most available in English—has seemingly not mitigated this problem, while the more integrative studies of this linguistic story such as Victor Durkacz's *The Decline of the Celtic Languages* (1983) and Michael Hechter's *The Celtic Fringe in British National Development* (1975, reprinted 1999) engage with paradigms on nationalism, integration, and culture now more than thirty years old.[8]

By contrast, a number of recent studies touching on the linguistic politics of administration within the British empire have taken up the question of languages directly, anchored by several well-crafted histories focused on South Asia.[9] These studies can be seen as part of a wider movement among cultural historians on the one hand and historical linguists on the other to retrieve the social history of languages around the world. As long ago as 1987 historian Peter Burke called for such an endeavor in response to the disciplinary divide that he perceived between history and linguistics.[10] Rather than a Saussurian emphasis on the logic and organization of communication systems rooted in structuralism—that is, the so-called "linguistic turn" in history and the social sciences with its emphasis on political-social discourse and communication strategies—the history of language as envisioned by Burke sought the application of sociolinguistic methods along the lines laid out by William Labov, Dell Hymes, John Gumperz, Joshua Fishman, and Peter Trudgill among others.[11] Language as an object of social or cultural history had, of course, figured prominently in older historical research on the standardization of languages in Renaissance-era Italy and the politics of language in France between the seventeenth and nineteenth centuries. In the case of Italy, this entailed the investigation of the Italian *questione della lingua*—ongoing debates about the standardization of the language—and the expansion of the Florentine dialect during the literary fertility of the fourteenth century and later.[12] For France, the study of efforts by, first, the Bourbon monarchs and, then, the republican movements of the eighteenth and nineteenth century to popularize and impose northern dialects of French at the expense of the other dialects and languages of the region originated in the massive *Histoire de la langue Française* (13 volumes, 1905–53) assembled by Ferdinand Brunot. Later, *Peasants into Frenchmen* (1976), Eugen Weber's classic study of the Third Republic, again drew attention to the relationship between language standardization and republicanism, a topic that has continued to be fleshed out by more recent studies of the intellectual and administrative origins of language policy launched by the Revolution and continually developed thereafter.[13] In the last decade, historians have continued to expand this field into topics like the history of global empires, diaspora, and nationalism, represented by multiple studies developing the history of language ideologies, programs of standardization, language and identity, and language contact.[14]

At the same time, a growing body of work among sociolinguists and linguistic historians has attempted to branch out beyond modern (usually twentieth-century) case studies to consider phenomena like language contact, bilingualism, code mixing, koineization, and standardization in a variety of historical contexts.[15] Built on searches for underused historical corpora and sociolinguistic data, as well as heroic attempts to reconstruct past speech using archival documentation, these studies have also yielded important methodological tools for the wider scholarly community. It is clear, for example, that modern understandings of the emergence of "standard" languages, heavily informed by the concept of the nation, frequently underestimate the past prevalence of language variation and diversity—sometimes even the existence of whole language communities—long after standardization was supposed to have occurred. Languages spoken by subaltern, lower-class, or otherwise marginalized communities have been especially prone to invisibility because of the nature of the historical record. But historical linguists have also been keen to present the historicized evolution of the concept of language itself, a process that was both influenced (and influenced by) major ideological developments in concepts like gender and race. For example, the idea that language was a marker of identity—and eventually, by the modern period, a distinctly *national* identity—was a key element of Western thought stretching back centuries. In the nineteenth century, however, as scientific developments contributed to ideas of biological race, language was increasingly considered a literal and physical marker of nationality in a way that often ignored the tendency toward linguistic heterogeneity in real life. Hence, in the classic case, newly colonized African societies were catalogued by linguistic characteristics and assigned to "tribes" and "nations" accordingly, contributing in a very material way to imperial administrative decisions by Europeans.[16]

A study of Ireland's sizable Irish-speaking community in the eighteenth and nineteenth centuries thus adds to a number of historical case studies already completed or still under way. Most of all, though, an account of the features and fortunes of the Irish-speaking community in this period contributes to an understanding of the history of Ireland. Given the intense scrutiny of the language as part of debates over strengths and failures of current language planning policy,[17] deliberations over Irish national identity,[18] and the acute awareness of Ireland's multilingual past in addressing its literary history,[19] this statement may initially appear so obvious as to be banal. But for the period in question here, the century before the first organized stirrings of language revival in the 1870s, the summary repeated by many historians has been more indifferent than engaged: the Irish language reached its nadir as a medium of literature, public discourse, and everyday language and was spoken by less than 15 percent of the population by 1901; at this time a vigorous revival movement brought it from the brink of death. As such, the period has not attracted nearly the interest accorded to medieval or early modern Ireland, when Irish was in a robust state and formal literary activity flourished widely, nor the years from 1870 onward, when the language revival movement and national independence together made Irish an increasingly visible aspect of political events. Indeed, there is much to say for Niall Ó Ciosáin's recent appraisal in a survey of the field that the history of the Irish language in the nineteenth century has only in the most recent years received any serious elucidation after more than forty years of Irish academic work.[20]

In reviewing this historiography, it quickly becomes evident that the problem has not simply been a lack of willingness to press deeply into the archives to find hidden traces of the language's story, or even to challenge certain presumptions about the chronology of Irish language history. Rather, deeper conceptual problems have arisen from the tendency by scholars to take on only a limited set of historical questions related to the history of Irish and to rely on an uncritical approach to the relationship between language and culture. One explanation for this lies in the long-term historiographical development of writings on the Irish language. A case can be made that this tradition dates as far back as the sixteenth century, when heightened awareness of the status of the language (and in particular, a perception that it was declining irreversibly) among Irish poets and prose writers made for a subject of repeated discussion.[21] As the priest and scholar Theobald Stapleton (ca. 1589–1647) wrote in justifying his 1639 Irish-language catechism, Irish was "chomh fueletheach, chomh mucht a sion, nach mór na deacha si as coimhne na nduinne" (so abandoned, so stifled as it is, that it has nearly been forgotten by the people)—a condition he blamed on the obscure literary products of the country's poets and the abandonment of the language by its nobility.[22] To consciously discuss the Irish language, as in the writings of the many subsequent Irish poets and prose writers whose manuscripts circulated throughout the eighteenth and nineteenth centuries, was thus to highlight first and foremost its diminished clout in the world of letters thanks to English colonization, the decline of native patronage for Irish, and the supposed growing disinterest of the Irish themselves in their own language. Séamus Ó Scoireadh (d. 1828), a scribe, translator, and grammarian, voiced this inherited historiographical stance clearly in his 1826 lecture before the Royal Irish Academy in which he advocated for preservation of Irish-language literature because "it is slighted at home, by our gentry abandoned, and by our literati, ignorant of its beauties, it has generally been but unmeritedly neglected."[23] Thus, long before the advent of modern scholarship, the history of Irish was linked first and foremost to an account of its decline and prospects of death.

The rise of modern, full-fledged political nationalism in the eighteenth and nineteenth centuries perpetuated this tendency to view the history of Irish largely through questions about its health. As the classic narrative account of this period will note, nationalists of a variety of goals increasingly sought to feature Irish and its restoration as a part of its agenda for independence. The interest in Irish taken up by certain members of the United Irishmen, notably Thomas Russell (1767–1803), and by other Belfast intellectuals who were close acquaintances of members of this political movement, such as Dr. James MacDonnell (1763–1845), demonstrated a definite dedication to the language if not a wholesale consideration of a revival project.[24] Later, in the 1840s, Thomas Davis (1814–45) and the Young Ireland movement began pressing for the restoration of Irish as a national language as part of any renewal of national culture under the banner of independence.[25] And in the late nineteenth century, the initial impetus for language revival provided by the Society for the Preservation of the Irish Language (founded 1876) and the Gaelic Union (founded 1880) merged with a larger cultural nationalism to produce the Gaelic League (founded 1893), the most visible and long-lasting advocate of the Irish language born in the nineteenth century.[26] It should be emphasized that this well-worn account has been rightfully challenged recently on the grounds that it ignores the contributions of Irish-language intellectuals of the early nineteenth century to concepts of nationality[27] and because it disregards discontinuities in the national ideology of earlier groups with those of the end of the nineteenth century.[28] Moreover, as Philip O'Leary and Brian Ó Conchubhair have ably shown in their path-breaking studies on the relationship between the Gaelic League intellectuals and modernism, no one voice spoke for all turn-of-the-century cultural nationalists.[29] But for the purposes of discussion here, what is important is the long-term shadow cast on academic writing of the early and mid-twentieth century by the received narrative about the history of Irish favored by revivalists that saw its endangerment and potential extinction as its primary feature.

That influence has proven very durable. It was further developed in the many public forums (generally, newspaper and pamphlet publications) sponsored by the Gaelic League that provided a place for a new historiography of the Irish language to emerge—one in which certain narratives about the language gained more traction than others. For instance, surrounded by a shrinking population of Irish speakers (most of whom, if native speakers, resided by this time in intensely rural and often poor areas), many nationalists had difficulty recognizing the heterogeneity of Irish-speaking communities of a century earlier. Others, like the scholar Énrí Ó Muirgheasa (1874–1945), emphasized the inherent Catholicism of Irish-speaking communities,[30] an interpretation encouraged in part by anger over the use of Irish by Protestant missionary groups in the early nineteenth century but that ignored the history of Irish-speaking Protestants in Ireland. Most of all, facing apathy in the 1890s and early 1900s about the language among politicians, certain Catholic bishops, and school administrators, revivalists also repeatedly cited a select few past villains in the decline of Irish who conveniently echoed those of their own time. One was Daniel O'Connell (1775–1847), the early nineteenth-century advocate of Catholic emancipation and Repeal, who had not only failed to press for language revival but could also be conveniently blackened by a late nineteenth-century movement that believed that political separation without assertion of cultural difference (as O'Connell appeared to have advocated) was worse than Union. A second guilty party was the national school system implemented under British rule in 1831. As was self-evident to those cultural nationalists doing battle in their own time period with recalcitrant administrators slow to remove barriers to integrating Irish with the school system, the national school could be retroactively assigned a significant portion of the responsibility for the decline of Irish in the first place. A third was the priests and bishops of the Catholic Church, whose eighteenth- and nineteenth-century varieties, if assumed to be like the twentieth-century versions hesitant to require Irish for matriculation at Catholic universities (as several were in the 1900s), could be labeled irretrievable forces of anglicization. Finally, as Ó Conchubhair has emphasized, the influence of racial and biological thinking at century's end made many in this generation wholly convinced of the inseparable spiritual connection between nation—even race—and language. The overall result was that the history of the Irish language became, in these circumstances, a recounting of Ireland's fight for political independence, a recitation of the litany of wrongs done by O'Connell, the priests, and the national school system, and the self-evident proposition that speaking Irish was a biological manifestation of certain features like rusticity, orality, and most of all, a deep—even biological—Irishness.

Echoes of these assumptions can be found in subsequent writings as late as the 1960s, and in some cases beyond. The first truly scholarly attempts to give an overview of the language, such as Daniel Corkery's *The Fortunes of the Irish Language* (1954), told the history of the Irish language as if it was the history of Irish nationalism—a stance that often anachronistically assigned linguistic significance to independence movements where none was evident. In the actions of seventeenth-century Gaelic aristocrats, eighteenth-century agrarian secret societies, the Fenians of the 1860s, and the Land League founded in 1879, Corkery saw evidence alike of the unchanging national aspirations of Ireland. While he acknowledged that not all these elements had been equally aware of the language issue (only with the founding of the Gaelic League in 1893 was the goal of revival actualized), he also portrayed the resistance of these groups to British rule as implicitly advocating an Irish-speaking culture over anglicization.[31] Even beyond Corkery, the history of the Irish language in the eighteenth and nineteenth centuries continued to be built—in some cases well into the last decades of the twentieth century, and even by authors with profound expertise in Irish literature and language—around the simplest of narratives as a language confined to the soon-to-be dispersed rural poor, its death a product of O'Connell's policies, the treacheries of the national school system, and the opposition of the clergy.[32] Other legacies of nineteenth- and early twentieth-century understandings of language, such as the tendency to focus on Irish-speaking communities in locations where the language was spoken in 1900 or in the subsequent Gaeltacht-designated regions of the independent state (in particular, western islands and coastal lands), still loom large today in studies that have nevertheless contributed considerably to the field.[33]

Such interpretations failed to absolutely dominate completely the study of the history of Irish, of course. Even within the revival movement of these early decades there were less visible voices offering alternative interpretations of the history of Irish and its decline. Take, for example, the curt response to a biographical sketch of the noted Gaelic Leaguer Tomás Ó Concheanainn (1870–1961) published in *An Claidheamh Soluis*, the voice of the League, in September 1899 that had cast blame on the national school system for undermining Irish. Noting the newspaper's clichéd account of Ó Concheanainn's inspiration to language advocacy as a product of the tyranny of a national school teacher who had administered "many a cut … for venturing, now and then, to speak a word in the only language he knew," the respondent—no less than Ó Concheanainn's national school teacher himself—denied vehemently that he had ever "punished Master Thomas Concannon nor any other pupil of mine for speaking Irish."[34] A more nuanced account of Irish in the eighteenth and nineteenth centuries was also provided in the final chapter of Douglas Hyde's *Literary History of Ireland* (1899), titled "The History of Irish as a Spoken Language." Conversant in Irish and familiar with manuscript sources, Hyde tentatively placed the beginnings of its decline in the mid-eighteenth century. He was also willing to highlight unconventional instances of Irish speaking, as in reports of the widespread use of Irish by members of the British army's Irish brigades.[35] Other challenges to accepted historiography appeared in responses to Corkery's initial revisionist study, *The Hidden Ireland* (1924), which sought to reinstate the history of eighteenth-century Irish-language poets left out by the exclusive focus of scholars on the Protestant Ascendancy. In a strikingly modern review submitted to a 1934 forum in *Studies*, the Ulster-born, Irish-speaking Protestant nationalist Aodh de Blacam (1891–1951), clearly sensitive to the complexities of language and identity given his background, argued that Corkery had replaced one single-dimension account (that of William Lecky's English-speaking Protestants) with another (Munster's Irish-speaking Catholic poets). No eternal connection between language and nation should be assumed given the historically determined nature of such concepts, wrote de Blacam in a tentative historicization worthy of today's scholarship on nationalism: "After all, the vital importance of a national language is a recent discovery."[36]

New directions and a push toward more scientific attention to the history of the language truly began, however, with the work of Brian Ó Cuív, Maureen Wall, and Seán de Fréine in the 1960s and 1970s. Ó Cuív's lectures on the history of Irish of the late 1940s and early 1950s, published in 1980 as *Irish Dialects and Irish-Speaking Districts*, provided a fresh and detailed synthesis of the legal, literary, and linguistic status of Irish over the course of several centuries, including some of the first systematic uses of the census data from the nineteenth century. Although Ó Cuív's research has not been so centrally accessible because his prolific output consisted largely of articles scattered throughout journals such as *Éigse*, *Ériu*, and *Celtica*, his later synthesis published as part of the multivolume *New History of Ireland* demonstrated his masterful familiarity with centuries' worth of archival sources.[37] When it came to the history of the eighteenth and nineteenth centuries, Ó Cuív greatly expanded the context for the fortunes of Irish in this period, noting both exceptions to the conventional explanations for its decline as well as ways in which institutions and individuals reinforced its secondary status. Ó Cuív's ability to marshal obscure archival sources, for instance, enabled him to present evidence of the still-vibrant literary community of scribes and poets in operation at this time—figures like Seán Ó Neachtain (ca. 1640–1729), a Dublin transplant and prolific poet-scribe, and the Kilkenny diarist Amhlaoibh Ó Súilleabháin (1783–1838). He drew attention to the diversity of church policy on Irish, highlighting its approach to teaching the Irish language in continental seminaries, and publications of devotional literature in the seventeenth and eighteenth centuries. And while he emphasized the role of religious and government educational policies in the nineteenth century as part of the story of decline, he was also keen to discuss the role of economic shifts—namely the advantage to speakers of learning English—and the potential contribution of demographic changes in the form of rural depopulation.

Wall's article on Irish, meanwhile, included as part of Ó Cuív's 1969 edited collection, has become one of the most frequently cited sources for the history of the language in this period and is notable for its reassessment of many of the tropes of the previous half-century. The idea that Daniel O'Connell, the Catholic Church, and the national schools together single-handedly destroyed Irish had become, as Wall memorably described it, an "over-simplification" of the history of the language in school textbooks perpetuated "in the manner of a catechism answer." The so-called Catholic hedge schools that had predated the national system, Wall pointed out, had already been teaching English literacy long before, and the position of the church on Irish in the nineteenth century had been one of pragmatic neglect. Most importantly, like Ó Cuív, Wall emphasized the broader context of a linguistic hierarchy in Ireland (dating back to the seventeenth century) in which English had replaced Irish in the administrative, legal, and commercial life of the country. Acquiring English, she argued, was a way for Irish speakers to gain access to this world, especially in the nineteenth century when the political life of the country revolved around electioneering, mass meetings, and a public sphere conducted in English. Financial opportunities through employment in teaching, the civil service, and the police force also required English, as did immigration to English-speaking countries abroad.[38]

This focus on large-scale shifts, particularly broader cultural change, also dominated another highly influential work on the history of Irish in the eighteenth and nineteenth centuries, de Fréine's *The Great Silence* (1965). In many ways, today's studies of the period remain locked in the framework built by de Fréine. Crude notions that the English had legislated Irish out of existence, de Fréine argued, could not withstand historical scrutiny. Rather, imperial rule created a context that led the Irish themselves to reject their own culture—and with it, the Irish language—because of their desire to seize the advantages of official largesse and commercial advancement being offered by the English-speaking world. De Fréine, who had actually devised the study as a way to explain persistent population loss, often used the image of psychological trauma and pathological abandonment to describe this cultural transformation—a break from the past, as he portrayed it, fueled by the Great Famine and reflected in the mass emigration of the nineteenth century. The Irish language in this account was a framework for shared values and customs, the missing adhesive that had once bound communities through an awareness of their common past. In short, Irish speakers and the Irish nation gave up the language as the price of gaining modernity, but with the heavy cost of losing their culture and way of life.[39]

De Fréine's linking of loss of language with cultural decline was an elaboration of an axiom that has become unassailably lodged in subsequent Irish historiography, even in works not focused on the language. This approach holds that culture is a distinct and bounded entity that can "decline" or be "lost" (rather than constantly subject to change and contestation), and that language shift and cultural transformation in Ireland were the same phenomenon, entailing an abrupt and powerful break with the past in the nineteenth century. This concept of disruption, for example, features heavily in Emmet Larkin's influential accounts of the nineteenth-century Catholic "devotional revolution," in which the newly enforced religious orthodoxy of the Catholic Church was portrayed as a replacement for a prefamine culture that included, most visibly, the Irish language.[40] Rupture figures in the more recent description by Angela Bourke of the nineteenth century as a time of "rich resources of imagination, memory, creativity, and communication that were jettisoned when the Irish language and its oral traditions were denigrated and discarded throughout much of the country."[41] Likewise, studies of the language itself have almost universally viewed Irish through the lens of cultural conflict and departure. Thus, Brighid Ní Mhóráin's study of the Irish language in Iveragh, Co. Kerry, conveys its history in terms of a "comhlint chultúrtha idir dhá theanga" (cultural conflict between two languages) and a substitution of one culture for another. Máirín Nic Eoin, writing of the decline of Irish in an important study of the Irish language in County Kilkenny, similarly asserts that "a rejection of the traditions of the county implies also a rejection of the language which carried those traditions in its literature and lore."[42]

There are questions raised by this approach to culture and language, however. It should be emphasized that this notion of disjuncture is in many ways a literary-based interpretation of Ireland's linguistic past: the declining output of original writings in Irish over the course of the seventeenth and eighteenth century, combined with the near-cessation of most Irish-language scribal activity by the end of the 1840s, represents the sunset of one era, followed by the beginning of a new one with the reappearance of Irish-language literary work during the revival of the 1890s. That the Irish-speaking community continued to have a history between 1840 and 1893 does not remain clear in this scheme. The deployment of terms like "tradition" and "culture" in many studies are also far from clear-cut, especially where the issue of the relationship between language and the social and the cultural is concerned. Would not some sectors of Irish-speaking society have shared more cultural practices with certain English speakers than with other Irish speakers? Was Irish-speaking culture simply a homogenous entity locked in struggle with its English-speaking opposite? The problem, as Ó Ciosáin has noted, is that scholars have often treated the relationship between social context and the Irish language as "self-evident rather than as requiring to be elucidated,"[43] a problem shared by a historical discipline in general that all too often regards the languages spoken by their historical subjects to be an intrinsic and unproblematic marker of cultural identity (i.e., that all Irish speakers by definition share a singular identity not accessible to speakers of other languages). This lends itself to easy histories of language contact, language shift, or language death in which the encounter or transformation is presented as a simple interaction between two distinct and well-defined language communities, and language change the replacement of one culture for another.

Of course, the relationship between culture and language is not easily elucidated, given more than a century of theoretical discussion on the question combined with the complexities of the debate over the nature and function of culture and identity among historians, sociologists, and anthropologists in the past thirty years. But certainly some attempt to grapple with the multivalent nature of identity and the capacious functions of language in both reflecting and establishing culture should be made. Languages have the potential to play a role as both a marker of social categories (subject to the perceptions of its speakers who may or may not recognize differences in identity based on language) and, simultaneously, a behavioral action that itself generates the subculture (or cultures) of speech communities broadcasting class, gender, nationality, and more subtle identities like occupation group, age cohort, and education level. Mindful of several decades of historical investigation that have revealed the contingent nature of culture—that is, culture not as an independently defined entity but as a sum of a series of practices and discourses by a community—it is important that any treatment of language similarly elucidate not only the use of speech to build bonds of solidarity but also the use of internal variation to index multiple cultural identities within the community.[44]

One place to look for guidance in this regard is, of course, the field of linguistics. But historians who venture here seeking to find vindication of any notion that language behavior can be explained with recourse to concepts like disappearance of a culture, or that languages transparently mark out a distinct culture for its speakers, should beware. Mid-twentieth-century concepts of linguistic relativity by Edward Sapir and Benjamin Lee Whorf, for instance, have not been accepted without serious reservation since the 1960s, and a symposium as long ago as 1991 seeking to assess the state of Sapir-Whorf found that a consensus had emerged that only a selective use of the thesis could be used to supplement a field fundamentally transformed by cognitive-based explanations of language behavior.[45] Since then, even sociolinguists have been increasingly cognizant of the ways language (particularly, language change) is determined not by outside social factors alone but first and foremost by the physical process of conversational interaction, child-parent relationships, speech networks, and interactive accommodation—in other words, cognitive and behavioral explanations—with broader external factors providing indirect influence by setting context for speech to take place. The well-known study by William Labov of the social class reflected in the dialects and registers of the speakers at Martha's Vineyard—supposedly an indication of how changes in spoken language could be driven by class, with upper and lower classes modifying their speech to either mimic or distinguish themselves from the other—has been modifiedy Labov himself, who has concluded that social class (gender, nationality, and other categories could be substituted here) is actually a poor predictor of many kinds of language innovation.[46] On the other side of the coin, case studies examining the ways languages establish identity (i.e., culture) have not only emphasized the multiple overlapping identities created by language but have also revealed that speakers themselves may or may not recognize a linguistically based identity at all.[47] The contingent nature of cultural identity, in other words, applies where language is concerned and should be treated as such in any history of the subject.

Unpacking the connection between culture and language is no small project, but taking the points made by linguists and cultural theorists alike into consideration provides a start. One solution presents itself in simply building a more detailed understanding of where and when Irish speakers interacted, to whom they spoke, and how both legal and cultural structures facilitated or prevented those conversations from taking place—an endeavor akin, in some ways, to describing the "ecology" of language as it has been phrased by the linguist Salikoko Mufwene to refer to the interactions between speakers that shape communal language.[48] A proliferation in the past two decades of focused studies of certain aspects of the Irish-speaking world of the eighteenth and nineteenth centuries has in many ways produced the building blocks for such an investigation in a way simply not available to a researcher like Wall or de Fréine working twenty or thirty years ago. Eighteenth- and nineteenth-century Ireland produced a ready-made corpus of more than four thousand Irish-language manuscripts, produced by hundreds of Irish-speaking scribes consisting of school teachers, farmers, laborers, and artisans. They offer, with some caveats, a strikingly in-depth look at the attitudes of many of the middling and lower-class intellectuals of the time.[49] Through Herculanean efforts, many of these manuscripts are in fact better cataloged than their English-language counterparts, enabling several detailed and revelatory studies of the content, ideology, and context of these poets and scribes. The publication of Breandán Ó Conchúir's *Scríobhaithe Chorcaí 1700–1850* (1982) provided a powerful contribution in the form of a biographical and archival reference work for the scribes working in the region of the largest concentration at the time, County Cork.[50] Profiles of individual poets, including Mícheál Óg Ó Longáin (1766–1837), Aodh Buí Mac Cruitín (ca. 1680–1755), Aodh Mac Domhnaill (1802–67), and Peadar Ó Gealacáin (1792–1860), have joined extended studies of the evolution of Jacobitism, images of women and femininity, and the deep interplay of English and Irish in songs and verse.[51] Another recent study by Bláthnaid Uí Chatháin expands a field all too often confined to just a small number of literary figures (particularly the Ó Longáin family) by highlighting twelve hereto lesser-known poets and writers from southwest Cork of the eighteenth and nineteenth centuries.[52] Pádraig de Brún, who has long tracked the identities of the many teachers involved with the evangelizing society known as the Irish Society for Promoting the Education of the Native Irish through the Medium of Their Own Language (founded 1818), has recently published a full listing of these individuals.[53]

All of these studies, even those predominantly interested in literary developments, have repercussions for the study of the history of the Irish language itself. In the 1970s, for example, it was still possible to assert that the Irish-speaking community of the eighteenth and nineteenth centuries was essentially apolitical—indeed, as one scholar put it, politics were supposedly a source of language decline: "Another crucial factor which hastened the decline of Irish was the involvement of the Irish people from the end of the eighteenth century in politics. Up to then, they did not take part in political matters—they were politically isolated and impassive."[54] Nothing could be farther from the truth, as a review of the intensely political and historically aware writings of this period explored in research by Morley, Lesa Ní Mhunghaile, Breandán Ó Buachalla, Peter McQuillan, and Cornelius Buttimer shows.[55] Meidhbhín Ní Úrdail's study of the Ó Longáin family, while ostensibly about the methods and fortunes of the scribe-poets themselves, has brought new revelations about the practice of translation and the interrelations of scribal and print culture, a subject also developed earlier in Ó Ciosáin's *Print and Popular Culture* (1997).[56] Simply recovering the identity of many of these individuals from the obscurity created by a largely anglophone record, as has been done by de Brún and Ó Conchúir, changes current concepts of the social classes, aspirations, and assumptions of the Irish speakers of the time. But for all this work, composite studies of the history of the Irish-speaking community as a whole in the eighteenth and nineteenth centuries remain limited in their reach. Two studies by Máiréad Nic Craith and Ní Mhóráin assembled a powerful array of references to Irish in the archives, presenting in detail the social context of Irish-speaking southwest Munster.[57] Investigations of the ideology of language advocacy and the history of language-based nationalism, as in the work of Tony Crowley, also remain popular.[58] The framework used in these latter studies of the broader Irish-speaking world, as well as the ultimate goal, however, remains virtually unchanged from that of Corkery or Hyde a century ago: to investigate when and why Irish declined as a spoken language, to review the literary history of the language, and to reconstruct the use of the language as a potent symbol of either nationalist or language revivalist debate.

By contrast, a different aim is offered by the present study. It is not an exploration of language shift or the declining number of Irish speakers, nor of language revival as part of political or cultural ideology. To be sure, the fact of the declining proportion of Irish speakers in the general Irish population and the rise of bilingualism provide a backdrop to the developments outlined here, and its findings may in some way contribute to larger understandings of the shift toward English. But a reader seeking a history of Irish nationalism or national identity will find it relegated to the background. Rather, the aim of this research is threefold. First, it seeks to present the viewpoints of everyday Irish-speaking communities on their language as much as possible given the limitations of the historical evidence, focusing on the period from 1770 to 1870. Its findings convey a sense of the continued vitality of this speech community during a time that scholars have almost universally regarded as a moribund gap between the early modern literary activities of poets and continental theologians and the revivalism of the late nineteenth century. Second, part I of this study (chapters 1–3) will examine the multiple identities—some national, some local—maintained by Irish speakers on the basis of the language itself, its contact with English, and recognized variations of dialect within Irish. These chapters show that Irish speakers drew on the language as a marker of shared religious and historical identities, setting up a contrast with English-speaking outsiders, even as they recognized internal divisions within the Irish-speaking community based on dialect. The rise of bilingualism complicated this picture further, as chapter 3 will demonstrate, as those with the ability to interact linguistically with English-speaking outsiders could claim a mastery of the linguistic landscape not available to either Irish or English monoglots. The geographic scope in these initial chapters, as it is throughout this study, is all of Ireland and not just the regions that ultimately retained Irish into the twentieth century. Justification for this decidedly nonlocal approach can be found in the fact that Irish speakers lived throughout the island, making a history of those individuals necessarily all-encompassing. Slightly better coverage of Munster and Connacht—a product of the archival sources utilized—will be detected in the evidence that follows, leaving room for much future work. But in the end, the result is a fairly wide-ranging catalog of the cultures existing within the umbrella of the Irish-speaking community as a whole, as well as an attempt to understand the specific circumstances of the late eighteenth and early nineteenth centuries that gave rise to new attitudes toward the language.

The third and final goal is to trace the interaction between Irish speakers and authorities represented by church and state, with the object of overturning usual depictions of the former as passive respondents to uniformly anglicizing initiatives from above. Chapters 4 and 5 start by seeking to modify usual treatments of the language policies of the state as an unchanging drive toward anglicization in Ireland, without any variations in intensity, tactics, or aims. This section proposes that after an initial period of intense anglicization during the Tudor and Stuart periods, driven by an intense desire to ensure above all that Ireland's ruling classes spoke English, the eighteenth century had been comparatively quiet on the linguistic front, as authorities could rest comfortably with a firmly English-speaking Protestant ruling class in place. But in the nineteenth century, with the expansion of the modern state in the forms of new educational, legal, religious, and political institutions, the language question arose again as Irish speakers, much more numerous and vocal than expected by authorities, made it difficult to enforce an all-English administrative regime. The result was short-term compromise, especially at the local level and on an ad-hoc basis, fueled by the active participation of Irish speakers in these systems. This was followed by a gradual return by the last quarter of the nineteenth century to indifferent anglophone policies as the number of Irish speakers declined.

Chapters 6 and 7 demonstrate a parallel rise of the language question within the Catholic Church, built once again not just on policies enacted on high by clerical and episcopal authorities and thrust onto the laity but, rather, established in the give-and-take with parishioners at the local level. The choice of the one hundred years between 1770 and 1870, at odds with usual periodizations of the Irish language that often try to fit its history into a framework borrowed from literary or political events, is of relevance here as this choice was driven by the need to consider major developments in the Catholic Church. This was the revival and devotional reform of the Catholic Church, a development that has been increasingly dated by historians not to 1850 and the Synod of Thurles but to the stirrings of church building and parish reforms of the last quarter of the eighteenth century. Like the Irish state, transformed in the century after 1770 by its overall expansion and increasing presence in everyday lives, the Catholic Church, through its increasing insistence on church-centered worship and regular sacramental interaction, ensured that its body of lay members would be addressed collectively in an institutional setting where reform and regulation could take place. But this also meant addressing linguistic diversity in a way not necessary when clerical contact had been limited and even individualized. The long-term participation in some quarters of the Irish-speaking community in shaping Catholic reform, as shown in chapter 6, made this language question all the more visible. The cumulative effect of this study, it is hoped, will be a new perspective on the functions and everyday ideologies associated with the Irish language and a recognition that for the Irish-speaking community of this period, decline and obsolescence were not the all-encompassing considerations that they have been for modern historians.

PART I

IDENTITIES

Language Bonds and the English-Speaking Other

THE NOTED IRISH-LANGUAGE REVIVALIST, AUTHOR, AND PRIEST Peadar Ó Laoghaire (1839–1920), reflecting in his autobiography on the shock he experienced on first arriving at St. Patrick's College, Maynooth, in 1861 and finding that many of his fellow students had been raised without learning a word of Irish, attributed his surprise to growing up in west Cork without knowledge of the national picture:

> An fhaid a bhíos-sa sa bhaile agus gan taithíghe ná eólus agam ach ar na cómharsain a bhí am' thímpal i bparóiste Chluandrochad agus i bparóiste Bhaile Múirne, níor tháinig lá d'á chuimhneamh riamh chúgham go raibh aon bhaoghal ar an nGaeluinn.[1]
>
> [For as long as I was at home, knowing and experiencing only the neighbors I had around in the parishes of Clondrohid and Ballyvourney, it never once occurred to me that there was any danger to the Irish language.]

At once, Ó Laoghaire realized the possibility of the language disappearing, and he felt an intense loneliness and sorrow descend upon him ("tháinig uaigneas thar bárr orm agus brón"). Haunting in its description of the tragedy of language loss, Ó Laoghaire's recollection also reveals the importance of approaching the Irish-speaking community of these early years on its own terms. Put simply, an account of the history of the Irish language in the late eighteenth and early nineteenth centuries written from the perspective of an awareness of its subsequent linguistic fortunes—thus placing disproportionate attention on language decline, falling linguistic prestige, and the impact (or failure) of national revival movements—risks obscuring what were often very different views of the status of the language within still-robust local Irish-speaking communities.

The solution to this problem is to recover, as far as possible, the perspectives of Irish speakers themselves in these years, supplemented by an examination of social practices where the sources for recovering that viewpoint are absent. In addition, a fresh critical look at many of the outsiders—antiquarians, travel writers, and government officials—who commented on the state of the Irish language in these years can also assist in this endeavor if such sources are read against the grain so that glimpses of the everyday lives of Irish speakers can be disentangled from the prejudices and assumptions of such observers. Equally important is the awareness of differences among members of Irish-speaking communities over the status of the language in their daily lives. Such diverging perspectives, first as constituted by linguistic diversity within speakers of Irish, and second as initiated by varying levels of bilingualism, will be explored in chapters 2 and 3. But even here, although the focus will be on the continuities in the various attitudes of Irish speakers toward their language, attention is directed to differences in the motivations and convictions of specialized scholars of the language on the one side—the scribes who most often left a written record of their thoughts in Irish—and, on the other, the general population whose ideologies were more often displayed in their linguistic behaviors and routines rather than in any self-penned documents. Simply foregrounding Irish-language sources are not, in other words, sufficient on their own to capture any one perspective of the language, since, after all, such a one-dimensional viewpoint did not exist. Instead, an understanding must be gained of the range of views on the status of Irish possessed by a still-diverse community—a diversity that remained strong until the late-nineteenth and early-twentieth centuries when the strongest Irish-speaking areas of Ireland collapsed onto the rural, coastal regions of the far south, west, and northwest.

Finally, just as synchronic variations in the Irish community deserve attention, so, too, must the attitudes of Irish speakers toward their language be suitably historicized to account for changes that took place over time. Irish scribes of the late eighteenth century and throughout the nineteenth century most certainly drew on the ideologies of earlier literary accomplishments, including medieval creation tales, sixteenth- and seventeenth-century poetry, the prose of writers like the priest-scholar Seathrún Céitinn (ca. 1580–ca. 1644), and, more broadly, the cultural ideals passed down from generation to generation concerning the history and status of the Irish language. But they were not bound by those concepts, and they employed them for their own means. A wide range of new factors, from the impact of the rising Catholic middle class and consequent influence of Daniel O'Connell to the changing economic features of everyday life, all had a role to play in linguistic perspectives, and no history of this period would be complete without taking stock of their importance.

This need for awareness of historical change also applies to what is almost certainly the richest resource for recovering the views of everyday Irish speakers about their world: the Irish National Folklore Collection. Founded in 1935 by the Irish government to consolidate and formalize previous folklore initiatives, the Folklore Commission responsible for this archive employed a mix of full-time and part-time collectors who together amassed thousands of volumes of interviews transcribed from field recordings of local informants, most from the 1930s and 1940s but quite a number from the decades after. Far from just collectors of folklore, the commission also captured personal reminiscences, songs, religious material, and local histories. This material has been mined briefly for its potential revelations regarding the experience of Irish speakers of language shift, and it will be explored most deeply in chapter 3.[2] But when it comes to language attitudes in the eighteenth and nineteenth centuries, it is vital to keep in mind that the respondents of the folklore material were, in each and every case, interviewed long after the politicized revival of the Irish language had taken hold, at least a decade after the creation of the Irish state, and well after the entrenchment of a national history that had heavily emphasized certain aspects of Irish linguistic history—namely the seemingly irretrievable decline under English rule—to the exclusion of others. The experience of language shift as remembered by Irish speakers in Gaeltachtaí of the 1930s, 1940s, and 1950s, as in the often-cited collecting done by Michael Murphy in County Tyrone, cannot be simply back-projected to encompass the experience of speakers of the 1830s, 1840s, and 1850s, much less the 1770s, 1780s, and 1790s.[3] A more critical assessment of context and a more selective use of the folklore record is required, namely, an approach that uses pre-1900 sources to sift and highlight similar themes from the twentieth-century material while leaving aside items whose applicability to earlier years cannot be confirmed.

What follows is thus an effort to recover the attitudes and beliefs of ordinary Irish speakers about their language in this earlier time. Every effort will be made to acknowledge both historical change and, where apparent, variety in attitudes, although the evidence will also show certain constants over time in the ways that the Irish-speaking community as a whole interpreted the place of Irish in Ireland. Most importantly, these chapters seek to move beyond the inference that the declining number of Irish speakers alone set the central narrative of the fortunes of the language at what was admittedly a time of significant linguistic upheaval. Instead, the threads of alternate narratives will receive their due consideration in the hopes of providing a more complete understanding of the significance of the language in the minds of its people.

It was believed, first and foremost, that the Irish language possessed a deep antiquity and unusual fluency. This was one feature on which Irish speakers could concur, especially those within the scholarly community who reflected on the topic of the Irish language and who continued to circulate a remarkably consistent origin story up through the seventeenth, eighteenth, and nineteenth centuries. That history was given particular detail in two major surviving medieval texts that influenced subsequent Irish writers: the *Lebor Gabála Érenn*, a history of the peopling of Ireland and of the origins of the Gaels and their language, and the *Auraicept na nÉces*, a scholarly grammar and prosody that included an extended preface explaining the creation of Irish and its notable linguistic features. Multiple redactions and contradictory internal details, especially prevalent in the *Lebor Gabála*, make for inconsistencies, but the essential story told in these sources emphasized the Asian (or more specifically, Mesopotamian) setting for the creation of Irish, its assembly from the dispersed seventy-two languages of the world after the fall of the Tower of Babel, and the melding of Irish with the ancestors of the Gaels through the naming of the language after one of its creators. In this telling, after the flood God dispersed the original language spoken by the descendants of Noah, Gortighern (that is, Hebrew), in retaliation for the construction of Nimrod's Tower. The original language—and, in some tellings, Greek and Latin as well—survived under the protection of the descendants of Eibhear, hence the unbroken link of Hebrew with humans' first language.[4]

Some time later, according to the medieval accounts, the Scythian king Féinius Farsaidh (a descendant of Japhet, son of Noah and one of the three ancestors along with Shem and Ham who, in medieval European origin-legends, were believed to be the basis for the three fundamental divisions of the world's peoples) left his kingdom for the plain of Senair near the original site of the Tower of Babel. There, Féinius created a school from an assembly of scholars, including two principle *saoithe*: Gaedhil, son of a fosterling of Féinius named Eathór; and a second sage, Iar. This team of scholars then assembled the Irish language by taking the purest and most fluent forms from the various scattered languages, essentially building, in the memorable recent description of Joseph Lennon, the "reformed original language."[5] This language, all but Adamic in its purity, was claimed to encompass every subtle advantage of its component languages, however obscure, plus additional features brought to it by the poets; it was, therefore, more comprehensive than other languages and held pride of place in being the first language established after the fall of the tower. Irish was even described in the *Auraicept* as having survived the fall of the tower: scattered but still in existence in its seventy-two pieces, it awaited only Féinius and the poets to call it back into full view. Féinius named the language, referred to generically as *bérla Feni* (language of Féinius) or *bérla na nGaedel* (the language of the Gaels), after Gaedhil: hence, *Gaedelg* or *Gaedhilig*, thereby grafting linguistic identity onto an ethnic one.[6]

After returning to Scythia to impart the language to his subjects, Féinius bequeathed Irish to his scholar son Nél and to his descendants. From here, the accounts merged the history of Irish with the origins of the Milesian invasions of Ireland via Spain. Nél, summoned to Egypt where he married the daughter of the Pharoah, Scota, named his son Gaedhil Glas after the language. Described as "ár n-athair" (our father), Gaedhil Glas produced descendants who, following Moses and the Jews before them, left Egypt and embarked on an odyssey-like voyage over several generations throughout the Mediterranean and Asian worlds. Finally arriving in Spain, where Míl (or Mílid) had now taken over leadership, the band of Irish speakers made one last move to Ireland, where they formed the final invasion force featured in the *Lebor Gabála*—*gabh*, or "take," referring to successive conquests said to have peopled the island.[7]

It is difficult to overestimate the influence of this account of the inception and spread of the Irish language. Already well known in the scholarly community with access to the *Lebor Gabála* and the *Auraicept* before the seventeenth century, the noted historian Seathrún Céitinn in his monumental history of Ireland, *Foras Feasa ar Éirinn* (1634–35), drew directly from copies of these and other texts in a synthesis that simplified and further popularized some of the disparate strands of the earlier medieval histories.[8] Céitinn's contemporary, the well-known Franciscan scribe and chronicler Mícheál Ó Cléirigh (ca. 1590–1643), who edited a late redaction of the *Lebor Gabála*, performed a similar function in preserving and consolidating the essential features of the story. From this point, the origin story elicited interest from a range of subsequent writers in both Irish and English. Céitinn's *Foras Feasa*, as Vincent Morley has recently shown, remained incredibly popular among eighteenth- and nineteenth-century scribes for whom the text provided a baseline for collective understanding of Irish history. The creation of Irish on the plain of Senair, its exulted status, and the importance of Nél in bequeathing it to his son Gaedhil Glas also appeared in the Kerry poet Seán Ó Conaill's epic "Tuireamh na hÉireann" (ca. 1657), a second popular literary work among scribes that Morley has highlighted for its extensive circulation and impact on the Irish sense of nationality.[9]

From there, the influence of the linguistic origins legend can be traced in the Irish-speaking world through other noted historians like Ruaidhrí Ó Flaithbheartaigh (1629–1718), whose *Ogygia: Seu Rerum Hibernicarum Chronologia* (1685) repeated the story, albeit with a measure of skepticism.[10] Likewise, the account featured in the poem "Tuireadh na Gaedhilge agus Teastas na hÉireann" by the Sligo poet Seán Ó Gadhra (1648–ca. 1720), a rejoinder to certain earlier scholars like Giraldus Cambrensis (ca. 1146–ca. 1223) and Richard Stanihurst (1547–1618) for their distorted accounts of Irish history. Ó Gadhra reminded his audience:

> Is fíor gur teanga aosta an Ghaedhilg
> Ó aimsir an Tuir, mar scuir na féinnigh,
> Is do chuir a chumasc an chuideacht ó cheile.
> Do b'é Gaedheal mac Eathóir, fileoir tréitheach,
> Do chuir scoil scafairí ar mhachaire Shéanair
> Is do shaothruigh amach an Teanga Ghaedhilge[11]

> [It is true that Irish is an ancient language
> from the time of the Tower, as the warriors scattered
> and the company was separated.
> It was Gaedhil son of Eathóir, gifted poet,
> who established a school of strapping men on the plain of Senair
> and cultivated the Irish language]

This account, or at least garbled versions of it, was equally well known in the English- and Latin-language print world at an early date. Cambrensis knew of the linguistic creation story, and his account was repeated by Edmund Campion (1540–81) in his *A Historie of Ireland* (1571) and by Stanihurst in his *Treatise Containing a Plain and Perfect Description of Ireland* (1577).[12] But it was the eighteenth-century Irish-language scholar, grammarian, and poet Aodh Buí Mac Cruitín, conversant in the writings of Céitinn (and possessing a sympathetic ear), whose *A Brief Discourse in Vindication of the Antiquity of Ireland* (1717) probably most broadcast the story of Féinius Farsaidh to English readers, prompting reprinting of the tale in nineteenth-century publications like the *Transactions of the Gaelic Society of Dublin* (1808), Ursula Young's *Sketch of Irish History* (1815), John O'Donovan's *Grammar of the Irish Language* (1845), and Martin O'Brennan's *Ancient Ireland* (1855).[13]

Several aspects of this origin story need to be highlighted. First, it posited a birth location for Irish that was at a remove from the island itself, in the distant east, and in a manner that created a place for Irish at the beginnings of postdiluvian humankind. Irish, in this telling, was not autochthonous to the island. This was, in part, a product of the evolution of the *Lebor Gabála* (and to a lesser extent, the *Auraicept*) itself as subsequent copyists mixed native and nonnative histories. The results grafted European historical sources such as the *Chronicle of Eusebius* (379 AD), the writings of Isidore of Seville (ca. 560–636), and the Old Testament onto older native concepts.[14] The tension between this need to harmonize the origins of Irish with biblical understandings of linguistic history, and a deeper connection of the language with the island, was evident in occasional references to Irish speakers on the island prior to the arrival of the Milesians. Parts of the *Lebor Gabála*, for example, and subsequently Céitinn's interpretation in *Foras Feasa*, hinted that the descendants of Míl arrived in Ireland to find Irish speakers already present. These speakers consisted of the descendants of previous settlers Cessair, Partholón, Nemed, the Fir Bolg, and the Tuatha Dé Danann—the earliest of whom were said to predate Noah and the flood. Yet even here, the histories generally rounded back to the same outward-facing theme regarding the tower and postdiluvian language: the pre-Milesian language of Ireland was none other than Scoitbhéarla, the same Scythian language developed by Féinius at his school at Senair but brought to the island by Nemed (born of a collateral line of Japhet and thus related to Féinius) before the migration of Nél to Egypt.[15]

At the same time, this melding of linguistic origins and biblical pseudohistory placed the Irish legends firmly within the concepts of language history purveyed by other European intellectuals. The bare outlines of the Irish story echoed others across Europe as various protolinguists sought to reconcile the place of their own languages with biblical accounts of the tower. Speakers of Castilian thus believed their language had been created at the tower and brought to Iberia by Tubal, a grandson of Noah.[16] A parallel belief in the similarities between Hebrew, the purest of languages, and Welsh, brought by descendants of Noah to Wales, was visible in the early modern scholarly writings of John Davies in his *Antiquae Linguae Britannicae* (1621), Charles Edwards in his *Hebraismorum Cambro-Britannicorum Specimen* (1675) and *Y Ffydd Ddi-ffvant* (1677), and in the work of the eighteenth-century educationalist Griffith Jones (ca. 1684–1761).[17] Indeed, given that biblical views of ethnicity held sway over scholarly understandings of national histories well into the beginnings of Western Enlightenment, as Colin Kidd has emphasized, every language had its partisan in the early modern period seeking to demonstrate its affinity with an original Adamic common tongue. This fight was waged, for example, by Johannes Gropius Becanus (1519–72) on behalf of Flemish, Abraham Mylius (1563–1637) for Belgian, Georg Stiernhielm (1598–1672) for Swedish, and Andreas Kempe (1622–89) for Danish, along with a host of other writers for their own national languages.[18] In this regard, even if the Irish linguistic history placed the language's origins outside of Ireland, this story had the effect of reasserting both the essentially European origins of the Irish—like Welsh, Flemish, or Belgian writers, the Irish were descendants ethnically and linguistically of Japhet, supposed common ancestors of all Europeans—and the fundamentally ethnic identity of the language: Gael and Gaedhilg were inextricably linked in the same biblical past.

Second, this origin story firmly characterized Irish as a conquering (rather than conquered) language—one that had been passed down by a distinctly male lineage. This point is important because it sheds some light on the subsequent intensity of disappointment of poets and scribes of the sixteenth century and afterward who witnessed the language withering in the face of English conquest, and whose deeply gendered interpretation of failed Gaelic resistance as a matter of emasculated honor and a disruption of heteronormative bonds of male sociability—recently elucidated in research by Sarah McKibben—closely shaped their evolving response.[19] What disturbed these poets, in part, was the reversal of fortunes of a language, Irish, linked in these origin tales not with the feminine symbol of the land but with the triumphant male invaders who had peopled the island. As is well known, the female personification of Ireland has a deep history in the literary and scholarly past. As a representative of the land—as the goddesses that bequeathed names to the premodern Irish landscape, as the three queens Fódla, Banba, and Ériu from whom sovereignty over the island was seized by the descendants of Míl, and as the bride symbolically taken by the early Irish kings elected chief of their *tuatha*—the female figure has a long pedigree in representing the identity of Ireland.[20] And yet in the linguistic origin tale, the Irish language was created by male scholars, named for a male son, and was brought to Ireland by their male progeny who conquered and inhabited the island, slaughtering resisters. Although grammatically the name for the language was (and remains) feminine—*Gaedhilg*, represented by the pronouns *sí* and *í*—the scholarly divisions of Irish for the purpose of poetic composition, *béarla na féine*, *béarla na bhfileadh*, *béarla an eadarscartha*, *béarla teibidhe*, and *gnáithbhéarla*, all revolved around the masculine noun *bérla* or *béarla*, meaning "language."[21] Only in the seventeenth century did the word *béarla* acquire a more exclusive usage denominating the English language specifically.[22] In sum, the image of the language as passed along to early modern commentators was that of a conquering language, associated not with the "passive" female, in the patriarchal understanding of the time, but with the "active" male.

Finally, Irish was presented in these origin myths as distinctly scholarly in tone. It may have been a conquering language, but its martial speakers and its passage from father to son were not understood to be contradictory with its intellectual prowess. It was Nél, the scholarly master and sage who had mastered the world's language in order to distill Irish from the confusion that his father Féinius had charged with this responsibility; his brother, Nenual, was given only temporary charge of Scythia in his father's absence. Later, on his death, Féinius bequeathed the kingdom of Scythia permanently to Nenual, but to Nél he left the Irish language. That Nél's gift was of greater value was proven by subsequent events: invited by the Pharaoh to continue his linguistic work by setting up schools in Egypt, it was Nél's lineage that ultimately peopled Ireland.[23] Beyond its creation at the hands of scholars, Irish itself was believed to be a uniquely fluent arrow in the scholar's quiver. Thus the *Auraicept*, unsurprisingly given its intention as a grammatical treatise for prosodic teaching, depicted Irish first and foremost as a language for highly accomplished scholarly activity that had been selected and enriched by poets. Irish, it was emphasized, had been written ("roscrib") from the very beginning by Gaedhil for use "du ceastaib & du chaingnib domundaibh eter tuaith & eglais" (for worldly questions and law cases of both laity and church).[24]

Ancient, pure, scholarly, victorious in conquest, masculine, and intimately bound with Gaeldom—these, then, were the predominant views of the Irish language bequeathed to its early modern speakers, especially its poets. Some of these perceived aspects the Irish language were reinforced by the experience of Tudor and Stuart conquest starting in the late sixteenth and early seventeenth centuries, while others no longer fit comfortably with the political realities of the time. As the political function of classic praise poetry declined along with the prestige of the Catholic gentry displaced by Protestant conquest, the poet's power derived from the status of a Gaelic patron weakened accordingly. As a substitute for this prestige no longer bestowed by the Gaelic political order, as Joep Leerssen has noted, poets turned to their shared emphasis on perceived shared values of honor, scholarship, and aristocratic lineage.[25] This suited earlier medieval conceptions of the language as born of these same scholarly values, reinforcing the esteem associated with Irish and undoubtedly contributing to the contempt directed at speakers of the English language in poems of the seventeenth and eighteenth centuries, among them "Créacht do Dháil Mé im Árthach Galair" ("A Wound Has Made Me a Sickened Vessel") and "Is Olc an Ceart Fulang an Fhámuire" ("It Is an Evil Duty to Suffer the Course Man") by Dáibhídh Ó Bruadair (ca. 1625–98), "Tairngaireacht Dhuinn Fhírinne" ("Prophecy of Donn Firinne") by Aogán Ó Rathaille (ca. 1670–1729), and "Is Atuirseach Géar Mo Scéal" ("Sharply Sorrowful Is My Story") by Eoghan Rua Ó Súilleabháin (1748–84), in which *Béarla cruinn* ("exact"—even "antiseptic"—English) was contrasted with *Gaedhilig chaoin* (smooth Irish).[26] In the eyes of this highly literate class, not only was Irish being devalued in favor of an unscholarly tongue, but to add to the injustice, *parvenu* Protestant landowners and Irish boors feigning ability were positively clamoring to speak English, as in the anonymously authored satire *Pairlement Chloinne Tomáis* (ca. 1613).[27]

Meanwhile, the exclusive correlation between Irish language and Gael built into the origin stories, a feature linked to a larger binary divide between native Gael and foreign Gall, no longer proved workable in a society in which many descendants of the Old English, including Céitinn himself, had not only mastered the Irish language but also become proficient scholars in their own right. Bernadette Cunningham has detected an attempt in Céitinn's writings to unhitch this ethnic connection between Gael and *Gaedhilig* by playing up alternative aspects of the origins stories in the *Lebor Gabála*, particularly those that associated the language with Féinius's associate Gaedhil rather than his grandson Gaedhil Glas, and by highlighting the presence of Scoitbhéarla, the Irish-language forbearer, prior to the coming of the Milesian Gaels to Ireland.[28] To build this case, Céitinn leaned heavily on the notion that Milesian conquest by Irish speakers had not brought with it linguistic displacement, thus advancing another concept: a proper, "Christian" invasion (like that of the Old English) ended in assimilation and acquisition of the invaded nation's language rather than its displacement. In addition to the original Milesian example, Céitinn emphasized the survival of English among the Saxons after the arrival of the Norman William the Conquerer as an instance of legitimate invasion, an example that doubled in justifying the arrival of his own ancestors in Ireland owing to their willingness to accept Gaelicization.[29] By contrast, the very fact of the decline of Irish in the face of the English language pointed toward the illegitimacy of the Tudor and Stuart plantations. Tying these strands together, the Irish language could be portrayed as an inheritance of all the rightful heirs of Ireland and not just the Milesian progeny: Gaels, but also the Old English whose arrival had been legitimate because both Christian and linguistically accommodating.

If the Irish language had been perpetuated by patrilineal descent in these earlier texts, this concept of a masculine linguistic identity was no longer entirely sustainable in the face of plantation and dispossession from the late sixteenth century onward. That those in control of Ireland by the seventeenth century—the Protestant planters, Cromwellian soldiers, and Scottish adventurers—spoke English suggested, however painfully, that it was now this new language that had become the (masculine) conqueror, not Irish. The smashing of Catholic power and the older Gaelic order had brought with it the proliferation of the prophecy genre of *aisling* poems in the seventeenth and eighteenth centuries in which the Irish-speaking *spéirbhean* (beautiful woman) offered the poet a message of future deliverance from English rule. Capable of forging links with political ideologies of rebellion such as Jacobitism and built on new concepts of Irish nationality (as opposed to Gaelic, Old English, or even more local loyalties), the *aisling* focused on the dishonored woman or widow whom the heroes of Ireland were to redeem by ridding the county of English-speaking foreigners.[30] That Irish would be identified with the fallen female figure, who speaks that language when delivering her message to the poet, and English with the triumphant invaders represented a role reversal from a linguistic standpoint from the medieval accounts. This again hints at the reason for the depth of the downturn in fortunes perceived by Irish literati in a world where their language, although self-evidently pure, ancient, and intellectual, had nevertheless been shoved aside by the new ruling classes.

The injection of religious conflict into the Irish political landscape further transformed conceptions of identity of which language was a part. Older binary concepts were now modified in the minds of many Irish to include the Old English, and the conflict with the foreigner reimagined as a struggle between Catholic Irish and Protestant New English. Molded by dynamic Reformation writings asserting the diabolical error of Martin Luther and John Calvin, bolstered by coalescing concepts of a rightful central kingship in Ireland expediently linked to the arrival of the sometime-Catholic Stuarts on the throne, and together convinced that the fortunes of Catholicism and Ireland as a nation had become intertwined, this assertion of a primarily religious divide accorded well with the linguistic realities prompted by the arrival of the monolingual New English.[31] These ideas did not weaken in the eighteenth century—in fact, they were strengthened by the shared experience of the penal laws—so that a poet like Armagh-born Art Mac Cumhaigh (ca. 1738–73) could lay out a picture of the religious-linguistic landscape in the clearest of terms: his "Tagra an Dá Theampall" ("The Disputation of the Two Churches") featured a dialogue between a newly constructed Protestant church in Forkhill, Co. Armagh, which speaks in English, and a neighboring Irish-speaking Catholic chapel. While the English-speaking church revels in the thriving state of Protestant peoples, the virtues of Luther, and the errors of popery, the Catholic chapel derides "clann Liútair" (followers of Luther) and laments the passing of the Gaelic order "sa teanga fuair Gael mac Eathair ar Mhaigh Séanair óireac" (in the language Gaedhil, son of Eathór, received on the illustrious plain of Senair).[32] If the feminine identity traditionally ascribed to the Catholic Church is taken into account, Mac Cumhaigh in his poem can be seen to have expertly woven together all the central markers of the language as viewed by its speakers (or at least its scholarly community) at the end of the eighteenth century: the scholarly language of Gael created at the tower; the language associated with the victims of illegitimate conquest; the language, literally, of the Catholic Church; and the voice of a feminine entity (the Catholic Church, or Ireland herself).

Together, these strands identifying the characteristics of the Irish language served as one source for the vocabulary on which the Irish speakers of the late eighteenth and nineteenth centuries drew to formulate their own attitudes toward the language. In fact, this sense of the magnificence and antiquity of Irish—albeit a reputation under attack—was the predominant belief of this period, especially among Irish-language scribes and poets. As the most prolific scribe of the time, Mícheál Óg Ó Longáin of Cork, wrote in an English-language essay in 1817, Irish was "a gift of the Creator" and "one of the most truly original and unmixed on Earth." Not only did it stand alone as the "least adulterated branch of the Celtic," but it was far more pure than the "mixed" languages of English, French, Italian, and Spanish. According to Ó Longáin, only the ancient languages of Greek, German, and Hebrew stood in comparison, and the last was said to be less "copious" than Irish.[33] A former United Irishman, Ó Longáin's sentiments here were inseparable from the political themes he developed in his wider poetic corpus in which English-speaking churls and fanatics were portrayed as the antagonists of a dispossessed Irish people who would one day be released (that is, achieve *saoirse*, freedom) from their bonds.[34] Linguistic and political fortunes were similarly intertwined in the words of the Cork scribe Mícheál Mac Cártha, who wrote in a lengthy treatise sent to John O'Daly in 1846, "Now that almost all Irishmen know their duty and are ready to wrench off the shackles of slavery with the unwearied arms of peace and persistence, our harmonic melifluent [sic] language will soon reach the highest pitch of glory, and our bards, as of yore, will become the envy, the example, and the admiration of the whole world."[35]

Poems extolling the virtues of Irish composed in the mid-eighteenth century or earlier continued to circulate in the late eighteenth and early nineteenth centuries, often accompanied by scribal notes indicating hope that such a peerless language would return to its former status within the community. A poem by Mac Cruitín (d. 1755), for instance, "A Uaisle Éireann Áilne" ("To the Noblemen of Beautiful Ireland"), called on the Catholic gentry, Gaelic and Old English alike, to protect their literary heritage by reminding them of the purity, breadth, and sophistication of Irish:

Nír dhealbh an domhan uile
Teanga as milse mór-thuile
De bhriathraibh as briocht-shnuite blas
Caint as cian-tuilte cúntas[36]

[The entire world did not form
as full-flowingly sweet a language
of words of most magically hewn sound
a speech of most long-running account]

These lines elicited ongoing interest from scribes and antiquarians, who included the poem as an exhortation in favor of the language in various works over the next century.[37] Similar sentiments could be found in "A Ghaoidhilge Mhilis" ("O Sweet Irish"), composed by Peadar Ó Doirnín (ca. 1700–69), and "Do Tharlaigh Inné Orm" ("I Met Yesterday"), a bawdy macaronic piece written by Liam Inglis (ca. 1709–78) about a lusty Irish speaker who—in a yearning for a return to the older linguistic gender roles—sexually conquers an English-speaking maiden and convinces her to learn Irish.[38] In Inglis's poem, the man's initial response to her English, a flippant retort to hearing it spoken, was popular enough that the landlord and Irish scholar Thomas Swanton (1810–ca. 1865) of Ballydehob in west Cork could still find it in circulation in his area in 1855:

Béarla ní'l agam
Ní chleachtaim a shord
Ach gaodhaillainn liom labhair
'Us freagradh gheóbhair[39]

[I don't know English
I don't make a habit of its sort
But speak Irish to me
And an answer will be given]

Also notable was the short poem "Milis an Teanga" ("Sweet Is the Irish"), often ascribed to Céitinn, that placed Irish on an equal level with Latin and Hebrew: "Gidh Eabhra teanga is seanda / Gidh Laidean is léigheanta / Uatha uirthi níor fríth linn / Fuaim nó focal do chomaoinn" (Though Hebrew is the oldest tongue / Though Latin is the most learned / We did not find in them / A sound or word to enhance it).[40] Later copies have been traced to the mid-eighteenth century and later, among them a Galway manuscript by the shepherd-scribe Brian Ó Fearghail (1715–ca. 1788) and a composite Belfast copy by the teacher and musician Séamus Mac Óda from 1818.[41] Yet another such example in this vein, "Mola na Gaodheilge," a short, unattributed poem from the Waterford-Kilkenny area copied by the scribe Finghin Ó Scannaill in the nineteenth century, began simply: "Teanga mhin bhog mhilis celmhur a seaid an Gaoidheilge" (A smooth, soft, sweet, sensible language is the Irish).[42]

Although the story featuring the Tower of Babel to account for the age of Irish remained current in the nineteenth century, an alternate narrative placed the language back even further in time, as the tongue granted to Adam and spoken by Eve in the Garden of Eden—or even the language preferred by God. For Nioclás Ó Cearnaigh (ca. 1800–1865), priest and Irish scholar from County Louth, Irish-language poetry he had collected and preserved offered proof that "the Irish language is the natural one, nay, the language through which the omnipotent Creator spoke all things animate ... into existence."[43] An advertisement to give instruction in Irish from *Saunders's Newsletter*, reproduced in the *Bristol Mercury* in 1833, not only claimed that Japhet had been a speaker of Irish but also hinted that the language was spoken in paradise and possibly in heaven.[44] An anonymous extended poem, copied in the early nineteenth century and titled "Cómhnúadh na Gaeilge" ("The Memory of Irish"), reminded its readers about the virtues of Irish and its one-time dominance in all aspects of Irish life. But the verses also contended that the roots of Irish lay further back, in the speech of Adam and Eve:

> Is í laibhair Adhamh,
> Ann a pharrus fein
> Is ba siubhlach gaeillic
> O bheaul allainn Eabha.[45]
>
> [Adam spoke it
> in his own paradise
> and Gaelic strolled
> from the beautiful mouth of Eve]

Even sober-minded antiquarians and writers of the eighteenth and nineteenth centuries like Charles Vallancey (ca. 1725–1812), the Catholic advocate and Irish-language scholar Charles O'Conor (1710–91), the president of St. Jarlath's College, Uileog de Búrca (1829–87), and contributors to the *Nation* wrote of the language "spoken by Adam and Eve" in their assessments of the antiquity of Irish.[46]

Similar sentiments could be found beyond the scholarly world. Describing a visit to a local cabin in Moneymore, Co. Londonderry, in 1846, for example, one Protestant missionary noted that "all said there was no language so pure and holy as the Irish."[47] Another was told by an Irish-speaking teacher that Irish was "not only the language spoken before the flood [and] by Adam in the garden of Eden, but he could prove it was the language spoken by the angels in heaven."[48] One might dismiss such evidence as a mere puff piece for missionary societies—the funding of the Irish Society, the missionary society at issue here, depended on convincing its patrons that speakers had a desire to learn how to read religious texts in Irish[49]—if it were not for strikingly similar opinions expressed in folk sources. According to Seánín Uí Flathartha, a Galway farmer born in 1880, "Deireann daoiní go rá teangachaí ann roimhe. Ní chreidim-se sin!" (People say that there were languages before it. I don't believe that!). On the contrary, he claimed, Adam and Eve spoke Irish: "Dhá reir sin, níl duine na daoine 'n-ann a rádh nach í'n Ghaedhilg' is sine" (Accordingly, nobody can say that Irish isn't the oldest).[50] Another Galway informant, born in 1852, made a similar boast about Irish when relating the story of the Tower of Babel and the origins of human languages: "Agus sin an chaoi a dtainich na teangaidheachaí amach ar dtúis, ach, cúpla ceánn a bhí ariamh ann. Tá sé raidhte go raibh an Ghaedhilge ariamh ann" (And that's the way the languages came out in the beginning, except a few of them that had always been there. It is said that Irish was always there).[51]

Eighteenth- and nineteenth-century attitudes toward the language were not just echoes of long-standing accounts of its antiquity, however. Two new developments of the time, the sectarian tensions unleashed by a resurgent Protestant proselytism among Catholic communities (especially in the heavily Irish-speaking west) starting in the late 1810s and the meteoric rise of Daniel O'Connell, both helped elaborate on older notions of a religiously tinged linguistic divide as well as the connection between Irish and aristocratic honor. The evidence of the first of these two links, largely found in the records of the Protestant missionaries, must be taken with some caution: those commenting on attitudes toward Irish were also eager to prove the religious overtones ascribed by its speakers to the language. One supposed feature of the Irish language in particular, that the devil could not speak it (and hence that Irish and holiness were, conversely, linked), likely originated not within the Irish-speaking community but among commentators with condescending views. Stanihurst, for instance, had written in the seventeenth century that Irish was too difficult a language for the devil to speak, a pronouncement still being remembered centuries later, in 1877.[52] Furthermore, the perception of a connection between Catholicism and Irish speaking, although prevalent among many Catholics of the time, did not accurately reflect a speech community that in fact included sections of the Protestant population.

These caveats aside, a link between Catholicism and Irish speakers, and between Protestantism and English-speaking usurpers, had currency. Credence must be given to reports from nineteenth-century sources that locals believed Saint Patrick himself had rendered the devil incapable of speaking Irish, that the Irish saints had all spoken the language, or that Bibles written in English were deemed, by definition, Protestant.[53] One contemporary, a Protestant convert from Catholicism, remembered Martin Luther's reputation as the supposed author of the "black book," written in English by a man who was a "duine malluidhe droch bheathach" (a cursed, immoral person).[54] A Protestant clergyman reported from County Clare in 1817 that children in his parish "look with suspicion on everything having the stamp of English, as savouring of Protestantism, in which they were much encouraged by their priest."[55] Reverend Edward Jones Alcock, speaking of the Bantry area of west Cork, likewise affirmed the persistence of these attitudes in 1830: "[English] is the language of their conquerors; it is the language of a church which they have always been led to consider as heretical and oppressive; every early prejudice is against it, counteracted only by the desire of worldly advancement; and every effort is exerted on the part of the priesthood to take advantage of these circumstances."[56] Even the American Protestant and traveler Asenath Nicholson (1792–1855), an outsider less prone to one-sided views of the families she visited in the 1840s, likewise wrote of a family in Bantry, with whom she left an Irish-language Bible that "the peasants in this part of the country are not so afraid of the scriptures if they speak Irish because they attach a kind of sanctity to this language."[57] Whether a widespread belief or not, Protestant missionaries certainly acted on this concept of trust among Irish speakers of anything written in their own language. As late as 1880, a landlord seeking advice from the Achill Missionary Society on obtaining cheap devotional material in Irish remarked that he had heard that Catholics alleged that "the devil never tells lies in Irish."[58]

As for the second development, a long-standing connection between the language as a tool of defense and the heroic aristocratic figure motif in popular storytelling may have been transferred to O'Connell as his stature in Ireland grew. As Niall Ó Ciosáin has shown, stories of famous Irish rogues and highwaymen enjoyed strong popularity in the world of cheap *colporteur* texts, where such tales combined the bandit-hero common to western European literature with the image of the aristocratic tory created by the displacement of the Irish Catholic gentry in the seventeenth century. Accounts depicted the tory as a dashing character who evaded capture from pursuers and who represented a legal system that lacked full legitimacy,[59] but there were also versions of these tales in which the bandit-hero used his knowledge of Irish to cleverly exploit the English monoglotism of his pursuers. At least one version of the life of the tory Ned Ryan recorded in 1849 has the hero discover his enemy's plan by secretly listening to their English: "An English officer and his party went in search of him—he was apprised of the approach of some person by the barking of a dog, and coming out of the house stealthily to listen, he heard some persons talking, and on drawing near, he discovered the foe by their English gibberish, which betrayed their intent."[60]

So, too, can this motif of the Irish speaker evading danger through the clever use of the language be found in the popular tales of the nineteenth century featuring a heroic O'Connell. Scholars have long emphasized O'Connell's position as a messianic figure for Catholics representing not just political goals—like Catholic emancipation and the abolition of tithes—but a much wider peasant conception of deliverance from poverty, exorbitant rents, English conquest, and other onerous grievances.[61] O'Connell, these studies show, enjoyed a reputation and acclaim among many Irish men and women unrivalled in its intensity; it is therefore significant that a number of stories recovered by collectors featured the Irish language as the means by which O'Connell was able to outsmart or evade the deceit of the English. Folklore scholar Ríonach Uí Ógáin has presented a number of such anecdotes in which a young servant tips off O'Connell or one of his allies to impending danger by using Irish to conceal the communication from English speakers. In one story, a servant girl saves O'Connell from death in a blind duel by revealing the intended treachery of a steersman who is supposed to aim the man's weapon. Similar accounts related how O'Connell had been warned by a servant girl or boy that the English lords with whom he was feasting aimed to poison him, as in a dialogue submitted by "S.O.C." to the Gaelic League newspaper *An Claidheamh Soluis* in 1901:

A Dhomhnaill Uí Chonaill an dtuigeann tú Gaedhilg?
Tuigim a chailín 'gus a bhfuil beo dem' ghaoltaibh
Tá rud in do chopán a mharbh na céadta
Má's fíor sin a chailín, béidh tusa liomsa go hÉirinn[62]

[Daniel O'Connell, do you understand Irish?
I do, girl, as do those of my kin still alive
There's something in your cup that would kill hundreds
If that's true, girl, you'll be along with me to Ireland]

O'Connell's life is saved, enabling him, in some tellings, to switch his cup discreetly with a nearby guest. In this same vein were often-repeated stories of O'Connell using Irish around English-speaking newspaper reporters at mass meetings to prevent arrest for treason.[63] Overall, such stories were far from ephemeral: Uí Ógáin notes that 144 accounts of the tale about O'Connell outwitting death using Irish have been documented in Irish folklore and that it represents "the best-known and most widespread of all the O'Connell anecdotes."[64]

These positive portrayals of Irish should not obscure the fact that some contemporaries possessed a very real indifference, shame, or reticence about the Irish language and, conversely, a drive to speak English. The MP J. C. Curwen declared in 1818 after traveling in County Galway: "Probably a century will not pass away before the Irish will become obsolete. We met with few who did not understand English, and who seemed to have a pride in being able to speak it."[65] A time could be envisioned, according to the school teacher Amhlaoibh Ó Súilleabháin, making an entry in his diary in 1827, "go n-imeochaidh an teangadh Gaodhalach so an a bhfuilim-se ag scriobh" (that this Irish language in which I am writing will be gone).[66] Thomas Swanton, corresponding in 1846 with the antiquarian John Windele (1801–65), observed of Irish speakers in his part of Cork that "the people here seem desirous to give it up," and folklorist Robert MacAdam (1808–95) believed that a "false shame" had kept some Irish speakers from admitting to knowledge of the language at the time of the 1851 census count.[67] The Irish scholar Proinsias Ó Catháin, reflecting in 1873 on the language shift underway in Ulster, noted that the drive to learn English so as to avoid the embarrassment of not being able to answer a question in that language was "discouraging the use of the ancient native language."[68] The verdict reached by national schools inspector P. Newell at the end of the century was that "false shame, however, a disposition to ape so-called superior ways, and an ignorant belief that Irish is a badge of inferiority and of no educational or other value, have kept parents and children from cultivating it as much as they ought for a long time past."[69]

Indeed, the weakening status of Irish had become central to the overall discourse surrounding the language from the seventeenth century onward as poets and scholars, who most acutely felt the deterioration of its standing, made a discussion of this development central. To talk about Irish was to talk about its decline, and it was this commentary on the tragedy of Irish speakers abandoning their language that continued to circulate among scribes throughout the eighteenth and nineteenth centuries. Thus, a poem like Dáibhídh Ó Bruadair's "Nach Ait an Nós" (ca. 1643), which complained of the men of Ireland who sought to learn the "codes of foreign clerks" (códaibh gallachléire) by acquiring a "ghost of course English" (gósta garbhbhéarla), was circulated by scribes Uilliam Mac Cairteáin (ca. 1668–1724) and Ríghrí Mac Raghnaill (fl. 1760–82) of Cork in the eighteenth century and by Mícheál Óg Ó Longáin in the nineteenth century.[70] The grammarian Froinsias Ó Maolmhuaidh's poem of 1677, "Truagh Daoine ar Dhith Litri" ("Pity People Who Lack Letters"), similarly complained that "ni thuig Gaoidhil Gaoidhealg fein . . . treighid ni fhaghaid onoir" (the Gaels themselves don't understand Gaelic . . . they abandon [it], they forsake honor), a sentiment that evidently remained current among the scribes of subsequent centuries who continued to copy it.[71]

But the existence of these negative views of Irish by its speakers should not be elevated so that alternate views are drowned out. When reflecting on language shift, Irish speakers were just as apt to blame outside forces, particularly English conquest, rather than contempt for Irish. According to Amhlaoibh Ó Súilleabháin:

> Tá an Bearla Sasanach ag breith barr gach la air ár tteangain dilis bunudhasach fein, seo agus mile miliún aineamh nó easnamh eile ata orainn ón ló ar rug na Sasanaig greidhm air ár nduithche dilis fein .i. Éirionn bocht chraite.[72]

> [The English language is everyday overtaking our own dear native language. This and a thousand million other disfigurements and deficits that have befallen us from the day the English got a hold of our beloved country, that is, poor tormented Ireland.]

The poet and scribe Micheál Ó hAnnracháin (ca. 1801–ca. 1876) complained that it was "the priests and the national schools [that] helped on the designs of the government to quench our language."[73] Particular caution must also greet claims that Irish speakers were abandoning their language because they believed it was vulgar, course, or backward, since many such observations originated with those—even some with close local connections—of a higher social class and background. These observers transferred their own negative opinions regarding Irish onto its speakers to explain why they might—self-evidently—be abandoning it. The priest John Kiely, for example, testifying before an 1825 select committee on the possibilities for improving the education and economic situation in his home parish of Mitchelstown, Co. Cork, linked the potential for manufacturing advances with the arrival of English, while admitting his belief that "those who understand the Irish only are more rude in their manners," and that they were "courser" and less educated.[74] The assumed link between desire for education and a demand to learn English, as if the latter was self-evidently the social currency desired by such a goal, led even as sympathetic an observer as national schools head inspector Patrick Keenan (1826–94) to explain the passion for schooling in the remote islands of Donegal in terms of "one predominant desire—the desire to speak English." Thus: "They may love the cadences, and mellowness, and homeliness of the language which their fathers gave them, they yet see that obscurity and poverty distinguish their lot from the English-speaking people; and accordingly, no matter what the sacrifice to their feelings, they long for the acquisition of the 'new tongue,' with all its prizes and social privileges."[75] Even the comments and writings of Irish-language poets and scribes cannot be taken to express the views of all Irish speakers, since the rural intelligentsia of school teachers and artisans of whom many were members greeted the decline of literary output in Irish as a particularly regrettable sign of neglect—a conclusion that may not have been shared by Irish speakers who lacked the same interest in such scholarship.

In any event, evidence for a contrasting attachment to the Irish language can be found for every incidence of contempt. Like the Scots and the Welsh, the Irish speakers were "fond of their own language to [the point of] enthusiasm," according to the Scottish missionary Daniel Dewar in 1812. Dewar argued that attempts at religious conversion in English, coupled with the decline of the vernacular since the sixteenth century, had in fact produced the opposite effect of isolating and deepening the attachment of speakers to Irish.[76] According to an Anglican missionary active in teaching literacy in Irish in 1818: "We find that the Irish peasantry are almost to veneration attached to their own language; and while they are in numerous instances indifferent to learn[ing] the English language, we find them, with great attention and almost incredible perseverance, apply[ing] themselves to learn the Irish language."[77] Surveys filled out by clergymen in 1817 and returned to the Association for Discountenancing Vice, a proselytizing society established at the end of the eighteenth century, reported that "a crowd of Irish peasants would listen more willingly to anything read to them in Irish than if read to them in English, even if they understood the latter."[78]

This attachment to Irish expressed itself quite literally through a passionate devotion to the manuscripts symbolizing its literary heritage—much to the consternation of antiquarians and scholars increasingly seeking out such texts for study and deposit in academies and libraries. To be sure, there were instances of indifferent destruction of manuscripts, including a case in which a stack had been flung into a fire by an irate wife.[79] But Irish speakers were in other cases loath to give up their Irish books. The Irish scholar John O'Daly (1800–78) found his efforts in 1844 to procure a book of Irish songs from a widow in Kilkee, Co. Clare, frustrated despite his employment of a local intermediary, Michael O'Sullivan, to persuade her to give it up. In frustration O'Sullivan reported:

> Mr. Griffin and I have been at Kilkee on Sunday last, the second time, and can get no account of the book, yet I am sure the widow has it but does not like to part with it. Joseph Kett has certainly taken a transcription of it, and I am sure he has a good collection besides. Kilkee is a post town and the widow Collins is the owner of the book. She lives about two miles outside the village, and as to writing to her about it, believe me that I have done all that could be done both by word and otherwise to get it. In fact, I have tried everything in my power to get it but no use.[80]

Seán Pléimeann (1814–96), a national school teacher and, later, editor of *Irisleabhar na Gaeilge*, reported to the Royal Irish Academy in 1873 that emigrants, despite the obvious difficulty of transporting property overseas, insisted on taking their Irish manuscripts with them. In the north it was noted that those departing received Irish manuscripts as a gift: "The emigration from Ulster of the Irish speaking peasantry during the past 50 years deprived that province of many valuable and curious manuscripts, which either belonged to the emigrants or were presented to them by friends as a parting token of affection."[81] It is difficult to imagine a situation in which books in a language supposedly held in low regard would be carried off on such an odyssey, unless they did in fact possess an emotional significance to their owners.

A recovery of the ideology of Irish speakers can only go so far in presenting the role of the language in the everyday lives of its speakers, making an account of the sociolinguistic practices associated with Irish necessary to move more deeply into its history in this period. Here, no concept has tended to obscure the understanding of scholars of this period more than the idea that eighteenth- and nineteenth-century Ireland was characterized by diglossia—that is, a high-prestige language (English) had a claim on key high-status domains like the public sphere, politics, schools, and modernized economic relationships, while a low-prestige language (Irish) was confined to the private sphere and the home.[82] As an academic term, "diglossia" was borrowed by Charles Ferguson in 1959 to describe societies in which two language varieties, a "high" and a "low" register or dialect, coexisted. The examples foremost in the mind of Ferguson were Swiss-German cantons in which high German was reserved for certain situations involving prestige and learning while low German was the language of the home everyday socialization; classical and spoken forms of Arabic; Haitian Creole and French; and literary versus spoken forms of modern Greek. Later, John Gumperz and Joshua Fishman elaborated on Ferguson's framework, with Fishman providing a more schematic summary of four possible scenarios involving diglossia and bilingualism: cases of both diglossia and bilingualism, in which an entire speech community spoke both languages and reserved the use of one language for high, prestigious domains, while the low language was reserved for less prestigious situations; diglossia without bilingualism, where two or more languages exhibited a hierarchical difference in prestige but access to both languages (that is, bilingualism) was not available to all members of the speech community; bilingualism without diglossia, in which two languages enjoyed equal prestige; and instances of absences of both diglossia and bilingualism, in which all individuals shared the same language repertoire—that is, their ability to use all dialects, registers, and other variations in relation to a single language or languages.[83]

One might start by asking where eighteenth- and nineteenth-century Ireland falls in Fishman's scheme. The answer is not clear cut. Excluding scenario 4 as inapplicable, one might describe Ireland in this period as falling under scenario 1: both diglossic and bilingual. But as Fishman noted, the answer actually depends on how a scholar defines a speech community. If the speech community is taken to encompass the entire nation, because bilingualism was not universal, Ireland might better be characterized under scenario 2: diglossic but not bilingual (since English-Irish bilingualism was not, and has never been, universal). Alternatively, if just the Irish-speaking community is taken as the focus, near-universal bilingualism and diglossia (scenario 1) might seem more applicable once again; or perhaps scenario 3 (bilingualism without a language hierarchy) would apply, a label that dismisses the presence of diglossia in Ireland. The issue is further complicated by the question of stability. Fishman, like Ferguson before him, noted that in societies where different linguistic domains were not separated, bilingualism and diglossia would be unstable because one language would displace the other. As a result, simultaneous bilingualism and diglossia (scenario 1) existed only in certain specific cases: "Wherever speech communities exist whose speakers engage in a considerable range of roles (and this is coming to be the case for all but the extremely upper and lower levels of complex societies); wherever access to several roles is encouraged or facilitated by powerful social institutions and processes; and finally, wherever the roles are clearly differentiated (in terms of when, where, and with whom they are felt to be appropriate), both diglossia and bilingualism may be said to exist."[84] In short, a stable scenario 1 is dependent on sharply defined roles and domains, since this situation differentiates high from low languages, and it is reliant on a widespread ability in the speech community to speak all languages or varieties of a language (otherwise, there will simply be multiple speech communities, each potentially having its own high- and low-prestige domains). Neither of these applied to Ireland, as will be shown below: first, there is significant evidence that domains were not in fact stable or clearly defined in Ireland during the period in question—a phenomenon referred to by linguists as "leak."[85] Indeed, this was probably a significant reason for the success of English in taking over (that is, language shift), since no clear domain existed—high or low—where one language could thrive. Second, regarding the question of how widespread bilingualism had become in Ireland, the answer becomes academic since it depends on which speech community (national, regional, local) in Ireland one selects.

There are further difficulties in applying the concept, even if scenario 2 is selected and Ireland is taken to be diglossic but not bilingual. One problem arises in how to define "prestigious" domains, roles, and situations of language use. Modern scholarly definitions of what constitutes a prestigious domain will not do but must in fact be altered so that historically specific meanings of prestige and power held by ordinary Irish speakers in the eighteenth and nineteenth centuries are placed to the fore. Moreover, a close look at linguistic domains in action often reveals no clear divide between what is prestigious and what is not. Two examples, both from twentieth-century case studies of Scots Gaelic–speaking communities in the 1960s and 1970s, provide an apt perspective. Investigating the supposed diglossia of northern Scots Gaelic communities, linguist Kenneth MacKinnon observed that the usual markers of "high" and "low" prestige, public and private domains, did not account well for linguistic decisions in his subjects. One instance in particular, the use of English by Scots Gaelic speakers for counting and enumeration, revealed the inherent problem: an intimate and private activity (counting) had been completed using what was supposed to be the high-prestige language (English).[86] MacKinnon's conclusion that prestige mapped poorly onto public and private divides should urge caution on researchers—and this is without engaging in a discussion about the historically determined and ever-changing concepts of "public" and "private" in earlier societies. Nancy Dorian, examining the same Scots Gaelic speech community, further undermined the concept of diglossia by highlighting religious practices centered on prayer (private) and liturgy (public), both seemingly high-prestige activities involving speaking and listening to God. Yet these practices were conducted in Scots Gaelic. As Dorian insisted: "At the time when church Gaelic was still fairly widely used, it would clearly have been incorrect to suggest any diglossic relationship between Gaelic and English among the fisherfolk such that English served as the 'high' language and Gaelic as the 'low' language (as in Fishman's 1967 adaptation of Ferguson 1959), since a 'higher' use of language than the religious use could scarcely be found for this group."[87] One does not have to look hard to find the same problem in eighteenth- and nineteenth-century Ireland. Ferguson, for instance, defined a high (H) language as enjoying a reputation among its speakers as "somehow more beautiful, more logical, better able to express important thoughts, and the like."[88] As has been shown above, a more succinct description of the attitudes of many Irish speakers toward their language, even during its decline, would be difficult to envision.

The problem with the use of the term *diglossia* runs still deeper. Since the 1970s, and in particular through the work of Lesley and James Milroy, linguistic networks, not domains, have been the organizing concept more often applied by sociolinguistics to understanding the adoption and distribution of language variation and shift in speech communities. In contrast to domains, network-based models hold that language choice is based on the social relationship between interlocutors: who was speaking was more important than where a speech act took place. In many twentieth-century case studies—including one conducted in Ireland—a linguistic-network model has better described language choices among bilinguals, thus making it an attractive tool of analysis.[89] Where historical case studies are concerned, an approach like that proposed by Susan Gal in her detailed examination of early twentieth-century language shift in a bilingual town on the border of Austria and Hungary holds special relevance. Although the sources are simply not rich enough to offer a full accounting of Irish sociolinguistic behavior for the eighteenth and nineteenth centuries in the way that Gal was able to offer for the twentieth century, her focus on face-to-face communications and the strength of bonds within the community provides a more compelling determining factor in the spread of one language at the expense of another.⁹⁰ In short, at the very least the application of diglossia to Ireland should not be the starting point for understanding its speakers but rather one of several potential conclusions to be reached after investigation. It cannot be used casually to express the notion of an imbalance in prestige between two languages, as the presence of any hierarchy of domains cleanly denoting different linguistic behaviors in Ireland must be tested rather than presumed. In fact, after casting considerable doubt on the impact of domains on linguistic behavior, the analysis below emphasizes the presence of networks as a better way of explaining the Irish situation in the period under question.

Turning first to the various linguistic contexts for the lives of eighteenth- and nineteenth-century Irish speakers, it can certainly be said that English was far more visible, at least on a national level, within the realms of legal documents, books (although not absolutely), newspapers, pamphlets, and commercial advertisements. English governed the school curriculum intent on imparting literacy in that same language. Courtrooms, police barracks, and parliament all conducted business first and foremost through English. But a closer look at the actual involvement of Irish speakers in these spheres of authority reveals significant contestations of language dominance and examples of Irish carving out a niche for itself alongside English. One place at which this was evident was the numerous markets, fairs, and shops where important economic transactions occurred that transferred local produce to wider Irish and international markets and vice versa. Often depicted by historians as a source of anglicization, commercial transactions would be better described as a series of settings where the two languages met and intermingled. It is true, for example, that fairs provided an excellent opportunity for Irish speakers to learn and use English. The folklorist and first Irish president Douglas Hyde (1860–1949) recalled that an older Irish speaker from his youth had learned English later in life largely through practice at marketplaces.⁹¹ Yet there is no evidence that Irish was excluded from such domains, and much business was conducted through this language as well. As Irish scholar Edward O'Reilly (1765–1830) insisted in 1823, "The business of our fairs and markets is generally carried on in that language; a knowledge of it is therefore at least useful, if not absolutely necessary, to all who have occasions to buy or sell in those places."⁹²

Regional evidence confirms the ubiquity of Irish in the marketplace both in towns and cities as well as in the countryside. Take, for example, a number of accounts from Munster. One traveler, describing the market-goers whom he met on the road to Waterford city in 1810, remarked that "it is a little singular . . .

that some of those extensive pig breeders and dairy men cannot speak a single sentence of plain English."[93] The Methodist missionary Fossey Tackaberry reportedly passed through a market in Skibbereen in west Cork in 1822 without hearing any English spoken. City markets were also frequented by Irish speakers. As Methodist preacher James McQuige noted, "In some of the largest southern towns, including Cork, Kinsale, and even the Protestant town of Bandon, provisions are sold in the markets and cried in the streets in Irish." The Englishwoman Henrietta Chatterton confirmed the same during her travels in 1838; she described hearing Irish among the jostling pig sellers and cart drivers at the market in Tralee, Co. Kerry. As late as 1855, the trustee for the Cork corn market noted that Irish-speaking brokers were necessary to enable transactions between buyers and monoglot farmers arriving in the city.[94] What was true for Munster was also true for Connacht. Shepherds arriving at the sprawling Ballinasloe fair from Connacht in the 1830s were described as Irish monoglots who experienced no difficulty in transacting business. Uileog de Búrca asserted that Irish was still spoken at fairs and markets in the 1870s in heavily Irish-speaking areas like the region surrounding Tuam, Co. Galway, and even in 1898 the national school teacher Patrick Garvey observed that "90 percent buy and sell in the old vernacular" at the country fair in Headford, Co. Galway."[95]

Such a situation was inevitable given that commercial transactions brought buyers and sellers from a variety of surrounding areas, leading to a mixing of individuals of varying proficiency in one or the other of the two languages, and sometimes both. While monolingualism did not prove a barrier to selling or buying, bilingualism (and not just English) provided a distinct advantage in opening trade opportunities and guarding against unfair deals. This was equally true for those whose first language had been English. Patrick Forhan, a businessman and medical student from Dingle, Co. Kerry, and a native English speaker, began learning Irish in 1849 in order to conduct transactions with Irish speakers.[96] But monolinguals did not have to go to such lengths to ensure an advantageous bargain; a trusted bilingual interpreter would suffice just as well. The Donegal Irish speaker Micheál Mac Gabhann (1865–1948) recalled in his memoirs that the *fir mhóra an Lagáin* (big Lagan men)—the English-speaking strong farmers—at the Letterkenny hiring fair in the 1870s would bring along men to translate for them in order to hire the young boys newly arrived from the countryside.[97] Irish monoglots relied on bilinguals to help them in a similar fashion: "One in a village, at least, must be made capable to interpret for those who cannot speak English," reported a teacher in 1821.[98] Eighty-four-year-old Seámus Uí Riagáin, a farmer from the barony of Kiltartan, Co. Galway, born in 1853, told folk collectors that buyers approached sellers at fairs in English "if they were going to buy from you" (dhá mbeidíst a dul a cheannach uaidhit), but that many knew Irish and could switch when dealing with a monoglot.[99]

A similar situation could be found in the shops, post offices, and other urban settings in which commercial activity took place. This was especially true in cities with extensive Irish-speaking hinterlands, such as Limerick, Galway, Cork, and Waterford.[100] Evidence that a Dingle postmaster and his wife, for instance, conducted their business in Irish has survived thanks to a petty sessions dispute in which the couple were accused of cheating customers out of funds received by post-office money orders.[101] Shopkeepers, it was remarked in a report to the Irish Society in 1831, made a practice of hiring bilingual shop boys expressly for their ability to conduct business with Irish-speaking monoglots from the countryside.[102] Dublin papers like the *Freeman's Journal* were known to carry advertisements for such individuals on occasion, as in the call made in November 1844 for a "young man who has a perfect knowledge of the woollen trade, for a house in the west of Ireland," for which "it is necessary that he should speak the Irish language."[103] Such advertisements appear, if anything, to have become more common in later years as shopkeeper and supply networks replaced local homemade goods. A Galway draper named Semple, in advertising for an assistant in 1876, considered "a knowledge of the Irish language and good testimonials indispensable," a preference echoed in a search for a bookkeeper for a "house of business in the west."[104] Applicants presented the ability to speak Irish as an asset, too, when posting situations wanted advertisements, and one hopes that the bookkeeper who mentioned "seven years' practical experience . . . speaks Irish" was able to contact the aforementioned employer who had posted the bookkeeper vacancy only two months earlier.[105] Advertisements mentioning abilities in Irish can be found for individuals seeking jobs as accountants, correspondents, agents, salespersons, grocers, and sellers of liquor and hardware as well.[106]

A similar case for the presence of the Irish language in public settings as understood from the perspective of local communities can be made. Just as bilingual agents, brokers, and clerks found their way into shops and fairs, evidence exists for bilingual civil servants, policemen, and local administrators in public roles. Irish-speaking members of the constabulary in particular appeared in certain accounts of the period, especially in court cases in which the policemen's ability to understand Irish had enabled them to overhear the accused discussing particulars of the alleged crime or participating in a disturbance. A constable Egan, for example, called to testify regarding a murder case, was able to report the particulars of a conversation conducted in Irish between the accused, Silvester Sullivan, and a jail visitor named George Needham.[107] Another constable, a Mayo policeman named Larner, testified as to his ability to understand the Irish spoken by a priest in exhorting a crowd to vandalize an impound lot wall at Gorteenmore, Co. Mayo.[108] The police present at a threatening anti-tithe mob were described as Irish-speaking in testimony before a Lords' committee in 1832, and an editorial defending the force in 1864 emphasized that plain-clothes detectives relied on Irish as a means of ferreting out information.[109] The need to appoint Irish-speaking constabulary members to enumerate agricultural estimates (or to employ interpreters when such individuals could not be found) was emphasized in a report on the working of the land acts in 1887, further suggesting the presence of bilingual police in the force.[110] As for prison administration, awareness of the need to accommodate Irish speakers surfaced from time to time, and increasingly so as the nineteenth century wore on and centralized oversight of such institutions grew. A correspondence between a prison official and a Roman Catholic priest submitted as evidence to a parliamentary committee regarding the Richmond General Penitentiary in Dublin in 1825 included a denial by the administrator of the need to provide religious services in Irish; in 1884, however, another inquiry into prisons revealed the practice already in place of appointing Irish-speaking warders among non-English-speaking populations.[111]

These examples are not meant to suggest that the Irish state under the Act of Union was in any way saturated with bilinguals, or that the presence of bilingual figures of authorities somehow undermined the power differential between officials and the general population (see chapter 5). As a matter of fact, the ability to speak Irish could bestow significant power on such authorities. But to suggest, conversely, that the public realm represented by legal authorities was universally English speaking is to ignore the evidence to the contrary. The same could be said for public meetings such as those for local boards of guardians or for distressed tenantry. An account of a heartbreaking gathering of Ballinrobe, Co. Mayo, laborers on the eve of the disastrous winter of 1846–47 reveals that the distressed locals put their case in Irish to the meeting chair, parish priest Reverend John Morris, and two magistrates, John Fynn and John Lynch. Fynn and Morris, it was reported, also spoke in Irish at the meeting.[112] Such pleas recall an earlier surviving written petition to MP Thomas Spring-Rice, composed in Irish by schoolmaster and scribe Eoghan Caomhánach (1784–1849) on behalf of a Limerick laborer, Sémus Ó Cathasaigh, seeking help for the man and his family following a prolonged period of unemployment.[113] Participants spoke in Irish at meetings conducted under more ordinary circumstances as well. Newspaper correspondent Henry Coulter encountered a wealthy farmer from the district of Clifden, Co. Galway, in 1861 who sat on the "local board"—possibly the board of poor-law guardians or a local grand jury. This man, Coulter noted, was an Irish monoglot who insisted at meetings that an issue be explained to him in that language before he was obliged to cast his vote; indeed, he "rather pride[d] himself on his ignorance of the language of the Sasanach."[114] A similar situation unfolded at a meeting of the Tuam, Co. Galway, Board of Guardians in 1879, which nearly ground to a halt when the chair attempted to pass over the vote of a monoglot member, Patrick Concannon, when he was unable to respond to a resolution under question that had not been explained to him in Irish. Fellow members protested, an interpreter explained the resolution, and Concannon's vote was recorded.[115]

Newspapers have held pride of place among historians as a classic representative of the modern public sphere. But this was not a world sealed from Irish speakers despite the dominance of English as the language of the press. There is definite evidence that common Irish speakers also secured access. Historians of print culture have long noted that the practice of reading newspapers out loud in the eighteenth and nineteenth centuries helped to widen circulation otherwise limited by cost and illiteracy. This was as true of Ireland as elsewhere. Writing of south Cork in 1812, James Alexander observed, "The common people in and about Glanmire, especially those who can read, are, in their own little way, politicians and therefore prodigiously fond of newspapers."[116] The English traveler James Grant noted of the south of Ireland in 1844:

> In these rural districts where the population is too thinly scattered to admit of establishing Repeal reading rooms, the practice is for the peasantry in each parish to assemble every Sunday afternoon in the most convenient place in the parish to hear the Repeal weekly journals read.... The numbers who meet together every Sunday for the purpose of learning, in the way I have described, the progress of the Repeal question, vary according to the populousness, or otherwise, of the district, from fifty to one hundred and fifty.[117]

Adding one small step to this process—explaining the English-language content in Irish—brought world events easily to monoglot Irish speakers. Such a practice was probably common: an 1856 report on Spike Island prison explained that "those who have learned to read [English], and who also speak Irish, very generally translate the subjects and substance of their lessons into Irish for those who have failed to learn to read."[118] Michíl Pheaidí Dheann Uí Chonaill, a Kerry farmer born in 1868, recalled that locals would gather to hear the latest events concerning Charles Stewart Parnell appearing in the *Cork Examiner*, and that a bilingual reader summarized them in Irish; likewise, the Waterford resident "Donnchadh Ruadh" explained in *An Claidheamh Soluis* that his "earliest recollection of my own is that I used [to] sit listening while my mother read the report of the Invincible Trials, and tried to explain them in Irish to the workmen."[119]

Yet another public situation in which Irish was used often was, grimly, the executioner's platform. This location offers a prime example of a place regarded as public in its own time, but which would not make a likely candidate for assessing linguistic roles today. Indeed, it is possible that no domain offered a more regular site for public spectatorship and participation for ordinary individuals in the eighteenth and nineteenth centuries. Historian V. A. C. Gatrell, speaking of English executions in this same time period, has noted that crowds could swell into the tens of thousands. Assemblies in Irish assize towns reproduced this popularity on a smaller scale, as executions offered one of the most anticipated spectacles in the local calendar of events. The enactment of capital punishment in this period involved an orchestrated display of the condemned in a procession that began with a last show of conviviality in the prisoner's cell the night before, continued with the solemn transportation to the gallows, and ended with the victim hanged before the surging crowd. One of the customary, albeit informal, concessions made to the condemned was the ability to address the crowd from the scaffold. Gatrell observes that "although every effort was made to force them to public professions of guilt and penitence, they were not checked if they betrayed that role." In short, the scaffold speech offered to those capitally convicted one of the few opportunities to seek comfort in the face of his or her terrible end at the hands of the legal system—one best delivered in a language that the condemned person preferred and that the crowd, who might provide some support and solace, understood.[120]

Not surprisingly, many chose to do so in Irish. Four men condemned for murder in 1822 "ascended the platform [and] addressed the people beneath in Irish, wishing them ten thousand blessings and begging their prayers in return; imploring the deluded to avoid bad company," reported an account in the *Patriot* newspaper.[121] John Brewer, convicted of murder at the assizes in 1837, proclaimed his innocence in Irish to the "immense multitude who had assembled to witness the melancholy spectacle," before facing the final drop.[122] Also protesting his innocence was Timothy Magrath of County Clare, who "addressed the immense concourse who had assembled at the place of execution, in Irish, and in a firm and distinct voice protested that he had neither 'hand, act, part, or knowledge,' in the outrage."¹²³ Patrick Guiry, convicted in County Waterford in 1839 for conspiracy to murder, "spoke in Irish" on the platform to explain to the crowd that he had been convicted after refusing to turn informer and give evidence.¹²⁴ Another Waterford man, Mr. Christopher, executed for the murder of a bailiff in 1850, prompted astonishment "at the calm, firm, and confident way in which he proclaimed his innocence" in Irish.¹²⁵ Not all claimed innocence. Michael Coy, sentenced to death at the Galway assizes in 1830 for murdering his wife, "spoke to the assembled multitude for a few minutes in the Irish language, earnestly imploring their prayers, acknowledging his guilt and the justice of his sentence, and expressing his forgiveness of his prosecutors and of the world."¹²⁶ A man named Morahan, convicted in Castlebar for rape, "declared himself innocent of a murder for which he had formerly stood his trial, but acknowledged the justice of the sentence under which he was to suffer."¹²⁷ If anything, it was English speakers who needed to be accommodated: Patrick Lyden, convicted at Galway assizes of murdering Mary Lyden, a woman he had married following a seduction and rape charge, had his address in Irish simultaneously translated to the crowd by the priest.¹²⁸

One final domain possessing considerable prestige and yet subject to the intrusion of Irish into an otherwise English milieu was the schoolhouse. This finding is contrary to the position taken in most histories of the period, in which schools have been presented as the primary example of the dominance of the English language in key settings. This has much to do with the development of a historiography rooted in education as the primary battleground in the attempt to retake ground ceded earlier to English. As Senia Pašeta has confirmed for Irish secondary and university schools, education was a primary site for cultural contestations in late nineteenth- and early twentieth-century Ireland and an opportunity to wrest control away from the state in order to provide a platform for educating a new nationalist community—a process similar to that described by Partha Chatterjee with regard to Indian nationalism.¹²⁹ Primary schools were also targeted for reform as part of this broader cultural concern, with the demand to place Irish on the curriculum appearing as a central goal of the earliest stirrings of organized language revivalism. Given these concerns, it is no surprise that the case against the education system relied strongly on describing the exclusion of Irish from schoolrooms as absolute—especially from the national schools established in 1831.¹³⁰

To move beyond this black-and-white appraisal reveals considerable subtleties. To begin, the teaching of literacy in Irish and the popular memory of learning Irish from country schools and itinerant tutors still lingered decades into the nineteenth century and even beyond, defying conceptions of education as exclusively synonymous with English. A report to the central committee of the Irish Society in 1818 concerning south Munster noted that Irish had been taught in "a considerable number of schools" fifty years previously; in fact, the society initially relied on uncovering the remnants of these teaching networks in order to staff its schools.[131] Folk accounts from west Connemara could recall efforts such as a pay school in Moyrush that had offered Irish instruction around 1800, and in the parish of Clonmany, Co. Donegal, a clergymen in 1814 was well aware of a local man, "upwards of 70 years of age, who teaches the English, Irish, French, Latin, and Greek languages."[132] Visiting Kilkee, Co. Clare, in the 1830s, the traveler Mary Knott noted that teachers taught Irish to between sixty and seventy students in two of the six schools she encountered.[133] Parliamentary reports of the time, discussing conditions prior to the launching of the national system, made clear that in at least a few instances there were schools other than those connected to Protestant proselytizing societies teaching Irish, including twenty-four from 1834 uncovered by Pádraig de Brún, who has looked extensively into the subject.[134] On a less ambitious scale, John Kearns, a Sligo schoolmaster, made a practice in the late 1830s of teaching Irish to "a number of families every night," and as Proinsias Ó Catháin explained in 1873, "There is not a town in the province of Munster that had not its teacher of Irish over 20 years ago."[135] Even in the twentieth century, family memories preserved awareness of teachers of Irish in the early nineteenth century, like Meath resident Phil Lynch, who recalled that his grandfather had been "one of the best Irish and English teachers in Meath, if not in Leinster" at a school "before the Emancipation."[136]

Of course, regardless of any educational past in which literacy in Irish had a place, the nineteenth century increasingly cemented an understanding in the minds of Irish speakers that schooling meant learning how to speak and read English. English dominated the curriculum of both the informal pay schools and the national schools, and parents expected and indeed insisted that their children learn English by attending them. Teachers, charged with the task of ensuring English literacy, employed the pedagogical tools of the day—rote recitation and various forms of corporal correction—to meet this goal. Yet it must be emphasized that the predominantly English-only curriculum of schools failed to keep Irish from passing through the schoolhouse door, in part because it was nearly impossible to monitor the children's language use when they were outside of the teacher's presence. Even a teacher who was most adamantly opposed to any speaking of Irish as a barrier to learning English had to wage a constant struggle to keep children from using it. When Patrick Keenan visited a number of Irish-speaking communities on the islands off the coast of Donegal in 1856, he reported instances of teachers employing parents to monitor students' use of Irish at home.[137] But surveillance was probably of limited efficacy at best. Peig Ní Shítheacháin, born in southwest Cork in 1857, recalled from her school days that the teacher would rely on her daughter to listen in on other students' conversations, only to have the spy apparently collude in the deception:

> Is cuímhin liom ná bhíodh aon bhéarla dá labhairt againn nuair a bhídhimís amuigh linn fhéin. Do chuiread an mághaistríos a ingín féin amach ag éisteacht linn feuch a mbeidmhís a' labhairt béarla, agus do rithfidh sí isteach le'n a sgeul "She's talking English Mam."[138]
>
> [I remember that we wouldn't speak any English when we were off by ourselves. The mistress sent out her own daughter to listen to us to see if we were speaking English, and she would run in with the news, "She's talking English, ma'am."]

Michael Kinneally, a Clare farmer born in 1845 whose teacher had also employed spies, remembered, "We all spoke Irish around Corofin in my rising up. We spoke it at school but were forbidden by our teacher to do so."[139] In any case, not all teachers insisted that English be spoken outside of formal lesson time. According to Párthalán Ó Catháin, a Connemara teacher born in 1815 who had first conducted an informal pay school before coming under the national school system in 1842, students were allowed to use Irish during play time (*am súgraidh*), provided that English was spoken in the classroom.[140]

One of the best indicators that Irish infiltrated the classroom despite efforts to the contrary was the observation by many contemporaries that schools, especially in heavily Irish-speaking districts, struggled to adequately teach children to speak English. The slow progress in providing teacher training, the difficulties in sustaining schools in remote districts, and the constant struggle to keep parents in agricultural districts from removing students from class during the harvest season certainly contributed to the impediments that stood in the way of teaching English to Irish speakers.[141] But as the Anglican vicar Horatio Townsend, writing of County Cork in 1810, remarked, more was involved than simply time in school: "The greater part derive no eventual advantage from their schooling, being recalled at an early age, when their labor can be turned to some account. Mixing then with a family, who speak only Irish, even the little smattering of English they had acquired is soon lost."[142] Hugh Dorian (b. 1834), a memoirist from the Fánaid region of north Donegal who had been a teacher, wrote similarly of the failure of the informal schooling of prefamine times in imposing any kind of all-English front: "Another great disadvantage in the way of a learner in that district at that time was nearly the total want of knowledge of the English language. While at home the language spoken was Irish; on the way to and from school, and still worse while there itself, every word spoken, except what was taken out of a book, was Irish."[143]

Country schools in Irish-speaking regions struggled most to teach English to their pupils, as evidenced by the complaints made by parents about the quality of reading instruction in those areas. This situation carried over from the prior pay schools described by Dorian into the national schools, which evidently enjoyed an equally troubled reputation in this regard. As Ó Catháin noted, "Parents often object to send their children even to national schools which are situated in country districts in which the Irish language is generally spoken, stating as a reason that their children would learn nothing but what they term 'broken English' in these schools."[144] It certainly did not help, as more perceptive contemporaries noticed, that learning involved rote recitations from primers such as the infamous *Reading Made Easy*, with little regard for the acquisition of actual speaking skills. "For [the] several years he was at the National School," wrote a County Kerry teacher for the Irish Society in 1847 with regard to a local boy, "he never learned a word of English; I tried him and found he could not speak a word, though he could read English tolerably well."[145] Reporting to the commissioners of national education in 1855, Keenan agreed that advancement in English was slow going: "When the children go home in the evening they have to unlearn the learning of the day, and speak Irish again to their relatives, to return with Irish only on their tongue to school in the morning."[146] As a later contributor to *An Claidheamh Soluis* in 1900 observed in looking back on seven decades of the national primary school system:

> The language and the nation have both suffered grievously by the exclusion of Irish from the schools. Yet the language has survived this treatment for three generations, because it has been part of the life of the people. On the other hand, the English language could never have been spread by mere school teaching if it had not at its back a large and dominant population using it as the language of their lives.... Cases could be cited of parents who, not content with having English taught at school to their children, also compelled them at home to speak only English, and yet these children have grown up knowing very little English, and using Irish as their natural language, because their surroundings were not English-speaking, but entirely Irish-speaking.[147]

In other words, insofar as social domains in eighteenth- and nineteenth-century Ireland implemented any kind of linguistic hierarchy in which English was employed in formal, public, high-status contexts, it did so in a way that was clearly incomplete, if not subject to outright challenge. Irish speakers were willing to use their language in visible, public settings and were unable (or unwilling) to exclude it from high-status domains.

By contrast, considering the role of interlocutors and networks of speaker relationships reveals a much more consistent division of labor in terms of linguistic deployment. If anything jumps out from the observations made in this time period, it was the often-remarked-upon preference among Irish communities to speak their language among themselves, while employing English to speak to outsiders. Some bilinguals were even distinctly hostile to the idea of using English, according to the Anglican clergyman John Richardson (ca. 1669–1747), writing in 1712, an observation still salient 140 years later when Owen Connellan (1797–1871), professor of Celtic languages and literature at Queen's University, Cork, testified in 1857 that in Munster, "those that speak the English language fluently, prefer speaking the Irish language, that is, among themselves."[148] Consider also the evidence from agricultural and social surveys conducted early in the century by the Dublin Society in order to get a grasp on the economic resources of the country and from the contemporary parochial appraisals collected by the statistician William Shaw Mason (ca. 1774–1853) on behalf of the Royal Irish Academy. These reports have been cited by historians as revelatory for the geographic distribution of Irish speakers and their mention of language switching as evidence of transitory bilingualism before the permanent shift to English.[149] But an alternate reading suggests that an extended, stable period of bilingualism existed in many areas in which Irish functioned as an internal community language and English was reserved for outsiders. In east Kilkenny, according to Mason's respondent, "All the inhabitants of this parish can speak English, but among themselves they speak Irish mostly," and William Tighe noted of the same area in 1800 that although English was "understood by most of the younger part of the lower classes," when it came to Irish, "the common people seldom speak any other language among themselves."[150] In Meath "the language used by the people in addressing each other is Irish, but there are very few who do not speak English well," and "when together, the peasants all converse, and if they have a story to tell, or a complaint to make, they still wish to be heard in Irish."[151] Nearby, in the parish of Clonmore, Co. Louth, "most of the inhabitants speak the English language, but they prefer the Irish among themselves," similar to findings in Queen's County and in County Cork.[152]

Analogous reports were made for areas in which Irish-speaking pockets survived in largely anglicized counties. From Killegney parish in County Wexford, Mason's respondent reported in 1814 that "the language among the peasants, except the Protestants, in their discourse with one another is mostly Irish, but they all speak English."[153] In the parish of Clonmacnoise in King's County, "the general language is English, though they sometimes speak Irish to one another," an observation confirmed by Charles Coote in his Dublin Society survey of the barony of Clonlisk in King's: "The English language is spoken by all sorts; but the peasants, when conversing together, speak in their native tongue only."[154] James MacParlan in his survey of County Leitrim likewise noted that children addressed in Irish by outsiders such as himself would reply in English.[155] Even in the city of Waterford, English "is generally used, but the country people, in dealings and communications with each other, constantly speak Irish."[156] With few exceptions, the observers of this period pointed time and again toward a common practice of switching from Irish to English only with outsiders.

Another strong indicator that communities maintained Irish as an intergroup form of communication was the near-invisibility of the language to some contemporary outside observers. Visitors to even the most heavily Irish-speaking districts—including those who claimed to have spoken to locals—mistakenly believed that Irish had disappeared. Hely Dutton, writing in his survey of County Galway in 1824, claimed that "the use of the English language is increasing rapidly all through the county, but in no part more than in Connemara, and generally with a good accent."[157] This was a dubious claim, of course, given that Connemara sustained the highest concentration of Irish monoglots in the country well into the twentieth century. Indifference to the regions and peoples speaking Irish explains some of this lack of awareness, but such an explanation cannot cover those who had explored Ireland on foot. Both Henry Monck Mason (1778–1858), Trinity College librarian and bilingual advocate of education through Irish, and Daniel Dewar had ready explanations. Dewar observed: "I have always found that in places where gentlemen hostile to this tongue [Irish] assured me there was not a word of it spoken, in these very districts I heard very little English. The truth is, a great part of Ireland is not much explored by such gentlemen; and when they do travel, it is not through the valleys and recesses of the mountains, but along the roads, where they must, at the inns, see those whose interest it is to speak the language of strangers."[158] Monck Mason agreed, noting that "travelers may be deceived by the circumstance that they are generally understood when speaking English wherever they visit; but let them remember that the road, the inn, the market, and the town are just the places where the improvement is to be expected."¹⁵⁹ Such oversight speaks strongly to the vibrancy of Irish as a form of intercommunication, with English reserved to networks of outsiders.

Rare examples describing the actual phenomenon of switching between Irish and English also give greater support to the notion of the interlocutor as a determinant of language used, not domain. A "gentleman residing in the County of Westmeath" reported to the Irish Society in 1823: "English is the language that we hear generally spoken; but I have often observed that when any of their superiors have been present, conversation changed to Irish; and I know that in their private meetings, Irish is the language used in general."¹⁶⁰ Similarly, the traveler Henry Inglis noted on a visit to patron-day celebrations in the mountainous district of Maam, Co. Galway, in 1834 that upon the instigation of a faction fight between two groups at the gathering, "the language which, in compliment to me, had been English, suddenly changed to Irish." The land agent W. Steuart Trench, on a seal-hunting trip with a hired crew of Irish-speaking boatmen off the coast of Kerry in 1856, witnessed the boat captain switch from English to Irish whenever shouting orders to his men.¹⁶¹ Even beggars, a writer for the Poor Law Inquiry of 1835 reported, "apply in English to the better orders for alms; but it is Irish they use to the lower orders, and they always curse in Irish."¹⁶² In each of these cases the interlocutor rather than the domain determined the point of linguistic switch.

Linguistic proficiency may have had some role to play in this, but it cannot explain all of these choices. Many of these same reports in fact emphasize that full bilingualism had been achieved in these areas in which Irish was retained for communication within the community; the residents of these localities, as the travel writer Thomas Newenham noted of west Cork, "spoke the English as fluently as the Irish language."¹⁶³ Rather, Irish continued to serve, even for perfect bilinguals, as a preferred language for communicating within the community, that is, within local networks of familiarity that distinguished insiders from outsiders. In engaging in this practice, these communities used the language to build solidarity and to confirm the same long-standing sense of identity built around not just linguistic but religious and historical difference as well—built heavily, in fact, on the defined sense of identity inherited from the early modern period and transformed by new developments of the eighteenth and nineteenth centuries. As a Limerick priest, Father MacCloghan, succinctly explained it to the German traveler Julius Rodenberg during his visit in the 1850s, there were "entire districts, especially towards the west, where the people, living on wild mountains and in fishing cabins on the flat sea-coast, regard English as the language of the nobles, the strangers, the detested oppressors.... We have other districts about here, from the Kerry mountains to the mouth of the Shannon, in which the people understand just sufficient English to visit the markets and appear before the magistrate, but they revert to their native language so soon as they return to their huts, or kneel before the altar in prayer."[164]

Such a divide was encapsulated by the application of the term *Sasanach* (or in Ulster, *Albanach*: Scotsman) by Irish speakers interchangeably to anyone, whether born in England or not, identified through their Protestantism or their English tongue as an outsider. Describing the Irish-speaking communities of County Clare in the 1820s, police inspector and former magistrate George Warburton claimed the term was in wide use to refer to Protestants, Englishmen, and "strangers."[165] No higher an authority than Daniel O'Connell claimed during his Repeal campaign, when he came under fire for using the term, that there was no other word in Irish to refer to Englishmen. As O'Connell explained at an 1843 meeting of the Loyal National Repeal Association:

> During the struggle for Catholic emancipation the expression was very frequently used, and, singular to remark, there was no other expression in the Irish language whereby an Englishman could be designated except by styling him a "Saxon." There was no other Irish for an Englishman and it also implied the idea of the person in allusion to whom it was used being a Protestant. It meant both an Englishman and a Protestant, and nothing could exceed the surprise of some of his huntsmen when they found that an Englishman, or "Saxon," who came on a visit to him at his country residence, was not a Protestant, but an English Catholic gentleman. They called him the Catholic Sassenagh, the Irish of which meant Protestant Catholic.[166]

These terms—Saxon, Scots, Sasanach, Albanach—were linguistic as much as national in their scope. As Edward Wakefield observed in 1812 of the inhabitants along the coast of Donegal, most "do not know a word of English, which they call Scotch," a finding echoed by the Englishwoman Charlotte Elizabeth when visiting Letterkenny in Donegal in 1844.[167] Irish-born English speakers were also susceptible to the label, according to the German traveler Johann Kohl, who noted in 1844 than Leinster residents were called "Saxons" in Connacht in part because of the prevalence of English in the east.[168] Sensitivity toward, and awareness of, terms like *Sasanach* and *Albanach* still registered as late as 1901, when Earnán de Siúnta, an Irish-speaking Protestant from Mayo who wrote under the penname "An Buachaillín Buidhe," defended his support for the language in a letter to *An Claidheamh Soluis*:

Cuirthear "Albanaigh" ar mhuinntir mo chreidimh-féin i gConnachtaibh, & cuirthear "Sasanigh" orra i gCúige Mumhan & is fíor an sgéal é. Is Gaill iad go léir, acht corrcheann aca amháin. Is i Sasana amháin atá dúil & spéis a gcroidhe, & ní'l spéis aca ins an tír bhuicht so, ná i rud ar bith bhaineas le fíor-náisiuntacht na hÉireann ... Is mór an truagh sin, acht do b'fhéidir, má's é toil Dé, go dtiocfaidh an lá áthasach ann fós, a mbéidh Gaedhil & Gaill ag oibriughadh gualainn ar ghualainn le chéile.[169]

[It is true people of my faith are called *Albanachs* in Connacht, and *Sasanachs* in Munster. They are all foreigners, except the odd one. The desires and interests of their hearts are with England only, and they have no interest in this poor country here, nor in anything that deals with the true Irish nationality.... It is a great pity, but perhaps, God willing, the happy day will yet come, when Gael and Gall will work shoulder to shoulder together.]

Although eager to move beyond the concepts of "native" and "foreigner" given his own knowledge of Irish at a time when language revival had moved to the center of nationalist discourse, the contributor remained aware of older religious- and politically based understandings of insider and outsider, and indeed still saw them as relevant in his own time.

That Irish retained such a revered status as the language of insiders after bilingualism became common emphasizes its deeply embedded status within its communities even after language shift was well under way. Still considered the language of learned scholarship, of Catholicism, and of common oppression at the hands of English-speaking outsiders, Irish competed openly with English in high-status domains. Although aware of the power and access afforded to speakers of English, bilinguals' choice of language was more often dictated by their relationship to their audience than by incompatibility with certain settings. How long the language commanded this status would have differed from parish to parish, and from decade to decade as the number of English monoglots increased. Eventually, as in the recollection made by Douglas Hyde in 1884 about his youth in County Roscommon, the ties of communication needs between Irish speakers were broken in deference to English monoglots:

Is minic chonnaic mé, má tá aon duine ann san bhparáiste gan Gaeidhlig, labhóraidh uile dhuine Beurla nuair a bhfuil seision 'nna bh-fiadhnuise, acht má tá fear nach labhras acht Gaedheilg ann, labhóraidh siad beurla go minic ann a fhiadhnuise-sion, agus rud aon rud a bheir conghnamh do bhás na Gaedheilge.[170]

[Often I saw, if there was anyone in the parish without Irish, everybody would speak English when they were in their presence, but if there was a man who only spoke Irish there, they would often speak English even in his presence, and little by little it contributed to the death of Irish.]

And even where Irish remained strong, as will be seen in the next two chapters, regional linguistic identities and contact with English brought complications to this binary picture. Nevertheless, it must be remembered that the use of Irish for intimate social relations persisted into the twentieth century and beyond. As Denis Gallagher, a national school teacher from Achill, Co. Mayo, testified in 1903, "we speak English only when we meet strangers or when we are at school."[171]

Peasant Etymologies

IN 1939 THE FOLK COLLECTOR Seán Ó Flannagáin interviewed locals of the parish of Tulla, in east County Clare, about the names of fields, gardens, and lakes in the area. Although born less than thirty kilometers away in Gort, Co. Galway, just across the Clare-Galway border, Ó Flannagáin marveled at the number of Irish-language place-names known only to locals—including English monoglots—for virtually every little rock and agricultural feature, and he took great care to note the meaning of names as understood by his respondents in addition to their variations in pronunciation. Speaking with James Meany, a farmer born in Glendree in 1883, Ó Flannagáin learned that a garden known as *garrdha na h-igine* was alternately pronounced as *garrdháin na h-igine* and was "supposed locally to mean Quigney's Garden." Locals also had a specific word for fields "shaped like a person's thigh," namely *más*, a word for the human anatomical feature that had been co-opted for topographical purposes. Many names also had a story attached to them about local events and personalities, as in Meany's explanation of the lake known as *locháin a cholltair* (Mod. Ir.: *coltar*, a plough colter): "A poor man's cow was drowned in Lochán a Cholltair, and the Good People had a hand in her. Father Foley—a native of Gleann Draoi—was PP [parish priest] of Tulla at the time. When he heard of the poor man's loss, he came, blessed the coulter of a plough, and threw it into Lochán a Cholltair and remarked, 'Nothing will ever be drowned in Lochán a Cholltair again.'"[1] Such place-name lore could be found frequently in Ireland and was common enough elsewhere to have regularly appearing features identifiable by modern folk scholars, including single, recurring plot motifs and the purpose of providing an explanation for names that would otherwise lack meaning other than as a spatial referent.[2]

Ó Flannagáin's finds serve as a reminder that Irish was inscribed by its speakers on their surrounding landscape and that this language, expressed both in place-name and lore, was made local by differences in pronunciation and shared meaning. This localism was bolstered by a more general presence of dialects within the Irish-speaking community, a fact that served to create an alternate conception of Irish-speaking identity driven not by a binary divide with an English-speaking "other" but by a language-established localism. Thus, the meta-geography of an Irish-speaking Ireland sharing a common history of dispossession and Catholicism provided only one of many paradigms in popular understandings of self and community. Ireland could also be understood as a collection of provinces, counties, parishes, townlands, and even more refined distinctions leading in increasingly localized directions toward the individual and his or her immediate vicinity. The Irish language played a significant role in settling the frontiers of these smaller geographical areas in two interrelated ways: through its speakers' recognition of dialect and through onomastic lore.

Linguists classify Irish into three main isoglosses, or areas of common dialect, that roughly correspond to the three provinces out of the four in which it is still spoken. These isoglosses include a southern or Munster dialect, a western or Connacht dialect, and a northern or Ulster dialect, an arc of gradual change that can be roughly traced from south to north and continuing past northeast Ulster to the Isle of Man and Scotland.[3] The precise geographical extent of each isogloss has often been a subject of debate among linguists, and scholars emphasize that these linguistic divisions have been subject to continual modification, but the basic differences in pronunciation and vocabulary that characterize each region have been well documented.[4] As important as this linguistic work has been, however, the focus here will be on the perceptions of Irish speakers themselves of dialect difference rather than on the objective boundaries of isoglosses as established by dialectologists. In this regard, the concepts of iconization and erasure as proposed by the scholars Judith Irvine and Susan Gal have a particular relevance. Relations between linguistic forms and social identities, Irvine and Gal note, are constructed by speakers for their own purposes, so that linguistic features are said to reflect social differences that are in fact contingent rather than inherent (iconization), while other linguistic features may be rendered invisible so as to conceive of a given population as culturally homogenous (erasure).[5] Both of these tactics, and particularly the first, were in play among eighteenth- and nineteenth-century Irish speakers, who often identified subtle distinctions in language that served to closely tie individuals to specific regions and communities. In recognizing these speech-driven differences, Irish speakers were no different than any other language community, including that of Welsh speakers, which drew similar linguistic boundaries.[6]

Nowhere was evidence of this localism better revealed than in the records of the Ordnance Survey, the nineteenth-century body most closely concerned with Irish names of place and with the complexities of affixing them to the landscape. Initiated in 1824 under a select committee chaired by Irish MP Thomas Spring-Rice, the Ordnance Survey of Ireland was primarily conceived as a means of improving the accuracy of tax valuations by making a detailed cartographic survey of Ireland on a scale of six inches to the mile. The Irish project was particularly vibrant in that it incorporated a memoir project and a specially convened topographic team with Irish-language expertise in order to provide not only surveys and maps but also published information on the geology, economy, population, artifacts, and ancient sites of historical interest found in the course of the survey. The devotion of the Ordnance Survey topographic team to place-name etymology and its willingness to solicit information about those names from locals ensured that issues surrounding pronunciation and meaning figured heavily in the endeavor. This interest in deciphering the significance of names arose out of the uniquely bilingual situation in Ireland: the maps produced by the Ordnance Survey were intended for an English-speaking audience, but the majority of place-names to which it referred originated in the Irish language. This created a challenge for a survey interested in both accuracy and consistency in depicting those names while making them legible or accessible to English readers. Thus, the individual placed in charge of the Irish Ordnance Survey, Thomas Colby (1784–1852), had familial connections to Wales and lived there in his youth—an experience that may have contributed to his attentiveness to the language issue when he went on to direct Survey work in Ireland, and the topographic team included some of the most qualified Irish scholars of the period—Edward O'Reilly, John O'Donovan (1806–61), and Eugene O'Curry (1794–1862)—in order to help research place-names and apply some kind of orthographic discipline to the mapping system.[7]

In placing the work of the Ordnance Survey within the context of previous and ongoing surveys of England, Wales, Scotland, British North America, and India, historians have rightly characterized the Irish Ordnance Survey as an essential aspect of larger imperial initiatives to gather information and statistics—that is, to know the landscape.[8] However, this scholarship has tended to overplay the role of the survey in enacting translation and anglicization, resulting in an overemphasis on the propriety of representing Irish words in English orthography.[9] As a result a more relevant issue has not received its due: the fundamental differences between the object of the survey in establishing a fixed, orthographically standard, and cartographically depicted landscape (whether in the Irish or English language) and the unfixed, variable, and largely non-cartographic conceptions of place of the local Irish population that the surveyors solicited for pronunciation and etymology of place-names. It was in this fluidity, dependent as it was on local dialects and onomastic lore, for which the Irish language functioned as an instrument in establishing the bounds of local identity—much to the frustration of the topographic team. The Ordnance Survey records thus provide a basis from which to consider the interrelatedness of speech, identity, and place.

Local loyalties were central to Irish identity in the nineteenth century, as the ongoing presence of regional rivalries attested. One of the deepest divides revolved around provincial loyalty and the allegedly significant differences between inhabitants of Connacht, Ulster, Leinster, and Munster. Connacht, and in particular the Connemara region, had a reputation for wildness in other parts of Ireland. "In Leinster," one English visitor noted in 1843, "hell and Connaught are terms synonymous, and the dwellers among these wild districts are looked upon as something out of the pale of civilisation."[10] Asenath Nicholson was made aware of these distinctions by the innkeepers and cottagers she visited in the late 1840s: "I found that the district of Connemara, through all Ireland, was considered as a distinct item altogether. This people are pointed out to strangers as the Americans would point you to the wildest tribes of their Indians."[11] A widely circulated set of song verses found in Irish-language manuscripts and print sources in the late eighteenth and early nineteenth centuries, occasionally given the title "Moileamh na gCeithre Chúige" ("Praise of the Four Provinces"), extolled the respective virtues of each of the four provinces, highlighting their most noted qualities of hospitality, good cheer, and genealogical pedigree. The explicitly competitive context for this piece was evident in the introduction to the verses given by Muiris Ó Gormáin (d. 1794), the eighteenth-century Dublin scribe from County Monaghan, in an undated manuscript. Ó Gormáin framed the verses with a story about four old women who go to a mill to process their grain but are asked by the miller to praise each of their respective provinces so that he can decide which of the women would be allowed to mill first.[12] Provincial differences even made their way into the institutional politics of the Catholic Church, as competition for church resources and places in continental colleges pitted members of both the secular and regular clergy of the four regions against each other.[13]

Such rivalries were sharpened in spaces where intermingling occurred, such as fairs and fields, especially as internal migration for seasonal agriculture work and to seek jobs in cities increased. A study of prefamine mobility has found that as many as one-third of the sampled population it utilized had changed their county of habitation in their lifetime, and the majority of this group had moved more than 35 miles from their county of birth.[14] Migratory harvesting reached a peak in the first decades of the nineteenth century, leading to tensions and often violence when workers—especially nonlocal "strangers"—sought scarce jobs and competed with locals for their livelihood.[15] Similar conflict was heightened at fairs because regional origins often coincided with respective roles of buyer and seller, as when western cow and sheep breeders transacted business with the big cattle men of the midlands. In such instances, even dress could serve to mark difference. An observer at the Ballinasloe fair in 1835 noted that Connachtmen, clothed in dark brown and arriving to sell, would jeer at their Leinster buyers, dressed in light gray frieze, who "look[ed] upon themselves," even when laborers, "as much superior to the Connaught men, whom they always slight, and attempt to turn to ridicule."[16] Tellingly, provincial rivalries continued overseas where Irish emigrants, abruptly thrown into close proximity, still recognized differences based roughly around a north-south and east-west axis. Evoked through terms like "far down," used to describe northerners, labor conflicts centering on competition for canal and railway employment revealed the often violent intensity of these geographic loyalties.[17] Micheál Mac Gabhann, an Ulsterman who traveled extensively in the United States in the late nineteenth century, recalled one such encounter with a Connachtman that ended in physical confrontation: "Ba é an t-ainm a bheireadh na Connachtaigh ar mhuintir na contae seo thall ansiud na 'Far-Downs' agus nuair a chuir mise eisean san abhainn deirimse leatsa gur chuir mé 'far down' é!" (The name that the Connachtmen used to give the people of this county who were over there was "Far-Downs," and when I put that man in the river I tell you that I put him "far down!").[18]

Within larger provincial differences Irish men and women recognized finer distinctions based on county, parish, and townland. In the districts comprising the northern region of Donegal, for example, those living in the Fánaid, the peninsula located on the northeastern edge of the barony of Kilmacrenan, were reported in 1835 to consider the residents of the Inishowen region on the opposite shore of Lough Swilly as "debased and demoralised." The inhabitants of the Fánaid, for their own part, were considered a "rude people" by outsiders—even by residents of the towns of Milford and Rathmullan, located at the southern edge of the same peninsula.[19] Understandings of regional differences had little to do with marked, official boundaries and everything to do with perceptions of what characteristics distinguished local residents as opposed to outsiders. Attempts by surveyors to determine local boundaries, for instance, ran aground on the complexities of these distinctions, as in this report, also from Donegal:

> It is impossible to get the country people to agree upon the extent of any of these local territories, some making them too small, others too large. The most strange inconsistencies are had recourse to, by the natives of small villages to the outside limits of these local territories. The town of Letterkenny is in the middle ... of Glensoolie, and yet the inhabitants deny that they are Glensooliemen, that appellation being applied only to the wild yet distilling inhabitants of that glen from Scarve Sollus to the source of the river; the inhabitants of Carrickeen are not Laganmen in their own conceit, though they are always so styled by their more western neighbours.[20]

So central was local identity that there were country dwellers who did not know their county of residence, as evident by the witness from Erris who was reportedly unable to identify County Mayo as his home to the judge at trial.[21]

Language played a major role in determining these boundaries in Ireland. Once again, Irish speakers identified differences in their speech first and foremost on a provincial basis. As John Corrydon, a Kerry Irish speaker, put it when giving testimony at a Fenian trial in 1867, "I would give a good guess as to the province from which a person speaking Irish came from his accent."[22] An awareness of these dialect differences was on display in a poem by the Limerick-born Eoghan Caomhánach, composed, according to a note in the margin of the manuscript, on New Year's Day, 1829. Written by Caomhánach in reference to a slight he had received from a Galway priest who had rescinded a promise of a teaching post, the poem mocked the speech of the clergyman by accentuating at the end of each line his pronunciation of words such as *gnóthaidh, taithaidh,* and *staraidh,* which would have been provided with an extra syllable in the Munster Irish of the author: *gnóthaidhe, taighaidhe, staraidhe.*[23] Hence, almost the entirety of the twenty-six-line poem revolved around the rhyming of glaringly "mispronounced" Connacht speech.

Proverbs reinforced the respective merits of each provincial dialect of Irish, as in an often-repeated comparison of the various ways of saying the word "potato," which was pronounced *fataí, prataí, potátaí,* or *tataí,* depending on one's place of origin. Amhlaoibh Ó Súilleabháin recorded one such version of this adage in his diary in 1827: "Bheadh tataí nighte bruithte ite ag Conachtaoi, an fhaid bheadh Laigheanach ag radh potátaoi" (The Connachtman would have a *bhataí* washed, boiled, and eaten in the time a Leinsterman would say *potátaí*).²⁴ In a west Galway version it was two women from Connacht and Munster who argue over the correct form of the word: "Dubhairt an bhean Chonnachtach go mbeadh na fataí nighthe, bruithte, is ithte aici fhéin chúns bheadh an bhean eile a' rádh 'prátaí'" (The Connacht woman said that she could wash, boil, and eat a *fataí* before the other woman could say *prátaí*).²⁵ A saying comparing the accents of the four provinces that had been in circulation from at least the late sixteenth century likewise favored one province over the others, as in this version collected in the 1880s in County Galway:

Tá blas gan ceart ag an Muimhneach,
Tá ceart gan blas ag an Ulltach,
Ní'l ceart nó blas ag an Laighneach,
Tá ceart agus blas ag an gConnachtach²⁶

[The Munsterman has the right accent but wrong speech
The Ulsterman has the right speech but wrong accent
The Leinsterman has neither the right speech nor the right accent
The Connachtman has both the right speech and the right accent]

It is unclear whether this was actually a popularly known saying among native speakers, as surviving versions tended to crop up in chronologies and printed sources where they were likely repeated from earlier writers. The phrase appeared in Richard Stanihurst's writings, for instance, and again in Peter Lombard's *De Regno Hiberniae Commentarius* (1632) and Richard Cox's *Hibernia Anglicana* (1689).²⁷ Nevertheless, John O'Donovan, who also repeated this phrase in his 1845 grammar, noted that it was at that time "current in most parts of Ireland," suggesting that it did indeed circulate in the Irish-speaking community.²⁸

Recognized dialect variations between the provinces ranged from slight differences in phonology and morphology to fundamental distinctions in semantics. Commenting on a song that he was submitting for publication in the *Nation*, an anonymous Irish scribe remarked in 1844 that Munster speakers often added a third syllable to words like *calma* (brave), pronouncing it *calama*—"improperly," the scribe added.²⁹ The Cork-born Robert King (1815–1900), later appointed a Protestant curate in the area of south Londonderry and northern Tyrone, was amazed by the differences in the Ulster dialect of the north, particularly their unique pronunciations of basic prepositions and variations in verb endings.³⁰ The amateur linguist Charles Percy Bushe (ca. 1829–98), assembling a glossary of Irish words in 1886, recorded that *diabhal* (devil) was pronounced "dhioul" in Connacht but "dhowl, dheel, or dhowk" in Munster, and he remarked on the provincial differences in the word used for the language itself: *Gaedhilge, Gaedhilinn,* and *Gaedhilic*.[31] Patrick Lynch (1754–1818), a native Munster Irish speaker born in County Clare, observed semantic differences in the words *macánta* and *cneasta* between Connacht and the rest of Ireland: "It is curious to observe that while in Munster, Leinster, and most parts of Ulster, the word *macánta* signifies honest, and *cneasta*, mild; in Connnaught their acceptation is quite the contrary, as among the people of that province *macánta* signifies mild, *macántact* mildness and *cneasta, cneastacht*, honest, honesty, &c."[32] Not surprisingly, such variety could hinder understanding when speakers intermingled. Mac Gabhann reported that he and his fellow Ulstermen could make out the Irish of Connacht speakers but he had real difficulties initially with the Munster dialect that he encountered while traveling in Alaska in the 1890s:

> Tá cuimhne mhaith agam ar oíche amháin gheimhridh a bhí muid inár suí thart sa chábán s'againne. Bhí muid scaifte mór ann—daoine as achan chearn d'Éirinn. Tá mé ag fágáil go rabh scór uilig istigh agus déarfainn nach rabh os cionn ceathrair den scór sin nach rabh tuigbheáil acu ar an Ghaeilg, agus Gaeilg a bhíthear a labhairt. Cha rabh sé deacair againne Gaeilg na gConnachtach a thuigbheáil ach chuireadh muintir uachtar na hÉireann cruaidh go leor orainn in amannaí. Mar sin féin, d'éirigh muid comh cleachtaithe leo fá dheireadh agus nach rabh moill ar bith orainn iadsan a thuigbheáil comh maith le duine.[33]
>
> [I remember well one winter night when we were sitting around in our cabin. We were a big crowd—people from every corner of Ireland. I'd say there would have been about twenty in all inside, and I would say that there were not more than four out of twenty that didn't understand Irish, and it was Irish that was being spoken. It wasn't hard for us to understand the Irish of Connacht but the Irish of the men from the south of Ireland gave us difficulties at times. Even so, we were able to get accustomed to them at last and we were not prevented from understanding them as well as anyone.]

Irish speakers were thus well aware of such dialect differences and conceived of provincial boundaries as marking out those distinctions.

Provincial linguistic identities were also subdivided in the minds of Irish speakers into smaller regions, further grounding identity in the local. This, at least, was the finding of outsiders who had traveled or had firsthand knowledge of these areas. In publishing his Irish-language catechism in 1742, Andrew Donlevy (d. 1746) himself had observed the tendency of counties and baronies to "differ in the pronunciation," adding that "some cantons pronounce so oddly that the natural sound of both the vowels and the consonants, whereof, even according to themselves, the words consist, is utterly lost in their mouths."[34] The Irish scholar James Hardiman (1782–1855)—a native speaker—pointed out in 1820 that the Irish spoken by members of the Claddagh fishing community on the western edge of Galway city was "pronounce[d] in a harsh, discordant tone," making them "scarcely intelligible to the town's people."[35] Hely Dutton said much the same of the Claddagh in 1824: "Few speak any language but a harsh sounding Irish, scarcely intelligible to the inhabitants of Galway."[36] Patrick Knight observed differences within the Erris peninsula of County Mayo, itself a relatively isolated district perched on the western edge of the county, asserting that the nearby Ballycroy district differed "not only from its detached situation, and almost disconnection from the other part of Erris, but from the difference between its inhabitants in customs, manners, habits, dialect of language, and the aborigines of this part of Mayo."[37] In Munster, "each county has its own dialect," noted one contributor to the *Freeman's Journal* in 1856, so that "in one county the Irish for 'pot' is 'corcan' [corcán], in another it is 'crocan'"—although this same observer also cautioned that such differences were not, of course, insurmountable.[38] Other differences were as much occupationally based as geographical: O'Donovan recognized the existence of what was known as a *bearlagar na saer* ("tradesman's jargon") in parts of Munster, which he referred to as a slang preserving otherwise obsolete words.[39]

Pronunciation varied noticeably within even a very small area. The border between the counties of Clare and Galway, for instance, straddled considerable linguistic differences according to the comments of observers. O'Donovan, in his visit to the parish of Killeenadeema in southwest Galway in 1838, noted that Clare residents referred to its celebrated local mountain as Sliabh Eachtaídhe, while Irish-speakers in Galway called the same feature Slia Bachthe.[40] Such differences long persisted: a century later, Seán Ó Flannagáin visited the same area and noted that residents in the parish of Killanena, Co. Clare, pronounced the name of the village Dubhghleann as "Dú-ghleabhann," whereas "three miles west in County Galway they pronounce it Dú-ghleánn." *Gaineamh* (sand) was pronounced "gainiv" in Clare, but "gaine" just across the border in south Galway.[41] Another folklore collector active in the Swinford area of County Mayo, in speaking with an inhabitant born around 1860, noted that locals pronounced the past-tense form of the verb "to be," *raibh*, like the English word "row" (i.e., a quarrel).

His own mother, however, living just three miles away, pronounced *raibh* like the Irish word *roth* (wheel), in which the final consonant became silent.[42]

Once again, mobility heightened the awareness of these subtle dialect differences, even within what were otherwise relatively uniform isoglosses. Peadar Ó Laoghaire complained about the failure to use synthetic forms of verbs—a particularly strong feature in Munster Irish—among Irish speakers he encountered outside of County Cork. Before leaving Liscarrigane, Ó Laoghaire recalled, he had never heard phrases such as *tá mé, bhí mé*, and *bhí siad*; he was accustomed to *táim, bhíos*, and *bhíodar*. This, he insisted, was a small but important difference: "Neithe beaga iseadh iad san, ach is neithe beaga iad a thagan isteach go mion minic sa chaint" (These are small things, but they are small things that are making their way into the speech very often).[43] A Cork fisherman born in 1869, recollecting for a folklorist in 1943 a trip he had once taken to Kinsale, remembered being struck by the dialect differences in phrases like "Conas go bhfuileann tú?" (How are you?). "Níor airígheas an chaint sin in aon áit riamh ach i gCion Sáile" (I didn't hear that phrase in any place but Kinsale), he asserted.[44] Language could serve as marker in the aforementioned labor competitions pitting laborers from one county against another, as reported by John O'Daly in 1847. Tipperary laborers, he claimed, displeased at the competition from Kerry *spailpíní*, converged on the houses of farmers who employed such laborers, confronted the sleeping migrants, and made them pronounce the word *gabhar* (goat). Those who pronounced it in a Kerry accent would be intimidated into leaving the area.[45]

Irish therefore served to situate speakers within a specific geographic identity that was not just national but local. Dialects of the language could be very subtle to identify, but they nevertheless indicated a world of difference to Irish speakers, who recognized contrasts between inhabitants of the four provinces as well as between communities originating in various sub-divisions of these larger regions. But the role of language in marking the bounds of the local did not stop there. Irish speakers recognized far more refined distinctions between locations based not just on abstract notions of "parishes" or "counties" but also on a closer interpretation of the landscape itself. Onto this landscape, the Irish language was used to imprint names of place and other signifiers that told a complete story of the area and served to distinguish a shared membership in the local community.

The late twentieth-century geography of the townland of Kilgalligan, Co. Mayo, which was extensively studied by the folklorists Séamas Ó Catháin and Patrick

O'Flanagan in the 1970s, serves as a vivid entry point for understanding how landscape and language intermingled in nineteenth-century Ireland. Located in the extreme northwest corner of the Erris region, Kilgalligan, like much of this part of Mayo, was characterized by low population density and relative isolation. Nevertheless, Ó Catháin and O'Flanagan were able to record 805 place-names from among the eighty-five people living on the 852 acres of the townland—most of them from a handful of informants. The place-names encompassed a variety of different types, with varying relationships to the landscape and to the history of the local community. Ó Catháin and O'Flanagan identified seven main categories of names. Toponyms included all names that referred to natural features, such as rivers, reefs, bogs, cliffs, and rocks. Another large number of place-names originated in the "cultural landscape" of the area, including names referring to houses, ditches, fields, and other features that had been created or altered by human hands. Place-names based on the supernatural referred to areas associated with fairies, cairns, and locations considered haunted. Some names indicated ownership or possession, as in Garraí Mhicín Shiobháin (Garden of Micín Shiobháin). Others commemorated past events by attaching the name of a historical person. Still another set of names communicated the metaphorical significance of a location based on the shape of the natural landscape or a past event, such as the use of the name An Doras Mór (The Big Door) to refer to a cliff face. Last, Kilgalligan residents used place-names based on plants and animals, as in An Crann Critheach (The Aspen Tree) or An Cuirdín Mín (The Dutch Rushes).[46] If the inhabitants of the other townlands of Ireland—there were more than 60,000 in the nineteenth century—recognized even half as many place-names as Kilgalligan, then the immensely detailed understanding of the landscape possessed by Irish men and women becomes strikingly clear.

For the most part such names were not remembered based on any pictorial representation such as a map but instead were created and affixed through folklore. Most were known only within a small radius of any given location. As Ó Catháin and O'Flanagan noted, "The place-names of Kilgalligan have been created primarily to serve the interests of its own inhabitants, and thus few of its place-names are known to people living outside the confines of the townland." The two researchers collected a number of stories that established the significance of place-names and indicated how and why they had obtained their appellations. Some stories could be long and detailed, involving archetypes and motifs common to international folktales, but for many names their significance could be encapsulated in a very short narrative. In Kilgalligan, for example, the name Na Curraigh (The Currachs) referred to a set of currach pens where boats were anchored in summer months and laid up for the winter.[47] This brief and seemingly innocuous description actually offered a world of information enclosed and encapsulated within the Irish-language name: knowledge of the seasonal cycle attached to this location, its purpose in terms of the local fishing economy, and the daily activities of the community. To know both the lore and the significance of place-names was thus to "read" the landscape through language and storytelling, enabling an individual to project membership in the community. Those who did not know those names or folklore were by definition outsiders.

Two other features of the place-names of Kilgalligan stand out. First, as the two folklore researchers realized, although most names were shared by locals, even within the community not all place-names were used or understood by every inhabitant. Indeed, while ignorance of a place-name might indicate one's outsider status to the local community, it might also identify one's occupation, gender, or status within the region. Ó Catháin and O'Flanagan observed that women and children had applied certain names to places associated with activities such as washing and drying clothes that were unknown to other members of the community.[48] Fishermen and farmers possessed varying sets of names that differed on the basis of their distinct interactions with the landscape, with the former knowing more names for features of the shorelines and the sea and the latter being well versed in field names. Thus knowledge of local names also encompassed subsets of place-names that helped to establish one's individual status within the local region.

Second, many place-names were not affixed permanently but rather changed over time. Over half the names from Kilgalligan fell into categories such as historical or cultural names that were subject to the volatility accompanying human interactions with the landscape over time. A new event might create a new name for a location, or, conversely, a change in local activities might render a name anachronistic. A shipwreck or another unfortunate accident might lead to a fresh name for a rocky promontory on the sea, or the transfer of wasteland into a productive farming use might convert a toponym into a name indicating possession. The abandonment of a certain type of economic activity such as spinning or weaving might change the relationship of a place-name referring to a location associated with that industry. Likewise, changing patterns of land use in the nineteenth-century had an ongoing effect, as reclamation of wastelands and bogs, the volatility of tenancy, and the process of enclosure meant constant change in the countryside.[49] When John O'Donovan tried in 1839 to locate an ancient trench in County Kilkenny that he had found marked on a centuries-old Mercator map of Ireland, he discovered that recent enclosures had effaced any remaining evidence of it.[50] Under such circumstances, place-names changed or were forgotten accordingly. Ó Catháin and O'Flanagan used the term "process" to describe the naming of places in Kilgalligan—an apt description to keep in mind in approaching earlier periods.[51]

Evidence from the nineteenth century indicates that a similarly dynamic relationship between place-names, local inhabitants, and the landscape thrived in communities more than a century earlier. Animals provided one of the most common motifs in Irish onomastic lore. The name of the townland of Glenturk, Co. Galway, for instance, was known by its Irish speakers as Gleann Tuirc, signifying "Hollow of the Wild Boar." According to local residents in 1838, the townland received its name from a wild boar that had formerly terrorized the district and, with its tusk, carved out the valley that featured in the local landscape.[52] Menacing pigs featured in the place-name lore of other locations as well, including Gleann na Muice Dubhe (Hollow of the Black Pig), a name for the area of Newcastle West, Co. Limerick, connected by locals to a story about a boar killed by a hero named Darby Dunn.[53] Some such onomastic lore shocked collectors like William Hackett of County Cork, who recoiled at the story of Gil Greine current in 1860 near Killaloe, Co. Clare. Gil Greine, Hackett was told, was the name of the young daughter of a local gentlemen who had the unfortunate habit of "getting out of her comfortable warm bed every night and going down to the kitchen and ... lick[ing] every plate or dish she could find and then going to sleep on the floor in the kitchen." Eager to dissuade his daughter from continuing this habit, Gil's father admitted to his daughter that her mother was a greyhound, leading Gil to drown herself in a local lake. Inhabitants of the area thus applied the name Tuama Greine (Greine's Tomb) to a local geographical feature where the unfortunate woman was said to have committed suicide.[54]

As in twentieth-century Kilgalligan, names in nineteenth-century communities commemorated the misfortunes of locals. A water hole located on a point near Glencolumbkille was known as Poirtín Liath-Bháin, according to a visitor, because of a misfortune that had befallen a man fishing at the spot one day:

> Tháinig an taoile isteach air. Thosuigh sé ag spáncaireacht ag dul suas an poll gur mhothuigh sé bó ag géimeadh ar an bhruach. Tháinig sé aníos an poll, [agus] thug siad Poirtín Liath-Bháin air, mar is é an t-ainm bhí ar an fhear, Liath-Bhán.[55]
>
> [The tide came in on him. He started to struggle to get out of the hole when he perceived a cow lowing on the edge. He came up out of the hole, and they called it "Little Landing Place of Liath-Bhán," because the man's name was Liath-Bhán.]

Undisturbed trees and erected stone piles were also assigned grave significance. An ash tree planted in the parish of Boyounagh, Co. Galway, for instance, was said to commemorate an old woman's corpse that had fallen from the shoulders of its bearers en route to the church. To ward off the bad luck associated with this event, locals had erected a pile of stones around the tree known as Leacht Mhaire Ní Thuathail (Mary O'Toole's Monument) in reference to the deceased woman.[56] The deeds of local Irish saints received equal attention for their role in literally imprinting their presence on the landscape. Natural rock formations, noted marks or impressions in stones, and other geological features, for example, provided reminders of noted events in the lives of these saints. A stone cairn located in the townland of Ballygaddy, Co. Galway, was called Altoir Phadraig (Patrick's Altar) in 1838 by locals, who claimed that Saint Patrick had once read Mass at the site.[57] A stone in the townland of Drumbride, Co. Meath, was known to locals as Leach na n-Glún (Stone of the Knees) because two impressions in it were believed to have been left by a local saint kneeling in prayer.[58] Saint Columcille in particular was believed to have left marks in stones at sites all over Ireland. The impressions of the fasting saint's ribs left in a stone on the Aran Islands were asserted by locals to have been created when his emaciated body was thrown to the ground in a battle with another local eminence, Saint Enna.[59] Columcille's name was also connected to a stone in Templemore parish, Co. Londonderry, allegedly bearing his footprints.[60]

An even deeper understanding of the connections between place-name variability and linguistic identity emerges out of the interactions between the members of the topographic branch of the Ordnance Survey and the informants they relied on to gather cartographic details. Two challenges in particular posed themselves to Colby and Thomas Larcom (1801–79), his fellow officer in charge of the Ordnance Survey in Ireland. First, to establish a single name and spelling, the survey needed to select only one from the many current and previous names in use both in the local area and in previous maps, surveys, and bureaucratic documents such as grand-jury presentments and land conveyances. Once this had been done, there remained the goal of rendering Irish-language names in an English orthography faithful to the original meanings and pronunciation of the words. This meant using the etymology of original Irish-language names—often in conjunction with place-name lore—to assist in determining the best name to place on the final Ordnance Survey maps. Thus Colby and Larcom instructed their surveying officers in the field to cast a wide net in accumulating information on ancient and former names, local pronunciation, and features of the landscape to which they referred in the hope of shedding as much light as possible on the original Irish versions—a means, it was hoped, to more accurately providing a new spelling in English. This information collected in the field was supplemented by any names of places produced by a separate boundary survey being conducted at the time by the surveyor and geologist Richard Griffith (1784–1878). Finally, experts like O'Donovan were set to work interpreting the names that had been collected by surveyors in the form of field-name books that poured in regularly to the Ordnance Survey headquarters in Mountjoy Barracks in Dublin.[61]

It is revealing, however, that O'Donovan and the topographic team assembled by Larcom (including George Petrie, Eugene O'Curry, and James Clarence Mangan) began this research not by turning first to contemporary onomastic lore but by pouring through the growing manuscript archives of Trinity College, Marsh's Library, and the Royal Irish Academy, where they attempted to conciliate the field-name books with the historical and textual sources of the libraries. From a scientific and cartographic standpoint, this search for a documentary history of place-names made sense in that it sought to establish original designations and to eliminate "corruptions" that had entered over time. Such research was conducted in the hope of linking one proper name to each location, taking care to standardize its meaning (in Irish), its pronunciation (in both Irish and English), and its spelling (in English). The project favored names possessing the authority created by years of use and a universally shared meaning. But this paradigm also brought along with it a number of assumptions about the representation of the landscape. It privileged, for instance, the place-names preferred by the literate classes of earlier centuries—whether Irish or English speaking—who recorded those names in manuscripts left at the various libraries consulted by the topographic team. Even more significantly, it meant that if the name of a site varied among locals, its ultimate cartographic designation would still consist of one name displayed in printed form on a map. This, of course, reflected the specific goal of the map, which was designed to give not only locals a common reference when speaking of a geographic designation but also outsiders (including the government and the authorities), who could now understand the landscape of an area without actually visiting it physically.

In short, a place could no longer possess a different name depending on one's relationship to that area, since this would undermine the purpose of a map. To O'Donovan and the Ordnance team place-names were not a "process" but rather a label that the passage of time had merely obscured. When research into written documents proved inadequate on its own (historical records could be incomplete, and the information collected by the surveyors in the field often proved contradictory), this cartographic mandate carried over into attempts to elicit similar information directly from informants in the countryside. O'Donovan himself headed these efforts by taking to the road to hear pronunciations and place-name etymology from local Irish speakers.[62] Examining local accounts of the origin and meaning of the parish names of Killursa, Killeany, and Kilcuana in County Galway, for example, O'Donovan had been told by locals that Saint Fursa and his brothers Eidhne and Cuana had erected churches at the dawn of Christianity in Ireland. Thus the names of the parishes had been derived from these saints. But O'Donovan, who had visited these churches, pronounced them far more recent in origin: "A person skilled in the styles of old churches will, however, at once come to the conclusion that the present walls of Kill-Fursa, Kill-Einy, and Kill-Cuana, are all modern (i.e., Gothic), with the exception of a small part of the western gable of Kill-Fursa, which contains a doorway which is at least, 1,200 years old."[63] Similarly, in the parish of Kilnamanoge, located near the town of Portumna, Co. Galway, residents explained that the word was pronounced Cill na mBan Óg (Church of the Young Women), but O'Donovan, armed with a seventeenth-century written source, contested this pronunciation and meaning: "This is in all probability a modern corruption, as it is called Kilmonology in an inquisition taken in the reign of Car I [Charles I], and I incline to think that it may have been corrupted like Dunnamanoge near Carlow, which has been proved to be a corruption of *Moghna Moshenog*. If the name of this parish be similarly corrupted, it may be inferred by analogy that the true name is *Cill Mo Shenog*."[64] The name, O'Donovan suspected, originally came from a saint for which the church had been named, rather than from the phrase "young women." But whether O'Donovan was correct on this point is immaterial, for his dismissal of these place-names as understood by locals in 1838 in favor of a two-hundred-year-old historical source highlights contrasting purposes between the search for an established and documented name by the survey team and the semantic flexibility of such names in the community over time.

Such indications of fluidity, along with the parochial nature of place-name etymology, pepper the accounts of the members of the Ordnance Survey team detailing their encounters with locals. In the parish of Kells, Co. Meath, a round tower was called a *clogcás* by some inhabitants who understood this to mean a "belfry," but a *claightheach* by others in the same area, meaning a "steeple"—a subtle but notable difference.[65] In County Galway, O'Donovan found that the name of Boyounagh parish near Templetogher was pronounced in three different ways by locals: "bwee-ounagh," "bwee-oonagh," and "bwee-vannagh" for Buidheamhnach, thus making it impossible for him to determine its meaning.[66]

Thomas O'Conor, his young assistant, had similar complaints. In Oranmore parish, east of Galway city, he discovered that the name of a local holy well was pronounced in at least four different ways, again making it impossible to decide on one Irish meaning. "It appears from the various pronunciations of the name of this well, as above given, that there is no fixed sound of it among the people, which might decide the meaning," lamented O'Conor.[67] Elsewhere, the Irish speakers of the parish of Killygarvan in Donegal believed that the name referred to the "church of St. Garvan," while for others it meant the "burial place of the Garvans"—two distinct understandings based on the ambiguity of the word *cill*. To further confuse matters in this instance, older land records supplied a different name entirely.[68] In some cases locals might agree that a place-name referred to a saint, but differ on the identity of the individual in question. In the parish of Kilgeever in Mayo a local church was called Teampull na Naomh (Church of the Saints) by some, but Teampull Phadruig (Church of Saint Patrick) by others.[69] Even at a place as well known and significant as Croagh Patrick, an international pilgrimage site in use for centuries, locals consulted by O'Donovan provided more than one name for the final penitential station located at a short distance from the summit of the mountain. Some referred to this station as Roilig Mhuire (Virgin's Cemetary), but others called it Garrae Mór (Great Enclosure).[70]

Understandably, this ambiguity led to considerable frustration on the part of the cartographic workers and to a tendency to see the onomastic lore attached to place-names as transient or even deliberately misleading. When conducting research on the history of the parish of Aghagower in Mayo, O'Donovan had been told by locals that its Irish name was Achadh Chabhair, signifying the "Field of Assistance." This name, according to the local understanding, had originated in the stations performed in the area by pilgrims seeking relief from bodily afflictions. But O'Donovan, relying on the medieval *Tripartite Life of St. Patrick*, believed that the name had once been Achadh Fobhar, or "Field of the Spring." The pilgrim story, he noted in a tone of annoyance, "is one of those ridiculous derivations which peasant storytellers invent to account for the name in such a manner as to please and instruct their auditors."[71] The meaning of the name of the parish of Conra in Westmeath had been equally "corrupted" by its inhabitants so that it conflicted with the name given in the Book of Armagh (dated to the ninth century): "The huge rock on this hill of Uisneach, a part of which was split and formed into a cromlech, is now called 'the Cat's Rock' from (as the peasantry believe) a supposed resemblance between it and a cat sitting and watching a mouse; but this name is of peasant origin and its Irish name Carraig an Chait is a corruption of Carraig Choitrigi, which it is called in the Book of Armagh."[72]

It was not only the Ordnance Survey employees who looked on the explanations of Irish speakers as inadequate. Antiquarians like Hackett complained equally of "peasant etymologies." Approaching one local about the meaning of the name Kilmeen, Hackett became impatient when the Irish speaker insisted that "-meen" could not refer to anything but the Irish word *mín* (smooth or level). Such individuals, Hackett complained, insisted on their own appraisals of the meaning of words: "Here I must remark that the class of people who are best instructed in the Irish language are unfortunately poorly informed in other matters, and one prevailing feature may be recognized among them, that is, an overbearing contempt for any suggestion as to the etymology of words or names of places except such as they themselves originate."[73] Like O'Donovan, Hackett saw place-names as an unchanging entity with stable meanings external to the passage of time. Thus failures by locals to recognize ancient etymologies and pronunciations were regarded as corruptions—not to mention as symptoms of the decline of Irish-speaking and of "tradition" in Ireland—rather than a result of the living process of naming the landscape.

The parochialism in the pronunciation and meaning of Irish-language names was also indicated by complaints made by the Ordnance Survey team about the sheer number of place-names and their recognition in the community. Originally, Colby had instructed the surveyors to label everything "attached to the ground," a vague instruction that left considerable discretion to the surveying teams. Not surprisingly, the type of place-names deemed appropriate by the survey team for collecting and recording differed from location to location and was subject to the level of detail preferred by individual officers in the field. These variations left Larcom at headquarters with the task of deciding which features should be included in the final engravings. The six-inch maps produced by the Ordnance Survey marked a number of elements, including lakes, rivers, springs, wells, waterfalls, large houses, mills, pastures, woods, orchards, ruins, and churches. For all the detail of the final maps, however, it is clear that a number of names could not be included owing to the volume involved. By the time that O'Donovan took up the task of refining the entries in the name books, he found that the multiplicity of names collected precluded any additional inquiries on his part into more detailed descriptions of local areas.[74]

This was especially the case once he visited those localities and compared the names collected by the surveyors before his arrival to the information being given by community members. O'Donovan found that some names were not recognized by the locals whom he consulted, or were understood by only a small section of the population. The geographer J. H. Andrews, in his concise account of the Ordnance Survey, has followed O'Donovan's own logic in concluding that the discrepancy arose because the original surveyors had incorrectly recorded names of such an ephemeral and fleeting nature that they had no currency in local communities. But an alternate reading is indicated by the evidence of O'Donovan's letters. As O'Donovan himself noted, these names often referred to recent individuals or events and had not been in use for long: "There are hundreds of little names of nooks, holes, and corners in the name books which are not known to the people generally, and many of which I am quite persuaded are arbitrary and called after [i.e., were chosen by] the present inhabitants. Many of these are scarcely worth attention as they will not be retained for half a century. The people deny several of them to be names at all!"[75] O'Donovan was not encountering inaccuracy or a lack of discretion by the surveyors in recording place-names but instead was experiencing the highly localized and chronologically variable use of names by the community itself. Thus the names provided to surveyors differed depending on the person interviewed. O'Donovan had witnessed this phenomenon directly in County Donegal when he had secured the assistance of a "celebrated Irish-scholar," Mr. O'Gallagher, to point out the townland names in Clondavaddog. O'Gallagher, though aware of many names, had "never heard half of the names of the rocks, clefts, holes, waves, heads, or points on the coast," but he recommended that O'Donovan consult with the local fishermen who would know all of them. To O'Donovan such names were "so arbitrary and of such recent imposition that it is very difficult to find any eight persons able to pronounce with certainty what they ought to be." Yet to the fishermen a shared knowledge of them established both their common occupational status and their relationship to the local landscape.[76]

It may be tempting to attribute the suspicion of O'Donovan and other scholars toward folk etymology to a disdain for popular culture, but this was not the issue here. In fact, O'Donovan and Petrie were unique among the staff of the Survey in encouraging the writers of Ordnance memoirs and the surveyors to take such information into consideration.[77] On many occasions O'Donovan, O'Curry, or O'Conor accepted popular place-name lore, although they tended to prefer accounts for which historical sources provided corroboration.[78] In any case, O'Donovan was equally dismissive of the instability of the names applied by the Irish gentry to their manors and estates. He rejected the fashion of the time for applying ecclesiastical names to manor houses in an attempt to acquire prestige; he complained that "it is highly pedantic to call a house erected on a spot where there was never an ecclesiastical establishment by the name of abbey." Any such designation, O'Donovan insisted, was accurate only if an actual religious community had once existed there.[79] From a cartographic perspective such naming practices on the part of the gentry were as inaccurate as the geographical inconsistencies of the humble farmer.

The Ordnance Survey endeavor thus revealed the distinct uses and natural mutability of place-names in Ireland as well as the importance of language and dialect in the interpretation and understanding of those names. Surveyors and topographers insisted on durability, consistency, and the weight of history in determining the choice of names and in fixing labels to the landscape. But such expectations ran contrary to the very nature of place-names, which arose out of collective perceptions of local history, continually shifting local personalities, and in short, the contemporaneousness of the living landscape. Even without such volatility, however, the surveyors and local informants would have been at an impasse because place-names communicated far more than simply geographic location to the residents of the area: shared pronunciations and etymologies defined membership in the community by providing the stories and word derivations necessary to interpret the landscape. In this fashion place-names (as well as language difference) found their basis in the geographically local and the chronological present, reinforcing a regional identity for Irish speakers grounded in their immediate community and in recognized differences between their own speech and that of outsiders.

Bilingualism and the Humor of Language Contact

THE LOCAL AND REGIONAL IDENTITIES built around speaking Irish, however stoutly built on recognized linguistic variations and shared understandings of a common confessional and political history, nevertheless faced a significant challenge in the eighteenth and nineteenth centuries as communities increasingly included not just bilinguals but also members with full fluency only in English. While it is estimated that between one-third and one-half of all Irish speakers knew only one language in the first decades of the nineteenth century, census records indicate that by 1851 only 21 percent were monoglots, and in 1901 fewer than 4 percent spoke only Irish. The 1911 census recorded that a mere 5 percent of those born between approximately 1811 and 1851 spoke only Irish. This figure suggests that even in 1851 those who spoke only Irish predominated mostly among the older generations and that many younger monoglots went on to acquire English in subsequent decades.[1] At the same time, the presence of monoglot English speakers within the confines of a language community, already a fact of life in some areas in the eighteenth century, became more prevalent as the overall percentage of Irish speakers declined. Even for those who continued to speak Irish, English had thus made extraordinary inroads into daily life, and popular attitudes reflected a response to these trends.

Scholars have traced in increasing detail the impact of this language contact on the literary and intellectual output of the Irish-speaking world, emphasizing in particular the ambivalence of Irish speakers who absorbed a variety of loan words and concepts from an English-speaking context even as they remained deeply suspicious of the political changes that they associated with that language's ascendancy.² But given the intimacy of the contact between English and Irish—it is worth emphasizing again that linguistic mixing and divides took place even within single households—a closer look at popular attitudes using the largest single source for such an investigation, the folklore collected in the early twentieth century from Irish-speaking communities, has considerable merit. This source reveals, however, an unexpectedly dominant form used to express the experience of language contact in modern Ireland: humor. Of at least 450 documented allusions to the Irish language that can be identified among the oral interviews collected by the Irish Folklore Commission in the 1930s and 1940s, more than half consisted of jokes and humorous short stories centering on a foolish character whose mishaps in negotiating a world of two languages provided occasion for laughter. The following anecdote, told by a fisherman born in 1869 from south County Cork, is typical of much of this material. It involves an Irish-speaking butcher who, selling pigs at a market with his wife, is approached by an English-speaking buyer:

1

Tháinig ceannuightheóir. Bhí sé ag ceannach na muice uaidh. D'fiarthui sé dhe an muar a bhí uaidh. Do freagair sé i nGaoluinn é mar ní raibh a mhalairt aige. "Ah, nonsense man," adubhairt an ceannioghtheóir. Ghlaoidh an fear eile ar a mhnaoi léithreach. "Toir anso," ar seon, "Tá sé ag ceannach na muice uaim." "An muair a thúbharfadh sé dhoith?" ar sise "Nonsense adubhairt sé," ar sion, "agus ní fheadar an muar é sin!"³

[A buyer came up. He was buying the pig from him. He asked him how much he wanted. He [the seller] answered him in Irish as he had nothing else. "Ah, nonsense, man," said the buyer [in English]. The other man called off to his wife. "Come here," he said, "He is buying a pig from me." "How much would he give you for it?" she said. "He said *nonsense*," he said, "and I don't know how much that is!"]

Most of these jokes were cataloged according to the Aarne-Thompson (AT) international folktale index under Type 1699—stories based on a "misunderstanding because of ignorance of a foreign language."⁴

As noted earlier, the use of folklore collected in the early twentieth century as an indicator of late eighteenth- and nineteenth-century attitudes demands considerable caution. But in the case of these particular tales, there is a strong case for considering them as representative of orally circulated stories addressing language contact in the years prior to 1900. First, there is clear continuity between the early-twentieth-century jokes and the few examples that have survived from the nineteenth century. The Irish scholar Robert MacAdam, for instance, recorded one such story around midcentury in County Meath that centered on linguistic misunderstanding about two Irish speakers visiting a town market. In the story, the Irish speakers engage an English speaker in a conversation about local events. Struggling to make out the meaning of the English phrases, the Irish speakers mistake the English word "agony" for the homophonous Irish word *eagnaidheacht* (argue, dispute), creating a comic misinterpretation of an otherwise tragic story of a child's death.[5] A highly popular tale about Irish-speaking card players who use a linguistic ruse to win a hand of cards was also widespread in the mid-nineteenth century: a version featuring the poet Donnchadh Rua Mac Conmara (1715–1810) as the Irish-speaking trickster was known to scholar Standish Hayes O'Grady (1832–1915).[6] Humorous stories about attempts to use English have been found in a string of tales about the adventures of a Connemara hackler recorded in Irish by an American immigrant born in County Galway in 1832.[7] Douglas Hyde encountered a number of such stories when he collected oral source material in the last decades of the nineteenth century in Galway and Mayo, and he identified a Leinster story about the stupidity of Connacht migrant laborers in a Meath manuscript written by Peadar Ó Gealacáin in 1851.[8] The language revivalist David Comyn (1854–1907) published an example in 1880 featuring a woman who speaks in overly literal broken English, presumably taken from popular sources, while a Gaelic League publication of folk tales published in 1901 included several such jokes, also of a popular provenance.[9] Similar anecdotes heard in Scotland in the 1860s featuring Scots Gaelic speakers help corroborate the pre-1900 provenance of this oral material.[10]

Moreover, the majority of these stories, as with the work of the Folklore Commission in general, were collected from older men and women who were born in the nineteenth century and had thus acquired many of their oral tales at that time. Unlike personal observations on the language, which were subject to dramatic change (especially after the first quarter of the twentieth century) along with the status of Irish in the general population, jokes, because more akin to the typical formulaic techniques of storytelling, would have been more resistant to variation over time. Certain plot details, for example, imply that the stories found in the twentieth-century folklore collection were more strongly associated with the nineteenth century: references abound to Daniel O'Connell (1775–1847), the Battle of Trafalgar (1805), the construction of London Bridge (rebuilt in 1831), Queen Victoria (1819–1901), and the second Boer War (1899–1902). The same conclusion is suggested by references to datable features like "peelers" (members of the Irish police force established by Sir Robert Peel), dispensary doctors, and emigrant letters from abroad, all aspects of Irish life appearing—or becoming more prominent—in the nineteenth century.[11]

Although the AT 1699 stories have not been the subject of an extended investigation, the folklorists Séamas Ó Catháin and James Stewart did take note of them in the 1970s by tracking versions of certain tales and identifying a number of key features of the genre.[12] More recently, Liam Mac Mathúna has highlighted their linguistic complexity as part of his detailed study of code mixing and bilingualism in Irish literature and folklore.[13] Among key findings, Ó Catháin keenly observed that some of the Irish tales depended on highly localized pronunciations of both Irish and English for their humor, thus limiting their circulation not only to Ireland but also within the country to areas of specific regional dialects. He also pointed out cases of overlap in motif between the AT 1699 tales that focused on language difference and two other types: AT 1698, a group of stories centering on misunderstandings arising from deafness, and AT 1697, which refers to a specific international tale known as "We Three; For Money" that also involved linguistic miscommunication.

At first glance, the Irish jokes appear rather straightforward in their meaning and function. Many of them, as in example 1, revolved around the misunderstandings and broken English speech of Irish speakers. A Galway farmer from the barony of Clare recalled another such story, one that had also been collected and published by *An Claidheamh Soluis* in 1903. It involved an Irish speaker named "Éamuinn a' tSléibhe" (Éamonn of the Mountain), an old man who heads down to the local fair to listen to English speakers in order to pick up a few words of their language. On returning home, he describes his day in Irish before attempting the same in English:

2

Dúirt sé mar seo leofa: go ra sé ar aonach na h-Éille & go dtainic sé abhailí i n-aon chos i n-áirde amháin, nó go dtainic sé go dtí ghabhail-éadain a thighe h-éin; go dtug sé amach a' bórán & go dtug sé isteach a lán caorán, nó gur chuir sé síos tine in' fhíanaisí héin.[14]

[He said it like this to them: that he was at the Éille fair, and that he galloped home until he came to the end-rafters of his own hip-roofed house, that he put out the dried cow dung and that he brought in a lot of small sods of turf, so that he lit up a fire before him.]

Éamonn then translates this same story into English using his new abilities in the language, yielding an absurd result:

"I went to the fair o' the fong," he said. "I came home on the one leggedy high, intil [sic] I came to the fork o' the face o' me own house. I brought out the cow-bread an' I brought in the full ood [sic] of sheep-bread, intil I put down a fire in me own witness."

With its ridicule of broken English speech, this joke seems to exemplify the explanation offered by Seán de Fréine for the decline of the Irish language in the nineteenth century. The Irish, de Fréine argued, had "accepted the ethnocentric Ascendancy viewpoint that Irish was a backward language, and that even to speak it was a positive hindrance to progress."¹⁵ Scholars citing folklore as evidence have understandably reached similar conclusions, arguing, as does Grace Neville, that Irish speakers "had internalised the possibility of a link between stupidity and the Irish language."¹⁶

But when the body of stories found in the Folklore Commission's National Folklore Collection is considered as a whole, this interpretation becomes problematic. Of 186 jokes uncovered here from the folklore collection, 25 percent either featured English speakers as the target of ridicule for their inability to communicate in Irish or else depicted an Irish speaker triumphantly deflecting an insult back onto the English speaker.¹⁷ The most common example of such stories involved two Irish speakers who challenge two English speakers (often soldiers) to a card game and then make fools of them by using Irish in order to secretly win the hand.¹⁸ Similarly, in an anecdote told about Daniel O'Connell, the famous Irish politician debates the merits of the English and Irish languages with an Englishman. The Englishman compares Irish to the barking of dogs, prompting O'Connell to retort by drawing parallels between English and a bleating goat.¹⁹ Overall, 14 percent of the stories involved either an insulted or tricked English speaker, or an Irish speaker who was rewarded in some fashion despite experiencing a linguistic misunderstanding. Another 12 percent made the Irish speaker the butt of the joke but, all the same, included some kind of witty retort that reverses the ridicule (see table 1).

Even in the remaining 74 percent of the jokes, the stories in which the Irish speaker is depicted as the fool, the message conveyed could be uncertain. As the sociologist Christie Davies has argued, verbal humor is often ambiguous precisely because it involves wordplay and texts and can thus be subject to a number of interpretations.²⁰ Consider again example 2. Éamonn speaks in broken English, but the English is actually an overly literal translation of the Irish phrases: for instance, "i n-aon chos i n-áirde amháin," an idiomatic phrase meaning "gallop," is rendered word for word into English as "on the one leggedy high."

This joke may have invited ridicule of Éamonn for his mistranslation, but an equally viable interpretation might have been that English could not describe the basic elements of everyday rural life as fluently as Irish. Rather than a rejection of Irish, the story, on the contrary, might have prompted solidarity with Éamonn for contrasting the expressiveness of Irish with the absurdity of English. This is not to say that an unlimited number of readings of these jokes lay open to nineteenth-century audiences. But the objective in approaching humor, as suggested by the researcher Wladyslaw Chlopicki, should be to establish a limited set of credible interpretations by conducting a closer reading both of the joke texts themselves and of their specific cultural and historical circumstances.[21]

There is a danger in assuming, moreover, that these jokes simplistically mimicked contemporary views denigrating the Irish language in an increasingly English-speaking Ireland. On the contrary, one would expect to find what the anthropologist James Clifford has underscored in discussing dominated communities: authoritative cultural forms are often actively reformulated "in complex, oppositional contexts."[22] Research on the projection of cultural power has provided empirical evidence of this recasting of authority—a "production," in the description of the historian Michel de Certeau, that has a formal, discernible

TABLE 1: Plots of Irish Aarne-Thompson type 1699 jokes in National Folklore Collection

Target and source of humor	Number of jokes	Percentage of sample
English speaker is tricked or insulted, or Irish speaker is rewarded for misunderstanding	26	14
Irish speaker is tricked or misunderstands English but makes a retort that deflects the insult	22	12
Irish speaker is the target of humor, and joke centers on:		
Absurd conversation between Irish and English speakers	40	22
Irish speaker's failed attempt to speak English	49	26
Irish speaker's use of English in the wrong context	15	8
Irish speaker's "buying" English as an object	4	2
Irish speaker's misinterpretation of English words as a threat or insult	26	14
English speaker's misunderstanding of Irish, leading to difficulty for Irish speaker	4	2
Total	186	100

structure.²³ Indeed, it is arguable that once a prominent discourse emphasizing the power associated with the English language came into existence, the use of Irish itself became, by definition, a challenge to that very discourse. If these jokes represented a rejection of the Irish language, why tell them in Irish? An answer to this incongruity lies in the recognition that popular culture does not straightforwardly assimilate the goals and tactics of elite culture. Approaching these jokes as a formal site for negotiation and reinvention of the status of the Irish language provides a first step in resolving this seemingly incongruous and lighthearted popular response to language contact.

In explaining why humor figured so prominently in Irish responses to language contact, it is worthwhile to start by confirming that these jokes were intended to be funny. Humor is, after all, culturally determined, and we cannot be certain about the purpose of these stories without reference to their reception in their own time. Indeed, some of these anecdotes might well seem more cruel than humorous to a modern audience. In one story from County Clare, an old man is taunted by a gang of boys who purposely encourage him to discuss his broken wheelbarrow in English even though they know that his mastery of the language is poor.²⁴ In a similar Galway story an old fisherman's boat is vandalized by another band of schoolboys; the incident leads him to confront their teacher about punishing them. Lacking English, the old man struggles to explain the episode to the schoolmistress, who has only a little bit of Irish:

3

"It is terrible," adeir an mháighistreás nuair a thuig sí céard a bhí i gceist aige.

"Ná bí ag cur an mhilléain uilig ar *Terrible*" adeir seisean, "bhí chuile dhiabhal gasúr acu chomh dona le *Terrible* bocht."²⁵

["It is terrible," said the mistress when she understood what had happened.

"Don't be putting all the blame on *Terrible*," he said. "Every damn one of them was as bad as poor *Terrible*."]

The misunderstanding punctuating the end of the anecdote lightens the mood, but it hardly undermines the tragic tone of the story overall.

It is nevertheless clear that Irish speakers themselves believed these stories to be humorous and intended them as jokes. Tellers referred to them as *scéal grinn* or *scéal greannmhar* (a funny story).²⁶ That these stories induced considerable laughter can be inferred from the humor surrounding the episodes that make up the tale of the Connemara hackler introduced earlier. Among these anecdotes is an instance in which an Irish-speaking rent collector named Conán attempts to make conversation with an English-speaking water guard (coastguard officer) named Murphy, who tries to buy some buttermilk from him. Murphy can understand Irish but not speak it, while Conán struggles to understand his English replies to questions about sightings of the British army in the area. The result is a misunderstanding of the word "nonsense" similar to the joke in example 1:

4

"A Mhurphy," arsa Conán, "an bhfaca tú an tArm Dearg anseo inniu ag pressáil na bhfear?"
 "Nonsense," arsa Murphy.
 "Ní neansa ná nápla," arsa Conán, "ach an tArm Dearg ag pressáil na bhfear."
 "No, no, what nonsense," arsa Murphy, "Fetch me the milk."

["Murphy," said Conán, "did you see the Redcoats here today press-ganging the men?"
 "Nonsense," said Murphy.
 "It's not *Neansa* (nonsense)," said Conán, "but the Redcoats, pressing the men."
 "No, no, what nonsense," said Murphy. "Fetch me the milk."]

There is no doubt that the hackler episodes were meant to be humorous, as demonstrated by the often-repeated description of the response of characters to events: "You could have put a live bird down the throat of every man in the house, as they laughed."[27] Clearly, tellers considered these absurd dialogues and misunderstandings to be very funny.

Ireland was not, in fact, unique in featuring humor in the response to language change. Contact between languages has sparked joking stories for centuries, and examples have been found in almost every national context. Among the staples of the Irish repertoire was the story "We Three; For Money," a tale that, although classified as AT 1697, shares many features with the AT 1699 stories. This anecdote centered on the attempt by three travelers to speak a foreign language by memorizing stock phrases. In an Irish-language version collected in southwest county Kerry in the late 1920s, three Irish speakers learn three English phrases—"We three," "A purse of money," and "Right and good reason!"—by following a group of English-speaking gentlemen and discreetly listening in on their conversation. Satisfied that they have picked up enough English, the three travelers continue down the road. Later, the men come across a dead body and are approached by a local gentleman who interrogates them in English:

5

"Who killed the man?" said the gentleman.
"We three!" said the first man.
"For what?" said the gentleman.
"A purse o' money!" said the second man.
"You'll be hanged!" said the gentleman.
"Right an' good reason!" said the third man.[28]

The three men are then arrested and sentenced to be hanged. This and similar anecdotes have long been circulating in both printed and oral forms for at least six hundred years. One of the earliest examples in the European context appeared in the medieval compendium *Summa praedicantium* (ca. 1348) by John Bromyard, in which it is three Welshmen traveling in England who are arrested for wrongdoing because of their misapplication of English. Later versions appeared in the French writer Philippe de Vigneulles's *Cent nouvelles nouvelles* (1505–15)—here, German speakers try to learn French—and in the *Nouvelles récréations et joyeux devis* (1558) by Bonaventure des Périers, in which it is three French-speaking brothers whose efforts to learn Latin land them in trouble.[29] The motif also appeared in other formats, such as the English jest-book tradition, as in the early sixteenth-century collection of humorous tales known as *Scoggin's Jests* and said to have been written by the physician Andrew Borde. Here, the witty trickster Scoggin teaches three stock Latin phrases to his clerical student in order to enable the pupil to fraudulently receive his deaconship from the ordinary of the diocese without fluency in that language.[30]

Internationally, "We Three" and a variety of similar language-based jokes circulated widely in the nineteenth and twentieth centuries. In the United States, the jokes were told about—or even by—immigrants of Irish ancestry: black communities of the late nineteenth and early twentieth centuries told "We Three" stories about Irish immigrants unable to speak English, while another version about recent Irish arrivals who "could speak only a few words of English" was collected in 1938 from an Indiana woman who had heard it, of all places, from her elderly Irish-born aunt.[31] In Latvia, under Russian control in the 1870s, attempts to teach the Russian language in state schools spawned a story about students confused by a Russian-speaking school inspector. As told by a Latvian American immigrant born in 1886, the joke featured an inspector holding a penknife who asks a schoolboy to repeat a phrase he has uttered: "Povtari" (repeat), says the inspector in Russian, frightening the boy, who thinks that he has said in Latvian, "Paut ar ir?" (Do you have testicles?).[32] British folktales presented encounters between Englishmen and Scotsmen afflicted by misunderstandings of Scots English or Scots Gaelic. In one story an English boat captain queries a Highland counterpart: "Where are you bound for?" To this question the Highlander, referring to his cargo, replies, "Potatoes."[33] Worldwide, AT 1697 and AT 1699 stories about language misunderstanding have been found in virtually every continent.[34]

The similarities in setting and plots of the Irish jokes and the international stories are evident. Spanish-speaking communities on the New Mexico–Colorado border, for instance, told jokes in the 1930s about Spanish speakers bargaining with English-speaking shopkeepers in broken and pun-filled conversations, as in the following example featuring a Mexican man who is sent to purchase gloves from a shop owned by an American:

6

Los cajeros eran americanos y le dice el cajero:
"What you want?"
"Sí, guante," le dice él.
"What you say?" le dice.
"Sí, pa José."
"Oh, you fool!"
"Sí de ésos de la correita azul."
"Oh, you go to hell!" le dice.
"Sí, de esos me mandó él."[35]

[The cashiers were Americans and one cashier says: "What you want?" "Yes, glove," he (the customer) says to him. "What you say?" he says. "Yes, for José." "Oh, you fool!" "Yes, those with the blue thongs." "Oh, you go to hell!" he says. "Yes, he sent me for those."]

There are unmistakable similarities between this story and a number of tales circulated in Ireland dealing with exchanges in shops. In one Irish anecdote the use of the English word "sick" by a shopkeeper is misinterpreted to be the Irish word *saic* (sacks) by an Irish speaker looking for material to make clothes:

7

"Paddy," arsa seisean, "are ye sick?"
"Leóga," arsa Padaí, "Ní ádhbhar saic nó saic atá dhe dhith orm ach ádhbhar léineadh dó Máire!"[36]

["Paddy," he (the shopman) said, "are you sick?" "Indeed," said Paddy, "it isn't any sacks or material for sacks that I need, but shirt material for Mary!"]

India under British rule produced stories similar to the many Irish jokes featuring broken English, as in the story of Kalachand Babu, an Indian staff assistant to the lieutenant governor. This story, published in 1924 from an oral source, featured broken English as Kalachand Babu attempts to serve his master:

8

   Kalachand Babu: "Sir, You Honour—Your humble has Benaresing [coughing]—whole night benaresing—benaresing, no little eye-shutting, Sir."
   Lieutenant governor: "How could you go to Benares and return in a night, Kala Babu?"
   K B: "No going Benares, Sir. Throat, Sir, here—Sir—impatient Sir, whole night, Sir."
   L G: "Oh, you had a sore throat. You must go to a doctor."
   K B: "Sir, Sir—I will eat you, Sir!"
   L G: "Hello! Eat me? What do you mean, Kalachand? How will you digest me?"
   K B: "No, Sir. I will give you a eating [i.e., feed you], Sir.[37]

Likewise, in an Irish example the master is a tyrannical landlord named Ivy whose servant boy, Séamus Bán, innocently insults him through his inability to speak English:

9

   Ceann de na maidineachaibh a thánaig sé isteach agus d'fiafruigh sé connus a bhí sé, agus dubhairt Ivy leis ná raibh sé foghnamh in ain chor. Dubhairt Seámus bán "God keep you so," agus cheap sé go raibh an ceart aige á rád leis mar ná raibh ach beagán béarla aige, agus rud éigin, mar "God relieve you" a mheas sé a rádh.[38]

   [One of the mornings he came in and asked him how he was, and Ivy said to him that he was not well at all. Séamus Bán said, "God keep you so," and he thought that he was correct to say it because he didn't have a lot of English, and something like "God relieve you" was what he thought to say.]

As these examples show, the close connection between humor and language misunderstanding was a very common historical phenomenon, and not just in Ireland.

   If the net is widened to include stories about deafness that share many elements with the anecdotes about language difference, then the international context for the Irish stories becomes even clearer. As Ó Catháin has noted, language misunderstanding mimics deafness in many ways, and it is likely that jokes based on one disability were easily adapted to another. Consider the following Norwegian story first collected in the 1840s about a deaf ferryman confronting a bailiff sent to repossess his house. Seeing the bailiff approaching, the ferryman plans out his side of the conversation and tries to anticipate responses; he guesses that the visitor will question him about the axe handle that he is whittling and about his boat. The conversation is immediately derailed:

10

"Good day, fellow!" said the bailiff.
"Axe handle!" said the ferryman.
"Ah so—," said the bailiff. "How far is it to the inn?" he asked.
"Up to this knot!" said the man, and pointed a bit up the axe handle.
The bailiff shook his head and stared hard at him. "Where's your old woman, fellow?" he said.
"I'm going to tar her," said the ferryman. "She's lying down on the shore, cracked at both ends!"[39]

A similar Irish tale current in the 1890s (if not earlier) featured a man who is both deaf and an Irish speaker. The Irish speaker is selling potatoes at a market when a buyer approaches him:

11

Buyer: "Good morrow, John!"
John: "Selling potatoes I am."
Buyer: "How is all at home?"
John: "Two-pence halfpenny a stone."
Buyer: "How is the wife and child?"
John: "The finest you ever boiled."[40]

Like stories about language misunderstanding, such jokes about deafness have been found in a number of countries, including Spain, England, Chile, and the United States.[41]

Another source lay in the Irish literary landscape itself. Early modern Irish literature, especially the *dánfhocail* verse epigrams, was heavily steeped in puns and wordplay.[42] The mocking of broken speech by upstart lower-class Irish speakers attempting to adopt English speech figured prominently in seventeenth-century writings, as did stories of Irish speakers misunderstanding English. Examples can be found in Seathrún Céitinn's *Trí Bior-Ghaoithe an Bháis*, a seventeenth-century homily on death in which an illustrative anecdote has a group of Munster soldiers travel to England, only to find themselves confused at their lodging house by the phrase "make reckoning" (i.e., make payment). The soldiers understand this as "Mac Raicín," a person. Other instances were known from Irish-language works of the seventeenth and eighteenth centuries, including *Pairlement Chloinne Tomáis* (ca. 1613), the anonymous satire *Lucht na Simléirí* (ca. 1684), another derivative from the previous two known as *Eachtra Áodh Mhic Goireachtaidh* (ca. 1707–27) by Eamonn Oig Mhac Anaosa of Armagh, the poems of Aogán Ó Rathaille, and Seán Ó Neachtain's mock heroic tale *Stair Éamuinn Uí Chléire* (ca. 1710).[43] Ó Neachtain featured an episode in *Éamuinn Uí Chléire* in which a garbler of English (*fleangach an Bhéarla*) arrives at a school to deliver an absurd story in broken English. A possible antecedent for example 2 above, Ó Neachtain's telling has the hero, Éamonn, sarcastically remark that the stranger's speech sounds like Hebrew, and he accepts a bet that the speaker cannot translate his own speech into Irish. The garbler succeeds, demonstrating that his original English had been an overly literal translation of Irish idiomatic phrases.[44] Among the works of Ó Rathaille, "Seanchuimhne ar Aodhagán Ua Rathaille" relates an episode in which an Irish speaker mocks an English-speaking minister's son caught in a tree, disguising the ridicule behind Irish verse and making a fool of the minister.[45] From the opposite end of the ideological spectrum, there was the impact of English literature circulating in Ireland: the plays of Shakespeare contained numerous examples of the puns and broken speech of foreigners—many of them Irish, Scots, and Welsh.[46] Since the plays of Shakespeare appeared more often than any other work in the repertoire of Ireland's fledgling provincial theaters starting in the eighteenth century, this influence cannot be discounted.[47]

These international and historical examples provide more than potential sources for the Irish tales. They also offer important clues as to why language contact elicited humor. In analyzing jokes, most researchers employ variations on the concepts of *incongruity* and language *scripts*—the semantic and cognitive information attached to language and shared by its speakers—as the central defining feature of verbal humor. Borrowing from linguistic theory, scholars have argued that all such humor features the juxtaposition of two scripts that are revealed by the punch line. These two distinct, or incongruous, categories of understanding are suddenly elucidated, thus leading the listener to jump from one meaning or expectation to another and, ultimately, to laugh.[48] In example 3 above, for instance, the understanding that the teacher has expressed sympathy that may placate the aggrieved old man ("It is terrible," she laments) is suddenly punctured by the realization that he believes she has named one of the perpetrators: he does not actually understand the meaning of the word "terrible." The joke plays with two distinct scripts attached to the word "terrible": first, an adjective denoting dread and misfortune, and, as used by the teacher, an indication of sympathy; second, for those unfamiliar with syntactical and lexical usage in English, a proper name suggesting that the teacher is trying to identify a person. Humor is sparked by the jump from an expected meaning to an incongruous alternate meaning of a word.

The notion of incongruity is even clearer in jokes relying on puns, as in the story of the sick man whose Irish-speaking wife sends for the doctor:

12

"How are the bowels?" do cheistig an dochtúir go Gallda.
"Yearra a'dhochtúir, a ghrádh" adeir sí go h-úmhail, "deamhain boul ná sácer agam; bhris an cat iad."[49]

["How are the bowels?" asked the doctor, in a foreign fashion. "Well, doctor, my dear," she said humbly, "I have not a bowl or saucer; the cat broke them."]

The homophonous connection between "bowels" and "bowls" sets up a punch line revealing two incongruous interpretive frames: a doctor inquiring after the symptoms of a patient, and a doctor who is ridiculously asking about a woman's crockery. Puns are particularly efficient in setting up these scenarios because they enable two scripts to emerge from a single word. And their potential is especially heightened when they involve two languages—as in examples 7 and 12 above—since similar phonological units will in almost every case involve disparate linguistic scripts. Given the abundance of homophony in language contact and the centrality of double meanings to verbal humor, it would have been more surprising if jokes had not played a part in popular responses to the encounter between Irish and English in Ireland.

Nevertheless, while this explains the presence of jokes in Ireland, the universality of humor in response to language contact does not account for the specific features of the anecdotes found in Irish folklore or for their function in their own time and place. Earlier jokes featuring language misunderstanding in Irish literature, as in the writings of Ó Rathaille and Ó Neachtain, largely portrayed English (especially as spoken in Ireland)—not Irish—as the inferior vernacular. The versions datable to the late nineteenth century, however, added the ridicule of Irish speakers to ongoing jokes about monoglot English speakers. The humor employed by the Irish-speaking community had clearly taken on new meanings under the different linguistic circumstances of subsequent years in which fluency in English, with or without Irish, was becoming increasingly prevalent. This prompts an examination of the jokes within the specific context of Irish-speaking communities and the significant changes experienced by their members in this period.

On one level the jokes explicitly connected the inability to speak English with a failure to engage with the changes affecting rural Ireland in the nineteenth century. This was done, for instance, in several jokes featuring the difficulties of communicating with an English-speaking doctor. Rural medical needs were being increasingly met in the nineteenth century by professionally trained representatives of the network of public dispensaries established in 1805. By the 1840s the number of such facilities had grown substantially to 650. The Irish system was unique in that it was state-supported and largely designed to serve the poor.[50] This put such professional medical care within the reach of rural communities at a very early stage. For those unable to speak English, according to the jokes, the need to seek medical advice was fraught with the frustrations of trying to describe symptoms and to convey the cause for illness. In some instances a man or woman seeking help for a spouse describes the sickness in broken and profane English: "What she put in she put out. She turn wheel about. She's half a 'grug' in the bed. She couldn't shit nor stand. She's always *tachta* [choking] *dochtúir*," explains one man about his wife in a Kerry anecdote from Dunquin parish.[51] Aside from embarrassment, joke tellers warned of the potential for miscommunication when patient and doctor did not share a language. In one tale the death of a woman's husband brings her to the dispensary only to find that the regular doctor, who speaks Irish, has been temporarily replaced by an English monoglot physician. "Satharn Cásca" (Easter Saturday), responds the woman to the doctor's inquiry about the time of death, leading the doctor to reassert, "Don't mind your *Cásc*, but when did he die?"[52]

Another motif exploited by joke tellers depended on the heightened contact with the world outside of Ireland brought to rural communities by the realities of large-scale emigration and by Irish participation in the newly aggressive British imperialism of the nineteenth century. The direct and immediate exposure to a foreign and English-speaking world ushered in by an emigrant letter from an overseas destination like America was undoubtedly a disorienting experience for some rural inhabitants, and one with humorous potential in folk accounts. In one joke an emigrant who has successfully become a town mayor writes in English to his Irish-speaking sister back home in Donegal. When the letter is read to her, she confuses the word "mayor" with "mare" and concludes that her brother has turned into a horse.[53] In other examples it is the returning emigrant herself who sets in motion the humor rather than a letter, as in the case of a daughter who visits her mother after marrying in America. "Do you have any children?" asks the mother in Irish, to which the daughter responds in English, "I have a pretty little 'bowee' [boy]." "My goodness! You have a little cow [bóín], and God willing, you'll have a calf soon," exclaims the mother in Irish.[54] Other jokes played on the issue of young Irishmen serving in the British army. Most popular was a joke about a Boer War soldier who writes home to his Irish-speaking mother. When the mother hears the letter read to her, she picks up on the phrase "We are now making a shift for Ladysmith" in her son's letter—a reference to the famous South African town besieged by Boer forces in 1899: "Heavens! And he hadn't even sewed a button on a pair of trousers before," comments the mother, introducing puns on the words "shift" and "Ladysmith" (i.e., Lady Smith).[55]

Another situation joke tellers connected to the language issue was that of the Irish speaker in the courtroom. While the difficulties of multiple languages in the courtroom played a central role in setting up humor, few jokes suggested absolute disadvantages faced by Irish speakers. Instead, it was often the judge or translator who was left perplexed. A popular joke from the second half of the nineteenth century centered on an English-speaking judge who overhears a witness make an utterance in Irish. Pressing the witness to translate the statement, he is told that the remark had been an insult of the judge's appearance.[56] In another case an Irish-speaking witness testifies that her attacker followed her from *Cómhartha Mór* to *Cómhartha Beag*, a reference to two local Irish place-names. Confused, and assuming that she means *cófra* (chest), the translator tells the judge that the man followed the witness from "the big chest to the small chest." This convinces the magistrate that the dispute had been merely domestic—that the man had followed her from one part of the room to another.[57] In a story titled "An Gúistúis nár thuig cad dúbhairt fear" ("The Justice who didn't understand what a man said"), an Irish-speaking witness reports to the court that he had observed several men fighting "tré na ceile" (i.e., all fighting each other). Perplexed and believing that the man is talking about yet another witness, the judge adjourns the court because he needs to "hear *tré na ceile*'s evidence."[58]

Consumer goods, which also began to infiltrate rural communities in much greater quantities in the second half of the nineteenth century, likewise featured prominently in the stories. Already by the 1830s, even in the most rural and impoverished sections of Irish society, the evidence shows that consumption of certain products like tobacco, sugar, and tea was on the rise.[59] The truly dramatic change came after the famine when increasing incomes (an index of real wages shows a jump of 60 percent in the two decades before 1877), along with evolving rural retail markets, meant an even greater rise in the acquisition of consumer goods. This entailed changes not only in the quantity of goods sold but also in their form and distribution. Itinerant dealers and their wares were increasingly replaced by mass-produced retail goods sold by shopkeepers.[60] Accordingly, jokes featured the town shop as a setting for language misunderstanding, with the confused Irish speaker as perplexed about the English phrases of the shopman as about the process of purchasing goods itself. The intimidating nature of shopping appeared in the setup of one anecdote in which an Irish speaker, unable to ask the clerk for what he needs, paces the floor silently until approached so that he can point to the things he will buy: "Agus ba é sin an dóigh a dteárn siad á gcuid margaidh" (That's how they did their shopping), affirmed the storyteller.[61] Most stories turned on a punch line featuring a misunderstanding of the English uttered by the clerk or the inability to recall the English word for an item. In one story an Irish speaker tries to ask for a "shirt" but pronounces it "church"; this leads the shopman to direct him to a chapel down the street.[62] In a popular Kerry joke an Irish speaker is told to wait for his or her change: "I don't need 'change,'" retorts the shopper, "just directions to the Blarney road."[63]

No consumer good, however, was more closely associated with English speaking and social advancement than tea. Already a well-established item in the diet of upper-class households by the eighteenth century, tea became a universal drink in rural households in the nineteenth century and especially in the two decades after 1850.[64] By 1884, according to the traveler Alexander Shand, reporting from Gweedore, Co. Donegal, "bad tea" had completely replaced illicit whiskey, the earlier drink of choice among peasants.[65] For rural inhabitants the arrival of tea served as a bright marker of the boundary between the past and present. Accounts like Tomás Ó Criomhthain's *An tOileánach*, the memoir of a Blasket Islander born in 1865, returned repeatedly to the subject of tea. As Ó Criomhthain recalled, he was a grown man before tea came to the island, and even then it was confined to times like Christmas, when it was used sparingly so that some could be stored up (*cuirfaí i dtaisce í*) for the holiday again the following year.[66] Another famous Irish-language memoirist and resident of the Blaskets, Muiris Ó Súilleabháin (1904–50), recalled his grandfather evoking the lack of tea as a symbol of the past: "Is beag an bhróg ná an stoca a bhí á chaitheamh san am san, ná fiú amháin braon té le fáil" (It was rare we had shoes or stockings to wear at that time, nor a drop a tea to be had).⁶⁷

Not surprisingly, the subject of tea appeared frequently in nineteenth-century folk accounts discussing its first appearance in a community. Such recollections emphasized the confusion about preparing tea, especially among women of an older generation not accustomed to it. A Galway respondent born in 1863 remembered, "Our parents who had gone through the famine were not accustomed to tea. They frequently strained away the tea from the leaf. To the tea leaves they added salt, pepper, and butter and eat [sic] them with bread, using the tea as drink."⁶⁸ A humorous story circulated at the time involved a woman visited by a distinguished person, such as a priest or a gentleman, who produces a packet of tea and asks the woman to prepare it for him. The woman boils the tea leaves, throws out the water, and serves the tea on a plate.⁶⁹ Similar stories were found by folk collectors in Scotland, as in a tale discovered on the Isle of Skye about a young man returning from Edinburgh with tea for his mother.⁷⁰ Tellingly, in some Irish examples the connection between the novelty of preparing tea and speaking Irish was made explicit: In a Donegal version of this anecdote the visitor is an Irish soldier returning from service in England who produces the tea for a confused Irish-monoglot keeper of a lodging house.⁷¹ The connection between tea and modernity emerges in the AT 1699 jokes as well, notably in a story about an Irish-speaking traveler who is given his first cup of tea at a lodging house while on the road away from home. Served a presweetened first cup and told in English that it is "Congo tea," the man drinks it down approvingly. The lady of the house returns with a second, unsweetened cup and tells him, "Sweetin to your likin'." Not understanding the instructions, the man drinks it plain and balks at its bitter taste: "Well, my love forever for *Congo tea*," he remarks in Irish, "but devil take this *Sweetin to your likin'*."⁷²

Yet for all the importance placed by joke tellers on the connection between speaking English and engaging with change in rural society, not all humorous anecdotes conveyed an allegory about modernity and language based on the clumsy exposure of Irish speakers to the new institutions of retail consumption, law, and medicine. On the contrary, when the settings of these stories are considered as a whole, they show that the gap between speaking English and speaking Irish was more likely to exist within the quotidian context of the local community. Table 2 summarizes the settings used in the jokes. From this vantage point it becomes clear that the largest category of jokes dealt not with the difficulties of Irish speakers away from home and encountering the novel institutions of modernity but, rather, with the interaction with English speakers in their own communities. Nearly one-half (46 percent) of all stories dealt with language misunderstanding in the home, neighborhood, or local fair. Even the next most-used setting—a country road or a lodging house away from home (together totaling just under 20 percent of the jokes)—represents a relatively localized, unmarked site. The majority of jokes did not rely on settings often viewed by scholars as factors in language decline: schools, churches, shops, military barracks, courtrooms, and overseas travel.

That language contact was understood in largely local terms is supported by the types of English speakers who appeared in the jokes. These included not just the expected representatives of economic and educational advancement but also many who were not far removed in class or occupation from the Irish-speaking characters themselves. English-speaking landlords, doctors, soldiers, shopkeepers, policemen, middling farmers, judges, teachers, and, of course, Englishmen made their appearance in many tales. But so too did English speakers of more humble backgrounds: market-goers, keepers of lodging houses, fishmongers, feather mongers, tailors, pub-goers, and even a beggar. One consistent feature seemed to be their outsider status: English speakers almost always arrived from beyond the Irish community, even if they did not always represent developments associated with modernity. English speakers in these stories were strangers and visitors—unknown people met in town, at the fair, or out on a road,

TABLE 2: Joke settings and situations

Setting or situation	Number of jokes	Percentage of total
Church	1	0.5
Military barracks	2	1.0
Ship or vessel	2	1.0
School	5	2.7
Courtroom	5	2.7
Pub	5	2.7
Home of gentry or other upper-class individual	6	3.2
Doctor's visit	8	4.3
Shop	9	4.8
Overseas (England, Scotland, America)	14	7.5
Lodging house while traveling	16	8.6
On the road while traveling	21	11.3
Fair or market	30	16.1
Local home or community	59	31.7
Unspecified	3	1.0
Total	186	100

or individuals encountered in bigger towns and cities. In other cases, they are locals who had moved abroad and then returned after spending time in the outside world.

Along with this outsider status attributed to English speakers, the English language itself was objectified as something bought or sold. In one example, a foolish young man is sent out by his father with money to attend school, but he ends up "buying" the English phrase "Good morrow" from a man he meets on the road. A Kerry version describes a group of Irish speakers who learn the phrase "Good morrow" but later claim to have "lost" it in the mud.[73] Another joke centered on an Irish-speaking stonemason who achieves success both at home and as an itinerant worker in England. When asked how he had done so well abroad without learning English, he retorts in Irish, "If I didn't have English, my hammer did!"[74] In anthropomorphizing the hammer and giving it the ability to speak, this anecdote thus turned the hierarchy of languages upside down: English was associated with economic success, but also with the clanking blows of a dull, blunt instrument. Irish, by contrast, appeared organic. While these jokes undeniably portray English as desirable, it nonetheless was seen as originating outside and beyond the limits of the Irish community as a tool or an object to be bartered and exchanged.

The AT 1699 stories were thus only partially about new rural institutions and the tendency for English to dominate in those anglicized, modern domains. The outsiders featured in the anecdotes were English-speaking doctors and judges, but they were also English-speaking tailors and beggars. The jokes therefore leave the impression that tellers wished to incorporate a wide variety of everyday motifs centered on language contact but that they saw no one type of linguistic encounter—including the confused Irish speaker in an anglicized setting—as the sole representative of the language change they were experiencing. Nor was the utility of English represented as anything more than a means to repair broken lines of communication with outsiders who, in a strong reaffirmation of the vitality of Irish, remained extraneous to the linguistic bonds created by those who still spoke the language.

The line between the Irish-speaking and English-speaking worlds was not the only divide indicated by the jokes. A far more important division existed between the monoglot characters in the jokes (both English and Irish) and the bilingual audience and joke tellers. This is illustrated by a closer examination of the storytelling itself. The Irish anecdotes fell somewhere between formality and informality. While short in length—most consisted of between five and ten sentences—they were not short enough to constitute "conversational joking" as examined by the linguist Neal Norrick. Conversational jokes, like most of today's jokes, are one or two lines in length and consist of a short buildup and punch line; they are easily fitted into conversations and can function like proverbs or a gloss in adding commentary to the subject under discussion.[75] The Irish stories, by contrast, were too long for casual insertion into a dialogue and included fairly elaborate introductions like character sketches and descriptions of settings. Moreover, as indicated by Ó Catháin and by the example of the hackler's tale, a number of these anecdotes could be strung together to create a longer story; this suggests that they were intended for longer storytelling sessions. At the same time, they were much shorter than the usual fairy lore, international tales, and Irish-hero cycles that lay at the center of the oral corpus in Ireland. This indicates that they "traveled" better than long stories; it was possible to enjoy them not only in more formal settings—in the home, for example, on winter evenings—but in other, less formal social spaces occupied by a range of individuals. Shorter, more informal stories also did not require advanced memorization and story-organizing techniques, and thus they were available to a wider number of storytellers.

Furthermore, unlike formal joking relationships—humor strictly confined to interactions between certain members of a family or community—that have long occupied anthropologists, there seems to be no indication that the Irish jokes were similarly restricted to specific audiences or joke tellers.[76] Many reported hearing the stories from their parents or relatives. As a Donegal man explained it simply, "Seo scéal beag eile a chualaidh mé fá 'n am nach rabh béarla" (This is another little story I heard about the time there wasn't English).[77] The folklore material does suggest a gender imbalance among joke tellers: of 164 stories in which the storyteller's gender can be determined, 73 percent were male and 27 percent were female. This difference, however, may reflect the greater number of males employed in collecting folklore rather than any trend in how the jokes were originally told. All full-time collectors were male, as were nearly all the part-time collectors of the Folklore Commission.[78] There is also the question of dialect. As Ó Catháin noted, a number of these tales rely on regional pronunciations of certain words to make the puns sensible. This would have limited their circulation to certain sections of the country, in most cases within one of the three major dialect divisions of Munster, Connacht, and Ulster.[79] Gender imbalance and dialect concerns aside, however, these jokes were probably shared widely in a number of settings and by a wide range of individuals.

But such audiences would not have been unlimited. As the anthropologist Mary Douglas has pointed out, jokes are subject to the bounds of what is permissible in a given social context. A joke is unlikely to be told in a context in which the audience does not share in the sentiments expressed by the joke teller.[80] The Irish anecdotes often conveyed the necessity of mastering the English language and the ridiculousness of Irish speakers who had not. It is therefore doubtful that these tales were told to audiences who did not have at least some abilities in speaking English. To tell these stories to a monoglot Irish-speaking audience would be to compare its members to the victims of the jokes and to violate the acceptability of the tales. Instead, these anecdotes drew joke teller and audience together in a shared community based on their knowledge of both languages.

In fact, many of these jokes were linguistically impossible to understand outside of a bilingual context. Adapting the useful categories for linguistic jokes and translatability proposed by the researcher Robert Lew, it could be said that Irish anecdotes relying on syntactic, lexical, or phonological ambiguity required a knowledge of all languages employed in the punch line to "get" the joke— that is, they were not translatable into Irish or English alone. Example 2, for instance, depends on syntactical and lexical ambiguities to set up the humor. Examples 7 and 12 rely on phonological similarities between English and Irish, much like another example that featured the resemblance between the pronunciation of the English word "charity" and the Irish word *seargtha* (withered) as pronounced in Connemara (*seargthaí*). This similarity leads to frustration for an English-speaking tramp who comes to the door of an Irish speaker:

13

"Have you any chairty [i.e., charity], Miss?"
"Níl aon fhata seargthaí sa teach agam," arsan cailín.[81]
["I don't have a withered potato in the house," said the girl.]

None of these jokes could have been adequately told without using both languages, nor could they have been understood other than by a bilingual audience. Other jokes, such as examples 1, 3, and 4, are not easily categorized, but the humor of the punch line would have been seriously stunted without the contrast created by a bilingual rendering. Fully half the stories told bilingually fall into these categories. Only jokes that relied on what Lew calls "pragmatic ambiguity," or a violation of the conventions of conversation or discourse, worked regardless of the languages used. This is the case in example 5, which, although often told using both Irish and English, could be narrated using either language alone, or another language altogether.[82] But while this last category of tales could have been tailored to suit the language abilities of the audience, few informants appear to have done so: 85 percent of the sampled stories had been told to the collectors using both English and Irish. In sum, these jokes were largely told by bilinguals and for bilinguals.

This conclusion regarding the audience for jokes is important because it reveals a subtle difference in Irish society between those Irish speakers who could also speak English and those who could not. By the second half of the nineteenth century there were very few Irish-speaking communities where bilingualism had not become predominant. But while some kind of facility in both languages had become the norm, full proficiency in English varied. There were some who undoubtedly attained complete fluency in both languages. As a Cork slater born in 1885 recalled in discussing his parents and his cousin David, "They all had brains and they were great talkers. David could converse in Irish and English: It was all the same to him, and my father was the same way.... My mother couldn't read or write, but she had Irish and English."[83] Others, however, struggled to attain adequate fluency in English—a source of embarrassment as the number of English speakers both inside and outside the community grew.

This divide is critical to understanding the function of the Irish humor considered here. Scholars have long been aware that minority communities tell jokes featuring negative stereotypes of members of their own group. In much the same way, Irish-language jokes target an Irish-speaking minority within a majority English-speaking Ireland. But close examination of such humor outside of Ireland has disproved the notion that such jokes represent evidence of self-hatred or self-ridicule. Detailed readings reveal that minority communities often employ stereotyped cultural features of their own group, but in a manner that manipulates these caricatures so that they celebrate group identity rather than denounce it. In some cases minority groups will even reverse joke targets and circulate humor directed at the majority community. Furthermore, jokes that appear to target one's own group may in fact focus on just one subset of the larger whole. Jewish humor has long been the most frequently cited evidence of this phenomenon, but other examples, including the emergence of Scottish self-directed humor in the nineteenth century, confirm these findings. In the latter case, for instance, research has revealed that overly zealous religious observance by certain Scottish Presbyterians became a subject of mockery, but not Scottishness itself. Impressed by such examples, scholars have rejected the concept of self-hatred and emphasized the importance of recognizing variations within minority groups rather than treating them as homogenous units.[84]

In much the same way the Irish jokes reflect attempts by bilinguals to put distance between themselves and monolingual speakers rather than any rejection of the Irish language per se. It was Irish monoglots, never bilingual Irish speakers, who made fools of themselves in these stories. Bilinguals appear far less often in the jokes, but when such characters do show up, they smoothly manage affairs to their own advantage. They act as interpreters at fairs, in courtrooms, and lodging houses. They even deceive Irish monoglots. In one story a bilingual speaker tricks his gluttonous monoglot friend into accepting employment from an English speaker by convincing him that she is offering food.[85] In a Donegal story a bilingual speaker and his Irish-only partner are out selling secondhand clothes when the time comes to find lodgings. The bilingual mischievously teaches his oblivious friend to tell a female lodging-house keeper in English, "Dear madam, if you let me sleep with you tonight, I'll see you satisfied in the mornin'!"[86]

The gap between bilingual and monolingual Irish speakers was matched in the jokes by the difference between bilingual and monolingual English speakers, and in truth English monoglots hardly fared any better than those who spoke only Irish. In one County Galway story an English monoglot who moves into the area is constantly greeted by his Irish-speaking neighbors with *bail ó dhia* (may God prosper you) while he is cutting turf. Frustrated and uncomprehending, he finally responds, "To hell with yourself and your *bail ó dhia* bog."[87] In a Kerry story a "bean chliste i nGaoluinn agus i mBearla" (clever woman in Irish and English) visits a rich farmer's house and obtains a number of choice goods. In exchange she promises to give to the farmer's daughters a choice of fat hens from a flock at her own house. When the English-speaking daughters arrive, however, the old woman pretends not to know English or the purpose of their visit. "Perhaps she's asking for her son, Donal," exclaims one of the girls in exasperation at the woman's Irish.[88] Another story relates how a bilingual man steps into a pub in England and bets one of the customers that he cannot take down the dictation of a letter to the Irishman's wife. When the Englishman accepts, proud of his literacy, the bilingual speaker wins the bet by composing sentences that combine both languages.[89] The winning of a wager featured in another popular story in which an English monoglot, usually a landlord or other English figure in most versions, bets an Irish speaker that he cannot eat a dozen chickens at one sitting. Accompanied by his bilingual associate, the Irishman begins to eat the chickens but soon finds himself too full to continue. The Irish speaker whispers to his friend that he can't eat any more; the English speaker, overhearing this, asks the bilingual to translate and he does: "He says he'd ate twice as many if he had 'em," explains the bilingual, with the result that the English monoglot concedes the wager and pays up.[90]

Joke tellers even appeared to have been at a loss in deciding which type of monoglot was at a greater disadvantage, as in a County Galway story about an Irish-only old woman who approaches an English-only herring dealer at the Gort fair. The woman asks him to quote a price, and he replies in English, "Fivepence." Not understanding his reply, the buyer offers him sevenpence in Irish, to which the herring dealer responds, "I couldn't. I won't give them without fivepence." "Who was worse?" asks the teller in concluding the anecdote, as the two monoglots each in turn evade what would have been an advantageous deal.[91] Directionless conversations between monoglots abound in these jokes, often peppered with clever puns left undeciphered by the two speakers but openly available to a bilingual audience. A Kerry story collected from a farmer born in 1871 offers a prime example in the form of a conversation between a local and a Peeler. "Fine day," remarks the Peeler, prompting the Irish speaker, who mistakes the English word "day" for the Irish *tae* (tea [tay]), to answer in Irish, "Hell if I know where you could get some tea!" The Peeler persists by asking, "Where are you going?" to which the Kerry man, hearing *bróg* (shoe) for "going," announces, "I haven't had shoes for a while—I couldn't pay for them."[92]

Ultimately, the jokes offered neither Irish nor English as the triumphant language in these instances. Rather, these nineteenth-century jokes offered both languages as a spectacle to the only observers able to discern the absurdity in such conversations: the bilingual listeners. This marked a strong change from the mocking of upstart English speakers so central to seventeenth- and eighteenth-century Irish-language literature. Yet far from inverting earlier humor by shifting the focus to Irish speakers as the target of humor, these jokes in fact incorporated both varieties of monoglots as victims of misunderstandings. Only bilingualism, joke tellers argued, guaranteed immunity from being tricked or caught unaware. Acknowledging this distinctive viewpoint of bilingual Irish speakers helps uncover the meaning of these jokes in the context of Ireland in the decades before 1900. On the one hand, bilingual Irish speakers told jokes to affirm the importance of learning English. A starker message about the feelings of disability, inaptitude, and imprisonment created by monolingualism in Irish can hardly be imagined. Irish monoglots, according to these stories, appeared completely foolish when they tried to negotiate the transformations affecting their communities. To speak English was to come to terms with these changes and to control them. On the other hand, jokes enabled bilinguals to reassert the Irish-speaking culture that they shared with monoglots. Ridicule was thus directed toward English monoglots too, and while this language was portrayed as useful, it remained an outside force that had infiltrated the community but not yet to the full exclusion of Irish.

PART II

ENCOUNTERS

Education and Established Church

GIVEN THE NATURE OF ENGLISH conquest and rule in Ireland, the status of the Irish language among Irish speakers was inevitably molded by the policies and influences of the English-speaking state in everyday life. The scope of that presence varied considerably over the centuries, however, driven not only by changes in linguistic ideology as the early modern policies of the Tudors and Stuarts gave way to Protestant ascendancy and then to nineteenth-century Union, but also by the arrival of the modern liberal state in Ireland (and elsewhere) with its expansive view of the place of governance in the life of the individual. It is this latter phenomenon that historians of language have identified as having a major impact on the fortunes of minority languages, since the supplanting of local institutions by a central state focused on implementing standardized versions of law, education, bureaucracy, and, most importantly, language—a development that reached full stride in the nineteenth century—necessarily created new questions for authorities as to how interactions between government and governed could be negotiated where linguistic heterogeneity reigned.[1] It should also be recognized that even with this newly expanded presence of the state at both the national and local levels, the power of authorities to shape the linguistic landscape was not omnipotent but, rather, always potentially circumscribed by the actions of Irish speakers, who could either resist or accommodate the use of English within domains of the state, and by internal factions within governing powers that prevented any kind of policy unanimity on the question of language.

A new direction in the linguistic policies of authorities in Ireland was discernible in the late eighteenth and early nineteenth centuries, a change that cannot be understood without references to the preceding trends of the sixteenth and seventeenth centuries. The rough outline of this history was already discernible to contemporaries like Thomas Andrews (1813–85), professor of chemistry and vice president at the Queen's University of Belfast, who identified three major phases in Crown policy in Ireland at an address delivered at the annual meeting of the National Association for the Promotion of Social Science in Belfast in 1867. Speaking of the interrelation of educational, religious, and linguistic policy, Andrews observed that previous Irish administrations had always subordinated the expansion of education to "forced attempts to mould the character and alter the habits and opinions of a people." Under the Tudors and Stuarts, this had involved the explicit goal of anglicization, later to be supplanted in the eighteenth century by an overwhelming concern with eradicating Catholicism. Only with the publication of the final report of the second commission on Irish education, completed in 1812, had a final, and more neutral, stage been reached: "This report ... corresponds to the third phase or epoch in the educational history of Ireland. The aim of education was no longer the substitution of the English for the Irish language, nor the conversion of the people to the Protestant faith, but the training of the young of all creeds and opinions under one system and in the same schools."[2] Andrews was wide of the mark in assuming a liberality in the national education system arising out of this report. Not only were its avowedly nonsectarian goals eventually upended by the withdrawal of official Protestant support and the successful efforts by the Catholic hierarchy to reassert a measure of control over primary education through local clerical school managers but its potential linguistic inclusiveness also failed to materialize for Irish speakers, as will be shown below.

Nevertheless the schema described by Andrews is useful for a couple of reasons. First, his three-part periodization stands up well to scrutiny. A more active push by English and Irish authorities between 1537 and the early 1700s to explicitly favor the English over the Irish language was later superseded by a second stage—once an English-speaking elite had been guaranteed at the end of the Williamite war—in which a concern with language was replaced by a larger concern with ensuring a Protestant educational regime. This initially entailed a push between 1700 and 1740 toward concession on the use of Irish in the religious sphere. But by the end of the eighteenth century, this initial conciliatory stance had been replaced with a policy best described as agnostic: the state essentially became blind to the existence of Irish speakers, since its elites were now anglicized, leading to an abandonment of the grand statutory opposition to the Irish language favored by the Tudors and Stuarts. Policies subsequently either assumed that everyone in Ireland spoke English or quietly made temporary adjustments in anticipation of a future time when anglicization would be complete. This strategy, which of course could be just as harmful toward the fortunes of Irish in its nonacknowledgment of its speakers as an actively antagonistic policy, nevertheless ran into difficulties in the nineteenth century as the aforementioned growth of the state brought the issue of language more directly into the spotlight and highlighted the shortcomings of the Irish educational and religious regime being created under the Act of Union.

Second, Andrews was correct in linking the questions surrounding education and religion together with language, as it was in these two domains that state policy in Ireland was developed enough at an early date to follow this three-part history in its entirety. Although England—and by extension, its rule in Ireland—had embarked on one of the earliest efforts to centralize and consolidate the monarchical state in Europe, the intersection between most domains of authority and everyday life remained limited, decentralized, and decidedly local in nature until the end of the eighteenth century. This was true of the legal system and of politics (that is, voting and participation in the public sphere), both of which remained either restricted to those of financial means or else negotiated through purely local institutions—two characteristics that allowed local languages to survive unmolested. It was only with the emergence of the expanded modern state and the creation of new, nationalized domains in the legal and political arena that a change was triggered in policies toward local languages, whose presence was now considered a problem to be addressed. By contrast, realms of the state that had been established (with varying degrees of permanency) on a national basis much earlier, namely, the educational institutions and established Protestant church that emerged with Tudor conquest, had followed a longer timeline that only converged with the trajectory of legal and political realms when religion and education, too, experienced the transformative powers of the modern state. Thus, the longer history of the place of the Irish language in the established church and in Irish schools will be treated in this chapter, while the legal and political systems will be reserved for the next.

That education and the established church should be treated simultaneously in assessing the influence of the state on language should not be surprising. As Patricia Palmer has carefully traced out for the late Tudor period, achievements of imperial conquest, a Protestant national church, and English-language ascendancy in Ireland were all aligned in the minds of Elizabethan administrators.[3] As English rule expanded in Ireland, the question would repeatedly arise in the centuries after the Reformation as to how to secure the Protestant church in

Ireland and how concessions for language difference might be negotiated in a faith supposedly dedicated to worship in the vernacular. Debate over the use of languages other than English in religious settings—conducted not only in Ireland but also in Wales and Scotland—were in turn closely tied to debates over educational policy, since Protestant (and Catholic) denominations alike considered teaching to be a purview of the church. Primary education began—and sometimes ended—with catechetical instruction, and for Protestants in particular, learning to read meant acquiring an ability first and foremost to read the scriptures. Hence, it is impossible not to consider educational policies with regard to language in Ireland without simultaneously tracing the broader linguistic questions addressed by the Church of Ireland, and it is to this subject that this chapter will turn.

The reign of Henry VIII and the passage of the Act for the English Order, Habit, and Language (28 Henry VIII c. 15) in 1537, as has long been recognized, brought a new direction in language policy in Ireland. Prior to the sixteenth century, legal policy on language had been concerned with the Hibernicization of English speakers in the Pale and ideas of decline and degradation of English customs and law in areas infiltrated by the Irish language. Thus, the Statutes of Kilkenny, passed in 1366, insisted not only that "every Englishman do use the English language" also but that marriage between English and Irish be prohibited, that English fashion and modes of horse riding be followed, and that English common law be used throughout the Pale. Englishmen caught speaking Irish could be subject to forfeiture of their lands.[4] By the end of the fifteenth century, with the resurgence of Gaelic power, these proscriptions on Irish speaking were already unsustainable. Under the 10 Henry VII c. 8 (1495), the Statutes of Kilkenny were reaffirmed by Poynings's Parliament, but with the explicit exception of the clauses prohibiting the speaking of Irish and riding in a saddle.[5] In any case, neither the original statutes nor their 1495 confirmation was enforced beyond the Pale, and even within this area, their success was limited.[6] No such territorial limits were envisioned by the 1537 statutes, however. Instead, a more ambitious call was made to all the "King's subjects within this land," who, it was said, had been stricken by the "diversitie that is betwixt them in tongue, language, order, and habite" and divided by cultural differences that "perswadeth unto them, that they should be as it were of sundry sorts, or rather of sundry countries, where indeed they be wholly together one bodie." While addressed to the residents of the Pale who could call themselves subjects of the king, the act in principle could thus be extended to any territories in Ireland that fell to English rule.[7]

The solution offered to this pernicious diversity by the 1537 statute was that anyone "that will knowledge themselves according to their duties of allegeance to be his Highness true and faithfull subjects" was enjoined to use English, "without ceasing or returning at any time to Irish habite or language."[8] Acting through the Irish Parliament, Henry was thus laying out a bold statement of centralized monarchical power based around the allegiance of a linguistically unified populace.

Several aspects of this Tudor enactment on language stand out for signaling a new direction in policy. First, the 1537 act mirrored other moves by early modern states to actively promote a single vernacular for governance in the post-Renaissance period. Henry's contemporary and rival, Francis I of France (1494–1547), similarly lamented linguistic heterogeneity in his kingdom as an impediment to governance and a threat to the social fabric. The result was the Ordonnance de Villers-Cotterêts (1539), which explicitly reinforced a long-term trend toward the use of French rather than Latin by the Valois for administrative and judicial use. In Poland, a ruling in the same year by the Diet insisted on the use of Polish to publish all laws and edicts, while in Spain the Inquisition imposed Castilian on trials in Catalonia in 1561.[9] Closer to home, the first of the Welsh acts of union (1536) enshrined English as the language of the courts and of officeholders, once again part of a broader push by Tudor administrators—in this case, Thomas Cromwell—to both impose civility on Wales and ensure administrative uniformity.[10] The Henrician act of 1537 was thus a part of a new and larger trend, especially among more centralized states like England and France, to break with the heteroglossia of the Middle Ages in favor of linguistic ascendancy for the ruling vernacular in governance.

At the same time, the 1537 act pushed beyond the attempts made by other European states to exclude other languages (usually Latin) from administration and the law, and in fact, the unusually broad scope of Tudor policy in Ireland with respect to language has been recognized.[11] A whole range of Irish cultural practices were targeted for suppression, from how living quarters were kept to hairstyle, clothing, and dress. The pronouncements on language, moreover, were sweeping:

> And be it enacted by authority aforesaid, that every person or persons, the King's true subjects, inhabiting this land of Ireland, of what estate, condition or degree he or they be, or shall be, to the uttermost of their power, cunning, and knowledge, shall use and speak commonly the English tongue and language, and that every such person and persons, having childe or children, shall

endeavour themselfe to cause and procure his said childe and children to use and speak the English tongue and language, and … shall bring up and keep his said childe and children in such places, where they shall or may have occasion to learn the English tongue, language, order, and condition.[12]

This focus on undermining the use of Irish was inseparable from long-standing initiatives by various Dublin parliaments and officials to hinder the language's institutional support by ejecting Irish bardic poets from districts under English control during the fifteenth and sixteenth centuries.[13] Similar efforts were made in Scotland by way of the prohibition on poetic patronage enacted by the Statutes of Iona (1609).[14] Such policies went well beyond the language of law and administration to attempt to legislate, in effect, Englishness. The 1537 act also further developed a theme already established in earlier centuries, and soon to be repeated in writings by the likes of Edmund Campion and Richard Stanihurst in the 1570s, that those who lived without English customs, laws, and language were "rude and ignorant people," and that lack of linguistic uniformity had left many subjects of the king "in a certain savage and wilde kind and maner of living."[15] No concept of Irish speaking as compatible with civility was conceded, and indeed one of the most persistent perceptions of Irish throughout the sixteenth and seventeenth centuries was that speaking it was in itself a sign of disloyalty to the English Crown.[16]

The broader activism of the 1537 policy can also be understood through its provisions on education and religion, which in fact occupied a significant portion of the text of the act. Nominations for church dignities and offices were to be bestowed on English speakers first, and then on non–English speakers after a vacancy had not been filled for three months—provided the position had been announced at market towns adjoining the site of the benefice. The act insisted that attempts to prioritize non–English speakers for church office would result in the appointment being voided in favor of a selection by the king. Archbishops and bishops were instructed to bind appointed priests and deacons by oath to "endeavour himselfe to learne the English tongue and language, and use English order and fashions," as well as preach in English. Finally, church officials were bound to organize in their districts "a schole for to learne English, if any children of his paroch come to him to learne the same."[17] This last provision, too, marked a difference between Tudor policy, with its creation of new institutions (the parish schools) where English would be privileged, and undertakings elsewhere, as in France, where already-existing institutions were to be reformed so as to enshrine a specific language.

Notably, neither the 1537 act nor its successors outlawed Irish directly, and at no point in the subsequent centuries was a successful step taken of making English an official language in any of the constituent nations under English rule.[18] Instead, the act hoped to achieve the objective of making English universally known by favoring it from a legal and administrative viewpoint and by encouraging its use whenever possible. Clearly, the desired end result was the same: no role for Irish was envisioned, and all hopes were for a universal use of English. But it was also understood that a direct prohibition of Irish was impossible, given the numbers that spoke it and the fact that in the sixteenth century, and well into the seventeenth, a majority of Ireland's Gaelic and Old English families were bilingual or even monoglot Irish speakers.[19] Palmer in particular has drawn historians' attention to the widespread and sustained use of interpreters during the Elizabethan conquest of Ireland, noting that such provisions were all but mandatory given the existence of monoglots among even the top ranks of Irish society.[20] Furthermore, the English administration in Ireland simply lacked the institutional sites where Irish could be proscribed—hence the need for the 1537 act to first create those spaces (specifically, the parish schools and an established church), and then anglicize them. Tellingly, one of the few exceptions where an institution already existed from which Irish might be proscribed was the Irish Parliament itself, and even in this case the administration had to compromise linguistically, as evident in the Earl of Ormond's use of Irish in the 1541 session proclaiming Henry VIII king.[21]

As Brian Ó Cuív long ago argued, all of this points to the absolute importance of full conquest of Ireland through Elizabethan and Stuart initiatives to the creation of both anglicized institutional spaces and an anglicized ruling class.[22] Until this took place, English rule in Ireland was left with a contradictory set of policies and decisions, most of them touching on religious administration, that relied repeatedly on the use of Irish despite ambitions to eliminate the language. As early as the reign of Edward VI (1547–53), religious officials were already being allowed by the monarchy to translate the Protestant service into Irish as needed despite the letter of the 1537 act.[23] The unpreparedness of the newly created established church to deal with Irish-speaking congregations continued under Elizabeth when the Act of Uniformity (2 Eliz. I c. 2, 1560) addressed non-English-speaking congregations by permitting Protestant officials to translate and deliver the "mattens, even song, celebration of the Lord's Supper, and administration of each of the sacraments, and all their common and open Prayer" in Latin—a request made of the queen, the text of the act explained, because of the difficulty in getting the services printed since "few in the whole realm can read the Irish letters."²⁴ This provision revealed both the awareness among officials of the impracticality of providing the liturgy in English and the unpreparedness of the church to offer it in Irish—hence the decision to use Latin—up until Seon Carsuel published his *Foirm na nUrrnuidheadh*, a translation derived from the Book of Common Order, in 1567.²⁵

Ambiguity in the proper direction to take in administering a subject people speaking a language other than English continued in the late Tudor and early Stuart periods. Throughout the 1560s, 1570s, and 1580s, Elizabeth appointed, again in direct opposition to the 1537 act, a number of bishops and prebendaries who preached in both languages, among them the bishop of Meath, Hugh Bradie, and a number of officials assigned to the dioceses of Kildare, Down, and Armagh.²⁶ Sir Henry Sidney, who had encouraged Elizabeth to appoint Irish-speaking officials, reported in 1576 that only 18 of 102 vicars in Meath could speak English, and local landlords revealed that they were informally translating prayers and the church's articles into Irish for local ministers.²⁷ Elizabeth's own personal interest in knowing something of the Irish language, if only to better understand the methods by which souls were to be brought into her reformed church, was evident in her request for an Irish primer sometime in the early years of her reign. The resulting book, possibly compiled and presented by Chriostóir Nuinseann, Baron Delvin (ca. 1544–1602), of the powerful Westmeath family, used the opportunity not only to demonstrate the basic grammatical elements of Irish but also to recount the classic story of the language's postdiluvian origins in the east.²⁸ Under James I, such concessions continued. A commission convened by the king to report on the state of Ireland advised that translations of the New Testament (published by Uilliam Ó Domhnaill in 1602) and the Book of Common Prayer (published by Ó Domhnaill in 1608) be put into use "in the parishes of the Irishrie," and that nonresident (i.e., non-native) Anglican priests "there do constantly keep and continue one to read service in the Irish tongue." By all appearances, these recommendations were put into effect in 1623.²⁹ In 1634 a meeting of the Convocation at Dublin made even further provision for Irish, passing, at the urging of William Bedell, the provost of Trinity College, canons stipulating that "part of the service should be read in Irish where half or most of the congregation is Irish," and that "where most of the people were Irish, the Church-wardens should provide, at the charge of the parish, a Bible and two common prayer books in the Irish tongue." As in 1623, it was also ordered that an Irish reader be employed in parishes where the minister spoke only English.³⁰

Such policies were by no means the leading edge of a broader acceptance of linguistic pluralism under English rule, however. Despite the allowances by the

Crown noted above, the half-hearted attitude of a good portion of the established church in Ireland toward the use of Irish was noted by both contemporaries and by modern historians.[31] Reports that many of the five hundred copies of Ó Domhnaill's New Testament had still not been distributed after nearly thirty years gives a strong indication of the lackluster support of the Church in Ireland for Irish-language provisions. The problem stemmed, as Michael Cronin has argued, from a central paradox in the notion of providing translations of Protestant works in the Irish language: "Recurrent emphasis on the barbarous, uncivilised nature of the Irish, whose very language was seen as synonymous with sedition, did not sit happily with efforts to supply the Gaelic Irish with printed translations in their own language."[32] The equation of Irish speaking with a lack of civility—a status whose reversal was presumed to be the goal of weaning the Irish from Catholicism—nullified arguments by other, more progressive wings of the church that Protestant dedication to bringing the word of God to all humankind by any means possible trumped distaste for translation. Notably, a similar record exists for the established churches in Wales and Scotland. Despite the earliest push among the Celtic languages to translate and use Welsh-language Bibles (from 1563 on) and the use of Welsh-speaking ministers in monoglot areas, the established church—and its bishops in particular—remained lukewarm on the use of the vernacular until the explosion of Welsh printing by Methodists in the eighteenth century.[33] In Scotland, the Presbyterian established church built a similarly ambivalent record around the stated goal of anglicization, especially in highland parishes, combined with provisions for Gaelic-speaking preachers starting in the 1650s through the translation and use of Gaelic psalters, liturgical manuals, catechisms, and Bibles in the sixteenth and late seventeenth centuries.[34]

In the realm of education, this impasse between favoring English and permitting linguistic compromise was equally apparent, but the Crown and local authorities were less willing to compromise than they had been on the issue of religion. Since education was the means by which the rude and ignorant might be elevated to the ranks of the civilized, and since the English language had been powerfully contrasted in the minds of its speakers with the barbarism of Irish, the latter could not, by definition, be the means of educational attainment. The Elizabethan statute passed in 1570 by the Dublin parliament to create diocesan schools was less direct on the matter of language than the 1537 provision (which had specifically designated that the parish schools teach English), but the act did stipulate that the schoolmaster be English, or of "English birth of this realm," referring to those of Old English descent. The justification for the schools closely linked the purposes of education with pacification in Ireland, noting that "the greatest number of the people of this your Majestie's realm hath of long time lived in rude and barbarous states, not understanding that Almightie God hath by his divine laws forbidden the manifold and haynous offences which they spare not daily and hourely to commit and perpetrate."[35] By the early seventeenth century, according to the 1612 report of the Jesuit Richard Conway, only a few infant schools remained outside of the Protestant-based educational institutions in which authorities had insisted that students be taught English.[36] Parallels for this English-only ideology existed in Scotland, where in 1616 the Act for the Settling of Parochial Schools declared even more explicitly the goal of abolishing and removing Scots Gaelic as the principle cause of incivility in the Highlands and northern islands.[37] The only thing blunting the force of this all-English educational policy in Ireland was the paucity of state- and church-sponsored schools in Ireland until well into the eighteenth century. Parish schools, for instance, were few in number until the Anglican parish system was fully developed at this later period, and the diocesan schools never became anything like a tool for educating the wider Irish population.[38]

Following the disruption of the mid-1600s, during which few efforts either in favor or against the use of Irish in educational or religious spheres took place, a second stage of language policy emerged with the completion of the Williamite conquest and transfers. With Protestant victory in Ireland and the removal of any vestiges of a Catholic elite at the topmost echelons of power, no longer did Ireland's Protestant ruling classes need to concern themselves with attacks on wider cultural practices such as the fashion or dwelling choices of the Irish. The introduction of a bill in the Irish House of Lords in 1697 by Viscount Lanesborough (1650–1724) to directly suppress the Irish language was surely evidence, as historian James Kelly has argued, of ongoing antipathy in officialdom toward Irish.[39] But its failure was also indicative of the new ambivalence of ruling elites toward linguistic antagonism, especially when one considers the eagerness of an insecure Protestant government to otherwise countenance penal measures in the 1690s. In other words, with Ireland securely in control of English-speaking Protestant supporters of the Crown and parliament, the express need to undermine the Irish language was eclipsed by a more pressing objective of undermining Catholicism.[40]

This was a project in which some authorities were even willing to countenance the use of Irish, and ensuing policies and parliamentary acts touching on language thus framed their educational and religious provisions through the prism of this goal. The lectureship in Irish at Trinity College, introduced by Bedell in the early seventeenth century as part of the university's need to train ministers who could reach the Irish-speaking population, was revived after a lapse of several years when Charles Lynegar received an appointment in 1708.[41] Both the 2 Anne c. 7 (1703) and the 8 Anne c. 3 (1709), which called for the Catholic clergy to register with authorities under threat of transportation, also made concessions to the use of Irish by stipulating that priests who converted to Protestantism "shall publicly read the common prayer or liturgy of the church of Ireland in the English or Irish tongue in such places, and at such times, as the said archbishops or bishops shall direct or appoint."[42] The first decade of the 1700s also witnessed the beginning of a new series of attempts by certain factions within the Irish established church to use the Irish language in parochial care as a means to reach the broader Irish population and thus improve the chances of conversion. These proponents of Irish-language evangelizing centered around a number of ministers and rectors active in the lower house of Convocation led by Reverend John Richardson, a rector in the diocese of Kilmore and chaplain to the Duke of Ormond, and included Reverend Nicholas Browne, rector in the diocese of Clogher, Reverend Walter Atkins, treasurer of the cathedral of Cloyne, and Lynegar himself.

In 1703 the lower house proposed a resolution that, for the "speedy conversion of the papists of this kingdom," a number of preachers be employed by the bishops to deliver sermons in the Irish language in every diocese. This resolution earned a positive response in the upper house, although no specific statement of a plan of action was put forth. Similar efforts were proposed in 1709, including printing the Bible in Irish (full editions of both New and Old Testament had been available since 1685), the liturgy, and a catechism in Irish and English explicitly aimed at Catholic recusants. Once again, it was recommended that an Irish-language reader be appointed for each diocese to preach and catechize.[43] Not fully satisfied with the zeal of the response, in 1710 yet another push was made by various clergymen to have the complete Bible printed in Irish font and to make better provision for scripture readers in Irish. This time, a number of powerful Irish figures came to support the cause, including Francis Annesley (1663–1750), a Tory MP; Edward Southwell (1671–1730), Irish chief secretary; and Arthur Annesley, the fifth Earl Anglesey (ca. 1678–1737). A memorial was presented to the Duke of Ormond, Lord Lieutenant, urging the printing of church literature in Irish and advertising the popularity of providing divine service in Irish among its speakers, a recommendation that was then forwarded on to the Irish primates before being brought before the queen for consideration.

For reasons unknown, the version of the memorial presented to the queen omitted any reference to religious services through Irish.[44] Nevertheless, with the queen's approval, and despite the last-minute opposition of several high-ranking critics of the initiative, a committee was convened in the Irish House of Commons under the leadership of MP Charles O'Neill. It was this committee that recommended that "a competent number of ministers duly qualified to instruct them, and perform the offices of religion to them in their own language," be maintained for the Catholic Irish population. The resultant bill enacting these recommendations, however, was tabled indefinitely when the Commons adjourned.[45] Although occasional schemes to press for Irish-language preaching continued in the next two decades—Bishop Francis Hutchinson of Down and Connor (1660–1739) embarked on an Irish-language missionary effort based on Rathlin Island in 1722, and even Bishop George Berkeley of Cloyne (1685–1753) favored new initiatives—the 1710 proposed bill was the last attempt to establish the use of Irish as part of religious state policy in the eighteenth century.[46] By 1711 opposition forces had already organized enough that counter-proposals calling for English-only charity schools were floated and approved in Convocation.[47] As the Convocation of the established church in Ireland did not meet again for 150 years,[48] no serious formal institutional push on language policy could have manifested itself in ensuing years, even had there been interest.

Both continuities and discontinuities with late Tudor and early Stuart policies can be discerned in the failed 1710 endeavor. The push for the use of Irish within the Protestant mission showed recognition of the need to reconcile a religious institution claiming to be an extension of the English state with the linguistic heterogeneity of its subjects. As with the Tudors, this did not, however, mean the abandonment of the project to bring all Irish speakers ultimately into the English-speaking fold. While the overriding goal became the conversion of Catholics, because Catholicism was synonymous with ignorance and superstition, it was understood that once conversion took place, a more general movement toward English habits and English-speaking would follow. At the same time, the Irish-language proponents of the early eighteenth century began to display a much more accepting view of linguistic diversity than their precursors—at least where religious duty was concerned. Richardson, for example, argued that the provisions of the 1709 penal law permitting converted priests to preach in Irish had removed any restrictions on use of the language by Protestant ministers enacted by the 1537 Act for the English Order, Habit, and Language—in fact, he claimed the act "enjoined" its use. Taking his argument for linguistic tolerance further, Richardson noted that "difference of language doth not keep up difference of religion.... It is not the Irish language, but the popish religion, that is repugnant to the English interest;... the Irish language itself... hath not any marks of the Beast upon it."[49] Both the twenty-fourth of the church's Thirty-Nine Articles, with its insistence that no public prayers or sacraments be administered in a language not understood by the congregation, and the scriptures, specifically the insistence of Matthew 28:19 that the disciples of Christ spread his teachings to all nations, were cited as justification for approaching Catholics through whatever language necessary.[50]

On a deeper level, proponents of Irish-language evangelization began to question the assumption that language difference necessarily enforced national or religious divide. Scotland and Wales, where inhabitants spoke languages other than English and yet had been accepted as loyal Protestant subjects of the monarchy, were held up as evidence that linguistic difference need not enforce religious divide. Richardson even went so far as to assert that language was a fluid marker of reality: "Diversity of language doth not tend to keep up difference of religion and interest. There is not any language in the world that hath operation upon the nature of things. A language is only a certain arbitrary form or manner wherein men have either tacitly or expressly agreed to communicate their thoughts of anything to one another, and doth neither alter the thing itself, nor our thoughts and conceptions of it." Within Ireland, the irrelevance of language to religious loyalty was apparent: "We have English papists, and Irish Protestants, Irish papists and English Protestants."[51]

Further examples of linguistically (if not religiously) ecumenical attitudes appeared in Bishop Hutchinson's preface to his bilingual almanac, printed in Dublin in 1724 as part of his larger outreach scheme to convert Irish Catholics.[52] While it was conceded that uniformity of language in Ireland would help assist trade, business, and religion, Hutchinson dismissed notions that the production of printed material in Irish would prop up a language that, according to its critics, should be abandoned. Citing once again the examples of Scots Gaelic, Welsh, Manx, and Cornish, languages spoken by peoples who had nevertheless accepted the laws and Protestant religion of the English, Hutchinson declared: "For my part, I have not the least hope of [the native Irish] losing their language, nor do I apprehend it to be of any consequence either to church or state, whether they lose it or no. If they were but good Christians, good Protestants and good subjects, their speaking Irish would do no harm to anybody."[53] Undoubtedly, as has been recognized, these sentiments also foretold a wider interest in (and sympathy for) the Irish language in the scientific and antiquarian communities that gradually came to see Irish in a secular, rather than evangelizing, light.[54]

In strong contrast to this ongoing willingness, especially at the lower levels of the church, to engage with the island's Irish-speaking majority as a means of furthering the religious foundations of the state, no such compromises were envisioned in the realm of education. As James Kelly has observed, the insistence that any schooling provided in Ireland by authorities be conducted in English—even if only as a means of lessening hostilities between diverse parties in Ireland—was upheld by no less than James II, otherwise a nominal ally to the Irish cause.[55] The centerpiece of this renewed push for providing English instruction was the 7 William III c. 4 (1695), commonly known as An Act to Restrain Foreign Education. Its most important provision in terms of the eighteenth-century penal laws was the disability the act placed on Catholic education by prohibiting students from going abroad and Catholic masters from teaching in Ireland. This aspect of the statute was strictly confessional, not linguistic, and once again no interdiction on Irish was attempted. But anticipating objections to the ban on Catholic-led education on the grounds that insufficient Protestant schools existed, the 1695 statute also turned to the Henrician and Elizabethan provisions for schools made in 1537 and 1570, asking that they be enforced so that adequate educational resources be made. Although the Elizabethan diocesan schools were now referred to as "Latin free-schools," the 1695 statute clearly envisioned an anglicized education in the parish schools, described, as in the 1537 act, as "school[s] to learn English."[56] The aim of the 1695 statute in steering Irish students toward the English-speaking parish and diocesan schools thus marked a continuity with its sixteenth-century counterparts. The statute also echoed similar, if even more direct, policy in Scotland where, for instance, rents had been granted by William III to the Synod of Argyll for the explicitly stated purpose of building English schools to combat the use of the Scots Gaelic language, and where the 1616 Act for the Settling of Parish Schools was renewed again in 1696 with the purpose of extending it to the Highlands.[57]

The unwillingness to compromise on the issue of language and education was further sustained in subsequent statutes. The aforementioned 1709 act passed under Anne, in addition to its pronouncements on converted priests and attempts by Catholic landowners to dodge penal legislation, reaffirmed the 1695 statute while also heading off the practice of Catholic schoolteachers of uprooting their schools and moving them to adjoining counties when called before the county assizes. These teachers were to be treated in the same fashion as renegade priests. As noted above, attempts to enforce the creation of parish schools to teach English along the lines of 1537 were renewed by Convocation again in 1711, although in this case without any results.[58] More concrete were the 8 Geo. I c. 12 (1721) and 5 Geo. II c. 4 (1731), two statutes that made it easier for the Protestant hierarchy to provide glebe and other church lands and for landlords to bequest private lands for the use of Protestant schoolmasters "to teach the English tongue."[59] So anathema was the use of Irish in education that even John Richardson, otherwise so willing to accommodate and rely on Irish to further his religious goals, made no mention of the use of Irish in the charity schools he proposed in 1710 as a means of furthering the education of Catholics. Both the resultant memorial presented to the lord lieutenant in that year and the version offered to the queen spoke only of schools to teach English "that the whole nation may in time be made both Protestant and English."[60] It is these statutes, especially the 1695 and 1709 acts, that have prompted occasional claims among modern scholars that the eighteenth-century penal laws legislatively proscribed Irish, akin perhaps to those provisions by which Catholic land inheritance was undermined. This was, for example, the conclusion reached by the Jesuit scholar Edward Cahill, who saw no distinction between prohibitions on Catholic teaching and banning the study of the Irish language and who described the penal laws as an "active persecution" with an aim "in large part ... [of] suppressing the Irish language and nationality."[61] It should be emphasized, however, that no explicit ban on Irish was enacted. Instead, state policy involved a consistent push to create new educational institutions in which the vernacular used was English in the explicit hope of seeing it displace all others.

This course of action received further reinforcement in 1733 with the chartering of the Anglican-led Incorporated Society for Promoting English Protestant Schools in Ireland, an organization dedicated to creating charity schools to expand Protestant education to Catholics through the medium of the English language. This initiative is best understood within the wider British educational context at the outset of the eighteenth century. There was a growing realization that no advancement had been made in instilling even basic literacy, not only in Ireland, where it was recognized by the second decade of the 1700s that the previous parish, diocesan, and free schools had failed to attract the attendance of the vast majority of the population in non-English-speaking areas, but also in Scotland, where vast stretches of the Highlands had been left untouched by the Stuart-era parochial schools, and in Wales, where primary education consisted largely of the short-lived charitable schools set up by the Welsh Trust voluntary movement. The answer proposed during this last installment of active English-language educational policy was the charter (or charity) schools subsequently started in Scotland by the Scottish Society for Promoting Christian Knowledge (SSPCK, established 1709), the Welsh charter schools run by the original English SPCK starting in 1699 and their successors, the circulating schools founded by Griffith Jones in 1731, and finally, the Incorporated Schools of Ireland. A number of common features linked these initiatives, including a strong interest in proselytism of Catholic children (at least in the Scottish and Irish contexts), an emphasis on catechism as the first step in instruction, and the charitable basis of their financial support, although in the Irish case this was quickly supplemented by a £1,000 annual parliamentary grant and, later, an additional £1,000 annually provided by the assignment to the society revenues generated by issuing licenses to hawkers and pedlars. By the end of the 1700s, the size of the grant had increased so that Irish schools were receiving nearly £12,000 per year.[62]

Although at the outset the charter schools in all three areas shared a similar dedication to teaching English, the different directions taken by each with regard to Irish, Scots Gaelic, and Welsh are instructive in understanding the unique features of Irish policy. On one end of a spectrum in terms of enabling literacy in the Celtic vernacular were the Welsh schools. Initially wedded to an English-only environment, the SPCK schools quickly conceded on catechetical instruction in Welsh, undoubtedly as a result of a much longer tradition of religious printing and instruction in the vernacular in Wales. When the SPCK schools were deemed inadequate, the circulating school system led by Jones that replaced them were even more amenable to Welsh, relying on the language heavily to impart instruction.[63] By contrast, in Scotland the SSPCK schools were largely run by lay directors, many of them lowland lawyers and landlords, who did not share the interest in Gaelic of many of their counterparts in the religious field, and whose attitudes toward highland Gaelic speakers were marred by the Jacobite rebellions of 1715 and 1745. Thus, while concessions on using Scots Gaelic to catechize and in appointing bilingual teachers were made, the SSPCK schools insisted on teaching only English literacy right up until the 1750s. This put them somewhere on the other side of the vernacular-based spectrum, much closer to the end occupied by the Irish case, in which the Incorporated Society and its supporters, particularly those among the hierarchy like Archbishop Hugh Boulter (1672–1742), insisted on an English-only approach.[64]

A telltale variable—aside, of course, from the personal favor or disfavor of these schools' founders—can be identified here as a determinant of the use of the vernacular: the decision on whether to establish schools on an itinerant or a stationary basis. Teaching monoglot Welsh, Scots Gaelic, and Irish speakers to read English required far more time and depth to the educational process than simply teaching them to read in their own language. Thus, English-only instruction required the building of a school and a multiyear commitment by the teacher. This was an expensive proposition in regions where the goal was to cover vast expanses of often isolated and rugged areas with limited instructional resources. By contrast, using the local vernacular in instruction enabled students to acquire literacy much more quickly, enabling teachers to circulate widely by dedicating only a few months to each location. As a bonus, students could acquire the skills to read religious literature faster and thereby head off danger to their souls. Thus in Wales the circulating schools established by Jones operated for short, three-month intervals, usually in the winter when agricultural activity ceased—and relied on Welsh. They were also wildly successful: as many as 92 schools reportedly operated in 1741 in three counties alone, and over 3,300 schools had taught close to half the Welsh population by the late eighteenth century.[65] In Scotland and Ireland, by contrast, the schools were stationary and long term, enabling them not only to use English but even, for a time, to advantageously locate the schools at a physical distance from the students' home region so as to more easily loosen their bonds with their Irish- and Gaelic-speaking (but more importantly, Catholic) milieu. In the end, the Irish charity schools were avoided by Catholics in droves, and only 34 were still in operation in 1824. In Scotland, the English-only policy itself was reevaluated starting in 1754 and replaced with a much more tolerant policy toward the use of Gaelic scriptures and literacy. The Scottish schools survived, albeit in modified form, into the nineteenth century.[66] In other words, Irish educational policy remained stubbornly wedded to anglicization even in comparison to its nearest analog, Scotland.

The consistency with which education in English was pushed in state policy in Ireland, however, deserves further explanation. If administrative unity achieved through legal and cultural assimilation was the primary aim of sixteenth-century monarchies in Europe, then the primary goal of many states starting in the late seventeenth century was the purification and standardization of a single national language. Such undertakings were built on the idea of rationalization and on eradicating vestiges of superstition and illiteracy often expressed in local languages. This was to be done, in most cases, by enshrining literacy in a dominant vernacular language and by encouraging resultant literary activity in printed form. France, for instance, which had already embarked on a push for literary expansion in French based on the Italian model, furthered these efforts in the seventeenth century with the creation of the Académie Française (1635), whose dictionaries served to inculcate a certain written standard, and the Collège des Quatre Nations in 1688, whose purpose was to teach French in areas like Alsace, the Pays-bas, Rousillon, and Pignerol.[67] During the Revolution, these efforts took on a new urgency as not only administrative uniformity but also the spread of revolutionary ideals became paramount. The ability to read—specifically, to read French—was considered essential to combating counter-revolution.[68] These efforts were striking in their conviction, as not only were "patois" languages flagged—as the author of one of two key reports on the subject, the Abbé Henri-Baptiste Grégoire, put it—for "la nécessité d'anéantir" (the necessity to destroy) these dialects but even German and Italian, as the languages of "despots and slaves," were believed to be obstacles to the revolution's goals.[69] Schools were seen as the primary means of achieving this annihilation, although historians are clear that little headway was made at the time to enact such policies.[70]

Although eighteenth-century linguistic ideologies elsewhere lacked the politicized zeal of France during the Revolution, similar concerns have been identified in the intellectual climate of the time. The founding of linguistic academies accelerated in the eighteenth century, including new institutions in Madrid (1713), Copenhagen (1742), Lisbon (1779), Moscow (1783), and Stockholm (1786).[71] Most relevant was the situation in England and Scotland, where defensiveness about the international standing of the English language encouraged efforts toward literacy and a written standard. English was considered by its speakers to be a marginal language in Europe well into the eighteenth century, eclipsed by Italian, German, Spanish, and especially French, the language of diplomacy. Although English was in fact already quietly laying the groundwork for global ascendancy—the eighteenth century saw a rise in translations of important literary works into English, for instance, a sign of trends to come—few recognized this fact or else believed it was tenuous. Furthermore, when the English looked back to their literary history they found Old and Middle English texts that could no longer be read without a dictionary, leading to the conclusion that English had degenerated and would continue to do so in the future unless checked. To most contemporaries this decline and unintelligibility in English appeared incongruent with Enlightenment understandings that a first-rate, civilized nation would speak a comparably clear, pure, and comprehensible language, leading key writers of the period, including John Locke, Lord Chesterfield, Samuel Johnson, and Jonathan Swift to advocate reform of English. In Scotland, too, a similar consciousness was raised by commentators such as James Elphinston and Sylvester Douglas concerning Scots English, particularly with regard to making the language more genteel. Such linguistic awareness was heightened by the Jacobite rebellions of the eighteenth century and the subsequent hostility toward Scottishness they sparked in England. Swift, of course, raised similar concerns for the English spoken in Ireland, where the propriety of Hiberno-English received similar attention from Maria Edgeworth and John Keogh. Although no academy was founded to advocate a certain form of English—Tony Crowley has argued that conceptions of English liberty and the association with the French Académie doomed such a project—various initiatives to standardize and "improve" the language were contemplated throughout the seventeenth and eighteenth centuries in both England and Scotland, including a short-lived commission convened by the Royal Society in 1664.[72]

With these ideologies of language of the eighteenth century in mind, educational policy in Ireland can be seen as closely conforming to wider expectations regarding "non-elite" languages. Languages such as Irish were not only considered barbarous, backward, difficult, and uncivilized—as various commentators had been arguing for centuries—but were also believed to lack a written corpus, further condemning it in the eyes of eighteenth-century advocates of dictionaries, printed pamphlets, and high literature. That Irish possessed a long history of written practices was ignored or, more often, unknown until the revival of Celtic scholarship in the second half of the century, making it unsuitable in the eyes of some as a basis for imparting education. Moreover, enabling any instruction through a vernacular like Irish could only provide a drag on the project of elevating English and uniting its constituents that was so central to the Enlightenment project as envisioned by English speakers. No better formulation of this three-part goal of refining and fortifying English, encouraging it to compete with other world languages like French, and relying on it to unite the Scottish, Irish, Welsh, and English nations can be found than the writings of Thomas Sheridan (1719–88), the Irish-born actor and elocutionist. In *British Education: or, the Source of the Disorders of Great Britain* (1756), Sheridan complained that Britain had neglected the English language during the rise of the vernaculars during the sixteenth and seventeenth centuries, resulting in the inheritance of a second-rate language left to "chance and caprice" and incapable of "accomplishing an entire union" with the Scots, Irish, and Welsh who "made up a considerable part of British dominions, both in power and extent, who spoke in tongues different from the English, and who were far from being firmly united in their inclinations."[73] Given Sheridan's antidote—the study of English, the writing of dictionaries, and schemes to elevate English to a first-rate world language—it is no surprise that policymakers of the early eighteenth century saw no place for any other languages in any proposed system of education in Ireland.

Having been so active on the question of language in the realm of religious and educational policy for two centuries, from the 1740s until the end of the century the state and its established church lapsed into virtual nonrecognition of the presence of Irish as a living language. When the 1709 penal law against the clergy came up for renewal in 1757, for example, only its provisions for converted priests were confirmed, while later renewals in 1772 and 1780 amended the original wording regarding mandatory preaching so that the reference to the use of Irish was simply omitted.[74] Protestant printing of Irish-language religious materials, a field in which the church had been a leader in the sixteenth and seventeenth centuries, was notably absent from the 1730s onward, eclipsed by Catholic printers at home in Dublin, such as Ignatius Kelly, Patrick Wogan, and Bartholomew Corcoran, and abroad, where Andrew Donlevy's catechism was printed by James Guerin in Paris in 1742.[75] These actions were accompanied by claims that the number of Irish monoglots was already so low as to eliminate the need to accommodate such speakers. Referring to Ireland's "poor Catholicks," the Protestant clergyman Samuel Madden (1668–1765) proposed in his *Reflections and Resolutions Proper for the Gentlemen of Ireland* (1738) that "as the old affection of speaking only Irish is quite laid aside, there is now scarce one in twenty who does not understand and speak English well," a percentage not in fact reached until the twentieth century.[76] By the early nineteenth century, parliamentary commissions created to look into education felt confident that the Tudor-era parish schools were no longer necessary because English was so universal, and John McEvoy, writing in 1802 in his capacity as an observer for the Dublin Society, believed that English was rapidly displacing Irish throughout the country: "The Roman Catholics are the only sect, who are fond of speaking the Irish language, and with them too it is wearing off very much."[77] So widespread was this belief that Irish had already declined significantly that advocates for the use of Irish in religious missions felt compelled to state that the language had not, in fact, disappeared. Whitley Stokes, writing in 1799, reminded readers that, in his estimate, 2.4 million Irish speakers still could be found.[78] Yet such attitudes persisted: in the 1820s, the Protestant archbishop of Cashel—an ecclesiastical province encompassing a still largely Irish-speaking Munster—believed that English had become so prevalent that the requirement that an English school be kept by the clergy under the 1537 act had become obsolete.[79]

One contributing factor to this tendency to view the Irish language as having already passed into extinction was, ironically, the growth, starting in the second half of the eighteenth century, of antiquarian interest in the Irish literary past among educated elites. A variety of endeavors helped fuel this interest, from published works like Charles Vallancey's *An Essay on the Antiquity of the Irish Language* (1772), Joseph Walker's *Historical Memoirs of the Irish Bards*

(1786), Charlotte Brooke's *Reliques of Irish Poetry* (1789), and James Hardiman's *Irish Minstrelsy, or Bardic Remains of Ireland* (1831) to the founding of learned societies such as the Royal Irish Academy (1785), the Gaelic Society (1807), the Iberno-Celtic Society (1818), the Celtic Society (1845), and the Ossianic Society (1853). Although scholars have long modified their views of these endeavors as merely antiquarian by pointing to the many points of contact between eighteenth- and nineteenth-century Celtic research and the Irish-language scribes and intellectuals, from the Ó Neachtain family of the early 1700s to the contributions of Seosamh Ó Longáin (1816–80),[80] one strand of this "rediscovery" of the Irish language was the concentration by many of its participants on ancient Irish literature, ruins, and artifacts. The Irish language, though viewed in a positive light by these antiquarians, was lauded not for its present-day use but for its supposed affinity with ancient languages like Phoenician, Hebrew, Greek, and Latin.[81] Choices for texts to publish by the various antiquarian societies were invariably manuscripts and compositions dating no later than the songs of Toirdhealbhach Ó Cearbhalláin (1670–1738), and most predated 1600. Vallancey, for example, boasted in his Irish grammar published in 1773 of having learned "the old language of Ireland still fortunately preserved in ancient books" rather than from "any jargon yet spoke by the unlettered vulgar."[82] The reading public with an interest in the Irish language was presented with book titles by Brooke and Hardiman that, however undoubtedly close the personal connection of their authors to the living language, nevertheless spoke first and foremost of literary "reliques" and "bardic remains."[83] And the scholar of ancient languages and editor of a number of medieval and early modern Irish texts, Robert Atkinson (1839–1908), notoriously never learned to speak (in fact disdained proponents of) the modern language.[84] This was not a universally shared sentiment among scholars of Irish in this period, as the careers of Edward O'Reilly, who advocated the study of Irish both for its usefulness in unlocking the past as well as its practical use as a modern language,[85] or John O'Daly, the publisher and scholar who played such a vital role in the early development of the move to revive the spoken language, demonstrated. Advocates of the contemporary use of Irish for religious instruction, such as Thaddaeus Connellan (ca. 1775–1854) and Henry Monck Mason, also saw beyond the possibilities of the language as scholarly artifact, while local enthusiasts likewise saw the restoration of Irish as a daily language as a desirable goal. But a number of scholars undeniably took an interest in Irish (indeed, for many it was one of the prime reasons to take an interest in Irish) from the perspective that it was more akin to classical heavyweights like Greek and Latin than to modern languages.

This tendency to see Irish as a relic of the past rather than a living part of contemporary eighteenth- or nineteenth-century society becomes even more noticeable when it is contrasted with language attitudes elsewhere, especially in British colonial projects in other parts of the world. Consider for example, the different direction taken in Scotland from 1754, when SSPCK directors replaced earlier opposition to literacy in Gaelic in their schools with a new effort to inculcate basic catechetical and scriptural literacy in the vernacular. A full twenty Gaelic catechisms were printed and disseminated by the end of the eighteenth century.[86] While the Crown, parliament, and the religious hierarchy seemed incapable of recognizing Irish as a candidate for the Enlightenment project of standardization and grammatical description, in New Zealand British religious missionaries had embarked on an ambitious project starting in 1815 to encourage widespread literacy in the Maori language. By 1821 a Maori grammar had been published, and by the 1830s a first book of hymns and an edition of the New Testament—all accomplished despite the need to create a suitable orthographical convention from scratch.[87] In India, language was one of the lynchpins of colonial consolidation of power from the mid-eighteenth century onward as successive East India Company administrations sought to master for themselves the languages of the subcontinent while influencing those spoken by natives in their role as adjuncts to the colonial state. Orientalist scholars and company governors-general actively promoted Indian education in Sanskrit in strongholds of learning like Benares, where a college was founded in 1791, in a bid to first elevate preferred native intellectual and religious authority before utilizing it to fulfill British administrative goals. Study entailed a whole range of languages to improve administration: Persian initially, along perhaps with Sanskrit and Arabic, and later in the nineteenth century, regional languages like Urdu and Hindi deemed better suited to colonial rule at the local level. Colleges founded at Fort William, Calcutta (1800), and at Fort St. George, Madras (1812), helped enable British civil servants master these requirements.[88] Only in the third and fourth decades of the nineteenth century did a growing push for the use of English among Indian civil servants gain momentum, and even then regional languages—albeit in unified, standard written forms created with the assistance of British authorities—were seen as a key intermediary step.[89] This activism contrasts sharply with the assumed irrelevance of Irish to the logistics of running church and state in Ireland at the outset of the nineteenth century.

But linguistic agnosticism was not infinitely sustainable in Ireland. Irish could be safely ignored as long as an English-speaking elite could be relied upon to enact the more limited aims of early modern government. Once institutions of the state began extending their presence more dramatically into the everyday lives of nonelites, however, the linguistic issue resurfaced. For education and religion, the change manifested itself in the early nineteenth century as the state became increasingly interested after 1800 in how it could extend educational institutions, and the established church became concerned about threats to its claim to represent the Irish nation. This change was further boosted by the rise in the gross numbers of Irish speakers. Notably, this interpretation modifies the findings of historians of education, who have asserted that debates over the use of Irish in schools were brief, if not completely absent, both before and after the establishment of the national system of education in 1831.[90] Such readings have been a result, in part, of the tendency to rely exclusively on the official reports and records of the national commissioners of education rather than surveying the larger terrain on which not just educational but also religious authorities played a role. To be sure, such debates were not overtly visible, but the second decade of the century did in fact witness the issue of Irish abruptly resurface as part of a renewed debate—often along well-established lines—about how to accommodate the language. This concern becomes especially visible when the scope is widened to consider discussions within the wider Protestant missionary community, a vital, rather than expedient, shift of focus because of the overlapping goal among all Protestant denominations in imparting basic primary education: catechetical and scriptural teaching and literacy. The stakes were high in these discussions, especially for a Church of Ireland that was on the defensive by midcentury, and although no radical alteration in the overall final character of Irish education or religious institutions resulted, the debate did play a role in the course of state development and deserves to be highlighted both for the role Irish speakers played in prompting that debate and for the impact resultant policies had on Irish speakers.

The Westminster Parliament, charged with Irish oversight after the Act of Union, quickly turned to address education in Ireland, where a patchwork of schools run by religious and charitable institutions dominated the official educational landscape. The most visible of these schools, numbering over sixteen hundred by 1830, were those run by the so-called Kildare Place Society (f. 1811), an avowedly nondenominational and charitable institution whose board of directors at one time included Daniel O'Connell, but whose efforts came under fire starting in the 1820s for masking an underlying Protestant ethos. Most distressingly, the quality and number of schools in Ireland were low, as the majority of the Catholic population chose informal local pay schools over the thinly veiled Protestantism of the schools receiving state and charitable financing. Thus, from 1809 onward, appointed education commissioners provided a steady stream of reports soliciting plans for a more effective (and nondenominational) approach. Although sectarian issues dominated these discussions, from the beginning linguistic policy, too, was raised. For some, linguistic uniformity was one of the antidotes to the religious diversity the schools might ameliorate. This was the take of MP Henry Grattan, who in response to a call from the secretary of the national board for proposals on Irish education argued in 1811 that any new schools should teach and rely on English only: "I beg to add, that one great object of National Education should be to unite the inhabitants of the Island, and that such an event cannot be well accomplished, except they are brought to speak one common language. I think the diversity of language, and not the diversity of religion, constitutes a diversity of people. I should be very sorry that the Irish language should be forgotten; but glad that the English language should be generally understood."[91]

The majority of MPs undoubtedly shared Grattan's attitudes, but they were not universal. The Scottish radical MP Joseph Hume (1777–1855), debating the annual supply of educational grants to the Irish charters schools in 1823, complained that few Catholics were receiving instruction despite the huge financial outlay. Urging the size of the grant to the charter schools be reduced, Hume added: "Government could not be ignorant of the state of Ireland; and they ought to know that the demoralizing was, in no small degree, owing to the ignorance of the peasantry. To remove this they should have education in the Irish language; and parents and children ought not, as was the case with their schools, to be separated."[92] Older, sectarian arguments about the preferred effectiveness of Irish-language education in dispelling the "mists of delusion" from the eyes of Catholics also returned, pressed by observers such as the Anglican (later, Unitarian) minister and writer Thomas Kitson Cromwell (1792–1870) who denounced the effectiveness of English-only schools that taught "the poor natives, who are incapable of maintaining a conversation in any language but the Erse."[93] In this case, linguistic accommodation was seen as an antidote to Catholic educational shortcomings.

The most influential players in this debate, however, were the increasingly visible evangelical and Protestant dissenter organizations that placed vernacular literacy for scriptural reading at the forefront of their educational (and proselytizing) aims. The appearance of these societies on the Irish scene and the premium put by many of them on scriptural literacy in native languages raised the profile of the language question for religious and educational administrators alike for the first time in nearly a century. Here, Irish conditions merged seamlessly with the larger British colonial context already well developed elsewhere in which Protestant, and especially evangelical, interests had succeeded in openly grafting missionary efforts onto imperial expansion and administration. Hence William Wilberforce was among the architects of the East India Company Charter Act of 1813, which in addition to promoting Orientalist aims in developing native Indian educational institutions also opened up India to missionary work. But not coincidentally, Wilberforce was active in London in support of an auxiliary branch of the most active of the new organizations created by evangelicals at this time to promote education in Irish, the Irish Society for Promoting the Education of the Native Irish through the Medium of Their Own Language. Speaking in favor of the venture at a meeting in 1822, Wilberforce noted that the "aboriginal inhabitants of Ireland," as he referred to them, needed a system of education and the distribution of Irish-language primers, Bibles, and extracts from the scriptures.[94] Wilberforce's endorsement was representative of a wider Protestant movement that, in addition to the Anglican evangelicals, included sections of Baptist, Congregationalist, Ulster Presbyterian, and Methodist forces that sought a combination of vernacular missionary work and educational expansion. Among the Irish-language missionary initiatives launched by these denominations were the open-air sermons conducted by itinerant Methodist preachers Gideon Ouseley, James McQuige, and Charles Graham in the 1790s and early 1800s, the Congregationalist (but broadly interdenominational in membership) London Hibernian Society founded in 1806, the Baptist Society for Promoting the Gospel in Ireland founded in 1814, the Presbyterian Missionary Society launched in 1830, and the evangelical-led Irish Society itself. The question of whether to use Irish literacy as a tool for educational advancement was raised and debated repeatedly by organizations affiliated with each of these denominations, creating visibility for the issue among authorities charged with school policy.

The structure of these organizations and their methods for implementing their missionary designs have been well-researched in recent years by a number of historians.[95] Supported by donations and, in the Anglican instance, the patronage of high-profile evangelical bishops and archbishops, the London Hibernian Society, Baptist Society, Presbyterian Missionary Society, and the Irish Society set up a series of local schools on both permanent and temporary bases starting in the 1810s, 1820s, and 1830s. The goal of these schools, especially those of the Irish Society, was to impart scriptural literacy in Irish, an object for which Irish-speaking teachers—among them Catholics and Protestant converts who were native speakers—were paid capitation fees. To publicize and build public support for their aims, missionary advocates wrote a series of works weighing in on the question, including Daniel Dewar's *Observations on the Character, Customs, and Superstitions of the Irish* (1812), Christopher Anderson's *Memorial on Behalf of the Native Irish* (1815), J. S. Taylor's *Reasons for Giving Moral Instruction of the Native Irish through the Medium of Their Vernacular Language* (1817), W. S. Sankey's *A Brief Sketch of Various Attempts Which Have Been Made to Diffuse a Knowledge of the Holy Scriptures through the Medium of the Irish Language* (1818), Charles Orpen's *The Claim of Millions of Our Fellow-Countrymen of Present and Future Generations, to Be Taught in Their Own and Only Language; the Irish* (1821), and Irish Society founder Henry Monck Mason's *Reasons and Authorities and Facts Afforded by the History of the Irish Society Respecting the Duty of Employing the Irish Language as a More General Medium for Conveying Scriptural Instruction to the Native Peasantry of Ireland* (1829). Their advocacy of Irish was based on a small number of key tenets, many of them familiar from earlier efforts by John Richardson and others and can be summed up in three points: a rejection of claims that the population of Irish speakers was too small to justify addressing their educational needs, an identification of close parallels between Irish Catholics and native inhabitants of other regions who lacked "civility," and an understanding that Irish literacy was to be a bridge to English acquisition and English literacy.

On the question of numbers, it was warned that the Irish-speaking population had been grossly underestimated, and that even where a functional knowledge of English had been achieved, a high-order ability to read and absorb religious concepts usually had not.[96] Such arguments, which were repeated at meetings in an effort to build support for missionary projects, made headway, especially in England where knowledge about Ireland was low but money for Protestant charity work was plentiful. At a meeting in Southampton to form an auxiliary to the Irish Society attended by one of its founders, the Reverend Joseph D'Arcy Sirr, reservations were raised by Lord Ashton (1755–1840), who explained that he "doubted whether the hand-bill circulated to call this meeting had not overstated the actual number of persons speaking the Irish language," and while admitting that it was favored by many Irish, "it was only a colloquial dialect; very few could read it." Sirr, however, countered with estimates of millions of speakers and eyewitness accounts of Irish monolingualism, leading another attendee who previously "had not heard of this Society," a Mr. John Bullar, to conclude that "a case had been made out."[97] But others remained skeptical. An "absurdity," was the judgment of one commentator who wrote in response to

Anderson's claims that neglect of instruction in Irish had paradoxically prevented the spread of English.[98] A Dublin correspondent writing to the *Times* in opposition to Orange disturbances also took the opportunity to inveigh on missionary efforts in Irish, noting that while in favor of antiquarian scholarship, "I am far from attributing any importance to this ancient dialect, and I have always laughed at the hypocritical pretences with which the pockets of the credulous English have been picked by the canting missionaries, who go about collecting money for instructing the native Irish in the truths of the Christian religion in their own language." In all of Ireland, the correspondent continued, "there are not half a million of adults ... who do not speak English."[99]

Drawing connections with populations elsewhere purportedly in need of Christian education helped combat this dismissal of Irish speakers by reminding audiences of the difficulties of trying to build scriptural literacy in places like India where English was not spoken. To be sure, the application of such colonial paradigms to the Irish language was part of a broader ideology that had long linked Ireland with European perceptions of Asia, North Africa, and the East.[100] Newspaper and periodical writers made claims that Irish speakers had been observed communicating seamlessly with Tunisians and Moroccans, for instance, while a review of an early spelling book published in 1810 by the Reverend William Neilson explicitly paired the manual with a Tahitian language guide of the same year on the grounds that "these two small pamphlets are highly acceptable, as evidences of the rational zeal of our fellow subjects for the religious instruction of barbarous nations."[101] Scholarly pursuits of eastern origins for Irish were tracked: "Antiquaries say that there is much of the Oriental turn of expression in the Irish language," observed one such editorial.[102] But the application of colonial analogies also had an immediate practical effect for missionaries in building a case for imparting education in Irish. By playing up the similar linguistic boundaries impeding Protestant missionaries in Ireland, Africa, and Asia, a case could be better made for distributing the Bible in Irish or founding schools dedicated to its instruction. Anderson himself had complained of the neglect of vernacular scriptural education, noting, "It is to be deplored that in a populous district within the United Kingdom, the same policy has not been heartily and generally adopted, which the community at large has been applying (most laudably) toward the distant tribes of Heathen nations!"[103] Dewar, too, argued that overseas missions in the South Sea, India, and Africa had made the absence of such work in Ireland conspicuous, and local societies such as the White's Row auxiliary of Portsea, England, acted as affiliates to various missionary efforts using vernacular translations of the scripture around the globe, combining support for Asia and Africa with assistance for Ireland.[104] By the 1850s, the Irish case had come full circle, and advocates for the use of Indian languages in spreading the scriptures were in turn citing Ireland and Wales as evidence where vernacular proselytizing had proved advantageous.[105]

However, the goal for these societies, as they often reminded their audience, remained the achievement of literacy in English by Irish speakers. Time and again, they reiterated their belief that teaching literacy in Irish would not only fail to inhibit the spread of English but would also encourage the decline of Irish in the long term.[106] Toward this end, Irish texts were nearly universally provided with parallel English translation to enforce the hoped-for procession to literacy in the target language. Another indication of the limited role for Irish literacy foreseen by missionaries was the insistence on religious reading only. Virtually no secular material was provided, and even basic spelling books used passages from scriptures to illustrate their case. While intensive, single-text reading practices were typical of this time period, and while study of the Bible was seen by Protestants as the nonnegotiable minimum required in any education of children, the refusal to develop Irish literacy beyond a religious context revealed the true designs of the missionary societies. As Sankey wrote, the "very scantiness of Irish books is not altogether without its advantages, inasmuch as it affords an opportunity of communicating the benefits of religious instruction, free from the risk of corrupting the mind by the productions of a licentious and immoral press."[107] In part, as has been noted, this may have reflected the attitudes of many Irish speakers themselves, who may not have seen literacy in Irish as an asset.[108] Moreover, opposition to wider literacy in Irish also served to placate potential opposition to their plan among those, especially the Anglican hierarchy, the landlords, and the wider English-speaking public, who still saw Irish speaking as a threat to the state. Bishop Woodward of Cloyne, for instance, had been an especially vocal opponent of Irish-language instruction in the late eighteenth century, and according to McQuige, the belief that "teaching them Irish will increase their animosity to the existing government" was still a much used counterargument to scriptural education in 1818.[109] This link between speaking Irish and disloyalty was very persistent; cases of applications for gun possession being denied in part on the grounds of Irish monoglotism were well enough known to circulate in national newspapers.[110] For some opponents, no time devoted to instruction in Irish could be justified, even if it meant a bridge to English. As Richard Digby Neave framed it bluntly in 1852 in reference to such efforts, "It is a backward movement to teach the rising generation the dying tongue of an illiterate race, to the exclusion of the dominant language of civilization."[111]

This debate over whether to use Irish within the missionary movement could be dismissed as limited in scope and of little consequence to larger educational questions were it not for the visibility it raised for the language question in proposals elsewhere. A letter by "Philanthropos" submitted to the *Monthly Magazine* in 1816 proposed a large-scale system of circulating schools for Ireland on the model of similar successful efforts in Wales and Scotland at that time. According to the plan outlined by Philanthropos, Irish was to be the language of instruction given the enthusiasm for vernacular literacy being generated not only by the London Hibernian Society but also by "the attention which is paid to the language in Maynooth college, where M'Curten's grammar is used." Notably, an all-Irish educational atmosphere was envisioned by Philanthropos: "The schools to be opened should be for the sole and express purpose of teaching the inhabitants of those districts where Irish is spoken, particularly in the south and west, to read their native language. Alphabet boards, containing the letters of the Irish alphabet, in the Roman and Irish character in parallel columns, to be used in teaching the alphabet; and syllable boards of two and three letters to succeed these." Schools were to be conducted for six- to eighteenth-month terms, and classes were to be held in local homes.[112] An editorial letter by the *Belfast News-Letter* in 1828 also favored a broader encouragement of literacy in Irish. Lauding the efforts of the Irish Society, the *News-Letter* turned the usual missionary argument regarding the primacy of the scriptures on its head: Bible-reading, it was argued, would only be encouraged if a broader fondness (and ability) to read in Irish had been nurtured. After all, according to its editors, "there are numerous subjects on which the Bible was never intended to convey information," and so general knowledge might be built through "the establishment of a cheap periodical in the Irish language ... [as] one of the most likely methods of generating a taste for reading."[113] Less supportive were the members of the Clare Liberal Club, who, in April of 1828 at a quarterly meeting discussing the use of club funds, turned to the efforts of Reverend Robert Daly, rector of Powerscourt and central organizer in the Irish Society, to raise donations for his cause. According to member John Macnamara of Moher, Co. Clare, such efforts were "gull," designed to impose on the "pockets of John Bull." Another member doubted whether Irish literacy could be learned at all without recourse to some other intermediary language.[114] By contrast, an advocate for instruction in Irish appeared in the pages of the *Quarterly Journal of Education*, where an article in 1833 complained that neglect of Irish-language education among "the peasantry, who, in large districts of the country, understand no other language," had contributed to a wider loss of the country's literary history. Significantly, this article was cited in a later report of the education commissioners.[115]

The use of Irish by the missionary groups also prompted the question of the vernacular in education to be taken up by first, the Kildare Place Society and then, on a handful of occasions, by the national school commissioners after the founding of the new system in 1831. In its eighth report, for 1820, the Kildare Place Society (KPS) investigated the work being done by the Irish Society and London Hibernian Society and concluded that an approach using Irish had merit but that a lack of printed materials in Irish was holding the schools back. It recommended a continued focus on English-language schools, leaving the Irish-language work to the other two societies, but it did add that the KPS should support efforts under way to produce teaching materials—specifically, reading and spelling books—in Irish.[116] The national education commissioners revisited the question on their own starting in their 1825 report, when they collected evidence on all the schools then in operation in Ireland. This report confirmed that the practice of teaching through Irish was being used, even in some pay schools without missionary affiliation. Its investigation into the KPS, for example, revealed that among the books in use in their classrooms were a number of Irish texts: the O'Reilly catechism in Irish, James Gallagher's *Irish Sermons*, Tadhg Gaelach Ó Súilleabháin's *Pious Miscellany*, and a number of the society's own Irish-language spelling and reading books. The commissioners also called up witnesses like George Pringle of the London Hibernian Society, Reverend John West of the Baptist Society, and Henry Monck Mason of the Irish Society, who all testified as to the use of Irish-language scriptures and teaching in missionary (and some nonmissionary) schools.[117] That Irish speakers would make up a significant portion of any system with a national scope could not have escaped the notice of the commissioners.

As has been noted by historians repeatedly, the Stanley letter outlining the parameters for the national schools in 1831 made no mention of Irish as a means of instruction, neither banning nor prescribing its use. In effect, English was the only language of instruction envisioned, and the conclusion has been rightfully made that the board did not see it as a suitable goal for instruction. Moreover, not until Patrick Keenan, as a senior inspector, raised concerns starting in 1855 about the effectiveness of English-language instruction imparted to Irish monoglots was the issue meaningfully revisited.[118] But a few features of these first two decades of the national schools with regard to language deserve to be better highlighted. The first is that the question of Irish-language instruction did not disappear entirely from national-level debate, even after 1831. John Coolahan, for instance, has uncovered two instances, in 1833 and 1837, in which the commissioners received complaints that an English-only system was not taking into account the numbers of Irish monoglots.[119] The endlessly quoted dismissal of Irish by Daniel O'Connell in 1833, in which he spoke of its decline in favorable terms as a boon to ending language diversity and referred to the "superior utility" of English, provides another case of the visibility of the issue at the national level—one that proves more complicated on further investigation. Most historians take this quotation from the recollections of the MP William O'Neill Daunt (1807–94), who claimed that O'Connell had made it at a Saint Patrick's Day dinner party.[120] But O'Connell in fact made a similar statement, this time in specific response to the proposal that Irish be used in education, during a parliamentary speech in May of 1833. In this instance, O'Connell was responding to a petition by the Scottish Presbyterian Synods of Glasgow and Ayr, "praying for a system of education for the Irish in their native tongue." O'Connell's opposition was based not just on a utilitarian view of language—he noted again that he would "not regret its extinction"—but also on the claim that the numbers of Irish monoglots had been exaggerated. The petition, he noted, exemplified the ignorance about conditions in Ireland of which he was far more aware.[121]

O'Connell's reaction, as well as another case of opposition to teaching through Irish by the commissioners of national education, hints at another factor in the rejection of Irish-language teaching by the board. After an initial period of acceptance by Roman Catholics of efforts by the Irish Society and others to teach in Irish, by 1825 even the Irish Society was associated in Catholic minds with proselytizing and Bible-reading without supervision or commentary.[122] A similar association between Irish-language instruction and proselytizing was also undoubtedly forged in the minds of the education commissioners, who were under strong pressure in the 1820s and 1830s to emerge with a system that would be palatable to the Roman Catholic prelates. Notably, one of only two identified cases in which use of the Irish language was raised by teachers with the commissioners during this time period involved an attempt in 1834 by the Protestant Thaddaeus Connellan, who was intimately involved in the missionary organizations, to receive national school funds as a teacher of Irish.[123] This application was denied, just as the Scottish Presbyterian petition was tabled, indicating that neither Roman Catholics nor the commissioners could disentangle Irish vernacular instruction from a movement seen as an intrusion by proselytizing outsiders fanning the flames of sectarianism.

The second point to be made is that, especially in these first two decades of their existence, the language question was far less pressing on the school administrators than it might have been had the system's growth not been so slow in precisely the same regions where Irish speaking was strongest. Put another way, the commissioners could get away with ignoring Irish because of the uneven spread of the system. In 1841 after a decade in existence, of 2,337 national schools in operation, a full 1,647, or 70 percent of the total, were located in heavily English-speaking Leinster and Ulster, where just 53 percent of the Irish population and less than 13 percent of the Irish-speaking population (according to the 1851 census) resided. Connacht had 208 schools in operation in 1841, by far the lowest of all four provinces, and Mayo and Galway combined for a mere 102 schools (4 percent of the total) despite containing approximately 10 percent of the Irish population. Cork and Cork city, with 10 percent of the Irish population in 1841, could boast only 185 national schools, or less than 8 percent of the total.[124] In 1855, after over two decades in existence, little progress had been made, and Munster and Connacht still lagged behind. In that year, less than 39 percent of the 5,124 schools in operation were located in those two most heavily Irish speaking of the four provinces, and in Connacht in particular, with only 14 percent of the share of national schools but nearly 34 percent of all Irish speakers (in 1851), the system was least entrenched.[125] The reasons for this regional disparity are not difficult to ascertain. National schools were expected to be initiated using local organizers and money, to which the central authorities would add their own financial support and teacher salaries. This made poorer regions less able to offset such costs.[126] Moreover, in Connacht the opposition of Archbishop John MacHale to clerical participation in the national system until well into the 1860s and 1870s meant that priests, typically the local initiators of applications to add new schools to the rolls, were discouraged from participating. Instead, lay Catholics had to take up the task.[127] Ironically, given MacHale's additional objection to the national schools on the ground of their "antinational" approach, his tactic likely further cloaked from the attention of commissioners the unsuitability of English instruction in an Irish-speaking community.

Finally, it should be noted that Keenan, who famously condemned the English-only approach and recommended the use of Irish as a bridge to English literacy in the 1850s, was not the only one to see the virtues of introducing instruction through Irish. Indeed, at the local level some Irish-speaking teachers had already made this a practice regardless of the policy of the national commissioners who did not, after all, prohibit the use of Irish. For example, there is widely distributed evidence of the use of a mnemonic device, based on the use of Irish words to describe the shape or sound of each letter, to help bridge the language divide in learning the English alphabet. Attestations of their use exist for Cork, Donegal, Galway, Kerry, Leitrim, Mayo, and Roscommon, and they were likely used in other locations as well.¹²⁸ In this approach, the letter *A*, for instance, was remembered with the phrase *cúpla den teach*—"couple (i.e., roof joint) of the house"—referring to its pointed shape. The letter *J* was often connected to *camán* (hurley stick), while the letter *T* suggested *croisín* (a cross). The phrase *crú an asail*, the ass's hoof, applied to the letter *U*. Other letters used more indirect prompts. The letter *K*, not present in the Irish alphabet, could be remembered by *eochair* (key) because of its shape. The letter *F* was sometimes connected to *fata* (potato), provided that locals used this specific dialectical form of the word instead of *prata*, as spoken in other regions. Precisely how long this practice had been used is difficult to determine. The examples reported by contributors to *An Claidheamh Soluis* in the first decade of the 1900s and those collected by folklorists in the 1930s and 1940s were taken from Irish speakers born in the mid-nineteenth century who recalled it from their school days, suggesting that classrooms made use of the mnemonic device at least as far back as the 1850s and 1860s, if not earlier. One informant from Erris, Co. Mayo, recalled that they had been employed in that area right up until 1880.¹²⁹ Micheál Mac Gabhann, born in 1865, remembered being taught in this fashion by an old man using a willow rod blackened in the fire.¹³⁰ In the 1890s the newspaper editor and Irish scholar Seán Mag Fhlainn (1843–1915) recalled its use in the area of Tuam, Co. Galway, a number of years earlier,¹³¹ and Conchubhar Maguidhir (ca. 1861–1944), the translator, folk collector, and Gaelic League activist from Galway, also reported that he had been taught using the method when he had attended school.¹³²

Although Keenan claimed in his reports for Donegal in 1859 that neither managers nor teachers fluent in Irish seemed willing to countenance the use of the language in teaching English literacy,¹³³ there is evidence to the contrary that schoolmasters used Irish not only to help students learn the alphabet but also as a general teaching tool. Rhymed verses provided a particularly helpful aid to learning English. Mag Fhlaim remembered that Sean Phátruic Molloy, a Tuam teacher, would dismiss his students at the end of the day by saying, "T-H-A-T, march home to the *fataí*," a phrase that rhymed the letter *T* with the long *I* in *fataí* (potatoes).¹³⁴ A chant with such phrases as "A-B-C, *do bhrisfinn do chroí*" (I would break your heart) was reportedly sung in the barony of West Carbery in Cork and had become a sufficiently well-known part of Irish-speaking popular culture to appear in nineteenth-century storytellers' repertoires: the character in a midcentury tale from Clifden, Co. Galway, for example, jokes that he will teach a hackler English by reciting for him, "A-B-C *go mbristear do chroí*" (may your heart be broken) and "A-B, *go caora mhór bhuí*" (a big yellow sheep).¹³⁵ The use of Irish also helped when first introducing English words and concepts to Irish speakers. Keenan's own colleague, inspector John Edward Sheridan, testified before the Powis Commission that "some national school teachers use Irish for the purpose of explanation, to make themselves understood by the pupils."[136] Jeremiah O'Donovan Rossa (1831–1915), too, recalled from his school days in southwest Cork that the master used Irish in the course of teaching English, and Seán Pléimeann, who taught at Rathcormuck National School in County Waterford, attested, "About Cahirciveen in Kerry teachers often find it useful to explain in Irish to their pupils the meaning of words occurring in the lessonbooks."[137] It was reported in 1882 that a national school teacher in Cork "taught his bilingual pupils the meanings of declensions and conjugations of the English grammar through the medium of Irish."[138] And in Erris, Co. Mayo, it was noted in 1905 in *An Claidheamh Soluis* by Eoghan Cóir that "necessarily, but not as a recognized and essential part of his duty, [the teacher] uses Irish to teach English. When the child has acquired a sufficient smattering of English to follow the teacher, the use of Irish is gradually discontinued, and instruction is given through the medium of English."[139] Inaction at the national level in terms of addressing the educational needs of non-English speakers thereby prompted those at the local level to modify such policies to suit needs on the ground.

A reckoning of sorts for both the established church and the education system began with the publication of the results of the 1851 Irish census, the first to attempt an accurate measure of the numbers of Irish speakers then in existence. Although the figures did not indicate that Irish speaking was in a robust state— less than one quarter of the population was returned as speaking Irish—the gross numbers nevertheless undercut the long-standing claim that Irish speaking had already become extinct. "People are taken by surprise of the extent to which [Irish] is now spoken; and more curiosity about it is awakened than I ever knew before," reported Robert MacAdam to John Windele in 1857.[140] Windele pointed out that Irish had been, in the seventeenth century, "numerically far below what it is at the present day," making nonsense of claims of its extinction.[141] At a meeting of a Belfast branch of the Irish Society held in 1858, the annual report made clear that long-standing doubts had been affected: "As to the number of Irishmen who thus speak the ancient language of their country, there remains no longer any doubt, the latest census—1851—having announced the fact— a wonderful one, too, after nearly eight centuries of English connection with Ireland—that 1,524,286 of its inhabitants converse in the Irish tongue, and 319,602 neither converse in nor understand any other."[142] The bishop of Cashel,

Robert Daly, agreed, noting that the census data, while revealing a decline in speakers, had presented powerful evidence of a large enough number to justify the continuance of missionary efforts through Irish, and that even the national school system had been wrong in using an English-only approach.[143] Denials of the continued existence of a sizeable Irish-speaking population did not disappear, of course. The Belfast minister Reverend Edgar, observing that Presbyterian missionary schools teaching Irish had been discontinued in 1854, noted, "We preach in Irish to the old, who know it only; but Irish is dying, and should die. English is the language of our pulpit and our schools."[144]

Nevertheless the 1850s witnessed yet another reignition of debates that had both immediate and long-term ramifications. For the Church of Ireland, under increasing pressure for disestablishment from the 1830s onward, the news that so many of the Irish people continued to speak a language for which the church had made little or no accommodations (aside, that is, from the evangelical wing who had launched the Irish Society) was not welcome. By the 1850s and 1860s the argument that the established church had not made any progress among Roman Catholics made it all the more unpalatable that it would receive state support, and many Protestants began a process of self-criticism in search of reasons for the failure to expand. Language policy was seized on as one example of this failure and a weak spot in the church's claim to establishment. According to the dean of Exeter, "Instead of giving the Irish the Bible and the liturgy of the established church in their native tongue, we endeavoured almost to exterminate the Irish language, and introduce the English, which was a hopeless task and met with signal failure."[145] A lecture delivered by Reverend James Kelly of Saint George's church, Liverpool, in 1865 surveyed the entire history of the Reformation in Ireland and found the mission to the Catholics, especially the Irish speakers, similarly lacking. He blasted the unpreparedness of the Elizabethan church as revealed by its reliance on Latin when no Irish translation of the services had been made, and complained of the indifferent reception of the Upper House of Convocation ("nominees," Kelly added, "of the British government") to the call for Irish-language preaching in 1710.[146]

The casting of blame on British governance intensified as disestablishment, ultimately enacted in 1869, appeared increasingly inevitable. A lecture delivered by the Reverend Theophilus Campbell, rector of Finvoy, in May of 1868 defended the established church through a number of key rhetorical claims of the time, most importantly the assertion that the Irish church had never been fully Catholic in its early years, thus making the Reformation a return to its original antipapal roots. To this, Campbell added the mismanagement of disgraced

English bishops sent to serve as prelates in Ireland and, in a clear stab at the statutes of Elizabeth, the impossibility of pressing the Reformation among an Irish-speaking population when the English government insisted on English and Latin.[147] Late that year, a letter submitted to the *Hull Packet* newspaper insisted that it was the English administration that had undermined the church in Ireland through its attempts to stamp out the Irish language, a policy that linked conquest and linguistic imperialism in the minds of the Irish in a way reminiscent of nineteenth-century Russia. Refusal to allow services in English, the suppression of Irish literary activity, the blocking of plans for Irish-speaking ministers starting in 1703, and the appointment of English-speaking "younger members of influential English families" had all ensured the success of Catholicism.[148] Catholic commentators, for their own part, pointed out what they saw as a fallacy in this linguistic defense, as in a contributor to the *Freeman's Journal* who reminded readers that the persistence of English-speaking Catholics in the Pale undermined the notion that the Reformation had somehow been stalled by using English rather than the Irish language.[149]

Proponents of the language defense pressed their case on the hustings and during the debates over disestablishment itself in the House of Commons. MP Lord Claud Hamilton, speaking in the Commons in 1868 in opposition to plans to strip the Church of Ireland of its property, denounced those who believed a punitive settlement was necessary based on claims that the church "had totally failed to discharge its function." In his estimation, the Irish church had in fact been undermined by its use as a tool of English imperial expansion: "He was perfectly prepared to acknowledge that, for two centuries, the English government had made use of the Irish church as a political engine; that was no fault of the church, which resisted as much as it could the steps taken to employ it in such a capacity. For political reasons, it was not allowed to publish Prayerbooks in the Irish language, so that fair play was not allowed the church in its endeavours to reach the hearts of the Irish people."[150] It would be unfair, Hamilton concluded, to penalize the church for a situation caused by English linguistic conquest. This argument was flexible enough to suit the supporters of disestablishment as well. On the other side of the political aisle, the Liberal MP John Dent Dent (1826–94) also conjured this argument in defense of disestablishment during a campaign, noting that the Church of Ireland had been undermined by England's linguistic policies and that its advantageous transformation into a missionary church could only be furthered by releasing it from the state.[151] Meanwhile, as if to take matters into their own hands, the Church of Ireland adopted a new canon at its national meeting of April 1871 enabling ministers to "use such portions of the service in Irish as the ordinary should direct."[152]

Such arguments contained a grain of truth, but the recalcitrance of the established church itself on the language question over several centuries cannot be denied. Certainly, it was the Upper House of Convocation that, along with the Irish Parliament and the Crown, had pushed the key policies that had favored English at every turn: in the 1560 Act of Uniformity and in response to moves by the ministers acting in the Lower House to press for a missionary drive to the Catholics in Irish in 1710. Divide over the language question in the church also broke along a radical-conservative axis as much as one that separated the hierarchy from their ministers. By the nineteenth century, impetus for Irish in the Protestant context was coming firmly from one direction, namely, the evangelicals represented by the Irish Society and from outside dissenting groups like the Baptist Society, whose enthusiasm for Irish proselytizing prodded Anglicans to do the same. The fact that the language question had been raised during the debates surrounding the final years of church establishment at all revealed the extent to which missionaries, as well as the broader Irish-speaking population whose visibility had been heightened by the 1851 census, had been able to push the issue back into the spotlight in the most significant way since the early 1700s.

A reckoning of sorts arrived for the state's language policies in education as well. In a series of reports delivered to the national commissioners in the 1850s, Patrick Keenan pointed to the absolute deficiency of schools in which Irish speakers, and monoglots in particular, were expected to acquire English through rote recitation. Keenan never advocated learning Irish as more than a bridge to the ultimate goal of English literacy, but he did envision a far larger role for the language than had hereto been the case. By his own account, his reports urging the use of Irish in the classroom and his entreaties with teachers and school managers to allow the same had made an immediate impact by establishing, for the first time, "the unqualified right and incumbent duty of the teachers to use the vernacular freely whenever they themselves understood it, as an aid to the education of the children in English."[153] In his report for 1858, Keenan even went as far as recommending that a supplemental salary of £4 to £5 be paid to qualified teachers who used Irish in the classroom.[154] This recommendation was not adopted but had made a sufficient enough impact to be cited over a decade later when the first major efforts were well under way to petition the national commissioners to add Irish as an extra subject for results fees. As has been demonstrated, however, Keenan's recommendations were hardly novel: Irish teachers themselves had already integrated such practices into their classrooms, and although the full extent of this technique is difficult to measure, it was certainly known as a common practice by Irish speakers themselves.

Finally, it should be noted that this narrative changes the usual timeline presented by historians of the evolution of the appearance of Irish in the school curriculum by attributing a greater role to Irish teachers. A change in attitude toward Irish in the national schools has traditionally been dated to 1876 and the founding of the first national organization dedicated to the language, the Society for the Preservation of the Irish Language (SPIL). But even at a formal level, a new direction was already evident in 1869 when a resolution passed at the annual meeting of the Irish National Teachers' Organization called for a petition to the commissioners to pay gratuities to national schools teachers who taught Irish as a special subject in their classrooms.[155] This was followed by another resolution at the 1871 annual congress expressing support for teaching Irish as a special subject in the schools—a statement accompanied by strong condemnations by many members of the educational system's long-standing apathy toward Irish—and another expression of support in 1874 for Irish to be included in the results scheme being implemented by the Powis Commission.[156] The following year, a number of school managers signed a memorial urging administrators to "encourage the study of the country's language, by paying for the teaching of it in Irish districts as an extra subject,"[157] an approach that was eventually adopted by the commissioners in 1878 after SPIL had added its weight to the petitioning cause. By 1883 the use of Irish to teach English had been sanctioned by the commissioners,[158] and Irish was added in 1878 as an extra subject at the primary level and as a subject for results fees at the secondary level—a breakthrough that proved a starting point for the more expansive inclusion of Irish on the school curriculum under the Bilingual Program scheme introduced in 1904. The firm place of Irish in the schools by the eve of Irish independence was thus a product of a long-standing debate reaching beyond 1876 and waged outside of the reports of commissioners, and driven in no small part by the use of Irish by teachers without regard to its approval at the topmost level.

 5

Courtroom and Polling Booth

WHEREAS THE IRISH ADMINISTRATION and their English counterparts had been forced to address the question of language in the realms of education and religion as early as the sixteenth century, language did not become salient in two other key areas of intersection between governance and everyday life—the courts and the polling booth—until the mid to late eighteenth century. It was at this point that the expansion of the legal system vertically into the lives of middling- and even lower-class litigants through the expansion and formalization of new venues such as the petty sessions courts made the issue of language in the courts more visible than at any time in the preceding hundred years. Similarly, the transformation of Ireland's political system in the early nineteenth century into one more broadly based on popular movements, contested elections, and the support of coalitions of voters made the languages spoken by participants in the political process newly relevant in a way that it had not been under the restricted, aristocratically dominated seventeenth and eighteenth centuries. Irish speakers, meanwhile, helped drive these changes by seeking redress in the courts, by insisting on using Irish when giving testimony, by their presence at elections where oaths had to be administered, and by taking part in broad-based popular political movements such as the campaign for Catholic emancipation, the reform of the tithe system, and the repeal of the Act of Union.

At no time did Irish speakers, once placed under the English laws that had been extended in a gradual process largely completed in the seventeenth century, confront a legal system in which its written records, basic proceedings, or decisions were conducted in their language. While the same could be said for English speakers in England well into the early modern period—Latin and especially French served as the primary languages of the English courts even as late as the sixteenth century—a gradual process of anglicization of the legal system culminating in the early eighteenth century meant that vernacular access to law proceedings was increasing for some subjects of the king even as it remained inaccessible to others.[1] This transformation began as early as the reign of Edward III, when English statute permitted pleadings to be "shewed, defended, answered, debated, and adjudged in the English Tongue," provided that the decision be enrolled in Latin.[2] By the late seventeenth century, a push to use English for all written and oral components of law proceedings of inferior courts in England had emerged, and in the eighteenth century, the English statute 4 Geo. II c. 26 (1731) fully prohibited Latin and French in favor of English in both the English and Scottish courts.[3]

A series of statutes extended such provisions to Ireland and Wales, relegating subjects who spoke languages other than English to a court atmosphere more explicitly anglicized than before. In Wales, the acts of union (1536) insisted that English be the medium of the law, a move confirmed by the 6 Geo. II c. 14 (1733) that mirrored English statute by prohibiting Latin or French in the Welsh courts. This anglicization was not absolute: scholars have uncovered widespread evidence of bilingual officials and interpreters, which would have mitigated the exclusion of Welsh from the legal system, even at higher courts like the Great Sessions and the Council in the Marches.[4] But by the letter of the law, and no doubt often in practice, the vernacularization of the courts in Wales had not made proceedings for the average Welsh speaker any more transparent. In Ireland, a similar process of privileging English can be traced in Irish statutes permitting it to be used for pleadings and proceedings in all inferior courts of record (1697),[5] in prohibitions on attorneys and solicitors filing bills commencing suits in languages other than English (1733), and in stipulations that the transactions of the courts of exchequer be in English (1743).[6] Finally, an Irish counterpart to the 1731 and 1733 English acts, the 11 Geo. II c. 6 (1737) stipulated that all court proceedings in Ireland be "in the English tongue and language, and not in Latin or French" on the basis, ironically, that "great mischiefs do frequently happen to the subjects of this kingdom from the proceedings in courts of justice being in an unknown language."[7]

But the actual impact of the 1737 act and the language policy of the legal system in mid-eighteenth-century Ireland must be examined within the larger context of the time. Participation in a formal legal setting—as a judge, lawyer, jurist, or magistrate—was circumscribed by social status everywhere in Britain and Ireland, limiting access by the average individual to higher courts as anything other than defendant. As bilingualism or English monolingualism became the norm in Ireland's middling ranks, having previously become all but universal among the gentry, the impact of the anglicization of the courts was delayed. Likewise, the grip of the Protestant Ascendancy—who, even if occasionally bilingual, universally spoke English as a first language—on legal administration in the 1700s further deflected the direct impact of changes in court languages on the wider Catholic population that contained the majority of Irish speakers.[8]

The largely informal and localized nature of justice experienced by most Irish men and women in the eighteenth century (and to an extent, into the nineteenth) necessarily made language policy a parochial matter regardless of statutory guidelines. Scholars have emphasized that justice at the lower ends of the social spectrum often involved local mediators such as priests, village elders, and local gentry, especially in cases of petty theft and assault. Where legal settlement was required beyond this customary law, justice was often pursued through the assistance of local justices of the peace in "private chamber," or indirectly at higher courts through the assistance of these same magistrates. Legal access was also provided through nearby manor courts, patented by the Crown and headed by a seneschal.[9] In each of these cases, an argument can be made that language provided little barrier to Irish speakers seeking justice. The customary law provided by priests and local villagers in the eighteenth century was often dispensed in the languages spoken locally, and as Edward Wakefield noted for Irish-speaking Connacht in 1812, more than a few members of the local gentry spoke the language of their tenants and could therefore "assist them with advice."[10] Most magistrates likely had to rely on interpreters by the 1830s,[11] but Irish-speaking officials were not unknown and would have been even more common in the eighteenth century. The traveler John Carr reported in 1805 that justices of the peace in Meath either knew Irish or used interpreters, while a Tuam stipendiary magistrate, Tomkins Brew, who had also served as commissioner of the peace in Clare in the 1820s (and was briefly a member of the Orange Order in the 1790s), claimed to be able to speak Irish "a great deal better than I do the English" in testimony before a Lords select committee in 1839.[12] As late as 1858, bilingual magistrates such as Daniel John Cruice of Donegal were serving in official capacities.[13]

If the evidence of continuing practices in the nineteenth century is any indication, manor courts, too, had been conducted bilingually throughout much of their period of existence, either through interpreters or through Irish-speaking officials. Concerned with a wide array of noncriminal disputes over issues such as debts, wages, rents, and various conflicts between tenants, manor courts could be found in a large number of localities until the last decades prior to their abolition in 1859. In the late 1830s, for instance, thirty-four manor courts were still operating in the counties of Clare, Galway, Mayo, Roscommon, and Sligo—all heavily Irish-speaking areas—with particularly active courts in the first two. Monthly sessions were still being held at Killarney, Co. Kerry, in the 1840s.[14] The courts generally proceeded without attorneys, with the seneschal presiding and a jury sworn to hear testimony, and there is clear evidence that Irish was in use. An observer reported that a Galway manor court held near Oughterard in the early 1830s featured an all Irish-speaking jury as well as a bilingual seneschal.[15] Further north in Mayo, Irish-speaking juries also could be found, along with a seneschal, Reverend Joseph Seymour, who "understands it pretty well, but ... does not speak it."[16] To the south, in Cork, the seneschal of the Macroom, Kilcrea, and Blarney manor courts argued that country people preferred his venue where, instead of using interpreters, they could "tell their story in Irish, and to address the jury through [the judge], and to tell their story as they like themselves."[17] Even Irish monoglots could be found on manor court juries, much to the dismay of later parliamentary inquirers appalled that evidence given in English might not be understood by those offering verdicts.[18] The system was evidently also well supplied by interpreters—perhaps to a rising degree as this older system carried on into the nineteenth century under increasingly monolingual English-speaking seneschals. Colonel Foster, proprietor of estates at Collon, Co. Louth, mediated a case regarding a forged bank note in 1809 by way of an interpreter, and on the Wynne estates of Sligo, Irish monoglots at the local manor court, as Wakefield noted, "make known their case, which is often some trifling quarrel, through the medium of an interpreter."[19]

Such was the insistent presence of Irish in the administration of justice during a stage in which everyday mediation—especially those most encountered by the average individual in a lifetime, involving theft, debt, and tenancy disputes—was the purview of informal and semiformal localized arbitrators. But as scholars R. B. McDowell, Desmond McCabe, Richard McMahon, and Neal Garnham have established, this localized system was slowly supplemented in the eighteenth century, then supplanted in the nineteenth, by a more formalized and centralized system reliant on the older county assizes and quarter sessions (most established in the seventeenth or early eighteenth centuries) and, especially from the 1820s, on the new petty sessions courts. By increasing the frequency of court sittings and diversifying the locations where they met, administrators hoped to replace the less formal types of justice hereto largely enacted by single magistrates and seneschals with a more uniform system. In turn, the introduction of regular petty sessions, where litigants could expect standard fees and checks on unbridled expenses by magistrates, opened the formal legal system to the lower classes in even remote locations.[20] As contemporaries like Dean John Patrick Lyons of Erris, Co. Mayo, saw it, the addition of new court venues were "mainly for the purpose of bringing the administration of justice within the reach of the poor."[21] Thus state-administered legal institutions increasingly intersected with the lives of Irish men and women, including Irish speakers, starting in the late eighteenth century. This forced the question of how non–English speakers could function in English-speaking courts.

On one level, the anglicized nature of these new and more formal court proceedings was, like the earlier manor courts, softened by the presence of Irish speakers in the jury box, among counsel, and even occasionally on the bench. Oliver Burke, for example, who had direct knowledge of the working of the Connacht courts of the beginning of the nineteenth century, knew two bilingual lawyers: a solicitor named John Kirwan, who worked as an interpreter at assizes, and a Mayo Crown counsel named Walter Bourke, whose knowledge of Irish "gave him a power over [witnesses], which others, ignorant of that language, failed to command."[22] There were bilingual officials, like the Corofin, Co. Clare, petty-sessions clerk who translated the terms of a written agreement for an elderly Irish-speaking woman in an intrafamily dispute regarding a contested land purchase.[23] And while the evidence is less persuasive, there were claims that judges with Irish-language knowledge served on high courts or, more to the point, that some serving in the early nineteenth century felt pressure to learn it. Lord Chief Justice Hugh Carleton (1739–1826) was said to be an Irish speaker.[24] So, too, was Judge Barry Yelverton, 1st Viscount Avonmore (1736–1805), according to the journalist Maurice Lenihan (1811–95), writing of his time reporting on court proceedings for the *Tipperary Vindicator* in the 1840s. Lenihan also noted that Sir William Cusack Smith (1766–1836), baron of the exchequer and antagonist of Daniel O'Connell, had "learned Irish because he didn't trust the court interpreters."[25] His teacher, reportedly, was Irish scholar Edward O'Reilly.[26]

As for juries at the assizes and quarter sessions, Irish monoglots, not just bilingual Irish speakers, could be found. O'Reilly, writing in 1823, was concerned that juries, "little acquainted with the English," were unable to catch subtle errors in witness testimonies translated into English for the benefit of the judge.[27] The Juries (Ireland) Acts of 1833 and 1871–72, both major reforms that affected jury selection in the nineteenth century, elicited comments from observers—especially those eager to see the Irish legal system clamp down on certain disturbances like rural unrest—alleging both the presence of Irish monoglots on juries and the supposed inadequacies of the Irish justice system that such speakers produced.[28] Although neither of the two reforms proposed qualifications excluding Irish speakers, such critics seemed to believe that there was a connection among the property qualification to serve, the language of jurors, and the verdicts rendered. The pro-Protestant *Galway Advertiser*, for example, cheered the 1833 bill for expelling those from the rolls who "can neither read or write, and others of them [who] could not understand one syllable of the king's English."[29] The bar, set at between £10 and £20 ratable property qualification in 1833 and between £12 and £20 in the aftermath of the 1871–72 reforms, was evidently not high enough, however, to exclude all Irish speakers: an instance at the 1872 Clare spring assizes in which an Irish-monoglot juror had qualified for service was reported in the Dublin newspapers and prompted testy questions in the House of Commons directed at the chief secretary, the Marquess Huntington, about the lack of exclusivity created by the recent reforms.[30] Perhaps as a result, in 1876 the Juries (Procedure) Ireland Act added a new category of persons exempt from jury service in the form of those unable to read or write English—a qualification that would have affected monoglot Irish speakers.[31]

But interpreters were the primary means by which the increasingly pressing gap between Irish-speaking (especially Irish monoglot) participants and the newly expanding formal English-speaking legal system was bridged. At the higher echelons of the courts with local jurisdiction—the assizes and sessions—interpreters were already commonplace by the end of the sixteenth century.[32] Sir John Davies, for example, mentioned their use in the courts in his *A Discovery of the True Causes Why Ireland Was Never Entirely Subdued* (1619).[33] But specific provision for regularly paid local interpreters at assizes was likely not made until 1774, when such authority was granted to county grand juries, the bodies that dominated local administration in Ireland from the eighteenth through the early nineteenth centuries.[34] In that year, 13 & 14 Geo. III c. 32 (1773–74), amending the earlier 5 Geo. III c. 14 (1765) regulating grand jury presentments for road and bridge repair expenses, introduced a new provision stating that "it shall be lawful" to pay expenses of up to £5 per session for court interpreters at the county assizes. This statute probably recognized a practice of applying county rates to interpreting costs already being exercised in some areas: Donegal grand jury presentment books from the 1760s, for instance, already show a biannual salary of £2 for interpreters being paid for work at assizes.[35] But elsewhere, a particularly complete run of presentments that have survived from Meath covering 1761 to 1830 suggest that payments (at least as a formal and regular disbursement at the local level) started sometime around the mid-1770s. An entry for 1775 instructs that "£5 be raised as before and paid Nicholas Fitzsimmons as interpreter pursuant to Act of Parliament."[36]

Permission to present expenses for interpreters employed at the county assizes was confirmed in subsequent road repair statutes in 1796 and 1836.[37] Moreover, details of presentments from Waterford for 1830 demonstrate that, at least in this county, the grand jury understood the cost of interpreters to be a nondiscretionary item enforced under the Act to Regulate the Amount of Presentments of Grand Juries (1823). This was so despite the absence of any specific mention of interpreters in the 1823 act, which was designed to oversee payment of court officials.[38] Authorization to pay costs of interpreters at quarter sessions was added under Victoria in 1837 and 1851, along with the stipulation that each county's assistant barrister was to certify whether an interpreter was necessary and determine if one individual might suffice for the whole county or if interpreting should be divided among several sessions' districts. A limit of £15 per salary disbursement for interpreting at quarter sessions was stipulated by the 1837 and 1851 acts.[39] Because the 1836 act regulating expenses for assize interpreters had omitted Dublin, it received its own separate statutory provision in 1844 for court interpreters at a maximum £10 salary per grand jury session.[40]

In contrast to the higher courts, no statute authorized payments of interpreters at petty sessions on the justification that paid personnel were not needed—a volunteer could simply be sworn and relied on to interpret.[41] Despite this absence of formal statutory authorization, interpreters were certainly used at petty sessions. Henry Monck Mason, for example, specifically singled out petty sessions as a site where Irish speaking could be heard in the 1830s. Henry Inglis, visiting petty sessions in Westport, also found interpreters in use there in 1835, while Proinsias Ó Catháin could still report their employment at sessions held in remote places in Ulster in the 1870s.[42] Lesa Ní Mhunghaile has highlighted the eyewitness account of Scottish politician Robert Graham at the Kilrush, Co. Clare, petty sessions in 1835, where he reported that a majority of witnesses would insist on an interpreter when called upon to testify.[43] Mention of Irish-speaking witnesses in trial accounts, such as the two men who testified at the Maam petty sessions concerning an attack on a Protestant Bible reader, confirms the existence of interpreters at the lower courts as well.[44] As for justices of the peace, who represented the first step in almost all initiations of legal action through their role in issuing summons and taking initial information from witnesses prior to adjudicating, filing bills of indictment, or laying the groundwork (if necessary) for further action at trial, instructions on how to use interpreters to take testimony were laid out in legal handbooks along with the full text of the oath to be used to certify the translation.[45]

Employment of interpreters, which represented a relatively significant cost to the counties, involved both regular salaried individuals and individuals procured as needed by the officers of the court. Surviving Mayo presentments for the years 1792–95 record expenses for two different interpreters, Thomas Bennis and Matthew Waters, and indicate that they were paid £5 per term's work of interpreting, for a total cost to the county of between £10 and £20 annually. Thus, for example, Bennis had been paid £10 in the summer assizes of 1792 (likely for work at two sessions), another £5 in the summer of 1793, £5 in the spring of 1794, £10 in the summer of 1794 for service "to the two courts"—presumably assizes and quarter sessions—and another £5 at the spring assizes of 1795. Such salaries were less than those paid to the jailer (£15 for a half year's salary) and treasurer to the grand jury (£30), but matched that of the secretary to the grand jury and exceeded the £2 paid to the petty constable for a half year's worth of work.[46] Parliamentary investigations into grand jury costs for the year 1807 provide another snapshot of interpreting, this time for the country as a whole. In that year, fifteen of twenty-eight counties making a report, plus the cities of Limerick and Waterford, employed at least one interpreter, although five other counties that did not submit itemized returns listing individual expenses (Kerry, Galway, Leitrim, and Limerick) or did not report (Sligo) can safely be assumed to have done so as well. Among those making presentments for costs were predominantly English-speaking counties like Fermanagh, Westmeath, Wexford, and Wicklow, whose courts nonetheless found it necessary to supply an individual to translate despite lower percentages of resident Irish speakers.[47] Some interpreters listed in 1807, such as John Farrel of the Donegal assizes, whose longtime connection to the system extended to at least 1814 when he was recorded as receiving £5 at the summer assizes for "interpreting Irish at sessions," or George Ladley, who was listed as an interpreter for Meath in multiple years between 1801 and 1810, were likely considered professional providers of the service. Others, like Hugh O'Riely, who was also paid for supplying fire and candles to the Tyrone grand jury, or Michael Canny, who was also deputy clerk of the Crown, provided services in other capacities to the courts. Outsiders were brought in as well. Sheriffs, clerks, and judges' criers received payments for procuring interpreters, and one deputy clerk, John Bourne, was active in supplying interpreters to both the Wicklow and Wexford courts.[48] Among the notables who served as a court interpreter was the Irish scholar Pádraig Stúndún (c. 1820–1908), who was listed with that occupation in the census.[49]

Summaries of grand jury presentments for 1821–23 and for the 1830s offer less detail regarding expenses for courts—most counties simply lumped all their costs for salaries for officials together into one figure, making the employment of any interpreters invisible—but a few instances of providers of such services on the payrolls were evident. The city of Limerick compensated its sheriffs £5 for each of the spring and summer assizes in 1821 for providing an interpreter to its assize court.[50] The county of Cork reported £20 total spent on an interpreter for its assizes in both 1822 and 1823.[51] In 1830 the Clare grand jury registered £4 12s. 3d. in expenses for an unnamed interpreter employed at the spring assizes and again for the summer assizes, while the Waterford grand jury labeled the £5 in interpreting expenses at each of its assizes "imperative" under the terms of 4 Geo. IV c. 43.[52] In the town of Kilkenny, an outlay of £4 12s. 4d. was recorded for the 1832 spring assizes, and in Cavan, Patrick Smith was the interpreter retained at compensation levels similar to other counties for his work at the assizes and quarter sessions.[53]

It has been suggested that employment of interpreters at the courts was discontinued or discouraged as early as the mid-nineteenth century,[54] but in fact interpreters were still widespread in many counties late into the period. Interpreters were still required from time to time in Armagh in the mid-1840s, although reportedly to a lesser extent than in previous years.[55] Clare paid £40 in expenses for its two interpreters at assizes and quarter sessions in 1866, and in the same year Cork disbursed £60 in salary for three interpreters split between the county assizes and quarter sessions in the East and West Ridings. The grand juries of Donegal (one interpreter), Galway (two, plus one interpreter for the city of Galway), Leitrim (at least one), Limerick (two), Mayo (two), Sligo (two), Tipperary (four, one each for quarter sessions and assizes in the North and South Ridings), and Waterford (two) also reported presentments for interpreting expenses at this time.[56] This is a reduced list compared with 1807, to be sure, but aside from the omission of Kerry, it represents a sustained commitment to interpreters in core Irish-speaking areas past midcentury. This is especially notable in the face of reluctance in some quarters to take on such costs, as in 1859 in Mayo where an assize judge tried to refuse any expenses associated with Irish-speaking witnesses. This decision was lambasted in the *Limerick Chronicle* as violating the practice of providing for interpreters at "grand jury presentment by every county in Ireland for the purpose of examining witnesses before the courts."[57] Such opposition to the cost of interpreters may have been growing, but they were not universal. Interpreters were still being employed in Sligo, for instance, as late as 1876; the secretary of the grand jury is recorded in that year as asking that the salary be delayed until approved by the chairman of the quarter sessions.[58] The 1871 census lists seven anonymous interpreters for the province of Munster, including a female; another interpreter (also a female) for Connacht; one interpreter for Ulster (a male, for Donegal); and a female interpreter enumerated for Leinster.[59] In 1894 the national registrar of petty sessions clerk could report to Chief Secretary John Morley that 109 of 606 petty sessions districts in the country still made provisions for interpreters, and at the Waterford assizes, the position of permanent interpreter was discontinued only in 1898 when the policy was amended to bring in a translator from Dungarvan as needed.[60]

This last point regarding the use of ad-hoc interpreters prompts a need to carefully consider official records of the employment of such personnel. The omission in grand jury presentments of costs for interpreters may indicate a switch to translation on an informal basis, and these records underestimate the earlier scope of interpreting in lower-level settings like the petty sessions or magisterial inquiries for which no official provision for translation had been made. James McQuige, for example, was almost certainly not on the official rolls of the county when he served itinerantly in courts in Donegal, Fermanagh, and Londonderry in the late 1700s and early 1800s.[61] A petty sessions case in 1835 in Dingle involving a dispute between two fishing boat crews reveals that the magistrate relied on a local shopkeeper present in the bridewell, George Boyle, to convey a message to the Irish-speaking petitioners urging them to drop their case.[62] An even clearer sense of the improvised nature of interpreting can be illustrated by a case of vandalism directed toward a Catholic chapel heard at the Newport, Co. Mayo, petty sessions in 1841. The discovery at this session that witness Michael Mangan could not speak English prompted the magistrate, James Hillas, to propose that a "Mr. Gillespie be sworn as interpreter." When the prosecution, representing parish priest James Dwyer, challenged Gillespie's abilities, the justices simply turned to "a man named O'Boyle" to proceed with the translating.[63] Even high-profile cases relied on informal interpreters to make ends meet. An assistant to the clerk of the Crown was sworn to interpret for witness John Burke at the murder trial of George Robert Fitzgerald, held at Castlebar assizes in 1786.[64] The Court of Common Pleas in Dublin evidently did not have a regular interpreter on staff, either, but it had planned ahead for a witness brought in from Connemara for the case of *Hennon v. Andrew Henry Lynch, MP*, heard in 1839—an interpreter from Galway had been invited to accompany the witness.⁶⁵ In the libel case of *Bridge v. Casey* heard at the Court of Queen's Bench in 1877, at which Isaac Butt served as counsel for the defendant, an objection lodged against the interpreter initially sworn for a witness (the translator selected was a fellow witness) was solved when an observer, Reverend John Walsh, "proferred himself as an interpreter, and was sworn."⁶⁶

The presence of interpreters and Irish-speaking legal officials, however, does not offer a complete picture of the history of Ireland's legal system as it broadened its reach into the country's multilingual population in the nineteenth century. The use of interpreters, for example, was clearly subject to a significant degree to the discretion of the presiding officer at legal proceedings. Linguistic access was by no means guaranteed, as an Irish-speaking woman found when pressing an assault charge against the Mayo priest Patrick Lavelle at the 1861 Ballinrobe petty sessions. Her case was adjourned when the judge decided that no funds were available for an interpreter.⁶⁷ At an earlier case, also from Mayo, a judge at the 1834 Castlebar petty sessions, having concluded that a litigant had sufficient English to lay out his complaint, threatened to dismiss the suit when the man insisted on using Irish.⁶⁸ Furthermore, interpreters were not intended to make transparent the entire workings of the proceedings of the court. Despite occasional examples to the contrary, such as the 1864 prosecution of Mary Dougan for manslaughter at the Lifford, Co. Donegal, assizes where "the indictment and pleading were conducted through the medium of the Irish interpreter,"⁶⁹ available evidence emphasizes the use of interpreters almost exclusively to enable witnesses or litigants to give their testimony so that the case could proceed in English.

But it would be a mistake to see the place of Irish in the courtroom only in terms of the decisions and initiatives of judges, statutory provisions, and legal prerogative. Irish speakers exerted themselves within the confines of the system to press their ability to speak at court in the language that they preferred. Indication of an active, rather than a passive, participation starts with the nature of Irish speakers' point of entry into legal proceedings. Not all Irish speakers were merely "Irish witnesses," as they were called in accounts of trials in this period, brought in to testify through an interpreter and then turned away once their evidence had been registered.⁷⁰ Many initiated legal proceedings themselves, bringing action at petty sessions and at assizes for theft and assault; in fact, McMahon has proposed that a staggering one-third of the families of the county of Galway—one of the most Irish-speaking regions of the country, it should be added—were involved in petty sessions cases in one way or another in 1839 alone, and that the city of Galway contained perhaps the busiest petty sessions court in the country.[71] Examples from the courts of western counties are readily available: James Murphy, for instance, brought charges through an interpreter at the 1831 Mayo assizes against six individuals for entering his house at night and stealing "a quantity of potatoes," alleging that they had barged in after knocking.[72] Irish speaker John Grimes also brought charges in the Mayo assizes of that same month, offering testimony against Patrick Caulfield for having assaulted him when besieging his house alongside a large crowd.[73] A year later, yet another Mayo case arising from assault was brought by Michael Corcoran through Irish against defendant Luke Gibbons.[74] All three of these cases resulted in acquittals for the defense, but a pattern regarding the success rates of such prosecutions should not be inferred. A Westport petty sessions case of 1833 brought by Martin Heraghty, "a simple country man, who gave his testimony in Irish," against Edward Currigan for stealing his banknotes gained enough traction with the magistrates that they recommended the case be sent on to a jury.[75]

Even more compelling is the evidence of female Irish-speaking complainants, whose standing at a public forum such as a court would have been further circumscribed by gender in addition to those of language and class. An indictment for rape brought by Mary Connolly at Cork assizes in 1825 against John Hearne was conducted through an interpreter, if a slightly glib newspaper account of the trial is to be believed. Although the tone of this case is hard to gauge from the surviving account—the court report cynically suggested that the victim "appeared quite capable of defending herself" and recounted light-heartedly the resulting decision of the defendant to marry Connolly—the use of Irish by the litigant remains credible as she was able to build her case on an inability to have assented in English (as the defense had claimed) to the encounter.[76] A more creditable account of an abduction in 1805 yielded charges against Patrick Rood brought by Irish speaker Mary Conlan, who testified through an interpreter at Dundalk Crown court that Rood had helped a group of men carry her off in the night "with the intent of marrying her to one Patrick M'Ananey."[77] Similar cases of indictments for abduction or rape—undoubtedly overrepresented in surviving evidence of Irish speaking in the courtroom owing to the details available for public consumption in such cases—were heard at the Castlebar petty sessions in 1833, at the Mayo assizes in 1830 and 1845, and at the Galway petty sessions in 1837, all brought by Irish-speaking female complainants entirely or partly through an interpreter.[78]

But the central case for the ways in which Irish speakers helped shape the emerging legal system of the nineteenth century lies in the struggle that took place between bilinguals and the courts over the ability to give testimony in Irish even when capable of delivering it in English. From the point of view of the bench, Irish speakers often claimed nonproficiency in English so as to buy time under cross-examination to formulate a response while an interpreter needlessly translated. These concerns were not only directed at Irish witnesses: any foreigner in an English or Irish court, according to one treatment of the subject, might "modestly conceal his proficiency as a linguist, and avail himself of the assistance of an interpreter, which gives him an opportunity of preparing with due caution his answer to any inconvenient question."[79] Such complaints had been made regarding the manor courts, where, according to one attendee, bilinguals asked for questions to be put in Irish to "avoid a rapid cross-examination."[80] The same was alleged for witnesses at the assizes and sessions courts. A number of witnesses "professed not to understand English, in order to evade the direct and pertinent questions put on cross-examination in Irish through an interpreter," complained a trial report for Ennis assizes in 1832.[81] Even more neutral observers not directly connected with the judiciary, like Maurice Lenihan, believed that certain Irish speakers feigned misunderstanding of the interpreter—much to the embarrassment of that individual, who thus appeared incompetent—in order to avoid making a reply.[82] Such tactics could tip the balance in favor of either the prosecution or defense when either side presented a witness who could not be subject to examination on a level playing field.

Irish speakers, in turn, whether through an awareness of this stratagem or through a desire to give their evidence in the language they preferred, insisted on delivering their testimony through an interpreter. This could bring the justice system to a halt until accommodation could be provided. McQuige recalled a trial in Londonderry that was held up for hours while an interpreter was sought.[83] John MacHale's biographer, Bernard O'Reilly, claimed that the archbishop had specifically instructed his Irish-speaking flocks not to give testimony in English unless the language was thoroughly understood.[84] Unsurprisingly, judges were frustrated when attempts to force testimony in English failed, as in this 1829 report from Mayo:

> In courts of justice here the witnesses are constantly examined in Irish; and though a person appearing and anxious to give evidence on behalf of his nearest friend should be pressed to speak English, and threatened if he did not with punishment, or that he would [be] put down without having his evidence taken (it being ascertained that he could speak English, and was heard to do so), he would declare in Irish that he would not trust his soul to any other, and retire without giving his evidence, or submit to punishment sooner than do so.[85]

Judges do not appear to have been hesitant to dismiss or even pursue legal action against such witnesses on the grounds that they had heard them speak English.[86] But the legitimacy of such actions was doubtful, especially given that statements by witnesses as to their language proficiency were delivered prior to entering the dock under oath. A surviving text of an Irish-language oath used by a Galway interpreter, possibly a street cleaner named Séamus Morris of Spiddal, for instance, does not bind the witness as to language ability.[87]

Instead, the legitimacy of a stated need for an interpreter became embedded in the tactics of counsels at cross-examination in the early nineteenth century as attorneys tried to elicit evidence of the linguistic abilities of witnesses on the stand in order to impugn the reliability of their statements. Law enforcement personnel, who had often interacted with witnesses in the course of the proceedings, were summoned to contradict claimed inabilities to speak English. Thus, it was stated during the testimony of James Conmy at assizes in 1831 that "three of the police would prove that this man could speak very good English," and at the same sessions that witness Catherine Nelson had been heard speaking English by the governor of the jail.[88] Family members, too, could be brought to bear on witnesses regarding linguistic ability, as in the case of a father and brother who testified that complainant William Egan was no monoglot at Castlebar petty sessions, or Mary Conner, whose prosecution of her case was thwarted when her own "mother from the body of the court cried out" that she could speak English, prompted by the defense attorney.[89]

It is against this background that the 1858 legal decision of *R. v. Burke*, rendered at the Irish Court of Crown Cases Reserved, should be understood. The case centered on the admissibility of evidence by two witnesses who had been called by the Crown in the trial at the Mayo assizes of Martin Burke, subsequently found guilty of raping Margaret Sheridan. The witnesses, Sarah Anne Gorman and Bridget Reilly, had been summoned to attest to the linguistic capabilities of Martin Thornton, an Irish-speaking witness for the defense who had been given an interpreter when he had stated that he could not speak English. The two prosecution witnesses testified that Thornton had spoken to them and had been overheard singing "The Heights of Alma" in English, effectively undermining his credibility before the jury. On appeal at the Crown court, the judges were to decide whether such collateral facts could be used to challenge the reliability of an Irish-speaking witness—in essence, to pronounce on the legitimacy of the tactics that attorneys had been using at cross-examination to cast doubt on witnesses' professed inability to speak English. The majority, in a 7–3 decision, found against the admissibility of such evidence, claiming that at the very least, the linguistic ability of a witness should be ascertained immediately upon coming on the table rather than drawn out in subsequent examination. More centrally, the majority argued that while the credibility of a witness was subject to examination, this was true only insofar as such issues raised were directly related to the matter at hand (i.e., by showing bias or illustrating that prior statements by the witness about the events or persons in question were false). Previous case law on testimony, it was argued, showed that points of particular fact regarding the witness (in this case, language ability) that did not materially impinge on the questions at issue in the trial were not exceptions to this rule of inadmissibility, and to decide otherwise would be to open up cross-examinations to endless discussions on every aspect of an individual's life.[90]

It was this reasoning regarding the limits of admissible collateral evidence that also had most impact on subsequent legal understanding. Thus, as it was put in an 1892 treatise on evidence by Sidney Phipson, *R. v. Burke* illustrated that a witness's "credit cannot ... be impeached by contradiction on irrelevant matters," much as (according to Phipson) suggestions that a woman had had previous liaisons with men could not become a point of contention in a rape trial.[91] But while the ramifications of *R. v. Burke* were largely read in terms of evidence admissibility, it is important to note that the majority decision also based its reasoning on the notion that Irish speakers, like any non–English speaker at trial, should reasonably be allowed to give testimony in the language they preferred. No attempted strategy on the part of Irish speakers to undermine cross-examination should be assumed, they argued. As Judge Christian, writing the lead judgment, stated: "I apprehend it is perfectly possible that the witness was actuated by an honest motive in wishing to be examined in Irish. He may have wished to express himself in the language which he knew best, in which he could most clearly express his thoughts." English speakers, he cautioned, would do well to imagine the tables turned by picturing themselves convicted of perjury in a French or Italian court after a witness had been called to attest to their use of "some words of French or Italian on some previous occasion." Supporting statements by others in the majority took similar lines. Judge Monaghan noted that it was established practice for judges on circuit to ascertain the ability of a witness to testify in one language or the other immediately upon presentation and to even allow Irish speakers testifying in English to resort to Irish when they felt it was needed. Similar understandings were voiced by Judge Lefroy, who observed:

> The judge has always endeavoured to ascertain whether it was fit and proper to allow the witness to give his testimony in the Irish language, on the ground

that it was not justice to him to oblige him to give his evidence on oath in a language he was not certain of; and whilst we are so very anxious for the cause of justice, are we to have no regard to what is due to the conscience of the witness? Why are we to presume that when the witness tells us he cannot give his testimony in English that he does so from a bias?[92]

These pronouncements stood in stark contrast to assumptions by the minority legal opinion that the use of languages other than English was first and foremost an evasive tactic, and posited considerable legitimacy in the accommodation by judges of speakers' needs.

One final issue stands out in the *R. v. Burke* decision: the absence of case law specific to language or translation on which the judges could depend as a guide to their decision. Treatises on evidence and conduct of cross-examinations, court cases based around admissible testimony, and legal precedent for treatment of witnesses all provided backing for judges on both sides of the *R. v. Burke* decision. But as to precedent for permitting a witness to testify in a preferred language, neither majority nor minority opinions found traction in previous decisions. In short, the judges were guided to a significant degree by the logistics of conducting court proceedings, not by legal precedent. As Judge Christian summarily put it: "I venture to say, that if in every case during the last assizes in which a witness insisted on being examined in Irish, and his knowledge of English was suggested, there had been witnesses examined pro and con, it is a matter of very serious doubt to me, whether the spring assizes for the province of Connaught would be over at the present moment." By appearing in court to testify, and by litigating cases at petty sessions and assizes, Irish speakers themselves had created conditions in which the legal system had conceded the need to accommodate their language in order for the courts to conduct their business, however imperfect or limited that accommodation ultimately turned out to be.

A strikingly similar trajectory emerges for the intersection of Irish speakers and the political sphere of the first half of the nineteenth century. The period between the reinstatement of Catholic voting rights in 1793 and the Ballot Act of 1872 witnessed the abrupt reemergence of Irish speakers as significant participants in voting and politics for the first time since the beginning of the eighteenth century, if not earlier. This was the result of a number of shifting factors that aligned in the nineteenth century, namely changes in the electoral franchise, statutory modifications in voting practices, the decline of aristocratically dominated politics, and above all, the emergence of popular mobilization on key issues like emancipation, tithes, temperance, and repeal.

The Relief Act of 1793 (33 Geo. III c. 21) did not address any potential linguistic issues to be overcome in administering election-day oaths, but in extending the vote to Catholics it did initiate the eventual doubling of the number of forty-shilling voters in the counties (to 100,000). Catholics subsequently held the majority in the county franchises outside of Ulster by the late 1820s. This was further amplified by the Act of Union, which removed at a stroke a good number of the pre-Union corporation boroughs marked by Protestant dominance and left the county constituencies with even greater influence.[93] While 1793 may not have represented a stark change with regard to larger Catholic political fortunes—historians have well demonstrated the prior existing alternatives to voting that enabled political influence in the eighteenth century, from Catholic-propertied influence over Protestant tenant voters to parliamentary petitioning—the reforms of 1793–1801 nevertheless would have enfranchised for the first time since 1728 a significant bloc of Irish-speaking voters by adding both Catholics and county dwellers, two constituencies heavily represented by Irish speakers.[94] From there, the number of such voters, like the size of the franchise in Ireland in general, would have peaked in 1829 when the granting of emancipation was won at the cost of raising the county franchise to £10. At that point the number of voters (and with them, undoubtedly, the number of Irish-speaking voters) began to decline to less than one in eighty people at the end of the 1840s, a result of stricter registration requirements instituted in the Reform Act of 1832, the falling popularity of vote-qualifying leaseholds among landlords, wide disparities in property valuations, and the famine. This trend was finally halted with the Irish Franchise Act of 1850, which, by instituting a £12 county franchise and £8 borough franchise on a better-organized registration system and a more uniform property-valuation standard, reversed this trend and raised the number of county voters back to 135,000.[95] This, in turn, would have improved the number of Irish speakers on the rolls for a short time in the 1850s and 1860s, although as a percentage of the electorate their numbers would have been declining at this point along with their percentage of the overall Irish population.

The results of this addition of Irish speakers to the rolls were already evident in the first decade of the 1800s. A Donegal special election to fill the county seat left vacant by the death of Henry Brooke in January 1808 yielded a contested result when Major General George Vaughn Hart claimed that his opponent, Henry Conyngham Montgomery, with the assistance of the sheriff, had enlisted fraudulent freeholders—many "illiterate, and also wholly ignorant of the English language"—to give him a victory.[96] Such language might be dismissed as a mere example of the condescension of the time toward "unsuitably" lower-class voters, for which unfamiliarity with English become a proxy. Instances of dubious voters or freeholders created by propertied interests immediately prior to elections were in any case numerous under Ireland's notoriously chaotic franchise of this period.[97] But what is striking is Hart's further discussion of the means by which Montgomery had registered these voters and the ways in which this revealed the growing issue of Irish-speaking voters—especially monoglots—arriving at the polls. Both the affidavits of registry of freehold and their oaths, Hart noted, "were administered to [the voters] in the English language ... without being explained, interpreted, or made known to them in the Irish language, with which alone they were acquainted, contrary to the true spirit and effect, and in open evasion of the several election acts in force in Ireland."[98] For all the aspersion of Hart's petition regarding Montgomery's supporters, it was the absence of translation, and not only voter property qualification, that in his mind justified throwing out the case.

Hart's petition contains some ambiguity as to whether any laws current in 1808 specifically insisted on translation of the election oaths required to enable freeholders to cast their vote. Translation of the oaths may have already been a practice on an informal basis at the time. The earliest statutory provision for interpreting at poll booths, however, appears to have been the 57 Geo. III c. 131 (1817), which required returning officers presiding at elections to appoint an interpreter for each polling station to administer oaths in Irish on receipt of a written request from any of the candidates. This act, for example, is listed as the authority for paying an interpreter by the undersheriff of Queen's County, who employed one at the general election of 1818.[99] The 1817 statute also stipulated that interpreters themselves were to take an oath swearing to faithfully render their services and were to be compensated up to a half guinea (10s. 6d.) per day out of the election expenses paid by the candidates. As the act applied to both borough and county elections, such provisions were also required for town and city elections. The claim for the 1817 statute as the first to address Irish-speaking voters is bolstered by the fact that the laws on polling and oath administration that it replaced (from 1797 and 1811) do not mention interpreters, nor do the other statutes that these earlier laws replaced.[100]

The provisions laid out in 1817 were upheld by its replacement, 1 Geo. IV c. 11 (1820), which slightly reduced the salary of poll interpreters to 10s. per day. The 1820 statute also dropped specific demands that interpreting expenses be paid by candidates, a shift caught up in larger uncertainties of the time as to respective liabilities of returning officers, grand juries, or candidates for election costs. As with a number of expenses that were perceived to have spiraled upward to the detriment of candidates, the cost of interpreters—like the deputy sheriffs, clerks, and other required officials—was to be capped and placed in the hands of the returning officer under the 1820 provisions. The 1 & 2 Geo. IV c. 58 (1821), similarly intended to curtail expenses and shift responsibilities away from grand jury presentments, listed interpreters as the returning officer's liability at 10s. per day.[101] Provision for interpreters was confirmed on the same basis in the 4 Geo. IV c. 55 (1823) and in a proposed bill to regulate polls presented by William Smith O'Brien, Sir Denham Norreys, and Sir Thomas Wyse in 1839.[102] Only in 1872, when the 35 & 36 Vict. c. 33 imposed a secret ballot and repealed the 1820 and 1823 statutes, were Irish speakers left without specific statutory requirements of a poll interpreter. This omission likely arose from a lack of awareness of (and insensitivity to) the need for such provisions, combined perhaps with a sense that the new expectation of private voting necessarily precluded the presence of an interpreter. In any case, returning officers were recommended by a subsequent handbook for administering elections to take care, in light of the absence of sworn interpreters, that at least one presiding officer or assistant at a polling place should know Irish in areas where the language was spoken so that documents could be explained to Irish speakers who could not read English.[103]

Gauging the actual employment and use of interpreters, rather than their legal provision, suffers from the shortcomings of surviving records. Fleeting glimpses can be found, however, that also provide suggestive evidence about the types of Irish-speaking voters making their way to the polls. Reports to parliamentary inquiries of expenses incurred by sheriffs as returning officers offer some of the best details regarding interpreters at the polls, although the failure of some officers to make reports, the decision to report lump summaries of expenses, or the occurrence of uncontested elections makes impossible broad conclusions about when and where interpreters were used in any specific constituency. Returns nevertheless reveal considerable expenses for interpreting, and in seemingly unlikely places. An interpreter was employed in the Queen's County election in 1818, as has already been noted, and several in the county election for Tipperary at a cost of £55 14s. 9d. This sum was identical to the expenses paid for the fourteen interpreters employed in Limerick for seven days' worth of translation in 1818. But this paled in comparison to the expenses for the Galway election of that year, in which a staggering £293 15s. was paid for interpreters at a total of thirty booths—more than the entire election costs incurred by the city of Limerick.[104] By the 1840s and 1850s such tremendous expense—aided by efforts to shorten polling days—happened less often. But the use of interpreters remained robust. Four interpreters were employed in the summer 1841 contest in County Kerry for a total of £10, an expense split among candidates William Browne, Morgan John O'Connell, and Arthur Blennerhassett. Another was required for the contest in Tipperary that same year and was paid £2 for four days of work.[105] In the 1857 general election, county contests required interpreters in Clare, Galway, Sligo, and even Cavan, where Hugh Annesley specifically requested and paid for an extra booth with an interpreter to supplement thirteen interpreters already deployed in a contest where he was successfully returned.[106] Two years later, returning officials in Clare again employed five interpreters at a cost of more than £4.[107]

The scale of need for such interpreters should give pause in considering the social class of Irish-speaking voters, especially for the period after 1829. The basic requisite for the county voters participating in the pre-1829 elections was 40s., not an exorbitantly high qualification even if potentially onerous in Connacht and other western regions where valuations were lower. On the one hand, this suggests a relatively modest lower limit to the means of those qualifying, raising images of large numbers of Irish-speaking voters of marginal incomes marshaled, like their English-speaking counterparts, to the polls by their landlords. The sheer number of voters qualifying after 1800 supports this assertion of modest qualifications. For example, both Tipperary and Galway, where significant numbers of interpreters were used, have been flagged as standouts in the increase of the size of their electoral expansion; it has been estimated the number of Galway voters rose from 700 in 1803 to 13,000 in 1815, and in Tipperary from 1,700 to 16,000. Given that the law required that interpreters be provided on request of the candidate, the linguistic provisions at polls should be read in part as a tool for landlords to mobilize dependent voters.[108] The cynicism with which poorer voters greeted such efforts could be found in a song current in Cork in 1841 titled "Abhránan Bhoicht-Aontadhóra" ("The Poor Voter's Song"):

> Dob fhios dóibh mé bheith bocht
>   is do mheas siad mé go claon
> Is go bhfullangin leam thoil
>   bheith amhla ar feadh mo shaoghail.
> Do mheas siad mé is fíor
>   mar aon da mbuídhean fós

Do ghlacfadh breab is díol
   air mo *Vote*, air mo *Vote*.[109]

[They knew me to be poor
   and they thought I could be perverted
And that I would suffer my will
   to be thus for the duration of my life.
They thought me, it is true,
   to be one of their crowd yet
That a bribe and payment would be accepted
   for my vote, my vote.]

Of course, as this song hints, how these Irish speakers voted once at the poll—whether in lockstep with landlord, subject to clerical influence, or independently decided—was not a foregone conclusion. Indeed, they would have been subject to the usual conflict between deference and independence that scholars have identified for any tenant voters, whether English or Irish speaking.

On the other hand, not all Irish-speaking voters were modest tenants. The large numbers of county voters prior to 1829 obscures what must have been a varied electorate among Irish speakers, a finding that becomes much clearer for the post-1829 restricted electorate subject to a £10 qualification in 1829 and £12 in 1850. The continued use of interpreters after 1829 suggests the existence of a comfortably situated Irish-speaking electorate, an especially notable fact when one considers that the need for interpreters implies a monoglot or near-monoglot voter. Even taking into account K. T. Hoppen's warning that straightforward deduction of social class from property qualifications for the pre-1850 electorate is fraught with pitfalls—irregular registration and variations in property valuation across counties made the nonenfranchised broadly similar in social range to the franchised—it is safe to conclude that the interpreters needed in Kerry and Tipperary in 1841, as well as those in Clare, Sligo, and Galway in 1857, were administering to a relatively comfortable class of qualifying Irish-speaking voters. Tipperary's county electorate, for example, had dwindled to a rarified two hundred voters by 1849; later, in 1866, the middle-class nature of the electorate was revealed by the 48 percent of Connacht county voters and 63 percent of Munster voters in that year who had property rated at £20 or above.[110] Furthermore the post-1850 electorate in particular was known to be more homogenous, more dominated by farmers, and in sum, more broadly drawn from the middling agricultural classes. It was from this electorate that Irish speakers were qualifying and then relying on interpreters to vote.

Cork presents a case that stands out for its evidence of widespread use of interpreters on the socially restricted post-1829 electorates. A total of seven interpreters were employed in the five-day county contest of 1841 between Daniel O'Connell, Edmund Burke Roche, Nicholas Philpott Leader, and Robert Longfield. This meant an interpreter was provided for each of the seven booths set up that year, for a total cost of £9 13s. 10d. In 1857—again, it should be noted, on a more homogenous and middle-class county electorate of farmers—a full thirty-nine interpreters (at £39 total in salary) were needed in the field for the spring election to administer a total of forty polling booths.[111] But even this was dwarfed by the seventy-five interpreters salaried for the 1868 Cork election, as reported by the subsheriff. In part, the multiplication of polling booths to save costs by compressing voting time undoubtedly played a role in this increase in interpreters. Presiding officers operated under the 13 & 14 Vict. c. 68 (1850), which demanded that election administrators set up one polling booth per barony. This achieved its intended cost-saving effect: the army of interpreters employed in 1868 cost £37 10s., less than the expenses for half the number of personnel at the 1857 election. Nevertheless, returning officers and candidates, who shared expenses, were loath to take on unnecessary costs of any kind, and it is unlikely that such expansive interpreting provisions were generously brought on to serve nonexistent Irish-speaking voters.

Thus far, the focus has been on linguistic provisions made for voters in county constituencies. But officials provided interpreters in borough contests as well, although the story is more complex. Most boroughs, especially those drawn with tight, closed-in boundaries, were influenced by the corporate and electoral dominance of Protestant freemen both before and after the Relief Act of 1793.[112] The restitution of the Catholic vote therefore would not have provided a significant change to the numbers of Irish-speaking voters seeking to participate in borough elections. The exceptions to this rule, however, reveal striking instances of Irish-speaking voters. The most obvious cases were the counties of cities and towns, where sizeable borough franchises were drawn not just from the freemen of the city proper but also freeholders—of whom many were Catholic tenants and laborers—from the surrounding countryside. Of particular note here were the county cities of Limerick and Cork, where a significant Catholic freehold vote existed, along with Galway, where not only the freeholders but also the freemen were Catholic.[113] Limerick, for example, accrued over £7 in costs paid to one entrepreneurial interpreter who provided services over the course of twenty-one days at the 1818 borough contest between John Prendergast Vereker and Thomas Spring-Rice.[114] In that same year, the town of Galway employed three interpreters, comparable to the five interpreters employed in the same capacity much later at the 1857 general election. One of those Irish monoglots voting in the 1857 Galway election, in fact, was later summoned to give evidence through an interpreter when allegations of sums of money delivered for votes sparked the convening of a commission to look into the results.[115]

The city of Cork, like the county, provided another stark instance of an Irish-speaking constituency. The city contained a significant Catholic freeholder constituency that was evident from 1807 on, represented by a growing body of voters estimated at nine hundred by 1830—mostly residents in the city's liberties and consisting of small tenant farmers and manual laborers along with some merchants and shopkeepers.[116] Tellingly, interpreters were reported as expenses for both the 1818 and 1820 elections, and city officials testifying in 1838 agreed that freehold voters were not only indistinguishable in class from those of the surrounding county, but that they were unambiguously Irish speakers—most bilingual but some "unable to speak English, [and thus] obliged to have an interpreter," according to the town-clerk.[117] Even the smaller boroughs were not without their contests requiring interpreters, however. Kinsale, Co. Cork, with an electorate of less than three hundred between 1832 and 1847, nevertheless employed an interpreter at a cost of £2 6s. 1d. for five days' worth of service at the single polling booth required for the 1841 election, paid by candidates William Henry Watson and Mathias Wolverley Attwood.[118] Dungarvan, Co. Waterford, where Hoppen has noted that the retention of borough votes by forty-shilling freeholders after the Reform Act of 1832 made for a uniquely popular electoral force, similarly employed two interpreters in 1857. The first, at a cost of 9s. 2d., was paid through the joint expenses of the two candidates, John Francis McGuire and John Nugent Humble, but the second was charged to McGuire alone in response to his specific request for a second polling booth.[119]

In short, the enfranchisement of massive new numbers of county freeholders (and their counterparts in the large borough constituencies) brought Irish speakers to the polling booths in new numbers, although not without a few such voters in smaller town electorates as well. As to the interpreters themselves, little can be readily known about those who served at the polling booths. Election officers provided few names in returns of expenses, although some are known, such as Michael Crowe and Thomas Egan, who were named as providing services for County Limerick in 1820, and a Patrick Kelly, listed as an interpreter in Sligo in 1857.[120] There is definite evidence of overlap with scribal circles in at least one case, however. The texts of two translated oaths can be found bound in with the papers of the Ó Longáin family, and all three sons—Peadar, Pól, and

Seosamh—served in the 1852 and 1861 Cork elections.[121] The first surviving oath, rendered perfunctorily as *leabhar na breibe* (the bribe oath),[122] corresponds closely to the text prescribed in 4 Geo. IV c. 55 (1823) to bind a voter not to receive any reward in exchange for a vote. The second consists of a direct translation of the oath mandated by the Irish Reform Act of 1832 affirming one's eligibility to vote and verifying that no previous vote had been cast.[123] Notably, both render the act of voting as *guth a thabhairt* (to give voice, i.e., a vote) rather than an English loan such as *vótail*. Such a meaning of *guth* can be found readily in modern Irish and was common enough in the nineteenth century, but it stands out nonetheless for striking a decidedly plebeian note in evoking phrases like *guth na ndaoine* (the voice of the people).[124]

How far this "voice" translated into political presence and to what extent vested political interests in the country had to address this expanded Irish-speaking element within their midst are another question. The Irish political realm itself changed significantly in the late eighteenth and early nineteenth centuries in response to developments such as the American and French Revolutions, Daniel O'Connell's drives for Catholic emancipation and repeal, the mobilization against tithes, agitation in opposition to the Poor Law, and the temperance movement. Meanwhile, older forms of popular mobilizations like the bread riot and agrarian agitation continued to thrive. These features of everyday life both altered constitutional definitions of Irish political representation to include previously excluded religious groups (Catholics and Dissenters) and pressed home the possibilities of popularly based political mobilization to force reform. Voting was only one of many ways in which a newly emboldened popular participation in the political sphere took place. Processions, songs, scribal prose and poetry, and large-scale meetings were other salient features of popular political awareness in this period, as a number of scholars have emphasized.[125] Despite the obviously broader scale in which Irish politics was operating by this period, however, as some scholars have noted the use of the Irish language at such events and to express popular opinion has remained stubbornly invisible in the majority of historical accounts of this period.[126]

In fact, evidence of Irish speakers at public meetings or of the use of Irish to communicate with the crowd can be found for every popular movement of this period. Speakers addressed local temperance meetings in the vernacular, as in the speech given in 1841 by Dean Lyons at Binghamstown chapel "in the Irish language in plain, but impressive terms."[127] Father Theobald Mathew (1790–1856), the head of the national antidrink movement that flowed from his Cork

Total Abstinence Society, administered his temperance oaths in both languages, much to the acclaim of the pupils of the St. Jarlath's Gaelic Literary Institute, who commended his approach at a meeting in 1844. The overlap between an interest in Irish, if not fluency in speaking it, could be found in the Galway branch of the famed temperance society, which resolved in 1844 to set up "a school for instruction in the Irish language" under the leadership of Reverend B. J. Roche.[128] Beyond the temperance movement, the passage of the Poor Law in 1838 and the subsequent outcry in 1843 over the tax burdens it implemented also prompted the use of Irish for public address. This is all the more notable when one considers the attendance of ratepayers at such events, who would have been tenants or landowners of some means.[129] An 1843 meeting in Ballyhaunis, Co. Mayo, of anti–poor law dissidents chaired by Michael Blake Germingham, Esq., consisted of "clergy, gentry, and other ratepayers of the parishes of Annagh, Bacon [Bekan], Aughamore, and Knock." With these Irish-speaking taxpayers in mind, the Reverend Coyne, parish priest of Annagh, "addressed the meeting in the Irish language, and dwelt forcibly on the effects of the poor law on the country, and the probable increase of the rates."[130]

But the popular movements most closely associated with Irish-speaking public addresses were the Catholic emancipation, anti-tithe, and repeal agitations of the 1820s, 1830s, and 1840s. That this was the case should not surprise given the overlap between all three campaigns: Anti-tithe sentiments were well integrated into broader popular misgivings about Protestant rule in Ireland during the emancipation campaign of the early 1820s, while repeal agitation of the late 1830s and 1840s shared with the earlier emancipation movement an emphasis on subscription fees, or Catholic "rent," to help finance candidates. All three sought political reform through broad-based support built by leaders through an appeal to crowds in public speeches. This common thread should not obscure the many differences between the three with regard to geographic and social differentiation. Anti-tithe meetings, for example, appealed to Catholic Irish of all social backgrounds through a vague sense of grievance, but it specifically took hold among tithe-payers of the more prosperous Leinster and Munster midlands where the 1824 change in agistment brought tithes onto grazing land for the first time. Tithes thus had a particularly strong appeal to small and middling farmers as well as grazers with enough means to own the cattle being distrained by the hated tithe proctors. By contrast the penny-a-month rent of the Catholic Association, founded in 1823 with the goal of emancipation, and the adoption of this approach again during the repeal movement, made for near-national campaigns involving participants of both the lower and middling ranks.

These movements also encompassed social differences between the middle- and gentry-class leaders, the voters being marshaled to the polls in highly disciplined campaigns, and the general population attending monster meetings and participating in processions. The shared use of public addresses by all three movements does not, therefore, elide differences between them, or the possibility of alternate forms of popular participation via the Irish language—as yet invisible to historians—that were specific to each.

Setting these differences aside, however, it is clear that the Irish language had a presence among anti-tithe, emancipation, and repeal meetings alike. Priests were among the most visible deliverers of public addresses in Irish at meetings during the 1820s through 1840s, whether because of individual convictions, pressure from parishioners, or the wider politicization of the church to push for Catholic interests in this period. Priests were also natural candidates to deliver such speeches because they were among the few with both a firm experience in delivering addresses in Irish from the pulpit and a direct connection with locals. Aside from purely religious discourses, priests had long made a practice in speaking in Irish to their flocks on more secular concerns such as the involvement of parishioners in secret agrarian societies.[131] The continuity between Sunday addresses delivered by priests and popular mobilization was reinforced by the use of chapels for large meetings. In late January of 1825, the parish priest of Newcastle, Co. Limerick, Reverend William Fitzgerald, addressed a crowd in Irish said to number "nearly 5,000 persons" who had gathered at the parish chapel for a rent meeting. Fitzgerald spoke following several English-language speeches by a Mr. B. Sharkey, Mr. B. O'Dwyer, Mr. Therry, and another priest, Reverend Cassin.[132] It is likely that this is the same Reverend Fitzgerald of Limerick known to have assisted candidates on campaign and for his "popular eloquence, particularly in the Irish language," as reported by a Dublin correspondent.[133] The Dungarvan parish chapel provided the setting in June for a meeting in support of Henry Villiers-Stuart during the famous Waterford election of 1826. Addressing "the freeholders and inhabitants of the town and its vicinity," Reverend Murphy of Kilrossanty provided "a nervous and energetic harangue in the Irish language, which brought forward frequent peals of applause."[134] Two years later, the chapel of Feenagh, Co. Limerick, hosted a meeting to enact Catholic Association prohibitions on faction fights at which the parish priest, Reverend Kelly, spoke in Irish prior to an address in English by association leader Thomas Steele.[135] Country chapels similarly provided a convenient location for repeal meetings, especially those called to host deputies from the national organizations in search of donations and statements of local support. A deputation of repeal advocates visiting Shanbally, Co. Cork, in 1839 were met in the local chapel by the curate, Reverend R. Walsh, who then advocated their case to his congregation in Irish.[136] Likewise, the Reverend Fitzmaurice, curate of Dromid parish, Co. Kerry, hosted MP Maurice O'Donnell and a contingent of repeal officers at the parish chapel in 1845. More than £12 was reportedly collected from the assembled audience, who listened to Fitzmaurice deliver an address "in the venerable and heart-moving Irish tongue."[137]

But clerical addresses in Irish were not always given from the altar, especially during the anti-tithe campaign. The size of attendance also had a hand in this venue shift. An unnamed priest was said to have spoken in Irish at a nine-parish anti-tithe meeting—presumably held outdoors—in Mayo in 1838, one of three members of the clergy to address a crowd estimated at thirty thousand.[138] That same fall, another anti-tithe meeting consisting of thousands of "men of Oranmore, Ballynacourty, Carrabrown, and Clare-Galway" was held at the Kiltullagh, Co. Galway, race course. Speaking from an erected platform, the Reverend Hosty "addressed the meeting for a considerable time in the Irish language, which had visibly a great effect upon the multitude."[139] A 14 December 1838 outdoor gathering in Iveragh, Co. Kerry, to launch O'Connell's Precursor Society, forerunner of the Repeal Association, included Irish addresses by two priests: Reverend E. Fitzgerald, parish priest of the parishes of Cahirciveen and Filemore, and Reverend Jeremiah O'Sullivan, parish priest of Prior and Killemlagh. Fitzgerald, it was reported, spoke "with great ability and effect," describing tithes "as an enormous quadruped that, having for centuries consumed the produce of the country, was grown so formidable that no person could be found daring enough to attempt its destruction," and noting that one man (O'Connell) would "undertake the task, . . . having succeeded in taking one leg from the beast."[140]

Priests also spoke at repeal gatherings held outdoors, in meeting halls, and in courthouses during election events. The Clare priest, Reverend Patrick Quaid of Callaghan's Mills, delivered a speech in Irish to the pro-repeal partisans who had gathered at the Ennis courthouse in response to the nomination of the conservative candidate, Crofton Moore Vandeleur (1808–81), at a bitter election meeting in June 1841.[141] Quaid was also one of the featured speakers later at a massive repeal procession for MP William Smith O'Brien held in the city of Limerick in 1846. Speaking at an open-field meeting immediately before O'Brien himself addressed the crowd, Quaid proclaimed that "he did not intend to address them in the language which they had previously heard at the meeting. He considered that language an alien language to the Irish people, and he conceived that he was not transgressing any law when he stated so." Continuing, according to an abstract of his speech, Quaid told the audience in Irish, "Children of the bygone heroes victory was yours in days of old and victory will be yours again. The enemy came and took your blood. He took your country and he imprisoned your friends.... The ball is up! Repeal is demanded. Prosecute your demand."[142] A meeting held "near the residence" of another Repeal Association notable, William O'Neill Daunt, at Enniskean, Co. Cork, in December of 1842 featured the local parish priest, Father O'Donovan, who both presided and addressed the audience in Irish.[143] An election gathering of "freeholders of the baronies of Murrisk and Burrishoole" at Westport, Co. Mayo, in 1846 to secure the nomination of Joseph Myles McDonnell as a repeal candidate also featured an Irish address by the local curate, Reverend Curran, who spoke following a series of motions and speeches in English.[144]

But among priests, Reverend John Murphy (ca. 1790–1831) of Corofin, Co. Clare, stands out for his active public speaking in support of O'Connell and emancipation at the famous county election campaign of 1828. A native speaker—English was, according to him, "the language I am least accustomed to speak"—Murphy was the son of a blacksmith who attended Maynooth before being ordained for the parish of Doora in the diocese of Killaloe, most likely in 1812.[145] He was later appointed to Corofin, where he was known prior to the emancipation campaign for his efforts in the 1820s to establish schools in the area amenable to Catholics and for taking on Edward Synge, a local land agent who had actively encouraged proselytizing efforts by the Hibernian Society. Murphy became active in the months before, during, and after the Clare summer election, speaking in Irish at a Catholic Association meeting at Dysert in January of 1828, for instance, using the language "which the Rev. Gentleman at all times wields so ably."[146] Murphy later addressed his own parishioners in Irish after Mass on the Sunday immediately before the election.[147] At Dysert, Murphy spoke in Irish again during a pro-emancipation meeting in late September 1828 to induct new members into the Order of Liberators, this one attended by a number of local gentry as well as an "immense multitude" of "public-spirited and patriotic residents of the barony of Inchiquin."[148] The manner in which speeches in English and Irish comingled at such events can be gauged from Murphy's performance at another ceremony investing new members of the Order at Saint Munchin's chapel in the city of Limerick in September 1828. Reportedly attending, along with the bishop of Limerick, John Ryan, and Catholic Association leader Thomas Steele, were "numbers of the trades of the city, with several of the labouring classes," who had processed earlier with trees to decorate for the occasion, as well as "respectable citizens." Commencing in English, Murphy was said to have turned to Irish when addressing "the dense crowd in the middle of the aisle" before returning to English once again.[149]

Outreach to Irish speakers at these politicized events was not confined to priests. Members of the laity also mounted the hustings to connect with Irish speakers and draw them into the wider popular movement. The most notable of such speakers, of course, was O'Connell himself, although separating facts from hearsay in this instance can be difficult. The story that he had used Irish to disguise treasonous statements from government-backed reporters at his meetings was popular even in his own time, although accounts differ as to the occasion when he had done this—both Cork and Clare were floated as settings for this ruse.[150] A firmer case can be made for O'Connell delivering a speech in Irish to an audience in Tralee during the general election campaign of 1835[151] or in 1843 in Sligo where, by his own admission, he "addressed there 150,000 Connaughtmen in the Irish language."[152] Aside from O'Connell, it was suggested at the time of his declaration as a candidate at the Clare election of 1828 that "an honest substantial £10 freeholder, who cannot speak English," be selected to second the motion of the Liberator's candidacy in Irish.[153] Lay speakers were especially prevalent during the tithe agitation. A meeting in Ballinrobe, Co. Mayo, at the parish chapel in February of 1832 reportedly consisted entirely of speeches in Irish. Attended by "the landholders of Ballinrobe," a "crowd of peasantry," and "a number of our fair and fashionable countrywomen," the gathering included speeches against tithes by Mark Corcoran of Kilkeeran, James Mellet of Cloonenagh, John Fahy of Ballyjennings, Anthony Higgins of Knocklahiff, and Denis Henilly of Cloengowls. The audience, too, it was said, "made sensible observations" in the Irish language."[154] Likewise, every member making or seconding a motion at a similar anti-tithe meeting held near Castlebar, Co. Mayo, in 1838 was said to have addressed the audience in Irish.[155] Meetings at Headford, Co. Galway, in November of 1838, where a "genuine patriot, Patrick Hanley, Esq., of Kilroe" gave an address in Irish to the assembled "landed proprietors, clergy, and inhabitants," and at Dunmanway, Co. Cork, later that same month at which "two respectable farmers" spoke in Irish, hint further at the middling social status of the Irish speakers involved.[156] Such addresses were not only known to take place in heavily Irish-speaking Connacht and Munster, however. At a May 1838 meeting at Ballyhale, Co. Kilkenny—a town near the regional heart of the original anti-tithe agitation—a number of locals, described as "some farmers," delivered speeches in Irish at the close of the gathering.[157]

One of the more visible instances of public addresses delivered in Irish took place during a series of anti-tithe demonstrations in and around the town of

Ballyduff, Co. Kerry, in July 1832. An attempted sale of distrained cattle, seized as payment for tithes, brought forth one Jeremiah O'Connor, who urged the crowd on a number of occasions not to buy any of the property. According to evidence given later at his trial at assizes for conspiracy, O'Connor addressed the crowds in Irish, referring to the tithe system as a tyranny and suggesting that anyone who purchased the cattle be marked with "red letters of blood." What made this case so public was the decision of Daniel O'Connell to offer his legal services as defense for O'Connor and his three other codefendants, Gerard O'Connor, Reverend Andrew Sullivan, and William MacCarthy, and the spirited attack made by O'Connell on the entire tithe system in the course of the trial.[158] A transcript of one of O'Connor's Irish-language addresses appears to have survived.[159] In it, O'Connor, like Reverend O'Sullivan in 1838, attributed animal-like characteristics to the oppressive tithes, reminding the crowd that they and their mothers before them for three hundred years had been under the claws of the ministers (*faoi cruba na ministeirighe*) and that the English (*na Sasanaig*) had imposed a monstrously inequitable system whereby the fruits of the labor of the majority—achieved by the sweat of their brow (*le allas ar mailighe*)—was extracted for the benefit of the few. Addressing the crowd as *Clanna Gaodhal* (the Gaels), the speaker commended the heroic efforts of the men of Kilkenny for standing up against tithes, called for loyalty to Daniel O'Connell, predicted the return of a parliament to Ireland, and foresaw the English, rather than tithe proctors, supporting their own church (*coimeadach na Sasanaig suas a dteampuil fein*).[160]

Full texts of speeches delivered in Irish at other significant political events have survived as well. An address by a Thomas Harney to the freeholders of the parish of Kilbarrymeaden during the famous Waterford county election of 1826 was translated into English and preserved in writing by the Irish scholar Séamus Ó Scoireadh. Urging absolute support for Henry Villiers-Stuart against the "contemptible enslaving and bloodthirsty Beresford" (as Ó Scoireadh rendered the Irish original), Harney detailed a long history of unremitting conquest of "the aboriginal inhabitants" of Ireland by the English. Ireland, according to Harney, was left "seven thousand times worse" than before arrival of the English—and yet this was "no more than the play of children in comparison with what happened at the period of the Reformation, in the reign of Elizabeth and afterwards." The eighteenth-century penal legislation came in for particular scorn by Harney, who observed that they had remained in effect "until the dread of foreign war constrained England reluctantly to repeal a part of it." Emancipation, he concluded, would help dismantle the vestiges of the code.[161] Ballyhale, Co. Kilkenny, was also the site of an earlier anti-tithe speech, this time delivered by Amhlaoibh Ó Súilleabháin in 1832 to a crowd he estimated at a hundred thousand.[162] Like Harney, Ó Súilleabháin outlined a history of Catholic grievances at the hands of the English (*na Sasanaig*), starting with the plantation of Ulster and continuing on through the Cromwellian conquest, the missteps of the Stuarts, the betrayal of the Treaty of Limerick, and finally, the loss of parliament under the Act of Union. And like O'Connor, Ó Súilleabháin addressed his Irish-speaking crowd as *clanna gaodhal* or as *Caitilicidhe* (Catholics) and urged them to band together against landlord exploitation, Orange violence, and unreasonable taxation in the same way as the voters of Waterford had cooperated to elect Villiers-Stuart in 1826.[163]

A repeal speech delivered in Irish has survived as well, this one delivered—according to its modern editor, Breandán Ó Buachalla—by the Protestant minister Reverend Robert King at Dundalk, Co. Louth, in 1843. Not surprisingly, unlike those who delivered the surviving emancipation and anti-tithe speeches, King did not make appeal to a common Catholicism in opposition to English rule; given King's own faith and the more religiously based grievances of the emancipation and anti-tithe campaigns, this was expected. He did, however, couch his calls for repeal in terms of Ireland's historic grievances at the hands of the English and relied on a cultural touchstone for his Irish-speaking audience in the form of a reference to lines by the seventeenth-century poet Fearflatha Ua Gnímh. Addressing his speech to those in the gathered crowd "nach dtuigionn acht fírbheagan de'n tSacs-Bhearla in air labhaireadh libh ceana" (who do not understand but truly little of the English in which you were addressed previously), King described Daniel O'Connell as a latter day Moses, set to lead the Irish people (through the repeal campaign) out of Egypt and the bondage of "pharaoh" Robert Peel.[164]

King's speech points to one last point to be made about the use of Irish in the major popular political movements of the 1820s, 1830s, and 1840s. While it is clear that occasional instances of meetings conducted entirely in Irish can be found, very few of the surviving references to public events at which Irish was spoken did not also involve English-speaking speeches. King clearly delivered his Irish address after an English speech, as did a number of the speakers throughout the period. These were mixed events, in other words, bringing together those most proficient in one or the other of the two languages to pass along the message of emancipation, repeal, or tithe reform. Given these circumstances, it is difficult to see how these political movements can be interpreted as a product of one language community or the other. Rather, they were a product of both, as their leaders could ill afford to couch their message in just one language given the presence of speakers of both languages at the polls, on the grounds before the hustings, and in the chapels where many meetings occurred. Moreover, the influence of both language communities continued well into the 1850s and 1860s, even after the demise of the popular movements of the 1840s, as evidenced by the presence of Irish speakers (including monoglots) at the polling booth during those years. The modern Irish political scene that emerged in the second half of the nineteenth century was thus forged not just in English-speaking Ireland but in its Irish-speaking communities as well.

Language and Catholic Devotional Reform

IN PUBLISHING HIS IRISH-LANGUAGE Catholic instructional manual, *The Catholic Children's Religious Primer* (1825), the Waterford schoolteacher and chapel clerk Pádraig Denn (1756–1828) noted that his new work would join a crowded field of Irish catechisms to be found, he observed, "in every town." Fifty years later, Seán Pléimeann, also from Waterford, could still report that at least one copy of an Irish-language religious publication, whether a catechism, Tadhg Gaelach Ó Súilleabháin's *Pious Miscellany*, or James Gallagher's *Sixteen Irish Sermons*, was "to be found with every Roman Catholic who can read Irish."[1] Irish-speaking Catholics had not always been so well supplied with devotional instruction, however. After a respectable output of Irish-language religious tracts and catechisms from the Irish continental colleges of the seventeenth century, a downturn of production followed in the early decades of the eighteenth century. In 1742, the year Andrew Donlevy published his bilingual catechism in Paris, religious reading was in short enough supply that he justified the publication on account of the "great scarcity of those large Irish catechisms, published upwards of a hundred years ago, by the laborious and learned Franciscans of Lovain [sic]; and the consideration of those great evils, which arise from ignorance, partly for want of instructive books."[2] But following these lean years, a rebound in printed Irish-language Catholic material took place starting in the 1770s and 1780s, an increase that was paralleled in the manuscript world. By 1800 about a dozen new or reprinted religious titles in Irish had appeared, a pace sustained into the 1840s. Scribal production of religious material, although more steady in its output over the years, also exhibited signs of greater productivity by the early nineteenth century: of the manuscripts containing religious content in the collections of the Royal Irish Academy—the largest such corpus that has been fully cataloged—the number surviving from the years 1800–1820 outnumber those written in 1780–1800 by a ratio of about three to one.[3]

What has not been made clear by modern scholars is the relationship of this Irish-language religious output to the broader transformation of Irish Catholicism starting in the late eighteenth century and continuing through the final decades of the nineteenth century. While the features of this change—variously described by researchers as an institutionally driven "devotional revolution," a long-term attempt to impose Tridentine orthodoxy by reformers, or a lay-driven mix of orthodox and unorthodox religious practices arising out of negotiation with clerical authorities—have been repeatedly debated and refined,[4] the Irish language (where it has been addressed at all) has been consistently portrayed as the vehicle for a spirituality that remained antithetical to the new version of Catholicism conveyed in English. Emmet Larkin, whose initial analysis in 1972 popularized the concept of a dramatic introduction of modern devotional forms that had accelerated after the appointment of Paul Cullen as archbishop of Dublin in 1852, proposed that the new Catholicism was a substitute for a culture that had been disappearing even before the Great Famine. Loss of language was a part of that cultural loss, he noted, concluding that the devotional revolution had been built on anglicization. This understanding was reinforced by research that explicitly connected the Irish language with religious practices—especially unorthodox prayers—that were no longer favored in the postfamine Irish church. The folklorist Seán Ó Súilleabháin, surveying the vast field of prayers found among the nineteenth-century laity, concluded that "none of them went over into English" when language shift occurred, while Diarmuid Ó Laoghaire, writing of the Irish-language prayers he had published in 1975 as *Ár bPaidreacha Dúchais*, agreed that "few of those prayers found their way into English."[5] This stance in fact echoed the earlier conclusion reached in one of the main sources for nineteenth-century religious culture used by Ó Laoghaire and Ó Súilleabháin, Douglas Hyde's study of the folk prayers and religious songs of Connacht, *Abhráin Diadha Chúige Connacht* (1906). Hyde contended that the Irish-language religious material he encountered had disappeared wherever a shift to English had occurred, an appraisal in turn echoing even earlier nineteenth-century folklorists like William Wilde, who suggested that as the Irish had "taken to reading bibles and learning English," native beliefs had declined.[6]

The sense that modern Irish Catholicism emerged out of the twin pillars of language shift and devotional reform has retained its strength in current historical research, although not without some challenges. The work of Donal Kerr has most clearly presented religious reform as a consequence of anglicization, arguing that new forms of Catholicism were carried first and foremost by way of printed prayer books in English. While acknowledging that a few of these publications were available in Irish, Kerr proposed that it was literacy that truly provided the entryway for the new devotions contained in the manuals. Since the acquisition of literacy at the time meant learning English, he argued, it was this language that opened the door to new Catholic practices.[7] Underpinning this argument have been wider scholarly conceptualizations of the deeper transformations in Irish society said to have paved the way for religious change. This was the emergence of a strong farming class and their mercantile counterparts in the Catholic "core" consisting of the wealthier agricultural lands and growing urban trade centers of south Munster and Leinster. Although not always stated outright, the inference has been that these social classes—and the spirituality that developed among them—was conveyed in English, whereas any devotional forms that continued to circulate in Irish in these areas have been described as archaic and conservative in nature.[8] In other words, as middling farmers and urban merchants reached for English as a means of economic advancement in modern Ireland, the new Catholicism they developed as part of their advancement would have been, according to these studies, a creation of an English-speaking world.

By contrast, alternate interpretations have highlighted the problems with mapping this linguistic divide so neatly onto religious change. Desmond Keenan, in an early response to the devotional revolution thesis, argued for a relatively direct correspondence of Irish-language and English-language prayers and catechisms—the former usually consisting of supplications rooted in Latin originals, and the latter usually translations from the English into Irish—and concluded that formal, orthodox Catholicism during the reforms of the nineteenth century had not differed in the two languages.[9] Elsewhere, investigations of local beliefs in heavily Irish-speaking areas and of Irish-language religious print culture by Eugene Hynes and Niall Ó Ciosáin, respectively, have highlighted the ways in which the rigid definition of terms like "orthodoxy" and "modernity" by scholars (who are eager to connect such terms with anglicization) often mask the linguistic diversity of Irish belief at the time of this extensive transformation.[10] In truth, the challenge in assessing the role of Irish speakers in Catholic devotional change requires even greater complexity, because this analysis depends ultimately on how that religious evolution is defined by scholars. And yet no consensus has emerged on this question. Larkin's original concept of the devotional revolution was of a phenomenon that had been driven, on the one hand, by the institutional growth of the Catholic Church in the wake of the famine and by the improved ratios of priests to parishioners in the second half of the nineteenth century. On the other hand, Larkin believed that the devotional revolution was marked by forms of worship that were both new and Italian—or at least continental European—in form. These included new devotions introduced by Cullen in the Dublin archdiocese such as the rosary, forty hours, novenas, blessed altars, stations of the cross, vespers, and dedication to the Sacred Heart, all pushed by newly formed sodalities and confraternities.[11] Larkin's sense of the generically international characteristics of the new Irish Catholicism has in many ways been confirmed by the findings of recent investigations into topics like the rise of mass-produced statuaries and stained-glass windows of mid-nineteenth-century Catholicism.[12] If such Dublin-based practices are taken, in very narrow fashion, to define the emerging devotional characteristics of Irish belief, then the evidence for a strong impact of the Irish language on devotional revolution becomes harder to sustain.

On the other hand, a less constricted view of the primary features of the new Catholicism advocated by the laity and church officials has been far more acceptable to most of today's historians. Scholars have questioned Larkin's findings by showing that a number of these devotions, including the rosary and the Stations of the Cross, were present in Ireland long before Cullen's time.[13] Others have warned that not only were Irish religious interests more closely attuned to prayer books like the *Key of Heaven* that could hardly be described as ultramontane but also that many devotions (like the Stations of the Cross) were in fact geographically widespread in western Christianity and therefore cannot be treated as exclusively Italian in their origin.[14] These interpretations hold that the devotional changes affecting Ireland started as early as the last quarter of the eighteenth century and that they involved an essentially Tridentine emphasis on the Mass within a chapel (as opposed to outdoors or at "stations" held in private home settings that became a necessary expedient during the population boom of the prefamine decades), meeting sacramental obligations, and the use of devotional manuals, prayer books, and catechisms to educate the laity about such practices. Larkin himself, in fact, although continuing to draw contrasting interpretations as to timing, embraced these points in one of his last publications on the topic.[15] The remaining questions to be resolved have been regarding the exact nature of the orthodoxy being sought by reformers at any given time. How frequent was Mass attendance intended to be in the eyes of church officials, and what range of devotional practices were they willing to sanction? How much power did the laity have in determining the face of Irish Catholicism, and to what degree did that vision differ from those of clerical authorities?[16] In fact, a strong case can be made for the role of the Irish language in building this new orthodoxy as defined in this fashion. Furthermore, a perspective that incorporates the contributions of Irish-speaking communities helps answer these lingering questions while building a more complete picture of the devotional transformation of this period.

Surveying the religious landscape as it stood in the final decades of the eighteenth century and first quarter of the nineteenth century, Irish Catholicism was represented by a greater diversity of Irish-language devotional, catechetical, literary, and hagiographical works in both print and manuscript than at any time since the beginning of the seventeenth century. Although religious material as a percentage of the content of manuscripts declined slightly from the eighteenth to the nineteenth century, the overall number of religious manuscripts increased significantly (as with manuscripts in general), while the volume of printed religious works in Irish increased dramatically. When this corpus is combined with the range and variety of prayers, hymns, canticles, and religious stories that circulated orally, a full sense of the dynamism of Irish-language religiosity right on the eve of the language's lowest point becomes evident. Anything more than a superficial accounting of this oral content for the decades before the end of the nineteenth century is nearly impossible, dependent as historians are on the few near-contemporaries like Hyde who published collections of them and on traces of these practices in the twentieth-century recordings of the Irish Folklore Commission. By contrast, the written record of Irish-language written material of the eighteenth and nineteenth centuries is relatively well preserved in the manuscript and print collections of various archives in Ireland and abroad, and they can provide a start for an analysis of how Irish-language devotional material played a part in shaping Catholic orthodoxy.

Turning first to manuscript output, nearly forty-three hundred hand-written Irish-language texts have survived in various holdings in Ireland, England, Scotland, and Wales, with an additional hundred or so residing in other public and private collections in North America, continental Europe, and Australia. Of these, approximately four thousand date to the eighteenth and nineteenth centuries.[17] It is the catalog summaries of these manuscripts—along with the contents themselves of seventy-five representative manuscripts—that provide a basis for this study in an approach that follows that of Vincent Morley in his recent examination of this same corpus for different purposes.[18] It is believed that the small number of texts not considered do not differ from those included here. The central challenge posed by these manuscripts is the criteria by which to identify their contents as "religious" in nature. In keeping with the time period of their creation, Irish-language literary works being copied and composed in the eighteenth and nineteenth centuries had a far more expansive understanding of the place of religion in society. Thus, references to God, and Christian precepts in particular, were common in written texts without such content being understood to be conspicuously religious or tied to devotional practices. For example, one of the most popular tales among scribes of this period was the medieval morality story *Fís Mherlino* about the encounter of a sinful Bohemian with hell.[19] But just as nineteenth-century editions of Dante's *Inferno* would not be a primary focus of the researcher seeking to discern the religious practices of Victorian England, such tales have not been included here. Likewise, general references to God, salvation, and sin were common themes in Irish-language prose and poetry (as they were in other languages), and while religious verse has been included in the analysis below, content with incidental Christian themes has not. Finally, scribes commonly included scribal prayers in their texts as a coda to their work. These, too, have been excluded as they were intended to be embedded in the writing act itself, rather than in everyday religious practice. In the end, a substantive body of hagiographical material, prayer books, devotional guides, meditative instructions, hymns, missals, catechisms, religious verse, and sermons yield strong evidence of the religious preferences of the scribes who assembled these texts and beyond them, their coreligionists.

Irish scribes possessed clear interest in including religious material in their texts: approximately one in five manuscripts contain at least one item of religious content either in isolation or in combination with secular writings. This percentage, based on surviving manuscripts, is almost certainly a minimum proportion of what was originally created: the preservation of religious texts like catechisms and prayer books was undermined by their ephemeral nature and their susceptibility to transportation overseas by emigrating owners, while the preference of many mid-nineteenth-century scholars and librarians who collected these texts to obtain epic poetic cycles and older secular material rather than religious items with a popular provenance meant that some manuscripts undoubtedly fell by the wayside.[20] Moreover, if we take the example of the body of Irish texts in the Royal Irish Academy, the percentage of manuscripts with religious content remained at about 20 percent through both the eighteenth and nineteenth centuries. But because manuscript production (as measured by the number of surviving manuscripts) increased in the nineteenth century—about two manuscripts have survived for every one from the eighteenth century—this steady one-in-five proportion meant an increase in the amount of manuscript religious material being copied and circulated.

Naturally, manuscript circulation could not match that of print in terms of sheer volume, but historians are clear that these texts did not simply sit in the homes of scribes, limiting their impact. Rather, they were lent to fellow readers in ongoing exchanges that often became the focal point of scribal correspondence, especially in earlier decades before antiquarian patronage increasingly came to overshadow the production and transmission of manuscripts in the second and third decades of the nineteenth century.[21] Scribes compiled and updated book lists to track books borrowed by others as well as texts (including religious material) that interested readers might seek to obtain from them, as exemplified by the inventories compiled by Mícheál Óg Ó Longáin in response to inquiries from interested buyers.[22] Jottings and other marginalia tell a similar story, as a few illustrative examples show. The scribe Tomás Ó Hóidh lent a text containing the life of Christ to a fellow scribe, probably Nicholas Reid, in 1778, while a note by a James Sullivan on a late-eighteenth-century collection of poems and catechetical material reveals that "James Tobin at Achill" had lent the book to him.[23] A surviving letter written in 1832 from a J. Courtney describing his return of two texts and requesting the loan of a literary miscellany can be found among another of the Ó Longáin manuscripts, and Mícheál Óg himself penned an application—in verse form, no less—seeking to borrow a copy of the religious text *Trí Bior-Ghaoithe an Bháis* from one of his contacts.[24]

Alongside this uptick in manuscript materials, printed religious works increased too. The stark record of Irish-language printing in terms of volume and number of titles, in comparison not only to the vast new numbers of English-language Catholic texts that appeared in this period but also to Welsh, Breton, and Scots Gaelic printing, has been closely studied,[25] but such findings do not tell the whole story. First, while dwarfed by the numbers of titles being produced in other languages, printing in Irish undoubtedly increased and diversified starting in the late eighteenth century, and it was Catholic religious titles that deserve recognition for nearly the entirety of this growth. An Irish speaker looking to engage in devotional reading or obtain a catechetical guide in the mid-eighteenth century had only a handful of titles that had been printed within the last half century to choose from, and the period between 1750 and 1780 had been an especially barren time in printing. There were a few catechisms and instructional texts, including Archbishop Michael O'Reilly's *An Teagasg Criostuidhe, agus na Gnáth-Úrnaighthe* (ca. 1727), Sylvester Lloyd's *Doway Catechism in English and Irish* (1738), and Reverend James Pulleine's *An Teagasg*

Criosdaidhe Angoidhleig (1748), published domestically, as well as two published abroad: a reprint of Giolla Brighde Ó hEodhasa's 1611 catechism (Rome, 1707) and Andrew Donlevy's *An Teagasg Criosduidhe do Reir Ceasda agus Freagartha* (Paris, 1742). Two short religious tracts were published: a history of the Loreto church appended to the 1707 Ó hEodhasa catechism, *Tosach agas Aistriugha Míorbhuileach Theampoll Mhuire Loreto*, and a reprinting of Seán Ó Dubhlaoich's seventeenth-century publication, *Suim Bhunudhasach an Teaguisg Chriosdaidhe*, inserted at the end of Aodh Mac Cruitín's *The Elements of the Irish Language, Grammatically Explained in English* (1728). To this could be added a 1736 translation of Giovanni Pietro Pinamonti's *La Vera Sapienza* (1677) and multiple runs of Bishop James Gallagher's *Sixteen Irish Sermons* starting in 1736.[26] Beyond this, as Donlevy had observed, one had to depend on an increasingly dwindling supply of surviving seventeenth-century prints. By contrast, the Irish reader of the 1820s was supplied with a much wider range of titles: Irish-language versions of the two catechisms possessing a multiregional market at the time (the O'Reilly catechism and the Butler catechism), a number catering to local instructional needs (the Coppinger catechism for south Munster, the Pulleine catechism in the north, the Kirwan and Loftus catechisms circulating in Connacht, and the Young catechism of Limerick), as well as reprints of old favorites like the Donlevy. Alongside these texts were at least twenty-two new devotional titles between 1770 and 1870—with seven new publications appearing in a particularly active stretch between 1818 and 1825—and a constant stream of new editions of Gallagher's *Irish Sermons* and Ó Súilleabháin's *Pious Miscellany*.[27]

Second, while strikingly outpaced by the number of devotional works in other languages, the bulk of printing in the Irish language during this expansion was of precisely the type of texts that were most poised to be shared with the widest possible audience: catechisms, pious song collections, and sermons. A single printed catechism, for instance, even at a low level of circulation, might be used by a Sunday schoolmaster or priest to impart religious knowledge orally in Irish to thousands of locals over many years. Catechisms also had the virtue of acting as basic reading primers, reinforcing their own use while acting as a possible bridge to wider reading in Irish, as evidenced by locals who explained to Protestant missionaries that they had acquired literacy through such a method.[28] Likewise, the two most-often reproduced printed texts in Irish in this period, Gallagher's *Irish Sermons* and Ó Súilleabháin's *Pious Miscellany*, both featured content that traveled seamlessly between oral and literate worlds. A single edition of Gallagher's *Irish Sermons* could reach scores of parishioners on a single Sunday or holy day by way of a priest or curate who chose to rely on it as part of his address. Ó Ciosáin, who has provided an extensive analysis of the *Pious Miscellany*, has similarly emphasized its mobile qualities by noting the simultaneous existence of its songs in three different forms in the nineteenth century: print, manuscript, and oral.[29] These qualities enabled the *Pious Miscellany* and similar devotional texts like those of Pádraig Denn to circulate well beyond their original regional home in south Leinster and southeast Munster to regions like west Clare, where the Kilrush poet Micheál Ó hAnnracháin, for example, knew them well enough to argue that "Tádhg Gaodhlach and Patrick Denn's productions were the most suitable for the people and set forth good language and style of composition."[30]

Even without this multiplier effect, the most-often printed Irish-language religious material had a visibly large circulation on its own. The *Pious Miscellany* had at least eighteen editions printed in its heartland of east Munster and south Leinster in the first half of the nineteenth century and, as Ó Ciosáin has noted, was the most frequently reissued publication in Irish prior to the twentieth century.[31] A new edition of Gallagher's *Sixteen Irish Sermons* appeared in almost every decade during a century-long run between 1736 and 1841. As for catechisms, Protestant observers of the 1820s, possessing a sharp eye for any potential literary competition with the scriptures, calculated the number of readers of Irish to be between twenty and thirty thousand solely on the basis of the number of catechisms they had seen in the homes of Catholics.[32] This was undoubtedly an underestimate, as fifteen thousand copies alone of the first edition of the local catechism sanctioned by Archbishop John MacHale of Tuam and assembled in 1839 by his associate, Father Martin Loftus, were distributed in the west of Ireland, while Uileog de Búrca observed that later editions of this same text were still selling six thousand copies per year in 1874.[33] This output looks respectable in comparison with the initial distribution in 1827 of forty-three thousand catechisms by the Catholic Book Society, an institution whose offerings consisted exclusively of English-language texts.[34] Even a catechism produced within the context of antiquarian interest in the language (and hence at a disadvantage in reaching a popular audience), the 1863 version of the O'Reilly catechism printed by William Williams of the Keating Society, reportedly sold five thousand copies in the Waterford area.[35] Catechisms also secured a long afterlife in Irish material culture. Writing of the catechism sanctioned by Bishop John Young for Limerick and printed in a single edition in 1811, Daniel McCarthy noted over a half century later that the work was "still in use throughout part of the diocese."[36] National schools inspector Patrick Keenan was exaggerating when he testified before a Royal Commission in 1870 that "in the south and west the catechism is almost universally learned by the children in the Irish language," but the impression of ubiquity when it came to certain Irish-language texts like the catechism was certainly shared by others, as Pléimeann's comments cited above demonstrate.[37] Thus, although outnumbered by religious texts in English, Irish-language religious material—because strong in certain genres like catechetical works—was experiencing a growth in this period that was poised to reach a wider audience than a mere title count would otherwise suggest.

The dynamics of this market of manuscript and printed religious works, and especially the workings of its suppliers, reveals much about the relationship between the Irish language and the changes taking place within Irish Catholicism. It is possible to detect a two-tiered (but not necessarily mutually exclusive) audience within this market: one interested in cheaper printed (or occasionally handwritten) texts like catechisms and devotional works such as the *Pious Miscellany* designed for a general readership and the other in pursuit of more sophisticated and extended meditative prose tracts, religious poetry, and prayer books that were more often (although not exclusively) available in manuscript form. Although Irish speakers of all social backgrounds served as consumers of each of these types of texts at various times, this second market for higher-order texts skewed toward strong farmers, church officials, and other individuals with the financial means to contract for handmade reading material in Irish, as can be glimpsed in the commentary of a contributor to the *Freeman's Journal*:

> Catholic clergymen have been known to give five pounds for a transcript of a few pages of Irish sermons.... Still more remarkable are the well authenticated cases of the farmers, one of whom paid seventeenth shillings to a person that he employed to copy a small Irish Catholic prayer-book, such as, if it had been an English book, would have been sold then for eighteen pence, and would now, perhaps, be worth but sixpence. Another farmer paid five pounds for a transcript of a larger Irish prayer-book, but which in English would certainly not cost more than three shillings.... A farmer's son, on getting one hundred pounds from his father as a provision, instantly set apart twenty-five pounds of it to purchase Irish books, sending in every direction, and to any distance for them.[38]

A manuscript valued at five pounds may have been unusually expensive, but it was not atypical for scribes to charge several shillings for a well-copied prayer book or poetry miscellany in Irish. Micheál Ó hAnnracháin, for instance, was asking between 2s. and 5s. each for his manuscripts in 1876.[39] Moreover, a demand for manuscripts did exist at this price, as scribes like Tomás Ó Iceadha (1775–1856), a former agricultural laborer from Tipperary who went on to teach Irish at St. John's College, Waterford, found when a missal he translated into Irish for his own use drew the attention of a Clonmel cloth seller, James O'Meara, who subsequently commissioned several devotional works for his own use starting in 1819. Ó Iceadha soon discovered that a number of people had an interest in such books ("[tá] ainmhian eugmhaiseach aig morán daoine chuige"), and he subsequently procured sponsorship for decades from a number of lay and clerical patrons in the Waterford region, including Risteard Ó Domhnaill, Risteard Ó Faoláin, and several local priests: Father Pádraig de Bhal, Father Pattruig Ó Domhnald, and the future bishop Father Dominic O'Brien.[40] Put directly, not all users and patrons of these texts were marginal or struggling tenant farmers and cottiers, the social classes presumed by historians to be the sole holdouts against an anglicizing class of middle-class Catholics.

To be sure, some of these devotional tracts and extended meditative prose works were available in cheaper print formats, enabling their reach to extend beyond just financially secure priests and farmers. A handwritten note by its former owner in the back of the Newberry Library's copy of Pádraig Denn's translation of Richard Challoner's *Think Well On't*, published by John Hackett in Clonmel in 1819 as *Machtnuig go Maih Air*, explains that it was purchased in 1842 for only 7d.[41] The Clonmel priest William Heffernan similarly noted in 1845 that "small prayer books ... printed in the Roman letters"—presumably works like Matthew Kennedy's *The Spiritual Rose* (first edition, 1800) or the publications of Denn—could be found for 4d. a piece.[42] But where a certain title was not available, had fallen out of print, or simply had never been produced in Irish (as was the case with Ó Iceadha's missal), contracting with a local to hand-write a copy of a desired text was the preferred option. This meant greater expense in most cases, but with a smaller market for buyers—those literate in Irish were outnumbered by those who could read English, and scribes often operated in relatively local circles[43]—the cost in time and effort of pursuing subscribers in order to secure a print run was often outweighed by the convenience of simply having a text copied out to order from a locally procured scribe.

There were even advantages to scribal-produced texts over their printed counterparts that reveal some of the purposeful planning that went on between selective patrons and responsive scribes into the creation of religious manuscripts. Printed texts could not be individually personalized for an owner, whereas manuscripts offered endless possibilities for uniquely selecting and ordering content, enabling scribes and patrons alike to choose the religious material deemed most appropriate for inclusion. In fact, the vast majority of manuscripts containing religious material from the eighteenth and nineteenth centuries consisted of more than one genre, with hagiographical material adjoined to excerpts of seventeenth-century Franciscan publications and religious verse interspersed with prayers and morality tales. Oftentimes, secular and religious material was placed together in large miscellanies. Mícheál Óg Ó Longáin, for instance, in assembling a manuscript in 1820 for one of his main patrons, Cork banker and one-time wine merchant James Roche, chose to combine a passage from Seathrún Céitinn's *Trí Bior-Ghaoithe an Bháis* with a psalm, a religious poem, the thirteenth-century dialogue *Agallamh an Chuirp agus an Anam*, a hagiographical passage, and a sermon on the Passion.[44] The eighteenth-century Cork scribe and poet Seán Ó Murchadha na Ráithíneach (1700–1762) included a life of Columcille in a manuscript he copied for a clerical patron, Father Domhnall Ó Cearbhaill, because the priest wanted "nídh éigin do bheatha threas phatrún na hEireann .i. naomh Coluim Cille do sgríobhadh ann so" (something on the life of the third patron of Ireland, i.e., St. Columcille, to be written here).[45] These virtues undermine modern historians' emphasis on the impact of high-volume printed publications, revealing the ways that past patrons benefited from the intellectual selectivity and uniqueness in the assembly of manuscripts that ensured that the Irish collections of no two religious readers were alike.

Manuscripts, like printed texts, also traveled between the oral and written world, and this could in many cases mitigate the more limited circulation and higher costs of obtaining hand-written texts. The reading of manuscripts out loud in eighteenth- and nineteenth-century Ireland is well attested, whether by scribes themselves or by subsequent owners of the texts. Scribal notes uncovered by Breandán Ó Conchúir, for example, refer to manuscripts being read to children and used for the amusement of "cluinteoirí" (listeners) and "do gach duine [ag] éisteacht" (to everyone listening).[46] Liam Ó Danachair of Athea, Co. Limerick, who had grown up in Ballyallinan, recalled such itinerant figures from among his grandparents' generation of the prefamine period. One such visitor, known as "Páid na hAbhann," read from "a roll of Irish manuscript and a few books of his own making—sheets of clean paper cut to book shape, and stitched in a cover of cloth or soft leather with wax-end."[47] As with texts in any language, in other words, the ability of handwritten material to jump barriers of social class normally created by literacy divides should be kept in mind.

The mobility of manuscript content between all social classes and literary abilities should not distract from the central point, however: religiously themed texts of the eighteenth and nineteenth centuries did find audiences among middling farmers and priests, and not just poor tenant farmers and laborers. While scribes themselves were of modest (sometimes even precarious) backgrounds, a survey of the patrons, subscribers, and sponsors of this Irish-language religious output suggests a mix of clerical and lay supporters, many with the means to afford subscriptions for multiple copies of printed works or the cost of a manuscript priced at several shillings. The largest single act of patronage for religious texts involved Bishop John Murphy (1772–1847) of Cork, who supported the writing of more than one hundred Irish manuscripts starting in 1814 by a circle of Cork scribes surrounding Ó Longáin and consisting of his sons, Peadar and Pól, as well as Tadhg Ó Conaill, Seán Ó Dreada, Éamann Ó Mathúna, Seán Ó Muláin, Seán Ó hUghbhair, Eoghan Tóibín, and two priests, Fathers Dónall Ó Súilleabháin and Donncha Ó Ceallacháin.[48] As an example of patronage of devotional texts for purely practical purpose, Murphy offers a slightly uncommon profile for a typical patron since he was also a bibliophile with an interest in amassing the texts themselves as much as their deployment; the German traveler Johann Kohl's often-cited description of the bishop's home packed to the ceilings with volumes belies an interest in the books as much as their content.[49] But Murphy was not the only supporter of devotional reading to come from top echelons. Bishop of Waterford and Lismore Dominic O'Brien (1798–1873), a patron to Tomás Ó Iceadha, was also the president of St. John's College, Waterford.[50] A translation of Thomas à Kempis's *Imitation of Christ* completed by an unknown clerical scribe, possibly Reverend Pulleine, sometime before 1762 attracted the support of Bishops Antonius Garvey of Dromore and Theophilus Mac Cartan of Down and Connor, who were among the committed subscribers for a print edition that never made it to press.[51] Other officials sanctioned more successful printings and even provided the Irish text itself in some cases. The catechism named for Archbishop Michael O'Reilly (ca. 1690–1758), probably compiled when he had been a priest, appeared first sometime in the 1720s or 1730s and remained in circulation well into the nineteenth century. Archbishop John Carpenter of Dublin (1729–86), who played a prominent role in shaping the form of orthodox Irish-language religiosity at the turn of the century, commissioned Charles O'Conor to provide Irish versions of common prayers in a guide for the Mass, *Rituale Romanorum* (1776).[52] Later, Bishop William Coppinger of Cloyne and Archbishop John MacHale of Tuam encouraged the production of the aforementioned catechisms that circulated throughout the early and mid-nineteenth centuries, while Thomas Bray, Archbishop of Cashel, adapted a set of prayers and instructions in Irish from Coppinger's *True Piety* (9th ed., 1813) and published them as *Oideas Athchoimir agus Urnaighthe* (1807).[53] The leap from manuscript to print form by the hymns of Ó Súilleabháin's *Pious Miscellany* also owed some debt to the support of high officials, with subscriptions from the bishop of Ossory and a number of priests from the Tipperary, Kilkenny, and Waterford areas documented in the original 1802 edition.[54]

As in the case of the *Pious Miscellany*, however, clerical involvement in the production of religious texts was more often conducted at the local level by interested priests. The Reverend Jonathan Furlong (1800–1857), a Clare priest originally from Limerick, produced two prayer books and an abridged Butler catechism that were printed in Dublin between 1839 and 1842. Prior to this, he commissioned the scribe Mícheál Píocóid to write out a copy of Seathrún Céitinn's *Eochair-Sgiath an Aifrinn* (written ca. 1610) in 1836.[55] Labhrás Ó Fúartháin, a schoolmaster like many scribes of the time, produced a copy of part of *Eochair-Sgiath an Aifrinn* in 1777 for Father Matha Paor of Ardeenloun, Co. Waterford, while Ó Dreada, a stonecutter, worked for two Cork priests: the aforementioned Father Dónall Ó Súilleabháin of Enniskean and Father Eoin Ó Céileachair of Muntervary, Co. Cork (the latter was evidently a Repeal supporter, as the words "Hurrah for Repeal!" appear below his signature in an 1833 prayer book).[56] The Cork priest Father Muiris Ciniféic commissioned manuscripts containing *Trí Bior-Ghaoithe*, religious verse, a sermon, and a copy of *Míorbhuileach Theampoll Mhuire Loreto* from Éamann Ó Mathúna in 1841–42.[57] Scribes themselves were no doubt aware of the potential market among priests for purchasing copies of religious material, as an 1832 letter from Mícheál Óg Ó Longáin to an unnamed priest soliciting his services in copying a number of religious texts attests.[58] Other priests purchased manuscripts or printed texts without necessarily directly patronizing their production. An auction list of the books of Dean John Patrick Lyons of Mayo from 1845 revealed that he owned copies of Ó hEodhasa's catechism (described as "O'Hussey's prayers, &c. in Irish," probably the 1707 edition) and Froinsias Ó Maolmhuaidh's *Lucerna Fidelium* (1676). The names of clerical owners that appear scattered throughout surviving manuscripts, such as the nineteenth-century Kilkenny priest John Gorman who at one time appears to have possessed an eighteenth-century text containing hagiographical material written by Ruisdeard Cais, confirms the popularity of Irish-language religious material among this constituency.[59]

The majority of the patrons of religious texts were not clerical, however. Ó Ciosáin's review of subscribers to the first edition of the *Pious Miscellany*, for example, has demonstrated that clerics made up no more than one-fifth.[60] Within the scribal world of religious manuscripts surveyed here, of forty-five scribal patrons who could be identified, only eighteen were of clerical background. Unfortunately, these patrons left few clues as to their identity or social situation, an evidentiary problem that afflicts historical understanding of scribal work in general, not just the world of religious texts.[61] Occasionally, some basic biographical information has survived. Muiris Ó Gormáin, who worked in Dublin, wrote out a copy of *Trí Bior-Ghaoithe* for a medical doctor, Sean Ó Fheargusa, in 1752.[62] Other patrons were businessmen and urban professionals, as the examples of James Roche of Cork and James O'Meara of Clonmel cited above attest. The domestic context in which lay patrons used these texts can be glimpsed from examples such as the copy of *Eochair-Sgiath an Aifrinn*, written by the scribe Donochadh Mhurchoideach Ua Sganuill in 1830 for the use of Peadar Ó Riordann and his children.[63] Likewise, Aindrias Mac Cruitín (ca. 1650–1738) of County Clare produced a manuscript containing the life and history of Saint Senán in 1721 for Éamonn Ó Maolruanáigh and his wife Seabhán Ní Conmara.[64] Other patrons may have lacked the economic basis to put them among middling farmers and businessmen yet were part of professions such as school teaching that placed them in a more ambitious social context than their income might otherwise suggest. Seán Builléad and Seán de Bhailis, Cork schoolmasters for whom Seán Ó Murchadha na Ráithíneach worked in the eighteenth century, provide two such potential illustrations. Of course, recipients of manuscripts also came from more modest backgrounds, among them the ship's carpenter Muiris Ó Conchúir, who requested a text containing religious verse in 1758 from Ó Murchadha.[65]

Perhaps the most common patrons of religious texts, however, were scribes themselves, who often wrote copies for their own use or else encouraged fellow scribes to produce copies for them. In addition to serving as a patron, Father Ó Súilleabháin was himself an active scribe, translator, and publisher of religious material, including an edition of the *Imitation of Christ* (1822), a dual role also taken up by Uilliam Ó Duinnín of East Muskerry who copied a composite manuscript of verse and prose for his own use while also soliciting religious texts from Mícheál Óg Ó Longáin.[66] Ó Longáin wrote a large number of texts for his own library, including a copy of *Eochair-Sgiath an Aifrinn* written in 1799, as well as catechetical material, presumably to assist in his Sunday school teaching.[67] Tadhg Ó Conaill, a gardener from Cork, commenced writing a copy of *Trí Bior-Ghaoithe* in 1819 for himself, and the schoolmaster-scribe Peadar Ó Gealacáin wrote a collection of religious material for his own "use and profit" (*úsáid agus tairbhe*) between 1845 and 1846.[68] As with the patrons, it would be a mistake to presume that clerical affiliation somehow encouraged production of religious texts. Twenty-six clerical scribes can be definitively identified from among the eighteenth- and nineteenth-century religious manuscripts surveyed here, while 125 scribes can be identified as part of the laity. Among the lay scribes were some of the best-known producers of Irish material from throughout Ireland of this period, including in addition to those named above, Dáibhí de Barra (ca. 1757–1851) of Cork; Tadhg Ó Neachtain (ca. 1671–ca. 1749), Risteard Tuibear (fl. 1710–30), and Muiris Ó Gormáin, who all worked in Dublin; Art Mac Bionaid (1793–1879) of Armagh; Aodh Buí Mac Cruitín of Clare; and Amhlaoibh Ó Súilleabháin of Kilkenny.

The social basis for patronage and consumption of Irish-language religious material was not, therefore, incompatible with the very same forces that supported the devotional reforms considered central by historians to the emergence of modern Catholicism. The individuals creating and using these texts were often literate, of middling or even comfortable means, and especially in the case of priests, had direct ties to the institutional church. The circulation of these texts was made possible by lay users as well as clerical, just as historians have emphasized the ground-up drive to define religious practices in Ireland as much as any imposition from church officials above. The cost of patronizing manuscripts, especially in the eighteenth and very early nineteenth centuries before the temporary collapse of the market for scribal work in the third and fourth decades of the 1800s (a downturn later mitigated by patronage by antiquarians and museum libraries), would have put many of these Irish-speaking devotional readers squarely in the ascendant middling classes identified by scholars like Hynes as having benefited from the chapel-centered, morally restrictive teachings of the new Catholic orthodoxy.[69] Geographically, although religious manuscripts were produced in all four provinces of Ireland, south Munster (particularly Clare, Limerick, Tipperary, Cork, and Waterford), south Leinster (Kilkenny and even heavily anglicized Wexford), and Dublin provided particularly visible homes for the printers and scribes involved in producing these texts—regions that coincide directly with the areas identified by scholars as providing an initial stronghold for devotional reform.[70] In short, the social basis for a role for Irish-speaking readers to participate in the forging of modern Catholicism was undoubtedly present, leaving the question of what type of religious texts were being read by these Irish speakers and how those texts contributed to devotional change.

When seeking to characterize the predominant ideological strains guiding Irish-language Catholic devotional writings as they emerged in the nineteenth century, scholars have turned to a number of sources: the Irish-language religious productions of the seventeenth-century Irish continental seminaries, especially St. Anthony's in Louvain; the English-language publications of eighteenth-century insular Catholics; and an older and uniquely Gaelic religiosity believed to have been antithetical to a new anglicized orthodoxy. There are elements of truth to each of these conclusions, but it should be stated that too much focus on the sources of devotional writings risks missing the distinct and dynamic ways in which late eighteenth and early nineteenth-century Irish-speaking advocates of certain Catholic practices reshaped the religious ideologies inherited from the past. This is particularly important given the high proportion of translations and scribal reproductions at the heart of the prescribed Catholicism of the Irish-speaking world. A failure to recognize the act of production at the heart of translation and copying of texts—in other words, a tendency to see such activities as merely parroting earlier ideologies—encourages dubious interpretations of modern Irish-language spirituality as something forged entirely in another context (particularly one that is English-speaking) and then imposed on passive Irish speakers.[71] In any case, translation played a huge role in the ideological development of all religious texts, particularly in the Catholic context where international exchange was so prominent. It is impossible to find a Catholic devotional text in any of the major European languages—including English—not built at least in part on translation.

Historians' portrayal of passivity among Irish-speaking communities in the devotional development of modern Catholicism extends beyond the issue of translation and reproduction to the question of relative size of influence. As pointed out above, the number of English-language religious texts outnumbered those in Irish by a considerable margin (although not, perhaps, to such a degree as has often been assumed). This has undoubtedly contributed once again to interpretations of Irish religious history that see modern Catholicism as a product molded by the English-speaking world and then imported into an Irish-speaking one. But Irish-language advocates of Tridentine-based reformed Catholicism can be found just as easily as those operating in an anglophone context. Even if less visible, that Irish-language contribution to the newly emerging understandings of what constituted Catholic orthodoxy must be accounted for in order to create a full and accurate picture of the history of this period.

One starting point for untangling this history lies in a comparative glance at the devotional and instructional texts available to Irish- and English-speaking readers of the nineteenth century—individuals, it should be remembered, who were often one and the same in an increasingly bilingual society. Consider the English-language reading lists of two institutions often associated with the new Irish Catholicism: the Christian Brothers, a teaching confraternity founded in 1802 that fit the mold of nineteenth-century organizations often associated with devotional revolution; and the *Irish Catholic Penny Magazine*, a short-lived periodical founded in 1834 through the efforts of William Joseph Battersby, one of the founders of the Catholic Book Society.[72] In 1825 the head of the Hanover Street Christian Brothers School presented a summary to the national education commissioners of the religious books used in the school. Topping the list were general prayer books, with seventy-two copies, followed by Alban Butler's *Lives of the Saints* (twenty-four copies), Richard Challoner's *Think Well On't* (twenty-one copies), the controversialist work *A Net for the Fishers of Men: The Same which Christ Gave to His Apostles* (fourteen copies), another titled *Fifty Reasons, or Motives, Why the Roman Catholic, Apostolic Religion, Ought to be Preferred to All the Sects this Day in Christendom* (thirteen copies), Giovanni Pietro Pinamonti's *Hell Opened to Christians* (twelve copies); John Gother's *Instructions for Confession and Communion* (twelve copies), Giovanni Manni's *Four Maxims of Christian Philosophy* (twelve copies), the work of an unnamed author titled *Lives of the Irish Saints* (twelve copies), and Joseph Reeve's translations of the histories of the New and Old Testament, at twelve copies each.[73]

This snapshot of anglophone reading practices was echoed by a similar list presented by the editor of the *Catholic Penny Magazine* in 1834 under the heading of "A Religious Library for Each Individual." The young, according to the magazine, as well as uninformed adults, should start with Butler's catechism or its equivalent before taking up more advanced summaries of doctrine in works like William Gahan's *The Complete Manual of Catholic Piety*, Henry Turberville's summary of the Douai catechism titled *Abridgement of the Christian Doctrine*, Claude Fleury's *Short Historical Catechism*, and Edward Glover's *An Explanation of the Prayers and Ceremonies of the Holy Sacrifice of the Mass*. Advanced individuals were to move on to reflective works examining the Christian life such as *An Introduction to a Devout Life* by Francis de Sales, the *Imitation of Christ* by Thomas à Kempis, Charles Gobinet's *Instruction of Youth in Christian Piety*, and Reeve's histories of the Bible, while truly ambitious readers might take up controversialist tracts and meditative works of piety, among them translations of Lorenzo Scupoli's *Spiritual Combat* and Challoner's *Thirty Meditations*.[74] In terms of content, such reading programs worked in a progression from catechisms and abridgments of Catholic doctrine to instructive material on sacramental and liturgical participation, followed by historical readings and exemplars for spiritual living, and completed by meditative and combative works aimed at defending the faith in a world of competing Christian interpretations. Newer titles from the seventeenth and eighteenth centuries from authors like Manni, Gahan, Gother, and Challoner mixed with older classics like the *Imitation of*

Christ. In all, the two lists provide a useful snapshot of prescribed reading practices in English advocated by two of the institutions regularly identified as forgers of modern Irish Catholicism.

How did this body of texts compare to their Irish-language counterparts? Taking into account both Irish-language manuscripts and printed texts, a picture emerges of slightly diverging genres (although often not religious ideologies) at the level of more sophisticated reading material but closely overlapping preferences when it came to general-use manuals such as catechisms and prayer books. Of the 713 eighteenth- and nineteenth-century manuscripts found to contain at least one item of religious provenance, hagiographical material (present in 28 percent of texts), religious verse (40 percent), and prose tracts (53 percent) were the three most dominant genres in Irish-language religious texts. Addressing first the hagiographical material, it was certainly true that English- and Irish-language readers alike were interested in the lives of saints and martyrs, a subject that provided, as the popular English devotional author Alban Butler claimed, "models for our imitation."[75] For English-speaking readers able to afford access, the most popular option was clearly the multivolume Dublin editions of Butler's *Lives of the Fathers, Martyrs, and Other Principal Saints* (1st ed., 1756–59), which had been reedited and reissued in Dublin between 1779 and 1780 by Archbishop Carpenter with the assistance of Charles O'Conor and Father Bernard MacMahon. New editions succeeded this revision in later decades by Dublin printers Hugh Fitzpatrick (1802), Richard Coyne (1836), and James Duffy (1866).[76] Although dominated by internationally known saints, Carpenter's Irish edition reworked Butler's text by adding a calendar of Irish saints; an abridged version consisting of extracts of Irish lives published by John Coyne in Dublin in 1823 contained more than two hundred pages of specifically Irish lives for the Hibernian-minded reader. An examination of the sources used by Butler and Carpenter show strong roots in the seventeenth century, when some of the first serious attempts to collate medieval lives and to publish them had taken place. The 1823 Coyne abridgement, for example, lists among its sources the works of John Colgan, James Ussher, James Ware, Jean Bolland, and Louis-Sébastien le Nain de Tillemont. To this, the *Lives* had added supplemental medieval material from Giraldus Cambrensis, Jocelin of Furness, and more recent publications like Richard Challoner's *Britannia Sancta* (1745).[77]

Irish-language hagiography, although differing in that it existed exclusively in manuscript form, contained significant overlaps in sources, if not in actual versions of the lives that circulated. For example, Bolland's *Acta Sanctorum* (1643) and Colgan's *Acta Sanctorum Hiberniae* (1645) provided source texts for Irish translations of the lives of Saints Juliana and Gelasius, respectively, found in several eighteenth-century texts.[78] The life of Patrick written by Jocelin of Furness in the twelfth century experienced continual popularity among both language communities throughout the eighteenth and nineteenth centuries. First repopularized for an Irish audience in Thomas Messingham's *Florilegium Insulae Sanctorum* (1624), Jocelin's life subsequently could be found in an English translation by the Franciscan Robert Rochford as *The Life of the Glorious Bishop S. Patricke, Apostle and Primate of Ireland* (1625); another English translation was published by Edmund Swift in Dublin in 1809.[79] In Rochford's publication, Patrick's life was also paired with a life of Bridget assembled from a composite of the Latin account by Cogitus of AD 680 and a second account (also medieval, and often ascribed to Saint Ultan) taken from the revision by John Capgrave and Wynkyn de Worde of John of Tynemouth's medieval collection, the *Nova Legenda Angliae* (1516).[80] Rochford's English translation, as Bernadette Cunningham and Raymond Gillespie have pointed out, was immensely popular in Ireland in the seventeenth century and afterward, where it was translated into Irish and circulated in manuscript form.[81] Indeed, these two lives—that of Jocelin and Cogitus—dominated the hagiography in circulation among eighteenth- and nineteenth-century scribes. In particular, Jocelin's life of Patrick—who as a subject was in turn the most often cited in these Irish-language texts, about twice as often as Bridget—made up approximately half of the surviving lives of this saint in this time period.[82]

Not all Irish- and English-language hagiographical material in the eighteenth and nineteenth centuries intertwined so closely. The second-most popular life of Saint Patrick was a version taken from the so-called *Tripartite Life* in Irish that can be traced to either the ninth or tenth centuries and that had robust, early modern scribal transmission in Ireland.[83] Moreover, it served as a basis for the life of Patrick in the Book of Lismore, the fifteenth-century compilation written in Irish containing lives of Patrick, Bridget, and Columcille, as well as those with a distinctly local flavor: Senán, Finán of Clonard, Brenán, Ciarán of Clonmacnois, and Mochua of Balla. Although the original vellum manuscript was lost between the seventeenth century and its rediscovery in 1814, material derived from the saints' lives in the Book of Lismore were circulated in places like Clare and Cork in the late eighteenth and early nineteenth centuries, including several lengthy copies of the text starting in 1816.[84] Perhaps more notable, however, was the fact that the most copied saint's life among the nineteenth-century manuscripts surveyed here was that of Saint Margaret of Antioch, specifically an Irish translation by the fifteenth-century writer Pilip Ó Dálaigh of a Latin original. With more than fifty-five versions surviving, the Ó Dálaigh life was circulating largely in Munster scribal circles by the eighteenth and nineteenth centuries. Numerous early copies were made in the Clare-Limerick-Tipperary region, including versions by Aindrias Mac Cruitín of Clare in 1719 and Dáibhí Ua Mohir of Limerick in 1726, while others appeared in Cork scribal circles, among them two by Seán Ó Murchadha na Ráithíneach, written at the beginning and end of his career.[85] In the nineteenth century, the Cork scribal circle centered on the Ó Longáins and the associates of Bishop Murphy added considerably to the Ó Dálaigh exemplars in circulation, as did a handful of Waterford scribes including Denn, Ó Iceadha, and Uilliam Criostamhar Jr.[86] So ubiquitous was this tale that Eugene O'Curry, annoyed at the popularity of a nonnative saint, surmised that its unparalleled "high esteem among the peasantry and seafaring people" of Munster was the result of a concerted effort to displace Irish saints by Old English clergy.[87] Its popularity, however, was more likely rooted in its Irish literary features: Ó Dálaigh's version, according to cataloguer Robin Flower, worked the life into a bardic romance, thus rooting in the wider Gaelic literary canon a story that might otherwise have taken the form of a standard church biography.[88]

After hagiography, manuscripts containing instances of devotional verse were the next most common type of religious material in the Irish-speaking world. There was much less overlap between the two language communities with regard to verse, a genre that was very well represented among the higher-order texts of the Irish-speaking world but much less known in Ireland's devotional readers in English by the nineteenth century. In circulating this devotional verse so widely, Irish scribes and printers compressed and repackaged a long and dynamic history of religious poetry that had evolved over several centuries but was especially influenced by developments in the seventeenth century. This history included the work of medieval devotional poets like Donnchadh Mór Ó Dálaigh (ca. 1175–1244), whose poems were among the most commonly reproduced in the eighteenth and nineteenth centuries. Medieval Irish devotional verse, as on the continent, focused on the Virgin Mary, the Passion, eternal judgment, the Trinity, and other symbolic tenets of the faith, yielding sophisticated reflection on Christian ideals for the interested.[89] Equally popular among later scribes were the poems of the late sixteenth and early seventeenth century, a period that witnessed changes in the themes and forms of Irish religious verse as new trends in art, the experiences of the Renaissance and Reformation, and the political upheavals in Ireland itself had an impact. Most often represented by the work of Aonghus Fionn Ó Dálaigh (ca. 1548–ca. 1602) and Giolla Brighde Ó hEodhasa (d. 1614) among the eighteenth- and nineteenth-century scribes, this early modern devotional poetry was marked by its meditative approach, its focus on the perceived sins of the Irish people as a cause of political conquest, its exaggerated and extensive reflection on death (often as a prelude to redemption), and its transference of the concept of patronage from the declining secular patrons of past years to divine figures like Christ and Mary. Adopting the baroque styles of the time (much like their English and continental counterparts, as Tadhg Ó Dúshláine has argued), these poets contributed to a loosening of the previously strict classical meter and its replacement with a more emotional approach that drew heavily on the prose writers of the time—especially Louis de Granada and Thomas à Kempis—to convey the transitory nature of life.[90] Again, most notably in the poems of Aonghus Fionn, these seventeenth-century poems focused often on Mary, even repurposing the older genre of courtly love poetry, now derided in favor of the seriousness of devotional poetry, to replace esteem for aristocratic women with dedication to the Blessed Virgin.[91]

To the poems of these older periods, eighteenth- and nineteenth-century scribes and patrons added the new forms practiced in their own times, an era marked by a further loosening of metrical conventions, the intermingling of poetry and song styles, and an overall blurring of lines between verse, hymns, ballads, and devotional music. Accentual meters known as *amhrán*, built on assonating rhyme schemes, became predominant in this time period, replacing the earlier syllabic meters that had dominated classical poetry.[92] The devotional verse of the seventeenth-century poets had certainly circulated among a more popular audience, particularly by way of intersection with printed prose tracts produced in the continental Irish colleges. Thus, an author like Céitinn cited a number of devotional poets in *Trí Bior-Ghaoithe an Bháis*, a work with some aspirations to the general audience envisioned by the preacher, while the writings of Ó hEodhasa, who combined prose and poetry in his catechism, has been said to have reached a broader audience (often through oral circulation) than had hereto been believed.[93] But these earlier connections between poetry, prose, print, and a wider general audience were superseded by even closer ties in the eighteenth century. Two compositions by the Monaghan poet and scribe Father Brian (or Bernard) Ó Cathaláin (d. 1804), for instance, "Duan an Duine Dhosgaidh" ("Poem of the Reckless Person") and a translation of the hymn *Dies Irae*, appeared in the 1825 edition of the aforementioned *The Spiritual Rose*, a work with catechetical overtones that spoke to a broad audience.[94] Similarly representative of eighteenth-century trends in religious verse was the Munster poet Tadhg Gaelach Ó Súilleabháin (ca. 1715–95), another favorite of nineteenth-century devotional readers. The *Pious Miscellany*, popular in both manuscript and print, offered verse set to popular tunes by musicians such as Toirdhealbhach Ó Cearbhalláin. While rooted to some degree in earlier Irish poetic traditions in its deployment of certain verse motifs, the *Pious Miscellany* also reflected new ideological directions in its push to improve religious observance like Mass attendance as an antidote to sin and in its inclusion of songs dedicated to the Sacred Heart ("Duain Chroidhe Iosa") and to the Rosary ("An Paidrín Páirteach").[95]

But while devotional verse remained a part of popular tastes and, in the special case of the *Pious Miscellany*, was attuned to certain trends in Catholic ideology such as the rising popularity of the Rosary, there were signs that religious poetry in the eighteenth and nineteenth centuries no longer had the status it once had among Irish-language readers. For instance, the diversity of religious poems, the *duanta diadha*, included in the *duanairí*, or poem books, of later decades declined. Thus, whereas Ó Longáin and his son Pól managed in a typical manuscript from 1817 to gather together poems from Tadhg Mac Dáire, Dómhnall Mac Dáire, Tadhg Ruadh Ó Conchúbhair, Cormac Mac Cuilionnán, Aodh Mac Cruitín, Muiris Mac Gearruilt, Eoghan Mac Craith, Gofradh Fionn Ó Dálaigh, Fearghal Óg Mac an Bhaird, and the usual favorites Aonghus Fionn Ó Dálaigh, Donnchadh Mór Ó Dálaigh, and Ó hEodhasa, other scribes made do with only poems from the latter three.[96]

Another indication of the changing status of religious verse lies in the evolution of the form and format of *duanairí* themselves. As Meidhbhín Ní Úrdail has pointed out in examining the corpus of the Ó Longáin family, a familiarity with the conventions of print culture such as title pages, organizing of text into paragraphs, use of headers, and tables of contents became an increasingly visible feature of scribal work by the second decade of the nineteenth century.[97] This was a change from the earlier *duanairí* that lacked such features and conformed to older ideals of the classical *filidh*, who had presented such writings in formal fashion to their patrons.[98] The new forms, which approximated the layout of printed texts (and may in some cases have been intended to be sent to press should an opportunity arise), did accommodate intentions to provide patrons with full collections exclusively of verse. But a shift in the treatment of religious verse can be detected in the practice of some scribes of slipping such poems into what were otherwise prose texts rather than creating a single dedicated book of secular and nonsecular poetry along the lines of the older *duanairí*. The apparent ornamental intention of this use of religious poems is confirmed by their truncated placement as introductions to extended prose tracts, as when scribes placed excerpts from Ó hEodhasa or Ó Dálaigh between copies of *Eochair-Sgiath an Aifrinn* or Richard Challoner's *Garden of the Soul*.⁹⁹ It is notable that this practice extended to the print world, where Pól Ó Longáin supplemented his translation of Challoner, *Gairdín an Anma* (1844), with verses by Ó hEodhasa.¹⁰⁰ This point should not, however, be overdrawn. Religious verse continued to be an active part of religious reading and oral culture throughout the nineteenth century. Mícheál Óg Ó Longáin himself composed religious verse, as did Pádraig Denn.¹⁰¹ Two extended dialogue poems centering on a sinner's encounter with death, "Aighneas an Pheacaigh leis an mBás" and "Siosma an Anma res an gColuin," were extremely popular, with the former cited by Thomas Crofton Croker in 1824 as one of the common dialogues to be found in manuscripts of the time. In fact, both were popularized by Denn in print in the nineteenth century to such an extent that they were remembered by Waterford inhabitants as late as the 1930s.¹⁰²

But the single-largest genre represented in Irish-language manuscripts and printed works of the late eighteenth and early nineteenth centuries was devotional prose, not unlike the favored reading material of English-language readers (who, again, were in some cases also Irish-language readers). Preferred titles for both language communities had many similarities, and increasingly so among the newer works being circulated as the nineteenth century arrived. Eighteenth- and nineteenth-century scribes selected from the corpus of seventeenth-century devotional works more often than from any other period, and in particular Céitinn's *Eochair-Sgiath an Aifrinn*, written on the virtues of the Mass, was the most popular text among these later Irish readers. Approximately one in six religious prose tracts copied during these two centuries consisted of this work, with a disproportionately large number of exemplars created in the Munster and south Leinster areas. Céitinn's *Trí Bior-Ghaoithe an Bháis* possessed a similar popularity in the eighteenth century, although it was copied less often after that time. Popular, too, was *Scáthan Shacramuinte na hAithridhe*, a handbook for the clergy on penance published by Aodh Mac Aingil (or Mac Caghwell) in 1618, and *Parrthas an Anma* (1645), a manual for prayer, sacraments, and doctrine by Antoin Gearnon—but in both cases less so than the works of Céitinn, which held unparalleled sway over Irish-speaking interests in the eighteenth and nineteenth centuries. The later decades were not simply a repeat performance of the prose of the seventeenth century, however. Nearly as frequently copied as *Eochair-Sgiath an Aifrinn* were even older exemplars, as in a prose version of a medieval poem, usually titled in the Irish texts *Agallamh an Chuirp agus an Anam*, consisting of a dialogue between a body and a soul. The piece, which circulated extensively in Europe in a variety of languages, centered on the relative culpability of soul and flesh in the sins of this world, framed as the dream of a sleeping man about a spirited debate between a soul that has temporarily returned from hell to discuss blame for the tortures of the afterlife with a body eager not to be assigned culpability.[103] Scribes from a number of counties reproduced various versions of this dialogue, including Galway, Roscommon, Cork, Kerry, Tipperary, Clare, Waterford, Wexford, Meath, and Dublin, demonstrating its strong popularity.[104]

None of these core Irish-language texts had a direct counterpart among the most recommended books on the English-language lists of the Christian Brothers or the *Catholic Penny Magazine*, although at least one, the medieval dialogue, could be found in English translation, usually in verse form, by Protestant translators.[105] But this does not mean that there was not ideological overlap in the common post-Tridentine roots of both the English- and Irish-language works. And in any case, it is possible to detect a shift in the preferred prose tracts of eighteenth- and nineteenth-century scribes, printers, and readers that provided a supplement to the above-listed Irish texts of the seventeenth century. These texts hewed much more closely to the lists of works also popular in the English language. This change involved a considerable diversification of the prose tracts available, supplied by new translations of published works of the fifteenth through eighteenth centuries from Latin, Italian, Spanish, French, and English originals. These new prose translations were provided by a handful of translators, some of them unidentified, with connections to all the major Irish-language circles of the eighteenth century, including the Dublin scribes centered on the Ó Neachtain family, the Ó Longáin networks of Cork, and the northern scribes of the Monaghan-Cavan-Armagh region. Copyists ensured that these translations continued to circulate in manuscript form, and a few of them made the leap to print in the nineteenth century.

A good example of this trend was the translation of Giovanni Pietro Pinamonti's *La Vera Sapienza*, consisting of weekly meditative devotions organized by day. Pinamonti, an Italian Jesuit missioner with a reputation for confessional and catechetical work, exemplified wider trends in post-Reformation Catholicism toward an emphasis on preaching, instructional writings, and meditational reading.[106] While often overshadowed by the French strand in this movement, Italy, too, contributed to the flood of Catholic writings (especially in the seventeenth century) seeking a lay audience. Many of these Italian writers infiltrated both language communities in Ireland in the eighteenth and nineteenth centuries. The first English translation of *La Vera Sapienza* has been dated to 1699,[107] with a subsequent 1798 Dublin printing by Richard Cross.[108] Three copies were among the aforementioned collection of the Christian Brothers in 1825. Meanwhile, Seán Ó Neachtain translated this work into Irish sometime before 1717 when his son Tadhg made a copy of the work.[109] Another Irish translation by Father Seán Mac Diarmada Ó Briain (d. 1752) was completed by 1736 when it was printed in Cork; printer John Connor offered yet another Cork edition in 1795, this time translated by Father Seán Ó Conáill, that attracted more than eighty subscribers, including three of the Munster bishops who contracted for one hundred copies each.[110] It also lived on in manuscript form: Ó Briain's contact with Seán Ó Murchadha na Ráithíneach meant that this translation went on to be recopied a number of times by the Ó Longáin circle of Carraig na bhFear.[111]

The popularity of *La Vera Sapienza*, with its daily instructions on how to avoid sin through meditation and prayer, were emblematic of new directions in Catholicism among Irish-language scribes and printers that reached a high point with the translations of similar works by Archbishop Carpenter, Séamus Ó Scoireadh, Tomás Ó Iceadha, Father Dónall Ó Súilleabháin, John MacHale, and Mícheál Óg Ó Longáin (the last, specifically, under the patronage of Bishop Murphy). Pinamonti's *L'Inferno Aperto al Cristiano* (1688), first translated into English as *Hell Opened to Christians* in 1715 and published in London, focused on the torments awaiting the impenitent, organized into daily reflections. Printed in Dublin in English in 1753, it was published repeatedly by Richard Grace and by James Duffy in the nineteenth century and became visible enough in Irish popular consciousness that James Joyce drew on it when writing *A Portrait of the Artist as a Young Man*.[112] But it had currency in the Irish-speaking world as well: Ó Longáin completed an Irish translation from the English for Murphy in 1818.[113] Another work of weekly meditations with an Italian provenance, *Testamento o Ultima Voluntad del Anma* (ca. 1576), a Spanish-language title by Charles Borromeo, the Bishop of Milan, appeared in English translation no later than an edition published at Saint-Omer in 1638. Yet this title, too, had been rendered into Irish by the fourth decade of the eighteenth century, when Archbishop Carpenter owned a manuscript copy that may have been his own translation.[114] Pinamonti's Jesuit predecessor, the preacher Giovanni Battista Manni (1606–82), attained after his death a ready audience in Ireland for his *Quattro Massime di Christiana Filosophia* (1643), a discursive work on the concepts of body, soul, heaven, and hell. First translated into English no later than 1675 as *Four Maxims of Christian Philosophy*, the work reached a fifth impression by 1700 and continued on to multiple reprintings in Dublin by the early nineteenth century.[115] Two simultaneous translations of this work into Irish appeared between 1819 and 1820, both translated from English editions. The first, a manuscript by Ó Longáin for Bishop Murphy, was paired with a translation of a biography written by Bishop Coppinger of Nano Nagle (d. 1784), founder of the Ursuline and Presentation Sisters.[116] The second, printed in two editions by John Bull in Waterford in 1820 and 1825, was translated by Ó Scoireadh, who also provided translation work for James Hardiman (1782–1855) and Bishop James Warren Doyle (1786–1834) of Kildare and Leighlin.[117]

By the 1840s, yet another Italian spiritual writer, Redemptorist founder Alphonsus de Liguori (1696–1787), was receiving attention from Irish translators. His collection of Marian discourses organized around the hymn *Salve Regina*, titled *Le Glorie di Maria* (1750), was published in English by a number of Dublin printers in the nineteenth century and translated into Irish and copied into three different manuscripts between 1846 and 1848 by Ó Iceadha. One of these manuscripts was written on the request of Dominic O'Brien and Martan Mac Reamoinn of St. John's College, where, Ó Iceadha reported, the popularity of the work had prompted his translation not for learned folks but "don comharsa aig nach fuil leughann" (for those friends who were not educated).[118] In Liguori, Ó Iceadha and his Waterford patrons had found the voice of a much more contemporary Catholicism based very closely on observation of the Eucharist, prayer, and collective devotions such as those dedicated to Mary; it is also noteworthy that his Redemptorists conducted their first mission in Ireland—a development considered by historians to be unambiguously a part of the devotional revolution—soon after, in 1853.[119] Liguori's popularity was further extended through the four editions of a translation of his *Esercizio della Via Crucis* (1761) by Archbishop MacHale, published between 1854 and 1873. MacHale in his introduction was clear that he intended his translation to be an encouragement to those Irish speakers who were new to the practice of the stations of the cross devotions: "The Way of the Cross has been long a favourite devotion with the people of Ireland.... This devotion is daily spreading, and the Stations of the Cross are crowded with followers who were not accustomed to tread them before.... It is to facilitate this devotion, and to make it familiar to the humblest, that I have translated the Way of the Cross, left us by St. Alphonsus Ligouri, into our own native language."[120] MacHale's translation could not have been more closely attuned to modern nineteenth-century Catholics with its choice of devotion, inclusion of musical notation for the hymn, and detailed illustrations to guide participants.

Once again, it should be remembered that while these Irish-language devotional works fit closely with the needs of orthodoxy as understood by sponsors like Murphy, MacHale, and O'Brien, the translations were not merely *post facto* attempts by the hierarchy to impose a completed religious reform on Irish speakers. Irish translation and interpretation of international Catholic works possessed a long history that had come of age along with a modern Irish Catholicism that encompassed both Irish and English languages. Take, for example, the case of *Introduction à la Vie Dévote* (1608), an incredibly popular work of seventeenth-century Catholicism by Francis de Sales. An extended reflection on the nature of piety and devotion built around a series of meditations, the work articulated the new Tridentine emphasis on practical and didactic approaches to encouraging spirituality in everyday life, using language that was accessible and inviting to a broad audience. It became, in many ways, a model for subsequent Catholic writings on the subject to appear in the seventeenth, eighteenth, and nineteenth centuries. These qualities also created an immediate demand for its translation, including a first English translation in 1613 and an Irish translation by Pilib Ó Raghallaigh, a Franciscan at the Irish College in Prague, between 1647 and 1650.[121] A 1709 scribal copy of this translation was made in Flanders, and new translations into Irish from English texts were completed in 1773 by a Clare schoolmaster, Dermod Ó Maolchaoine, and in 1840 by Ó Iceadha.[122] Other post-Reformation devotional texts had similarly entered the Irish-speaking world long before the end of the eighteenth century. The Kerry Carmelite Father Tadhg Ó Conaill (d. 1779), for instance, translated two extended devotional tracts, Antonio de Guevara's *Misterios del Monte Calvario* (1542, as *Rúindiamhair Chnuic Chealbhair*) and Antoine Yvan's *La Trompette du Ciel* (1661, as *Trompa na bhFlaitheas*); these works continued to be copied by scribes in Limerick, Waterford, and Cork as late as the 1830s.[123] An Irish translation of Pedro da Lucca's sixteenth-century contribution on preparation for death, *Dottrina del Ben Morire*, appeared among Waterford scribes as early as 1762, when Labhrás Ó Fúartháin made a copy; subsequent transcriptions were made by scribes Ó Iceadha and Uilliam Cnoc.[124]

By the 1830s and 1840s, prose translations in Irish had converged with their English counterparts so that almost every one of the top titles (or at least their authors) named in the English-language titles favored by the likes of the Christian Brothers and *Catholic Penny Magazine* mentioned above had an equivalent in the Irish-speaking community. Challoner's *Think Well On't* (1728) was translated by Uilliam Mac Coitir, a Cork schoolteacher, in 1817, by Pádraig Denn in 1819, and by Eoghan Caomhánach in 1820.[125] An Irish translation of Challoner's other major work, *Garden of the Soul* (1740), circulated by manuscript some time before it appeared in print, including what appears to be a partial copy made as early as 1806 by Seán Ó Muláin of Cork. A more complete translation was made in 1821, the date of another Cork manuscript by Uilliam Hógáin, two decades before the appearance in print of the translation attributed to Pól Ó Longáin.[126] The fourth most common text in the Christian Brothers list, *A Net for the Fishers of Men* (1686), a late Restoration-era Catholic apology that had been anonymously authored and published in London, received a translation by Father Dónall Ó Súilleabháin while a student at Maynooth in the early 1820s. This text survives in a copy for Bishop Murphy made by Mícheál Óg Ó Longáin, who also had made a translation from the work of John Gother, another favored author in the Catholic English-speaking world.[127]

These similarities between the preferred prose of the two language communities in Ireland had their limits. Many of the more sophisticated and complex translated devotional prose tracts in manuscript form did not circulate beyond the exchanges between local scribes and readers, and there was a distinct lack of translation in the other direction: neither of two very popular works among scribes, Céitinn's *Trí Bior-Ghaoithe* and *Eochair-Sgiath an Aifrinn*, appeared in English translation. But in moving on to consider the last religious genre represented in the Irish-language corpus, prayer books and catechisms, the differences between English- and Irish-speaking religious practices disappear. This is notable as it means that the texts most poised to influence a wide portion of the population—prayer books and catechisms were simpler in content, enabling a wider readership, and they were used orally by priests and school teachers as Sunday school instructional manuals—did not differ from their English counterparts. As with devotional tracts and poetry, the Irish-language prayer books and catechisms were rooted in the seventeenth century, when continental currents in religious instruction shaped by the Council of Trent, Jesuit educational ideals, and the popularity of preaching reached their fullest development. Catechetical works and manuals of religious practice were in fact the earliest type of text targeted by the Irish seminarians at Louvain, Prague, Rome, and the other Catholic colleges, yielding in Irish a whole stable of publications and manuscripts: a translation of a Spanish-language compendium of Christian doctrine by Flathrí Ó Maolchonaire (1593), the Ó hEodhasa catechism (1611), the Stapleton catechism (1639), Ó Dubhlaoich's *Suim Bhunudhasach an Teaguisg Chriosdaidhe* (1663), Ó Maolmhuaidh's *Lucerna Fidelium* (1676), a translation of Jacques Marchant's catechetical *Hortus Pastorum* completed by Father Conchubhar Mac Cairteáin (ca. 1700), two different translations of Diego de Ledesma's *Doctrina Christiana* (ca. 1720), Donlevy's bilingual catechism (1742), the Lloyd (i.e., Douai) and Pulleine catechisms (1738 and 1748), and, by 1800, both major catechisms also in use among English-speaking Catholics

(Butler and O'Reilly).[128] To this could be added more extended works steeped in catechetical approaches, like Antoin Gearnon's *Parrthas an Anma* (1645).

Not surprisingly, given the purposes of catechisms in the eyes of the church, none of these favored manuals of the Irish-speaking realm diverged in anything other than minor details from their counterparts in other language communities or from the Catholic orthodoxy envisioned by church reformers.[129] In fact, to a certain degree, English- and Irish-language catechetical texts had become indistinguishable by the eighteenth century, as evidenced by the domination by Lloyd's bilingual Douai catechism of bibliographies of Catholic religious texts for the first half of the century, and the ubiquity of bilingual editions of Butler—the most popular catechism in the English-speaking Catholic Atlantic world, it should be added—and O'Reilly in the second half.[130] Perhaps the only discernible trend in Irish-language catechetical text was the rise of the shorter catechisms (namely, the Butler, O'Reilly, Kirwan, and Coppinger catechisms) in high-volume print runs, displacing any print copies of the earlier catechisms of the seventeenth centuries. Nevertheless, full copies or extracted portions of all of these earlier catechetical texts lived on in manuscript form throughout the eighteenth and nineteenth centuries, including several that have survived from the early eighteenth-century Dublin Ó Neachtain network, more than a dozen from the nineteenth-century Ó Longáin and Bishop Murphy Cork circle, a handful made by the Waterford scribes, including Riocard Paor and Ó Iceadha, and scattered additional catechisms copied in Cavan, Clare, Westmeath, Wexford, Donegal, Limerick, and Tipperary.[131]

Turning finally to the last genre of popular religious texts, Irish-language prayer books, like catechisms, replicated a short list of common orthodox prayers found in any Catholic linguistic community of the time, with occasional additions specific to the Irish context. The books, intended by and large for the use of priests and educated members of the laity, provided instructions for conducting morning and evening prayers; attending and understanding the Mass; reciting litanies, vespers, and confession; keeping canonical feasts and holy days; and practicing devotions to the Sacred Heart.[132] A few were printed, if the genre is expanded to consider the Irish-language instructional prose manuals that overlapped in content, such as the summary of Christian doctrine contained in a short tract by Bishop Thomas Burke published in 1775 for the diocese of Ossory, Kennedy's *Spiritual Rose*, or the various similar texts published by Archbishops Butler, MacHale, and Bray, and by Denn and Furlong.[133] But most prayer books lived in manuscript copies for the immediate use of their owner and had either been translated directly from popular English-language prayer books of the time or, more often, mixed and matched universal prayers taken from any number of sources. And unlike certain religious manuscript libraries—such as that of Bishop Murphy—that probably did not see extensive use, surviving prayer books exhibit features of intense and practical deployment such as being well thumbed and compact in size, as well as in some cases having been taken abroad by their owners (as in the case of one of Dáibhí de Barra's prayer books owned by Father John Barry in Melbourne, Australia).[134]

Among the favored source texts for the Irish prayer books were those popular in the English-speaking world, namely *The Poor Man's Manual of Devotion*, later known as *The Key of Heaven* (published in earlier iterations as early as the seventeenth century but widely available in Ireland in the nineteenth century), *The Key of Paradise* (first published around 1623, but also printed several times in Dublin in the 1780s and 1790s), and *The Path to Paradise* (in print in Dublin by 1760 at the latest).[135] The manuscript assembled by the weaver-scribe Séamas Mac Donnchadha Ó Caoindealbháin of Limerick in 1846, for instance, relied on both *The Path to Paradise* and a later edition of John Clarkson's *An Introduction to the Celebrated Devotion of the Most Holy Rosary* (1737) for its content. Two similar manuscripts completed in the eighteenth century by scribes Seadhan Ó Laochadh and Eadhbhart Ó Troih, complete with title pages headed "Eochair Phairthais" ("Key of Paradise"), drew on the Dublin-printed publication of that same name. An 1830 manuscript by Tadhg Mac Cártha of Cork borrowed heavily from *The Poor Man's Manual of Devotions*, while adding an indigenous hymn in the form of the "Sgiathluithreach na Maighidine" (Breastplate of the Virgin Mary). In a gesture to the cross influences of print culture on these later prayer books, Ó Caoindealbháin inserted into the inside cover fronting his title page a colorized lithograph illustration of Christ cut from a English-language printed text.[136]

It may be tempting to dismiss these prayer books as mere derivatives of English-language approaches to devotional manuals that had already spearheaded reform in Ireland, but while these titles clearly were a heavy influence, a more nuanced appraisal recognizes the parallel track of the English- and Irish-language developments in Catholicism that had merged to provide a unified take on religious orthodoxy. Irish scribes were no strangers to prayer books: several examples from early eighteenth-century scribes Tadhg Ó Neachtain, Seadhan Ó Laochadh, Risteard Tuibear, Archbishop Carpenter, and Seadhan Ó Heidein were all written before 1750.[137] Furthermore, the content of the eighteenth- and nineteenth-century prayer books, consisting of the *Pater Noster*, the *Ave Maria*, the Apostle's Creed, the prayers on the Acts, Litanies of Jesus and Mary, the

Confíteor, the Nicene Creed, and many other universally known aspects of Catholic worship, had been available in Irish for a long time, notably in Ó hEodhasa's catechism. The ideology and emphasis in the Irish-language Catholic devotional manuals, catechisms, and prose tracts of the eighteenth and nineteenth centuries had shifted from the concerns of the seventeenth century, but they were still, like their English-language counterparts, the end point of an evolving post-Tridentine interest in building an orthodoxy that started to take firmer root in the 1770s and 1780s.

Turning last to the application of this body of devotional work in the field, Catholic reformers of the eighteenth and nineteenth centuries focused on two particular aspects of worship and devotional practices in implementing a new orthodoxy. The first of these two targeted practices was attendance at Mass and its attendant sacraments, confession and communion, now expected to take place in a proper chapel and not at rough Mass houses, at outdoor altars, or in private homes as stations. The second of these practices was prayer, in which purveyors of institutional orthodoxies pushed universal prayers that were to be recited during daily routines, litanies delivered in a family setting, and participation in certain public devotions like the Way of the Cross. Time and again, many of the Irish-language texts outlined above, particularly the prayer books and catechisms, took up both of these concerns as features of everyday religiosity in need of change enacted through educational efforts and clerical leadership.

Consider first the approaches to Mass being advocated. Reformers addressing the Irish-speaking community were united in their belief in the need for participants to understand the various components of the liturgy, be aware of its significance as a reenactment of Christ's sacrifice, and attend to the sacraments such as confession and communion in conjunction with one's presence at the chapel. As the schoolteacher Uilliam Ó hAodha (d. 1836) of Cork wrote in the colophon of his transcription of *Sochar an Aifrinn*, a medieval tract on the virtues of the Mass, "nach ceart et nách cóir do neach san mbith dearmad do dhéanamh don Aithfrinn, óir as adhbhal na sochar do leanann Aithfrinn déisteacht go ceart" (it isn't right or proper for anybody to omit Mass, as the advantages that follow listening to it correctly are immense).[138] Among the novel practices introduced in the eighteenth century designed to focus the minds of participants on the requirements of Christian belief was the set of prayers dedicated to the theological virtues. Known as the "Acts," and propagated in both English- and Irish-language catechisms and prayer books, these prayers were each dedicated to the virtues of faith, hope, and charity. The prayers were first indulgenced in 1728 by Benedict XIII and confirmed in 1756 by Pope Benedict XIV; among the early advocates was Donlevy, whose bilingual catechism of 1742 included a section devoted to them. Assigned an indulgence by Benedict XIV of "seven years and seven quarantines every time the faithful devoutly make them in their heart and say them with their lips," the prayers did not, however, crystallize in form and number until the 1770s.[139] A guide to participating in the papal jubilee published in Dublin in connection with the election of Clement XIV to the papacy in 1769 included them with the recommendation that they be said "when one visits the Chapel or Chapels to gain the Jubilee," and Clement officially extended the indulgence attached to the Acts to Ireland in 1772.[140] By the end of the eighteenth century, the exhortations of bishops and devotional literature in both English and Irish alike stressed the importance attached to their recitation by the laity, especially before Mass, and in 1810, their recitation as part of Mass attendance was made official.[141]

Catechisms and prayer books in both print and manuscript almost universally included the Acts in their sets of essential prayers. A pamphlet treatise on the subject by Frainsias Bizzarrini Comarec was reprinted bilingually in Dublin by Bartholomew Corcoran as *Acts of the Three Theological Virtues and Contrition Absolutely Necessary to Salvation/Gniomharta na nTri Subhailce Diadha agus Croidh Bhruighidh Ro Riachtanacha chum Slainte* (ca. 1780).[142] The prayers devoted to the theological virtues also could be found at this time in the liturgical manual *Ordo Administrandi Sacramenta* (1785), commissioned by Archbishop Carpenter for the purpose of establishing common standards of ritual in the Dublin archdiocese. Charles O'Conor was once again entrusted with the duty of translating the Acts into Irish; his efforts appeared in the appendix of the work alongside instructions for priests on administering the sacraments and preparing congregations for their Easter duties. The *Ordo Administrandi Sacramenta* remained in use in the archdiocese of Dublin, where reprints appeared in 1804, 1812, 1820, 1835, and in a twelfth edition as late as 1847. The work was also printed in Cork in 1829.[143] The Acts appeared in Irish-language devotional manuals like the *Spiritual Rose* and in the O'Reilly, Butler, Kirwan, Donlevy, Loftus, and Coppinger catechisms. By 1800 bishops actively called for the inclusion of the Acts in Sunday services in their dioceses. Carpenter's successor in Dublin, Archbishop John Troy, instructed his clergy in 1791 to recite the acts of contrition, faith, hope, and charity before every Sunday Mass and holy-day service. Subsequent diocesan statutes reaffirmed this custom in Meath in 1829, Dublin in 1831, Ardagh in 1834, and Kilmore in 1834.[144] In the Munster archdiocese of Cashel and Emly, Archbishop Bray stipulated that a prayer before the

Acts, then the Acts of contrition, faith, hope, and charity, and finally a special prayer before Mass be recited in Irish and English by the priest on all Sundays and holy days "in an audible and solemn tone," while "the congregation is to join most devoutly in reciting them on their knees. And immediately after the prayer before mass, the Angelus Domini is to be said in English or Irish on all Sundays and holy days of obligation in the diocese of Cashel and Emly."[145]

Another devotion attached to Mass services advocated by the authorities in Irish as much as in English was the recitation of litanies. Prayed in statement-and-response format, with a leader's call answered by a set reply from the congregation, litanies lent themselves well to participation by people of all class, educational, and linguistic backgrounds. A variety of litanies addressed to various saints and holy personages had been a feature of medieval Catholicism, but there was an increasing popularity of prayers offered specifically to one subject. Litanies addressed to the Virgin Mary or devoted to aspects of the divinity of Christ became particularly popular, the former especially as a Marian devotion associated with the Loreto shrine.[146] These were the forms that made their way to Ireland and became common in the nineteenth century. Their inclusion as part of Sunday services varied; they were more often presented as part of morning and evening prayers. But there is clear evidence that it was the practice in some chapels to recite the litanies before Mass.[147] The laity certainly had ample opportunity to become familiar with this form of devotion, as litanies to the Blessed Virgin and to the Holy Name of Jesus could be found in most of the Irish-language catechisms of this period, intended either as a familial devotion or for communal use. The Loftus and O'Reilly catechisms, for example, included both the litany of the Blessed Virgin and the litany of Jesus in Irish, and most manuscript prayer books supplied one or another of these devotions.[148]

The recitation of the Acts and litanies before Mass on Sunday and holy days represented one means of educating parishioners and heightening their participation in church services. But attention was also directed to the content of the Mass itself, conducted almost entirely in Latin. The Mass had been a particularly sensitive point for the Catholic church since the Reformation, as Protestants eagerly directed their criticisms at the use of a language not understood by the general congregation. This concern was renewed in the 1820s with the ramping up of the so-called Second Reformation, in which Protestant missionary efforts in Ireland increased significantly. On the one hand, the ritual of the Mass, focused as it was on the reenactment of the Lord's Supper by the priest at the altar, hardly invited lay participation regardless of their vernacular. The practice in Ireland did not differ, as Patrick Corish has noted: "Mass attendance was 'passive' in the sense that people said their prayers and allowed the priest at the altar to get on with what was seen as his business."[149] On the other hand, church officials desired a popular understanding of the meaning of the Mass and the ability to make occasional responses in Latin, as in the response *et cum spiritu tuo* to the priest's greeting, *dominus vobiscum*.[150] Unfortunately, lay understanding left much to be desired. A native of Achill, Co. Mayo, who grew up in the 1830s and 1840s recalled that his father had been the only person in the entire congregation who could satisfactorily make the Latin responses. Even in this case the answers may have exhibited more rote learning than mastery: "My father knew nothing of Latin, but being otherwise a scholar, he was able to go through the performance to the priests' satisfaction."[151]

A number of concerned Catholics, including those outside the clergy, sought ways to improve this liturgical knowledge in a way that would include Irish speakers. In 1835 William O'Neill Daunt, a convert to Catholicism and advocate for preserving Irish, expressed concern that the lack of understanding of the Mass among his fellow Catholics left the faith exposed to Protestant criticism in a flurry of letters to Bishop John Cantwell of Meath, Bishop John Murphy of Cork, Bishop Michael Collins of Cloyne and Ross, and Archbishop Daniel Murray of Dublin. Writing to Murray, Daunt affirmed, "Your Grace does not need to be informed that many, too many, of our peasantry are immersed in a state of awful frightful ignorance upon religious subjects." The problem, according to Daunt, was twofold: priests failed to provide adequate religious instruction on Sundays, and prayers given out on Sunday were in Latin, a language not understood by the general population. While affirming that the Latin content of the Mass could not be changed, Daunt suggested another solution: instructive prayers in the vernacular—"to be translated into Irish for the districts where that language prevails." By making these supplementary vernacular prayers mandatory, Daunt believed that the bishops could bypass clerical indolence and improve lay understanding of the faith.[152]

Daunt was not the only one eager to raise awareness of the meaning of the Mass among those attending. Indeed, there was a long-standing focus on this aspect in Irish-language religious publications (and their manuscript extensions) dating to at least the seventeenth century. Céitinn's *Eochair-Sgiath an Aifrinn* contained an extended discussion on the symbolism of the vestments and actions of the priest during the liturgy, while two of the catechisms of that era, the Ó hEodhasa catechism and Ó Maolmhuaidh's *Lucerna Fidelium*, contained short pieces on the meaning of the Mass and the significance of communion and confession.[153] Because none of these works would have qualified as a truly universally accessible text—they would have found first and foremost a young clerical student audience and, second, an educated Catholic lay audience—their influence on Mass practices would have been limited. However, a fourth text of the time to extensively address the Mass, Gearnon's *Parrthas an Anma*, took on a much more simplified dialogic format with content that later catechetical and devotional writers of the eighteenth and nineteenth centuries echoed closely. Having explained in the eighth section of the manual the basic significance of the Mass as reaffirming the principles of Christ's sacrifice, Gearnon in chapter 3 turned to the responsibilities of those listening to the Mass:

> C: Cionnas iomchras tú thú féin a n-aimsir an aifrinn?
>
> F: Anoim ar mo ghlúinibh ach an úair bhíos an soisgéul ga rádh; ní chuirim búaidhreadh ar an tshagart iná ar an muinntir oile éisdeas an t-afrionn.[154]
>
> [Q: How should you conduct yourself during the Mass?
>
> A: I remain on my knees except when the Gospel is being recited; I do not disturb the priest or the other people listening to the Mass.]

By the eighteenth century, such advice for comportment, combined with a rigorous explanation for what the Mass, communion, and confession signified, could be found in a number of key Catholic texts with a popular appeal. Challoner's ever-popular *Garden of the Soul*, for instance, offered "instructions and devotions for hearing mass," placing the liturgy within the context of the Old and New Testament understandings of sacrificial rite, the Passion, and redemption. Participants were to mentally prepare themselves on their way to chapel, focusing their thoughts before entering, taking holy water, and making the sign of the cross.[155]

Irish scribal manuscripts paralleled many of these same concerns. A manuscript copied by Risteard Tuibear and Tadhg Ó Neachtain in 1716 included an Irish-language breviary, prayers to be said during Mass, and a collection of common prayers and psalms in Irish, while a mid-eighteenth-century prayer book written by scribe Seághan Úa h-Úmhair provided a series of prayers to be said as the priest conducted the liturgy from the altar.[156] In the nineteenth century, this interest continued. An early text by Tadhg Ó Conaill, the scribe who worked for Bishop Murphy, prescribed personal meditation on the way to Mass on terms almost identical to those in Challoner:

> An tan bheigh tú ag dul chuim an aithfrion do éisdeacht, dein díthchioll air chuimhneamh ort féin chómh maith & is féidir riot é, re do smúainte mearbhathalach do ghláodhach chuim stoidéir, & a ttógbhail ó gach uile ghnó & ócáide eile.[157]

[When you are heading to listen to Mass, do your best to remember as best as you can to recall your confused thoughts for study, and take them away from all other business and concerns.]

Scribal texts urged readers (or their pupils) to learn basic prayers timed to the various components of the Mass, filling a void that might otherwise be left to distraction or passive listening. A prayer structured around Judas was to be said "Ann oúar poagus an seagart ann altar ata Crísta malltale poag" (at the time when the priest kisses the altar, as Christ was deceived by a kiss), noted an 1810 manuscript filled with illustrations of the Virgin and events in the life of Christ by the scribe Aodh Mac Ceagan.[158] The 1823 prayer book Ó Dreada copied for Father Eoin Ó Céileachair urged Mass listeners to direct one's attention to the "Páise & bás ár Slánuightheóra Iosa Críosd, & gan stad cuir ós cómhar do shúl an Naomh Ógh Muire Mhagdeléna & na Muireadha oile ag dul go sliabh Chalbharaoi chum amharc ar Chríosd dá chéusa" (Passion and death of our Lord Jesus Christ, and to put perpetually before your eyes the Virgin, Mary Magdelene, and the other Maries going to Mount Calvary to see Christ be crucified).[159]

Although written in some cases for the use of priests, the content of these prayer books with their prescribed devotions for the Mass did not remain locked away in clerical libraries. The laity, too, participated in the diffusion of their contents. Denn, for instance, along with a group of parishioners from the Cappoquin, Co. Waterford, community, introduced the practice of reciting the rosary and litanies before Mass as well as delivering Sunday vespers in Irish. Accounts confirm that this custom remained common in Cappoquin, located in the heavily Irish-speaking barony of Coshmore and Coshbride, for three decades after his death.[160] Not content merely with his chapel innovations, Denn took direct aim at improving knowledge of the Mass through his numerous publications intended for the priests, schoolteachers, and educated laity responsible for instructing Irish-speaking children—the "country scholar who can read English," as Denn described it, but who spoke Irish fluently and could read it in Roman letters. In a section titled "D'on Aifrionn Naomhtha" ("On the Holy Mass"), the *Catholic Children's Primer* proposed these basic requirements of attendees:

C: Cia hiad an drong na eisdeas e mar is coir?
   F: Ata an drong do chodlas aige, do bheir aire do neithibh saodhalta, do bhios aig feachuin a nunn agus a nall, do bhios aig comhradh re cheile, agus aig luighe air leath-ghlun, &c.[161]

[Q: Who are those who do not listen as they ought?

A: Those who sleep, who pay attention to worldly things, who look here and there, who converse together, and who half-kneel, etc.]

Preferably, respectful listening could be supplemented by reading or personal prayer. In cases of illiteracy Denn recommended a substitute:

An te na fuil abalta air leabhar paidreacha do leagabh, abareach se Coroin Iosa na dtri ndeithniur, agus deineach se machtnamh a nait a cheile air gach pairt do phais Chriosd mar ata minighthe annso leabhar beag so.[162]

[Those who are not able to read a prayer book, say the Rosary of Jesus in three decades, and reflect in each part on the Passion of Christ as it is explained in this little book.]

Denn then laid out for his reader each part of the Mass, explaining its significance and relation to the larger tenets of belief. A later reprint of Denn's work indicated that it was a custom in the Decies area of Waterford to have this explanation of the Mass read aloud before Sunday services by selected members of the congregation, with each taking turns asking and answering the explanatory questions.[163]

Perhaps the only issue on which these prayer books and manuals were silent, despite their minute level of detail in explaining the Mass and seeking to enrich the experience for Mass-goers, was the question of how often to attend. Although conveying the importance, for instance, of scrutiny of one's conscience and fulfilling confession, there was no concerted effort by these Irish-language texts to assert a specific frequency for attendance. On the other hand, the extensive sets of common prayers offered by the texts, many of which explicitly stipulated daily recital, implied that the priests, patrons, and scribes whose envisioned religious practices were contained within believed that Mass attendance, confession, and communion would also be at least regular, if not weekly or even monthly. In truth, the real concern displayed by these Irish-language texts was the level of understanding of liturgy and the need for Christological focus during Mass attendance—in other words, to provide a regimen of purposeful participation rather than overt concern with frequency.

This interest in a structured, orthodox routine of religious practice extended within these prayer books, catechisms, and devotional manuals to include the personal prayers they prescribed, the final aspect of everyday religiosity that dominated the reform envisioned by this strand of the Irish-speaking community. What made this focus on prayer urgent was the fact that outside of the chapel, there were abundant opportunities for Irish practices that conflicted with the preferences of reformers, namely in the form of folk prayers and supplications. Some of these prayers had their origins in medieval petitions of wider European provenance,[164] and they shared a basic acceptance of fundamental Christian beliefs including a collective understanding of the role and power of saints, the importance of the universal church, the significance of the Virgin Mary, and the existence of God. But many of the prayers confronted by reform-minded individuals of the eighteenth and nineteenth centuries also risked shifting the focus of belief away from core concepts about the sacrifice of Christ and the means to salvation, and in particular the simple and direct professions of belief central to prayers like the *Pater Noster*, the *Ave Maria*, the *Credo*, and litanies to Mary and Jesus. As such, the prayers presented in devotional instructions, both in English and in Irish, pressed for a simple and straightforward use of these universal prayers during daily business. Catechisms and prayer books also took an interest in the timing and deployment of these prayers, laying out a consistent regimen of morning prayers to be said upon waking and dressing, prayers before and after meals, prayers in the evening and on retiring to bed, and prayers to be said before and after sacramental duties like confession and communion. This meant a much more narrowly defined sacred sphere, drawing a contrast with lay practices that included prayers said when lighting a fire, churning butter, making bread, before eating the year's new potatoes, lighting or extinguishing a light, putting a child to sleep, milking a cow, and a variety of other special times, not to mention the use of *orthaí*, or charm supplications, to heal sick people or animals and to ward off bad luck.[165] Ambiguity as to the form and content of these prayers heavily saturated these practices, arousing suspicion from the vantage point of officials even if they had not been employed to obtain profane ends.

Catechisms and devotional manuals instead proposed a specific structure to prayer in daily life, particularly as it was conducted in the home, in order to reinforce the connection of prayer and belief. All catechisms at this time, in English or Irish, thus shared a similar content that encompassed the *Pater Noster*, the *Ave Maria*, the *Credo*, and the *Confiteor*, continued with litanies (usually the Litany of Jesus and the Litany of Mary), and the hymn *Salve Regina*, and concluded with important daily prayers for morning, evening, and meals. The O'Reilly catechism, for example, presented its first lesson in two parts: prayers for the morning and prayers for the evening. The object of these prayers made their purpose explicit from the beginning by calling for morning Acts of adoration, thanksgiving, love, and offering. Having professed conviction in the power of

God, the Irish Catholic man or woman continued with the *Pater, Ave, Credo,* and the Litany of Jesus. In the evening a similar schedule was proposed, with further professions of faith, a reflection on sin and contrition, prayers for protection, and the Litany of the Virgin Mary.[166] The litanies, which were conducted in call-and-response format, particularly lent themselves to a communal or household setting in which each member of the family could take a turn in reciting and answering.

The opportunity provided by evening household gatherings prompted further possibilities to reshape the religious landscape of the community. Rural inhabitants congregated in homes in the evenings, particularly during the long and inactive winter nights, to tell stories, exchange gossip, sing songs, and recite poetry. This involved not just the immediate family or household but also neighbors and friends. Communities already devoted these evenings to both secular and religious content, but Denn, for instance, sensed a greater opportunity for reflection and moral teaching. He urged owners of his *Stiúratheoir an Pheacuig* (1824) to "frequently read it for the family of his house, and also for his neighbours, particularly on winter nights when they can spare more time and have more leisure to assemble together, in order to hear it read for them."[167] The most important evening devotion endorsed by the Catholic Church was the family rosary. A medieval practice associated by tradition with the Dominican Order, the repetition of the *Pater Noster* and the *Ave Maria* while meditating on the events of the life of Jesus and Mary became an increasingly common aspect of lay devotion in European Catholicism. Rosaries could be offered to Christ alone, but especially from the time of the Council of Trent they became closely associated with Marian devotion. The rosary took root early in Ireland as well—probably through international monastic connections—and subsequently spread among the laity. As John Kilduff, soon to be bishop of Ardagh, reported to Archbishop Cullen in 1852 from Oughterard, Co. Galway, there were "sets of beads with large silver decade stones which are supposed to have been made about two centuries ago" among even the poorest members of his flock. "These beads," he noted, "have been transmitted in regular succession from mother to daughter."[168] But it was in the nineteenth century, with the growth of Marian devotions and the establishment of organizations like the Sodality of the Living Rosary, that the practice made large strides.

Like the litanies, the rosary worked well as an evening group prayer, with each person present in the household reciting a decade in turn at a set time every night.[169] The rosary, or *paidrín*, dedicated to the Virgin Mary was particularly popular, especially by the second quarter of the nineteenth century. The Donlevy catechism included instructions on how to pray the rosary, as did the Butler, Pulleine, and Loftus catechisms.[170] Readers of the *Pious Miscellany* found two poems on the rosary, and the devotion took center stage in *The Spiritual Rose*.[171] Both Denn and MacHale included instructions for the rosary in their prayer books, the latter on the reasoning that the "Rosary of the Blessed Virgin, so popular in Ireland, especially since the time that reading and writing became penal, ought to be again made accessible to the people in their native language." To drive home the Marian connections of its inclusion, MacHale appended to the rosary a commemoration of the 1854 Vatican pronouncement on the Immaculate Conception.[172] Rosary prayers also appeared in manuscript prayer books. A copy of an original eighteenth-century Archbishop Carpenter manuscript made by Finghin Ó Scannail included rosaries to Mary and Jesus, as did later manuscripts such as the expansive 1830 prayer book made by Tadhg Mac Cártha, in which the scribe noted that the rosary to Mary was particularly well suited to those who could not read.[173]

Several other devotions that made their appearances in these prayer books deserve mention, in that they placed Irish-language texts firmly within the bounds of currents driving modern Catholic reform. As has been noted, devotions to the Sacred Heart were featured in a number of printed works and manuscripts. In addition to the poem dedicated to the devotion in the *Pious Miscellany*, prayers for the festival of the Sacred Heart were copied into an Irish manuscript from the late eighteenth and early nineteenth centuries by an unknown scribe of northern provenance, and a litany to the Sacred Heart of Jesus was included in an 1824 manuscript by Séamas Mac Donnchadha Ó Caoindealbháin.[174] Another devotion included in Irish texts was the Thirty Days' Prayer, to be said "an am doghruing et trioblóidhíghe" (at a time of hardship and troubles), according to another manuscript by Ó Caoindealbháin.[175] The Thirty Days' Prayer appeared in a number of Irish-language manuscript translations from the popular prayer books *The Path to Paradise* and *The Poor Man's Manual of Devotions*.[176] Finally, there was the series of devotions to the Way of the Cross, previously mentioned as a feature in Irish-language printed materials, such as Kennedy's *Spiritual Rose* and, most visibly, MacHale's translations of Liguori's work dedicated to that subject. This devotion was also perpetuated in humble manuscript form, where some scribes, like the copyist of an early-nineteenth-century text, Michael Mhac Domhniel, included elaborate ink illustrations of the scenes from the Passion associated with each station. The well-thumbed condition of this text is an indication of its practical application in regular practice.[177]

The form of orthodoxy contained in these Irish-language texts was but one facet of a wide and diverse Irish-speaking religious community, one that coexisted with other communities of religious practice that did not conform to this new vision of Catholicism. It should be kept in mind that within these orthodox Irish-language texts, there were mixed genres of religious practices that made each manuscript or printed manual unique in its preferred vision. Even in manuscripts that were direct translations of earlier texts, scribes did not hesitate to add older prayers or poems if they saw fit to do so. Moreover, this is to say nothing of the process by which the orthodoxies represented by these texts made their way into the religious spaces of the everyday life of Irish men and women. These prayers and litanies by no means erased popular forms of piety and may even have presented opportunities to combine old Irish-language devotions with new: the rosary, for example, could be accompanied by older prayers already recited in the evening. Seán Mac Gearailt, a Waterford laborer born in 1874, recalled that his grandfather had the following routine before bed: "Deireadh sé an Paidrín i nGaoluinn. Ansan, nuair a bheadh sé sa leaba, bheadh paidreacha eile aige" (He would say the rosary in Irish. Then, when he would be in the bed, he would have other prayers).[178] Similarly, Catholics combined the rosary with older religious songs like "The Seven Dolours of the Virgin Mary," sung in Irish after the rosary, and it could be combined with older (unorthodox) circumstances calling for prayer before the herding of cattle, the beginning of a journey, the appearance of a storm, or holy-well ceremonies.[179]

But regardless of the ways these devotions were applied by Irish Catholics, Irish-language texts pressing a new orthodoxy built around Mass attendance and universal personal prayers did have a role to play in the emerging Catholicism of the period. In fact, no better indication of the long shadow cast by these earlier Irish-language religious works on modern Catholicism can be found than the prayer books that appeared as part of the revival movement at the end of the nineteenth century and beginning of the twentieth century. With firm roots in both turn-of-the-century cultural revival and modern Catholicism, works like Eoin Ó Nualláin's *An Casán go Flaitheamhnas: Láimhleabhairín Urnuighe* (1882) and *Leabhar-Urnuighe Naoimh Pádraic/St. Patrick's Prayer Book* (ca. 1894), and the anonymous *Leabhar Urnaighthe* compiled by a priest and published by the Catholic Truth Society in 1904, all replicated exactly the prayers found in manuscript and print prayer books throughout the first half of the nineteenth century.[180] It was these prayer books that provided an early basis for the forms of Irish-speaking Catholicism to emerge from the formative period of twentieth-century nationalism and would continue to play a role in Irish religiosity for decades afterward.

Priests, Pastoral Care, and Catholic Policy

Although the ideology of reform expressed in the Irish-language manuscripts and printed texts of the eighteenth and nineteenth centuries depended in no small part on the efforts of lay scribes, translators, and publishers, the modern Irish Catholic Church was still a product of the policies and decisions made by its institutional representatives. In terms of impact on linguistic policy, there was a striking parallel in this period between the Westminster government and the Catholic Church, both of which expanded into the lives of its members on a new scale starting in the late eighteenth century. For the latter, this trend encompassing a newfound emphasis on attendance at Mass in newly constructed chapels, participation in family prayers, and interaction with church authorities more often via the fulfillment of sacramental obligations. This necessarily brought greater linguistic diversity into religious spaces like the chapel, not only because Irish communities themselves were becoming increasingly mixed, but also because the simple fact of bringing larger sections of the community together in one place for common worship necessarily entailed a more varied congregation. Thus, as with the state, the need for more regular contact with multiple parishioners required church authorities to confront language questions in a way not required earlier in the eighteenth century, when local priests could simply administer to a more homogenous linguistic population in private homes and small Mass houses—if such gatherings happened at all. As Seán Ó Briain, bishop of Cloyne and Ross, recognized as early as 1764 in a letter to the prefect of the Sacred Congregation of Propaganda, it was imperative that the clergy preserve their ability to administer to their flocks in Irish, since this was the language used by the majority of Catholics in learning their catechism, praying, and confessing. As such, "the parochial clergy and other missionary priests must be sufficiently well acquainted with Irish in order to administer the Sacraments, to teach the people Christian doctrine, to instruct them in moral truths and in truths of the Gospel."[1]

Already it has been seen that some sections of both the church and laity—that is, various scribes, priests, schoolteachers, merchants, and artisans of its Irish-speaking communities—had taken an interest in (and were practicing) the devotional reforms that had also gripped parts of English-speaking Ireland. But the question remains as to what organizational efforts were taken by the church to ensure that personnel decisions, clerical education, and liturgical accommodations responded to this need to address the Irish speakers now expected (as with all Irish Catholics) to interact differently with Catholic institutions. While acknowledging individual clerical and episcopal support for Irish-language scholarship, most historians have portrayed Catholic authorities as indifferent, if not actively hostile toward the Irish language by the nineteenth century. These arguments can be summed up in three major propositions. First, it is said that the Catholic hierarchy failed to pursue an active policy of ensuring the use of Irish by its personnel, presumably by way of a central decision to ensure the proficiency of its priests in Irish. As Brian Ó Cuív concluded, "There seems to be no evidence that the Irish hierarchy ever planned collectively to ensure that the clergy would be competent in both Irish and English."[2] Second, a great deal of significance has been attributed to a perceived decline in clerical participation in (and patronage of) Irish scholarship, most evident in the appearance of phonetic Irish texts based on English spelling, rather than native scribal spelling, in the hands of priests. Related to this, scholars have dismissed evidence of the use of Irish by priests and bishops to broadcast episcopal instructions as exceptional and expedient, as opposed to deeply embedded in long-standing (presumably, scholarly) use of the language. Finally, much blame has been assigned to clerical education in the decades after 1782, when most of the official prohibitions on domestic Catholic education ended, sparking the founding of a number of new seminaries. Among these, St. Patrick's College, Maynooth, established in 1795, has been seen as a particularly important development not only because of its perceived weak devotion to teaching its students Irish but also because of the supposed anglicizing sensibility imparted to its students that made them hostile to the language. The result, according to Maureen Wall, was that "English-speaking priests often went to minister in Irish-speaking districts" and thus abetted or even provoked language shift.[3]

Even before considering the evidence, however, certain difficulties with these interpretations arise. The first point immediately prompts a reminder that church policy was just as often decided at the local rather than the national level. The absence of centralized policy on language does not preclude the accommodation of Irish in one fashion or another at the parish level by individual priests. In any case, it is not clear why the domination of first Latin and then English in the official life of the church should be taken as a sign that Irish was by definition on an insecure footing. After all, Catholicism had long accommodated a two- and three-tiered difference between the languages of its bishops and priests and the local vernacular of the laity. Among Irish ecclesiastical officials, English was merely the latest newcomer to a number of higher-level languages reflecting the cosmopolitan nature of the larger European church, including Spanish, Italian, French, and above all Latin—none of which had contributed to a decline in the use of Irish by the laity in previous centuries. As far as language shift is concerned, the choice of bishops to correspond in English or to publish synodal decrees in Latin and English mattered far less than the language used by priests from the altar, spoken by the catechetical teacher on Sunday, printed in catechisms and prayer books, and recited in the prayers learned from parents. The second point regarding literary patronage among priests holds even less salience. While greater interest in Irish scholarship among priests would have indicated a clear interest in the health of the language, it does not follow that absence of widespread participation in scribal activity points to opposition to the use of Irish in parochial duties or to parishioners speaking Irish. That priests relied on written texts in Irish based on English spelling conventions confirms that few members of the clergy had been schooled in scribal literary conventions, but that can hardly be taken as indicative of their respect for the use of Irish. Rather, the fact that they had such texts (and it should be kept in mind that the commitment to providing sermons and catechetical training that required such texts was itself only gaining ground in Ireland) and were committed to using them in their parochial work says much about clerical concern that their message be heard by Irish and English speakers alike.

The persistent focus on Maynooth in many historical accounts as the source of anglicizing priests also raises questions. Although Irish was taught at Maynooth, English undoubtedly dominated student life. The same could be said of the other new colleges founded in the late eighteenth and early nineteenth centuries in Kilkenny, Carlow, Thurles, and Tuam, as well as in the many minor seminaries taking root in places like Cork, Wexford, Navan, Newry, Armagh, and other towns around the country. But it is a significant leap to move from the prevalence of English in clerical education to arguing that Maynooth made English-speaking priests out of Irish speakers. Collegial training occupied a mere six to seven years in the life of newly ordained priests, making it an unlikely candidate to have induced a language shift among students who had grown up with Irish. Even assuming that Maynooth and other new colleges represented a new direction in clerical language proficiency, a problem of timing still presents itself. As Sean Connolly has cautioned, the impact of Maynooth before 1850 was considerably reduced by the prosaic fact that it took decades for the generations of priests educated before 1800 to be replaced. As late as 1853, Maynooth-trained priests made up only 53 percent of the entire Irish priesthood.[4] This suggests that the impact of these domestically trained priests on the Irish language should have been delayed until the second half of the nineteenth century. The identification of Maynooth and the late eighteenth century as a turning point in clerical education also problematically severs Irish clerical education in 1795 from its antecedents in the Irish colleges of France, the Netherlands, Spain, Italy, and Bohemia. Research on the curricula at these schools in the past few decades has considerably expanded historians' knowledge of the context for the intentions of Irish instruction at the time of the founding of Maynooth, revealing considerable continuities rather than a sharp break.

Finally, there has been a tendency to oversimplify the choices faced by priests, even those who spoke Irish and favored its continued use as a part of pastoral care. Many parishes confronted an extended period of language transition as English became first a growing second language, then a primary, and finally an exclusive means of communication for a significant portion of Catholic congregations. How did officials carry out pastoral duties among multilingual congregations? This point has not been raised by historians, who have often portrayed the language transition as a simple and straightforward choice between Irish and English. Contemporaries, by contrast, understood the overlapping linguistic complexities of the time. These were vividly captured by the novelist William Carleton (1794–1869) in his fictional description of an outdoor Mass in the short story "Ned M'Keown" (1830): "Up near the altar, hemmed in by a ring of old men and women, you might perceive a *voteen* repeating some new prayer or choice piece of devotion—or some other, in a similar circle, devouring with sanctimonious avidity Doctor Gallagher's Irish Sermons, Pastorini's History of the Christian Church, or Columbkill's Prophecy—and perhaps a strolling pilgrim, the centre of a third collection, singing the *Dies Irae*, in Latin, or the Hermit of Killarney, in English."[5] One can hardly imagine a richer representation of the composite nature of language use, Catholic ritual, and indeed Irish culture as a whole than the picture sketched here: not two, but three languages play a role in the religiosity of the laity. A full assessment of the place of Irish in the institutional life of the nineteenth-century Catholic Church thus requires a more rigorous exploration of these questions.

This chapter will start first by reviewing the evidence of the use of Irish by clergy in their everyday duties, keeping in mind the growing emphasis in the late eighteenth century and throughout the nineteenth on activities (sermons, catechetical training, and conducting Mass) that required a larger public participation. From here, it will consider the larger experience of mixed-language congregations and the challenges presented by language shift to clerical administration. Emphasizing the less-than-ideal situation faced by priests in these situations, the chapter offers a closer look at the justification behind priests' decisions to favor one language over another. Next, the linguistic backgrounds of parish priests and their preparation for the needs of ministering to Irish-speaking parishes will receive attention. Although the male and especially female religious orders that experienced significant growth in this century also played an important role in the daily piety of the laity—one that deserves to be explored—the focus here is on parish priests as the primary link between church and people. The proportion of nineteenth-century priests who spoke Irish, the timing of the transition to English monolingualism, and the steps, if any, taken to ensure that church officials could speak the language of their own parishioners will be the primary objects of investigation. Finally, the form and intent of clerical training will be considered, including the causes and timing of trends toward English in the newly founded Irish colleges of the period.

Early eighteenth-century priests, subject to penal legislation, often conducted Mass on the edge of public visibility, in truncated forms of worship performed in private and hidden spaces where the attendance of parishioners had been small-scale and covert. But the church of the late eighteenth and the nineteenth centuries was slowly moving toward chapel-centered worship and full attendance by parishioners. The practice of holding stations in private homes, an expedient measure that had arisen in the late eighteenth century as a means to accommodate spectacular population increases that had not been met by sufficient new chapels and clergy, were also gradually replaced by a new emphasis on worship in Catholic chapels.[6] Stations in private homes were attended by those living in the immediate vicinity and were therefore more likely to share a common language. Parish chapels, by contrast, housed larger and more heterogeneous congregations drawn from a number of localities whose members may or may not have used the same language in everyday life. The expectation of priests was that they would not only meet their congregations more regularly to provide Mass and confession but that they would also instruct, namely by giving a sermon and encouraging catechetical training in the community, and hear confessions. All of these endeavors raised the question of the language that would be used in communicating with this expanded lay presence.

The nature of the surviving evidence for clerical use of Irish, which tends to be found in scattered anecdotal references in diocesan records, correspondence, and newspaper reports, has no doubt obscured the extent to which sermons, portions of the Mass, and pastoral addresses by bishops during visitations and confirmations were given in Irish. But it is clear that a good many priests and curates did in fact provide regular preaching, instruction, and confessions in Irish, and that some acquired a considerable reputation in doing so. John Murphy, for instance, the parish priest of Corofin already identified for his political speeches in Irish, was known as a powerful deliverer of sermons in Irish who also made a practice of translating into Irish extemporaneously from Challoner's *Think Well On't* and Thomas à Kempis's *Imitation of Christ*.[7] The parish priest of Darrynane, Co. Kerry, the home region of Daniel O'Connell, preached in Irish: agricultural commissioner Jonathan Binn witnessed a crowd of 200 listen to such a sermon during a visit to the area in 1836.[8] Another Kerry priest, Father Eugene O'Sullivan of Dingle, reportedly made a practice of addressing the congregation in Irish after the communion, often using it as an occasion to explain the duties of the faith and to inveigh against Protestant converts.[9] James Walsh, the parish priest of Ballinvana and Bulgaden, in County Limerick, was described at the time of his death in 1858 as "an eloquent and impressive preacher in English and in his dear native tongue."[10] Father Ignatius of Mount Melleray Abbey, a Cistercian who immigrated to the United States, was known as "one of the best preachers in the Irish language, perhaps in the kingdom," according to an account reporting his departure in 1860.[11] Beyond Munster, John Doherty, parish priest of Carrigart, Co. Donegal, was known to deliver sermons in Irish, as evidenced by such an address offered at the funeral of a fellow priest in 1869.[12]

The frequency of sermons delivered in Irish in the western archdiocese of Tuam has been particularly well documented. Spanning the heavily Irish-speaking province of Connacht, Tuam under Archbishop MacHale witnessed regular Irish sermons delivered during episcopal visitations, at confirmations, and during regular weekly Masses. No less than four Mayo priests delivered sermons in Irish during a jubilee celebration at Ballindine parish, including parish priest Father Mullins, Father Carr the prior of Ballinsmaula, the Annagh curate P. Prendergast, and his fellow Annagh parish priest, Father Eugene Coyne.[13] Father Micheal Gallagher, a curate of the parish of Islandeady, Co. Mayo, was known to address his parishioners in Irish, as was Father Patrick Duggan of Cummer, who addressed a crowd assembled in Clifden on the occasion of a visit by MacHale in 1852.[14] During this same tour, in which MacHale made stops in Ballinakill and Tully, Co. Galway, it was reported that curate Father Edward Gibbons provided an Irish sermon during confirmations attended by hundreds.[15] Father Michael Mulkerrin, parish priest of Annaghdown, was capable of providing sermons in Irish, as he provided one during a confirmation for 600 locals in 1855.[16] Yet another confirmation tour in 1859 brought out the curate of Moylough parish, Father Patrick Fitzgerald, to preach in Irish, along with Reverend Duggan, who once again spoke in Irish.[17] The parish priest of Kilmain, Co. Mayo, John MacHugh, was known to preach in Irish "in his own peculiarly impressive and happy style," as he did during a confirmation visit to Ballinrobe in 1860.[18] At Spiddal in the same year, 190 parishioners gathered for confirmation received a sermon in Irish by Father R. Quinn, and throughout the 1860s and 1870s reports of similar visits reveal that Father James Browne, parish priest of Ballintober, Father James Flannelly of Roundstone, Father Austin O'Dwyer of Killour, and curate Mathias Lavelle of Errislanan were all willing to preach in Irish.[19] In addition to confirmation visits, it is clear that Lenten observances and Saint Patrick's Day were occasions for sermons in Irish in Tuam. During Good Friday celebrations in Clifden in 1864, Father Patrick MacManus provided a "suitable Irish discourse" under instructions from MacHale, and four years later Flannelly provided the same during Holy Week ceremonies in Roundstone.[20] MacHale stipulated in his Lenten pastorals in 1869 and again in 1872 that Good Friday sermons were to be in Irish in the "several churches" in the archdiocese, a practice that brought the attention of the Protestant archdeacon of Achonry, who admired what he saw as its effectiveness in bringing tenets of the Christian faith to the Irish-speaking community.[21]

It was not only during routine gatherings in rural parishes where Irish sermons could be found. Both Edward Wakefield and Philip Dixon Hardy confirmed that sermons in Irish regularly accompanied the Mass said at the international pilgrimage site at Lough Derg, Co. Donegal. According to Wakefield, one of the clerical administrators "says mass the whole day in Irish, while the others are engaged in confessing."[22] Even city chapels were settings for Irish-language addresses. Speaking of the city of Galway, for example, Wakefield reported that "preaching is performed here in Irish," and in Dublin there had been a practice in some chapels between 1776 and 1847, initiated by Archbishop John Carpenter, of having portions of his *Rituale Romanorum* read out in Irish at the first Mass on Sundays.[23] Johann Kohl observed in 1844 that two churches in Cork city provided Irish sermons, although he believed this was underserving the substantial Irish-speaking population in the area.[24] Irish sermons also began to be provided during parish missions, a new development closely linked to the devotional revolution and particularly well represented by the Jesuits and the Vincentians. Considered a means of reaching out to the laity to encourage their participation in spiritual life and to spread new devotional practices, Catholic mission efforts emerged in the wake of Protestant proselytizing of the 1820s and 1830s and involved several weeks of religious processions, Masses, sermons, catechetical instruction, and the administering of the sacraments of confession and the Eucharist. In 1842 and 1843 the Vincentians commenced missions starting in Athy and Carlow, while the Jesuits conducted their first missions in New Ross and Waterford city in 1850.[25] It appears that neither group had initially considered the problem of language use before beginning their work, despite the request of local parish priests such as Father Michael Meehan of Carrigaholt, Co. Clare, to send Irish speakers for the 1854 Jesuit mission.[26] But both orders took subsequent later steps to provide Irish-speaking missioners or, failing that, to involve local priests and curates who could provide Irish addresses. The Vincentians sent two Irish speakers, Fathers Leyden and O'Grady, on their first mission to Dingle in 1846, and the Jesuits first sent two Irish-speaking brothers on their mission to Miltown Malbay in 1864: Father Patrick Corcoran and Father Thomas O'Malley, both of Tuam. Accounts of missions in Tuam in the 1850s and 1860s record efforts to teach the Forty Hours Adoration of the Eucharist and devotions to the Blessed Virgin, combined with Irish sermons, and although O'Malley left mission work after a year, Corcoran and another Irish-speaking colleague from Tuam, Father William Ryan, continued to provide sermons in Irish on subsequent missions into the 1870s.[27]

Even where there was a willingness to preach in Irish, however, two difficulties stood in the way in this period: the availability of Irish-language written material from which to deliver a sermon and the growing number of parishioners proficient in only one language, making it difficult to accommodate both. On the first count, printed sermon books in Irish, while not unknown, did not approach the publication distribution of English-language texts.[28] Of the collections of sermons in Irish that did make it into print at this time, Gallagher's *Sixteen Irish Sermons* undoubtedly enjoyed a sustained and widespread print run and was joined briefly in later years by a text with more limited circulation printed by the Waterford language enthusiast Philip Barron, Father John Meany's *Irish Sermons with Translations* (1835).[29] But even with its immense popularity and wide dissemination, Gallagher's work hardly offered an adequate source for sustained and more regular preaching in Irish by priests. Other efforts to press sermons in Irish into print appear to have gained momentum but ultimately stalled, including a collection of fifty-two sermons by a Macroom priest named Father Roche that was recommended to Archbishop Bray in 1808 for print patronage.[30] Church administrators themselves recognized the problem of supplying sermon books, and some recommended the possibility of relying on reading substitute printed discourses in cases where preaching ability did not meet minimum standards, as when the diocesan statutes of Dublin in 1831 advised the use of simple catechetical discussion during instructions at Mass.[31]

Manuscript collections of sermons, however, clearly filled in some of this void. These consisted of both original compositions and also material translated from other languages. In some cases priests themselves were capable of producing these manuscripts, but in other instances they relied on local scribes. As with devotional writings, the sources and models for such texts were rooted securely in the Counter-Reformation, particularly the tradition of preaching developed in seventeenth-century France, with further influence by later printed English-language sources of the eighteenth and early nineteenth centuries developed by the same popular authors who dominated the output of English-language sermon books such as William Gahan, Richard Hayes, Joseph Morony, Barnaby Murphy, and the bishop of Ossory, James Lanigan.[32] Tadhg Ó Dúshláine has identified many of the continental writers used by subsequent Irish composers, including French preachers Pierre De Besse (1567–1639), Claude Joli (1610–78), Louis Bourdaloue (1632–1704), and Jean-Baptiste Massillon (1663–1742). Among the active churchmen drawing on these authors in assembling sermons were Bishop Seán Ó Briain (1700–1769) and the Reverend Seán Ó Conaire (1739–73), both of Cloyne.[33] At least five dozen sermons or fragments of sermons from eighteenth-century manuscripts have survived, either included as part of wider collections on devotional material or as part of sermon books produced by scribes.[34] Among the more prolific of such eighteenth-century composers was Father Conchubhar Mac Cairtéain (ca. 1658–1737) of Cork, noted earlier as a translator of devotional prose tracts, who produced a number of sermon translations and compositions that were still known a century later.[35]

By the nineteenth century, a small but vital tradition of composing, translating, and distributing prose sermons existed, especially in Munster, where networks of scribal activity had lasted longest. Many copyists were members of the same Cork circle active in producing devotional literature under the patronage of Bishop Murphy.[36] Other surviving *prônes* include the set of sermons written in the late eighteenth or early nineteenth century by an unknown writer, possibly a Father T. Donelan, on the subjects of cursing, stealing, and the duties of parents to raise virtuous children.[37] Pádraig Denn, another active participant in the production of devotional work, assembled several manuscript sermons, including a single collection of sixteen lessons on topics ranging from sin and confession to the virtues of humility.[38] Maurice Power (1791–1877), the parish priest of Lady's Bridge in east Cork, made his own translations of French sermons between 1832 and 1836.[39] The Waterford priest Pádraig de Bhal depended in part on Tomás Ó Iceadha to translate a handful of sermons from William Gahan's *Sermons and Moral Discourses for All the Sundays and Principal Festivals of the Year* (1799).[40] Father Jonathan Furlong, the devotional author, relied on Mícheál Píocóid, who copied out a sermon on baptism in 1836.[41]

Lack of access to formally trained scribes, however, did not prove to be a barrier, as evidenced by the number of sermon collections using nonscribal spellings based on English phonetics. This was even true for Munster, despite the strength of manuscript production in that province. Phonetically spelled sermon texts have been found among the papers of Diarmaid Ó Maoldomhnaigh, a priest of Rosscarbery, Co. Cork, and from a Tipperary priest, Michael Meighan.[42] A phonetically spelled sermon from County Kerry, written in the 1840s, has survived tucked away in the baptismal register.[43] Elsewhere, in Leinster, a surviving *prône* in phonetic spelling assembled by the parish priest John Heely (1759–1831) of County Louth between 1796 and 1816 relied for its sources on a familiar corpus of English-language devotional works including Robert Plowden's translation of *The Elevation of the Soul*, Dr. Hay's *The Sincere, Pious, and Devout Christian*, and Joseph Morony's *Sermons and Exhortations for the Whole Year*.[44] Connacht examples included a late eighteenth-century collection of phonetically spelled sermons found among the papers of Nicholas Archdeacon, the bishop of Kilfenora and Kilmacduagh.[45] And an extended near-contemporary set of instructions to accompany Mass, written by Father Myles Gibbons of Burrishoole, Co. Mayo, was clearly intended for the use of his fellow priests and curates who knew English but spoke Irish fluently and could use the collection to passably read using an English-based spelling. The collection offered instructions for the curate or priest in English, interspersed with lessons in Irish on the rosary, prayers, vestments, the elements of the Mass, the Acts, and litanies, all to be read, according to one passage, "to workmen and those of different occupations, etc."[46] This output of manuscript sermons was robust, as

Uileog de Búrca revealed in 1873: "There are several copies (say four to five) of sermons, containing some half hundred discourses, in the hands of several Catholic clergymen" in the Connacht region.[47]

Where a priest was not prepared to provide a full sermon in Irish, there was the simpler alternative of delivering the scriptural readings during the Mass in Irish. Scattered evidence suggests that this was the practice in some areas. William O'Neill Daunt alluded to a priest in Dunmanway in west Cork who customarily used an Irish text for the Epistle and Gospel portions of the Mass. He also noted that the bishop of Kildare and Leighlin, James Doyle, had insisted on vernacular readings for the same purposes.[48] Presumably, this prompted the use of an Irish-language Bible where appropriate. Bishop George Plunket of Elphin reported in 1826 that he had instituted a similar requirement regarding the reading of the Epistle and the Gospel "in the vernacular tongue."[49] The practice was probably more widespread, as Professor Patrick Murray of Maynooth confirmed as late as 1853. He noted that it was customary to quote scripture during services in Irish in those parts of Connacht and Munster that required it.[50]

As for the second problem, the increasingly diverse linguistic abilities of the congregations faced by curates and priests under pressure to provide instructions in the faith as the push for reform took hold, in no case was this more pressing than in the matter of providing sermons. While more and more young congregants were capable only of hearing a sermon in English, the old were more comfortable with Irish, while many parishioners lay somewhere in between. To accommodate the old, in this scenario, was to risk losing the young who represented the future direction of the church. One solution was to binate, offering Mass in English and another in Irish on the same day, or else to vary the language used at Mass on alternating Sundays, and indeed some priests chose these options. Writing on the Irish-speaking areas of south and west Kilkenny in 1800, William Tighe noted that "priests often preach alternatively in Irish and English."[51] Father Stephen Walsh, curate of the parish of Rath and Kilnaboy in the 1820s, also preached in both Irish and English, as did the dean, Father Terence O'Shaughnessy. The assistance of a curate considerably helped parish priests under pressure to offer two sermons at one sitting. For example, an instruction on the sacrament of confirmation delivered in English by a Kilkee curate in 1840 was followed up by the parish priest, who repeated the address in Irish.[52] The Limerick priest Father MacCloghan, encountered by Julius Rodenberg, similarly explained that "the priest in this country is compelled to preach in Irish here, in English there, and on the same Sunday to say mass in both languages."[53] William Heffernan, parish priest of Clerihan, Co. Tipperary, reported in 1852 that he offered two Masses on Sunday, one at 8:00 and another at 11:00, and that "instructions [were] always at Mass in English or Irish."[54] As Seán Pléimeann summarized it in 1873: "From Tramore in the county of Waterford all round to Galway Bay, i.e., in the three-fourths of Waterford, Cork, Kerry, and Clare, and in the portion of Tipperary in the diocese of Waterford and Lismore, preaching alternately in Irish and English is the rule wherever the clergyman knows Irish fairly."[55] The clergy generally followed this same practice in Connacht, according to Uileog de Búrca, who observed that the clergymen preached in Tuam cathedral "by order alternately in English and in Irish."[56]

But there were also drawbacks to this approach, beyond the obvious downside of dividing the congregation rather than addressing them as one body. Given the notoriously high parishioners-to-priest ratios in Ireland in the years before the famine, officials were hard-pressed, especially in rural areas, to provide one Sunday Mass per congregation, let alone two. In fact, the church discouraged granting permission to priests to binate in order to emphasize the unified gathering of a community for devotions.[57] Unless advantaged with one or more curates to assist him, many priests also had to say Mass at two or three chapels each Sunday—a necessity made more onerous by horse transportation and by the requirement that a priest fast until the completion of his duties. Facing such choices, and in particular the option of targeting the older, Irish-speaking parishioners or their younger English-speaking cohorts, many priests chose to rely on English. As the Galway farmer Seámus Uí Riagáin, born in 1853, heard his parish priest explain the situation: "Is minic a dubhairt sé linn go dtabharfadh sé na seanmóirí uaidh sa nGaeidhilge acht go mb'eagal leis ná tuigfeadh an mhuinntear óg a chuid chainnte mar ná raibh a ghaedhilge acub" (He often told us that he would give out his sermons in Irish, except that he was afraid that the young people wouldn't understand his speech because they didn't have Irish).[58] Among areas that had once featured sermons in both languages, the evidence seems to suggest that by the 1870s priests were no longer making such accommodations. As Proinsias Ó Catháin put it in 1873, "The custom of preaching sermons in Irish has not been so much practised in the present day as it had been in former times, for this reason, that a great many of the old people who understood that language have passed away."[59] Ó Catháin had much the same to say for Ulster: "Preaching in Irish had been much practised about 50 years ago, but the discouragements and hindrances which have since arisen with regard to the native tongue, together with the great cultivation of the English language among the people, have rendered it almost unnecessary to preach in Irish."[60] Facing congregations in which fluent Irish speakers made up an ever-shrinking proportion, priests became hesitant, as one observer put it, to endure the added burden of composing Irish sermons.[61] Indeed, parishioners may have, in some cases, even outstripped their clergy in terms of language shift. Bishop John O'Doherty of Derry, responding to inquiries on the subject, affirmed in 1894 that although a "considerable number" of his diocesan clergy knew Irish, they no longer preached in it because English predominated in the region.[62]

In making this decision, some clergymen no doubt favored the simplicity of providing one instruction instead of two. But for other priests, however practical the decision to shift from Irish to English, it was a choice made with some regret. "In my chapels I am, very much against my will but still yielding to a hard, a sad necessity, obliged to address my flock in English," reported Father Thomas T. Murray of Kilcolman, Co. Cork, in late 1856.[63] Bishop William Keane of Cloyne, speaking of his confirmation sermons, expressed similar feelings a few years later after visiting Clondrohid chapel: "I found it necessary to speak Irish to the congregations in Kilnamartara [Kilnamartery], Ballyvourney, and Clondrohid, as in those parishes many don't speak or understand English. In all the other parishes English was more necessary; and in only a few of them was it necessary to say some things in Irish." As Keane lamented at the end of his visitation season in 1864, "The Irish language is disappearing. Proofs of this sad loss are met with everywhere."[64] Nevertheless, some priests no doubt continued to try to bridge the gap. Father Ó Conghaile, for example, the priest mentioned by Uí Regáin, delivered his sermons to the general congregation in English before "he would explain the sermons in Irish to the old people who didn't have the English" (Mhínngheadh sé na seanmíurí i nGaedhilge dos na sean-ndaoine ná raibh a[n] bearla acu).[65]

Such accommodation was also emphasized for confessions, in which the desirability of satisfying this sacramental obligation in the language most comfortably spoken was readily apparent. Here the problems were not nearly so manifest as with delivering sermons, since any bilingual priest could adequately hear confession and provide absolution to members of both linguistic communities. But problems arose as the number of English monoglot priests increased, especially among the younger ranks of the clergy who gradually replaced their bilingual antecedents. Older priests who still spoke Irish became especially valuable in this regard, as was reported by Ó Catháin in the 1870s: "In regard to the clergy themselves very few of them are competent to preach a sermon in Irish; and whenever such becomes necessary, an old priest or clergyman is generally selected for the purpose.... The Church of Rome has been obliged to supply her various districts with a sufficient number of clergy who are eligible for the purpose of hearing confessions in Irish."[66] The linguistic limitations of many of the younger priests also attracted the disapproving notice of John O'Donovan, who remarked pessimistically to his longtime friend John Windele in 1850, "The young priests are doing more to extinguish the old language than any other class in the community, because they neither preach nor hear confessions through the medium of it."[67] Inevitably, the supply of older, Irish-speaking priests began to dwindle, too, and by the 1870s some parishes were failing to find adequate confessors in Irish. According to Ó Catháin, "Whenever a priest is not available for this purpose, the party confessing is (I am informed) obliged to make his or her confession even to a priest who is ignorant of the Irish language!"[68] Yet the problem was not universal and varied from parish to parish. Speaking for his parish of Glenville, Co. Cork, in 1894, Father O'Mahony reported that "the majority of the parish priests of this diocese possess a practical knowledge of the Irish language and make use of it occasionally in hearing the confessions of the comparatively small number of old people who cannot express themselves intelligently in English."[69]

As the availability of Irish-speaking priests contracted, there were ways for the elderly to make confessions in their own language, subject to some inconvenience. The folklore collector Michael Murphy, speaking to informants in Omagh, Co. Tyrone, in 1951, encountered elderly residents whose grandparents had been able to confess in Irish by waiting until a particular priest made his rounds of the parish: "I was told by Mary Meenan of Crockanboy [aged 78] that before the district of Rousky-Greencastle was divided into two separate parishes, the parish priest resided at Rousky. One such priest was Father Peter McGeown, a Gaelic speaker. She said her own people, especially her grandmother, 'would have to wait until Father Peter came up to make her confession; the other curates didn't know Irish.'" In cases where an Irish-speaking priest or curate did not make his rounds of a particular community, Irish speakers overcame this difficulty by traveling to adjacent parishes to secure absolution: "I was told by Pat McCullagh (Pat Micky Brian) of Seskinshule, Greencastle, and [a] native of Formil townland [about 70 years old], that either his mother or grandmother, his mother I think, had to go from Formil to Carrickmore to a priest to make her confession, because no Gaelic speaking priest resided any nearer to her."[70]

Outside of delivering sermons and confessions, the final aspect of clerical duties that was most impinged upon by the language question was catechetical instruction. In addition to the general post-Reformation emphasis on catechizing the young, pressure to attain basic religious understanding fell especially strongly on parishioners and their priests, because understanding the faith was directly tied to suitability for confirmation, a ceremony that took place during the annual visitation of the bishop. For the parish this occasion was a highly anticipated public event that included a special sermon in addition to the presentation of children to be tested for their grasp of the essentials of the faith. The format of this test, in which children (and unconfirmed adults) answered questions in front of the congregation, undoubtedly offered a nerve-wracking experience that represented a trial not only of the children but also of the parish priest himself and of his attention to his spiritual duties. If the children had been taught by a local schoolteacher, then the capabilities of that instructor came under scrutiny as well. Recollections of confirmation reveal the excitement and stress of the occasion, as was evident in the experience of a Donegal farmer born in 1854:

> Tá mé corradh agus ceithre sgór anois acht ma tá féin níor chaill mé mo dhóigh no mo chuimhne. Tá cuimhne mhaith agam ar an lá a chuaidh mé chuig an Easbóg.... Bhí achan ndúine ag fanacht go cruaidh le lá an Easbóig mar bhéad cat ag dúil le lucóg, cearthaidh ar chuid aca ar eagla na n-éireochadh leo ins an scrudú a bhí rompa.... Bhí na sloighthe annsin romhainn eadar fir, mna, agus paistí, chuaidh muid fhéin isteach agus crith eagla orainn ar eagla nach mbíodh a fhios againn an Teagasg Críost nuair a chuirfheadh an Sagairt Mór Ó Domhnall ceist orainn, ach ní muid a ba mheasa agus cluinfhidh sibh. Ba í scoil Pholl A' Gharraidh bhigh an chead scoil ar sgairteach uirthí. Tháinig mo *thurn* fhéin agus chuaidh mé go dtí an altóir go ceannasgach os comhair an áthair Mhóir Uí Domhnaill grast ó Dhia ar anamh. Ca méad cineal peacaidh ann ars seiséan.[71]

> [I am more than eighty now, but even if I am, I haven't lost my judgment or my memory. I remember well the day I went to the bishop.... Everyone was waiting keenly for the bishop's day like a cat would wait for a mouse; some of them terrified from the fear that they wouldn't pass the test that was before them.... Then the crowds were there before us, men, women, and children; we went in quaking with fear that we didn't know the catechism when big Reverend O'Donnell would ask us questions, but we were not the worst you will ever hear. It was the little Poll A' Gharraidh school that was first called on. My own turn came, and I went boldly to the altar before the big Father O'Donnell, God bless his soul. "How many kinds of sins are there?" he asked.]

This pressure would increase as bishops took a more visible role in diocesan administration in this period, a trend aided by easier travel and improved communications.[72]

By the end of the eighteenth century and first decades of the nineteenth century, the Irish Catholic church had already begun taking institutional steps to ensure better catechetical training. Dublin diocesan statutes required parishes to employ at least one schoolmaster to teach religious doctrine in 1730, a trend that sharpened after 1733 when the government-instituted charter schools set up under the Incorporated Society for Promoting English Protestant Schools in Ireland threatened to usurp church authority in this area.[73] One of the most important developments was the encouragement of Sunday-school teaching either before or after Mass, an initiative with deep roots in the eighteenth century so that, already in 1800, many Irish dioceses already had a system of proto–parish schools in existence that foreshadowed the large-scale efforts of the Catholic Church to exert control over education in the nineteenth century.[74] In these schools the clergy, or more often a lay schoolteacher, provided the necessary religious instruction for the literate and illiterate alike. No doubt because of this strong overlap between day schoolteachers and Sunday school instructors, in some cases catechism was supplemented by additional basic subjects, as Archbishop Murray explained in 1825: "There is generally a moral school in the chapels either before Mass or after Mass, where a number of pious people, men and women, teach; the men take charge of the boys, and the women of the girls, and teach them the catechism; sometimes they read for them a moral book according to the zeal of the pastor, and there are some instances where other instruction in reading and arithmetic are also given."[75] Similar arrangements were common in Connacht, according to Archbishop Oliver Kelly of Tuam. In Westport, for example, a large crowd of students received instruction as follows: "At Westport chapel on each Sunday there are 800 children instructed for at least an hour or an hour and a half. They are divided into different classes; those who cannot read are instructed apart by themselves; those who can read have certain lessons in the catechism marked out to them, which they are to learn in the course of the week; and on Sunday they are examined in their respective classes in the parts of the catechism that are marked out for them."[76] Both Murray and Kelly agreed that it was common for lay teachers to instruct the children—more than forty in Westport and Castlebar, for example, including both men and women. In country districts, Kelly noted, these duties often fell on Catholic weekday schoolteachers.[77] As weekly schooling became better established in Ireland under the national school system, and especially by midcentury when the Catholic Church had asserted *de facto* control over individual schools, catechetical education became a common aspect of regular school attendance as well.

Part of the driving force behind the catechetical work of Sunday-school teachers was the Confraternity (or Sodality) of the Christian Doctrine, a lay organization first founded in the sixteenth century in Italy—Charles Borromeo was an early proponent—with branches for both men and women in many (perhaps most) Irish parishes by the second half of the eighteenth century.[78] Strongest in the towns and more densely populated rural regions of Ireland—in the "populous parishes of the south and west," according to the 1825 education inquiry—the confraternity was clearly well established by 1800 in dioceses such as Kildare and Leighlin and well known to the bishops from Connacht and Munster.[79] The members of the confraternity devoted themselves to providing catechetical teaching on Sundays throughout Irish parishes. Individual branches even maintained a lending library in their locality to provide religious material. To help supply the Catholic population with the necessary devotional works and teaching manuals essential to improving religious education, the bishops founded the Catholic Book Society in 1827 at the urging of Bishop Doyle. This society printed, according to its own claims, five million copies of religious material, including catechisms, for wide circulation at cheap prices. In 1835 a second association called the Catholic Society for Ireland began similar work by distributing printed works to lending libraries and religious confraternities engaged in religious education.[80]

The place still accorded in some areas to the Irish language in this religious instruction was revealed in inquiries made by the commissioners of education in 1824 and 1825. Surviving returns from south Cork, for instance, confirm the use of "Butler's catechism, 2 Irish catechisms..., [an] Irish testament, Irish and English spelling book," and "no English version of [the] bible or testament" at the school run by Daniel Sullivan out of a private house in the town of Skibbereen. Another school in Skibbereen run by Owen MacCarthy relied on Butler and "one Irish catechism by Dr. Coppinger." The Coppinger Irish-language catechism was in use in another school in the same parish of Creagh run by Jeremiah Collins. At John Fitzgerald's school in the parish of Tullagh both English- and Irish-language catechisms could be found.[81] Notably, this evidence also confirmed that schoolteachers used Irish and English simultaneously in their catechetical instruction, accommodating students regardless of their language preference. Further information collected by the school commissioners, while exclusively concerned with the use of Bibles in the classroom, nevertheless suggested indirectly that the Irish language was used for general religious instruction in many day schools run by Catholics. A County Meath Catholic teacher named Peter Sheridan reportedly read the scriptures in Irish to his ninety-six students, a habit that probably encouraged the Irish Society to put him on its payroll as a scriptural instructor.[82] Charles Hanly, a schoolteacher at Stonehall, Co. Clare, read to his students from a copy of the scriptures in Irish, as did Charles McCarthy of Kilkerran parish in County Cork. Similar returns confirmed that the Bible was read by Catholic schoolteachers in Irish in schools in Kerry, Limerick, Leitrim, Roscommon, and Sligo.[83]

Nothing was more revealing, however, of the prevalence of catechizing in the Irish language than the recorded numbers of students presenting themselves to the bishop for confirmation requiring questioning in Irish. For example, Daniel Coughlan, a national school teacher from Kilbrittain, in southwest Cork, affirmed in 1881, "Until within about 30 years ago, the priests and schoolmasters of the rural districts here used the Irish language as the medium of religious instruction; so that, until then, not more than about one percent would be presented to the bishop for examination for confirmation, to answer in English."[84] Visitation records have survived particularly well for the diocese of Cloyne and Ross in County Cork and show that significant numbers of children were confirmed in Irish well into the late 1870s and early 1880s. Reporting from the parish of Banteer in June 1828, for example, Bishop Michael Collins noted that the "catechism[s] taught are the short English and Irish." Both were in use in the united parishes of Inishcarra and Cloghroe in that same year, as well as in Ballynamona, Grenagh, Liscarroll, Churchtown, Tullylease, Kilbolane, Milford, Ballyhooly, Castletownroche, Rathcormack, Conna, and Aghada parishes. Catechetical teaching societies imparted instruction in Irish in some cases, as evidenced by the details from the parish of Mallow, where "the catechism is said to be taught by a society of pious persons," and yet a number of the children were confirmed in Irish. Just after midcentury, catechizing in Irish still remained strong. In 1862 in the parish of Cloyne, 117 out of 203 children answered in Irish, and at Youghal in that year, 73 out of 439 did the same. In 1871 in the parish of Kilnamartery 89 out of 101 youths (and two adults) who presented for confirmation recited their catechism in Irish. In the parish of Barryroe half the children answered in Irish as late as 1880, and in Ardfield parish in that same year more than one-fifth responded in that fashion. Even in overwhelmingly English-speaking parishes a handful had been instructed in Irish. In Macroom in 1873, of the 119 children confirmed, 7 boys and 4 girls had to be examined in Irish. In other words, far from an unknown practice, Irish continued to be the language through which teachers imparted catechetical knowledge to Irish-speaking students in this region for the better part of the nineteenth century.[85]

The question of willingness to provide pastoral care in Irish brushes up against the closely related matter of language proficiency among Irish priests and bishops and the extent and timing of the emergence of clerical monolingualism in

English. As late as the end of the seventeenth century, it is likely that many Irish priests still had a weak command of English. When Father Bernard McGorke, accused of exercising Roman jurisdiction as dean of Armagh, was brought before a justice of the peace in 1682 to testify, he pleaded that "he the examinate hath not the English tongue well," and that his prior conversations with a justice of the peace should be understood in the light of his "not being able to express his mind fitly in English."[86] Many priests were more comfortable in Latin than in English, as was evident from the report of a government spy in 1667 concerning a secret meeting of priests with their bishop—a meeting at which "they spoke nothing but Latin."[87] Others, however, already had a strong enough command of all three languages to translate written works. The Killala priest and vicar general Father Paul Higgin, for example, who converted to Anglicanism in 1680, was recommended by the Protestant bishop of Ossory for a job at Trinity College in translating "into Irish [a] practical book of divinity [in] Latin or English adequate to the understanding of the poorer Irish."[88] By the eighteenth century, if the expectations of the government regarding the ability of priests to deliver addresses to their congregations in either English or Irish are a gauge, clerical proficiency in both languages had become the norm. The acts passed during the reign of Queen Anne concerning converted priests acknowledged explicitly their ability to read the liturgy in either language, while the proposed penal bill of 1755 insisted that "registered priests shall be bound at each Mass they celebrate to exhort their congregation in English or Irish to pray for King George and his successors by name."[89] For most priests, bilingualism was the norm by the late eighteenth century.

The story for eighteenth-century bishops was broadly similar, with the added feature that most, if not all, would not have been Irish monoglots by the seventeenth and eighteenth centuries given the Old English background of many members of the hierarchy and the prelates' status as members of Ireland's ruling class families. As has been shown, among them were several who were not only bilingual but also capable of producing religious texts and language reference materials in Irish. It should not be assumed, however, that the subsequent hierarchy of the late eighteenth century and throughout the nineteenth century were English monoglots. On the contrary, quite a few bishops of these years were clearly bilingual—and long before the well-known bilingual prelates of the late nineteenth-century language revival years like Dublin archbishop William Walsh (1841–1921) and Cardinal Michael Logue of Armagh (1840–1924). Denis Conway, bishop of Limerick from 1779 to 1796, spoke Irish and was indeed capable of haranguing a crowd in Irish for two hours in opposition to Whiteboy disturbances, as he attested in a letter to the archbishop of Cashel.[90] Bishop Theophilus Mac Cartan of Down and Connor (served 1761–78) was known to preach in Irish.[91] Bishop Matthew McKenna, who served Cloyne and Ross from 1769 to 1791, was a friend of Seán Ó Briain and a proficient Irish speaker, according to his obituary: "He was very partial to the mother tongue which he spoke upon almost every occasion and in every company. He always preached in this polite language."[92] Thomas Bray, archbishop of Cashel from 1792 to 1820, studied Irish while in Paris, as his instructions from Cardinal Marefoschi in transferring him from the Sainte Garde college at Avignon to France informed him that he was to study it along with English while there.[93] William Coppinger, bishop of Cloyne and Ross from 1791 to 1831, produced an Irish-language catechism and had a sufficient reputation among Irish scribes to merit a praise poem written in 1788 by Dáibhí de Barra of Cork.[94] Nicholas Archdeacon, who served Kilmacduagh and Kilfenora from 1800 to 1824, was likely the author of a set of Irish sermons found among his papers, as noted above, having learned the language later in life at the hands of a fellow priest.[95] Bishop John Young of Limerick (served 1796–1813) produced the Irish-language catechism that saw considerable use in his diocese.

Of the early- and mid-nineteenth-century bishops, there is clear evidence that David Walsh of Cloyne and Ross (served 1847–49),[96] Patrick MacMullan of Down and Connor (served 1793–1824),[97] Cornelius Egan of Kerry (served 1824–56),[98] William Abraham of Waterford and Lismore (served 1830–37),[99] William O'Higgins of Ardagh (served 1829–53),[100] Thomas Coen of Clonfert (served 1831–47),[101] Bartholomew Crotty of Cloyne and Ross (served 1833–46),[102] William Keane of Cloyne and Ross (served 1857–75), Patrick Durcan of Achonry (served 1852–75),[103] Timothy Murphy of Cloyne and Ross (served 1849–56),[104] John Derry of Clonfert (served 1847–70), Bishop Hugh Conway of Killala (served 1872–93),[105] Archbishop of Armagh Daniel McGettigan (served 1870–87),[106] Patrick Duggan of Clonfert (served 1872–96),[107] Archbishop of Tuam John MacEvilly (served 1881–1902),[108] and, of course, John MacHale of Tuam (served 1834–81) all spoke Irish fluently and delivered sermons in the language. Less certain, but within the realm of possibility, was that Bishop James Doyle had at least some knowledge of Irish.[109] Tellingly, other bishops of the generation born around the turn of the century had not been raised as native Irish speakers but became convinced of the need to learn it later in life as a means to administer their dioceses. This included John Murphy of Cork, patron of the large-scale scribal initiative of the late 1810s and 1820s, who commenced learning Irish at the age of forty after discovering upon his consecration as bishop that he "felt it was a duty of conscience to learn that language, and thereby to be able to examine, in the Irish catechism, such persons as should be presented to me for confirmation."[110] Another late learner was Michael Collins of Cloyne and Ross, who was able to acquire sufficient Irish to preach by the time of his death in 1832.[111] Michael O'Hea of Ross (served 1858–76), born in 1808, did not learn Irish until after his ordination as a priest but became proficient enough to preach.[112] Less successful in learning Irish but similarly concerned that duties as a bishop in the nineteenth century required it was Bishop George Brown of Galway, who reported "making some attempts to read the Irish catechism" in 1835.[113]

More systematic evidence is available for levels of Irish speaking among the nineteenth-century clergy. Of course, the natural source for this type of query—the Irish censuses—did not address the matter of language prior to 1851,

TABLE 3: Male Irish speakers in the Barony of North Salt, Co. Kildare, 1851–91

Year	Male Irish speakers, North Salt	Male population, North Salt	Percent Irish Speaking	Total male Irish speakers, Co. Kildare	Total male population, Co. Kildare	Percent Irish speaking
1851	227	4,123	5.50	422	48,528	0.86
1861	273	3,652	7.48	478	48,960	0.98
1871	104	3,418	3.04	209	44,946	0.47
1881	158	3,065	5.15	444	40,701	1.09
1891	132	2,746	4.80	279	38,407	0.73

SOURCE: *Census of Ireland for the Year 1851. Part I: Area, Population, and Number of Houses, by Townlands and Electoral Divisions. Part IV: Report on Ages and Education*, pp. 16–17 [2053], H.C. 1856, xxix; *Census of Ireland for the Year 1851. Part I: Area, Population, and Number of Houses, by Townlands and Electoral Divisions. Part VI: General Report*, p. 58 [2134], H.C. 1856, xxxi; *Census of Ireland for the Year 1861, Part II: Report and Tables on Ages and Education, Vol. 1*, pp. 107, 337 [3204-I], H.C. 1863, lvi; *Census of Ireland for the Year 1861, Part II: Report and Tables on Ages and Education, Vol. 2*, pp. 990–93 [3204-I], H.C. 1863, lvii; *Census of Ireland for the Year 1871. Part I: Area, Population, and Number of Houses; Also the Ages, Civil Condition, Occupations, Birthplaces, Religion, and Education of the People. Vol. I: Province of Leinster*, pp. 213, 298 [C. 662], H.C. 1872, lxvii; *Census of Ireland for the Year 1881. Part I: Area, House, and Populations; Also the Ages, Civil or Conjugal Condition, Occupations, Birthplaces, Religion, and Education of the People. Vol. I: Province of Leinster*, pp. 213, 298 [C. 3042], H.C. 1881, xcvii; *Census of Ireland for the Year 1891, Part I: Area, Houses, and Population: Also the Ages, Civil or Conjugal Condition, Occupations, Birthplaces, Religion, and Education of the People. Vol. I: Province of Leinster*, pp. 213, 298 [C. 6515], H.C. 1890–91, xcv.

and since very few of the original census returns prior to 1901 have survived, it is very difficult to get at the level of clerical proficiency at an individual level. Nevertheless, a picture of the language proficiency of nineteenth-century Irish priests can be gleaned from a number of smaller representative samples taken from the aggregate census tables of 1851–91 and from diocesan records. The most fruitful of these sources is data on the language proficiency of clerical students attending seminary. Brian Ó Cuív first examined such figures in regard to the percentage of young clerical students possessing Irish at Maynooth in 1851.[114] Because of the location of the college in the barony of North Salt in County Kildare, a county with very few Irish speakers (1 percent or less of its population between 1851 and 1891), the presence of any significant number of male Irish speakers under the age of thirty stands out in the published census

TABLE 4: Estimated levels of Irish speaking at Maynooth, 1851–91

Year	Male Irish speakers aged 10–29, North Salt	Estimated number of students at Maynooth[a]	Percent Irish speaking	Percent Irish speaking (all of Ireland)[b]
1851	204	520	39.2	23.3 (est: 32.6)
1861	254	521	48.8	19.1 (est: 26.7)
1871	97	372	26.1	15.1 (est: 21.2)
1881	132	500	26.4	18.2
1891	116	520	22.3	14.5

[a] As there are no figures for the exact years, these are estimates based on data from the visitations of trustees at comparable times. There were 525 students in 1847 according to the visitors' report of that year, and 519 were noted in the 1853 report. The figure of 521 for 1861 is taken from the 1860 report; there were 372 students in 1873 according to Corish (*Maynooth College*, 228), which may have been an even larger number than for 1871. Corish also offers 500 as the number for 1881; the figure of 520 for 1891 represents an estimated full return to pre-1869 levels and was close to the size of the student body in 1901, when the comparable figure stood at 525.

[b] As has been long accepted, the 1851–71 censuses underestimated the real number of Irish speakers because the format of the census questionnaire relegated the language question to a footnote. The figures from 1881, which record an apparent jump in Irish speakers, actually reflected a more accurate count. Reg Hindley estimates that the earlier censuses understated the real number by as much as 40%. A recalculation based on this assumption would put the figure for 1851 at 2,134,000 speakers, or 32.6% of the population, 26.7% for 1861, and 21.2% for 1871—still lower than the percentages of Irish-speaking students at Maynooth in those years. See Hindley, *The Death of the Irish Language: A Qualified Obituary* (London: Routledge, 1990), 15–19.

reports. Expanding on Ó Cuív's method, table 3 compares the level of Irish proficiency among males in North Salt between 1851 and 1891.

With levels of Irish speaking several percentage points above the norm for the surrounding areas, North Salt clearly had a disproportionately high number of persons proficient in Irish. In fact, around one-half or more of all the Irish speakers found by census takers in County Kildare each year were located in this barony. Not only was the Irish-speaking population of North Salt unusually high, but with nearly all of these speakers concentrated in the younger male cohorts aged between 10 and 29, it is clear that this group represented more or less directly the number of students claiming Irish-language proficiency at Maynooth.[115] Table 4 summarizes the data for this age group and compares its members to the estimated size of the student body at large. Enrollment at Maynooth varied from year to year, but after 1850 the college generally maintained between 500 and 525 students, as 500 was the number of free spaces funded by the 1845 annual grant. The student body reached a peak of 533 in the 1869–70 school year, declined after government financial support ended with the passage of the Church of Ireland Disestablishment Act in 1869, and returned to 500 in 1881–82.[116] For the sake of comparison, the final column in table 4 offers the percentage of Irish speakers (bilinguals and monolinguals combined) returned each year for the island as a whole.

From these figures it is clear that between two-fifths and one-half of the student population spoke Irish at midcentury and in the decade immediately afterward, that the proportion fell to one-fourth or less thereafter, and that the number of Irish speakers fluctuated rather than declined in any linear fashion. Evidence from Maynooth visitations and parliamentary education inquiries confirms this finding. Testifying in 1826, Father Philip Dowley, a senior dean at Maynooth, believed that "something over one-half" of Maynooth students could converse in Irish at that time.[117] A former student who matriculated at Maynooth in 1838, on the other hand, recalled that in that year Irish speaking "was confined to the students of the west and south, and even of these, some spoke it but indifferently. Supposing the [entering] class to be about forty in number, I would say ten or twelve spoke it vernacularly."[118] This estimate would have put Irish on a weaker footing for matriculating students in 1838—at 25 to 30 percent—but certainly within the bounds of later census figures.

If the student body at Maynooth is taken to be fairly representative of the type of students entering the priesthood in general, then the proportion of Irish speakers becoming priests in Ireland after midcentury ranged between 25 and 50 percent, with higher levels (closer to 40 or 50 percent) up until the 1860s, before a decline to 20 or 25 percent thereafter. At first glance this would seem to indicate a weakness in the language among the clergy, as Ó Cuív himself argued in reference to the 1851 figures. Indeed, Irish-speaking clerical students would probably have been in the minority for most of the nineteenth century. Yet a second look suggests a different perspective. Kevin Collins, for example, reacting to Ó Cuív's findings for Maynooth students in 1851, has noted that the percentage speaking Irish in that year exceeded the reported national percentage of only 23 percent.[119] Even given the undercount of Irish speakers in the censuses before 1881, the percentage of Irish-speaking students at Maynooth outpaced the estimated percentage of Irish speakers in the country as a whole throughout the second half of the nineteenth century (see column 5 in table 4 above). Moreover, again it must be kept in mind that the Maynooth cohorts of the mid-nineteenth century and after were replacing an older clerical set whose Irish proficiencies would have been higher. This would indicate an even better ratio of Irish-speaking clergy to Irish-speaking parishioners in earlier decades than the proficiencies of the younger priests represented in the Maynooth numbers suggest.

The comparison of Maynooth Irish speakers to the country as a whole has some weakness in that it ignores the reality that the priesthood was not evenly distributed over the entire country. A more apt comparison can be made between the percentage of new clergy speaking Irish and the overall percentage of priests assigned to dioceses in Irish-speaking regions. In 1845 the areas with the largest number of Irish speakers were located in the ecclesiastical provinces of Cashel (with 738 parish priests and curates) and Tuam (with 407 parish priests and curates) and in the diocese of Raphoe (with 54 parish priests and curates)—a total of 1,199 out of 2,393, or 50 percent of all priests in Ireland.[120] If it is assumed that significant pockets of English speakers within these areas were offset by Irish speakers outside of these dioceses in the ecclesiastical provinces of Armagh and Dublin, it is reasonable to conclude that one-half of all priests in Ireland at midcentury ministered to parishes with significant numbers of Irish speakers. About 50 percent of the new students emerging from Maynooth and from the other clerical colleges would also have needed to be Irish speaking to replace these priests. From this perspective it appears that the Irish-speaking 40 to 50 percent of young clerical graduates would have been fairly proportional to—but certainly not in excess of—the language needs of the church at midcentury.

Such aggregate estimates, however useful, demand still closer inspection of the language abilities of priests at the local level. In particular, how well did the language capabilities of priests match up with the language proficiency prevalent in their home dioceses, to which they often returned as pastors? Fortunately, a set of records from the diocese of Cloyne in Co. Cork, which lists the young candidates proposed for clerical training and ordination, sheds light on this topic for numerous years between 1849 and 1871. In Cloyne, as in many dioceses at that time, the practice had emerged of holding an annual formal concursus to test the classical training of prospective candidates for the priesthood and to rank them for the purpose of establishing their seminary of destination. In the records surviving from this period the Cloyne authorities also included an indication of the level of the Irish-language proficiency of their candidates, along with their home parish, age, and in some cases the ultimate college or seminary destination. Moreover, because Cloyne, with a population of almost 437,000 and more than 120 priests in 1834, was the most populous diocese in Ireland at this time,[121] the concursus records can be taken as strongly representative of the Irish-language proficiency of a group of priests ministering to a large section of the population of the country as a whole. Altogether more than 200 prospective clerical students are represented in the sample, as summarized by concursus year in table 5.

While language proficiency, as well as the number of candidates, varied from year to year, the Cloyne records demonstrate a few clear trends. First, although by the end of the 1860s a decline had begun in the number of young men able to use Irish, up to that time between two-thirds and three-quarters (or more) of the candidates spoke Irish. The percentage of the population as a whole who spoke Irish in County Cork, which constitutes the closest unit of analysis with which to make a comparison with the diocese of Cloyne, provides a useful context for these figures. The count in Cork returned 52 percent of the population as Irish speaking in 1851, 42 percent in 1861, and 34 percent in 1871. If these figures are revised upward by 40 percent, as proposed by Reg Hindley to rectify the undercounting of Irish speakers in those years, one arrives at the following figures for County Cork: 73 percent speaking Irish in 1851, 59 percent in 1861, and 48 percent in 1871.[122] On this basis it appears that the speaking of Irish among Cloyne clerical students fairly closely matched that among the population as a whole until around 1864. Numbers fluctuated from year to year, with certain clerical cohorts far more Irish speaking than the general population in this region, and other cohorts slightly less. After 1864, however, Irish speaking among students dipped, as in only two years (1866 and 1868) was the percentage of Irish speakers higher than in the population at large (the level for the general population remained closer to one-half). This shift around the mid-1860s is also revealed if one compares the average percentage of Irish-speaking candidates for the period 1849–64 with that for 1865–71. Up to 1864 the percentage of Irish-speaking candidates per year had averaged about 70 percent. Thereafter the average fell to about 35 percent for the years 1865–71.

On the assumption that the slate of candidates gathered at the concursus each year strongly mirrored the eventual makeup of ordained priests who returned to their home dioceses, it is clear that in Cloyne the proportion of Irish-speaking priests matched the proportion of the population speaking Irish until the last two decades of the nineteenth century at the earliest. Even the drop in Irish-speaking

TABLE 5: Language and candidates at Cloyne diocesan concursus, 1849–71

Year of concursus	Number of Irish speakers	Number of candidates	Percent Irish speaking
1849	6	12	50.0
1850	10	14	71.4
1852	7	11	63.6
1856	13	15	86.7
1858	11	12	91.7
1859	6	9	66.7
1862	10	16	62.5
1863	15	20	75.0
1864	13	20	65.0
1865	6	14	42.9
1866	7	11	63.6
1867	4	13	30.8
1868	5	9	55.6
1869	1	8	12.5
1870	1	9	11.1
1871	3	12	25.0
Total	118	205	57.6

SOURCE: Murphy Papers, Cloyne Diocesan Archives, 1795.10/1/1849, 1795.05/64/1850, 1795.05/19/1852, 1795.05/14/1856; Keane Papers, Cloyne Diocesan Archives, 1796.05/198/1858, 1796.05/178/1859, 1796.05/170/1862, 1796.05/187/1863, 1796.05/144/1864, 1796.05/190/1865, 1796.05/172/1866, 1796.05/148/1867, 1796.05/225/1868, 1796.05/244/1869, 1796.05/96/1870, 1796.05/249/1871. The language proficiency of candidates was assessed by the use of a variety of descriptions, including "good," "very good," "yes," "fair," "middling," "med," and "mediocre" (counted here as having Irish) and "little," "none," "scarcely any," "no," and "very little" (counted here as not having Irish). Of 118 candidates counted here as speaking Irish, only 7 were described as anything other than "good," "very good," or "yes."

prospective priests after the mid-1860s would have been delayed in its effects. If these young men returned to serve in Cloyne parishes after five to eight years at Maynooth, and if they spent an initial period of time as curates to older priests, many of whom spoke Irish, then the growing numbers of English monolingual priests would not have started to become a serious problem until the 1880s or later. The Cloyne evidence also addresses an issue raised by Collins. He has suggested, in reaction to Ó Cuív's figures for the level of clerical Irish speaking at Maynooth, that the robust percentage of language proficiency in Irish there represented a divide in the type of clerical education received by English speakers on the one hand and Irish speakers on the other. Wealthier families, Collins argued, would have been more likely to be English speaking and able to afford to send their sons to continental seminaries rather than to Maynooth or another domestic college.[123] This would suggest that a divide in language as well as in wealth separated priests educated in Ireland from those educated overseas and that perhaps Maynooth-educated priests comprised a comparatively higher proportion of Irish speakers. If this notion were correct, it would also challenge the adequacy of the cohorts of newly ordained priests to meet the language needs of Irish Catholics, as the foreign-educated clergy (about 20 percent of the total each year)[124] would not have been supplying its share of Irish-speaking priests to meet the basic needs of the church as a whole.

The data from Cloyne, in which officials identified the seminary or college destination of forty-eight candidates, challenge this proposition that there was any distinction between foreign and domestic students. Table 6 summarizes the destination and Irish-language abilities of these young men. Conclusions regarding trends at individual institutions cannot be established because of the small size of the sample, particularly for the domestic seminaries apart from Maynooth.[125] But if one considers the domestic and foreign colleges on the whole, the notion of a divide on the basis of collegial location is strongly undermined. Cloyne diocesan students were equally split between those destined for continental schools and those headed for Irish colleges and seminaries, with the percentage speaking Irish actually higher for those who traveled to Rome, Louvain, or Paris. This finding lends further credibility to the use of the Maynooth student population as a strong indication of overall clerical proficiency in Irish, since students attending foreign colleges likely exhibited few linguistic differences.

The fact that this data was collected by the bishops of Cloyne and Ross at all, of course, points to another significant feature of church administration, at least in the case of this locality: concern about the language abilities of its priests

TABLE 6: Language and Cloyne diocesan candidates by destination

Destination	Number of Irish speakers	Number of candidates	Percent Irish speaking
Domestic colleges			
All Hallows	1	1	100
Carlow	1	4	25.0
Castleknock	0	1	0
Maynooth	9	15	60.0
St. Colman's	0	2	0
Thurles	0	1	0
Total	11	24	45.8
Foreign colleges			
Paris	9	10	90.0
Louvain	3	7	42.9
Rome	3	7	42.9
Total	15	24	62.5

SOURCE: Murphy Papers, Cloyne Diocesan Archives, 1795.10/1/1849, 1795.05/64/1850, 1795.05/19/1852, 1795.05/14/1856; Keane Papers, Cloyne Diocesan Archives, 1796.05/198/1858, 1796.05/178/1859, 1796.05/170/1862, 1796.05/187/1863, 1796.05/144/1864, 1796.05/190/1865, 1796.05/172/1866, 1796.05/148/1867, 1796.05/225/1868, 1796.05/244/1869, 1796.05/96/1870, 1796.05/249/1871.

they were appointing to their parishes. Bishops could overlook English monolingual candidates provided they received appointments in places where lack of bilingualism was not a hindrance—after all, given the demand for clergy, few could afford to turn away priests ready and willing to serve. But bishops were also aware of the need to send Irish-speaking candidates to cover the Irish-speaking congregations, and they took definite steps to address this problem. How systematic was this decision making? To understand how bishops approached the question of language in their growing congregations, it is necessary to examine the larger context of church administration and clerical education.

Church policy on language did not emerge from any central decision-making process, as few courses of action taken by the Irish hierarchy, especially in the years prior to the Synod of Thurles in 1850, followed such planning. A central decision-making body did not formally exist apart from the possibility of convening an all-Ireland synod, and no such meeting was called in the decades before 1850. Archbishops did convene irregular synods in each of the four ecclesiastical provinces, however, and "official policy," insofar as this term can be applied appropriately to this case, remained the overall result of the distinctly decentralized policies of each archdiocese and, to an even greater extent, the outcome of the individual preferences of each bishop. Institutional attitudes toward the Irish language were formulated at the diocesan level, largely by the bishops whose interests lay with producing adequately trained clergy and proper diocesan guidelines for priests and laity alike.

Bishops, for instance, had for years devoted attention both to the appointment of newly ordained priests to their respective missions and to the proficiency of those clergymen in the necessary language. This concern with diocesan management can be traced back to the early eighteenth century, when the greatest threat to Irish came not from English but from the other languages acquired by clerical students studying on the continent, especially French. The language problem tended to arise in these years in conjunction with periodic conflicts over the presence of previously ordained students at the Irish colleges in Paris. These ordained students—who were over age twenty-four and had therefore lived in Ireland longer—mixed uneasily at the two Paris colleges with young seminarians aged eighteen or younger. Bishops preferred to send ordained students because they could be more assured of their devotion to the priesthood and to their mission back in the home dioceses than the clerical students (or *écoliers*, as they were known). Thus, as Emmet Larkin has explained, when the authorities threatened to close the colleges to ordained students, the bishops immediately took the side of continuing the education of already ordained priests in the name of ensuring a reliable cohort of new priests.[126] But this was not the only reason, for it was not an affinity for French living or service in the French army that alone made young *écoliers* unsuitable for the Irish priesthood. According to a petition sent in the late 1730s by the ordained students to the provisor of the Irish College in Paris, "The *écoliers* acquire perfect French but lose their Irish which renders them incapable of serving on the Irish mission."[127] The ordained students, by contrast, had generally experienced life on the mission in Ireland, a task requiring, as the bishop of Killaloe described it in 1748, ministering to the "common people who can't speak a word but Irish."[128] Concern that the Paris-educated priests would not return to Ireland with proficiency in Irish—or worse, would not return at all—extended to the qualifications attached to the burses used to fund students. Thus three burses established for the united diocese of Cloyne and Ross in 1764, and set to be administered by the provisor at the Collège des Lombards, mandated above all that recipients "know how to speak Irish" and "take an oath to return to mission in Cloyne or Ross."[129]

This concern with language abilities continued into the nineteenth century, although it was now English that had become the biggest issue for bishops eager to assign Irish-speaking priests to Irish-speaking parishes. Bishop Crotty found it necessary in 1845 to reassign a priest whose lack of Irish had rendered him unfit for the needs of the predominantly Irish-speaking parish of Bartlemy. Writing to the priest's temporary replacement, Crotty emphasized the need to communicate with parishioners in their own language: "Take them coolly and quietly—speak Irish to them and prepare the children for their first communion by instructing them well in the Irish catechism, and you will get them to do whatever you wish."[130] Outstanding abilities in other aspects of parish administration were no substitute for speaking Irish, as a young deacon not yet in orders from County Waterford found in 1856. Bishop O'Brien refused to appoint him to any country parishes on account of his lack of Irish, and without any vacancies in Waterford city, the young man turned to Dublin in the hope of securing an appointment there. Writing on his behalf to Archbishop Paul Cullen, his bishop lamented, "I should ordain him for this diocese immediately if I had any suitable employment to give him."[131] Expectations that clergymen have Irish where necessary extended beyond parish priests to curates as well. Bishop Collins expressed concern about the parish of Mallow in 1830, as the ill health of the regular parish priest prevented him from performing his duties. Collins noted on his summer visitation: "The present curate, though a good and able young man, [is] unfit for this parish on account of his inability to speak Irish."[132]

In other cases, bishops had to respond to demands at the local level that Irish-speaking priests and curates be appointed, or consider assertions by clerical candidates that their linguistic abilities made them especially suitable for a certain parish. Father Heffernan of Clerihan, already noted above for his bilingual instructions at Mass, specifically requested of Archbishop Michael Slattery that an Irish-speaking curate be sent to his parish in 1841 to assist him, noting that "it is in Irish the greater part of the people confess their sins."[133] A letter from Dr. Edward Ffrench to then-president of Maynooth Laurence Renehan sought help in procuring two Irish-speaking graduates from the clerical college at Thurles for ordination, as such knowledge was "indispensable in this diocese."[134] Meanwhile, clerical aspirants underscored their Irish-speaking abilities when seeking university bursaries or pastoral appointments. It was reported to Archbishop Bray in 1797 that the Kerry clergy had endorsed Father Charles Sughrue to succeed as bishop of Kerry in part because he was an "eminent preacher in

English and Irish."¹³⁵ In 1855 in the diocese of Cloyne, Father Robert O'Riordan, the parish priest of Milford, drew attention to his nephew's Irish abilities in seeking an endorsement from Bishop Murphy to allow him to continue his studies at Maynooth and to gain holy orders. The student, a young man named Ahern, had attended the Irish College at Paris but was forced to return home for health reasons and intended to finish his studies in Ireland. Noting that Bishop Murphy had demanded a positive recommendation from the college superior that Ahern "be fairly acquainted with the Irish language," O'Riordan affirmed that "he has a competent knowledge of the Irish language and made every effort in that way."¹³⁶

In cases where clerical aspirants lacked Irish, bishops, particularly those in dioceses with significant Irish-speaking populations, at times required candidates to acquire the language either before attending university or in the course of their studies there. In other cases, they issued exemptions to allow those without Irish to receive appointments anyway. Bishop Edward Kernan of Clogher insisted in 1828 that a clerical candidate learn Irish, recommending that he "lay down his shoulders to acquire it."¹³⁷ Surviving correspondence show that Bishop Keane of Cloyne was disposed to require candidates to obtain sufficient Irish before being ordained. One such student, John Wigmore, found that a recommendation to advance to Carlow College at the 1858 Cloyne diocesan concursus meant that he had "to make himself as well acquainted with the Irish language as possible."¹³⁸ Another student, John Barry, seeking a place at the Irish house in Paris, struggled throughout November 1857 to improve his Irish enough to satisfy Keane. Although he was eventually given permission to take up his position, Barry was warned that he would have to continue to work on his Irish while in France and pass another exam upon his return.¹³⁹ As for exemptions, Father Peter Quin was appointed curate by MacHale to a parish in Killala in 1839 despite not knowing any Irish, a concern that, combined with his reputation for drink, led the diocesan vicar and parish priest of Kilmore, John Patrick Lyons, to complain to Archbishop Murray that he "does not speak Irish sufficiently well for a Killala priest."¹⁴⁰ Bishops, too, might receive appointments over complaints that they did not speak Irish. The ascension of David Moriarty to the office of coadjutor bishop of Kerry was initially challenged in 1853 by promoters of the campaign of Irish speaker Father John Sullivan, parish priest of Kenmare, in part because of Moriarty's lack of Irish. Fortunately for Moriarty, Sullivan's weak qualifications—his main pursuit in life according to his detractors had allegedly been "teaching his dog Paddy to smoke, eat sugar, and wear spectacles"—made the language question moot, and Moriarty eventually enjoyed a successful career as bishop.¹⁴¹

None of these concerns about the appointment of priests emerged out of any central church policy; instead, they reflected personal decisions made by bishops. This process extended beyond clerical appointments to include the formulation of pastoral policies, in which differences could be found from diocese to diocese. In the diocese of Meath, Wakefield observed in 1808, Bishop Patrick Joseph Plunkett (d. 1827) "obliges the people to attend prayers and to confess in English."[142] But in the ecclesiastical province of Cashel, bishops not only permitted Irish to be used in acts of lay religiosity but also encouraged priests to use that language to provide pastoral care. A synod convened in 1813 under Archbishop Bray yielded a published set of statutes, the *Statuta Synodalia pro Unitis Dioecesibus Cassel et Imelac*, intended to set guidelines for priests ministering in that province. In addition to a detailed and comprehensive overview of the proper rules and obligations for priests in administering their parishes, the *Statuta* consistently made it clear that Irish was to be employed as needed to ensure proper orthodoxy in the Cashel dioceses. The instructions at Mass, for example, condemning wakes and intemperance on pattern days—the favored targets of religious reformers of the period—were to be read in Irish. The catechism was to be taught "in English and Irish, every Sunday and holyday, in the chapels." The *Statuta* even provided an entire set of exhortations to be read to Cashel congregations covering nearly all the central aspects of the faith, from confession and communion to marriage and Lenten practices. These addresses were designed to be read in either English or Irish in accordance with a predetermined program to match the annual events of the Catholic religious year.[143] The dedication of the archdiocese of Cashel to providing proper pastoral care in Irish was confirmed again at a provincial synod held in 1853: bishops, the published decrees of the synod remarked, needed to ensure that the priests they appointed in their parishes knew Irish for the purpose of guiding divine worship.[144]

The bishops in the Cashel archdiocese were not alone in their attempts to make certain that sufficient material was available to facilitate the religious devotions of the Irish-speaking populations of their dioceses. In the province of Dublin, too, despite the prevalence of English in the area, Irish had for a number of years maintained a place as part of the institutional necessities of the church. Eager to mitigate the problem of priests unable to give proper instruction after Mass, the bishop of Ossory, Thomas Burke, relied on his printed abridgement of the Catholic faith he had assembled for the diocese titled *A Summary of the Christian Religion* (1773). Intended to be read by priests after the gospel on Sundays, and initially accompanied by instructions encouraging priests to translate its content into Irish for their congregations, Burke later issued a formal Irish translation, *Suim Athchumuir an Chreideimh Chriostamuil*, in 1775.[145] This tactic of providing written exhortations in both English and Irish for the use of priests continued to be employed well into the nineteenth century. Thus the *Ordo Administrandi Sacramenta*, still in print at midcentury, also furnished the full text of an exhortation outlining the essential precepts of Christian belief in both English and Irish for the use of parish priests.[146]

The situation in the archdiocese of Tuam, where the long tenure of John MacHale as archbishop from 1834 to 1881 affected all official pronouncements on language use, has generally been held up by historians who perceive it as the one bright spot in what is considered an otherwise dismal church record on Irish. It is true that MacHale exhibited an unusual ferocity in defense of the Irish language in comparison with his contemporaries, and he displayed unique energy in producing a number of Irish-language translations in his lifetime. Among these projects he devoted more than twenty years to two ambitious secular works—translations of *Moore's Melodies* and the *Iliad* into Irish.[147] Traveling in Ireland in 1842, Johann Kohl had been singularly impressed with the work of MacHale and his close associate Father Martin Loftus, the former professor of Irish at Maynooth, on behalf of the Irish language in Connacht.[148] Kohl, however, had been speaking of MacHale's literary work rather than of the pastoral life of the region. In the absence of any documentation of MacHale's policy making—his correspondence has not survived—his official record in ensuring adequate pastoral care through Irish remains somewhat uncertain.[149] MacHale himself preached in Irish regularly throughout his years in Tuam, sponsored the publication of the Irish Tuam catechism under the direction of Loftus, and circulated his pastorals in Irish.[150] Yet the skepticism of Gearóid Ó Tuathaigh, who has argued that it is unclear whether MacHale's enthusiasm extended to taking care to appoint Irish-speaking priests to Irish-speaking districts, seems appropriate.[151] Absent his diocesan records of clerical appointments, a clear picture may not be possible.

At least one church initiative on behalf of the Irish language, however, was definitely conducted on something approaching an all-Ireland basis. This was the attempt in 1842 by a number of Irish prelates to sponsor the translation of an official Roman Catholic version of the Bible into Irish. Protestant versions of the Bible, translated as part of the larger conversion efforts of the Anglican church, had been in circulation since the seventeenth century. But the need for an acceptable Catholic version remained unfulfilled. Consequently, in 1842 a number of bishops met in Dublin and sanctioned a special translation of the

Douai New Testament by Father Martin Loftus, resulting in an immediate subscription for nearly 1,300 copies by the hierarchy.[152] In the end this project never came to fruition, possibly because of the death of Loftus sometime in 1847. The topic remained the subject of comment, however, with the County Louth priest Nioclás Ó Cearnaigh writing to Archbishop Cullen in 1850 of the need for a translation on account of the "numberless corrupt Irish bibles, testaments, tracts, etc., [that] have been, and still are, in the hands of Catholics."[153] Nevertheless, the failed translation initiative reveals a rare exception to the largely localized decision making with regard to language use.

The concern among bishops about the proficiency of the candidates being put forward for appointments in their dioceses raises one last salient issue in assessing the role of the Irish language in the church, namely, the clerical colleges producing these young priests. Maynooth has received the largest share of attention, no doubt assisted by the memorable description by Father Walter McDonald, a student at Maynooth in the 1870s and later a professor at the college, of the aged Irish professor James Tully—concluding at the time an impressive fifth decade of teaching Irish—half-heartedly reprimanding his students.[154] Alongside this, the overall milieu at Maynooth has been described as unusually proficient in anglicizing and transforming its students into middle-class opponents of the Irish language. Cardinal Tomas Ó Fiaich, for example, writing in 1972 of life in Maynooth more than a century earlier, believed that "bhréag-ghalántacht" (false affectation), wealth, and dandyism ran rampant in the student body: "Bhíodh an ceathrú cuid acu gan Béarla ag teacht isteach dóibh ach ba ghairid gur fhoghlaim siad Béarla breá" (A quarter of them had no English on entering, but in a short time they learned fine English).[155] Leaving aside the assumption in such claims that the Irish language was incompatible with a middle-class outlook, not to mention the contrasting images of unheated rooms, strict rules on student socialization, and grueling daily schedules offered by Patrick Corish in his more recent portrait of daily life in the college, a closer look at the colleges is certainly warranted to uncover the context for the expectations of clerical students as they left their educational institutions for vocations at their respective parishes.

Policies concerning the teaching of Irish in the clerical colleges did not spring into existence with the inclusion of language instruction at the time of the creation of Maynooth in 1795. Rather, the intent and purpose of instruction in Irish at Maynooth emerged out of long-standing approaches to the language that first developed in the continental schools of the seventeenth and eighteenth centuries. As early as 1650 the Congregatio de Propaganda Fide in Rome had made Irish a requirement for all priests on the continent intending to take up missions back in Ireland. Exceptions were made for students from regions where Irish was deemed unnecessary, but the language generally became an established part of clerical training in many schools. Surviving daily schedules for students—from the seminary at Tournai in Belgium, for instance—make it clear that individual colleges encouraged proficiency in the language and that the practice of speaking Irish at certain times had become entrenched over the years. At Lille, clerical students had developed a long-standing custom since 1635 of speaking only Irish on Tuesdays and Thursdays, a custom that survived into the eighteenth century. Indeed, it was reported in 1764 that students at Lille were often forbidden to speak English in order to improve their Irish, Latin, and French.[156]

Clerical students defended their ability to gather and speak Irish within their college walls as a unique and vital aspect of their education. The attempt by the University of Paris, whose colleges often allowed clerical students to attend their lectures and share burses, to insist that *boursiers* from the Collège des Lombards be integrated into its Collège de Lisieux was thus met with oppositional student petitions in 1762. The seminary living experience, argued the students from Ireland, with its shared spaces and its encouragement of the use of shared vernaculars (they mentioned both English and Irish), made it essential that they be permitted to remain segregated at the Collège des Lombards. A similar situation arose in 1774 when administrators threatened to redistribute the burses established for the Irish Jesuit College of Poitiers to non-Irish students in other colleges. The Irish students demanded that these burses be retained for the use of clericals from Ireland alone, citing in defense the need to sustain their community in Paris since "Irish is spoken constantly there and almost all the exercises are done in Irish. If placed elsewhere, *boursiers* would not be able to preach, catechize, or confess in Ireland."[157]

A number of features about this Irish-language instruction stand out. First, it is doubtful that it envisioned imparting Irish fluency to those who could not already speak the language in some capacity. The limited amount of time spent at the colleges and the breadth of learning required in both general study and in learning other languages made such acquisition unrealistic. Hence care was taken from the very beginning to exempt those for whom the language was not deemed necessary, as a means of freeing up time for studying other things. For students who did need Irish for their dioceses back home, moreover, the concern was to sustain fluency in Irish in the face of their collegial exposure to languages like French, Spanish, and Italian, not to mention the extensive time devoted to Latin, Greek, and even Hebrew. Given the greater preponderance of ordained priests who were being educated at these colleges—Larkin has estimated that approximately thirty-five out of forty students returning from education on the continent in the eighteenth century were of the group that had received orders prior to matriculating—the possibility that the clerical colleges intended to create Irish speakers out of English monolinguals becomes even more remote.[158] In short, these students had already spent a handful of years in their home dioceses as deacons on the mission; they had relied on the vernacular in their pastoral duties before leaving for Paris, Salamanca, Rome, or one of the other continental destinations to finish off their theological training; and it would have been impractical to expect these young men in their midtwenties (the youngest canonical age for ordination was twenty-four), who in all likelihood had already become familiar with pastoral duties, to devote their limited time abroad to acquiring Irish for the first time.

On the contrary, it was probably expected that most priests who returned to minister in Irish-speaking districts already knew the language, and that what they lacked was the ability to read and write for the purposes of catechizing, preaching, and translating. These literacy skills dominated the curriculum in these classes, not basic speaking. This was evident, for example, in the stipulations attached to burses founded to support Irish. The Collège des Lombards in Paris received perhaps the single greatest financial support for language training in Irish when Philipes Joseph Perrotin, a *garde des registres des finances*, pledged the interest on a sum of 12,000 livres in 1736 to establish a school in the college to teach Irish and to award prizes for composition in the language. The intention to produce literacy was evident in the guidelines stipulated by Perrotin, who asked that the school be dedicated to teaching "the Irish language to the students of the other sciences who do not know how to read or write it." The endowment dedicated awards to translations and catechetical responses.[159] The Irish language was therefore a firmly established part of clerical education by the end of the eighteenth century, but for the purpose of sustaining and polishing the ability to use the language in providing pastoral care and not for the goal of reversing large-scale language shift.

These modest but vital needs demanded by bishops of Irish-speaking priests strongly influenced the curricula of the new colleges established in Ireland by émigrés during the upheaval of the French Revolution. From its beginnings in 1795 Maynooth was expected to educate students from all over Ireland—including those destined to furnish pastoral care in Irish-speaking parishes; a chair of Irish was operative from the outset. Although not glamorously endowed in comparison with the other professorships, the Irish chair did receive fresh funding from an endowment of £1,000 granted in a contested will and made available to the college in 1820.[160] The annual interest earned on this bequest (just over £42 in 1826) helped to bring the annual income for the professor of Irish to £74 a year—a low sum but probably commensurate with the duties of an instructor who was expected to teach Irish only in evening classes to second-year theology students. The first candidate selected to fill the chair, Father John McLoughlin, turned down the appointment, but a second candidate, Father Paul O'Brien (1763–1820), accepted the chair in July 1802.[161] A poet from County Meath and a former Maynooth student, O'Brien took a proactive interest in teaching the language during a tenure that lasted until 1820 and that included the publication of *A Practical Grammar of the Irish Language* in 1809.[162] Father Martin Loftus himself succeeded O'Brien from 1820 to 1826, when the chair was filled by Father Tully, which he held until his death in 1876. Thereafter the professorship was temporarily left vacant until 1891, although Cardinal Logue, who had taught the Irish class at the Irish College in Paris in 1866, was among the instructors who fulfilled the duties on a short-term basis in the late 1870s.[163]

The situation in the other newly founded Irish clerical colleges varied. Neither of the first two schools to open—St. Kieran's, Kilkenny, in 1783, and St. Patrick's, Carlow, in 1793, founded as diocesan colleges for Ossory and for Kildare and Leighlin, respectively—felt the need to include Irish instruction in their original prospectuses. This may have reflected the student body initially envisioned at these colleges—to be drawn from these two less Irish-speaking dioceses of Leinster and to include not just clericals but also lay students interested in the professions. In the case of St. Kieran's, located in Ossory, where pockets of Irish speaking persisted in south and west Kilkenny, this may have been an oversight that later bishops wished to rectify. Certainly, Bishop William Kinsella (d. 1845) took notice of the attempt by Philip Barron to set up an Irish-language college in County Waterford in 1835, expressing interest in sending Ossory priests to receive Irish instruction at the school. In any event, St. Kieran's and Carlow were soon superceded by Maynooth in ordaining priests for Ireland, and by the post-famine years they had become dedicated to providing English-speaking priests for missions abroad.[164]

By contrast, St. John's College, Waterford, founded in 1807 in a more heavily Irish-speaking diocese, did include a chair of Irish, as did St. Jarlath's, founded in 1800 to educate the students of Connacht. At St. John's, the appointment of a professor of Irish likely came from a combination of interest from Bishop Abraham, who asserted in 1835 that he had become so concerned about the supply of Irish-speaking priests in his diocese that he directed the college not to advance any students without Irish, and Dominic O'Brien, president of the college and patron of several Irish religious translations by Tomás Ó Iceadha.[165] Although it is unlikely he was replaced after his death, it is clear that Ó Iceadha, who held the position from 1835 to 1854, performed effectively in his duties. Among those who credited his instruction with imparting an ability to read in Irish was the priest Gearóid Ó Maonadh (nephew of sermon writer Father John Meany), who reported to his brother in 1848 that "atáim anois ábalta air mhórán de leabharaibh clodhbhuilte Gaoidheilge ... do leughadh fá stiuradh ár n-Oide" (I am now able to read many printed Irish books under the tutelage of our Mentor).[166] At St. Jarlath's, definitive evidence points to Uileog de Búrca, appointed to the faculty following his ordination in 1858, as the first instructor of Irish.[167] But there is also a strong possibility that John MacEvilly, who served as professor of Sacred Scripture and Hebrew between 1842 and his selection as president of the St. Jarlath's in 1852, taught an Irish class identified by the *Freeman's Journal* in November of 1842 as having been established by the college.[168]

The aim of this Irish instruction and its roots in the experience of the continental colleges was evident from the curriculum at Maynooth, where instruction was heavily based on the essentials of acquiring proper literacy skills in order to write sermons and read catechisms. Paul O'Brien, for example, taught Irish grammar, Bible reading, and translation practice in 1808. Such work, conducted in evening classes, hardly represented the basis for a nonnative speaker to acquire enough Irish for the mission. It did, however, meet the pastoral needs of bishops and other officials who made the Irish-language class mandatory for all "students from those parts of the country where the Irish language is prevalent."[169] Any exceptions to the Irish requirement for ordination required dispensation from the appropriate bishop. The rarity of such a dispensation was indicated by the comments of the president of Maynooth, Bartholomew Crotty, in seeking an exemption for a recent graduate whose Irish had been disadvantaged by the temporary vacancy in the chair at the end of Father Loftus's tenure. Crotty wrote to the candidate's bishop, William Coppinger of Cloyne and Ross, in 1827:

> In my last, by Mr. Duggan, I requested your Lordship would favor me, as soon as your convenience would admit, with the necessary powers for presenting your subjects here for orders, and with any particular exception you might wish to have made on. I allude particularly to a former restriction, on the score of ignorance of the Irish language, which has never been recalled, unless in

particular instances. I believe if now insisted on, it might interfere with the advancement of Mr. Verling; but as your Lordship allowed him to take subdeaconship, I presume the dispensation included the other orders.[170]

By contrast, language dispensations for students from northern dioceses had already become commonplace in the 1820s. Nevertheless, as Bishop William Crolly of Down and Connor noted at the time, not all Ulster students could shirk this responsibility if they hailed from "rough districts, where the people are confined to mountains and places of that kind," and demand for Irish instruction remained robust enough that in 1826 the class numbered around fifty students.[171] It was only in the mid-nineteenth century, according to Corish, that complaints began to surface that the Irish requirement was not being enforced, although even in 1847 it was reported that fifty students—no change from twenty years earlier—had attended the Irish class that year.[172]

Once again, the ability to speak Irish natively prior to entering college would have been a crucial advantage as the range of subjects required for timely ordination left little room for extensive language training. The entire Maynooth curriculum required an average of six years. The first two years for most students involved fundamental training in mathematics and the humanities—subjects like algebra, geometry, chemistry, basic philosophy, ancient history, and of course, classical texts—followed by a year of rhetoric, with the humanities courses designed to ensure an appropriate level of skill in both reading and composition. Having completed this program, students passed to the core of their education, two years given over to logic and natural philosophy, followed by two or three years devoted to theology. Officials preferred a total of three years of such theological training, but as Corish has emphasized, the pressures to ordain and appoint new priests meant that the luxury of additional years and subjects beyond the fundamentals had to be foregone. Under these circumstances it would have been unreasonable to expect the university to offer enough Irish training to transform English monolingual speakers into fluent priests with a working pastoral use of the Irish language. If anything, professors and college administrators in the nineteenth century repeatedly noted the difficulty of meeting even the core demands of the curriculum, let alone studies beyond a handful of nonclassical languages—English, French, and Irish—all offered as mere evening classes at Maynooth.[173]

Attempts to inculcate Irish fluency through collegial instruction may even have proven counterproductive when second-language learners tried to employ Irish in front of native-speaking congregations. Learning Irish grammatically brought the risk of transgressing local dialect variations and inviting ridicule when priests tried to preach. This was precisely the situation reported by one priest, Father P. J. Moran of Mullingar:

> He was sorry to say that often, in the parts [of the country] where it was a necessity of the clergy (he did not refer to any particular denomination) to speak the Irish language, they spoke it imperfectly because it was with them, in many cases, purely a literary acquirement. They learned it in college and not from their mother's lips; the result being that they did not take to it naturally and dispensed with it whenever they could do so. These people felt diffidence, especially when they found that those who spoke the language habitually as their mother-tongue (particularly in the county of Mayo, west Galway, and County Clare) had a great natural taste, as well as intelligence, which made them very apt to ridicule the clergyman's mistake or mispronunciation.[174]

Becoming comfortable with local dialectical variations may have been conquerable with patience and determination. But it would have required far more than the time that could realistically be carved out of the six to seven years spent in learning philosophy, rhetoric, and theology at the clerical colleges.

At the same time, the nature of the education required of prospective priests *prior* to entering college also worked against attaining proficiency in Irish and even, given new developments in this realm in the nineteenth century, against the emergence of candidates with native language abilities. Those precollege years were dominated by the overwhelming need for clerical aspirants to acquire enough Latin (and some Greek) to read at least the literary mainstays of a classical education. In this regard priests were no different from their lay counterparts interested in a university education for the purpose of a career in the professions. The 1826 entrance requirements for the lowest humanities class at Maynooth, for example, demanded a familiarity with the Latin works of Virgil, Caesar, Horace, Sallust, and Cicero, along with Greek abilities for Lucian's *Dialogues*, Xenophon's *Cyropaedia*, and the Gospel of Saint John.[175] Classes at Maynooth and other colleges were conducted in Latin and required their students to submit their work in that language. This made the acquisition of a classical education crucial to becoming a priest—a necessity that crowded out devoting any significant time to learning Irish as a second language.

Time devoted to learning Irish as a second language meant time spent away from learning the classics, a situation that also favored native speakers. Moreover, major hardships awaited the young clerical candidate who undertook this endeavor. The experience of John Barry, required to learn the basics of Irish in 1857 at the request of Bishop Keane of Cloyne before leaving for seminary training in Paris, demonstrated the obstacles to acquiring the language too late in life. Barry's mother was an Irish speaker herself. Yet even with her help he struggled to learn the language. His parish priest, Father J. Fitzpatrick, explained:

> I examined him a few days ago in the principal parts of the Irish catechism, and he answered as well as could be expected from one who speaks but a few words of the Irish language and pronounces rather incorrectly what he does speak. He is getting off the prayers and Acts, and is, I am sure, doing all he can to acquire a knowledge of the language, but it is a great disadvantage to him that he cannot find any person here who reads the Irish correctly. He told me that he speaks or attempts to speak it at home with his mother, who speaks it well. He answered correctly enough in the catechism, and if he had some person to teach him who could read the Irish correctly, he would in a short time know it pretty well—in a word, he is doing his utmost, and under his present disadvantages he has made a fare [*sic*] proficiency.[176]

Even in the best of circumstances schooling may not have been able to create a native proficiency, and in any event, Ireland in the nineteenth century offered very little opportunity to learn Irish institutionally in the crucial younger years before entering college.

But unrelated changes in classical and secondary schooling at this time militated against native speakers as well. Larger trends in the founding of Catholic schools made it increasingly easier for urban dwellers—rich and poor—to obtain a primary and a classical education than their rural counterparts. Following the passage of Gardiner's Act in 1782, and especially after the subsequent repeal in 1792 and 1793 of penal disabilities that required schools to obtain licenses from Protestant bishops, formal Catholic schooling in the classics and basic humanities in Ireland blossomed.[177] Up to that time clerical aspirants had obtained their classical education at Protestant academies designed to prepare students for Trinity College, through personal tutors, or by becoming one of the "poor scholars" who attended the informal classical schools—many of them taught by Irish-speaking scribes and poets—existing predominantly in Munster.[178] Even after 1793 and well into the nineteenth century, because of the delay in creating new classical academies, many clerical aspirants obtained their schooling in Latin and Greek informally in rural schools that were in reality no more than extensions of the Catholic free schools and "hedge" schools that dominated primary education until the 1830s. While uneven in their quality, these country classical schools had the virtue of providing education at a lower cost, and they were diffused in sufficient numbers around the country to enable students from more isolated areas to attend.

Starting at the end of the eighteenth century, bishops began to establish formal preparatory schools with the financial contributions and moral support of Ireland's strengthening Catholic middle classes. These institutions represented better formal schooling but at a higher cost of attendance to scholars. Evidence of the impact of this educational transition was already apparent in interviews conducted at Maynooth in 1826. The president of the college, Father Bartholomew Crotty, recalled the past prevalence of so-called poor scholars and classical education obtained more cheaply; he noted that there were "poor scholars in almost every Greek and Latin school through [sic] the country," and that "only 5s. a quarter was paid in some good schools; that is forty or fifty years ago."[179] As the Maynooth professor Father James Browne remarked, things had changed:

> In some parts of the country a person can obtain a competent knowledge of Latin and Greek at a very small expense when he is enabled to live at his father's house; but at present some change has taken place in that respect; there are seminaries now established in many dioceses, and the bishops think it useful that all the young men that are sent to college should be prepared in those seminaries. Their expenses there are much more considerable than they would be if they had been educated at the country schools.

Browne estimated the cost of attending the Wexford seminary, for example, at £25 per year, with additional room-and-board expenses bringing the total up to £40.[180] This was far more costly than the one-guinea admission fee plus one guinea per quarter (i.e., £5 5s. per year) charged at that time in many of the country classical schools, and the extra expense was compounded if a student needed to travel and live away from home.

Both the aims and the locations of these schools discouraged ability in vernacular languages like Irish. As David Moriarty testified in 1853, the curriculum of these various preparatory secondary schools focused on "combining with classical education a more extensive study of English and mathematics."[181] The diocesan schools tended to cluster in larger towns and cities, thus raising the cost of attendance and making these schools susceptible to the predominantly English-speaking atmosphere of these localities. As was typical given the classically influenced views about what constituted a proper education, the fundamentals of Greek and Latin provided the central core of the curriculum—a result, as Peter Birch has noted with reference to the history of St. Kieran's, Kilkenny, of the influence of the Jesuits' educational objectives on European Catholic education. Even where languages other than Greek and Latin were taught, the vernaculars deemed acceptable were most often English and French, the two languages mentioned, for example, in St. Kieran's first prospectus.[182] There were exceptions: St. Mary's College, Cork, for example, founded by Bishop Francis Moylan in 1813 as a diocesan seminary, employed the scribe and Irish scholar Charles Field (ca. 1748–1831) as an Irish instructor.[183] The Errew Monastery school in County Mayo reportedly had "classes taught in the Irish language" at the time of its opening in 1842.[184] But overall these new academies offered little opportunity for maintaining or developing Irish-language ability.

While the diocesan schools conferred a boon on the wealthier urban middle class and on those in rural areas who could afford to board their sons in town, the urban poor also received a leg up over their rural counterparts when it came to education. Religious orders, male and female, began providing education at both the primary and secondary levels at this time. The principal orders included the Presentation Sisters, founded in Cork city in 1775, the Sisters of Mercy, founded in Dublin in 1828, and, of greatest significance for clerical education, the Christian Brothers, whose founder Edmund Rice launched his first school in 1802. In time the Christian Brothers would become the most widespread option for Catholic males seeking secondary education in Ireland, including those students intended for the priesthood.[185] But as with the diocesan academies, the Christian Brothers tended to found schools in the large mercantile centers: three schools in Dublin and one each in Cork, Limerick, Carrick-on-Suir, Thurles, Dungarvan, Ennistymon, and Cappoquin.[186] Irish eventually became a school subject at the Christian Brothers' schools, and their students dominated the Celtic exams offered by the Intermediate Education Board at the urging of later revivalist groups like the Society for the Preservation of the Irish Language starting in the 1870s.[187] In the first half of the nineteenth century, however, while a number of Irish speakers held staff positions in their schools, the language was not initially part of its formal curriculum.[188]

The growth of urban diocesan seminaries and teaching brothers' schools probably played a significant role in the decline of the older country classical schools whose rural location and low tuition may have provided easier access for Irish-speaking aspirants to the priesthood. By the mid-nineteenth century classical education in rural areas had all but died out in favor of the new schools located in larger—and less Irish-speaking—towns and cities. The real turning point was the Great Famine, according to Moriarty, who reported that mass death and emigration had significantly undermined the small country classical schoolteachers.[189] Bishop George Butler of Limerick (d. 1886) summarized the situation gravely in a letter to Archbishop Cullen in 1867:

> We are sadly off in most provincial towns, especially the smaller ones, for want of schools where the rudiments of Latin would be taught. These schools have wholly disappeared, and no one can now even commence to learn Latin unless he enters the seminary or comes to lodge in some great town where there is a classical day school. The parents in the class of life where vocations are found cannot afford this, and hence many vocations are lost, and the supply for the priesthood is becoming day after day less select than scanty. The disappearance of the primary classical schools has been occasioned by the establishments of the monks' schools in most of our county towns. The monks attract to their schools the great bulk of the youth, and no one will attend the classical school except the few who are destined for the professions. There are too few to support a teacher.[190]

English-speaking candidates from rural areas, of course, would have been equally disadvantaged. But given the national distribution of Irish speakers, who were more likely to be found in rural rather than in urban areas, the rise of the diocesan and teaching orders' schools must have had a negative impact on the number of Irish-speaking students able to obtain the necessary classical education to become priests, especially after 1850. It is this later point in time, rather than the founding of Maynooth, that provides a much better candidate for a shift in clerical education.

The clergy, in sum, reflected the linguistic makeup of Ireland as a whole. The church was no more immune to the declining numbers of Irish speakers among their ranks than any corner of the country. As younger cohorts of Irish men increasingly were raised without Irish, and as the epicenter of secondary education shifted to more formal town and city settings, the overall body of matriculating students for the clerical colleges that represented the future of pastoral care were more and more likely to exhibit weak abilities in the language. This was a slow and gradual change, however, built on the long-term turnover of older priests. Meanwhile, that earlier generation of priests and bishops who had arrived on the scene in the first half of the nineteenth century faced a clear challenge: either reach out to parishioners in the languages they spoke, or risk stalling the religious reforms desired in many corners of the church. This was a challenge by and large met on a case-by-case basis, subject to the larger pressure facing the church at the time of appointing enough priests to cover basic sacramental and liturgical duties regardless of whether linguistic considerations were met. This no doubt fell short of any expectations that the church should act as a bulwark against language shift, or that its officials should have mandated an all-Irish environment for worship. But by the more practical standards of implementing reform, the church undoubtedly exhibited a keen awareness of the need to administer to their flocks in Irish if devotional revolution was to make any headway.

Conclusion

Summarizing the challenges to administering the Austrian empire posed by linguistic diversity, a contributor to the 6 September 1866 issue of the *Pall Mall Gazette* contrasted the ease with which the British could govern at home. Conveying a sense of relief, it was noted: "It is almost impossible for an Englishman, who knows absolutely nothing of language questions, or of race questions determined by language—for the Irish language is virtually extinct—to realize such a state of things as one in which not only have ten languages got to be learnt and mastered by the aggregate central government, but they actually serve to denote ten separate political questions, each of which is more or less menacing to the very existence of empire."[1] Britain and Ireland in the years under the Act of Union were not, of course, as linguistically complex as Austria-Hungary. But to modern ears, the sentiments expressed in this editorial come off as strikingly ill-informed as to the realities of governing conditions. There is the assumption that language death brought with it certain advantages through its streamlining of the process of administration, a pronouncement not unknown today but most directly reflective of the centralizing urges of the rise of the modern liberal state of the nineteenth century. That language unity necessarily ensured survival of the imperial state through the quelling of "political questions" would prove equally inaccurate, as events in Ireland were to show in the early twentieth century. Leaving aside these ideological underpinnings, however, the statement is striking even in its own historical context for its ignorance of the situation in Ireland. More than one million men and women still spoke Irish in 1861, a fact brought home to officials by the cartographer and statistician Ernst Georg Ravenstein (1834–1913), who assembled a summary of the linguistic diversity of the two islands for the Royal Statistical Society in 1879. Ravenstein offered a clear verdict: "The reign of one universal language appears to be more remote than ever before."[2] For anyone who cared to look, as Ravenstein and a range of commentators from Henry Monck Mason and Robert MacAdam to John Windele and Mícheál Óg Ó Longáin were quick to point out, the existence of a large Irish-speaking community was evident.

In the century before 1870, as has been shown here, Ireland was not by any means an anglicized kingdom and, indeed, was quite capable of articulating the forms of modernity—whether religious, political, or economic—in the Irish language. This was especially so in the unusually dynamic period for the Irish language between the first decades of the nineteenth century and the *R. v. Burke* decision of 1858, a time when Irish speakers helped define new directions in Ireland's religious, political, and administrative ideologies. The dynamism of this Irish-speaking society prior to the formal stirring of language revivalism was in part a natural outcome of the millions of speakers present on the island in those decades. It could hardly have been otherwise: increasing population overall had brought with it a swell of Irish speakers, and by simply going about their daily lives through the medium of that language—transacting business, cultivating the land, participating in religious activities, teaching school, and socializing with neighbors—this community necessarily participated in the larger changes to Irish society well underway by the third and fourth decades of the nineteenth century.

It was not only the sheer number of Irish speakers that defined the community in the century before 1870, however. The nature of the relationship between Irish speakers and the various representatives of institutional power in Irish society—basically, the state and its religious arm, the established church, as well as the Catholic Church—changed considerably in this same time period, resulting in a mutual shaping of both sides. Scholars have long recognized one side of this equation, namely, the influence on Irish speakers caused by the growing power of church and state in the everyday lives of individuals. But that power has also been problematically depicted as unlimited and uncompromising, involving a simple absorption of Irish speakers into new, anglicized domains by religious and secular authorities, yielding the supposed triumph of the English language as the proof of the one-sided nature of this relationship. Conceptualizing the linguistic landscape using terms like diglossia has helped bolster this sense of the passivity of Irish speakers, leading to descriptions of a broad swath of formal, institutional domains in Irish society as self-evidently English speaking, while referring to the settings of Irish-speaking homes and private life as doomed Gaelicized holdouts. Yet evidence presented not just by this study but also by others in an increasingly active field of scholarship in the past five years has shown that Irish speakers subjected this divide, where it existed at all, to ongoing challenge. Courtrooms, as mounting scholarship has confirmed, were well known to Irish speakers, and not just through their roles as witnesses, prosecutors, or defendants but as jurors and occasionally attorneys and judges as well. Irish could be heard in classrooms and at public gatherings, in marketplaces and during religious activities. No history of the Emancipation campaigns, anti-tithe demonstrations, or even run-of-the-mill elections of the post-1793 period—at least not where county electorates in the west or south are concerned—can be honestly written without acknowledging the pressure on candidates to employ interpreters to mobilize supporters who spoke Irish at the local level. And if certain Irish speakers—whether elites or nonelites—saw Irish as a barrier to engagement with the modern world, others retained an older understanding of the language as the epitome of scholarly virtue and the expression of a displaced indigenous identity with deep roots. These attitudes, too, challenged the concept of power and prestige in Ireland as being constituted only where English was spoken.

The linguistic compromise involved in secular settings was replicated in religious realms. Catholic Irish speakers taught the catechism in Irish and said their prayers in Irish at home and in conjunction with attendance at Mass. They preferred, and sometimes even demanded, that Irish-speaking priests deliver sermons and hear confessions in their chosen language. Nor was it possible for Church authorities to ensure proper catechetical training, as they fervently wished in these early decades, without catering to the young Irish speakers who arrived in their Sunday schools and day-school classrooms needing instruction that would be clear enough in their language to ensure that they could pass the test posed by confirmation. Even among the Protestant denominations, as has become clear through research done by a number of scholars over the years, an ongoing, multicentury struggle was waged regarding the question of how to secure the faith in Ireland among a population speaking a language in which the church's ability to operate was chronically limited.

What of the other side of the equation—the influence of the existence of Irish speakers on the institutions of church and state? Here, a long view of the situation is helpful. An active period by the English administration in Ireland in trying to shape the linguistic landscape in Ireland among its elites arrived as part of extending Tudor and Stuart governance, marked by outright legislation to try to bolster the fortunes of English as well as by forced compromises in the form of deploying interpreters and learning Irish in order for administrators to govern. But although early modern states—the Tudor and Stuart administration was no exception—were eager to build kingdoms that were unified linguistically, and while speaking Irish continued to be viewed suspiciously by administrative elites in Ireland, the absence of key contact points between subjects and the state made the language question in Ireland—once the matter of the country's ruling classes was decided in favor of an English-speaking Protestant elite by the early eighteenth century—a less pressing matter. Absent a large presence of many of the domains in which subject and administrators could interact, such as a widespread centralized system of petty sessions courts, a formalized mass education system, or a right to the franchise by wide sections of the population, there simply was no pressure on the state to worry about language questions.

This linguistic agnosticism that had taken hold by the eighteenth century was also true in a sense of the Catholic Church, but for different reasons. The slow recovery of the church from the blows to the hierarchy in the early seventeenth century, combined with the delayed return of Catholic wealth with which to finance institutional expansion, meant that it was not until the end of the eighteenth century that participation in the church entailed more than informal, local activities for the majority of the Irish population. In other words, although there certainly were discussions around the topic of improving religious participation through Irish-language outreach, there was no need for the Catholic Church to really consider how to provide Irish-language sermons, catechizing, or confessions so long as such activities remained rare and could be handled in their own way by local clergy.

But on all sides, the language question came to a head starting in the 1770s and especially by the second and third decades of the 1800s as the immense growth and formalization of state and church entities made the issue of what language or languages would be used to implement those institutions more urgent. Irish speakers made this question more urgent, as noted above. They participated in court proceedings and arrived at voting booths, even when monolingual or simply unwilling to speak English. They insisted on using Irish for religious devotions and sacramental obligations, particularly personal ones, even after language shift had taken place in their community. And they showed up in schoolrooms speaking a language that was not on the curriculum. This had real consequences on all sides. It meant that the legal system had to make accommodations at the local level for interpreters and the costs associated with them. The court system also had to take up the increasingly urgent question of how to handle linguistic preference in the witness box, leading to the settling of the question in favor of Irish speakers in the *R. v. Burke* decision in 1858. As for the state church, it no longer seemed feasible in the climate of the nineteenth century to use the language barrier as an excuse for why more conversions were not taking place, contributing to disestablishment on the one side and the formal approval by the Church of Ireland of the use of Irish in worship in 1871 on the other. The decisions by Catholic bishops as to where to post priests, whether to produce religious texts and clerical manuals in Irish, and how best to prepare clergy at seminary were also made with the Irish-speaking population in mind.

Of course, for some elites the possibility of simply riding out language shift until English prevailed held considerable attraction—an attitude that can be seen in certain quarters of the commissioners of education, for example, and in both churches. But others took active steps to enable those institutions to function in Irish, by learning the language, for example, as several bishops and judges did, by requiring priests be able to read and catechize in Irish, or through statutory decisions at the parliamentary level to deploy interpreters to enable the political and legal process to operate. These developments meant not only access to power by Irish speakers: they were concessions that Ireland was not a universally English-speaking realm by an administration and a Catholic Church that had been able to function for much of the eighteenth century (indeed, at times the nineteenth century as well) without succumbing to that reality.

Those concessions did not disappear at the end of the nineteenth century, and this is where the developments of the eighteenth and nineteenth century offer a different perspective on the history of Irish and of language policies in the twentieth century. Again, as with anglicization, the process of language revival has been portrayed by scholars as a top-down process driven by a select few patriotic activists who pressed the Catholic Church and the British (later, the Irish) state to acknowledge a bilingual society. There is some truth to that depiction. But the bilingual educational program that became the cornerstone of the independent Irish state, for example, and the formerly acknowledged place of Irish as a part of both Protestant and Catholic worship in the twentieth century, were built on long-standing questions about how far an English-only policy for these realms could be sustained in the face of regular use of these institutions by Irish speakers. The rising awareness by Patrick Keenan and others among the inspectorate in the national system of education by the 1850s and 1860s that an English-only curriculum was not working in some areas of Ireland coincided with increasing interest in including Irish on the curriculum by teachers who had long been using it as an informal tool of instruction in the classroom. Irish, although certainly never the predominant language through which Catholicism was articulated in the nineteenth century, nevertheless was always present in the church, and it even carved out a role for itself in molding the devotional literature that helped carry new forms of orthodoxy. That continuity was clearly visible in the early twentieth century Catholic publications, particularly prayer books, that derived from (in some cases, were simply new editions of) earlier nineteenth-century printings by individuals such as Pádraig Denn. Even Protestant denominations, for all their fraught relationship with the language question given the missionary activity of the early nineteenth century, could draw in later years on a considerable body of religious texts in Irish made necessary over four centuries because of the pressure to reach Irish speakers in their language.

Literary scholars have long discussed the creation of modern Irish literature in terms of the contributions of Irish-language writing to that process. By contrast, historical interpretations of the wider place of Irish speakers in the making of modern Irish culture have tended to avoid that question or else assumed, given language shift, that no role for Irish existed. This position is untenable. Evidence of Irish speakers participating in the shaping of eighteenth- and nineteenth-century cultural and political processes demonstrates to the contrary that this was a speech community that, so long as it existed, was fully capable of negotiating the changes shaping the Ireland that emerged at century's end. Indeed, if some officials felt that the administration of Ireland under the Union had been easy in comparison with other multilingual states such as Austria-Hungary, as was suggested by the contributor to the *Pall Mall Gazette*, then this was also a testament to the ways in which the expansion of the modern state had been translated, absorbed, reformulated, and then perpetuated in its own unique way at the local level by Irish speakers. This is not to say that this process of modernization was seamless, as historians have long been at pains to demonstrate. As events before and after the mid-nineteenth century were to prove, Ireland could hardly be characterized as a placid place for governance as various challenges to replace or alter the relationship between Ireland and Britain repeatedly took aim at union. Nor was Ireland a classless society in which opposition to elite control failed to leave its mark through, for instance, successful opposition to tithes or the threats posed by rural agitation and violence. But the point is that these features, so central to the story of Ireland as it emerged at the end of the nineteenth century, cannot be simplistically characterized in terms of linguistic divides.

And yet, in taking final stock of the features of the Irish-speaking community highlighted here, one cannot discount the very real bonds of identity and difference from English-speaking society forged by a shared language and acknowledged by its members. Received understandings of the language and its connection to Ireland made it clear that Irish speakers saw the language as constituting a bright line marking a contrast with an illegitimate English-speaking conqueror. This was true even as internal divisions built by dialect, as well as the influx of bilingualism, complicated the Irish-speaking community on one side of that distinction. It was also true even if the exact identity of that English-speaking other—whether an actual foreigner or simply an English-speaking Irish person—was not always the same in every Irish-speaking community on the island. Rather, centuries of received understanding about conquest and dispossession had marked English as a threat to Catholicism, Irish sovereignty, and national well-being. To speak Irish was to neutralize that threat while affirming membership in the local community. A significant contingent of language revivalists of the end of the century recognized this dynamic and used it to frame their understanding of how to resolve the question of Ireland's independence—that is, by linking separation to a society built around the Irish language. Even if these activists built their notion of the characteristics of the Irish-speaking population as it existed at the end of the century, rather than the diverse society that existed one hundred years previously, this notion of an oppositional Irish-speaking voice was not entirely devoid of truth. It was, however, only one part of a more complex picture.

Source Abbreviations

ainm.ie	Máire Ní Mhurchú, Diarmuid Breathnach, and Fiontar, DCU, *ainm.ie*. Dublin City University and Cló Iar-Chonnacht, 2011. http://ainm.ie.
BL	British Library.
BL Cat.	S. H. O'Grady, Robin Flower, and Myles Dillon, *Catalogue of Irish Manuscripts in the British Museum* [British Library]. 3 vols. London, 1925–26, 1953.
CC	St. Kieran's College (Coláiste Ciaráin) Library, Kilkenny.`
CE	St. John's College (Coláiste Eoin) Library, Waterford.
CF	St. Colman's College (Cólaiste Colmáin) Library, Fermoy.
CL Cat.	Pádraig de Brún and Máire Herbert, *Catalogue of Irish Manuscripts in Cambridge Libraries*. Cambridge, 1986.
C MPH Cat.	Breandán Ó Conchúir, *Clár Lámhscríbhinní Gaeilge Choláiste Ollscoile Chorcaí: Cnuasach Uí Mhurchú*. Baile Átha Cliath, 1991.
DON	Collection of Father Lúcás Ó Dónnalláin (Donnellan), now at National University of Ireland, Maynooth.
Fenning 1–7	Hugh Fenning, "Catholic Imprints of Catholic Interest," *Collectanea Hibernica* 39–48 (1998–2006): 1701–39 (1), 1740–59 (2), 1760–69 (3), 1770–82 (4), 1783–89 (5), 1790–95 (6), 1796–99 (7).
FLK	Franciscan Library, Killiney (Irish manuscripts now held at University College Dublin).
FLK Cat.	Myles Dillon, Canice Mooney, and Pádraig de Brún, *Catalogue of Irish Manuscripts in the Franciscan Library Killiney*. Dublin, 1969.
IL	Jesuit Archives (Leabhlann na nÍosánach), Leeson Street, Dublin.
ISOS	Pádraig Ó Macháin, Dublin Institute for Advanced Studies, and Dublin City University, *Irish Script on Screen/Meamram Páipéar Ríomhaire*. 1999. http://www.isos.dias.ie.
KIL Cat.	Pádraig de Brún, *Catalogue of Irish Manuscripts in King's Inns Library Dublin*. Dublin, 1972.
LCM Cat.	Pádraig Ó Fiannachta, *Clár Lámhscríbhinní Gaeilge: Leabharlanna na Cléire agus Mionchnuasaigh*. Fascúl I–II. Baile Átha Cliath, 1978–80.

ML	St. Mel's College (Coláiste Naomh Mel) Library, Longford.
MM	Mount Melleray Abbey Library, Waterford.
MM Cat.	Pádraig Ó Macháin, *Catalogue of Irish Manuscripts in Mount Melleray Abbey, Co. Waterford*. Dublin, 1991.
MYN	National University of Ireland, Maynooth.
MYN Cat.	Paul Walsh and Pádraig Ó Fiannachta, *Lámhscríbhinní Gaeilge Choláiste Phádraig Má Nuad*. Fascúl I–VIII. Má Nuad, 1943–80.
NFC	National Folklore Main Collection, Belfield.
NFC S	National Folklore Schools Collection, Belfield.
NLI	National Library of Ireland.
NLI Cat.	Nessa Ní Shéaghdha and Pádraig Ó Macháin, *Catalogue of Irish Manuscripts in the National Library of Ireland*. Fasc. I–XIII. Dublin, 1967–96.
NLI Hayes	National Library of Ireland and Richard J. Hayes, *Sources: A National Library of Ireland Database for Irish Research*. 2007–12. http://sources.nli.ie.
NLI p.	National Library of Ireland Microfilm, positive reels.
NN	Archives of the monastery of New Norcia, Australia.
OX Cat.	Brian Ó Cuív, *Catalogue of Irish Language Manuscripts in the Bodleian Library at Oxford and Oxford College Libraries*. 2 vols. Dublin, 2001, 2003.
RIA	Royal Irish Academy.
RIA Cat.	Thomas F. O'Rahilly, Kathleen Mulchrone, et al., *Catalogue of Irish Manuscripts in the Royal Irish Academy*. Fasc. I–XXVII. Dublin, 1926–70.
SLV	State Library of Victoria, Melbourne, Australia.
SPIL	Society for the Preservation of the Irish Language, *Annual Reports*, 1878–1914.
T Cat.	Pádraig de Brún, *Clár Lámhscríbhinní Gaeilge Choláiste Ollscoile Chorcaí: Cnuasach Thorna*. 2 iml. Baile Átha Cliath, 1967.
TCD	Trinity College, Dublin.
TCD Cat.	T. K. Abbott and E. J. Gwynn, *Catalogue of the Irish Manuscripts in the Library of Trinity College, Dublin*. Dublin, 1921.
Torna	National University of Ireland, Cork, University Library, Torna Collection.
UWM	University of Wisconsin–Madison Library.
UWM Cat.	Cornelius G. Buttimer, *Catalogue of Irish Manuscripts in the University of Wisconsin–Madison*. Dublin, 1989.

Notes

INTRODUCTION

1. Garret FitzGerald, "Estimates for Baronies of Minimum Level of Irish Speaking amongst Successive Decennial Cohorts: 1771-1781 to 1861-1871," *Proceedings of the Royal Irish Academy*, Section C, 84, no. 3 (1984, repr. 2004): 117-55; Máirtín Ó Murchú, *The Irish Language* (Dublin: Department of Foreign Affairs and Bord na Gaeilge, 1985), 26.

2. *Census of Ireland for the Year 1851. Part VI: General Report*, pp. 231, 293, 349, 535 [2134], H.C. 1856, xxxi; Breandán Ó Madagáin, *An Ghaeilge i Luimneach, 1700-1900* (Baile Átha Cliath: An Clóchomhar Tta, 1974), 15-16; Seán Beecher, *An Ghaeilge in Cork City: An Historical Perspective to 1894* (Cork: Goldy Angel Press, 1993), 50-53.

3. Liam Mac Mathúna, *Dúchas agus Dóchas: Scéal na Gaeilge i mBaile Átha Cliath* (Baile Átha Cliath: Glór na nGael, 1991), 50-57; Máirín Mooney, "Irish in the Liberties (1850-1911)," and Liam Mac Mathúna, "Pobal Gaeilge Bhaile Átha Cliath: Oidhrí agus Ceannródaithe," both in *An Ghaeilge i mBaile Átha Cliath*, ed. Ciarán Ó Coigligh (Baile Átha Cliath: Saotharlann Staire Bhaile Átha Cliath, 1985), 12, 37; Fionntán de Brún, "The Fadgies: An 'Irish-Speaking Colony' in Nineteenth-Century Belfast," in *Belfast and the Irish Language*, ed. Fionntán de Brún (Dublin: Four Courts Press, 2006), 101-13.

4. *Freeman's Journal*, 11 Dec. 1843; James McQuige, *The Importance of Schools for Teaching the Native Irish Language Demonstrated in a Letter from James McQuige to the Rev. Joseph Ivimey, Secretary to the Baptist Irish Society* (London: Button and Son, and Whittimore, 1818), 12.

5. "Recollections of Parochial Work in Ireland," *The Monthly Packet* 26 (Feb. 1868): 197.

6. Historical figures for Britain and Ireland necessarily require estimation, given that no languages were enumerated before the count in Ireland in 1851. But relying on contemporary observers in the Irish case such as Christopher Anderson (1782-1852), along with estimates by scholars for Scotland and Wales based on population counts for areas known to be predominantly Welsh or Gaelic speaking, historians provide figures

for 1841 of 4 million Irish speakers, 800,000 Welsh speakers, and 300,000 Gaelic speakers, plus a small number of Manx speakers. That suggests a combined figure of 5.1 million Celtic language speakers out of a population just over 26.8 million. See Reg Hindley, *The Death of the Irish Language: A Qualified Obituary* (London: Routledge, 1990), 15; Dot Jones, *Statistical Evidence Relating to the Welsh Language, 1801–1911* (Cardiff: University of Wales Press, 1998), 221–22; and Charles W. J. Withers, *Gaelic in Scotland, 1698-1981: The Geographical History of a Language* (Edinburgh: John Donald Publishers, Ltd., 1984), 83.

7. Vincent Morley, "The Idea of Britain in Eighteenth-Century Ireland and Scotland," *Studia Hibernica* 33 (2004–2005): 101–2; Nicholas Canny, "Writing Early Modern History: Ireland, Britain, and the Wider World," *Historical Journal* 46, no. 3 (Sept. 2003): 738.

8. Geraint H. Jenkins, ed., *The Welsh Language before the Industrial Revolution* (Cardiff: University of Wales Press, 1997); Geraint H. Jenkins, ed., *The Welsh Language and Its Social Domains, 1801–1911* (Cardiff: University of Wales Press, 2000); Gwenfair Parry and Mari A. Williams, *The Welsh Language and the 1891 Census* (Cardiff: University of Wales Press, 1999); V. E. Durkacz, *The Decline of the Celtic Languages: A Study of Linguistic and Cultural Conflict in Scotland, Wales, and Ireland from the Reformation to the Twentieth Century* (Edinburgh: J. Donald, 1983); Michael Hechter, *Internal Colonialism: The Celtic Fringe in British National Development, 1536–1966*, new ed. (New Brunswick, NJ: Transaction Publishers, 1999).

9. Thomas R. Trautmann, *Language and Nations: The Dravidian Proof in Colonial Madras* (Berkeley: University of California Press, 2006); Michael S. Dodson, *Orientalism, Empire, and National Culture: India, 1770–1880* (Houndsmill, UK: Palgrave Macmillan, 2007); Alyssa Ayres, *Speaking Like a State: Language and Nationalism in Pakistan* (Cambridge: Cambridge University Press, 2009); Lisa Mitchell, *Language, Emotion, and Politics in South India: The Making of a Mother Tongue* (Bloomington: Indiana University Press, 2009); C. A. Bayly, *Empire and Information: Intelligence Gathering and Social Communication in India, 1780–1870* (Cambridge: Cambridge University Press, 1996); Bernard S. Cohn, *Colonialism and Its Forms of Knowledge: The British in India* (Princeton, NJ: Princeton University Press, 1996); Farina Mir, "Imperial Policy, Provincial Practices: Colonial Language Policy in Nineteenth-Century India," *Indian Economic Social History Review* 43, no. 4 (2006): 395–427; Katherine Prior, Lance Brennan, and Robin Haines, "Bad Language: The Role of English, Persian, and Other Esoteric Tongues in the Dismissal of Sir Edward Colebrooke as Resident of Delhi in 1829," *Modern Asian Studies* 35, no. 1 (2001): 75–112.

10. Peter Burke, "Introduction," in *The Social History of Language*, ed. Peter Burke and Roy Porter (Cambridge: Cambridge University Press, 1987), 1.

11. Burke, "Introduction," 3–4; William Labov, *The Social Stratification of English in New York City*, 2nd ed. (Cambridge: Cambridge University Press, 2006); Dell Hymes, "Models for the Interaction of Language and Social Life," in *Directions in Sociolinguistics: The Ethnography of Communication*, ed. John J. Gumperz and Dell Hymes (New York: Holt, Rinehart, Winston, Inc., 1972), 35–71; John J. Gumperz, *Discourse*

Strategies (Cambridge: Cambridge University Press, 1982); Joshua Fishman, *Language and Ethnicity in Minority Sociolinguistic Perspective* (Philadelphia: Multilingual Matters, Ltd., 1989); John Edwards, *Language, Society, and Identity* (Oxford: Basil Blackwell, 1985); Peter Trudgill, *On Dialect: Social and Geographical Perspectives* (New York: New York University Press, 1983); Ralph Fasold, *The Sociolinguistics of Society* (Oxford: Basil Blackwell, 1984).

12. E.g., Robert A. Hall, "The Significance of the Italian 'Questione Della Lingua,'" *Studies in Philology* 39, no. 1 (Jan. 1942): 1–10.

13. Eugen Weber, *Peasants into Frenchmen* (Stanford: Stanford University Press, 1976), 67–94; Caroline Ford, *Creating the Nation in Provincial France: Religion and Political Identity in Brittany* (Princeton, NJ: Princeton University Press, 1993), 10–28; David Bell, "Lingua Populi, Lingua Dei: Language, Religion, and the Origins of French Revolutionary Nationalism," *American Historical Review* 100, no. 5 (1995): 1403–37; Herman Van Goethem, "La politique des langues en France, 1620–1804," *Revue du Nord* 71, no. 281 (1989): 437–60; R. D. Grillo, *Dominant Languages: Language and Hierarchy in Britain and France* (Cambridge: Cambridge University Press, 1989); François Rouget, "La langue français: Obstacle ou atout 'de l'état-nation'?," *Renaissance and Reformation/Renaissance et Réforme* 29, no. 1 (2005): 7–23; Patrice Higonnet, "The Politics of Linguistic Terrorism and Grammatical Hegemony during the French Revolution," *Social History* 5, no. 1 (1980): 41–69; Peter Flaherty, "'Langue Nationale/Langue Naturelle': The Politics of Linguistic Uniformity During the French Revolution," *Historical Reflections/Réflexions Historiques* 14, no. 2 (1987): 311–28; and Martin Lyons, "Politics and Patois: The Linguistic Policy of the French Revolution," *Australian Journal of French Studies* 18, no. 3 (1981): 264–81.

14. To take just those studies available in English, recent publications include Pier M. Larson, *Ocean of Letters: Language and Creolization in an Indian Ocean Diaspora* (Cambridge: Cambridge University Press, 2009); Peter Mackridge, *Language and National Identity in Greece, 1766–1976* (Oxford: Oxford University Press, 2009); Friederike Baer, *The Trial of Frederick Eberle: Language, Patriotism, and Citizenship in Philadelphia's German Community, 1790–1830* (New York: New York University Press, 2008); Hiraku Shimoda, "Tongues-Tied: The Making of a 'National Language' and the Discovery of Dialects in Meiji Japan," *American Historical Review* 115, no. 3 (June 2010): 714–31; Victor Zhivov, *Language and Culture in Eighteenth-Century Russia*, trans. Marcus Levitt (Boston: Academic Studies Press, 2009).

15. Stephan Elspaß, Nils Langer, Joachim Scharloth, and Wim Vandenbussche, eds., *Germanic Language Histories "from Below" (1700–2000)*, Studia Linguistica Germanica Series, vol. 86 (Berlin: Walter de Gruyter, 2007); Donald N. Tuten, *Koineization in Medieval Spanish*, Contributions to the Sociology of Language 88 (Berlin: Mouton de Gruyter, 2003); Margarita Hidalgo, "Sociolinguistic Stratification in New Spain," *International Journal of the Sociology of Language* 149 (2001): 55–78; María Irene Moyna and Magdalena Coll, "A Tale of Two Borders: 19th Century Language Contact in Southern California and Northern Uruguay," *Studies in Hispanic and Lusophone Linguistics* 1, no. 1 (2008): 105–38; Judith T. Irvine, "The Family Romance of Colonial

Linguistics: Gender and Family in Nineteenth-Century Representations of African Languages," *Pragmatics* 5, no. 2 (1995): 139–53; Judith T. Irvine, "Subjected Words: African Linguistics and the Colonial Encounter," *Language and Communication* 28 (2008): 323–43; Urszula Okulska, "Historical Corpora and Their Applicability to Sociolinguistic, Discourse-Pragmatic, and Ethno-Linguistic Research," *Poznań Studies in Contemporary Linguistics* 41 (2006): 47–109; Theodore R. Weeks, "Religion and Russification: Russian Language in the Catholic Churches of the 'Northwest Provinces' after 1863," *Kritika* 2, no. 1 (Winter 2001): 87–110; Tom Priestly, "Denial of Ethnic Identity: The Political Manipulation of Beliefs about Language in Slovene Minority Areas of Austria and Hungary," *Slavic Review* 55, no. 2 (Summer 1996): 364–98; Zygmunt Szultka, "Le polonais comme langue écrite en Poméranie occidentale depuis le XVIe siècle jusqu'au XVIIIe," *Polish Western Affairs* 31, nos. 1–2 (1990): 81–95; Susan Gal, *Language Shift: Social Determinants of Linguistic Change in Bilingual Austria* (New York: Academic Press, 1979).

16. Irvine, "Family Romance," 144–49, and Irvine, "Subjected Words," 336–38.

17. Pádraig Ó Riagáin, *Language Policy and Social Reproduction: Ireland, 1893–1993* (Oxford: Clarendon Press, 1997); Diarmait Mac Giolla Chriost, *The Irish Language in Ireland: From Goídel to Globalization* (New York: Routledge, 2005), 111–98.

18. Diarmuid Ó Donnchadha, *Castar an Taoide* (Baile Átha Cliath: Coiscéim, 1995), 1–96.

19. Declan Kiberd, "Irish Literature and Irish History," in *The Oxford Illustrated History of Ireland*, ed. Roy Foster (Oxford: Oxford University Press, 2000), 297–308; Joep Leerssen, *Mere Irish and Fíor-Ghael: Studies in the Idea of Irish Nationality, Its Development and Literary Expression prior to the Nineteenth Century* (Notre Dame, IN: University of Notre Dame Press, 1997).

20. Niall Ó Ciosáin, "Gaelic Culture and Language Shift," in *Nineteenth-Century Ireland: A Guide to Recent Research*, ed. Laurence M. Geary and Margaret Kelleher (Dublin: University College Dublin Press, 2005), 136–39.

21. Brian Ó Conchubhair, *Fin de Siècle na Gaeilge: Darwin, an Athbheochan, agus Smaointeoireacht na hEorpa* (Indreabhán: An Clóchomhar Tta, 2009), 54–55.

22. Theobaldum Stapletonium, *Catechismus, Seu Doctrina Christiana, Latino-Hibernica, Per Modum Dialogi, Inter Magistrum et Discipulum* (Bruxelles: Huberti Anthonii, 1639), prologue, xi.

23. James Scurry [Séamus Ó Scoireadh], *Remarks on the Irish Language, with a Review of Its Grammars, Glossaries, Vocabularies and Dictionaries. To which is Added, a Model of a Comprehensive Irish Dictionary* (Dublin: Graisberry, 1827), 4.

24. Breandán Ó Buachalla, *I mBéal Feirste Cois Cuain* (Baile Átha Cliath: An Clóchomhar Tta, 1968), 26–27, 34, 37; Peter Froggatt, "MacDonell, James," and James Quinn, "Russell, Thomas," in *Dictionary of Irish Biography*, ed. James McGuire and James Quinn (Cambridge: Cambridge University Press, 2009), dib.cambridge.org/viewReadPage.do?articleId=a5184 and dib.cambridge.org/viewReadPage.do?articleId=a7846.

25. John Hutchinson, *The Dynamics of Cultural Nationalism: The Gaelic Revival and the Creation of the Irish Nation State* (London: Allen and Unwin, 1987), 101.

26. Such is the classic account provided by Hutchinson in *The Dynamics of Cultural Nationalism* and Tom Garvin in *The Evolution of Irish Nationalist Politics* (New York: Holmes and Meier Publishers, Inc., 1981). There was a time when the contributions of the Society for the Preservation of the Irish Language and Gaelic Union were not recognized in this narrative. See Máirín Ní Mhuiríosa, *Réamhchonraitheoirí. Nótaí ar Chuid de na Daoine a bhí Gníomhach i nGluiseacht na Gaeilge idir 1876 agus 1893* (Baile Átha Cliath: Clódhanna Teoranta, 1968), xi.

27. Vincent Morley, *Ó Chéitinn go Raiftearaí: Mar a Cumadh Stair na hÉireann* (Baile Átha Cliath: Coiscéim, 2011), 4–8.

28. Ó Conchubhair, *Fin de Siècle na Gaeilge*, 1–4.

29. Philip O'Leary, *The Prose Literature of the Gaelic Revival, 1881–1921: Ideology and Innovation* (University Park: Pennsylvania State University Press, 1994), 19–90; Ó Conchubhair, *Fin de Siècle na Gaeilge*, 1–9, 36–38, and passim.

30. Henry Morris [Énrí Ó Muirgheasa], "The Loss of the Irish Language and Its Influence on the Catholic Religion in Ireland," *Fáinne an Lae* 1, no. 13 (1898): 8–9.

31. Daniel Corkery, *The Fortunes of the Irish Language* (1954; repr., Cork: Mercier Press, 1956), 64–77, 102–17, 122–28.

32. Pádraig Ó Fiannachta, *Milis an Teanga: Stair na Gaeilge ó Thús* (Corcaigh: Cló Mercier, 1974), 51–52; Proinsias Mac Aonghusa, *Ar Son na Gaeilge: Conradh na Gaeilge 1893–1993, Stair Seanchais* (Baile Átha Cliath: Conradh na Gaeilge, 1993), 25–26. In other cases, general histories simply ignored the language altogether, and little change can be detected in the historiography over time: James O'Connor, *History of Ireland, 1798–1924*, 2 vols. (London: Edward Arnold & Co., 1925), affords it only two paragraphs (1:38, 221–22), while fifty years later, Oliver MacDonagh's *Ireland: The Union and Its Aftermath* (1977; repr., Dublin: University College Press, 2003) does not mention Irish at all.

33. Máire Ní Chiosáin, "Meath na Gaeilge i gCléire," in *Aistí ar an Nua-Ghaeilge in Ómos do Bhreandán Ó Buachalla*, ed. Aidan Doyle and Siobhán Ní Laoire (Baile Átha Cliath: Cois Life, 2006), 85–93; M. Ó hEarcáin, "Meath na Gaeilge i gCluain Maine agus in Iorras," *Donegal Annual* 47 (1995): 106–12; Brighid Ní Mhóráin, *Thiar sa Mhainistir atá an Ghaolainn Bhreá: Meath na Gaeilge in Uíbh Ráthach* (An Daingean: An Sagart, 1997).

34. *An Claidheamh Soluis*, 7 Oct. 1899.

35. Douglas Hyde, *A Literary History of Ireland from Earliest Times to the Present Day* (London: T. Fisher Unwin, 1899), 621.

36. Aodh de Blacam, "The Other Hidden Ireland," *Studies* 23, no. 91 (Sept. 1934): 446.

37. Brian Ó Cuív, *Irish Dialects and Irish-Speaking Districts: Three Lectures by Brian Ó Cuív* (Dublin: Dublin Institute for Advanced Studies, 1980); Ó Cuív, ed., *A View of the Irish Language* (Dublin: Stationery Office, 1969); Ó Cuív, "The Irish Language in the Early Modern Period," in *A New History of Ireland*, vol. 3, *Early Modern Ireland, 1534–1691*, ed. T. W. Moody, F. X. Martin, and F. J. Byrne (Oxford: Clarendon Press, 1976), 509–45; Ó Cuív, "Irish Language and Literature, 1691–1845," in *A New History of Ireland*, vol. 4, *Eighteenth-Century Ireland, 1691–1800*, ed. T. W. Moody and

W. E. Vaughan (Oxford: Clarendon Press, 1986), 374–423; Ó Cuív, "Irish Language and Literature, 1845–1921," in *A New History of Ireland*, vol. 6, *Ireland under the Union, Part, II, 1870–1921*, ed. W. E. Vaughn (Oxford: Clarendon Press, 1996), 385–435.

38. Maureen Wall, "The Decline of the Irish Language," in Ó Cuív, *A View of the Irish Language*, 81–90.

39. Seán de Fréine, *The Great Silence* (Dublin: Foilseacháin Náisiúnta Teoranta, 1965), 3–5, 53–64, 83–104, 123–64.

40. Emmet Larkin, "The Devotional Revolution in Ireland, 1850–1875," *American Historical Review* 77, no. 3 (June 1972): 649.

41. Angela Bourke, "'The Baby and the Bathwater': Cultural Loss in Nineteenth-Century Ireland," in *Ideology and Ireland in the Nineteenth Century*, ed. Tadhg Foley and Seán Ryder (Dublin: Four Courts Press, 1998), 79.

42. Ní Mhóráin, *Thiar sa Mhainistir*, 9; Máirín Nic Eoin, "Irish Language and Literature in County Kilkenny in the Nineteenth Century," in *Kilkenny: History and Society; Interdisciplinary Essays in the History of an Irish County*, ed. William Nolan and Kevin Whelan (Dublin: Geography Publications, 1990), 479.

43. Ó Ciosáin, "Gaelic Culture," 42.

44. William H. Sewell, "The Concept(s) of Culture," in *Beyond the Cultural Turn: New Directions in the Study of Society and Culture*, ed. Victoria E. Bonnell and Lynn Hunt (Berkeley: University of California Press, 1999), 52–55; Sherry Ortner, "Theory in Anthropology Since the Sixties," *Comparative Studies in Society and History* 26, no. 1 (1984): 144–56.

45. John J. Gumperz and Stephen C. Levinson, "Rethinking Linguistic Relativity," *Current Anthropology* 32, no. 5 (Dec. 1991): 613–15.

46. William Labov, *Principles of Linguistic Change*, 2 vols. (Oxford: Blackwell, 1994), 2:13–33; Peter Trudgill, "Colonial Dialect Contact in the History of European Languages: On the Irrelevance of Identity to New-Dialect Formation," *Language in Society* 37, no. 2 (2008): 241–80; Deborah Cameron, "Demythologizing Sociolinguistics: Why Language Does Not Reflect Society," in *Ideologies of Language*, ed. John E. Joseph and Talbot J. Taylor (London: Routledge, 1990): 79–93; Peter Auer, "A Postscript: Code-Switching and Social Identity," *Journal of Pragmatics* 37 (2005): 403–10; Joseph Gafaranga, "Demythologising Language Alternation Studies: Conversational Structure vs. Social Structure in Bilingual Interaction," *Journal of Pragmatics* 37 (2005): 281–300; James Milroy, "On the Role of the Speaker in Language Change," in *Motives for Language Change*, ed. Raymond Hickey (Cambridge: Cambridge University Press, 2003), 143–46; Leonie Cornips, "Loosing Grammatical Gender in Dutch: The Result of Bilingual Acquisition and/or an Act of Identity?," *International Journal of Bilingualism* 12, nos. 1–2 (2008): 105–24.

47. Judith T. Irvine and Susan Gal, "Language Ideology and Linguistic Differentiation," in *Regimes of Language: Ideologies, Polities, and Identities*, ed. Paul V. Kroskity (Santa Fe, NM: School of American Research Press and Oxford: James Currey Ltd., 2000), 35–83.

48. Salikoko Mufwene, *Language Evolution: Contact, Competition, and Change* (London: Continuum International Publishing Group, 2008), 15–26; Salikoko Mufwene,

The Ecology of Language Evolution (Cambridge: Cambridge University Press, 2001), 15-24, 153-57.

49. There has been less agreement, however, on what social class and ideologies these scribes—particularly in the eighteenth century—represented. See L. M. Cullen, *The Hidden Ireland: Reassessment of a Concept* (Mullingar: Lilliput Press, 1988), 50-52; Vincent Morley, *Washington igCeannas a Ríochta: Cogadh Mheiriceá i Litríocht na Gaeilge* (Baile Átha Clíath: Coiscéim, 2005), xiii-xvi; Breandán Ó Buachalla, "From Jacobite to Jacobin," in *1798: A Bicentenary Perspective*, ed. Thomas Bartlett et al. (Dublin and Portland, OR: Four Courts Press, 2003), 88.

50. Breandán Ó Conchúir, *Scríobhaithe Chorcaí, 1700-1850* (Baile Átha Cliath: An Clóchomhar Tta, 1982).

51. Meidhbhín Ní Úrdail, *The Scribe in Eighteenth- and Nineteenth-Century Ireland: Motivations and Milieu*, Studien und Texte zur Keltologie 3 (Münster: Nodus Publikationen, 2000); Rónán Ó Donnachadha, *Mícheál Óg Ó Longáin, File* (Baile Átha Cliath: Coiscéim, 1994); Vincent Morley, *An Crann os Coill: Aodh Buí Mac Cruitín, c. 1680-1755* (Baile Átha Cliath: Coiscéim, 1995); Fionntán de Brún, "Expressing the Nineteenth Century in Irish: The Poetry of Aodh Mac Domhnaill (1802-67)," *New Hibernia Review* 15, no. 1 (Spring 2011): 81-106; Ciarán Dawson, *Peadar Ó Gealacáin: Scríobhaí* (Baile Átha Cliath: An Clóchomhar Tta, 1992); Máirín Nic Eoin, *B'Ait leo Bean: Gnéithe den Idé-eolaíocht Inscne i dTraidisiún Liteartha na Gaeilge* (Baile Átha Cliath: An Clóchomhar Tta, 1998); Liam Mac Mathúna, *Béarla sa Ghaeilge: Cabhair Choigríche; An Códmheascadh Gaeilge/Béarla i Litríocht na Gaeilge, 1600-1900* (Baile Átha Cliath: An Clóchomhar Tta, 2007); Diarmaid Ó Muirithe, *An tAmhrán Macarónach* (Baile Átha Cliath: An Clóchomhar Tta, 1980).

52. Bláthnaid Uí Chatháin, *Éigse Chairbre: Filíocht ó Chairbreacha i gCo. Chorcaí agus ón gCeantar Máguaird, 1750-1850* (Baile Átha Clíath: An Clóchomhar Tta, 2006).

53. Pádraig de Brún, *Scriptural Instruction in the Vernacular: The Irish Society and Its Teachers, 1818-1827* (Dublin: Dublin Institute for Advanced Studies, 2009).

54. Padraig Ó Loingsigh, "The Irish Language in the 19th Century," *Oideas* 14 (1974): 13.

55. Morley, *Ó Chéitinn go Raiftearaí*, 8-22; Lesa Ní Mhunghaile, "Bilingualism, Print Culture in Irish and the Public Sphere, 1700-c. 1830," in *Irish and English: Essays on the Irish Linguistic and Cultural Frontier, 1600-1900*, ed. James Kelly and Ciarán Mac Murchaidh (Dublin: Four Courts Press, 2012), 224-37; Breandán Ó Buachalla, *Aisling Ghéar: Na Stíobhartaigh agus an tAos Léinn, 1603-1788* (Baile Átha Cliath: An Clóchomhar Tta, 1996); Peter McQuillan, *Native and Natural: Aspects of the Concepts of "Right" and "Freedom" in Irish* (Cork: Cork University Press in Association with Field Day, 2004); Cornelius Buttimer, "Gaelic Literature and Contemporary Life in Cork, 1700-1840," in *Cork: History and Society; Interdisciplinary Essays on the History of an Irish County*, ed. Cornelius Buttimer, Patrick Flanagan, and Gerard O'Brien (Dublin: Geography Publications, 1993), 585-683.

56. Ní Úrdail, *Scribe*, 205; Niall Ó Ciosáin, *Print and Popular Culture in Ireland, 1750-1850* (New York: St. Martin's Press, 1997), 118-31. See also Ní Mhunghaile, "Bilingualism, Print Culture," 224 and passim.

57. Ní Mhórain, *Thiar sa Mhainistir*, 65–154; Máiréad Nic Craith, *Malartú Teanga: An Ghaeilge i gCorcaigh sa Naoú hAois Déag* (Bremen: Cumann Eorpach Léann na hÉireann, 1994). Hindley's 1990 study (*Death of the Irish Language*, 14–23) also provides a usable summary of Irish language statistics for the nineteenth century, but on its analysis, see the response by Éamon Ó Ciosáin, *Buried Alive: A Reply to "The Death of the Irish Language"* (Dublin: Dáil Ui Chadhain, 1991), to Hindley's explanation for decline and especially for his examination of the class dynamics of the Gaeltacht and language policy in the twentieth century.

58. Tony Crowley, *Wars of Words: The Politics of Language in Ireland, 1537–2004* (Oxford: Oxford University Press, 2005).

CHAPTER 1. LANGUAGE BONDS AND THE ENGLISH-SPEAKING OTHER

1. Peadar Ó Laoghaire, *Mo Sgéal Féin* (Baile Átha Cliath: Brún agus Nuallán, 1915), 99–100.

2. Grace Neville, "'He Spoke to Me in English, I Answered Him in Irish': Language Shift in the Folklore Archives," in *L'Irlande et ses langues: Actes du colloque 1992 de la Société Française d'Études Irlandaises*, ed. Jean Brihault (Rennes: Presses Universitaires Rennes, 1992), 19–32.

3. The Murphy material can be found in the National Folklore Main Collection, Belfield (hereafter NFC) 1219. Searching for a sense of how language shift was experienced, modern scholars have at times leaned disproportionately on Murphy's 1951 investigation of north Tyrone in which the collector, assisted by an Irish speaker, canvassed local views on Irish at the time and in their parents' and grandparents' generation. See Neville, "'He Spoke to Me in English,'" 21–28, 31, and Mac Mathúna, *Béarla sa Ghaeilge*, 226–29.

4. R. A. Stewart Macalister, ed., *Lebor Gabála Érenn: The Book of the Taking of Ireland*, 5 vols. (1938–41, 1956; repr., Dublin: Irish Texts Society, 1984–96), 1:140–43, 192–97; George Calder, ed., *Auraicept na n-Éces: The Scholars' Primer* (Edinburgh: John Grant, 1917), 4–5.

5. Joseph Lennon, *Irish Orientalism: A Literary and Intellectual History* (Syracuse, NY: Syracuse University Press, 2004), 29.

6. Calder, *Auraicept*, 2–5, 8–19; Macalister, *Lebor Gabála*, 1:36–39, 140–49, 194–97, 2:10–15, 52–59, 90–93.

7. Macalister, *Lebor Gabála*, 1:38–39, 2:14–45.

8. David Comyn and Patrick S. Dinneen, eds., *Foras Feasa ar Éirinn le Seathrún Céitinn, D.D./The History of Ireland by Geoffrey Keating, D.D.*, 4 vols. (London: Irish Texts Society, 1902, 1908, 1914), 1:78–81, 224–31, 2:2–51; Anne Cronin, "The Sources of Keating's Forus Feasa ar Éirinn," *Éigse* 5 (1945–47): 132.

9. Vincent Morley, *Ó Chéitinn go Raiftearaí*, 53, 64, 69–71, 111–38.

10. Roderic O'Flaherty [Ruaidhrí Ó Flaithbheartaigh], *Ogygia, or, a Chronological Account of Irish Events: Collected from Very Ancient Documents, Faithfully Compared with Each Other, and Supported by the Genealogical and Chronological Aid of the Sacred and Prophane Writings of the First Nations of the Globe*, 2 vols., trans. James Hely (Dublin: W. McKenzie, 1793), 1:92–93.

11. Séamus Mac Domhnaill, ed., *Dánta is Amhráin Sheáin Uí Ghadhra* (Baile Átha Cliath: Oifig an tSoláthair, 1955), 15. On Ó Gadhra, see also Joep Leerssen, *Mere Irish and Fíor-Ghael*, 208.

12. Tony Crowley, *The Politics of Language in Ireland, 1366–1922: A Sourcebook* (London: Routledge, 2000), 29, 35.

13. Hugh MacCurtin [Aodh Mac Cruitín], *A Brief Discourse in Vindication of the Antiquity of Ireland: Collected Out of Many Authentick Irish Histories and Chronicles, and Out of Foreign Learned Authors* (Dublin: S. Powell, 1717), 10–27; Vincent Morley, *An Crann os Coill*, 38, 52; *Transactions of the Gaelic Society of Dublin, Established for the Investigation and Revival of Ancient Irish Literature* (Dublin: John Barlow, 1808), vi–vii; Ursula Young, *A Sketch of Irish History, Compiled by Way of Question & Answer, for the Use of Schools* (Cork: J. Geary, 1815), 6; John O'Donovan, *A Grammar of the Irish Language, Published for the Use of the Senior Classes in the College of St. Columba* (Dublin: Hodges and Smith, 1845), xxviii–xxxi. O'Brennan reproduced Seán Ó Conaill's "Tuireamh na hÉireann" in *Ancient Ireland: Her Milesian Chiefs, Her Kings and Princes, Her Great Men, Her Struggles for Liberty, Her Apostle St. Patrick, Her Religion* (Dublin: John Mullany, 1855), 2–100.

14. R. Mark Skowcroft, "Leabhar Gabhála, Part I: The Growth of the Text," *Ériu* 38 (1987): 81–85; Skowcroft, "Leabhar Gabhála, Part II: The Growth of the Tradition," *Ériu* 39 (1988): 7–32; John Carey, "Native Elements in Irish Pseudohistory," in *Cultural Identity and Cultural Integration: Ireland and Europe in the Early Middle Ages*, ed. Doris Edel (Dublin: Four Courts Press, 1995), 45–60; John Carey, *A New Introduction to Lebor Gabála Érenn: The Book of the Taking of Ireland* (1993; repr., Dublin: Irish Texts Society, 2006), 2–3; Anders Ahlqvist, *The Early Irish Linguist: An Edition of the Canonical Part of the Auraicept na nÉces, with Introduction, Commentary and Indices* (Helsinki: Societas Scientiarum Fennica, 1983), 17–20, 31–35, 40; Lennon, *Irish Orientalism*, 7–8, 28–36.

15. Comyn and Dinneen, *Foras Feasa*, 2:52–53; MacCurtin, *Brief Discourse*, 28–29. In some instances, the histories spoke of Irish as the Scotic language brought from the tower by Rifath (or Riphat) Scot, also said to be an ancestor of Féinius in the Noachian line. See Macalister, *Lebor Gabála*, 1:36–37. Ó Flaithbheartaigh in particular had trouble rectifying these two stories and expressed skepticism that subsequent waves of invaders of Ireland would share a language. See O'Flaherty, *Ogygia*, 16–17.

16. Peter Burke, *Languages and Communities in Early Modern Europe* (Cambridge: Cambridge University Press, 2004), 22.

17. Eryn M. White, "The Established Church, Dissent and the Welsh Language c. 1660–1811," Eryn M. White, "Popular Schooling and the Welsh Language 1650–1800," and Geraint H. Jenkins, "The Cultural Uses of the Welsh Language, 1660–1800," all in G. Jenkins, *Welsh Language before the Industrial Revolution*, 235, 326, 373–79.

18. Colin Kidd, *British Identities before Nationalism: Ethnicity and Nationhood in the Atlantic World, 1600–1800* (Cambridge: Cambridge University Press, 1999), 30–32, 65; George J. Metcalf, "The Indo-European Hypothesis in the Sixteenth and Seventeenth Centuries," in *Studies in the History of Linguistics: Traditions and Paradigms*, ed. Dell Hymes (Bloomington: Indiana University Press, 1974), 233–37.

19. Sarah E. McKibben, *Endangered Masculinities in Irish Poetry, 1540–1780* (Dublin: University College Dublin Press, 2010), 5–6, 14–18, 24–36, and passim.

20. Nic Eoin, *B'Ait leo Bean*, 33–70; B. Ó Buachalla, *Aisling Ghéar*, 469–70; Máire Herbert, "Goddess and King: The Sacred Marriage in Early Ireland," in *Women and Sovereignty*, ed. Louise Fradenburg (Edinburgh: Edinburgh University Press, 1992), 264–75.

21. For example, Céitinn wrote, "Is ann sin tug Féinius fá deara ar Ghaedheal an Ghaedhealg do chur i n-eagar is i n-ordughadh do réir mar atá *sí* 'n-a cúig codchaibh..." (It is then that Féinius directed Gaedhil to order Irish as *she* is into five divisions). Comyn and Dinneen, *Foras Feasa*, 2:10–11, emphasis mine. But see also Calder, *Auraicept*, 16–17: "Berla Feni tra arricht sund & iarmberla & berla n-edarscartha etir na feadhaib & berla na filed a ceathramad & an gnathberla fogni do chach a coiced," in Calder's translation: "Now the language of the Irish was invented here, and the Additional [recte: Archaic] Language, and Language Parted Among the Trees, and the Language of the Poets is the fourth, and the Common Language that serves everyone, the fifth."

22. Tom Dunne, "Voices of the Vanquished: Echoes of Language Loss in Gaelic Poetry from Kinsale to the Great Famine," *Journal of Irish and Scottish Studies* 1, no. 1 (Sept. 2007): 31.

23. Macalister, *Lebor Gabála*, 2:10–11; Comyn and Dinneen, *Foras Feasa*, 2:10–13.

24. Calder, *Auraicept*, 4–5.

25. Leerssen, *Mere Irish and Fíor-Ghael*, 189.

26. Dunne, "Voices of the Vanquished," 31–41; John C. Mac Erlean, ed., *Duanaire Dháibhidh Uí Bhruadair: The Poems of David Ó Bruadair*, 3 vols. (1910–17; repr., London: Irish Texts Society, 1986), 1:36–37, 82–83; Patrick S. Dinneen and Tadhg O'Donoghue, eds., *Dánta Aodhagáin Uí Rathaille: The Poems of Egan O'Rahilly*, 2nd ed. (London: Irish Texts Society, 1965), 166–67; Patrick Dinneen, ed., *Amhráin Eoghain Ruaidh Uí Shúilleabháin*, 2nd ed. (Baile Átha Cliath: Connradh na Gaedhilge, 1902), 96; Bernadette Cunningham, "Loss and Gain: Attitudes towards the English Language in Early Modern Ireland," in *Reshaping Ireland, 1550–1700: Colonization and Its Consequences; Essays Presented to Nicholas Canny*, ed. Brian Mac Cuarta (Dublin: Four Courts Press, 2011), 164, 178–80.

27. Mac Mathúna, *Béarla sa Ghaeilge*, 131–36, 143–51; Leerssen, *Mere Irish and Fíor-Ghael*, 197–202; N. J. A. Williams, ed., *Pairlement Chloinne Tomáis* (Dublin: Dublin Institute for Advanced Studies, 1981), 40, 97.

28. Bernadette Cunningham, *The World of Geoffrey Keating: History, Myth, and Religion in Seventeenth-Century Ireland* (Dublin: Four Courts Press, 2004), 130.

29. Comyn and Dinneen, *Foras Feasa*, 1:36–37; Dunne, "Voices of the Vanquished," 29.

30. Leerssen, *Mere Irish and Fíor-Ghael*, 216–20, 236–41; B. Ó Buachalla, *Aisling Ghéar*, 574–650; B. Ó Buachalla, "From Jacobite to Jacobin," 79–85.

31. Leerssen, *Mere Irish and Fíor-Ghael*, 213–16; Dunne, "Voices of the Vanquished," 32. On the concomitant development of Irish kingship, Jacobitism, and Catholic Reformation ideology, see B. Ó Buachalla, *Aisling Ghéar*, 3–8, 24–28.

32. Andrew Carpenter, ed., *Verse in English from Eighteenth-Century Ireland* (Cork: Cork University Press, 1998), 324.

33. National Library of Ireland (hereafter NLI) MS G 96, pp. 189–97. Although unsigned, this essay is believed to be the work of Ó Longáin. See Nessa Ní Shéaghdha and Pádraig Ó Macháin, *Catalogue of Irish Manuscripts in the National Library of Ireland*, fasc. I–XIII (Dublin, 1967–96) (hereafter NLI Cat.), fasc. III, 70.

34. Dunne, "Voices of the Vanquished," 41; B. Ó Buachalla, "From Jacobite to Jacobin," 86–96; McQuillan, *Native and Natural*, 203–13.

35. Mícheál Mac Cárthaigh to John O'Daly, 22 May 1846, published by Torna [Tadhg Ó Donnachadha] in "Congantóirí Sheáin Uí Dhálaigh," *Éigse* 2, no. 3 (Fall 1940): 215.

36. Tomás Ó Flannghaile, ed., *Duanaire na Macaomh: A Selection of Irish Poetry for Schools and Colleges* (Dublin: M. H. Gill and Son, 1910), 40–43, 177–79. See also Leerssen, *Mere Irish and Fíor-Ghael*, 207–8.

37. Examples include Royal Irish Academy (hereafter RIA) MS 23 O 35 (55), p. 355, transcribed by Brian Ó Fearghail in the 1770s; British Library (hereafter BL) MS Egerton 158, f. 157, transcribed by Séamus Ó Broin, 1736–39; NLI MS G 46, p. 87, transcribed by Séamus Banburi in 1820; and Thaddaeus Connellan, trans., *Reidh-Leighin air Ghnothuibh Cearba, Trachtail, Tuarasdal, Reic & Ceannach, &c &c. Chum Feidhme na ttAosóg, is do Gach Duine Lánaosda. Tairtheangtha Anois maille re Biseach le Tadhg O Coinniallain* (Dublin: R. Graisberridhe, 1835), 19.

38. Éamonn Ó Tuathail, ed., *Rainn agus Amhráin: Cnuasacht Rann agus Amhrán ó Chonndae na Midhe, ó Chonndae Lughmhaidh agus ó Chonndae Árdmhacha* (Baile Átha Cliath: Brún agus Ó Nóláin, Teor., 1923), 26–27; Carpenter, *Verse in English*, 327. For the dynamics of this sexual conquest by the Irish-speaking male, see McKibben, *Endangered Masculinities*, 89–98.

39. Thomas Swanton to John Windele, 31 Mar. 1855, RIA MS 4 B 15, 57 (i), corresponding to stanza 2 of the Inglis poem.

40. John C. Mac Erlean [Eoin Mac Giolla Eáin], ed., *Dánta Amhráin is Caointe Sheathrúin Céitinn* (Baile Átha Cliath: Connradh na Gaedhilge, 1900), 17; B. Cunningham supplies a translation in *World of Geoffrey Keating*, 128.

41. RIA MS 23 O 35 (55), p. 12; NLI MS G 199, p. 5. For Mac Óda, see Ó Buachalla, *I mBéal Feirste Cois Cuain*, 51.

42. NLI p. 442 (BL MS Egerton 126), f. 38a. See also Thomas F. O'Rahilly, Kathleen Mulchrone, et al., *Catalogue of Irish Manuscripts in the Royal Irish Academy*, fasc. I–XXVII (Dublin, 1926–70) (hereafter RIA Cat.), fasc. XXV, 3162 (RIA MS 24 C 44 [1174]).

43. Nicholas Kearney [Nioclás Ó Cearnaigh] to John O'Daly, 19 Jan. 1845, NLI MS G 389, pp. 267–69.

44. *Bristol Mercury*, 21 Sept. 1833.

45. NLI MS G 199, p. 280.

46. Tony Crowley, *Language in History: Theories and Texts* (London: Routledge, 1996), 99, 107–9.

47. Irish Society, "Twenty-Eighth Report, 1846," in *Reports of the Irish Society for Promoting the Education of the Native Irish through the Medium of Their Own Language* (Dublin: M. Goodwin, 1846), 23.

48. Irish Society, "Quarterly Extract, No. 49," in *Quarterly Extracts from the Correspondence of the Irish Society for Promoting the Education of the Native Irish through the Medium of Their Own Language* (Dublin: M. Goodwin, 1835), 298.

49. Nollaig Ó Muraíle, for example, notes that the society's estimates of the Irish-speaking population were influenced by its desire to bring the status of the language before the attention of Protestant charitable donors. See "Staid na Gaeilge i gConnachta in Aimsir Sheáin Mhic Héil," in *Leon an Iarthair: Aistí ar Sheán Mac Héil, Ardeaspag Thuama, 1834–1881*, ed. Áine Ní Cheannain (Baile Átha Cliath: An Clóchomhar Tta, 1983), 50–51.

50. NFC 829:20.

51. NFC 237:124; see also Grace Neville, "God's Own Language? Attitudes to Irish, Then and Now," *Etudes irlandaises* 26, no. 2 (2001): 85–86.

52. Crowley, *Wars of Words*, 23; *Freeman's Journal*, 28 Dec. 1877.

53. "Richard Whately," *Sunday Magazine* (1 Jan. 1867): 273; Irish Society, "Quarterly Extract, No. 8," in *Quarterly Extracts*, 61–62; Proceedings of the Committee, Irish Society Papers, Trinity College, Dublin (hereafter TCD), MS 7644, p. 7; *First Report of the Commissioners on Education in Ireland*, appendix 242, p. 686, H.C. 1825 (400), xii.

54. James Mullaney, untitled autobiographical manuscript, ca. 1856, John Rylands Library, MS 56 (NLI p.1713).

55. Proceedings of the Committee, Irish Society Papers, TCD, MS 7644, p. 7.

56. Irish Society, "Thirteenth Report, 1831," in *Reports of the Irish Society for Promoting the Education of the Native Irish through the Medium of Their Own Language* (Dublin: M. Goodwin, 1831), 30–31.

57. Asenath Nicholson, *Ireland's Welcome to the Stranger, or Excursions through Ireland in 1844 and 1845 for the Purpose of Personally Investigating the Condition of the Poor*, ed. Maureen Murphy (1847–51; repr., Dublin: The Lilliput Press, 2002), 203.

58. A. M. Disney to Paul Askin, 11 June 1880, Achill Island Mission Papers, NLI, MS 410.

59. Niall Ó Ciosáin, *Print and Popular Culture*, 84–99; Dáithí Ó hÓgáin, *The Hero in Irish Folk History* (Dublin: Gill and Macmillan, 1985), 178–92.

60. Unknown correspondent to John Daly, 23 Jan. 1849, NLI MS G 389, pp. 353–75. This motif, in which the speaking of English alerts a fugitive speaking another language, is also found in at least one Scottish tale. See "The Herring Fisher and the Press Gang," in Cuthbert Bede [Edward Bradley], *The White Wife, with Other Stories Supernatural, Romantic, and Legendary* (London: Sampson, Low, Son, and Marston, 1865), 92–93.

61. Gearóid Ó Tuathaigh, "Gaelic Ireland, Popular Politics and Daniel O'Connell," *Galway Archaeological and Historical Journal* 34 (1974–75): 21–34; Caoimhín Ó Danachair, "Dónall Ó Conaill i mBéalaibh na nDaoine," *Studia Hibernica* 14 (1974): 40–66; Diarmaid Ó Muirithe, "O'Connell in Irish Folk Tradition," in *Daniel O'Connell: Political Pioneer*, ed. Maurice R. O'Connell (Dublin: Daniel O'Connell Association, 1991), 72–85.

62. *An Claidheamh Soluis*, 8 June 1901.
63. *Mayo Constitution*, 19 Oct. 1841. This story would appear to have been recycled during the Land League agitation and ascribed to Michael Davitt. See Eugene Hynes, *Knock: The Virgin's Apparition in Nineteenth-Century Ireland* (Cork: Cork University Press, 2009), 133.
64. Ríonach Uí Ógáin, *Immortal Dan: Daniel O'Connell in Irish Folk Tradition* (Dublin: Geography Publications, 1995), 29–30, 150–54. Such findings belie claims by historians that O'Connell's personal ambivalence toward Irish exercised a negative impact on popular attitudes.
65. J. C. Curwen, *Observations on the State of Ireland, Principally Directed to Its Agriculture and Rural Population*, 2 vols. (London: Baldwin, Cradock, and Joy, 1818), 1:346.
66. Michael McGrath, ed., *Cinnlae Amhlaoibh Uí Shúileabháin/The Diary of Humphrey O'Sullivan*, 4 vols. (London and Dublin: Irish Texts Society, 1936–37), 1:54–55.
67. Thomas Swanton to John Windele, 12 June 1846, RIA MS 4 B 6, 43 (iii); Robert MacAdam, "Six Hundred Gaelic Proverbs Gathered in Ulster," *Ulster Journal of Archaeology* 6 (1858): 172, quoted in Crowley, *Wars of Words*, 126.
68. Francis Keane [Proinsias Ó Catháin], "Essay on the Present State of the Irish Language and Literature in the Province of Ulster," RIA MS 12 Q 13 (1126), pp. 128–29.
69. Society for the Preservation of the Irish Language (hereafter SPIL), "23rd Report, for 1900," in *Annual Reports* (Dublin, 1900), 24–25.
70. Mac Erlean, *Duanaire Dháibhidh Uí Bhruadair*, 1:18–19; RIA Cat., fasc. XVII, 2144 [RIA MS 23 H 18 (707), p. 88, 97], fasc. XXII, 2740 [RIA MS 23 H 15 (946), p. 200], fasc. VI, 743 [RIA MS 23 N 32 (259), p. 206], fasc VIII, 1012 [RIA MS 23 C 8 (373), p. 158].
71. Froinsias Ó Maolmhuaidh [Francisco O Molloy], *Grammatica Latino-Hibernica Nunc Compendiata* (Rome: S. Cong. de Propag. Fide, 1677), 277; Leerssen, *Mere Irish and Fíor-Ghael*, 205–6. Eighteenth- and nineteenth-century examples of Ó Maolmhuaidh's poem can be found in RIA MS 23 L 2 (100), p. 28, MS 24 L 29 (162), p. 54, MS 23 N 7 (660), p. 55, and MS 23 G 21 (917), p. 168. See RIA Cat., fasc. III, 302, fasc. IV, 468, fasc. XVI, 2043, and fasc. XXI, 2648. See also Dunne, "Voices of the Vanquished," 30, and Seosamh Watson, "Coimhlint an Dá Chultúr—Gaeil agus Gaill i bhFilíocht Chúige Uladh san Ochtú hAois Déag," *Eighteenth-Century Ireland/Iris an Dá Chultúr* 3 (1988): 98–100.
72. McGrath, *Cinnlae Amhlaoibh Uí Shúilleabháin*, 1:198–99.
73. Micheál Ó hAnnracháin to Maurice Lenihan, 26 Oct. 1871, NLI, MS 4726.
74. *Minutes of Evidence Taken before the Select Committee of the House of Lords, Appointed to Inquire into the State of Ireland, More Particularly with Reference to the Circumstances which May Have Led to Disturbances in that Part of the United Kingdom. 24 March–22 June, 1825*, p. 320, H.C. 1825 (521), ix.
75. *Twenty-Third Report of the Commissioners of National Education in Ireland (for the year 1856), With Appendices, Vol. 1*, appendix B, part iv, general reports, p. 143–44 [2304] [2304-I], H.C. 1857–58, xx.

76. Daniel Dewar, *Observations on the Character, Customs, and Superstitions of the Irish; and Some of the Causes which have Retarded the Moral and Political Improvement of Ireland* (London: Gale and Curtis, 1812), 89–96.

77. Proceedings of the Committee, Irish Society Papers, TCD, MS 7644, p. 29.

78. Ibid., p. 7.

79. Keane, "Ulster," RIA MS 12 Q 13 (1126), p. 139–40.

80. Michael O'Sullivan to John O'Daly, 7 Aug. 1844, NLI MS G 389, pp. 241–43.

81. John Fleming [Seán Pléimeann], "Essay on the Present State of the Irish Language and Literature in the Province of Munster," and Keane, "Ulster," RIA MS 12 Q 13 (1126), pp. 3–4, 138–40.

82. The term is used in, for example, Grillo, *Dominant Languages*, 2–6; Neville, "'He Spoke to Me in English,'" 21–22; and Ó Ciosáin, *Print and Popular Culture*, 6.

83. Charles A. Ferguson, "Diglossa," *Word* 15, no. 2 (1959): 325–40; John J. Gumperz, "Speech Variation and the Study of Indian Civilization," *American Anthropologist* 63, no. 5 (Oct. 1961): 976–88; John J. Gumperz, "Types of Linguistic Communities," *Anthropological Linguistics* 4, no. 1 (1962): 28–40; Joshua Fishman, "Bilingualism with and without Diglossia; Diglossia with and without Bilingualism," *Journal of Social Issues* 23, no. 2 (1967): 29–38.

84. Fishman, "Bilingualism," 32.

85. Fasold, *Sociolinguistics of Society*, 41; Edwards, *Language, Society, and Identity*, 71–72.

86. Kenneth MacKinnon, *Language, Education, and Social Processes in a Gaelic Community* (London: Routledge & Kegan Paul, 1977), 146–47.

87. Nancy Dorian, *Language Death: The Life Cycle of a Scottish Gaelic Dialect* (Philadelphia: University of Pennsylvania Press, 1981), 93.

88. Ferguson, "Diglossia," 330.

89. On networks, see Lesley Milroy, *Language and Social Networks* (Oxford: Basil Blackwell, 1980), 12–22, 40–108; Gumperz, *Discourse*, 38–58; Brian Imhoff, "Socio-Historic Network Ties and Medieval Navarro-Aragonese," *Neuphilologische Mitteilungen* 101, no. 3 (2000): 443–50. A study conducted by the Committee on Irish Language Attitudes Research between 1970 and 1975 on modern Irish-speaking communities found social networks to be a far more important determinant of language use than domains. See Ó Riagáin, *Language Policy and Social Reproduction*, 33–36.

90. Gal, *Language Shift*, 97–151.

91. An Craoibhín Aoibhinn [Douglas Hyde], "Sgeulta," *An t-Éireannach*, 13 Sept. 1884, John Glynne Notebooks, NLI MS G 733, p. 237.

92. Edward O'Reilly, "Essay on the Revival of Irish Language and Literature," 1823, RIA MS 24 K 4, p. 14.

93. A. Atkinson, *The Irish Tourist: In a Series of Picturesque Views, Travelling Incidents, and Observations Statistical, Political, and Moral, on the Character and Aspect of the Irish Nation* (Dublin: Thomas Courtney, 1815), 471.

94. Robert Huston, *Life and Labours of the Rev. Fossey Tackaberry; with Notices of Methodism in Ireland*, 2nd ed. (London: John Mason, 1860), 59; McQuige, *Importance of Schools*, 11; Lady Henrietta Chatterton, *Rambles in the South of Ireland during the*

Year 1838, 2 vols., 2nd ed. (London: Saunders and Otley, 1839), 1:228–30; *Fairs and Markets' Commission, Ireland. Report of the Commissioners Appointed to Inquire into the State of the Fairs and Markets in Ireland. Part II. Minutes of Evidence*, p. 180 [1910], H.C. 1854–55, xix. For McQuige, see P. de Brún, *Scriptural Instruction*, 6, 11–13, 109, and NLI Cat., fasc. II, 45.

95. *Belfast News-Letter*, 12 June 1835; Ulick Bourke [Uileog de Búrca], "Essay on the State of the Irish Language and Literature in the Province of Connaught," RIA MS 12 Q 13 (1126), p. 233; SPIL, "21st Report, for 1898," in *Annual Reports* (Dublin, 1898), 15.

96. Patrick Forhan to John O'Daly, 5 Jan. 1849, reproduced in Torna [Tadhg Ó Donnchadha], "Congantóirí Sheáin Uí Dhálaigh," *Éigse* 1 (1939): 262–63.

97. Micheál Mac Gabhann, *Rotha Mór an tSaoil*, ed. Proinsias Ó Conluain, transcribed by Seán Ó hEochaidh (Indreabhán: Cló Iar-Chonnachta, 1996), 35.

98. Irish Society, "Quarterly Extract, No. 1," in *Quarterly Extracts* (Dublin: M. Goodwin, 1821), 3–4.

99. NFC 434:85–91.

100. Henry Monck Mason, *Reasons and Authorities and Facts Afforded by the History of the Irish Society Respecting the Duty of Employing the Irish Language as a More General Medium for Conveying Scriptural Instruction to the Native Peasantry of Ireland* (Dublin: M. Goodwin and Co., 1835), 4; Reverend P. Fitzgerald and J. J. McGregor, *The History, Topography, and Antiquities of the County and City of Limerick; with a Preliminary View of the History and Antiquities of Ireland*, 2 vols. (Dublin: George McKern, 1826–27), 2:541.

101. *Freeman's Journal*, 14 May 1863.

102. Irish Society, "Thirteenth Report, 1831," in *Reports of the Irish Society* (Dublin: M. Goodwin, 1831), 20.

103. *Freeman's Journal*, 8 Nov. 1844.

104. Ibid., 7 June 1876 and 14 Feb. 1879.

105. Ibid., 14 Apr. 1879.

106. Ibid., 27 Aug. 1887, 12 Jan. 1888, 28 Nov. 1895.

107. Ibid., 17 Mar. 1842.

108. *Irish Times*, 13 Sept. 1861.

109. *Minutes of Evidence Taken Before the Select Committee of the House of Lords Appointed to Inquire into the Collection and Payment of Tithes in Ireland, and the State of the Laws Relating Thereto, and to Report their Observations Thereon to the House; and Who Had Leave Also to Report from Time to the House*, p. 128, H.C. 1831–32 (271), xxii; *Irish Times*, 27 May 1864.

110. *Land Acts (Ireland). Report of the Royal Commission on the Land Law (Ireland) Act, 1881, and the Purchase of Land (Ireland) Act, 1885*, p. 948 [C. 4969] [C.4969-I] [C.4969-II], H.C. 1887, xxvi.

111. *Richmond Penitentiary, Dublin. Report of the Commissioners Directed by the Lord Lieutenant of Ireland, to Inquire into the State of the Richmond Penitentiary in Dublin; Together with the Evidence and Documents Connected Therewith*, pp. 141–42, H.C. 1826–27 (335), xi; *Royal Commission on Prisons in Ireland. Second Report*, p. 21

[C. 4145], H.C. 1883, xlii. See also *Royal Commission on Prisons in Ireland, Vol. 1. Reports, with Digest of Evidence, Appendices, &c.*, p. 145 [C. 4233] [C. 4233-I], H.C. 1884–85, xxxviii.

112. *Freeman's Journal*, 12 Sept. 1846.

113. S. H. O'Grady, Robin Flower, and Myles Dillon, *Catalogue of Irish Manuscripts in the British Museum* [British Library], 3 vols. (London, 1925–26, 1953) (hereafter BL Cat.), vol. 1 p. 667 [BL MS Add. 27496, f. 3b].

114. Henry Coulter, *The West of Ireland: Its Existing Conditions and Prospects* (Dublin: Hodges and Smith, 1862), 125–27.

115. *Irish Times*, 28 May 1879.

116. James Alexander, *An Amusing Summer Companion to Glanmire, near Cork: Being a Picturesque Delineation of That Beautiful Village, Together with Certain Prospects of the Surrounding Country; to Which Are Added Strong Sketches of the Manners of the Inhabitants and Some Useful Observations and Reflections* (Cork: H. Denmead, 1814), 117–18.

117. James Grant, *Impression of Ireland and the Irish* (Philadelphia: G. B. Zieber and Co., 1845), 167–68.

118. *Third Annual Report of the Directors of Convict Prisons in Ireland, for the Year Ended 31st December, 1856; with Appendix*, p. 48 [2214], H.C. 1857, xxiii.

119. NFC 1200:151–56; *An Claidheamh Soluis*, 30 Sept. 1899.

120. V. A. C. Gatrell, *The Hanging Tree: Execution and the English People, 1770–1868* (Oxford: Oxford University Press, 1994), 36, 56–58. For a brief discussion of capital punishment in Ireland, see Raymond Gillespie, "And Be Hanged by the Neck Until You Are Dead," in *Hanging Crimes*, ed. Frank Sweeney (Cork: Mercier Press, 2005), 1–9. For evidence of the hanging of Irish speakers in London, see Peter Linebaugh, *The London Hanged: Crime and Civil Society in the Eighteenth Century* (Cambridge: Cambridge University Press, 1992), 291.

121. *Patriot* (Dublin), 6 Aug. 1822, quoted in Irish Society, "Quarterly Extract, No. 6," in *Quarterly Extracts* (Dublin: M. Goodwin, 1822), 42.

122. *Times* (London), 18 Aug. 1837.

123. *Mayo Constitution*, 1 Apr. 1830.

124. *Freeman's Journal*, 5 Aug. 1839.

125. Ibid., 13 Aug. 1850.

126. Ibid., 16 Aug. 1830.

127. *Mayo Constitution*, 25 Aug. 1834.

128. *Daily News*, 13 May 1858.

129. Senia Pašeta, *Before the Revolution: Nationalism, Social Change, and Ireland's Catholic Elite, 1879–1922* (Cork: Cork University Press, 1999), 1–4, 28–49; Partha Chatterjee, *The Nation and Its Fragments: Colonial and Postcolonial Histories* (Princeton, NJ: Princeton University Press, 1993), 3–13.

130. A similar case is presented by Michael Coleman in "'Eyes Big as Bowls with Fear and Wonder': Children's Responses to the Irish National Schools, 1850–1922," *Proceedings of the Royal Irish Academy*, Section C, 98 (1998): 177–202, and Caoimhe Máirtín, *An Máistir: An Scoil agus an Scolaíocht i Litríocht na Gaeilge* (Baile Átha Cliath: Cois Life, 2003), 209–14.

131. Proceedings of the Committee, Irish Society Papers, TCD, MS 7644, p. 7; Pádraig de Brún, "The Irish Society's Bible Teachers, 1818–1827," *Éigse* 19, no. 2 (1983): 286–88.

132. Brighid Bean Uí Mhurchadha, *Oideachas in Iar-Chonnacht sa Naoú Céad Déag* (Baile Átha Cliath: Oifig an tSoláthair, 1954), 44; William Shaw Mason, *A Statistical Account or Parochial Survey of Ireland, Drawn up from the Communications of the Clergy*, 3 vols. (Dublin: Graisberry and Campbell, 1814), 1:192.

133. Mary John Knott, *Two Months at Kilkee, a Watering Place in the County Clare, Near the Mouth of the Shannon, with an Account of a Voyage Down That River from Limerick to Kilrush* (Dublin: William Curry, Jr., and Co., 1836), 109–10. See also Alf MacLochlainn, "Social Life in County Clare, 1800–1850," *Irish University Review* 2, no. 1 (Spring 1972): 65.

134. P. de Brún, *Scriptural Instruction*, 65.

135. Comyn Papers, NLI, MS 8468, folder 14; Francis Keane [Proinsias Ó Catháin], "Essay on the Present State of the Irish Language and Literature in the Province of Munster," RIA MS 12 Q 13 (1126), p. 123.

136. NFC 1405:418.

137. *Twenty-Third Report of the Commissioners of National Education in Ireland (for the year 1856). With Appendices, Vol. 1*, appendix B, part iv, general reports, p. 145 [2304] [2304-I], H.C. 1857–58, xx.

138. NFC 52:242.

139. NFC 707:257–58.

140. Uí Mhurchadha, *Oideachas in Iar-Chonnacht*, 47.

141. Mary Daly, "Literacy and Language Change in the Late Nineteenth and Early Twentieth Centuries," in *The Origins of Popular Literacy in Ireland: Language Change and Educational Development, 1700–1920*, ed. Mary Daly and David Dickson (Dublin: Tony Moreau, 1990), 156.

142. Horatio Townsend, *Statistical Survey of the County of Cork, with Observations on the Means of Improvement; Drawn up for the Consideration, and By Direction of the Dublin Society* (Dublin: Graisberry and Campbell, 1810), "addenda," 62.

143. Hugh Dorian, *The Outer Edge of Ulster: A Memoir of Social Life in Nineteenth-Century Donegal*, ed. Breandán Mac Suibhne and David Dickson (Notre Dame, IN: University of Notre Dame Press, 2001), 118.

144. Keane, "Ulster," RIA MS 12 Q 13 (1126), p. 129.

145. Irish Society, "Twenty-Ninth Report, 1847," in *Reports of the Irish Society* (Dublin: M. Goodwin, 1847), 48.

146. *Twenty-Second Report of the Commissioners of National Education in Ireland, (for the Year 1855), with Appendices*, vol. 2, appendix G, p. 119 [2142-I] [2142-II], H.C. 1856, xxvii.

147. *An Claidheamh Soluis*, 13 Oct. 1900.

148. John Richardson, *A Proposal for the Conversion of the Popish Natives of Ireland to the Established Religion, with the Reasons Upon Which It is Grounded, and an Answer to the Objections Made to It*, 2nd ed. (London: J. Downing, 1712), 122; *The Queen's Colleges Commission. Report of Her Majesty's Commissioners Appointed to Inquire into the*

Progress and Condition of the Queen's Colleges at Belfast, Cork, and Galway; with Minutes of Evidence, Documents, and Tables and Returns, p. 196 [2413], H.C. 1857–58, xxi. Richardson's *Proposal* was issued bound, with consecutive pagination, with his *Short History of the Attempts That Have Been Made to Convert the Popish Natives of Ireland* (1712).

149. Breandán S. Mac Aodha, "Aspects of the Linguistic Geography of Ireland in the Early Nineteenth Century," *Studia Celtica* 20–21 (1985–86): 205–20.

150. Mason, *Statistical Account*, 1:419; William Tighe, *Statistical Observations Relative to the County of Kilkenny, Made in the Years 1800 & 1801* (Dublin: Graisberry and Campbell, 1802), 515.

151. Mason, *Statistical Account*, 3:391; Robert Thompson, *Statistical Survey of the County of Meath, with Observations on the Means of Improvement, Drawn Up for the Consideration, and Under the Direction of the Dublin Society* (Dublin: Graisberry and Campbell, 1802), 94.

152. Mason, *Statistical Account*, 1:198; Charles Coote, *General View of the Agriculture and Manufactures of the Queen's County, with Observations on the Means of their Improvement, Drawn Up in the Year 1801, for the Consideration, and Under the Direction of the Dublin Society* (Dublin: Graisberry and Campbell, 1801), 187–88; Townsend, *Statistical Survey*, 418–19.

153. Mason, *Statistical Account*, 1:456.

154. Ibid., 2:146; Coote, *General View of the Agriculture and Manufactures of the King's County*, 64.

155. James MacParlan, *Statistical Survey of the County Leitrim, with Observations on the Means of Improvement, Drawn Up for the Consideration, and by Order of the Dublin Society* (Dublin: Graisberry and Campbell, 1802), 85.

156. Mason, *Statistical Account*, 1:226.

157. Hely Dutton, *A Statistical and Agricultural Survey of the County of Galway, with Observations on the Means of Improvement, Drawn up for the Consideration and by the Direction of the Royal Dublin Society* (Dublin: R. Graisberry, 1824), 463.

158. Dewar, *Observations*, 96.

159. Mason, *Reasons and Authorities*, 4.

160. Irish Society, "Quarterly Extract, No. 10," in *Quarterly Extracts* (Dublin: M. Goodwin, 1823), 81.

161. W. Steuart Trench, *Realities of Irish Life* (London: Longmans, Green, and Co., 1868), 162–69.

162. *First Report from His Majesty's Commissioners for Inquiring into the Condition of the Poorer Classes in Ireland, with Appendix (A) and Supplement*, appendix A, p. 687, H.C. 1835 (369), xxxii. The bilingualism of mendicants is also mentioned in an account of the Ballinasloe Fair: *Belfast News-Letter*, 12 June 1835.

163. Thomas Newenham, *A View of the Natural, Political, and Commercial Circumstances of Ireland* (London: T. Cadell and W. Davies, 1809), xiv.

164. Julius Rodenberg, *The Island of Saints: A Pilgrimage through Ireland*, trans. Lascelles Wraxall (London: Chapman and Hall, 1861), 194.

165. *State of Ireland. Minutes of Evidence Taken Before the Select Committee Appointed to Inquire into the Disturbances in Ireland, in the Last Session of Parliament, 13th May–18th June, 1824*, p. 161, H.C. 1825 (20), vii.

166. *Freeman's Journal*, 17 Oct. 1843.

167. Edward Wakefield, *An Account of Ireland, Statistical and Political*, 2 vols. (London: Longman, Hurst, Rees, Orme, and Brown, 1812), 2:737; Charlotte Elizabeth, "Letters from Ireland, MDCCCXXXVII," in *The Works of Charlotte Elizabeth, with an Introduction by Mrs. H.B. Stowe*, 2 vols. (New York: M. W. Dodd, 1844), 1:479.

168. Johann Georg Kohl, *Travels in Ireland* (London: Bruce and Wyld, 1844), 57.

169. *An Claidheamh Soluis*, 27 July 1901. For de Siúnta, see *ainm.ie* (Máire Ní Mhurchú, Diarmuid Breathnach, and Fiontar, DCU, *ainm.ie* [Dublin City University and Cló Iar-Chonnacht, 2011], http://ainm.ie), s.v. "de Siúnta, Earnán (1874–1949)," http://ainm.ie/Bio.aspx?ID=17.

170. Hyde, "Sgeulta," NLI MS G 733, p. 237.

171. SPIL, "26th Report, for 1903," in *Annual Reports* (Dublin, 1903), 9.

CHAPTER 2. PEASANT ETYMOLOGIES

1. NFC 707:168–70.

2. W. F. H. Nicolaisen, "Place-Name Legends: An Onomastic Mythology," *Folklore* 87, no. 2 (1976): 146–51. This chapter will resist the conflation of nineteenth- and twentieth-century Irish onomastic lore with *dinnseanchas*, a specific branch of learning within the context of medieval Irish poetry. Clearly, onomastic lore has a strong literary continuity in Ireland, but to regard *dinnseanchas*, with its formal conventions as poetic genre, as synonymous with any Irish place lore without distinction risks anachronism. See Brian Ó Cuív, "*Dinnshenchas*—The Literary Exploitation of Irish Place-Names," *Ainm: Bulletin of the Ulster Place-Name Society* 4 (1989–90): 102–3.

3. Ó Murchú, *Irish Language*, 45–47; Ó Cuív, *Irish Dialects*, 34–39; Thomas F. O'Rahilly, *Irish Dialects Past and Present* (Dublin: Dublin Institute for Advanced Studies, 1976).

4. Heinrich Wagner, *Linguistic Atlas and Survey of Irish Dialects*, 4 vols. (Dublin: Dublin Institute for Advanced Study, 1958–69).

5. Irvine and Gal, "Language Ideology and Linguistic Differentiation," 37–38.

6. Geraint H. Jenkins, Richard Suggett, and Eryn M. White, "The Welsh Language in Early Modern Wales," in G. Jenkins, *Welsh Language before the Industrial Revolution*, 106–10.

7. J. H. Andrews, *A Paper Landscape: The Ordnance Survey in Nineteenth-Century Ireland* (Oxford: Clarendon Press, 1975), 56, 119–22; J. H. Andrews, "'More Suitable to the English Tongue': The Cartography of Celtic Placenames," *Ulster Local Studies* 14, no. 2 (1992): 7–21; Art Ó Maolfabhail, "An tSuirbhéireacht Ordanáis agus Logainmneacha na hÉireann, 1824–34," *Proceedings of the Royal Irish Academy*, Section C, 89, no. 3 (1989): 38.

8. Gillian Doherty, *The Irish Ordnance Survey: History, Culture, and Memory* (Dublin: Four Courts Press, 2004); Stiofán Ó Cadhla, *Civilizing Ireland: Ordnance*

Survey, 1824–1842: Ethnography, Cartography, Translation (Dublin: Irish Academic Press, 2007).

9. This debate has been more visible than the usual historical controversies, with Brian Friel's well-known play *Translations* (1980) using the Ordnance Survey as a context for exploring the issue of colonialism. For an overview of and response to this debate, see Lionel Pilkington, "Language and Politics in Brian Friel's *Translations*," *Irish University Review* 20, no. 2 (1990): 282–98.

10. R. D., *A Visit to the Wild West, or a Sketch of the Emerald Isles, Picturesque and Political, during the Past Autumn* (London: G. W. Nickisson, 1843), 19.

11. Nicholson, *Ireland's Welcome to the Stranger*, 143–44.

12. NLI p. 442 (BL Egerton MS 135), f. 7b. Other versions can be found in BL MSS Egerton 150, f. 364b, Egerton 155, f. 78b, Egerton 158, f. 48, Egerton 161, f. 29, and NLI MS G 193, p. 68, and repeated by Thaddeus Connellan in his Irish translation of Richard Whately's *Easy Lessons on Money Matters*. See Connellan, *Reidh-Leighin air Ghnothuibh Cearba*, 48; BL Cat., I, 606, and II, 81, 143, 223, 409; NLI Cat., fasc. V, 62.

13. F. X. Martin, "Provincial Rivalries in Eighteenth-Century Ireland," *Archivium Hibernicum* 30 (1972): 117–35.

14. Stephen Nicholas and Peter R. Shergold, "Irish Intercounty Mobility Before 1840," *Irish Economic & Social History* 17 (1990): 26–27.

15. Cormac Ó Gráda, "Seasonal Migration and Post-Famine Adjustment in the West of Ireland," *Studia Hibernica* 13 (1973): 58–59; Thomas Bartlett, *The Fall and Rise of the Irish Nation: The Catholic Question, 1690–1830* (Savage, MD: Barnes and Noble Books, 1992), 314.

16. *Belfast News-Letter*, 12 June 1835.

17. Matthew E. Mason, "'The Hands Here Are Disposed to Be Turbulent': Unrest among the Irish Trackmen of the Baltimore and Ohio Railroad, 1829–1851," *Labor History* 39, no. 3 (1998): 260–64; Peter Way, "Shovel and Shamrock: Irish Workers and Labor Violence in the Digging of the Chesapeake and Ohio Canal," *Labor History* 30, no. 4 (1989): 498–99; Jay Martin Perry, "Shillelaghs, Shovels, and Secrets: Irish Immigrant Societies and the Building of Indiana Internal Improvements" (MA thesis, Indiana University Bloomington, 2009), 11–13.

18. Mac Gabhann, *Rotha Mór an tSaoil*, 92.

19. John O'Donovan to Thomas Larcom, 30 and 31 Aug. 1835, *Ordnance Survey Letters, Donegal*, ed. Michael Herity (Dublin: Four Masters Press, 2000), 18–20; David Dickson and Breandán Mac Suibhne, "Introduction," in Dorian, *Outer Edge of Ulster*, 1–5.

20. John O'Donovan to Thomas Larcom, 30 Sept. 1835, *Ordnance Survey Letters, Donegal*, 69.

21. *Mayo Constitution*, 8 Aug. 1831.

22. *Freeman's Journal*, 14 Nov. 1867.

23. NLI p. 421 (BL MS Add. 27946), f. 45a; BL Cat., I, 703–4.

24. McGrath, *Cinnlae Amhlaoibh Uí Shúileabháin/The Diary of Humphrey O'Sullivan*, 1:48.

25. NFC 844:302.

26. Charles Percy Bushe Journal, NLI MS G 236, pp. 302–3. For a twentieth-century Mayo version, see NFC 109:282.

27. T. O'Rahilly, *Irish Dialects*, 249–50; O'Donovan, *Grammar*, lxxiv; Richard Cox, *Hibernica Anglicana, or the History of Ireland from the Conquest Thereof by the English to the Present Time* (London: H. Clark, 1689), 24; Crowley, *Politics of Language*, 88.

28. O'Donovan, *Grammar*, lxxiii.

29. RIA MS 23 O 47 (569), p. 4.

30. Robert King, *Sgéul Fa Bheatha agus Pháis Ár d-Tighearna agus ár Slanuightheóra, Iosa Críost* (Dublin: Goodwin & Co., 1849), iii–viii, quoted in Breandán Ó Buachalla, "Nótaí ar Ghaeilge Dhoire agus Thír Eoghain," *Éigse* 13, no. 4 (1969–70): 252–53.

31. Charles Percy Bushe Journal, NLI MS G 236, pp. 136, 302.

32. Patrick Lynch, *For-Oideas Ghnaith-Ghaoighilge na h-Eireand: An Introduction to the Knowledge of the Irish Language, as Now Spoken; Containing a Comprehensive Exemplification of the Alphabetic Sounds, and a Complete Analysis of the Accidents of the Declinable Parts; with the Pronunciation of Each Irish Word Employed in Illustration, So Far as Could Be Effected by the Substitution of English Characters; Systematically Arranged and Methodically Disposed, in Fourteen Short Synoptic Tables* (Dublin: Graisberry and Campbell, 1815), 13.

33. Mac Gabhann, *Rotha Mór*, 189.

34. Andrew Donlevy, *An Teagasg Críosduidhe do Réir Ceasda agus Freagartha, air na Tharruing go Bunudhasach as Bréithir Soilléir Dé, agus as Toibreachaibh Fíorghlana Oile* (Paris: Seumus Guerin, 1742), 505.

35. James Hardiman, *The History of the Town and County of the Town of Galway from the Earliest Period to the Present Time, Embellished with Several Engravings, to which is Added a Copious Appendix Containing the Principal Charters and Other Original Documents* (1820; repr., Galway: Connacht Tribune Printing and Publishing Company, 1926), 204.

36. Dutton, *Statistical and Agricultural Survey*, 198–99.

37. Patrick Knight, *Erris in the "Irish Highland" and the "Atlantic Railway"* (Dublin: Martin Keene and Son, 1836), 98. See also Charles R. Browne, "The Ethnography of Ballycroy, County Mayo," *Proceedings of the Royal Irish Academy*, 3rd ser., 4, no. 1 (1896): 91.

38. *Freeman's Journal*, 7 July 1856.

39. O'Donovan, *Grammar*, lxxiv–v.

40. John O'Donovan to Thomas Larcom, 1 Nov. 1838, *Letters Containing Information Relative to the Antiquities of the County of Galway, Collected during the Progress of the Ordnance Survey in 1839*, ed. Michael O'Flanagan, 3 vols. (NLI typescript, 1928), 2:9.

41. NFC 354:350; NFC 707:150–52.

42. NFC 227:94.

43. Ó Laoghaire, *Mo Sgéal Féin*, 31.

44. NFC 913:253.

45. Text of Lecture Delivered by John O'Daly on 8 Nov. 1846, John O'Daly Papers, NLI MS G 416.

46. Séamas Ó Catháin and Patrick O'Flanagan, *The Living Landscape: Kilgalligan, Erris, County Mayo* (Dublin: Comhairle Bhéaloideas Éireann, 1975), 1–5, 65–72.

47. Ibid., 7, 245.

48. Ibid., 245–46.

49. F. H. A. Aalen, *Man and the Landscape in Ireland* (London: Academic Press, 1978), 171–90; L. M. Cullen, "The Regions and Their Issues: Ireland," in *The Victorian Countryside*, ed. G. E. Mingay, 2 vols. (London: Routledge and Kegan Paul, 1981), 1:97–98.

50. O'Donovan to Larcom, 9 Sept. 1839, *Ordnance Survey Letters, Kilkenny: Letters Containing Information Relative to the Antiquities of the County of Kilkenny, Collected during the Progress of the Ordnance Survey in 1839*, ed. Michael Herity (Dublin: Four Masters Press, 2003), 83.

51. Ó Catháin and O'Flanagan, *Living Landscape*, 246.

52. Thomas O'Conor to Thomas Larcom, 3 Oct. 1838, in O'Flanagan, *Letters Containing Information Relative to the Antiquities of the County of Galway*, 1:131–32.

53. William Smith O'Brien manuscript, RIA MS 24 B 6 (313), p. 93.

54. William Hackett to John Windele, 26 July 1860, RIA MS 4 B 20/71.

55. *An Claidheamh Soluis*, 8 June 1901.

56. John O'Donovan to Thomas Larcom, 4 Sept. 1838, in O'Flanagan, *Letters Containing Information Relative to the Antiquities of Galway*, 1:39–40.

57. Unsigned letter to John O'Donovan, 9 Sept. 1838, in O'Flanagan, *Letters Containing Information Relative to the Antiquities of Galway*, 1:43.

58. Thomas O'Conor's appended notes, not dated (but ca. 1836), *Ordnance Survey Letters, Meath: Letters Containing Information Relative to the Antiquities of the County of Meath, Collected during the Progress of the Ordnance Survey in 1836*, ed. Michael Herity (Dublin: Four Masters Press, 2001), 46. The spelling of *leach* here has been preserved as in the original.

59. John O'Donovan to Thomas Larcom, 3 Aug. 1839, in O'Flanagan, *Letters Containing Information Relative to the Antiquities of Galway*, 3:180.

60. W. G. Wood-Martin, *Traces of the Elder Faiths of Ireland: A Folklore Sketch* (London: Longmans, Green, and Co., 1902), 256.

61. G. Doherty, *Irish Ordnance Survey*, 17–19; Andrews, *Paper Landscape*, 119–20.

62. G. Doherty, *Irish Ordnance Survey*, 20.

63. John O'Donovan to Thomas Larcom, 20 Sept. 1838, in O'Flanagan, *Letters Containing Information Relative to the Antiquities of Galway*, 1:68.

64. O'Donovan to Larcom, 3 Nov. 1838, in O'Flanagan, *Letters Containing Information Relative to the Antiquities of Galway*, 2:22.

65. O'Donovan to Larcom, 15 July 1836, in Herity, *Ordnance Survey Letters, Meath*, 18.

66. O'Donovan to Larcom, 4 Sept. 1838, in O'Flanagan, *Letters Containing Information Relative to the Antiquities of Galway*, 1:39.

67. Thomas O'Conor to Larcom, 3 Oct. 1838, in O'Flanagan, *Letters Containing Information Relative to the Antiquities of Galway*, 1:131–32.

68. Angélique Day and Patrick McWilliams, eds., *Ordnance Survey Memoirs of Ireland*, vol. 38, *Parishes of County Donegal I* (Belfast: Institute of Irish Studies, 1997), 36.

69. O'Donovan to Larcom, 13 July 1838, *Letters Containing Information Relative to the Antiquities of the County of Mayo, Collected during the Progress of the Ordnance Survey in 1838*, ed. Michael O'Flanagan, 2 vols. (NLI typescript, 1927), 1:233–34.

70. O'Donovan to Larcom, 9 July 1838, in O'Flanagan, *Letters Containing Information Relative to the Antiquities of the County of Mayo*, 1:217–18.

71. Ibid., 1:225–26.

72. O'Donovan to Larcom, 17 Sept. 1837, in *Letters Containing Information Relative to the Antiquities of the County of Westmeath, Collected during the Progress of the Ordnance Survey in 1837*, ed. Michael O'Flanagan, 2 vols. (RIA typescript, 1931), 1:41. Again, this example arose not out of anglicization—Carraig an Chait and "The Cat's Rock" mean the same in both languages—but out of changing pronunciations and meanings over time.

73. William Hackett to John Windele, 28 Apr. 1843, RIA MS 4 B 5/21/i–xviii.

74. Andrews, *Paper Landscape*, 86–87, 102, 120–24.

75. O'Donovan to Larcom, 5 June 1839, in O'Flanagan, *Letters Containing Information Relative to the Antiquities of the County of Galway*, 3:5.

76. O'Donovan to Larcom, 3 and 9 Sept. 1835, in Herity, *Ordnance Survey Letters, Donegal*, 22, 29.

77. Doherty, *Irish Ordnance Survey*, 122–29.

78. O'Curry, for instance, accepted the oral explanation given to him for the name of the parish of Rossconnell: "I believe they are right." See O'Curry to Thomas Larcom, 20 Aug. 1839, in Herity, *Ordnance Survey Letters, Kilkenny*, 27.

79. O'Donovan to Larcom, 17 May 1838, in O'Flanagan, *Letters Containing Information Relative to the Antiquities of the County of Mayo*, 1:34–35.

CHAPTER 3. BILINGUALISM AND THE HUMOR OF LANGUAGE CONTACT

1. Garret FitzGerald, "Irish-Speaking in the Pre-Famine Period: A Study Based on the 1911 Census Data for People Born before 1851 and Still Alive in 1911," *Proceedings of the Royal Irish Academy*, Section C, 103, no. 5 (2003): 204. FitzGerald's data, based on those alive in 1911, would include few if any individuals born before 1811.

2. Mac Mathúna, *Béarla sa Ghaeilge*; Ó Muirithe, *An tAmhrán Macarónach*; Dunne, "Voices of the Vanquished," 32–36; Ní Mhunghaile, "Bilingualism, Print Culture," 221–24; Charles Dillon, "*An Ghaelig Nua*: English, Irish and the South Ulster Poets and Scribes in the Late Seventeenth and Eighteenth Centuries," in Kelly and Mac Murchaidh, *Irish and English*, 149–50.

3. NFC 913:233.

4. Seán Ó Súilleabháin and Reidar Th. Christiansen, *The Types of the Irish Folktale*, FF Communications no. 188 (Helsinki: Suomalainen Tiedeakatemia, 1963), 302. References to the Irish language are cataloged under Section K in the National Folklore Collection, Delargy Center for Irish Folklore, University College Dublin. The content of this card index was consulted, and 219 overall references to the Irish language from oral sources were counted and examined. An additional 250 stories were

classified as AT 1699 by Ó Súilleabháin and Christiansen. Allowing for some overlap of stories cataloged in both places, that would indicate 250 instances of jokes out of approximately 450 total references to Irish.

5. Éamonn Ó Tuathail, "Meath Anecdotes," *Éigse* 4, no. 1 (Nov. 1943): 10–11.

6. Standish Hayes O'Grady, *Adventures of Donnchadh Ruadh Mac Con-Mara: A Slave of Adversity, Written by Himself, Now for the First Time Edited from an Original Irish Manuscript, with Metrical Translation, Notes, and a Biographical Sketch of the Author* (Dublin: John O'Daly, 1853), 12; James Stewart, "The Game of 'An Bhfuil Agat?—Tá,' or the Uses of Bilingualism," *Béaloideas* 45–47 (1977–79): 251–52.

7. The manuscript is believed to have been written by Patrick Lyden (1832–1929) of Faulkerraugh, Co. Galway, sometime after his immigration to the United States (he became a U.S. citizen in 1872). It is certain that Lyden acquired the stories in Galway before he emigrated. See Nancy Stenson, ed., *An Haicléara Mánas: A Nineteenth-Century Text from Clifden, Co. Galway* (Dublin: Dublin Institute for Advanced Studies, 2003).

8. Douglas Hyde, "Eachtra na gConnachtaibh," *Lia Fail* 1 (1927): 153–60; Séamas Ó Catháin, "'Butter, Sir . . . ' AT 1698 and 1699—a Typological Sandwich," *Béaloideas* 45–47 (1977–79): 84–85.

9. *Shamrock* (Dublin), 26 June 1880, clipping in David Comyn Papers, NLI, MS 4154; Énrí Ó Muirgheasa, "An Fear ag Díol na Muice" and "Fear Eile ag Déanamh Margaidh i mBéarla," in *Greann na Gaedhilge: An Chéad Chuid* (Baile Átha Cliath: Connradh na Gaedhilge, 1901), 6–7. Comyn was also the owner of at least one MacAdam manuscript containing such stories, as Hyde notes. See "Eachtra na Connachtaibh," 153.

10. Bede [Edward Bradley], *The White Wife*, 92–93, 100–103.

11. See, for example, NFC 394:4–5; NFC 52:189; NFC 913:235–36; NFC 1146:61–63; NFC 861:1060–61; NFC 1035:496; NFC 928:38–39; NFC 442:333.

12. Séamas Ó Catháin, "Dáileadh Roinnt Scéalta de Chuid AT 1699: Misunderstanding Because of Ignorance of a Foreign Language," *Béaloideas* 42–44 (1974–76): 120–35; Ó Catháin, "Butter, Sir . . . ," 84–117; Stewart, "Game," 244–58. Ó Catháin notes that unlike the other index designations, AT 1699 refers not to a specific international tale but to a *set* of tales connected by the motifs of humor and misunderstanding—an inconsistency in the Aarne-Thompson system that has led to ambiguity in differentiating between AT 1697, 1698, and 1699 in the cataloging of Irish tales.

13. Mac Mathúna, *Béarla sa Ghaeilge*, 239–66.

14. NFC 181:365–67; "Béarla 'Liam a' tSléibhe,'" *An Claidheamh Soluis*, 1 Aug. 1903.

15. Seán de Fréine, "The Dominance of the English Language in the Nineteenth Century," in *The English Language in Ireland*, ed. Diarmaid Ó Muirithe (1977; repr., Cork: Mercier Press, 1985), 84; see also de Fréine, *The Great Silence* (Dublin: Foilseacháin Náisiúnta Teoranta, 1965), 5.

16. Neville, "'He Spoke to Me in English,'" 30.

17. This sample consists of all tales cataloged via the Aarne-Thompson international folktale index under Type 1699 in the main manuscript collection from Counties

Clare, Cork, Donegal, Galway, Kerry, and Mayo, and of three-fourths of the AT 1699 tales from the same counties in the National Folklore Collection's Schools Manuscripts Collection. These locations were selected because of their more complete representation in the folk material—far fewer jokes were collected by the commission outside these counties. Only a portion of the tales from the Schools Manuscripts Collection was sampled since most consisted of shorter and less detailed versions of the same tales in the main collection. Finally, three additional tales (NFC 407:39–40; NFC 700:171–73; NFC 700:258–59) from Counties Tipperary and Carlow were included, as these had been found separately in the course of examining material identified elsewhere in the commission's index.

18. Several examples of this story have been found by James Stewart, including a version titled "Bhfuil agat? Tá," published in *An Claidheamh Soluis* in 1901; see Stewart, "Game," 250–51.

19. NFC 45:86–87.

20. Christie Davies, *The Mirth of Nations* (New Brunswick, NJ: Transaction Publishers, 2002), 5–11, and *Ethnic Humor around the World: A Comparative Analysis* (Bloomington: University of Indiana Press, 1990), 8–9.

21. Wladyslaw Chlopicki, "Review Article: The Mirth of Nations," *Humor* 16, no. 4 (2003): 415–24.

22. James Clifford, *The Predicament of Culture: Twentieth-Century Ethnography, Literature, and Art* (Cambridge, MA: Harvard University Press, 1988), 16.

23. Michel de Certeau, *The Practice of Everyday Life*, trans. Steven Rendall (Berkeley: University of California Press, 1984), xii–xvi. Moreover, this resistance to domination need not confine itself to direct opposition to the legal-political realm of the state (as in the classic example of peasant rebellions) and may be found in aspects of everyday life extraneous to both nationalist and colonial forms of political organization; see Partha Chatterjee, *Nation and Its Fragments*, 158–72, and James Scott, *Weapons of the Weak: Everyday Forms of Peasant Resistance* (New Haven, CT: Yale University Press, 1985), 26, 39–40, 308–9, 317, 320–21. Chatterjee proposes this concept of peasant resistance as a distinct South Asian anticolonialism, but its analytic strength makes it insightful in the Irish context as well.

24. NFC 538:13–14.

25. NFC 1235:290–91.

26. National Folklore Schools Collection, Belfield (hereafter NFC S) 32:127; NFC S 66:16, 261; NFC S 134:384–85; NFC S 85:39–40; NFC S 132:5–6; NFC S 327:314; NFC S 476:27.

27. Stenson, *An Haicléara Mánas*, 59–63, 154–56, 161, 168, translations by Stenson.

28. Séamus Ó Duilearga, "Cnuasach Andeas: Scéalta agus Seanchas Sheáin Í Shé ó Íbh Ráthach; Sean-Scéalta," *Béaloideas* 29 (1961): 38.

29. James Woodrow Hassell, *Sources and Analogues of the Nouvelles Récreations et Joyeux Devis of Bonaventure des Périers* (Chapel Hill: University of North Carolina Studies in Comparative Literature, 1957), 1:104–8; Bonaventure des Périers, *Nouvelles récréations et joyeux devis I–XC*, ed. Krystyna Kasprzyk (Paris: Librairie Honoré Champion, 1980), 99–101.

30. W. Carew Hazlitt, ed., *Shakespeare Jest-Books: Reprints of the Early and Very Rare Jest-Books Supposed to Have Been Used by Shakespeare*, 3 vols. (1864; repr., New York: Burt Franklin, 1964), 1:65–68; Adam Fox, *Oral and Literate Culture in England, 1500–1700* (Oxford: Clarendon Press, 2000), 69–70.

31. Richard M. Dorson, *Negro Folktales in Michigan* (Cambridge, MA: Harvard University Press, 1956), 79, 175–76, 183–84; Paul G. Brewster, "Folk-Tales from Indiana and Missouri," *Folk-Lore* 50, no. 3 (Sept. 1939): 297.

32. Inta Gale Carpenter, *A Latvian Storyteller: The Repertoire of Jānis Pļavnieks* (New York: Arno Press, 1980), 194–96.

33. Katharine M. Briggs, *A Dictionary of British Folk-Tales in the English Language*, 2 vols. (London: Routledge and Kegan Paul, 1970), 2:69.

34. Monia Hejaiej, *Behind Closed Doors: Women's Oral Narratives in Tunis* (London: Quartet Books, 1996), 166–67; W. H. Barker and Cecilia Sinclair, *West African Folk-Tales* (Northbrook, IL: Metro Books, 1972), 95–96; Nai-Tung Ting, *A Type Index of Chinese Folktales in the Oral Tradition and Major Works of Non-Religious Classical Literature* (Helsinki: Suomalainen Tiedeakatemia, 1978), 228–30; Henry Parker, *Village Folk-Tales of Ceylon*, 3 vols. (London: Luzac and Co., 1910), 2:76–79; Stith Thompson, *Motif Index of Folk-Literature*, revised and enlarged edition, 6 vols. (Bloomington: University of Indiana Press, 1957), 5:504; Hasan M. El-Shamy, *Types of the Folktale in the Arab World: A Demographically Oriented Tale-Type Index* (Bloomington: University of Indiana Press, 2004), 916–18; Dov Noy, ed., *Folktales of Israel* (London: Routledge and Kegan Paul, 1963), 97–98; Antti Aarne and Stith Thompson, *The Types of the Folktale: A Classification and Bibliography*, 2nd rev. ed. (Helsinki: FFC Communications, 1961), 482–84; Haim Schwarzbaum, *Studies in Jewish and World Folklore* (Berlin: Walter de Gruyter and Co., 1968), 338; Reginetta Haboucha, *Types and Motifs of the Judeo-Spanish Folktales* (New York: Garland Publishing, 1992), 672–73.

35. Juan B. Rael, *Cuentos Españoles de Colorado y Nuevo Méjico*, 2 vols. (Stanford: Stanford University Press, 1957), 1:119–20. As in many of the Irish examples, the terminations of the English and Spanish lines in the dialogue contain similar sounds: want/guante, say/José, fool/azul, hell/él. This rhyming is also prominent in other stories, especially those classified as AT 1698. See Ó Catháin, "Butter, Sir . . . ," 107–8.

36. NFC 1101:428–29.

37. Pandit Shyama-Shankar, *Wit and Wisdom of India: A Collection of Humorous Folk-Tales of the Court and Country-side Current in India* (London: George Routledge and Sons, 1924), 187–88. Shankar noted that "Benares is called Kashi by all Hindus, and *Kashi* in Bengal means *cough*. So Kala Babu translated coughing with the word Benaresing."

38. NFC S 309:185–86.

39. Peter Christen Asbjørnsen and Jørgen Moe, *Norwegian Folk Tales*, trans. Pat Shaw and Carl Norman (Oslo: Dreyers Forlag, 1960), 158–60.

40. NFC 433:74.

41. Aurelio M. Espinosa Jr., *Cuentos populares de Castilla y Leon*, 2 vols. (Madrid: Consejo Superior de Investigaciones Científicas, 1987–88), 1:304–6; E. M. Wilson, "Some Humorous English Folk Tales, Part One," *Folk-lore* 49, no. 2 (1938): 182–92;

Yolando Pino-Saavredra, ed., *Folktales of Chile*, trans. Rockwell Gray (New York: Routledge and Kegan Paul, 1967), 236; Vance Randolph, *Who Blowed Up the Church House and Other Ozark Folk Tales* (1952; repr., Westport, CT: Greenwood Press, 1972), 80–81; Charles F. Arrowood, "There's a Geography of Humorous Anecdotes," *Texas Folk-Lore Studies Publication* 15 (1939): 82–83.

42. Vivien Mercier, *The Irish Comic Tradition* (Oxford: Clarendon Press, 1962), 87–88.

43. Osborn Bergin, ed., *Trí Bior-Ghaoithe an Bháis*, 2nd ed. (Dublin: Hodges, Figgis, & Co., 1931), 117–18; Alan Harrison, ed., "Lucht na Simléirí," *Éigse* 15 (1973–74): 196–97; N. J. A. Williams, ed., "Eachtra Áodh Mhic Goireachtaidh," *Éigse* 13 (1969–70): 126; Mac Mathúna, *Béarla sa Ghaeilge*, 131–81; Leerssen, *Mere Irish and Fíor-Ghael*, 199, 241–42; Mercier, *Irish Comic Tradition*, 159–60, 171; Ó Catháin, "Dáileadh Roinnt Scéalta," 122.

44. Eoghan Ó Neachtain, ed., *Stair Éamuinn Uí Chléire* (Baile Átha Cliath: M. H. Mac an Ghuill & a Mhac, Teo, 1918), 52–53.

45. Reproduced in Crowley, *Wars of Words*, 76–78.

46. Dirk Delabastita, "Cross-Language Comedy in Shakespeare," *Humor* 18, no. 2 (2005): 161–84.

47. William Smith Clark, *The Irish Stage in the County Towns, 1720–1800* (Oxford: Clarendon Press, 1965), 286–91.

48. Victor Raskin, *Semantic Mechanisms of Humor* (Dodrecht: D. Reidel Publishing Co., 1985), 80–99; Charles F. Hockett, *The View from Language* (Athens: University of Georgia Press, 1977), 259–68; Arthur Koestler, *The Act of Creation* (New York: MacMillan Co., 1964), 32–51; Elliott Oring, *Engaging Humor* (Urbana: University of Illinois Press, 2003), 1–2.

49. NFC 41:250–51.

50. Oliver MacDonagh, "Ideas and Institutions, 1830–1845," in W. E. Vaughan, ed., *A New History of Ireland*, vol. 5, *Ireland under the Union, Part I, 1801–70* (Oxford: Clarendon Press, 1989), 209–10; Gerard O'Brien, "State Intervention and the Medical Relief of the Irish Poor, 1787–1850," in *Medicine, Disease, and the State in Ireland, 1650–1940*, ed. Greta Jones and Elizabeth Malcolm (Cork: Cork University Press, 1999), 199–206; Ronald D. Cassell, *Medical Charities, Medical Politics: The Irish Dispensary System and the Poor Law, 1836–1872* (Suffolk, UK: The Boydell Press, 1997), 8–10.

51. NFC 965:511–12.

52. NFC 928:38–39.

53. NFC S 1123:132–33.

54. NFC 627:292–94. Like many stories identified by Ó Catháin, this joke depends on both Hiberno-English and Irish for homophony. A dialectical pronunciation of the English word "boy" sounds like the diminutive form of cow (bóín) in Irish, with the final consonant dropped.

55. NFC 861:1066–67; NFC 197:14–15.

56. *Belfast News-Letter*, 19 Feb. 1876; Oliver Burke, *Anecdotes of the Connaught Circuit from Its Foundation in 1604 to Close Upon the Present Time* (Dublin: Hodges, Figgis, and Co., 1885), 186–87; NFC 700:258–59.

57. NFC 862:427-28.

58. NFC S 472:55-56.

59. K. Theodore Hoppen, *Ireland since 1800: Conflict and Conformity*, 2nd ed. (New York: Longman, 1999), 46.

60. Cormac Ó Gráda, *Ireland: A New Economic History, 1780–1939* (Oxford: Clarendon Press, 1994), 239–42, 265–66; R. V. Comerford, "Ireland, 1850–70: Post-Famine and Mid-Victorian," in Vaughan, *New History of Ireland*, 5:378–79.

61. NFC 1101:428-29.

62. NFC 512:26.

63. NFC S 476:27; NFC S 474:245; NFC S 477:499-502.

64. L. M. Cullen, *The Emergence of Modern Ireland, 1600–1900* (New York: Holmes and Meier Publishers, 1981), 174–76, 186–87.

65. Alexander Shand, *Letters from the West of Ireland, 1884* (London: William Blackwood and Sons, 1885), 35–36.

66. Tomás Ó Criomhthain, *An tOileánach*, ed. Seán Ó Coileáin (Baile Átha Cliath: Cló Talbóid, 2002), 19, 336.

67. Muiris Ó Súileabháin, *Fiche Blian ag Fás* (Baile Átha Cliath: Clólucht an Talbóidigh, Tta, 1933), 41.

68. NFC 463:140.

69. S. G. Ua Briain, "Sgéilíní Ó Chill Choca," *Irisleabhar na Gaedhilge* 11, no. 130 (1901): 115–16. Another version of this story type can be found in the collection of tales from Cosslett Ó Cuinn, *Scian a Caitheadh le Toinn: Scéalta agus Amhráin as Inis Eoghain agus Cuimhne ar Ghaeltacht Iorrais*, ed. Aodh Ó Canainn and Seosamh Watson (Baile Átha Cliath: Coiscéim, 1990), 57–58.

70. Mary Julia MacCulloch, "Folklore of the Isle of Skye," *Folk-Lore* 33 (1922): 384.

71. NFC 438:56-60.

72. NFC 1010:115. Versions of this tale can be found from Clare, Cork, Galway, and Kerry. See NFC 203:491–93; NFC S 32:127; NFC S 83:194–96; NFC S 279:5–6; NFC S 644:49, 396–87; NFC S 432:167–68; NFC S 474:245.

73. NFC 1010:179-81; NFC 227:538-40; NFC S 476:430-31.

74. *An Claidheamh Soluis*, 12 Sept. 1903, 1. Variant versions also circulated in County Clare (NFC 38:28) and in County Carlow (NFC 407:39–40).

75. Neal R. Norrick, *Conversational Joking: Humor in Everyday Talk* (Bloomington: University of Indiana Press, 1993), 20–42; Oring, *Engaging Humor*, 85–96.

76. A. R. Radcliffe-Brown, "On Joking Relationships," *Africa* 13, no. 3 (July 1940): 195–210; John G. Kennedy, "Bonds of Laughter among the Tarahumara Indians: A Rethinking of Joking Relationship Theory," in *The Social Anthropology of Latin America: Essays in Honor of Ralph Leon Beals*, ed. Walter Goldschmidt and Harry Hoijer (Los Angeles: University of California Press, 1970): 36–68; Phillip Stevens Jr., "Bachama Joking Categories: Toward New Perspectives in the Study of Joking Relationships," *Journal of Anthropological Research* 34 (1978): 47–71.

77. NFC 799:243.

78. Diarmuid Ó Giolláin, "Folk Culture," in *The Cambridge Companion to Modern Irish Culture*, ed. Joe Cleary and Claire Connolly (Cambridge: Cambridge University Press, 2005), 235.

79. Ó Cathāin, "Dáileadh Roinnt Scéalta," 125–33.
80. Mary Douglas, *Implicit Meanings: Essays in Anthropology* (London: Routledge and Kegan Paul, 1975), 98, 107.
81. NFC 1016:63. *Seargtha* (v. adj.): "withered, shriveled." This joke relies not only on a regional pronunciation of the Irish but also on a dialectical English pronunciation of "charity" as two syllables rather than three.
82. Robert Lew, "Exploitation of Linguistic Ambiguity in Polish and English Jokes," *Papers and Studies in Contrastive Linguistics* 31 (1996): 127–33. Lew's categories and examples are based on linguistic humor relying on one language and its translatability into another, but his analysis is equally applicable to the case of two languages used together. See also Christie Davies, "European Ethnic Scripts and the Translation and Switching of Jokes," *Humor* 18, no. 2 (2005): 151–52.
83. NFC 1592:120–26
84. Dan Ben-Amos, "The Myth of Jewish Humor," *Western Folklore* 32, no. 2 (Apr. 1973): 112–31; Christopher P. Wilson, *Jokes: Form, Content, Use, and Function* (London: Academic Press, 1979), 217–18; Davies, *Mirth of Nations*, 18–48.
85. NFC 913:233.
86. NFC 588:533–34.
87. NFC 413:305.
88. NFC 1125:2–3.
89. NFC 869:472–73.
90. NFC 203:10; NFC 809: 430–33; NFC S 47:240–41; NFC S 291:248–49; NFC S 398:157–58; NFC S 1093: 130–32.
91. NFC 474:582.
92. NFC 1035:496.

CHAPTER 4. EDUCATION AND ESTABLISHED CHURCH

1. Burke, *Languages and Communities*, 72–76; Robert J. W. Evans, "Language and State Building: The Case of the Habsburg Monarchy," *Austrian History Yearbook* 35 (2004): 17.
2. George Woodyatt Hastings, ed., *Transactions of the National Association for the Promotion of Social Science. Belfast Meeting, 1867* (London: Longmans, Green, Reader, and Dyer, 1868), 91–93; *Belfast News-Letter*, 21 Sept. 1867. The importance of this particular parliamentary report in influencing the eventual character of the national education system, though not language policy, is also noted in Donald Akenson, *The Irish Education Experiment: The National System of Education in the Nineteenth Century* (London: Routledge & Kegan Paul, 1970), 77–78.
3. Patricia Palmer, *Language and Conquest in Early Modern Ireland: English Renaissance Literature and Elizabethan Imperial Expansion* (Cambridge: Cambridge University Press, 2001), 14–15, 125–26. Palmer also traces the contrasts in this linguistic policy with the accommodation of native languages by the Spanish in their imperial holdings.
4. Crowley, *Politics of Language*, 15–16.
5. John Smith Furlong, *A Treatise on the Law of Landlord and Tenant, as Administered in Ireland*, 2 vols. (Dublin: Hodges and Smith, 1845), 1:11; Crowley, *Wars of Words*, 12; Palmer, *Language and Conquest*, 41.

6. Charles Runnington, *The History of the Common Law by Sir Matthew Hale, Knt.*, 4th ed. (Dublin: James Moore, 1792), 187; Leerssen, *Mere Irish and Fíor-Ghael*, 169.

7. This expansion of linguistic statutes from the Pale was also evident in 1588, when the Crown administration in Dublin ordered that the Statutes of Kilkenny be extended to Connacht and Thomond. See Brian Ó Cuív, "The Irish Language in the Early Modern Period," 513.

8. *The Statutes at Large, Passed in the Parliaments Held in Ireland*, 21 vols. (Dublin: George Grierson, 1786–1804), 1:120–21.

9. Rouget, "La langue française," 9–14; Grillo, *Dominant Languages*, 47; Burke, *Languages and Communities*, 73–74.

10. Geraint H. Jenkins, *A Concise History of Wales* (Cambridge: Cambridge University Press, 2007), 131–36; Peter R. Roberts, "Tudor Legislation and the Political Status of 'the British Tongue,'" in G. Jenkins, *Welsh Language before the Industrial Revolution*, 129–30.

11. R. J. W. Evans, *The Language of History and the History of Language* (Oxford: Clarendon Press, 1998), 20–21; Jenkins, Suggett, and White, "Welsh Language," 63.

12. *Statutes at Large*, 1:121–22.

13. Leerssen, *Mere Irish and Fíor-Ghael*, 254–55; Ó Cuív, "The Irish Language in the Early Modern Period," 520–21.

14. Durkacz, *Decline*, 2.

15. *Statutes at Large*, 1:120.

16. Nicholas Williams, *I bPrionta i Leabhar: Na Protastúin agus Prós na Gaeilge, 1567–1724* (Baile Átha Cliath: An Clóchomhar Tta, 1986), 9.

17. *Statutes at Large*, 1:125–26.

18. A point also made by R. Evans, "Language and State Building," 21.

19. Crowley, *Wars of Words*, 15.

20. Patricia Palmer, "Interpreters and the Politics of Translation and Traduction in Sixteenth-Century Ireland," *Irish Historical Studies* 33, no. 131 (2003): 259.

21. Palmer, *Language and Conquest*, 140; Crowley, *Wars of Words*, 15.

22. Ó Cuív, "The Irish Language in the Early Modern Period," 510–11.

23. *Belfast News-Letter*, 17 Apr. 1857; Williams, *I bPrionta*, 183.

24. *Statutes at Large*, 1:290. The use of Latin was interpreted by an eighteenth-century commentator as a response to the fact that "some of the Irish understood Latin, and therefore because ... they could not get the sacred offices in Irish ... it was deemed better to let them have them in Latin, than not at all." See *Preaching the Gospel in Irish Not Contrary to Law; But Enjoyned Expressly by Several Statutes and Canons Now in Force in this Kingdom, As Well As By the Word of God* (Dublin: J. Carson, 1713), 18. The nineteenth-century archbishop of Sydney, Patrick Francis Moran, even proposed that this use of Latin may have encouraged Catholics to unknowingly attend Anglican services for a short time. See Moran, *History of the Catholic Archbishops of Dublin, since the Reformation* (Dublin: James Duffy, 1864), 61.

25. Williams, *I bPrionta*, 11–16.

26. Risteárd Giltrap, *An Ghaeilge in Eaglais na hÉireann* (Baile Átha Cliath: Cumann Gaelach na hEaglaise, 1990), 8; Williams, *I bPrionta*, 10.

27. Moran, *History*, 71; Crowley, *Wars of Words*, 17–18.

28. Pádraig Ó Macháin, "Two Nugent Manuscripts: The Nugent Duanaire and Queen Elizabeth's Primer," *Ríocht na Midhe. Records of the Meath Archaeological and Historical Society* 23 (2012): 129–38; Williams, *I bPrionta*, 10–11.

29. Richardson, *Short History*, 18–19.

30. Ibid., 24. A. P. Perceval, who revisited this history in the early nineteenth century, described a similar set of policies arising out of Convocation, but gave the date as 1635. See Perceval, *The Amelioration of Ireland Contemplated in a Series of Papers. I: On the Use of the Irish Language in Religious Worship and Instruction*, 2nd ed. (London: W. J. Cleaver, 1844), 9–10.

31. Richardson, *Short History*, 24–25; Christopher Anderson, *Ireland, but Still without the Ministry of the Word in Her Own Native Language* (Edinburgh: Oliver and Boyd, 1835), 6–8; Palmer, *Language and Conquest*, 125–26.

32. Michael Cronin, *Translating Ireland: Translation, Languages, Cultures* (Cork: Cork University Press, 1996), 55.

33. White, "Established Church," 235–42, 264–65; Jenkins, Suggett, and White, "Welsh Language," 82–88.

34. Durkacz, *Decline*, 9–11, 15–23. The bible being used in this case was not a Scots Gaelic translation, but the Irish-language Bedell version (1685) distributed in part through the efforts of Andrew Sall, James Kirkwood, and the chemist Robert Boyle in 1687.

35. 12 Eliz. I c. 1, *Statutes at Large*, 1:361.

36. Walter McDonald, "Irish Ecclesiastical Colleges since the Reformation," *Irish Ecclesiastical Record*, new series, vol. 10 (Feb. 1874): 206; Crowley, *Politics of Language*, 60.

37. Durkacz, *Decline*, 5; Grillo, *Dominant Languages*, 85.

38. Akenson, *Irish Education Experiment*, 23–28. Akenson notes that even at their height around the late eighteenth and early nineteenth centuries, the 361 existing parish schools only educated approximately 11,000 students, while fewer than 20 diocesan schools were in existence in the 1800s. The third major pre-1700 educational initiative, the county-based royal free schools, were similarly unsuccessful.

39. James Kelly, "Irish Protestants and the Irish Language in the Eighteenth Century," in Kelly and Mac Murchaidh, *Irish and English*, 193.

40. For a parallel anglicization of the Stuart-era Welsh elite, see Jenkins, Suggett, and White, "Welsh Language," 80.

41. May H. Risk, "Charles Lynegar, Professor of Irish in 1712," *Hermathena* 102 (Spring 1966): 17.

42. *Statutes at Large*, 4:33.

43. Richardson, *Short History*, 30–41; Giltrap, *Eaglais na hÉireann*, 25–28.

44. Richardson, *Short History*, 44–54; Christopher Anderson, *Memorial on Behalf of the Native Irish, with a View to Their Improvement in Moral and Religious Knowledge through the Medium of Their Own Language* (London: Gale, Curtis, & Fenner, 1815), 24–25. Among the names listed on the memorial presented to the queen was a "Jonathan Swift." See Richardson, *Short History*, 53.

45. Richardson, *Short History*, 56–57; Anderson, *Memorial*, 25; Brian Ó Cuív, "Irish Language and Literature, 1691–1845," 375; Irene Whelan, *The Bible War in Ireland: The "Second Reformation" and the Polarization of Protestant-Catholic Relations, 1800–1840* (Madison: University of Wisconsin Press, 2005), 21.

46. Andrew Sneddon, "'Darkness Must be Expell'd by Letting in the Light': Bishop Francis Hutchinson and the Conversion of Irish Catholics by Means of the Irish Language, c. 1770–4," *Eighteenth-Century Ireland/Iris an Dá Chultúr* 19 (2004): 47–51; Edward Cahill, "The Irish Language in the Penal Era," *Irish Ecclesiastical Record* 55 (1940): 597–600.

47. Kelly, "Irish Protestants and the Irish Language," 199.

48. Donald Akenson, *The Church of Ireland: Ecclesiastical Reform and Revolution, 1800–1885* (New Haven, CT: Yale University Press, 1971), 29.

49. Richardson, *Proposal for the Conversion*, 10–11, 21.

50. *Preaching the Gospel*, 21–23; Richardson, *Proposal for the Conversion*, 3. Arguments based on the Thirty-Nine Articles were also used in Wales in the eighteenth century. See White, "Established Church," 243.

51. *Preaching the Gospel*, 24–25.

52. For the background to the almanac, see Sneddon, "Darkness Must be Expell'd," 51–54.

53. [Francis Hutchinson], *An Irish Almanack for the Year of Christ, 1724/An Almanack an Gaoidheilg arson Uliana an Tighearna Croisda, 1724* (Dublin: no printer, 1724), iv–v.

54. Leerssen, *Mere Irish and Fíor-Ghael*, 286–87.

55. Kelly, "Irish Protestants and the Irish Language," 193, quoting from J. S. Clarke, ed., *The Life of James the Second, King of England, &c. Collected Out of Memoirs Writ of His Own Hand, Together with the King's Advice to His Son, and His Majesty's Will*, 2 vols. (London: Longman, Hurst, Orme, and Brown, 1816), 2:636.

56. *Statutes at Large*, 3:259.

57. Durkacz, *Decline*, 17, 46.

58. Anderson, *Memorial*, 25–26; Durkacz, *Decline*, 73.

59. *Statutes at Large*, 5:63.

60. Richardson, *Short History*, 48.

61. Cahill, "Penal Era," 593–94.

62. Durkacz, *Decline*, 47; Akenson, *Irish Education Experiment*, 29–32; White, "Popular Schooling," 318–20; J. R. R. Adams, "Swine-Tax and Eat-Him-All-Magee: The Hedge Schools and Popular Education in Ireland," in *Irish Popular Culture, 1650–1850*, ed. James S. Donnelly, Jr., and Kerby A. Miller (Dublin: Irish Academic Press, 1999), 100.

63. White, "Popular Schooling," 322–24.

64. Durkacz, *Decline*, 49–52, 56–65, 73–74.

65. White, "Popular Schooling," 325–31.

66. Durkacz, 53–54, 66–68; Adams, "Swine-Tax," 100; Akenson, *Irish Education Experiment*, 34.

67. Flaherty, "Langue nationale/langue naturelle," 317–18; Burke, *Languages and Communities*, 90.

68. Scholarship on various aspects of this topic is extensive, but includes Michel de Certeau, Dominique Julia, and Jacques Revel, *Une politique de la langue: La Révolution français et les patois* (Paris: Gallimard, 1975); François Furet and Jacques Ozouf, eds., *Reading and Writing: Literacy in France from Calvin to Jules Ferry*, 2 vols. (Cambridge: Cambridge University Press, 1982); Lyons, "Politics and Patois," 264–81; Bell, "Lingua Populi, Lingua Dei," 1403–37.

69. Flaherty, "Linguistic Uniformity," 314–25; Frederic Hartweg, " 'Langue esclave et langue de la liberté': La révolution et la langue allemande," *Documents: Revue des questions allemandes* 4 (1989): 76, 79–80.

70. Lyons, "Politics and Patois," 270–71.

71. Burke, *Languages and Communities*, 90.

72. Richard W. Bailey, "The Ideology of English in the Long Eighteenth Century," *Linguistic Insights—Studies in Language and Communication* 7 (2003): 21–34; Charles Jones, "Nationality and Standardisation: The English Language in Scotland in the Age of Improvement," *Sociolinguistica* 13 (1999): 112–17; Crowley, *Language in History*, 60–63, 81; Tony Crowley, *Standard English and the Politics of Language* (Urbana: University of Illinois Press, 1989), 93–95; Crowley, *Wars of Words*, 80–85; Burke, *Languages and Communities*, 80, 115–16.

73. Thomas Sheridan, *British Education; or, the Source of the Disorders of Great Britain* (Dublin: George Faulkner, 1756), 159–60; Crowley, *Language in History*, 68–71.

74. 31 Geo. II c. 9 (1757); 11 & 12 Geo. III c. 27 (1771–72); 19 & 20 Geo. III c. 39 (1779–80). Note that this decline in attention paid to the Irish language in the eighteenth-century Anglican context was paralleled among the Ulster Presbyterians, for whom the issue similarly lost its prominence on the agenda at synod after an active interest in the 1710s and 1720s. See Roger Blaney, *Presbyterians and the Irish Language* (Belfast: The Ultach Trust, 1996), 27.

75. For this gap in Protestant Irish-language printing, see, for example, the bibliography in Malachy McKenna, "A Textual History of The Spiritual Rose," *Clogher Record* 14 (1991): 66–72.

76. Samuel Madden, *Reflections and Resolutions Proper for the Gentleman of Ireland, as to their Conduct for the Service of their Country* (Dublin: R. Reilly, 1738), 102–3; Ó Cuív, "Irish Language and Literature, 1691–1845," 383; Cahill, "Penal Era," 610.

77. *Eleventh Report from the Commissioners of the Board of Education in Ireland. Parish Schools*, p. 7, H.C. 1810–11 (107), vi; John McEvoy, *Statistical Survey of the County of Tyrone, with Observations on the Means of Improvement; Drawn up in the Years 1801, and 1802, for the Consideration, and under the Direction of the Dublin Society* (1802; repr., Belfast: Friar's Bush Press, 1991), 201.

78. Whitley Stokes, *Projects for Re-Establishing the Internal Peace and Tranquility of Ireland* (Dublin: James Moore, 1799), 45.

79. *First Report of the Commissioners on Education in Ireland*, appendix 255, p. 768, H.C. 1825 (400), xii.

80. See, for example, Ó Buachalla, *I mBéal Feirste Cois Cuain*, 29–37; Alan Harrison, *Ag Cruinniú Meala: Anthony Raymond (1675–1726), Ministéir Protastúnach, agus*

Léann na Gaeilge i mBaile Átha Cliath (Baile Átha Cliath: An Clóchomhar Tta, 1988), 56–61; and Leerssen, *Mere Irish and Fíor-Ghael*, 286–87.

81. Lesa Ní Mhunghaile, "Bilingualism, Print Culture," 237.

82. Charles Vallancey, *A Grammar of the Iberno-Celtic, or Irish Language* (Dublin: R. Marchbank, 1773), i.

83. Brooke learned the language in childhood, and Hardiman was a native speaker from County Mayo. See R. A. Breatnach, "Two Eighteenth-Century Irish Scholars: J. C. Walker and Charlotte Brooke," *Studia Hibernica* 5 (1965): 93, and *ainm.ie*, s.v. "Hardiman, James (1782–1855)," http://ainm.ie/Bio.aspx?ID=1084.

84. David Greene, "Robert Atkinson and Irish Studies," *Hermathena* 102 (Spring 1966): 14.

85. Edward O'Reilly, "Essay on the Revival of Irish Language and Literature," 1823, RIA, MS 24 K 4, pp. 5–18.

86. Durkacz, *Decline*, 74–75.

87. Don F. McKenzie, "The Sociology of a Text: Oral Culture, Literacy, and Print in Early New Zealand," in Burke and Porter, *Social History of Language*, 163–76.

88. Dodson, *Orientalism*, 41–60, 72–74; Bayly, *Empire and Information*, 284–300; Cohn, *Colonialism and Its Forms of Knowledge*, 20–48; Mir, "Imperial Policy," 398–405.

89. Prior, Brennan, and Haines, "Bad Language," 94–101.

90. John Coolahan, "Education as Cultural Imperialism: The Denial of the Irish Language to Irish-speakers, 1831–1922," *Paedagogica Historica* 37, no. 1 (2001): 18; Thomas O'Donoghue, *Bilingual Education in Pre-Independent Irish-Speaking Ireland, 1800–1922: A History* (Lewiston, NY: The Edwin Mellen Press, 2006), 31; Akenson, *Irish Education Experiment*, 380.

91. *Morning Chronicle*, 3 Feb. 1813; *An Claidheamh Soluis*, 10 June 1899; *Fourteenth Report of the Commissioners of the Board of Education, in Ireland*, p. 10, H.C. 1812–13 (21), vi; Crowley, *Wars of Words*, 100–101.

92. *The Morning Chronicle*, 12 Apr. 1823.

93. Thomas Kitson Cromwell, *Excursions through Ireland: Comprising the Topographical and Historical Delineations of Each Province*, 2 vols. (London: Longman, Hurst, Rees, Orme, and Brown, 1820), 1:11.

94. *The Morning Chronicle*, 26 Mar. 1822; *Caledonian Mercury*, 28 Mar. 1822.

95. See P. de Brún, *Scriptural Instruction*, 1–59; Blaney, *Presbyterians*, 75–81; I. Whelan, *Bible War*, 86–123.

96. W. S. Sankey, *A Brief Sketch of Various Attempts which Have Been Made to Diffuse a Knowledge of the Holy Scriptures through the Medium of the Irish Language* (Dublin: Graisberry and Campbell, 1818), 53–54; Mason, *Reasons and Authorities*, 4.

97. *Hampshire Telegraph and Sussex Chronicle*, 16 Oct. 1826.

98. *Caledonian Mercury*, 26 July 1828.

99. *Times* (London), 8 May 1829.

100. Lennon, *Irish Orientalism*, 59–61, 86–114.

101. *Morning Chronicle*, 16 Dec. 1823; "Extraordinary Fact," *Dublin Penny Journal* 2, no. 83 (Feb. 1, 1834): 248; "Taheitian and Irish Spelling Books," *The Eclectic Review* 6 (May 1810): 417.

102. *Morning Chronicle*, 18 Apr. 1838.

103. Anderson, *Memorial*, 27.

104. *Hampshire Telegraph and Sussex Chronicle*, 27 Oct. 1823.

105. *Belfast News-Letter*, 26 Sept. 1859; *Irish Times*, 27 Sept. 1859.

106. Sankey, *Brief Sketch*, 82–83; Mason, *Reasons and Authorities*, 14–15; Dewar, *Observations*, 97.

107. Sankey, *Brief Sketch*, 60.

108. I. Whelan, *Bible War*, 99.

109. McQuige, *Importance of Schools*, 9; Hyde, *Literary History of Ireland*, 620.

110. *Freeman's Journal*, 8 Jan. 1844 and 19 Apr. 1848.

111. Richard Digby Neave, *Four Days in Connemara* (London: Richard Bentley, 1852), 80.

112. "To the Editor of the Monthly Magazine," *The Monthly Magazine; or, British Register* 41, no. 280 (1 Mar. 1816): 112–13.

113. *Belfast News-Letter*, 4 Jan. 1828.

114. *Limerick Evening Post and Clare Sentinel*, 18 Apr. 1828.

115. "University of Dublin," *Quarterly Journal of Education* 6 (July–Oct. 1833): 19; *Twenty-Second Report of the Commissioners of National Education in Ireland, (for the Year 1855), with Appendices*, vol. 1, appendix G, p. 75 [2142-I] [2142-II], H.C. 1856, xxvii.

116. H. Kingsmill Moore, *An Unwritten Chapter in the History of Education. Being the History of the Society for the Education of the Poor in Ireland, Generally Known as the Kildare Place Society 1811–1831* (London: Macmillan and Co., Limited, 1904), 262–63; I. Whelan, *Bible War*, 113.

117. *First Report of the Commissioners on Education in Ireland*, appendix 221, pp. 553–54, 559, appendix 242, p. 682, appendix 249, p. 736, appendix 250, pp. 742–48, H.C. 1825 (400), xii.

118. T. O'Donoghue, *Bilingual Education*, 31; Coolahan, "Education as Cultural Imperialism," 18; Séamas Ó Buachalla, "Educational Policy and the Role of the Irish Language from 1831 to 1981," *European Journal of Education* 19, no. 1 (1984): 76; Akenson, *Irish Education Experiment*, 381.

119. Coolahan, "Cultural Imperialism," 19–20.

120. William J. O'Neill Daunt, *Personal Recollections of the Late Daniel O'Connell, M.P.*, 2 vols. (London: Chapman and Hall, 1848), 2:14–15.

121. *Morning Chronicle*, 3 May 1833. For the petition (but not the text of the speech), see 17 Parl. Deb. (3rd ser.) (1833) 842, hansard.millbanksystems.com.

122. P. de Brún, *Scriptural Instruction*, 91–93, 117–25.

123. T. O'Donoghue, *Bilingual Education*, 31; P. de Brún, *Scriptural Instruction*, 37; Ó Loingsigh, "Irish Language in the 19th Century," 10.

124. *Eighth Report of the Commissioners of National Education in Ireland, for the Year 1841*, appendix I, p. 13 [398], H.C. 1842, xxiii; *Abstract of the Census for Ireland, 1841*, p.1 [459], H.C. 1843, li; *Census of Ireland for the Year 1851, Part VI: General Report*, p. xlvi–xlviii [2134], H.C. 1856, xxxi.

125. *Twenty-Second Report of the Commissioners of National Education in Ireland, (for the Year 1855), with Appendices*, vol. 1, p. 3 [2142-I] [2142-II], H.C. 1856, xxvii.

126. Mary Daly, "The Development of the National School System, 1831–40," in *Studies in Irish History Presented to R. Dudley Edwards*, ed. Art Cosgrove and Donal McCartney (Dublin: University College Dublin, 1979), 159.

127. Bean Uí Mhurchadha, *Oideachas in Iar-Chonnacht*, 36; Maeve Mulryan Moloney, *Nineteenth-Century Elementary Education in the Archdiocese of Tuam* (Dublin: Irish Academic Press, 2001), 18–21, 25–27.

128. Examples include *An Claidheamh Soluis*, 15 June 1901 and 2 Nov. 1907; NFC 227:38–39; NFC 117:108–9; NFC 94:76; NFC 104:415; NFC 52:139–40; NFC 50:136; NFC 340:342–43; NFC 535:460–61; NFC S 398:213–14; NFC 374:294–95; NFC 464: 117–18; NFC 168:53–54; NFC 90:87; NFC 461:14; NFC 441:284–85; NFC 838:357; NFC 4:346; NFC 1266:64; NFC 609:499–500. Bean Uí Mhurchadha also cites an example collected and published in the 1930s and reiterates the widespread use of Irish as an aid in the classroom. See *Oideachas in Iar-Chonnacht*, 49–50.

129. NFC 90:678–79. The collector Pádraig Ó Conchubhair encountered children in the Dingle Gaeltacht even in 1952 who were still using the memory device when playing school. The children would select a "master" who would give out each letter and its "name," then call on the other students one by one to see if they could remember each phrase. See NFC 1262:1–2.

130. Mac Gabhann, *Rotha Mór*, 28.

131. Glynne Papers, Notebook no. 40, c. 1893, NLI, MS 7912.

132. *An Claidheamh Soluis*, 2 Nov. 1907; ainm.ie, s.v. "Maguidhir, Conchubhair (c.1861–1944)," http://www.ainm.ie/Bio.aspx?ID=459.

133. *Twenty-Fourth Report of the Commissioners of National Education in Ireland, (for the Year 1857), with Appendices. Vol. I*, p. 135 [2456-I] [2456-II], H.C. 1859, vii.

134. Glynne Papers, Notebook no. 40, c. 1893, NLI, MS 7912.

135. NFC S 398:213–14; Stenson, *An Haicléara Mánas*, 23.

136. *Royal Commission of Inquiry into Primary Education (Ireland). Vol. III. Containing Evidence Taken Before the Commissioners from March 12th to October 30th, 1868. Questions and Answers 1 to 17608*, p. 209 [C.6-II], H.C. 1870, xxviii.

137. Jeremiah O'Donovan Rossa, *Rossa's Recollections. 1838 to 1898. Childhood, Boyhood, Manhood. Customs, Habits, and Manners of the Irish People* (New York: Mariner's Harbor, 1898), 25; John Fleming [Seán Pléimann], "Essay on the Present State of the Irish Language and Literature in the Province of Munster," RIA MS 12 Q 13 (1126), p. 41; John Logan, "Book Learning: The Experience of Reading in the National School, 1831–1900," in *The Experience of Reading: Irish Historical Perspectives*, ed. Bernadette Cunningham and Máire Kennedy (Dublin: Rare Books Group of the Library Association of Ireland and Economic and Social History Society of Ireland, 1999), 173–76.

138. SPIL, *Report of the Proceedings of the Congress Held in Dublin, 15th–17th August 1882* (Dublin, 1884), 12–13.

139. *An Claidheamh Soluis*, 29 Apr. 1905.

140. Robert MacAdam to John Windele, 31 Aug. 1857, RIA, MS 4 B 17/65.

141. John Windele, "Present Extent of the Irish Language," *Ulster Journal of Archaeology* 5 (1857): 243.

142. *Belfast News-Letter*, 23 Mar. 1858.
143. *Bristol Mercury*, 19 May 1860; *Belfast News-Letter*, 21 Apr. 1865.
144. *Caledonian Mercury*, 18 Aug. 1860.
145. *Trewman's Exeter Flying Post or Plymouth and Cornish Advertiser*, 2 Dec. 1863.
146. *Liverpool Mercury*, 11 Apr. 1865.
147. *Belfast News-Letter*, 7 May 1868.
148. *The Hull Packet and East Riding Times*, 4 Sept. 1868. On this topic of Russian linguistic policy in Polish churches, see Weeks, "Religion and Russification," 95–102.
149. *Freeman's Journal*, 24 Oct. 1867.
150. *Belfast News-Letter*, 4 May 1868.
151. *Leeds Mercury*, 21 Sept. 1868.
152. *Freeman's Journal*, 26 Apr. 1871.
153. *National Schools (Ireland) (Teaching of Irish). Copy of Correspondence Between the Irish Executive and the Commissioners of National Education in Ireland, with Respect to the Teaching of Irish in the Irish National Schools*, p. 17, H.C. 1884 (81), lxi.
154. *Twenty-Fifth Report of the Commissioners of National Education in Ireland, (for the Year 1858,) with Appendices. Vol. I*, appendix B, p. 180 [2593] [2593-I], H.C. 1860, xxv; *Freeman's Journal*, 2 Feb. 1876; T. O'Donoghue, *Bilingual Education*, 35.
155. *Freeman's Journal*, 31 Dec. 1869.
156. *Belfast News-Letter*, 30 Dec. 1871; *Irish Times*, 30 Dec. 1871; T. O'Donoghue, *Bilingual Education*, 36.
157. *Freeman's Journal*, 10 June 1875.
158. Akenson, *Irish Education Experiment*, 382.

Chapter 5. Courtroom and Polling Booth

1. George E. Woodbine, "The Language of English Law," *Speculum* 18, no. 4 (Oct. 1943): 395–96, 425–33.
2. (Eng.) 36 Ed. III c. 15 (1362).
3. Burke, *Language and Communities*, 17; Mark Ellis Jones, "'An Invidious Attempt to Accelerate the Extinction of Our Language': The Abolition of the Court of Great Sessions and the Welsh Language," *The Welsh History Review. Cylchgrawn Hanes Cymru* 19, no. 2 (1998): 230, 236–37; J. A. Andrews and L. G. Henshaw, "The Irish and Welsh Languages in the Courts: A Comparative Study," *The Irish Jurist* 18 (1983): 7.
4. J. Gwynfor Jones, "The Welsh Language in Local Government: Justices of the Peace and the Courts of Quarter Sessions c. 1536–1800," in G. Jenkins, *Welsh Language before the Industrial Revolution*, 181–206; Mark Ellis Jones, "'The Confusion of Babel'? The Welsh Language, Law Courts, and Legislation in the Nineteenth Century," in G. Jenkins, *Welsh Language and Its Social Domains*, 587–614; Andrews and Henshaw, "Irish and Welsh Languages," 6–7.
5. 9 Will. III c. 38 (1697). See Edward Bullingbrooke, *An Abridgment of the Publick Statutes of Ireland, Now in Force and of General Use, and Also of Such English and British Statutes as Relate to and Bind Ireland, from Magna Charta to the Sixth Year of the Reign of His Present Majesty King George III, Inclusive*, 2 vols. (Dublin: Boulter Grierson, 1768), vol. 2, s.v. pleadings, entry xxv.

6. 7 Geo. II c. 14 (1733) and 17 Geo. II c. 8 (1743). The admiralty court, because not created until 1784, was instructed to substitute English for Latin as late as 1798. See 38 Geo. III c. 39 (1798) and R. B. McDowell, "The Irish Courts of Law, 1801–1914," *Irish Historical Studies* 10, no. 40 (Sept. 1957): 363–64.

7. *Statutes at Large*, 6:407. This statute is still in effect in Northern Ireland, prompting challenges to its legitimacy within the context of the 1998 Belfast Agreement and the European Charter for Regional or Minority Languages. See In the Matter of an Application by Caoimhin MacGiolla Cathain for Judicial Review . . . , (2009) NIQB 66, http//:www.courtsni.gov.uk.

8. For evidence of a confessional divide favoring higher numbers of Protestants seeking prosecutions at assizes between 1736 and 1795, see Neal Garnham, *The Courts, Crime and the Criminal Law in Ireland, 1692–1760* (Dublin: Irish Academic Press, 1996), 64–65.

9. Garnham, *Courts, Crime*, 54–55, 65. Garnham particularly emphasizes the role of courts-leet, part of the manor system, in the eighteenth century. See pp. 74–77 and Desmond McCabe, "Law, Conflict and Social Order: County Mayo, 1820–1845" (PhD diss., University College Dublin, 1991), 382–408.

10. Wakefield, *Account of Ireland*, 2:754; McCabe, "Law, Conflict," 196–97.

11. Circular by Maurice Fitzgerald and Charles Orpen, 5th ed., 1834, reprinted in appendix of Richard Whately, *Easy Lessons on Money Matters, Commerce, Trade, Wages, etc. etc. for the Use of Young People, as Well as Adults, of All Classes. Further Enlarged by Thaddaeus Connellan, Author and Publisher of the Works Mentioned in Pages v, vi* (Dublin: R. Graisberry, 1835), vii–viii.

12. John Carr, *The Stranger in Ireland, or, a Tour in the Southern and Western Parts of That Country, in the Year 1805* (London: Richard Phillips, 1806), 329; *Report from the Select Committee of the House of Lords, Appointed to Enquire into the State of Ireland in Respect of Crime, and to Report Thereon to the House; with the Minutes of Evidence Taken Before the Committee, and an Appendix and Index, Part I. Report, and Evidence 22 April to 16 May 1839*, pp. 1035–44, H.C. 1839 (486), xi, xii.

13. *Report from the Select Committee on Destitution (Gweedore and Cloughaneely); Together with the Proceedings of the Committee, Minutes of Evidence, Appendix, and Index*, p. 356, H.C. 1857–58 (412), xii.

14. *Mayo Constitution*, 14 Oct. 1833; John Windele, *Hand Book to Killarney, through Bantry, Glengariff, and Kenmare*, 2nd ed. (Cork: Messrs. Bolster, 1844), 37; *Report from the Select Committee on Manor Courts, Ireland; Together with the Minutes of Evidence, Appendix and Index*, appendix B, pp. 469–92, H.C. 1837 (494), xv; Richard McMahon, "Manor Courts in the West of Ireland Before the Famine," in *Mysteries and Solutions in Irish Legal History*, ed. D. S. Greer and N. M. Dawson (Dublin: Four Courts Press, 2001), 122–29; McCabe, "Law, Conflict," 401–8.

15. *Report from the Select Committee on Manor Courts*, p. 47, H.C. 1837 (494), xv.

16. *Report from the Select Committee on Manor Courts, Ireland; Together with the Minutes of Evidence, Appendix, and Index*, p. 113, H.C. 1838 (648), xviii.

17. *Report from the Select Committee on Manor Courts*, p. 69, H.C. 1837 (494), xv; McDowell, "Irish Courts," 377.
18. *Report from the Select Committee on Manor Courts*, p. 54, H.C. 1838 (648), xviii.
19. Wakefield, *Account of Ireland*, 2:167, 750.
20. McDowell, "Irish Courts," 371–72; Desmond McCabe, "Magistrates, Peasants, and the Petty Session Courts: Mayo 1823–50," *Cathair na Mart* 5 (1985): 45–53; McCabe, "Law, Conflict," 421–29; Garnham, *Courts, Crime*, 76–78; Richard McMahon, "The Court of Petty Sessions and Society in Pre-Famine Galway," in *The Remaking of Modern Ireland, 1750–1950: Beckett Prize Essays in Irish History*, ed. Raymond Gillespie (Dublin: Four Courts Press, 2004), 101–37.
21. *Mayo Constitution*, 23 Nov. 1841.
22. Burke, *Anecdotes of the Connaught Circuit*, 186, 284–85.
23. *Irish Times*, 8 July 1864.
24. McQuige, *Importance of Schools*, 13.
25. Maurice Lenihan, "Reminiscences of a Journalist," *Limerick Reporter and Tipperary Vindicator*, 1 Jan. and 19 Nov. 1867. For Lenihan's background, see Ignatius Murphy, *The Diocese of Killaloe, 1800–1850* (Dublin: Four Courts Press, 1992), 188.
26. Philip Barron, *Ancient Ireland. A Weekly Magazine* 1, no. 4 (Apr. 1835): 66.
27. Edward O'Reilly, "Essay on the Revival of Irish Language and Literature," 1823, RIA, MS 24 K 4, p. 16.
28. The ongoing efforts by administrators to control the compositions of juries in Ireland are explored in Níamh Howlin, "Controlling Jury Composition in Nineteenth-Century Ireland," *Journal of Legal History* 30, no. 3 (Dec. 2009): 233–43.
29. Quoted in the *Mayo Constitution*, 6 Feb. 1834, whose editors took the newspaper to task for being too anti-Catholic in its 4 Jan. 1834 edition.
30. *Freeman's Journal*, 24 and 28 Feb. 1873; 214 Parl. Deb. (3rd ser.) (27 Feb. 1873) 1036–37, hansard.millbanksystems.com.
31. Howlin, "Controlling Jury," 244.
32. Cunningham, "Loss and Gain," 171. For an even earlier fifteenth-century glimpse at interpreters and concessions to Irish speakers in municipal court settings, see Crowley, *Politics of Language*, 17.
33. John Davies, *Historical Tracts: By Sir John Davies, Attorney General, and Speaker of the House of Commons in Ireland* (London: John Stockdale, 1786), 215.
34. For the rise of the grand jury as local government body, see Virginia Crossman, *Local Government in Nineteenth-Century Ireland* (Belfast: The Institute of Irish Studies, Queen's University of Belfast, for the Ulster Society of Irish Historical Studies, 1994), 1–3, 25–40.
35. Garnham, *Courts, Crime*, 93–94.
36. John Brady, "Irish Interpreters at Meath Assizes," *Ríocht na Midhe. Records of the Meath Archaeological and Historical Society* 2, no. 1 (1959): 63.
37. 36 Geo. III c.55 (1796), 6 & 7 Will. IV c. 116 (1836).
38. 4 Geo. IV c. 43 (1823); *Grand Juries, Ireland. Returns of the Gross Sums Presented by the Several Grand Juries throughout Ireland, at the Spring and Summer Assizes 1830; Distinguishing the Amount of Such Presentments as Are Made Imperative by Law Upon*

Grand Juries, and over Which No Discretion Can Be Exercised by Them, p. 18, H.C. 1830–31 (324), xiv.

39. 1 Vict. c. 43 (1837) and 14 & 15 Vict. c. 57 (1851).

40. 7 & 8 Vict. c. 106 (1844); Charles H. Foot, *The Grand Jury Laws of Ireland: Comprising All the Statutes Relating to the Powers and Duties of Grand Juries, Including Orders in Council*, 2nd ed. (Dublin: Hodges, Figgis, and Co., 1884), 85.

41. *Times* (London), 11 Apr. 1894. Cf. 7 & 8 Geo. IV c. 67 (1827) and 14 & 15 Vict. c. 93 (1851), both key statutes in the evolution of petty sessions that do not mention provisions for interpreters.

42. Mason, *Reasons and Authorities*, 4; Henry Inglis, *Ireland in 1834: A Journey throughout Ireland, During the Spring, Summer, and Autumn of 1834*, 3rd ed. (London: Whittaker & Co., 1835), 2:104; Francis Keane [Proinsias Ó Catháin], "Essay on the Present State of the Irish Language and Literature in the Province of Ulster," RIA MS 12 Q 13 (1126), pp. 130–31.

43. Lesa Ní Mhunghaile, "The Legal System in Ireland and the Irish Language 1700–c.1843," in *The Laws and Other Legalities of Ireland, 1689–1850*, ed. Michael Brown and Seán Patrick Donlan (Farnham, Surrey, UK: Ashgate Publishing Limited, 2011), 333.

44. *Freeman's Journal*, 5 Oct. 1850.

45. Richard Nun and John Edward Walsh, *The Powers and Duties of Justices of the Peace in Ireland, and of Constables as Connected Therewith; with an Appendix of Statutes and Forms* (Dublin: Hodges and Smith, 1841), 176; Edward Levinge, *The Justice of the Peace for Ireland: Comprising the Practice in Indictable Offences, and the Proceedings Preliminary and Subsequent to Convictions; with an Appendix of the Most Useful Statutes, and an Alphabetical Catalogue of Offences*, 2nd ed. (Dublin: Hodges, Smith & Co., 1864), 81.

46. County Mayo Grand Jury Presentments, NLI, MS 10654, pp. 3, 38, 88, 104–5, 153, 189.

47. *(Ireland) Accounts, Presented to the House of Commons, of the Presentments Passed by the Grand Juries of Ireland, at the Spring and Summer Assizes, in the Year 1807*, pp. 3–447, H.C. 1808 (205), xiii. Counties reporting employment of interpreters in 1807 were Cavan, Clare, Cork, Donegal, Fermanagh, Kilkenny, Mayo, Meath, Roscommon, Tipperary, Tyrone, Waterford, Westmeath, Wexford, and Wicklow.

48. County of Donegal Grand Jury Book, Summer Assizes 1814, NLI, p. 5505 [2]; J. Brady, "Irish Interpreters," 63; *(Ireland) Accounts, Presented to the House of Commons, of the Presentments Passed by the Grand Juries of Ireland, at the Spring and Summer Assizes, in the Year 1807*, pp. 430, 433, 447, H.C. 1808 (205), xiii.

49. Ainm.ie, s.v. "Stúndún, Pádraig (c. 1820–1908)," http://ainm.ie/Bio.aspx?ID=475.

50. *Grand Jury Presentments, Ireland. Account of Presentments Made by the Grand Juries of the County of the City of Limerick, in the Year 1821*, pp. 1, 3, H.C. 1822 (306), vii.

51. *Grand Juries, Sums Levied. Returns to an Order of the Honourable House of Commons, Dated the 10th February 1824; For an Account of All Sums of Money Levied in the Several Counties of Ireland, During the Two Years Last Past, by Authority of*

Grand Juries; Distinguishing the County from the Baronial Charge, and Specifying the Heads of Account to Which Those Separate Charges Were Applicable, pp. 6-7, H.C. 1824 (287), xxii.

52. *Grand Juries, Ireland. Returns of the Gross Sums Presented by the Several Grand Juries throughout Ireland, at the Spring and Summer Assizes 1830; Distinguishing the Amount of Such Presentments as are Made Imperative by Law Upon Grand Juries, and Over Which No Discretion Can be Exercised by Them*, pp. 4, 6, 18-19, H.C. 1830-31 (324), xiv.

53. Ní Mhunghaile, "Legal System in Ireland," 332-33.

54. Brady, "Irish Interpreters," 63; Ní Mhunghaile, "Legal System in Ireland," 329, 333; Nic Eoin, "Irish Language and Literature," 471.

55. *Report from Her Majesty's Commissioners of Inquiry into the State of Law and Practice in Respect to the Occupation of Land in Ireland*, p. 52 [605] [606], H.C. 1845, xix.

56. *Courts of Law, &c. Return to an Address of the Honourable the House of Commons, Dated 7 August 1866; for, Return Showing in Detail, with a General Abstract, the Expenditure for the Year 1865-6, in Each of the Three Kingdoms, on Account of All Courts of Law and Justice and Legal Departments, Defrayed Wholly or in Part from Public Funds*, part ii, pp. 60-75, H.C. 1867 (223) (223-I), lvii.

57. From the *Limerick Chronicle*, quoted in *Liverpool Mercury*, 28 Mar. 1859.

58. Resolutions Passed at Assizes of the Co. Sligo Grand Jury, 1836-1871, NLI, MS 12912, p. 170.

59. *Census of Ireland, 1871. Part I: Area, Houses, and Population; Also the Ages, Civil Condition, Occupations, Birthplaces, Religion, and Education of the People. Vol. II: Province of Munster*, summary tables and index, table XX, pp. 1020 and 1028 [C.876], H.C. 1873, lxxii; *Census of Ireland, 1871. Part I: Area, Houses, and Population: Also the Ages, Civil Conditions, Occupations, Birthplaces, Religion, and Education of the People. Vol. III: Province of Ulster*, table XXIV, p. 444 and table XX, p. 990 [C.964], H.C. 1874, lxxii; *Census of Ireland, 1871. Part I: Area, Houses and Population: Also the Ages, Civil Conditions, Occupations, Birthplaces, Religion, and Education of the People. Vol. IV: Province of Connaught*, table XX, p. 641 [C.1106], H.C. 1874, lxxiv; *Census of Ireland, 1871. Part I: Area, Population and Number of Houses; Also the Ages, Civil Condition, Occupations, Birthplaces, Religion, and Education. Vol. I: Province of Leinster*, p. 167, 1206, 1214, 1268 [C. 662], H.C. 1872, lxvii. There are two interpreters listed for Leinster, but the male interpreter, resident in Dublin, is listed as foreign born, making it unlikely that he spoke Irish.

60. *Times* (London), 11 Apr. 1894; *Freeman's Journal*, 19 July 1898.

61. McQuige, *Importance of Schools*, 10.

62. *First Report of the Commissioners of Inquiry into the State of Irish Fisheries; with the Minutes of Evidence, and Appendix*, appendix xx, p. 129 [77], H.C. 1837, xxii.

63. *Mayo Constitution*, 23 Feb. 1841.

64. George Joseph Browne, *An Authentic Account of the Trials at Large, of George Robert Fitzgerald, Esq.; Timothy Brecknock, James Fulton, and Others, for the Procurement of, and for the Murder of Patrick Randall M'Donnell and Charles Hipson* (London: John Stockdale, 1786), 42.

65. *Freeman's Journal*, 15 June 1839.

66. *Full and Revised Report of the Eight Days' Trial in the Court of Queen's Bench on a Criminal Information Against John Sarsfield Casey at the Prosecution of Patten Smith Bridge; From November 27th to December 5th, 1877* (Dublin: Central Tenants' Defence Committee, 1877), 65.

67. *Morning Post*, 17 Sept. 1861.

68. Carney v. Clyde, Conry et al., *Mayo Constitution*, 3 Apr. 1834.

69. *Belfast News-Letter*, 27 July 1864.

70. For the term "Irish witness" referring to an Irish-speaking witness, see *Standard* (London), 14 Oct. 1837.

71. McMahon, "Court of Petty Sessions," 102.

72. *Mayo Constitution*, 8 Aug. 1831.

73. Ibid., 4 Aug. 1831.

74. Ibid., 11 Oct. 1832.

75. Ibid., 21 Jan. 1833.

76. *Royal Cornwall Gazette, Falmouth Packet & Plymouth Journal*, 27 Aug. 1825.

77. *Londonderry Journal and Donegal and Tyrone Advertiser*, 20 Aug. 1805.

78. *Mayo Constitution*, 25 Mar. 1830 and 27 May 1833; *Freeman's Journal*, 18 Mar. 1845; McMahon, "Court of Petty Sessions," 103.

79. John Pitt Taylor, *A Treatise on the Law of Evidence, as Administered in England and Ireland; with Illustrations from the American and Other Foreign Laws*, 2 vols., 2nd ed. (London: W. Maxwell, 1855), 1:65.

80. *Report from the Select Committee on Manor Courts*, p. 113, H.C. 1838 (648), xviii.

81. *Limerick Evening Post and Clare Sentinel*, 2 Mar. 1832.

82. Maurice Lenihan, "Reminiscences," *Limerick Reporter and Tipperary Vindicator*, 15 May 1868.

83. McQuige, *Importance of Schools*, 10.

84. Bernard O'Reilly, *John MacHale, Archbishop of Tuam: His Life, Times, and Correspondence*, 2 vols. (New York: Fr. Pustet & Co., 1890), 1:400.

85. Irish Society, "Eleventh Report, 1829," in *Reports of the Irish Society*, 14.

86. Examples include cases reported in the *Limerick Evening Post and Clare Sentinel*, 18 Mar. 1828, and *Mayo Constitution*, 16 Dec. 1833.

87. NLI MS G 236, p. 165. For Morris, see NLI Cat. fasc. VI, 41.

88. *Mayo Constitution*, 8 Aug. 1831.

89. Ibid., 28 June 1830 and 12 June 1834.

90. R. v. Burke, (1858) 8 Cox 44 (C.C.); Éanna Hickey, *Irish Law and Lawyers in Modern Folk Tradition* (Dublin: Four Courts Press in Association with the Irish Legal History Society, 1999), 95–96; Máire Ní Dhonnachadha, "Irish Language Interpreting in the Courts since the 1850s" (MA thesis, Dublin City University, 2000), 26–28. In the majority were judges Christian, Keogh, Greene, Ball, Richards, Monaghan, and Lefroy; in the minority were judges O'Brien, Pennefather, and Pigot.

91. Sidney L. Phipson, *The Law of Evidence* (London: Stevens and Haynes: 1892), 90. See also W. M. Best, *A Treatise on the Principles of the Law of Evidence; with Elementary Rules for Conducting the Examination and Cross-Examination of Witnesses*, 3rd ed.

(London: H. Sweet, 1860), 350; Charles Petersdorff, *A Concise, Practical Abridgment of the Common and Statute Law, as at Present Administered in the Common-Law, Probate, Divorce, and Admiralty Courts*, 6 vols., 2nd ed. (London: Simpkin, Marshall, and Co., 1861–64), 3:74; Edward W. Cox, *A Digest of All the Cases in All the Reports Decided by All the Courts Relating to Magistrates, Parochial, Ecclesiastical, Election, Municipal, and Criminal Law from 1856 to 1869* (London: Law Times Office, 1870), 94.

92. *R. v. Burke*, (1858) 8 Cox 44 (C.C.), 44–65.

93. J. H. Whyte, "Landlord Influence at Elections in Ireland, 1760–1885," *English Historical Review* 80, no. 317 (Oct. 1965): 742; P. J. Jupp, "Irish Parliamentary Elections and the Influence of the Catholic Vote, 1801–20," *Historical Journal* 10, no. 2 (1967): 184; P. J. Jupp, *British and Irish Elections, 1784–1831* (Newton Abbot, UK: David & Charles Holdings, and New York: Barnes & Noble Books, 1973), 166–67.

94. L. M. Cullen, "Catholics Under the Penal Laws," *Eighteenth-Century Ireland/ Iris an Dá Chultúr* 1 (1986): 26–27; Dáire Keogh, "The Catholic Church in Ireland in the Age of the North Atlantic Revolution, 1775–1815," in *Christianity in Ireland: Revisiting the Story*, ed. Brendan Bradshaw and Dáire Keogh (Dublin: The Columba Press, 2002), 157–60; Patrick Fagan, *Divided Loyalties: The Question of the Oath for Irish Catholics in the Eighteenth Century* (Dublin: Four Courts Press, 1997), 171. For evidence of late-seventeenth-century Irish-speaking voters, see J. G. Simms, "Irish Catholics and the Parliamentary Franchise, 1692–1728," *Irish Historical Studies* 23, no. 45 (1960–61): 29.

95. K. Theodore Hoppen, *Elections, Politics, and Society in Ireland, 1832–1885* (Oxford: Clarendon Press, 1984), 1–26; McCabe, "Law, Conflict," 395.

96. *Journals of the House of Commons*, 25 Feb. 1808, p. 104; William Hands, *The Proceedings on Election Petitions, with Precedents* (London: William Walker, 1812), 204–11; *Londonderry Journal and Donegal and Tyrone Advertiser*, 23 Feb. and 1 Mar. 1808.

97. Hoppen, *Elections*, 5–6, 10–11; Whyte, "Landlord Influence," 745–47.

98. *Journals of the House of Commons*, 25 Feb. 1808, p. 104.

99. *(Ireland) Sheriffs Charges and Expenses at Elections, 1818 and 1820. Returns to an Address of the House of Commons, of 13th June 1820; for an Account of All Sums of Money Paid to Sheriffs or Undersheriffs, at the General Election in 1818, and at the Last General Election, (1820) for Writs and Precepts, for Either Counties, Cities, or Boroughs, in Ireland . . .* , p. 11, H.C. 1820 (291), ix.

100. The starting point for the background to electoral laws in 1817 is the 35 Geo. III c.29 (1795), which attempted to create a blank slate by repealing a raft of polling and oath legislation from the time of the reign of George I through 1790. Post-1795, the relevant statutes are 37 Geo. III c. 47 (1797), 43 Geo. III c. 74 (1803), and 51 Geo. III c. 77 (1811). None of these statutes mentions provision for interpreters. See also *Report from the Select Committee Appointed to Inquire into the Expenses of Sheriffs and Other Returning Officers, At Elections in Ireland; and Also into the Laws for Regulating Elections in Ireland*, p. 3, H.C. 1820 (226), iii.

101. See 1 Geo. IV c. 11 §26–27; 1 & 2 Geo. IV c. 58 §7 and Schedule A; *Report from the Select Committee Appointed to Inquire into the Expenses of Sheriffs . . .* , p. 5, H.C. 1820 (226), iii.

102. 4 Geo. IV c. 55 §43; *Polls at Elections. (Ireland) A Bill to Regulate Polls at Elections in Ireland*, p. 6, H.C. 1839 (120), iii; 45 Parl. Deb. (3rd ser.) (5 Mar. 1839) 1286, hansard.millbanksystems.com.

103. 35 & 36 Vict. c. 33 (1872), Schedule 6; T.C.F. Battersby, *Carleton on Parliamentary Elections in Ireland: Together with the Practice in Election Petitions and an Appendix of Statutes and Forms*, 11th ed. (Dublin: Hodges, Figgis & Co. Ltd., 1892), 24, 240.

104. *(Ireland) Sheriffs Charges and Expenses at Elections, 1818 and 1820 . . .*, pp. 6, 8, 11–12, H.C. 1820 (291), ix.

105. *Election Expenses (Ireland). An Account of Expenses Incurred by the Returning Officer at Every Election for a County, or City, or Borough, in Ireland, During the Months of June and July 1841*, pp. 7–8, 13, H.C. 1843 (620), l.

106. *Election Expenses. Returns from Sheriffs and Other Returning Officers for Counties and Parliamentary Boroughs in Great Britain and Ireland*, pp. 191, 195, 203, H.C. 1857 (331), xxxiv.

107. *Clare Election. Minutes of Evidence Taken Before the Select Committee on the Clare Election Petition; with the Proceedings of the Committee*, evidence of sheriff Henry Green, 7 June 1860, p. 8, H.C. 1860 (178) (392), xi.

108. Jupp, "Catholic Vote," 184–87.

109. NLI MS G 430, p. 131, quoted in Pádraig A. Breatnach, "Meascra ar an Saol in Éirinn, 1841–44," *Éigse* 25 (1991): 105.

110. Hoppen, *Elections*, 16–17, 27.

111. *Election Expenses. Returns from Sheriffs and Other Returning Officers . . .*, p. 192, H.C. 1857 (331), xxxiv.

112. See the examples of Cork and Dublin, respectively, in Ian d'Alton, *Protestant Society and Politics in Cork, 1812–44* (Cork: Cork University Press, 1980), 88–101, and Jacqueline Hill, *From Patriots to Unionists: Dublin Civic Politics and Irish Protestant Patriotism, 1660–1840* (Oxford: Oxford University Press, 1997), 46–50, 195–96.

113. Hoppen, *Elections*, 2–5.

114. *(Ireland) Sheriffs Charges and Expenses at Elections, 1818 and 1820 . . .*, p. 8, H.C. 1820 (291), ix.

115. *Freeman's Journal*, 12 Oct. 1857.

116. Peter J. Jupp and Stephen Royle, "The Social Geography of Cork City Elections, 1801–1830," *Irish Historical Studies* 29 (1994): 16, 24.

117. *(Ireland) Sheriffs Charges and Expenses at Elections, 1818 and 1820 . . .*, pp. 4, 16, H.C. 1820 (291), ix; *First Report from the Select Committee on Fictitious Votes, Ireland; with the Minutes of Evidence, and Appendix*, pp. 11, 252–53, H.C. 1837–38 (259), xiii.

118. *Election Expenses (Ireland). An Account of Expenses Incurred by the Returning Officer . . .*, p. 5, H.C. 1843 (620), l; Hoppen, *Elections*, 2, 5.

119. *Election Expenses. Returns from Sheriffs and Other Returning Officers . . .*, p. 195, H.C. 1857 (331), xxxiv; Hoppen, *Elections*, 3.

120. *(Ireland) Sheriffs Charges and Expenses at Elections, 1818 and 1820 . . .*, p. 19, H.C. 1820 (291), ix; *Election Expenses. Returns from Sheriffs and Other Returning Officers . . .*, p. 203, H.C. 1857 (331), xxxiv.

121. Ní Úrdail, *Scribe*, 223.

122. For the use of *leabhar* to denote oaths, see Niall Ó Dónaill, ed., *Foclóir Gaeilge-Béarla* (Baile Átha Cliath: An Gúm, 1992), s.v. leabhar.

123. NLI MS G 96, p. 79; 4 Geo. IV c. 55 §48 and 2 & 3 Will. IV c. 88, Schedule B. For the Irish text of the oaths, see Buttimer, "Gaelic Literature," 610.

124. Daniel Foley, *An English-Irish Dictionary* (Dublin: William Curry and Company, 1855), s.v. vote; Patrick S. Dinneen, *Foclóir Gaedhilge agus Béarla: An Irish-English Dictionary*, new ed. (Dublin: Irish Texts Society, 1996), s.v. guth; Ó Dónaill, *Foclóir*, s.v. guth, vóta, vótail. No such understanding of *guth* appears to be found in early Irish texts, on the other hand. See *Dictionary of the Irish Language, Based Mainly on Old and Middle Irish Materials* (Dublin: Royal Irish Academy, 1913–76), s.v. guth.

125. Gary Owens, "Nationalism without Words: Symbolism and Ritual Behaviour in the Repeal 'Monster Meetings' of 1843–5," in Donnelly and Miller, *Irish Popular Culture*, 242–69; Cornelius G. Buttimer, "An Irish Text on the 'War of Jenkins' Ear,'" *Celtica* 21 (1990): 75–98; Buttimer, "A Cork Gaelic Text on a Napoleonic Campaign," *Journal of the Cork Historical and Archaeological Society* 95, no. 254 (1990): 107–19; Buttimer, "A Gaelic Reaction to Robert Emmet's Rebellion," *Journal of the Cork Historical and Archaeological Society* 97 (1992): 36–53; Buttimer, "Gaelic Literature," 588–89; Buttimer, "Cogadh Sagsana Nuadh Sonn: Reporting the American Revolution," *Studia Hibernica* 28 (1994): 63–101.

126. Morley, *Washington i gCeannas a Ríochta*, x–xxiii.

127. *Freeman's Journal*, 8 Oct. 1841.

128. *Freeman's Journal*, 13 Mar. and 25 Oct. 1844.

129. On popular opposition to the poor law, see Fred Powell, "The Irish Poor Law Controversy," *Social Policy & Administration* 15, no. 3 (Autumn 1981): 293–97; Mel Cousins, "Poor Law Politics and Elections in Post-Famine Ireland," *History Studies: University of Limerick History Society Journal* 6 (2005): 37; and Gerard O'Brien, "The Establishment of the Poor-Law Unions in Ireland, 1838–43," *Irish Historical Studies* 23, no. 90 (1982): 99–101.

130. *Freeman's Journal*, 28 Feb. 1843.

131. Examples of priests inveighing in Irish against secret societies can be found in Gearóid Ó Tuathaigh, "An Chléir Chaitliceach, an Léann Dúchais, agus an Cultúr in Éirinn, c. 1750–c. 1850," in *Léann na Cléire*, Léachtaí Cholm Cille 16, ed. Pádraig Ó Fiannachta (Maigh Nuad: An Sagart, 1986), 114; Pádraig de Brún, "Forógra do Ghaelaibh 1824," *Studia Hibernica* 12 (1972): 142–66; *Limerick Evening Post and Clare Sentinel*, quoted in the *Times* (London), 12 Nov. 1829 and 18 June 1831.

132. From the *Dublin Evening Post*, quoted in the *Morning Chronicle* (London), 2 Feb. 1825. This is undoubtedly the Rev. William Fitzgerald (d. 1826), who had a hand in the 1824 Irish-language proclamation noted above warning against secret societies. Fitzgerald himself was a poet and had close connections with Irish scribes Eoghan Caomhánach and Séamas Ó Caoindealbháin (see chapter 6). See P. de Brún, "Forógra do Ghaelaibh," 145–46.

133. *Times* (London), 30 Jan. 1830.

134. From the *Waterford Mirror*, quoted in *Glasgow Herald* (Scotland), 12 June 1826.

135. *Limerick Evening Post and Clare Sentinel*, 11 Nov. 1828.

136. *Freeman's Journal*, 14 Jan. 1839.

137. Ibid., 18 Nov. 1845.

138. *Belfast News-Letter*, 21 Aug. 1838. For commentary on the estimated size of such crowds, see Owens, "Nationalism without Words," 243–44.

139. *Freeman's Journal*, 20 Oct. 1838.

140. Ibid., 22 Dec. 1838.

141. *Times* (London), 14 July 1841.

142. *Freeman's Journal*, 13 June 1846.

143. Ibid., 13 Dec. 1842. An entry for this day does not occur in the published version of Daunt's daily log of repeal activities in this month. See William J. O'Neill Daunt, *A Life Spent for Ireland. Being Selections from the Journals of the Late W.J. O'Neill Daunt Edited by His Daughter* (London: T. Fisher Unwin: 1896), 20–21.

144. *Freeman's Journal*, 2 Mar. 1846.

145. *Limerick Evening Post and Clare Sentinel*, 24 Oct. 1828; *Mayo Constitution*, 19 Sept. 1831; Michael Denis Spellissy, *The Life of John Murphy, Priest and Patriot* (Dublin: M. H. Gill & Son, 1880), 11–16; Patrick Hamell, *Maynooth Students and Ordinations*, 2 vols. (Maynooth: Cardinal Press, 1982 and 1984), 1:127 (Murphy would appear to be entry no. 6615).

146. *Limerick Evening Post and Clare Sentinel*, 11 Jan. 1828.

147. Ibid., 10 Oct. 1828; I. Murphy, *The Diocese of Killaloe, 1800–1850*, 78. There is another account of a priest reported to have addressed a crowd of electors in Irish from the courthouse on the day of the 1828 election, although whether that was Murphy or another member of the clergy is unclear. See *Morning Chronicle*, 22 July 1828.

148. *Limerick Evening Post and Clare Sentinel*, 26 Sept. 1828.

149. Ibid., 2 Sept. 1828.

150. Accounts of O'Connell fooling reporters by using Irish can be found in *Mayo Constitution*, 19 October 1841; William Fagan, *The Life and Times of Daniel O'Connell*, 2 vols. (Cork: John O'Brien, 1847–48), 2:337–38; *Bristol Mercury*, 18 May 1850; F. Knight Hunt, *The Fourth Estate: Contributions towards a History of Newspapers, and of the Liberty of the Press*, 2 vols. (London: David Bogue, 1850), 2:285–86; *Hull Packet and East Riding Times*, 21 June 1861; and *Manchester Times*, 27 July 1861.

151. Fagan, *Life and Times*, 336–37; Gerald J. Lyne, "Daniel O'Connell, Intimidation, and the Kerry Elections of 1835," *Kerry Archaeological and Historical Society* 4 (1971): 84.

152. *Freeman's Journal*, 27 May 1843.

153. *Mayo Constitution*, 16 July 1829.

154. *Freeman's Journal*, 29 Feb. 1832.

155. Ibid., 16 Feb. 1838.

156. Ibid., 6 and 17 Nov. 1838.

157. Ibid., 23 May 1838. On the importance of this region, see Patrick O'Donoghue, "Causes of the Opposition to Tithes, 1830–38," *Studia Hibernica* 5 (1965): 8–9.

158. *Limerick Evening Post and Clare Sentinel*, 23 Oct. 1832; *Mayo Constitution*, 29 Oct. 1832.

159. The similarities between an anonymous anti-tithe speech preserved in NLI MS G 702 and the highlights of O'Connor's speeches given in trial reports have been used to suggest that this text records one of his addresses. See Séamus P. Ó Mórdha, "An Anti-Tithe Speech in Irish," *Éigse* 9, no. 4 (Winter 1960-61): 223-24.

160. Ó Mórdha, "Anti-Tithe," 225-26.

161. BL MS Egerton 113 (NLI p. 440), ff. 165-66.

162. Ó Súilleabháin recorded in his diary, "B[h]i cead mile fear ann, an cuid is lugha dhe" (There were a hundred thousand men there, at the least), consisting of attendees from Kilkenny, Waterford, Wexford, and Tipperary. McGrath, *Cinnlae Amhlaoibh Uí Shúileabháin*, 3:164-65.

163. Ibid., 4:109-15.

164. Breandán Ó Buachalla, "A Speech in Irish on Repeal," *Studia Hibernica* 10 (1970): 84-94.

CHAPTER 6. LANGUAGE AND CATHOLIC DEVOTIONAL REFORM

1. Patrick Denn [Pádraig Denn], *The Catholic Children's Religious Primer, Containing the Prayers, etc., Necessary for the Instruction of Youth, & Even for the Adult, Also the Lord's Prayer, and the Principal Parts of the Mass Expounded, with the Rosaries and Litanies of Jesus, Mary, and Joseph, the Rosary for the Dead; and the Recommendation of a Soul Departing, &c., &c.* (Cork: Daniel Mulcahy, 1858), vi; John Fleming [Seán Pléimann], "Essay on the Present State of the Irish Language and Literature in the Province of Munster," RIA MS 12 Q 13 (1126), p. 1.

2. Donlevy, *An Teagasg Críosduidhe*, xxxviii.

3. RIA Cat., fasc. I-XXVII.

4. For an outline of each of these respective points with an emphasis on more recent findings, see Emmet Larkin, "Before the Devotional Revolution," in *Evangelicals and Catholics in Nineteenth-Century Ireland*, ed. James H. Murphy (Dublin: Four Courts Press, 2005), 15-24; Emmet Larkin, *The Pastoral Role of the Roman Catholic Church in Pre-Famine Ireland, 1750-1850* (Dublin: Four Courts Press, 2006), 9-62; Nigel Yates, *The Religious Condition of Ireland, 1770-1850* (Oxford: Oxford University Press, 2006), 197-205; David W. Miller, "Landscape and Religious Practice: A Study of Mass Attendance in Pre-Famine Ireland," *Éire-Ireland* 40, nos. 1-2 (Spring/Summer 2005): 96-106; Dáire Keogh, "'The Pattern of the Flock': John Thomas Troy, 1786-1823," in *History of the Catholic Diocese of Dublin*, ed. James Kelly and Dáire Keogh (Dublin: Four Courts Press, 2000), 222-32; Ambrose Macaulay, *William Crolly, Archbishop of Armagh, 1835-1849* (Dublin: Four Courts Press, 1994), 93-141; Thomas McGrath, "The Tridentine Evolution of Modern Irish Catholicism, 1563-1962: A Re-Examination of the 'Devotional Revolution' Thesis," in *Irish Church History Today*, ed. Réamonn Ó Muirí (Monaghan: Cumann Seanchais Ard Mhacha, 1991), 91-94; Hynes, *Knock*, 98-108; and Cara Delay, "The Devotional Revolution on the Local Level: Parish Life in Post-Famine Ireland," *U.S. Catholic Historian* 22, no. 3 (2004): 41-60.

5. Larkin, "Devotional Revolution," 649; Seán Ó Súilleabháin, "Irish Oral Tradition," in Ó Cúiv, *View of the Irish Language*, 52; Diarmuid Ó Laoghaire, "Prayers and Hymns in the Vernacular," in *An Introduction to Celtic Christianity*, ed. James P.

Mackey (Edinburgh: T & T Clark, 1989), 269; Diarmuid Ó Laoghaire, *Ár bPaidreacha Dúchais: Cnuasach de Phaidreacha agus de Bheannachtaí Ár Sinsear* (Baile Átha Cliath: Foilseacháin Ábhair Spioradálta, 1982). See also Desmond Mooney, "Popular Religion and Clerical Influence in Pre-Famine Meath," in *Religion, Conflict, and Coexistence*, ed. R. V. Comerford et al. (Dublin: Gill and McMillan, 1990), 189.

6. Douglas Hyde, *Abhráin Diadha Chúige Connacht or the Religious Songs of Connacht. Being the Sixth and Seventh Chapters of the Songs of Connacht*, 2 vols. (1906; repr., Shannon: Irish University Press, 1972), 1:xi; William Wilde, *Irish Popular Superstitions* (1852; repr., Totowa, NJ: Rowman and Littlefield, 1973), 126.

7. Donal Kerr, "The Early Nineteenth Century: Patterns of Change," in *Irish Spirituality*, ed. Michael Maher (Dublin: Veritas Publications, 1981), 138–40. See also Thomas Wall [Tomás de Bhál], "Patterns of Prayers and Devotions, 1750–1850," in *Studies in Pastoral Liturgy*, vol. 3, ed. Placid Murray (Dublin: Furrow Trust and Gill and Son, 1967), 211–14.

8. Kevin Whelan, "The Regional Impact of Irish Catholicism, 1700–1850," in *Common Ground: Essays on the Historical Geography of Ireland*, ed. William J. Smyth and Kevin Whelan (Cork: Cork University Press, 1988), 270–71.

9. Desmond Keenan, *The Catholic Church in Nineteenth-Century Ireland: A Sociological Study* (Dublin: Gill and MacMillan, 1983), 21–22.

10. Hynes, *Knock*, 100–108; Ó Ciosáin, *Print and Popular Culture*, 198–202.

11. Larkin, "Devotional Revolution," 644–45; Ciaran O'Caroll, "The Pastoral Politics of Paul Cullen," in Kelly and Keogh, *History of the Catholic Diocese of Dublin*, 301–2.

12. Catherine Lawless, "Devotion and Representation in Nineteenth-Century Ireland," in *Visual, Material and Print Culture in Nineteenth-Century Ireland*, ed. Ciara Breathnach and Catherine Lawless (Dublin: Four Courts Press, 2010), 85–97; Ann Wilson, "Arts and Crafts and Revivalism in Catholic Church Decoration: A Brief Duration," *Éire-Ireland* 48, nos. 3–4 (Fall/Winter 2013): 5–48.

13. Hynes, *Knock*, 105–6; Kerr, "Early Nineteenth Century," 139–41.

14. Mary Heimann, "Catholic Revivalism in Worship and Devotion," in *The Cambridge History of Christianity*, vol. 8, *World Christianities c. 1815–c. 1914*, ed. Sheridan Gilley and Brian Stanley (Cambridge: Cambridge University Press, 2006), 79–80. See also Heimann, *Catholic Devotion in Victorian England* (Oxford: Clarendon Press, 1995), 16.

15. Larkin, "Before the Devotional Revolution," 15–16.

16. For a helpful discussion of these issues, see Hynes, *Knock*, 102–4.

17. Pádraig de Brún, *Lámhscríbhinní Gaeilge: Treoirliosta* (Baile Átha Cliath: Institiúid Ard-Léinn Bhaile Átha Cliath, 1988), 1–36; Ó Cuív, "Irish Language and Literature, 1691–1845," 391.

18. Morley, *Ó Chéitinn go Raiftearaí*, 111–14. The manuscript collections reviewed include: RIA Cat.; T. K. Abbott and E. J. Gwynn, *Catalogue of the Irish Manuscripts in the Library of Trinity College, Dublin* (Dublin, 1921; hereafter TCD Cat.); BL Cat.; National University of Ireland, Maynooth (hereafter MYN Cat.); Pádraig de Brún and Máire Herbert, *Catalogue of Irish Manuscripts in Cambridge Libraries* (Cambridge,

1986; hereafter CL Cat.); Brian Ó Cuív, *Catalogue of Irish Language Manuscripts in the Bodleian Library at Oxford and Oxford College Libraries*, 2 vols. (Dublin, 2001, 2003; hereafter OX Cat.); Pádraig de Brún, *Catalogue of Irish Manuscripts in King's Inns Library Dublin* (Dublin, 1972; hereafter KIL Cat.); Breandán Ó Conchúir, *Clár Lámhscríbhinní Gaeilge Choláiste Ollscoile Chorcaí: Cnuasach Uí Mhurchú* (Baile Átha Cliath, 1991; hereafter C MPH Cat.); Pádraig Ó Macháin, *Catalogue of Irish Manuscripts in Mount Melleray Abbey, Co. Waterford* (Dublin, 1991; hereafter MM Cat.); Pádraig Ó Fiannachta, *Clár Lámhscríbhinní Gaeilge: Leabharlanna na Cléire agus Mionchnuasaigh*, Fascúl I–II (Baile Átha Cliath, 1978–80; hereafter LCM Cat.); Pádraig de Brún, *Clár Lámhscríbhinní Gaeilge Choláiste Ollscoile Chorcaí: Cnuasach Thorna*, 2 iml. (Baile Átha Cliath, 1967; hereafter T Cat.); Cornelius G. Buttimer, *Catalogue of Irish Manuscripts in the University of Wisconsin-Madison* (Dublin, 1989; hereafter UWM Cat.); Myles Dillon, Canice Mooney, and Pádraig de Brún, *Catalogue of Irish Manuscripts in the Franciscan Library Killiney* (Dublin, 1969; hereafter FLK Cat.); NLI Cat.; National Library of Ireland and Richard J. Hayes, *Sources: A National Library of Ireland Database for Irish Research*, 2007–12, http://sources.nli.ie (hereafter NLI Hayes); Pádraig Ó Macháin, Dublin Institute for Advanced Studies, and Dublin City University, *Irish Script on Screen/Meamram Páipéar Ríomhaire*, 1999, http://www.isos.dias.ie (hereafter ISOS).

19. R. A. Stewart Macalister, "The Vision of Merlino," *Zeitschrift für Celtische Philologie* 4 (1903): 394.

20. Prayer books translated by the scribe Dáibhí de Barra, for example, are known to have once existed but can no longer be traced. See Ó Conchúir, *Scríobhaithe*, 251, and Seán Ó Duinnshléibhe, "'Mar is fánach mac a' teacht go cruinn mar 'athair': Dáibhí de Barra's Surviving Translations," in Breathnach and Lawless, *Visual, Material and Print Culture*, 259.

21. Ní Úrdail, *Scribe*, 77.

22. NLI MS G 95, p. 81–82, 149–50, 213.

23. NLI Cat., fasc. VI, 31 [NLI MS G 231, p. ii]; NLI MS G 70, p. 145.

24. NLI MS G 103, p. 17; NLI Cat., fasc. V, 34 [NLI MS G 180, p. 53–54].

25. Niall Ó Ciosáin, "Language, Print, and the Catholic Church in Ireland, 1700–1900," in *Which Direction Ireland? Proceedings of the 2006 ACIS Mid-Atlantic Regional Conference*, ed. Donald McNamara (Newcastle, UK: Cambridge Scholars Publishing, 2007), 127.

26. E. R. McClintock Dix and Séamus Ó Casaidhe, *List of Books, Pamphlets, etc., Printed Wholly or Partly in Irish, from the Earliest Period to 1820* (Dublin: An Cló-Chumann Teoranta, 1905), 5–14; McKenna, "Textual History of The Spiritual Rose," 67–69. This may even be an overestimate of the availability of such texts: a copy of this 1736 edition of *La Vera Sapienza*, translated as *Eagna Fhírinneach* and ascribed (as this title often was) to Father Paolo Segneri, has not been traced. Although Pinamonti was more likely the author of *La Vera Sapienza*, Segneri and Pinamonti often collaborated closely in writing these texts: F. Faber, *The Lives of Father Paul Segneri, S.J., Father Peter Pinamonti, S.J., and the Ven. John de Britto, S.J.* (New York: Edward Dunigan and Brother, 1851), 187, 191–92. See also Ní Úrdail, *Scribe*, 219.

27. Between 1818 and 1825, the following Catholic religious titles were published for the first time: Patrick Denn, *Leavar Beag na Rosaries, mar aon leis na Liodain, agus le Toirvirt Suas an Anama aig dul Deag, &c. &c.* (Clonmel: John Hackett, 1818); Richard Challoner, *Machtnuig go Maih Air, no Leismuainte air Fhirine Mhor an Chreidiv Chriosduvuil do Gach La Anso Mioy*, trans. Patrick Denn (Clonmel: John Hackett, 1819); Giovanni Manni, *Ceithre Soleirseadha de'n Eagnuidheacht Chriostuidhe, Tarraingthe o Cheithre Leur-Smuaintighthibh na Siorruidheachta. Air na Sgriobhadh go Bunnudhasach ann Iottailis le Eoin Baptista Manni, dhe Chomhluadar Iosa, agus Curtha a mBearla Sacsanach le W. V. agus Ionntoighthe o Shacs-bheulra, go Gaoidheilg le Seumas O'Scoireadh*, trans. James Scurry [Séamus Ó Scoireadh] (Portlairge: John Bull, 1820); Richard Challoner, *Smuain go Maith Air: No, Learsmuainteadh air Mhoirfhirinnidhe an Chreidimh Chriostaighe, do gach La san Mi*, trans. Eugene Kavanagh [Eoghan Caomhánach] (Dublin: John Coyne, 1820); Thomas à Kempis, *Searc-Leanmhain Chriosd. A gCeithre Leabhraibh le Tomas A Cempis*, trans. Domhnall O Suilliobhain [Dónall Ó Súilliobháin] (Dublin: Richard Coyne, 1822); Patrick Denn, *Stiúratheoir an Pheacuig* (Cork: printer unknown, 1824); Denn, *The Catholic Children's Religious Primer, Containing the Prayers, etc., Necessary for the Instruction of Youth & Even for the Adult, Also the Lord's Prayer, and the Principal Parts of the Mass Expounded, with the Rosaries and Litanies of Jesus, Mary, and Joseph, the Rosary for the Dead, and the Recommendation of a Soul Departing, &c., &c.* (Cork: Charles Dillon, 1825). An earlier text published in Carrick-on-Suir in 1796 by the scribe Pádraig Ó Néill, but for which a surviving copy has not been found, should also be mentioned in this context of turn-of-the-century printing: *Oific na hOighe Naomhtha Muire* (Carriug na Suire: Seaghan Stacy, 1796). See Eoghan Ó Néill, *Gleann an Óir: Ar Thóir na Staire agus na Litríochta in Oirthear Mumhan agus i nDeisceart Laighean* (Baile Átha Cliath: An Clóchomhar Tta, 1988), 40.

28. Irish Society, "Quarterly Extract, No. 20," in *Quarterly Extracts*, 62.

29. N. Ó Ciosáin, *Print and Popular Culture*, 123, 128–31.

30. Micheál Ó hAnnracháin to Maurice Lenihan, 24 Oct. 1876, NLI MS G 349.

31. N. Ó Ciosáin, *Print and Popular Culture*, 118.

32. *First Report of the Commissioners on Education in Ireland*, appendix 250, p. 744, H.C. 1825 (400), xii.

33. *Freeman's Journal*, 14 Nov. 1842; Ulick Bourke [Uileog de Búrca], "Essay on the State of the Irish Language and Literature in the Province of Connaught," RIA MS 12 Q 13 (1126), pp. 245–46. Antoine Boltúin argues that MacHale, as much as Loftus, should be given credit for the authorship of this catechism on the basis of its stylistic similarities to other Irish-language works by the archbishop. Boltúin, "Mac Héil agus an Ghaeilge: a Shaothar agus a Dhearcadh" (PhD diss., National University of Ireland, Galway, 1992), 130.

34. Sean Griffin, "The Catholic Book Society and Its Role in the Emerging System of National Education, 1824–1834," *Irish Education Studies* 11 (1992): 87.

35. Fleming, "Munster," RIA MS 12 Q 13 (1126), p. 1. For the history of this catechism and its printing, see Pádraig Ó Macháin, "Fr. Patrick Meany and the Dr. Keating Society, 1860–1865," *Studia Hibernica* 37 (2011): 183–89.

36. Daniel McCarthy, ed., *Collections on Irish Church History. From the Mss. of the Late Very Rev. Laurence F. Renehan, D.D., President of Maynooth College*, 2 vols. (Dublin: James Duffy and Sons, 1861–1874), 2:140.

37. *Royal Commission of Inquiry into Primary Education (Ireland). Vol. III. Containing Evidence Taken Before the Commissioners from March 12th to October 30th, 1868. Questions and Answers 1 to 17608*, p. 87 [C.6-II], H.C. 1870, xviii; Fleming, "Munster," RIA MS 12 Q 13 (1126), p. 1.

38. *Freeman's Journal*, 5 Mar. 1859. The contributor would appear to have been citing Philip Barron (ca. 1801–44), who recorded this same observation in his *Ancient Ireland. A Weekly Magazine* 1, no. 1 (Jan. 1835): 13.

39. Micheál Ó hAnnracháin to Maurice Lenihan, 31 Oct. 1876, NLI MS G 349.

40. Franciscan Library, Killiney (hereafter FLK; Irish manuscripts now at held at University College Dublin), MS A 38, f. 6b; Pádraig Ó Macháin, "Tomás Ó Iceadha's Translation of the Roman Missal," *Celtica* 24 (2003): 266; LCM Cat., fasc. I, 6–9, 31–32 [St. John's College (Coláiste Eoin) Library, Waterford (hereafter CE) MS 6 and CE MS 25]; NLI Cat., fasc. VII, 93, and fasc. IX, 18 [MS G 329 and MS G 388].

41. See writing by "Bat. Bower of the Commons of Cashel" on the back page of the copy of *Machtnuig go Maih Air*, Newberry Library, Chicago.

42. William Heffernan to John O'Daly, 13 Mar. 1846, NLI MS 8010, folder 2.

43. Ní Úrdail, *Scribe*, 218–19.

44. RIA Cat., fasc. XXII, 2824 [RIA MS F i 1 (984)]; Ó Conchúir, *Scríobhaithe*, 209–11; Ní Úrdail, *Scribe*, 73.

45. NLI p. 6042 (St. Colman's College [Cólaiste Colmáin] Library, Fermoy [hereafter CF] MS 24), p. 619.

46. Ó Conchúir, *Scríobhaithe*, 228.

47. Liam Ó Danachair, "Memories of My Youth," *Béaloideas* 17 (1947/49): 58.

48. Ó Conchúir, *Scríobhaithe*, 222–24.

49. Kohl, *Travels in Ireland*, 185; Máire Ní Mhurchú and Diarmuid Breathnach, *Beathaisneís a Sé: 1782–1881*, 2nd ed. (Baile Átha Cliath: An Clóchomhar Tta, 2008), 124.

50. LCM Cat., fasc. I, 6, 40 [CE MS 6 and CE MS 31]; John Keating, "Saint John's College Waterford: Beginnings and History," *Capuchin Annual* (1959): 343.

51. Domhnall Ua Tuathail, ed., *Tóraidheacht na bhFíreun air Lorg Chríosta, i gCeithre Leabhraibh. Tomás À Cempis a Sgríobh san Laidin. Aig so an Chéad Aistriughadh Gaedhilge. Sagart Éigin i n-aice le Dún Phádraig i gCo. an Dúin a d'Aistrigh, 1762* (Baile Átha Cliath: M. H. Mac Guill agus a Mhac, 1915), ix; Séamus P. Ó Mórdha, "Údar *Tóruidheacht na bhFíreun air Lorg Chríosda*," *Studia Hibernica* 3 (1963): 166–69; Ó Buachalla, *I mBéal Feirste Cois Cuain*, 13. The Protestant rector John Richardson had seen an Irish translation of the first part of *De Imitatione Christi* as far back as 1711, but its survival and relationship to the other translations has not been traced. See Ó Mórdha, "Údar *Tóruidheacht*," 171–72.

52. Pádraig Ó Súilleabháin, "Roinnt Caiticeasmaí Gaeilge," *Éigse* 11 (1965): 113–14; Michael Tynan, *Catholic Instruction in Ireland, 1720–1950: The O'Reilly/Donlevy Catechetical Tradition* (Dublin: Four Courts Press, 1985), 19–21; Ní Mhurchú and Breathnach, *Beathaisnéis*, 26. Carpenter may have even provided the original translation for

the 1762 version of *Imitation of Christ* circulating in County Down. See Brian Ó Cuív, "Irish Translations of Thomas à Kempis's *De Imitatione Christi*," *Celtica* 2, no. 2 (1954): 255.

53. Coppinger was assisted by Father Dónall Ó Súilleabháin, who also worked for Bishop Murphy: *An Teagasg Criostaidhe; do Reir Cheiste agas Fhreagraidh, Athraidhthe go Gaodhailge, le Oideas Uilliam Coppinger, Easbog Chluana agas Rois, ua'n nGeartheagash. A Scriobodh Se Fein a mBeurla, Ath-leighte leis an Athair Domhnald O'Suilliobhain* (Cork: Cormac Diolun: 1831). MacHale's catechism received the assistance of Father Martin Loftus: *An Teagasg Críosdaighe. Do Réir Chomhairle Ard-Easboig Thuama, agus Easbog na Cúige Sin* (Baile Átha Cliath: T. Codamhell, 1839); Thomas Bray and William Coppinger, *Oideas Athchoimir agus Urnaighthe do Dhaoine Eagcruadh agus Do'n Mhuintear Bhios ag Dul D'Eag, Maille re Gniomhartha Caoinduthrachta eile, a n-Gaoidheilg agus a m-Bearla, re Deagh Mholadh an Ollamahin, D.B. Ardeasbog Chaisil* (Cork: James Haly, 1807). For Bray's sources, which included Coppinger's *True Piety* (Cork, 1797), see his comments in the preface to the English version, *Short Instructions and Prayers for Sick and Dying Persons, with Other Acts of Devotion, in English and Irish, Recommended by D.B. Abp. C.* (Cork: James Haly, 1806), iii.

54. N. Ó Ciosáin, *Print and Popular Culture*, 124.

55. Jonathan Furlong, *Aithghearughadh. An Teagaisg Críosdaighe Geinearáilte: Molta le hArdeasboig Eireann, Chum Usáide na Mionaosóige, aig nach bh-fuil Fós Intleacht Chum Níos Mó d'Fhoghluim. Aistrighthe a n-Gaoidhilig, le Jonathan Furlong, Sagart Cathoilice* (Dublin: T. Coldwell, 1839); *Carad an Chríosdaigh; nó Leabharán iona bhfuil Urnuighthe Áirighthe Riachtanach chum Seirbhís Dhiadha do Chomhlionadh* (Dublin: no printer, 1842); *Compánach an Chríosdaigh; nó Tiomsúgh d'Urnaíghibh Cráibhtheacha Oireamhnach chum gach Dulgais do Bhainas le Creideamh, do Chomhlíonadh* (Dublin: Tegg & Co., 1842); NLI Cat., fasc. V, 69 [NLI MS G 194]; I. Murphy, *Diocese of Killaloe, 1800–1850*, 354–55. Furlong had less cordial relations with scribe Mícheál Ó hAnnracháin, who complained that the priest had "borrowed an Irish copy of Andalacha Inse Cathaigh [sic] from me and never returned it." Mícheál Ó hAnnracháin to Maurice Lenihan, 26 Oct. 1871, NLI MS 4726.

56. RIA Cat., fasc. XVII, 2129 [RIA MS 23 Q 8 (696)]; NLI Cat., fasc. VII, 53 [NLI MS G 317]; Eoghan Ó Súilleabháin, "Scríobhaithe Phort Láirge 1700–1900," in *Waterford: History and Society; Interdisciplinary Essays on the History of an Irish County*, ed. William Nolan and Thomas P. Power (Dublin: Geography Publications, 1992), 281; Ó Conchúir, *Scríobhaithe*, 61, 268. The repeal reference appears on the first page of the Jesuit Archives (Leabhlann na nÍosánach), Leeson Street, Dublin (hereafter IL) MS 6.

57. NLI p. 6037 (CF MS 1); LCM Cat., fasc I, 94 [CF MS 21]. Ó Conchúir, *Scríobhaithe*, 161, suggests that CF MS 5, a collection of religious verse made ca. 1842, may also have been made for Ciniféic; the priest was also a patron of Pól Ó Longáin. See RIA Cat., VII, 800 [RIA MS 3 C 9 (285)].

58. Ó Longáin to "Revd Sir," 1 Sept. 1832, NLI G 95, p. 231.

59. *Freeman's Journal*, 26 Aug. 1845; NLI Cat., fasc. VIII, 77 [NLI MS G 363].

60. N. Ó Ciosáin, *Print and Popular Culture*, 124.

61. Ó Conchúir, *Scríobhaithe*, 225.

62. NLI Cat., fasc. VIII, 4 [NLI MS G 333].
63. RIA Cat., fasc. XXV, 3172 [RIA MS 24 C 50 (1180)].
64. MYN Cat., fasc. V, 78–79 [National University of Ireland, Maynooth (hereafter MYN) MS C 41].
65. Ó Conchúir, Scríobhaithe, 225–26, 327. Ó Conchúir notes that the relationship between Ó Murchadha and Muiris Ó Conchúir was less one of a client and patron and more of a mutual intellectual exchange.
66. RIA Cat., fasc. XII, 1443 [RIA MS 23 B 26 (500)], and Ó Conchúir, Scríobhaithe, 64.
67. NLI MS G 320, pp. 7, 47. Catechisms and parts of catechisms copied by Ó Longáin can be found in NLI MS G 95, p. 27, NLI MS G 111, p. 97, RIA MS 23 G 27 (492), pp. 9–45, and RIA MS 23 C 18 (493), p. 89–103.
68. MYN Cat., fasc III, 65 [MYN MS M 76]; Ó Conchúir, Scríobhaithe, 49; Dawson, Peadar Ó Gealacáin, 27, referring to RIA MS 24 P 20 (1072), part iii.
69. Eugene Hynes, "The Great Hunger and Irish Catholicism," Societas 8 (1978): 141–43; Hynes, Knock, 99.
70. K. Whelan, "Regional Impact," 258–66. For an example of a Wexford scribe, there is Philib Ua Giobúin, who included religious material in RIA 23 D 8 (503), written 1740. See RIA Cat., fasc. XII, 1450.
71. The importance of translation as creation is emphasized in Michael Cronin, "Brollach," in Aistriú Éireann, ed. Charles Dillon and Ríona Ní Fhrighil (Béal Feirste: Cló Ollscoil na Banríona, 2008), x.
72. Dáire Keogh, Edmund Rice and the First Christian Brothers, 2nd ed. (Dublin: Four Courts Press, 2009), 102–5, 110–11, 170–88; Griffin, "Catholic Book Society," 94; Robin J. Kavanagh, "Pictures of Piety and Impropriety: Irish Religious Periodicals of the 1830s," in Breathnach and Lawless, Visual, Material and Print Culture, 115–28. Note that there were Irish speakers among the early Christian Brothers missionaries. See Aodh P. Caomhánach, "Na Bráithre Críostaí agus an Ghaeilge," in Gníomhartha na mBráithre, ed. Micheál Ó Cearúil (Baile Átha Cliath: Coiscéim, 1996), 123.
73. First Report of the Commissioners on Education in Ireland, appendix 252, pp. 756–57, H.C. 1825 (400), xii. There are two potential texts corresponding to the title of Lives of the Irish Saints: Patrick Lynch's Hibernia Sancta; or, Lives of Irish Saints (Dublin: Thomas Haydock, 1817), and, what is more likely to be the work identified here, the anonymously authored The Lives of the Irish Saints, Extracted from the Writings of the Rev. Alban Butler, and Now Placed in Order, with a Prefixed Callender; to which is Added, an Office and Litany in Their Honour, with a Defence of the Monastic Institute. By a Cistercian Monk (Dublin: J. Coyne, 1823).
74. Catholic Penny Magazine 1, no. 8 (5 Apr. 1834): 66–67.
75. Alban Butler, Lives of the Fathers, Martyrs, and Other Principal Saints: Compiled from Original Monuments, and Other Authentic Records: Illustrated with the Remarks of Judicious Modern Critics and Historians, 3rd ed., 6 vols. (Dublin: H. Fitzpatrick, 1802), 1:xi.
76. A. Butler, Lives of the Fathers, 6:281–92; Hugh Fenning, "Catholic Imprints of Catholic Interest," Collectanea Hibernica 39–48 (1998–2006): 1701–39 (1), 1740–59 (2),

1760–69 (3), 1770–82 (4), 1783–89 (5), 1790–95 (6), 1796–99 (7) (hereafter *Fenning*) 4, 192; Thomas Wall, *The Sign of Doctor Hay's Head, Being Some Account of the Hazards and Fortunes of Catholic Printers and Publishers in Dublin from the Later Penal Times to the Present Day* (Dublin: M. H. Gill and Son, 1958), 74–75.

77. [A Cistercian Monk], *The Lives of the Irish Saints, Extracted from the Writings of the Rev. Alban Butler*, 1–10 and passim.

78. RIA MS 23 O 35 (55), p. 249; RIA Cat., fasc. III, 363 [RIA MS 24 L 11 (124)]; MYN Cat., fasc. IV, 90 [MYN MS R 73, section b]; TCD Cat., 25 [TCD MS 1285]; Joseph Vendryes, "Betha Iuiliana," *Revue Celtique* 33 (1912): 311.

79. Thomas O'Connor, "Towards the Invention of the Irish Catholic *Natio*: Thomas Messingham's *Florilegium* (1624)," *Irish Theological Quarterly* 64 (1999): 165–66, 170–71; Bernadette Cunningham and Raymond Gillespie, "'The Most Adaptable of Saints': The Cult of St. Patrick in the Seventeenth Century," *Archivium Hibernicum* 49 (1995): 83, 101.

80. Robert Rochford, *The Life of the Glorious Bishop S. Patricke, Apostle and Primate of Ireland* (St. Omer's: John Heigham, 1625), 107; Carl Horstmann, ed., *Nova Legenda Anglie: As Collected by John of Tynemouth, John Capgrave, and Others, and First Printed, with New Lives, by Wynkyn de Worde A.D. MDXVI*, 2 vols. (Oxford: Clarendon Press, 1901), 1:ix–x, 153–60; BL Cat., II, 456; RIA Cat., fasc. IV, 500; Richard Sharpe, *Medieval Irish Saints' Lives: An Introduction to Vitae Sanctorum Hiberniae* (Oxford: Clarendon Press, 1991), 13–15.

81. Cunningham and Gillespie, "Most Adaptable of Saints," 97.

82. E.g., for Jocelin's Patrick, CF MS 24, p. 251; National University of Ireland, Cork, University Library, Torna Collection (hereafter Torna) MS T.xli, p. 67; BL MS Add. 39665, f. 55; NLI MS G 96, p. 151; NLI MS G 362, p. 283; RIA MS 23 K 6 (207), p. 1; RIA MS 23 G 20 (211), p. 1; RIA MS 24 C 1 (293), p. 159; RIA MS 23 M 8 (305), p. 97; RIA MS 23 A 38 (365), p. 88; RIA MS 23 E 9 (527), p. 1; RIA MS 24 A 22 (659), p. 1; and RIA MS 3 B 7 (810), p. 53. For the Cogitus/Capgrave life of Bridget, see CF MS 24, p. 329; MYN MS M 73, p. 258; MYN MS M 101, p. 247; Torna MS T.xl, p. 159; BL MS Add.18948, f. 56b; BL MS Add. 39665, f. 77; BL MS Add. 31876, f. 21; NLI MS G 220, p. 187; and RIA MS 23 B 30 (182), p. 57. Unlike the lives of Patrick and Bridget, however, the life of Saint Columba by Adomnán used by Rochford and Messingham was not widely reproduced by scribes in the nineteenth century.

83. Whitley Stokes, ed., *Lives of Saints from the Book of Lismore* (Oxford: Clarendon Press, 1890), v–vi; Kathleen Mulchrone, ed., *Bethu Phátraic: The Tripartite Life of St. Patrick* (Dublin: Royal Irish Academy, 1939), v–vi. For chronological dates, see Sharpe, *Medieval Irish Saints' Lives*, 20. Among the examples of the Tripartite life of Saint Patrick in later centuries are RIA MS 23 A 15 (46), p. 323, written by Sémus Mha Guidhir; RIA MS A iii 1 (969), p. 1, written by Tadhg Ó Neachtain; and TCD MS 1285, p. 95, written by Hugh O'Daly.

84. Cunningham and Gillespie, "Most Adaptable of Saints," 82; Ní Úrdail, *Scribe*, 161. Examples include MYN MS M 74, p. 1; NLI MS G 362, p. 7; RIA MS F iv 2 (268), p. 1; RIA MS 23 M 7 (287), pp. 193–94, 207–23, 243–45; and RIA MS 23 L 11 (553), p. 285.

85. Examples include FLK MS A 26, p. 28; CF MS 24, p. 477; MYN MS M 51, p. 330; MYN MS M 54, p. 265; MYN MS R 64, section b, p. 91; MYN MS R 66, p. 345; MYN MS C 49, p. 1, Torna MS T.xliii, p. 224; Torna MS T.lxvi, p. 1; BL MS Egerton 188, f. 118; NLI MS G 140, p. 163; NLI MS G 346, p. 78; NLI MS G 363, p. 33; NLI MS G 383, p. 156; NLI MS G 394, p. 85; NLI MS G 429, p. 99; RIA MS 24 B 26 (242), p. 1; RIA MS 23 C 7 (372), p. 66; RIA MS 23 L 31 (398), p. 132; RIA MS 23 I 35 (420), p. 137; RIA 24 B 17 (578), p. 56.

86. E.g., from County Cork: MYN MS M 39, p. 201; MYN MS M 73, p. 238; RIA MS 23 G 23 (256), p. 157; RIA MS 24 A 27 (661), p. 289. From County Waterford: CE MS 6, section a, p. 355; RIA MS 23 L 12 (105), p. 208; RIA MS 23 L 29 (109), p. 125. On the other hand, for a Galway example, see Cambridge Library MS Add. 6556, p. 179.

87. Quoted in "Antiquarian and Literary Intelligence: Cork Cuvierian Society," *Gentleman's Magazine and Historical Review* 2 (Sept. 1865): 343.

88. BL Cat., II, 531–32. This version is Recension A in Charles Plummer, *Miscellanea Hagiographica Hibernica* (Bruxelles: Société des Bollandistes, 1925), 264.

89. Tadhg Ó Dúshláine, *An Eoraip agus Litríocht na Gaeilge 1600–1650: Gnéithe den Bharócachas Eorpach i Litríocht na Gaeilge* (Baile Átha Cliath: An Clóchomhar Tta, 1987), 161.

90. Cunningham, *World of Geoffrey Keating*, 161; Ó Dúshláine, *An Eoraip agus Litríocht na Gaeilge*, 116–19, 123–51, 161–64; Terence C. Cave, *Devotional Poetry in France c. 1570–1613* (Cambridge: Cambridge University Press, 1969), 2–7, 24–26.

91. Lambert McKenna, *Dánta do Chum Aonghus Fionn Ó Dálaigh* (Dublin: Maunsel and Company, 1919), ix–xi; Ó Dúshláine, *An Eoraip agus Litríocht na Gaeilge*, 157–61; Ó Cuív, "The Irish Language in the Early Modern Period," 527.

92. Ó Cuív, "Irish Language and Literature, 1691–1845," 389.

93. Bergin, *Trí Bior-Ghaoithe an Bháis*, xii–xiii; Cunningham, *World of Geoffrey Keating*, 52–53, 161; Salvador Ryan, "Bonaventura Ó hEoghusa's *An Teagasg Críosdaidhe* (1611/14): A Reassessment of Its Audience and Use," *Archivium Hibernicum* 58 (2004): 263–66.

94. Malachy McKenna, ed., *The Spiritual Rose, or Method of Saying the Rosaries of the Most Holy Name of Jesus, and the Blessed Virgin, with Their Litanies* (Dublin: Dublin Institute for Advanced Studies, 2001), xvi–xviii; Énrí Ó Muirgheasa [Henry Morris], ed., *Dánta Diadha Uladh* (Baile Átha Cliath: Oifig Díolta Foillseacháin Rialtais, 1936), 142–46.

95. Patrick Denn, ed., *A New Edition of Timothy O'Sullivan's, Commonly Called Taidhag Gaodhlach's Pious Miscellany* [hereafter cited in notes as Denn, *Pious Miscellany*], 10th ed. (Cork: John Connor, 1829), 30–33, 49, 52–53; N. Ó Ciosáin, *Print and Popular Culture*, 125–27.

96. MYN Cat., fasc. III, 107–20 [MYN MS M 96].

97. Ní Úrdail, *Scribe*, 205.

98. For an examination of the role of written texts among early modern poets, see Pádraig Ó Macháin, "The Early Modern Irish Prosodic Tracts and the Editing of 'Bardic Verse,'" in *Metrik und Medienwechsel/Metrics and Media*, ed. Hildegard L. C. Tristam (Tübingen: Gunter Narr Verlag, 1991), 277–79.

99. FLK MS A 55, for example, written by an unidentified scribe around 1837, begins with five poems before a handwritten title page announcing Challoner's work, followed by an Irish translation of *Garden of the Soul*, before including four more poems. See FLK Cat., 125–26. Similarly, Seán Ó Muláin added verses from Dáibhí Ó Bruadair and Donnchadh Ó Dálaigh to a 1795 manuscript of *Eochair-Sgiath* that also included an introductory page and two additional prose tracts. MYN Cat., fasc. III, 92–93. These are just two examples of many.

100. Richard Challoner, *Gairdín an Anma: Iar na Sgríobhadh, le Pol Ó Longáin chum Úsaíde Speisialta Chaitillicidhe na hÉirionn*, trans. Pól Ó Longáin (Corca: Tadhg Ó Ceallacháin, 1844), 1–6.

101. Ní Úrdail, *Scribe*, 94; Risteárd Ó Foghludha, ed., *Duanta Diadha Phádraig Denn, 1756–1828 cct.* (Baile Átha Cliath: Oifig an tSoláthair, 1941), 1–16.

102. Thomas Crofton Croker, *Researches in the South of Ireland, Illustrative of the Scenery, Architectural Remains, and the Manners and Superstitions of the Peasantry* (London: John Murray, 1824), 331; NFC 259:626; Douglas Hyde, *Abhráin Diadha Chúige Connacht*, 1:86–95; Patrick Denn, *Aighneas an Pheacaig leis an mBás*, ed. Patrick Power (Waterford: Harvey & Co., 1899), 3. Denn included these two poems in his edition of the *Pious Miscellany* (see, from the 1829 edition, pp. 74–88), but there is uncertainty on whether he composed them or simply adapted them from an older poem known as "Eachtra an Bháis." See Denn, *Aighneas*, 5. Manuscript copies of "Aighneas" and "Siosma" exist in CE MS 30, MYN MS DR 4, and RIA MS 23 K 14 (195), p. 241. For other religious poems by Denn, see CE MS 16 and CE MS 29.

103. Michel-André Bossy, "Medieval Debates of Body and Soul," *Comparative Literature* 28, no. 2 (Spring 1976): 144–51; Thomas Wright, ed., *The Latin Poems Commonly Attributed to Walter Mapes* (London: Camden Society, 1841), 95, 321; Georges Dottin, "Une version Irlandaise du *Dialogue du Corps et de l'Áme*, attribué à Robert Grosseteste," *Revue Celtique* 23 (1902): 1–5; Henri Gaidoz, "Le Debat du Corps et de l'Áme en Irlande," *Revue Celtique* 10 (1889): 463–65.

104. E.g., Collection of Father Lúcás Ó Dónnalláin (Donnellan) at NUI–Maynooth (hereafter DON) MS 13, p. 1; MYN M 108, p. 405; NLI MS G 130, p. 19; RIA 23 E 7 (56), p. 137; RIA 23 D 8 (503), p. 203; RIA 23 Q 18 (573), p. 269; RIA 23 A 44 (971), p. 94; RIA F i 1 (984), p. 209; TCD 1367, p. 1.

105. William Crashaw, *The Complaint or Dialogue, Betwixt the Soule and the Bodie of a Damned Man*, 2nd ed. (London: G.E., 1622); Helen C. White, *English Devotional Literature (Prose), 1600–1640* (Madison: University of Wisconsin Press, 1931), 79. Crashaw claimed in his preface that he was the first to translate it into English, but it would appear that an earlier English version existed. See Bossy, "Medieval Debates," 144–45.

106. Faber, *Lives of Father Paul Segneri*, 172–76.

107. Ní Úrdail, *Scribe*, 219, quoting Robin Flower in BL Cat., II, 460.

108. Franz Blom et al., *English Catholic Books, 1701–1800: A Bibliography* (Aldershot, Hant., UK: Scolar Press, 1996), 270.

109. TCD MS 1364, as noted in TCD Cat., 216. Tadhg Ó Neachtain also mentioned his father's work as translator of this text in an elegy composed on his death. See

Cathal Ó Háinle, "Ar Bhás Sheáin Uí Neachtain," *Éigse* 19, no. 2 (1983): 386. See also NLI MS G 229, written by Seán Mac Solaidh (NLI Cat., fasc. VI, 25).

110. Hugh Fenning, "Cork Imprints of Catholic Historical Interest, 1723–1804: A Provisional Checklist," *Journal of the Cork Historical and Archaeological Society* 100 (1995): 142–43; Pádraig Ó Súilleabháin, "Clódóireacht Chaitliceach in Éirinn san Ochtú hAois Déag," *Irisleabhar Mhuighe Nuadhadh* (1964): 99.

111. Ní Úrdail, *Scribe*, 219–20.

112. Elizabeth F. Boyd, "James Joyce's Hell-Fire Sermons," *Modern Language Notes* 75, no. 7 (Nov. 1960): 563; James R. Thrane, "James Joyce's Sermon on Hell: Its Source and Its Backgrounds," *Modern Philology* 57, no. 3 (Feb. 1960): 173; James Doherty, "Joyce and *Hell Opened to Christians*: The Edition Used for His 'Hell Sermons,'" *Modern Philology* 61, no. 2 (Nov. 1963): 110–11.

113. MYN Cat., fasc. II, 98–99 [MYN MS M 50]; Ní Úrdail, *Scribe*, 216.

114. Charles Borromeo, *The Contract and Testament of the Soule* (St. Omer: no printer, 1638). Borromeo's title was also very popular among the English Catholic community and the wider international Spanish-speaking community. See James G. McManaway, "John Shakespeare's 'Spiritual Testament,'" *Shakespeare Quarterly* 18, no. 3 (Summer 1967): 197–204. Carpenter's manuscript is RIA MS 23 A 8 (354). There is another copy of the Irish version of Borromeo's text by an unidentified scribe: TCD MS 1407. See RIA Cat., fasc. VIII, 966–72, and TCD Cat., 267.

115. Thomas H. Clancy, *English Catholic Books, 1641–1700: A Bibliography* (Brookfield, VT: Ashgate, 1996), 106; Ní Úrdail, *Scribe*, 216–17; Boyd, "Hell-Fire Sermons," 562.

116. MYN Cat., fasc. II, 87–89 [MYN MS M 44]; Ní Úrdail, *Scribe*, 216.

117. Ainm.ie, s.v. "Ó Scoireadh, Séamus (?–1828)," http://ainm.ie/Bio.aspx?ID=1224.

118. CE MS 7, p. xxii. Ó Iceadha's other translations are in IL MS 3, and NLI MS G 1122. See also Frederick M. Jones, *Alphonsus de Liguori: The Saint of Bourbon Naples, 1696–1787* (Dublin: Gill and Macmillan, 1992), 269–71.

119. Michael Printy, "The Intellectual Origins of Popular Catholicism: Catholic Moral Theology in the Age of Enlightenment," *Catholic Historical Review* 91, no. 3 (July 2005): 443–46; Patrick Corish, *The Irish Catholic Experience: A Historical Survey* (Dublin: Gill and Macmillan, 1985), 202.

120. John MacHale, trans., *Toras na Croiche. Aistrighth le Seaghan Mac Hale, Ardeasbog Thuama* (Baile Átha Cliath: Seamus O Duibhthe, 1873), 6.

121. The original scholarly edition of Ó Raghallaigh's translation, edited by Mághnus Ó Domhnaill (*An Bheatha Chrábhaidh* [Baile Átha Cliath: Oifig an tSoláthair, 1938]), dated the translation to 1670, a result of an earlier confusion of two different manuscript copies of seventeenth-century translations. Subsequent investigation has confirmed an earlier date for the translation. See Anselm Ó Fachtna, "'An Bheatha Chrábhaidh' agus 'An Bheatha Dhiaga,'" *Éigse* 10, no. 2 (1962): 90–92; Charles Dillon, "An Beatha Chrábhaidh: A 'Popular' Translation," *Revue LISA/LISA E-Journal* [Online] 3, no. 1 (2005), par. 12, http://lisa.revues.org/2462, DOI : 10.4000/lisa.2462; and Dillon, "An tSeanmóir a Aistriú: Téacs agus Comhthéacs sa 17ú hAois," in *Aistriú Éireann*, 124–25.

122. CE MS 18, BL MS Egerton 120, and CE MS 2, respectively. On Ó Maolchaoine, see BL Cat., II, 593.

123. Cecile O'Rahilly, ed., *Trompa na bhFlaitheas* (Baile Átha Cliath: Institiúd Árd-Léinn, 1955), vii–x; White, *English Devotional Literature*, 104. Copies include, for Guevera, RIA MS 24 C 10 (929) from Limerick; for Yvan, MYN MS M 25 and M 75, NLI MS G 317, Torna MS T.ii, RIA MS 3 B 6 (277), and RIA 24 A 18 (662) from Cork, and NLI MS G 364 and CE MS 13 from Waterford.

124. NLI Cat., fasc. VII, 39 [NLI MS G 311]. The later copies are CE MS 6 and MYN MS B 2. For Ó Fhuartháin, see Eoghan Ó Suilleabháin, "Scríobhaithe Phort Lairge 1700–1900," in Nolan and Power, *Waterford: History and Society*, 282. An English translation was published in 1603 by Richard Verstegan: A. F. Allison and D. M. Rogers, *A Catalogue of Catholic Books in English Printed Abroad or Secretly in England, 1558–1640*, 2 vols. (1956; repr., London: Wm. Dawson & Sons, 1964), 2, no. 122.

125. MYN MS M 32 is a copy by Mícheál Óg Ó Longáin attributing the translation to Mac Coitir and supplying the date. See MYN Cat., fasc. II, 70–72; Challoner, *Machtnuig go Maih Air*; and Challoner, *Smuain go Maith Air*. There are also two later manuscript copies of the Ó Caomhánach translation: MS 686, held by a private collector, written by scribe Donachadh Ó Catháin of Cork, in the 1820s or 1830s—see Ronald Black, "Four O'Daly Manuscripts," *Éigse* 26 (1992): 67—and another, NLI MS G 368, pp. 79–233, written by scribe Aindrias Ó Suilliobhain of Cahirciveen, Co. Kerry, in 1852.

126. Ó Muláin's manuscript is MYN Cat., fasc. III, 66–67 [MYN M 78]. Its contents also seem to be drawn from Ó Dubhlaoich's *Suim Bhunudhasach*, and it differs significantly from the 1798 Dublin English-language edition of *Garden of the Soul* printed by Richard Cross. A similar manuscript can be found in FLK Cat., 126 [FLK MS A 55], also of Munster provenance, watermarked 1837 and by an unknown scribe. Both Torna MS T.xx, by Ó Hógáin, and RIA MS 24 A 30 (648), by Peadar Ó Longáin, were more faithful to the original. See T Cat., 68–69, and RIA Cat., XVI, 2015.

127. Ó Conchúir, *Scríobhaithe*, 179; Clancy, *English Catholic Books*, 29–30. *A Net for Fishers* can be found in Cambridge Library MS Add. 6475, p. 4b. The translation of Gother appears in MYN MS M 59. See CL Cat., 53–54, MYN Cat., fasc. III, 30, and Ní Úrdail, *Scribe*, 217, who also observes that these two manuscripts used to be one text.

128. Brian Ó Cuív, "Flaithrí Ó Maolchonaire's Catechism of Christian Doctrine," *Celtica* 1 (1950): 161–206; Pádraig Ó Súilleabháin, "Agallamh na bhFíoraon," *Éigse* 10, no. 1 (1961): 26–34; Ó Conchúir, *Scríobhaithe*, 32; Ó Háinle, "Bás Sheáin Uí Neachtain," 390.

129. Among the few examples are instructions inveighing against specific practices popular among Irish audiences deemed magical by the church, such as the use of charms and spells. See Thomas Hughes, *Doctor Kirwan's Irish Catechism*, ed. William J. Mahon, 8th ed. (Dublin: C. M. Warren, ca. 1850; repr., Cambridge, MA: Pangur Publications, 1991), 88–89.

130. Note the frequency of Lloyd's Douai catechism in *Fenning* 1, pp. 128–29, 153, and *Fenning* 2, pp. 70, 95, 97. For the domination of Butler and O'Reilly, see Tynan, *Catholic Instruction*, 14–18.

131. Of those that could be identified as one of the catechisms above: Donlevy, CF MS 27, MYN MS M 47, MYN MS M 109, NLI MS G 489, NLI MS G 1000, RIA MS 23 I 16 (406), RIA MS 23 I 44 (428), RIA MS 23 N 2 (558); Butler, MYN MS M 45, MYN MS M 89, RIA MS 23 G 27 (492); Stapleton, MYN MS M 45 and Torna MS T.xxiv; O'Reilly, FLK MS A 41 (possibly); Ó hEodhasa, St. Mel's College (Coláiste Naomh Mel) Library, Longford (hereafter ML), MS 6, MYN MS M 26, Torna MS T.iii, BL MS Egerton 192, RIA MS 23 L 27 (556); Ó Dubhlaoich, MYN MS M 47, BL MS Egerton 192, BL MS Add. 33196, FLK MS A 55; Pulleine, Cambridge Library MS Add. 3085, part b, p. 95; and Douai catechism, MYN MS M 45, MYN MS M 109.

132. Examples include IL MS 5, IL MS 6, MYN MS M 78, MYN MS M 80, MYN MS C 53, MYN MS C 73 (section i), MYN MS B 13, MYN MS MF 1, Archives of the monastery of New Norcia, Australia (hereafter NN) MS M 75 886, Torna MS T.xxviii, Torna MS T.xxix, Torna MS T.lxxiii, Torna MS T.lxxiv, Torna MS T.lxxv, Torna MS T.xxvi, MM MS 10, Cambridge Library MS Add. 6472, Bodleian Library Oxford MS Ir e 4, BL MS Egerton 139, BL MS Egerton 193, BL MS Egerton 198, RIA MS 23 A 22 (144), RIA 23 I 9 (149), RIA MS 23 A 37 (218), RIA 23 A 6 (219), RIA MS 23 A 7 (220), RIA MS 23 A 5 (221), RIA MS 23 A 8 (354), RIA MS 23 I 24 (411), RIA MS 23 I 43 (427), RIA MS 23 D 39 (518), RIA MS 23 N 2 (558), RIA MS 24 A 31 (1062), RIA MS 24 A 33 (1063), NLI MS G 107, NLI MS G 66, NLI MS G 203, NLI MS G 327, NLI MS G 415, NLI MS G 644, NLI MS G 850, FLK MS A 54, CE MS 10, CC MS 7, and State Library of Victoria, Melbourne, Australia (hereafter SLV) MS 10595.

133. Fearghus Ó Fearghail, "An Irish Instruction of 1775," *Ossory, Laois and Leinster* 3 (2008): 168–89; James Butler, *Suim Athghar an Teagasg Criosduidhe* (Dublin: J. Boyce, 1784); Bray and Coppinger, *Oideas Athchoimir*; John MacHale, *Craobh Urnaighe Cráibhthighte Tiomhsuigthe as an Sgriobhain Diadha, agus Rannta Toghtha na h-Eaglaise le Seaghan Mac Hale, Árdeaspog Thuama*, 2nd ed. (Baile Átha Cliath: Seamus O Duibhthe, 1857).

134. SLV MS 10595.

135. Pádraig Ó Súilleabháin, "Leabhair Urnaithe an Ochtú hAois Déag," *Irish Ecclesiastical Record*, ser. 5, 103 (1965): 299–302; Ó Madagáin, *An Ghaeilge i Luimneach*, 40; Blom, *English Catholic Books*, 163; Fenning 3, 87; Heimann, *Catholic Devotion in Victorian England*, 71–75.

136. NLI MS G 326; Torna MS T.xxviii; BL MS Egerton 193; and FLK MS A 54. Compare *The Path to Paradise: Being a Choice Manual of Devout Prayers, to which are Added the Psalter of the Most Holy Name of Jesus, the Rosaries, Vespers, Hymns, and the Manner of Serving Mass* (Kilkenny: T. Shearman, n.d. [ca. 1825]); *The Key of Paradise, Opening the Gate to Eternal Salvation. To this Edition is Added, a New Calendar. The Whole Revised and Corrected by the Reverend B[ernard] McM[ahon]* (Dublin: Patrick Wogan, 1796); and *The Poor Man's Manual of Devotions; or Devout Christian's Daily Companion, Containing Morning and Evening Prayer, Devotions for Sundays and Holydays, the Thirty Days' Prayer, Prayers at Mass, Prayers Before and After Confession and Communion, the Seven Penitential Psalms, the Psalter, Rosary and Litanies of Jesus* (Belfast: Thomas Mairs and Co., 1818). For a short discussion of a breastplate hymn related to Mary, see Breandán Ó Madagáin, "Ceol a Chanadh Eoghan Mór Ó Comhraí,"

Béaloideas 51 (1983): 73–75. Note that more than one Limerick scribe by the name of Séamas Ó Caoindealbháin was active in these years. The scribe of NLI MS 326 was a weaver. See Ó Madagáin, *An Ghaeilge i Luimneach*, 81–84, and Ní Mhurchú and Breathnach, *Beathaisneís*, 84–85.

137. BL MS Egerton 198, Torna MS T.xxviii, RIA MS 23 I 9 (149), RIA MS 23 A 8 (354), and RIA MS 23 A 22 (144), respectively.

138. NLI Cat., fasc. VII, 81 [NLI MS G 325]. On *Sochar an Aifrinn*, see BL Cat., II, pp. 555–56.

139. A. Maurel, *The Christian Instructed in the Nature and Use of Indulgence*, trans. Patrick Costelloe, 4th ed. (Dublin: M. H. Gill and Son, 1885), 99; John Brady, "Prayers before Mass on Sundays and Holydays in Ireland," *Irish Ecclesiastical Record*, ser. 5, vol. 69 (1947): 658; Donlevy, *An Teagasg Críosduidhe*, 252–59.

140. *Instructions for Gaining the Jubilee Granted by His Holiness Pope Clement XIV. Soon After His Election, which was on the 4th of June, 1769, Revised by Several Eminent Clergymen* (Dublin: Bartholomew Corcoran, 1770), 21.

141. Tynan, *Catholic Instruction*, 39.

142. This pamphlet is undated, but the year 1780 is proposed in Ó Casaidhe and McClintock Dix, *List of Books, Pamphlets, etc.*, 11. The original was published in Rome in 1764.

143. *Ordo Administrandi Sacramenta et Alia Quaedam Officia Ecclesiastica Rite Peragendi* (Dublin: P. Wogan, 1812), 177–210; J. Brady, "Prayers before Mass," 659.

144. J. Brady, "Prayers before Mass," 666.

145. *The Most Rev. Dr. James Butler's Catechism, Revised, Enlarged, Approved, and Recommended by the Four R.C. Arch-Bishops of Ireland as a General Catechism for the Kingdom*, 7th ed. (Cork: Charles Dillon, 1814), 65.

146. *New Catholic Encyclopedia*, 2nd ed., 15 vols. (Washington, DC: Catholic University of America in Association with Gale, Inc., 2003), 8:601–3.

147. William O'Neill Daunt to Daniel Murray, 16 Dec. 1835, Murray Papers, Dublin Diocesan Archives, file 31/4, ordinary, 1835, no. 149.

148. Loftus, *An Teagasg Críosdaige*, 7–14; Michael O'Reilly, *An Teagask Creestye, agus Paidreacha na Mainne, agus an Tranona* (Dublin: Richard Grace, n.d.), 5–11. Examples from manuscript prayer books include NLI MS G 107, p. 46, 54; FLK MS 54, p. 74–5, 83; NLI MS G 327, p. 19.

149. Corish, *Irish Catholic Experience*, 133.

150. These limited responses were occasionally dispensed with. In his study of late nineteenth-century Clare, Ignatius Murphy noted that altar servers were responsible for making the requisite responses on behalf of the congregation. See Murphy, *The Diocese of Killaloe, 1850–1904* (Dublin: Four Courts Press, 1995), 283.

151. Untitled autobiographical manuscript, NLI, MS 19,846, vol. 1, p. 11.

152. William O'Neill Daunt to Daniel Murray, 16 Dec. 1835, Murray Papers, Dublin Diocesan Archives, file 31/4, ordinary, 1835, 148–49; Daunt to Michael Collins, 17 Jan. and 8 Apr. 1832, Collins Papers, Cloyne Diocesan Archives, 1792.07/2/1832 and 1792.07/4/1832.

153. Patrick O'Brien, ed., *Eochair-Sgiath an Aifrinn, ar n-a Chnuasach agus arn-a Sgríobhadh le Seathrún Céitinn, Sagart agus Doctúr Diadhachta* (Dublin: Patrick O'Brien, 1898), 40–46, 118–21; Bonabhentura [Giolla Brighde] Ó hEodhasa, *An Teagasg Críosdaidhe*, ed. Fearghal Mac Raghnaill (Antwerp: Jacobus Mesius, 1611; Baile Átha Cliath: Institiúid Árd-Léinn Bhaile Átha Cliath, 1976), 79–86; Froinsias Ó Maolmhuaidh, *Lucerna Fidelium*, ed. Pádraig Ó Súilleabháin (Rome, 1676; repr., Baile Átha Cliath: Institiúid Árd-Léinn Bhaile Átha Cliath, 1962), 77–81.

154. Antoin Gearnon, *Parrthas an Anma*, ed. Anselm Ó Fachtna (Louvain, 1645; repr., Baile Átha Cliath: Institiúid Árd-Léinn Bhaile Átha Cliath, 1953), 137.

155. Richard Challoner, *The Garden of the Soul: or, a Manual of Spiritual Exercises and Instructions for Christians, Who (Living in the World) Aspire to Devotion* (Dublin: no printer, 1759), 77–83.

156. RIA Cat., fasc. IV, 423–26 [RIA MS 23 I 9 (149)]; NN MS M 75 886, pp. 35–77, http://www.isos.dias.ie.

157. NLI MS G 107, p. 89. This manuscript is not, however, a direct translation of *Garden of the Soul* but rather a miscellany of religious items including an Irish poem (p. 45).

158. RIA MS 23 I 43 (427), p. 12.

159. IL MS 6, p. 9. For other examples, all from the 1830s, see FLK MS A 54, pp. 296–309; NLI MS G 203, pp. 1–86; NLI MS G 415, pp. 17–50; SLV MS 10959, pp. 56–99.

160. Patrick Denn, *Urnaighthe an Tighearna, nó, "An Paidir," an t-Aifreann Naomhtha Fós, agus Aitheanta Dé Mínighthe. Mar Aon le hUrnaighthibh le Rádh do Dhuine & É ag Dul chum Báis, & tar éis Bháis Dó*, ed. Rev. Maurus Ó Faelan (Waterford: Gill, 1908), i; Peter O'Dwyer, *Towards a History of Irish Spirituality* (Dublin: Columba Press, 1995), 240.

161. Denn, *Catholic Children's Religious Primer*, 17.

162. Ibid., 22.

163. Denn, *Urnaighthe an Tighearna*, ii.

164. Examples of prayers with medieval and early-modern origins still circulating in modern Ireland can be found in Angela Partridge, "Ortha an Triúr Bráithre: Traidisiún Meánaoiseach i mBéaloideas na Gaeilge," *Béaloideas* 48–49 (1980–81): 188–203, and Gearóid Ó Murchadha, "Amhráin Bheannuithe agus Paidreacha ó Chorcha Dhuibhne," *Éigse* 3 (1941–42): 87. See also Keenan, *Catholic Church*, 21–22.

165. Nicholas M. Wolf, "Orthaí and Orthodoxy: Healing Charms in Nineteenth-Century Catholicism," in *Power and Popular Culture in Modern Ireland: Essays in Honour of James S. Donnelly, Jr.*, ed. Michael de Nie and Sean Farrell (Dublin: Irish Academic Press, 2010), 125–44.

166. M. O'Reilly, *Teagask Creestye*, 2–14; Tynan, *Catholic Instruction*, 35–36.

167. Denn, *Stiúratheoir an Pheacuig*, 29.

168. John Kilduff to Paul Cullen, 7 July 1852, Cullen Papers, Dublin Diocesan Archives, file 325/1, no. 120.

169. Patricia Lysaght, "Attitudes to the Rosary and Its Performance in Donegal in the Nineteenth and Twentieth Centuries," *Béaloideas* 66 (1998): 47–48.

170. Donlevy, *An Teagasg Críosduidhe*, 446–51; Tynan, *Catholic Instruction*, 91; Francis McPolin, "An Old Irish Catechism from Oriel," *Irish Ecclesiastical Record*, ser. 5, vol. 50 (1947): 513.

171. M. McKenna, *Spiritual Rose*, 56–87; Denn, *Pious Miscellany*, 30–32, 49.

172. Denn, *Catholic Children's Religious Primer*, 26–33; MacHale, *Craobh Urnaighe*, 7–8, 68–69, 74–88.

173. BL MS Egerton 195, ff. 18–19; FLK MS A 54, 317–25.

174. RIA Cat., fasc. VIII, 965–66 [RIA MS 23 A 2 (353)], fasc. IX, pp. 1055 [RIA MS 24 B 31 (384)]. A nineteenth-century manuscript by an unknown Cork scribe also contains prayers to the Sacred Heart, but in English. See MYN Cat., fasc. V, 99 [MYN MS C 53].

175. NLI MS G 326, p. 58

176. NLI MS G 107, pp. 60; FLK MS A 54, pp. 88–94.

177. M. McKenna, *Spiritual Rose*, 161–217; NLI MS G 644, pp. 96–119.

178. Mícheál Ó hAodha, "Seanchas ós na Déisibh," *Béaloideas* 14 (1944): 56.

179. Ó Murchadha, "Amhráin Bheannuithe," 88. See also Lysaght, "Attitudes to the Rosary," 37–39, 52.

180. Eoin Ua Nualáin [Eoin Ó Nualláin; John Nolan], *An Casán go Flaitheamhnas: Láimhleabhairín Urnuighe* (Dublin: M. H. Gill and Son, 1882) and *Leabhar-Urnuighe Naoimh Pádraic/St. Patrick's Prayer Book*, 5th ed. (Dublin: James Duffy and Co., n.d. [ca. 1900]); *Leabhar Urnaighthe. Sagart Righalta do Ghleas* (Baile Átha Cliath: Comhlucht na Fírinne Catoilice, 1904). On the interest of early revivalists in Catholic prayer books, see also Ní Mhuiríosa, *Réamhchonraitheoirí*, 3, 21.

Chapter 7. Priests, Pastoral Care, and Catholic Policy

1. Ó Briain to Cardinal Castelli, Nov. 1764, quoted in Wall, *Sign of Doctor Hay's Head*, 100.

2. Ó Cuív, "Irish Language and Literature, 1845–1921," 392; Ciarán Mac Murchaidh, "The Catholic Church, the Irish Mission and the Irish Language in the Eighteenth Century," in Kelly and Mac Murchaidh, *Irish and English*, 162–88.

3. Nic Eoin, "Irish Language and Literature," 468–71; Gearóid Ó Tuathaigh, "Maigh Nuad agus Stair na Gaeilge," in *Maigh Nuad: Saothrú na Gaeilge, 1795–1995*, ed. Etaín Ó Síocháin (Maigh Nuad: An Sagart, 1995), 14–17; Gearóid Ó Tuathaigh, "An Chléir Chaitliceach," 117–28; Wall, "The Decline of the Irish Language," 85.

4. Sean Connolly, *Priests and People in Pre-Famine Ireland, 1780–1845*, 2nd ed. (Dublin: Four Courts Press, 2001), 68.

5. William Carleton, *Traits and Stories of the Irish Peasantry*, 2 vols. (1830–33; repr., New York: Garland Publishing, 1979), 1:29.

6. Emmet Larkin, "The Rise and Fall of Stations in Ireland, 1750–1850," in *Chocs et ruptures en histoire religieuse: Fin XVIIIe–XIXe siècles*, ed. Michel Lagrée (Rennes: Presses Universitaires de Rennes, 1998), 21–31.

7. Spellissy, *Life of John Murphy*, 29–30.

8. Jonathan Binns, *The Miseries and Beauties of Ireland*, 2 vols. (London: Longman, Orme, Brown and Co., 1837), 2:347.

9. *Freeman's Journal*, 19 June 1851.
10. Ibid., 31 Dec. 1858.
11. Ibid., 15 Oct. 1860.
12. Ibid., 21 Jan. 1869.
13. Ibid., 6 Sept. 1842.
14. Ibid., 10 Aug. 1841 and 12 May 1852.
15. Ibid., 14 May 1852.
16. Ibid., 26 July 1855.
17. Ibid., 19 Sept. 1859.
18. Ibid., 25 July 1860.
19. Ibid., 14 Aug. 1860, 22 Sept. 1862, 31 July 1867, 15 Sept. 1871, 2 Sept. 1872.
20. Ibid., 31 Mar. 1864, 17 Apr. 1868, 18 Mar. 1876.
21. Ibid., 8 Feb. 1869, 12 Feb. 1872, 3 May 1876.
22. Wakefield, *Account of Ireland*, 2:604; Philip Dixon Hardy, *The Holy Wells of Ireland, Containing an Authentic Account of Those Various Places of Pilgrimage and Penance which are Still Annually Visited by Thousands of the Roman Catholic Peasantry, with a Minute Description of the Patterns and Stations Periodically Held in Various Districts of Ireland* (Dublin: P. D. Harvey, 1836), 6.
23. Wakefield, *Account of Ireland*, 2:610; Mac Mathúna, "Pobal Gaeilge Bhaile Átha Cliath," 37.
24. J. G. Kohl, *Ireland: Dublin, the Shannon, Limerick, Cork, and the Kilkenny Races, the Round Towers, the Lakes of Killarney, the County of Wicklow, O'Connell and the Repeal Association, Belfast and the Giant's Causeway* (New York: Harper and Brothers, 1844), 50.
25. Mary Purcell, *The Story of the Vincentians* (Dublin: All Hallows College, 1973), 109–16; Kevin Laheen, *The Jesuits in Killaloe, 1850–80* (Drumline, Newmarket-on-Fergus: O'Brien Book Publications, 1998), 8–11; Corish, *Irish Catholic Experience*, 202; O'Dwyer, *Towards a History of Irish Spirituality*, 233; Keenan, *Catholic Church*, 156–58. Other religious orders, newly established after the serious decline in such societies in Ireland in the eighteenth century, initiated similar efforts at about the same time: the Passionists in 1848, the Oblates of Mary Immaculate in 1851, and the Redemptorists in 1853. The Synod of Thurles in 1850 had specifically advocated imitation of the work of the Vincentians and the Jesuits in bringing the fruits of the rejuvenated post-penal Catholic Church to the neglected parishes of Ireland.
26. Reverend Michael Meehan to Cullen, 7 June 1852, Cullen Papers, Dublin Diocesan Archives, 325/4, no. 31.
27. *Freeman's Journal*, 30 May 1853 and 11 June 1867; Purcell, *Story of the Vincentians*, 116–17; Laheen, *Jesuits in Killaloe*, 73–74, 142, 148.
28. David Ryan, "Catholic Preaching in Ireland, 1760–1840," in Gillespie, *Remaking of Modern Ireland*, 77–79.
29. For Meany, his sermons, and the subsequent career of his nephew Patrick, see Pádraig Ó Macháin, "Fr. Patrick Meany and the Dr. Keating Society, 1860–1865," *Studia Hibernica* 37 (2011): 165, 173.

30. Dr. McCarthy of Cork to Bray, 11 Nov. 1808, Bray Papers, Cashel Diocesan Archives, 1808/23, microfilm, NLI p. 5999.

31. Corish, *Irish Catholic Experience*, 177.

32. Pádraig Ó Súilleabháin, "Catholic Sermon Books Printed in Ireland, 1700–1850," *Irish Ecclesiastical Record* 99 (Jan.–June 1963): 31–36.

33. Tadhg Ó Dúshláine, "Seanmóirí Mhaigh Nuad," in Ó Síocháin, *Maigh Nuad*, 63–72; Tadhg Ó Dúshláine, "Gealán Dúluachra: Seanmóireacht na Gaeilge, ca. 1600–ca. 1850," in *Léann na Gaeilge: Súil Siar, Súil Chun Cinn*, Léachtaí Cholm Cille 26, ed. Ruairú Ó hUiginn (Maigh Nuad: An Sagart, 1996), 87, 96; Ó Conchúir, *Scríobhaithe*, 51–53, 61–63, 86; Pól Breathnach, ed., *Seanmóirí Muighe Nuadhadh*, 4 vols. (Baile Átha Cliath: Muinntir Ghoill, 1906–11), vol. 1: nos. 2, 6, 11, vol. 2: nos. 1, 5, vol. 3: nos. 3, 7. See also Pádraig Ó Fiannachta, "Seanmóireacht Ghaeilge san Ochtú agus sa Naoú hAois Déag," *Irisleabhar Mhá Nuad* (1983): 141–49.

34. Cainneach Ó Maonaigh, ed., *Seanmónta Chúige Uladh* (Baile Átha Cliath: Institiúid Ard-Léinn Bhaile Átha Cliath, 1965); NLI p. 6042 (CF MS 24), p. 489; NLI MS G 435, p. 1. See also UWM Cat., 22–23 [University of Wisconsin–Madison Library (hereafter UWM) MS 177, section a, p. 5]; LCM Cat., fasc. II, 57–58 [ML MS 5, pp. 1, 95]; MYN Cat., fasc. 4, 30 [MYN MS M 109, p. 85]; MYN Cat., fasc. 4, 90–91 [MYN MS R 73, section b, pp. 137, 206]; MYN Cat., fasc. 4, 98–99 [MYN MS R 79a, section b, p. 46, section c, pp. 3–17]; MYN Cat., fasc. 6, 32 [MYN MS C 92, section d, p. 35]; CL Cat., 20 [CL MS Add. 3085, section b, p. 117]; NLI Cat., fasc. IX, 80–81 [NLI MS G 429, pp. 193, 203]; RIA Cat., fasc. I, 85 [RIA MS 23 L 24 (29), p. 181]; RIA Cat., fasc. IX, 1092–93 [RIA MS 23 I 3 (400), p. 1]; RIA Cat., fasc. XXII, 2821 [RIA MS 23 C 5 (982), pp. 31, 45, 58]; RIA Cat., fasc. XXV, 3154–55 [RIA MS 24 C 42 (1172), pp. 1, 14, 28, 42, 58, 71]; RIA Cat., fasc. XXVII, 3485 [RIA MS I i 1 (1268)].

35. Ó Dúshláine, "Seanmóirí Mhaigh Nuad," 64–66.

36. Pól Breathnach, *Seanmóirí Muighe Nuadhadh*, vol. 1: nos. 1, 3, 5, 7, 8, 13, 14; vol. 2: nos. 3, 4, 6, 7, 8, 11, 12; vol. 3: nos. 1, 4, 5, 6, 9, 10, 11; Ó Conchúir, *Scríobhaithe*, 61–63, 86, 165–66, 186–87.

37. NLI MS G 335, parts c–e. The scribe(s) here mix(es) phonetic and Roman-style spellings.

38. LCM Cat., fasc. I, 35–37 [CE MS 29].

39. Ó Dúshláine, "Seanmóirí Mhaigh Nuad," 72.

40. Pádraig Ó Súilleabháin, "Seanmóir ar an mBás," *Éigse* 13, no. 1 (1969): 11–25; P. Ó Súilleabháin, "Seanmóir ar Ghnáithchleachtadh an Pheacaidh," *Éigse* 13, no. 4 (1970): 279–90; P. Ó Súilleabháin, "Seanmóir ar Uimhir Bheag na bhFíréan," *Éigse* 14, no. 2 (1971): 107–20; P. Ó Súilleabháin, "Seanmóir ar an Meisce," *Éigse* 15, no. 4 (1974): 314–17. See also John Fleming [Seán Pléimeann], "Essay on the Present State of the Irish Language and Literature in the Province of Munster," RIA MS 12 Q 13 (1126), p. 4, who describes Ó Iceadha as making copies of John Meany's printed sermons while at St. John's College.

41. Mícheál Píocóid, "Seanmóin air an mBaisdhe," NLI MS G 217, p. 16.

42. Pádraig Ó Fiannachta, "Do Lochtuiv na Tangan," *Éigse* 12 (1967–68): 1–28; Ó Dúshláine, "Seanmóirí Mhaigh Nuad," 74–75; Anselm Ó Fachtna, "Seanmóir ar

Pháis Ár dTiarna Íosa Críost," *Éigse* 12 (1967–68): 177–98; Ó Conchúir, *Scríobhaithe*, 158.

43. Donal O'Sullivan, "A Sermon for Good Friday by Father Michael Walsh of Sneem," *Éigse* 4 (1943–45): 157–72.

44. Ó Fiannachta, "Seanmóireacht Ghaeilge," 146; MYN Cat., fasc. VI, 110–17 [MYN MS MF 4]; Seosamh Ó Labhraí, "Seanmóir ar Pháis Chríost," *Seanchas Ard Mhacha* 18, no. 1 (1999–2000): 100–16; Pádraig Ó Fiannachta, "Stíl na Seanmóireachta—Sampla," in *Léas ar Ár Litríocht*, ed. Pádraig Ó Fiannachta (Maynooth: An Sagart, 1974), 167–81; Ó Dúshláine, "Gealán Dúluachra," 102.

45. Archdeacon himself is believed to be the author of the three sermons, described by Gréagóir Ó Dúghaill in "Seanmóir ar an Troscadh," *Éigse* 15 (1973): 131–39. For the history of these papers, see also P. J. Murphy, "The Papers of Nicholas Archdeacon," *Archivium Hibernicum* 31 (1973): 124–31.

46. BL MS Egerton 129, f. 60a.

47. Ulick Bourke [Uileog de Búrca], "Essay on the State of the Irish Language and Literature in the Province of Connaught," RIA MS 12 Q 13 (1126), p. 254.

48. William O'Neill Daunt to Daniel Murray, 16 Dec. 1835, Murray Papers, Dublin Diocesan Archives, file 31/4, ordinary, 1835, 149.

49. Larkin, *Pastoral Role of the Roman Catholic Church*, 66–67.

50. *Maynooth Commission. Report of Her Majesty's Commissioners Appointed to Inquire into the Management and Government of the College of Maynooth, Parts I–II*, part II: minutes of evidence and answers to part K, testimony of Patrick Murray, p. 77 [1896] [1896-I], H.C. 1854–55, xxii.

51. Tighe, *Statistical Observations*, 515.

52. I. Murphy, *Diocese of Killaloe, 1800–1850*, 352–53.

53. Rodenberg, *Island of the Saints*, 194.

54. William Heffernan visitation report, 29–30 Sept. 1852, Slattery Papers, Cashel Diocesan Archives, 1852/51, microfilm, NLI p. 6003.

55. Fleming, "Munster," RIA MS 12 Q 13 (1126), p. 54.

56. Bourke, "Connaught," RIA MS 12 Q 13 (1126), p. 290.

57. Corish, *Irish Catholic Experience*, 159.

58. NFC 404:215.

59. Francis Keane [Proinsias Ó Catháin], "Essay on the Present State of the Irish Language and Literature in the Province of Munster," RIA MS 12 Q 13 (1126), p. 109.

60. Francis Keane [Proinsias Ó Catháin], "Essay on the Present State of the Irish Language and Literature in the Province of Ulster," RIA MS 12 Q 13 (1126), pp. 210–11.

61. "Servis Civilis," "Our Native Tongue," *The Nation*, 17 Feb. 1877, news cutting in Comyn Papers, NLI, MS 4154.

62. J. K. O'Doherty to Irish Language Congress, 15 Mar. 1894, NLI, MS 35,262, folder 14.

63. Thomas T. Murray to John Windele, 11 Nov. 1856, Windele Papers, RIA, MS 4 B 16, 81(i).

64. Visitation reports, 29 June 1863 and 18 June 1864, Keane Papers, Cloyne Diocesan Archives, 1796.00/4/1870.

65. NFC 404:215.
66. Keane, "Munster," RIA MS 12 Q 13 (1126), p. 109.
67. John O'Donovan to John Windele, 27 Feb. 1850, Windele Papers, RIA, MS 4 B 9, 74.
68. Keane, "Munster," RIA MS 12 Q 13 (1126), p. 109.
69. O'Mahony to Irish Language Congress, 21 Mar. 1894, Henry Dixon Papers, NLI, MS 35,262, folder 14.
70. NFC 1219:67, 70.
71. NFC 464:251–55.
72. Macaulay, *William Crolly*, 94.
73. Antonia McManus, *The Irish Hedge School and Its Books, 1695–1831* (Dublin: Four Courts Press, 2002), 20, 23; Mac Murchaidh, "Catholic Church," 166.
74. McManus, *Irish Hedge School*, 22–25.
75. *First Report of the Commissioners on Education in Ireland*, appendix 257, p. 792, H.C. 1825 (400), xii.
76. Ibid.
77. Ibid.
78. Martin Brenan, *The Confraternity of Christian Doctrine in Ireland: A.D. 1775–1835* (Dublin: Browne and Nolan, 1934), 3–5, 11–15.
79. *First Report of the Commissioners on Education in Ireland*, p. 88, H.C. 1825 (400), xii; Brenan, *Confraternity of Christian Doctrine*, 10, 17–22; McManus, *Irish Hedge School*, 24–25.
80. Macaulay, *William Crolly*, 99–100; Corish, *Irish Catholic Experience*, 172.
81. Education inquiry school returns for Jeremiah Collins and John Fitzgerald, Cloyne Diocesan Archives, 1792.05/22/1824.
82. P. de Brún, *Scriptural Instruction*, 452.
83. *Second Report of the Commissioners of Irish Education Inquiry*, appendix 11, pp. 108–9, appendix 22, 873, 954–55, 1048–49, 1076–77, 1082–83, 1098–99, 1244–45, 1252–53, 1302–3, 1330–31, H.C. 1826–27 (12), xii.
84. SPIL, *Report of the Proceedings of the Congress Held in Dublin, 15th–17th August 1882* (Dublin, 1884), 12–13.
85. Collins Papers, Cloyne Diocesan Archives, 1792.06/7/1828, 1792.06/7/1830; Keane Papers, Cloyne Diocesan Archives, 1796.00/4/1870, 1876.05/53/1873. See also Nic Craith, *Malartú Teanga*, 39–40.
86. William P. Burke, ed., *The Irish Priests in the Penal Times (1660–1760)* (Shannon: Irish University Press, 1969), 76–77.
87. Ibid., 18.
88. Ibid., 90–91.
89. Ibid., 204–5, 217.
90. McCarthy, *Collections on Irish Church History*, 2:130.
91. Séamus P. Ó Mórdha, "Údar Tóruidheacht," 163.
92. John Brady, "Catholics and Catholicism in the Eighteenth-Century Press," *Archivium Hibernicum* 20 (1957): 277. Proinsias Mac Cana, however, observes that

McKenna and Ó Briain corresponded in English. See *Collège des Irlandais, Paris and Irish Studies* (Dublin: Dublin Institute for Advanced Studies, 2001), 25.

93. M. Marefoschi to Thomas Bray, 3 June 1773, Bray Papers, Cashel Diocesan Archives, 1773/1, microfilm, NLI p. 5998.

94. NLI MS G 393, p. 61.

95. Mac Murchaidh, "Catholic Church," 179.

96. *Freeman's Journal*, 28 Sept. 1848.

97. Ó Mórdha, "Údar *Tóruidheacht*," 163.

98. Pádraig Ó Loingsigh, "Irish Language in the 19th Century," 8.

99. Letter from Abraham to Philip Barron, published in *Ancient Ireland. A Weekly Magazine* 1, no. 1 (Jan. 1835): 9.

100. James J. MacNamee, *History of the Diocese of Ardagh* (Dublin: Browne and Nolan Limited, 1954), 418.

101. Letter from Coen to Philip Barron, published in *Ancient Ireland. A Weekly Magazine* 1, no. 1 (Jan. 1835): 7; *Freeman's Journal*, 13 Aug. 1840.

102. Nic Craith, *Malartú Teanga*, 37.

103. *Freeman's Journal*, 11 Oct. 1859.

104. Nic Craith, *Malartú Teanga*, 37.

105. Ulick Bourke [Uileog de Búrca], *The Aryan Origin of the Gaelic Race and Language* (London: Longmans, Green, and Co., 1875), 87–92.

106. *Freeman's Journal*, 19 Sept. 1851.

107. John Glynne Papers, NLI MS G 754, p. 39; Bourke, *Aryan Origin*, 87–88.

108. *Freeman's Journal*, 14 Aug. 1860 and 4 Aug. 1863; *Irish Times*, 28 Mar. 1884.

109. Thomas McGrath, *Religious Renewal and Reform in the Pastoral Ministry of Bishop James Doyle of Kildare and Leighlin, 1786–1834* (Dublin: Four Courts Press, 1999), 176.

110. Letter from Murphy to Philip Barron, published in *Ancient Ireland. A Weekly Magazine* 1, no. 1 (Jan. 1835): 5.

111. Michael Collins's obituary, *Cork Mercantile Chronicle*, 12 Dec. 1832, Collins Papers, Cloyne Diocesan Archives, 1792/1/1832.

112. Nic Craith, *Malartú Teanga*, 36.

113. Letter from Browne to Philip Barron, published in *Ancient Ireland. A Weekly Magazine* 1, no. 5 (May 1835): 175.

114. Ó Cuív, *Irish Dialects*, 23.

115. By the second quarter of the nineteenth century most students at Maynooth fell between the ages of 18 and 25, but no smaller age span other than 10–29 can be derived from the published census reports. See Patrick J. Corish, *Maynooth College, 1795–1995* (Dublin: Gill and Macmillan, 1995), 112.

116. Corish, *Maynooth College*, 167, 228.

117. *Eighth Report of the Commissioners of Irish Education Inquiry. Dated London, 2d June 1827. Roman Catholic College of Maynooth*, appendix 16, p. 126, H.C. 1826–27 (509), xiii.

118. *Maynooth Commission. Report of Her Majesty's Commissioners Appointed to Inquire into the Management and Government of the College of Maynooth, Parts I–II,*

part II: minutes of evidence and answers to part K, testimony of Reverend John Harold, p. 43 [1896] [1896-I], H.C. 1854-55, xxii.

119. Kevin Collins, *Catholic Churchmen and the Celtic Revival, 1848–1916* (Dublin: Four Courts Press, 2002), 49.

120. These figures have been taken from Donal Kerr, *Peel, Priests, and Politics: Sir Robert Peel's Administration and the Roman Catholic Church in Ireland, 1841–1846* (Oxford: Clarendon Press, 1982), 33.

121. I. Murphy, *Diocese of Killaloe, 1800–1850*, 247.

122. Although County Cork and the diocese of Cloyne were not coterminous, Cork is taken as the most comparable geographical unit for which Irish-language data are available. These percentages exclude Cork city and have been taken from the 1851, 1861, and 1871 censuses.

123. Collins, *Catholic Churchmen*, 49.

124. Larkin, *Pastoral Role of the Roman Catholic Church*, 59.

125. Many of these domestic colleges and seminaries served as an intermediary step of a few years before students transferred to Maynooth. The destinations represented here are St. Patrick's College, Carlow, founded 1793; St. Patrick's College, Thurles, founded 1837; St. Vincent's School, Castleknock, founded 1830; St. Colman's College, Fermoy, founded 1858; and All Hallows, Dublin, founded 1859.

126. Larkin, *Pastoral Role of the Roman Catholic Church*, 30–36.

127. Liam Swords, "History of the Irish College, Paris, 1578–1800," *Archivium Hibernicum* 35 (1980): 69. See also François Eliot, "L'emigration irlandaise et les prêtes irlandais en France," in *The Irish French Connection, 1578–1978*, ed. Liam Swords (Paris: The Irish College, 1978), 89.

128. Quoted in Larkin, *Pastoral Role of the Roman Catholic Church*, 36.

129. Swords, "History of the Irish College," 109–10.

130. Bartholomew Crotty to Reverend O'Hea, 8 July 1845, Crotty Papers, Cloyne Diocesan Archives, 1793.05/2/1845.

131. Dominic O'Brien to Paul Cullen, 19 Sept. 1856, Cullen Papers, Dublin Diocesan Archives, 339/1, file 1, no. 118.

132. Collins Papers, Cloyne Diocesan Archives, 1792.06/7/1830, 20 June 1830.

133. William Heffernan to Michael Slattery, 25 Mar. 1841, Slattery Papers, Cashel Diocesan Archives, 1841/11, microfilm, NLI p. 6001.

134. Edward Ffrench to Laurence Renehan, 3 Feb. 1847, Slattery Papers, Cashel Diocesan Archives, 1847/14, microfilm, NLI p. 6002.

135. Michael Maher, ed., "Correspondence of Dr. Bray, Archbishop of Cashel," *Archivium Hibernicum* 1 (1912): 236.

136. R. O'Riordan to Timothy Murphy, 20 June 1855, Murphy Papers, Cloyne Diocesan Archives, 1795.05/6/1855.

137. John Forsythe, "Clogher Diocesan Papers, Part 2," *Archivium Hibernicum* 44 (1989): 25.

138. Reverend David O'Lery [sic] to William Keane, 22 Aug. 1858, Keane Papers, Cloyne Diocesan Archives, 1796.05/210/1858. Wigmore was the only candidate at the concursus in 1858 without Irish.

139. J. Fitzpatrick to William Keane, 8, 13, 23 Nov. 1857; Keane to Fitzpatrick 14 Nov. 1857, Keane Papers, Cloyne Diocesan Archives, 1796.05/134/1857, 1796.05/136/1857, 1796.05/137/1857, 1796.05/145/1857.

140. J. P. Lyons to Daniel Murray, 10 Apr. 1839, Murray Papers, Dublin Diocesan Archives, file 31/7, no. 60.

141. Anon. to Paul Cullen, 15 Oct. 1853; Edmund Walsh to Cullen, Oct. 1853 [no day listed]; J. Murphy to Cullen, 12 Nov. 1853, Cullen Papers, Dublin Diocesan Archives, 325/5, nos. 66, 67, 71; Report to Cardinal Fransoni and Michael Slattery, 26 Oct. 1853, Slattery Papers, Cashel Diocesan Archives, 1853/38, microfilm, NLI p. 6003. There is some uncertainty about whether Moriarty may have known Irish, or acquired it later. Uileog de Búrca claimed that Moriarty did in fact know Irish and used it to "speak and preach." See Bourke, *Aryan Origin*, 74.

142. Wakefield, *Account of Ireland*, 2:626.

143. *Statuta Synodalia pro Unitis Dioecesibus Cassel et Imelac: Lecta, Approbata, Edita, et Promulgata in Synodo Dioecesana*, 2 vols. (Dublin: Hugh Fitzpatrick, 1813), 1:108, 2:134–375. Quotation on page 2:243.

144. *Acta et Decreta Concilii Provinciae Casseliensis in Hibernia* (Dublin: Jacob Duffy, 1854), 80.

145. Fearghus Ó Fearghail, "An Ossory Instruction of 1773," *Archivium Hibernicum* 48 (1994): 25–28, and Ó Fearghail, "An Irish Instruction of 1775," 168–89.

146. *Ordo Administrandi Sacramenta*, 179–206.

147. Nuala Costello, *John MacHale, Archbishop of Tuam* (Dublin: Talbot Press, 1939).

148. Kohl, *Travels in Ireland*, 32.

149. On the MacHale archives, see Liam Bane, "Bishop John MacEvilly and the Catholic Church in Late Nineteenth Century Galway," in *Galway: History and Society; Interdisciplinary Essays on the History of an Irish County*, ed. Gerard Moran and Raymond Gillespie (Dublin: Geography Publications, 1996), 421–44.

150. N. Costello, *John MacHale*, 29, 143.

151. Ó Tuathaigh, "Maigh Nuad," 18–19.

152. *Freeman's Journal*, 14 Nov. 1842.

153. Nicholas Kearney [Nioclás Ó Cearnaigh] to Paul Cullen, 14 Aug. 1850, Cullen Papers, Dublin Diocesan Archives, 39/1, file 8, no. 66. On the translation initiative, see also Tynan, *Catholic Instruction*, 86.

154. Walter McDonald, *Reminiscences of a Maynooth Professor*, ed. Denis Gwynn (Cork: Mercier Press, 1967), 78–79.

155. Quoted in Ó Tuathaigh, "Chléir Chaitliceach," 126.

156. John Brady, "The Irish Colleges in the Low Countries," *Archivium Hibernicum* 14 (1949): 84–85; T. J. Walsh, "Compulsory Irish in France," *Journal of the Cork Historical and Archaeological Society* 58, no. 187 (1953): 2–4; Mac Cana, *Collège des Irlandais*, 21.

157. Swords, "Irish College, Paris," 105–6, 145.

158. Larkin, *Pastoral Role of the Roman Catholic Church*, 37–38.

159. Swords, "Irish College, Paris," 62; Liam Swords, "Collège des Lombards," in *The Irish-French Connection, 1578–1978*, ed. Liam Swords (Paris: Irish College, 1978), 55.

Perrotin's financing also helped to support the production of Andrew Donlevy's catechism of 1741.

160. Corish, *Maynooth College*, 32.

161. *Eighth Report of the Commissioners of Irish Education Inquiry*, appendix 64, p. 447, appendix 65, p. 449, appendices 72–73, pp. 453–54, H.C. 1826–27 (509), xiii.

162. For O'Brien, see Diarmaid Ó Muirithe, "An tAthair Pól Ó Briain," in *Maigh Nuad agus an Ghaeilge*, ed. Pádraig Ó Fiannachta (Maigh Nuad: An Sagart, 1993), 8–43.

163. Aisling Walsh, "Michael Cardinal Logue, 1840–1924, Part I," *Seanchas Ard Mhacha* 17 (1997): 113–17. Advanced students from the Dunboyne school at Maynooth taught the Irish class intermittently until the appointment of Eoghan Ó Gramhnaigh in 1891.

164. Peter Birch, *St. Kieran's College, Kilkenny* (Dublin: M. H. Gill and Son, 1951), 21–22, 37–38, 47, 168, 201, 222–30; John McEvoy, "Carlow College—Two Hundred Years of Education," *Carloviana* 40 (1992–93): 2–6; Larkin, *Pastoral Role of the Roman Catholic Church*, 48–52.

165. Letter from Abraham to Philip Barron, published in *Ancient Ireland. A Weekly Magazine* 1, no. 1 (Jan. 1835): 9.

166. Letter from Gearóid Ó Maonadh to Pádraig Ó Maonadh, 2 July 1848, reproduced in Pádraig Ó Macháin, "Litir Ghaelach, 1848," *Decies: The Journal of the Waterford Archaeological and Historical Society* 57 (2001): 89.

167. John Cunningham, *St. Jarlath's College, Tuam, 1800–2000* (Tuam: SJC Publications, 1999), 36, 97.

168. *Freeman's Journal*, 14 Nov. 1842. On MacEvilly's appointment, see Bane, "Bishop John MacEvilly," 423.

169. *Eighth Report of the Commissioners of Irish Education Inquiry*, appendix 16, p. 126, H.C. 1826–27 (509), xiii.

170. Bartholomew Crotty to William Coppinger, 7 May 1827, Coppinger Papers, Cloyne Diocesan Archives, 1791.05/1/1827.

171. *Eighth Report of the Commissioners of Irish Education Inquiry*, appendix 47, p. 378, H.C. 1826–27 (509), xiii.

172. Corish, *Maynooth College*, 53, 116; *Second Report of the Visitors of Maynooth College*, p. 5 [890], H.C. 1847–48, xxix.

173. Corish, *Maynooth College*, 29–30, 53, 74–79, 112–17.

174. SPIL, *Report of the Proceedings of the Congress Held in Dublin, 15th–17th August 1882* (Dublin, 1884), 25.

175. *Eighth Report of the Commissioners of Irish Education Inquiry*, appendix 8, p. 57, H.C. 1826–27 (509), xiii.

176. J. Fitzpatrick to William Keane, 8 Nov. 1857, Keane Papers, Cloyne Diocesan Archives, 1796.05/134/1857.

177. McEvoy, "Carlow College," 2–3.

178. William Mahon, "Scríobhaithe Lámhscríbhinní Gaeilge i nGaillimh, 1700–1900," in Moran, *Galway: History and Society*, 626.

179. *Eighth Report of the Commissioners of Irish Education Inquiry*, appendix 8, p. 58, H.C. 1826–27 (509), xiii.

180. *Eighth Report of the Commissioners of Irish Education Inquiry*, appendix 22, pp. 149–50, H.C. 1826–27 (509), xiii.

181. *Maynooth Commission. Report of Her Majesty's Commissioners Appointed to Inquire into the Management and Government of the College of Maynooth, Parts I–II*, part II: minutes of evidence and answers to part K, testimony of David Moriarty, p. 120 [1896] [1896-I], H.C. 1854–55, xxii.

182. Birch, *St. Kieran's College*, 21, 48.

183. Ó Conchúir, *Scríobhaithe*, 67–68.

184. *Freeman's Journal*, 11 Nov. 1842.

185. Norman Atkinson, *Irish Education: A History of Educational Institutions* (Dublin: Allen Figgis, 1969), 75–78.

186. *First Report of the Commissioners on Education in Ireland*, appendix 252, p. 749, H.C. 1825 (400), xii.

187. For example, of 210 "passes" in the Celtic examinations administered by the Commission for Intermediate Education in the year 1888–89, 151 were achieved by students of the Christian Brothers. SPIL, "11th Report, for 1888–89," *Annual Reports* (Dublin, 1889), 17–18.

188. Caomhánach, "Na Bráithre Críostaí agus an Ghaeilge," 123–24. For the curriculum and values imparted in the classrooms, see Keogh, *Edmund Rice*, 115–36.

189. *Maynooth Commission. Report of Her Majesty's Commissioners Appointed to Inquire into the Management and Government of the College of Maynooth, Parts I–II*, part II: minutes of evidence and answers to part K, testimony of David Moriarty, p. 120 [1896] [1896-I], H.C. 1854–55, xxii.

190. George Butler to Paul Cullen, 7 Sept. 1867, Cullen Papers, Dublin Diocesan Archives, 334/4, file 1, no. 55.

Conclusion

1. *Pall Mall Gazette* (London), 6 Sept. 1866.

2. E. G. Ravenstein, "On the Celtic Languages in the British Isles: A Statistical Survey," *Journal of the Royal Statistical Society* 42, no. 3 (1879): 579.

Bibliography

Unpublished Manuscript Sources

COBH: CLOYNE DIOCESAN ARCHIVES

Bishop Bartholomew Crotty Papers
Bishop Michael Collins Papers
Bishop Timothy Murphy Papers
Bishop William Coppinger Papers
Bishop William Keane Papers

DUBLIN: DUBLIN DIOCESAN ARCHIVES

Archbishop Daniel Murray Papers
Archbishop Edward McCabe Papers
Archbishop Paul Cullen Papers

DUBLIN: JESUIT ARCHIVES, LEESON STREET

IL MS 5: Anonymous prayer book once owned by Edmund Hogan S.J., 18th c.
IL MS 6: Seán Ó Dreada prayer book, 19th c.

DUBLIN: NATIONAL FOLKLORE COLLECTION,
UNIVERSITY COLLEGE DUBLIN, DELARGY CENTER

Main manuscript collection
Schools manuscripts collection

DUBLIN: NATIONAL LIBRARY OF IRELAND

Main Manuscript Collection

MS 194: Anonymous travel diary, ca. 1816
MS 410: Achill Island Missionary Society, letters and documents, 1872–96
MS 447: William Smith O'Brien Papers, 1860–62
MS 906: County Kerry register of persons convicted at the assizes and petty sessions, 1832–82

MSS 3253-54, MS 7912, MS 7929: John Glynne Papers and Notebooks, 1863-1906
MS 4154, MS 8468: David Comyn Papers, 1876-84
MS 4251: J. G. A. Prim correspondence, 1865
MS 4726: Michael Hanrahan correspondence, 1871-72
MS 5324: Brian O'Looney Papers, ca. 1888-89.
MS 5455: John O'Daly letters and newspaper clippings, 19th c.
MS 5653: Typescript summaries of Kinsale grand jury presentments, 17th-19th c.
MS 8010: Celtic Society Papers, 1845-54
MS 8145: Edgeworth Papers, 1813-52
MS 8612: Mary Hutton Papers, 1904-14
MS 10,654: County Mayo grand jury presentments, 1792-95
MS 11,949: County Louth grand jury presentments, 1713-32
MS 12,910: County Donegal grand jury presentments, 1772-98
MS 12,911 (NLI p. 3584): Lifford Assizes Records, 1823-99, and Stranorlar Petty Sessions Minute Book, 1851-1921
MS 12,912: County Sligo grand jury records, 1836-85
MS 13,631, folder 4: County Kerry grand jury presentments, 1819
MS 14,902: Westport petty sessions minutes, 1823-24
MS 16,233: County Dublin grand jury presentments, 1793-1803
MS 17,703: Land League Papers, 1881
MS 19,782: Sarah Selina Blakeney memoir, 1888-1901
MSS 19,846-47: Gallagher autobiography, ca. 1930
MS 21,999: Richard Gregory letters, 1818
MS 23,422: Patrick J. Dillon notebook, ca. 1855-68
MS 24,956: Robert McKinstry letter, 1904
MS 28,909: Douglas Hyde additional Papers, 1900
MS 35,262: Henry Dixon/Irish Language Congress Papers, 1894
MS 36,151: Thomas Colville Scott Papers, ca. 1853-68
NLI p. 975: Book of presentments of Donegal grand jury, 1768-83 and 1815-56 (copy of original at Donegal County Library)
NLI p. 5505: Donegal County grand jury queries, presentments, etc., 1772-1817 (copy of original in private possession)
NLI p. 6962: Letterkenny Petty Sessions records, 1849-51 (copy of original in private possession)

Gaelic Manuscripts Collection

MS G 36: James McQuigge manuscript, 19th c.
MS G 46: Séamus Banbury manuscript, 19th c.
MS G 70: Tadhg Ó Ferríghleo manuscript of poetry, catechism, etc., 18th-19th c.
MS G 73: Ó Longáin manuscript, religious and secular prose and poetry, 19th c.
MS G 79: Miscellaneous tales by scribe Uilliam Ó Heidirsgeoil et al., 18th c.
MS G 84: Cork manuscript of secular and religious poetry, 19th c.
MS G 93: Eóghan Tóibín manuscript of secular and religious prose and verse, 19th c.
MS G 95: Ó Longáin et al. manuscript, miscellaneous secular and religious items, 18th-19th c.

MS G 96: Ó Longáin et al. manuscript, miscellaneous secular and religious items, 19th c.
MS G 97: Ó Longáin et al. manuscript, miscellaneous secular and religion items, 18th–19th c.
MS G 99: Ó Longáin et al. manuscript, miscellaneous secular and religion items, 18th–19th c.
MS G 103: Ó Longáin et al. manuscript, miscellaneous secular and religious items, 19th c.
MS G 107: Unsigned manuscript of hymns and prayers by Tadhg Ó Conaill, 18th–19th c.
MS G 110: Schadhgthan Mhic Charrtha manuscript, secular tales and hagiography, 19th c.
MS G 111: Ó Longáin et al. manuscript, miscellaneous secular and religious items, 19th c.
MS G 154: Peadar Ó Longáin et al., miscellaneous secular prose and verse, 19th c.
MS G 183: Composite manuscript of verse, miscellaneous scribes, 19th c.
MS G 199: Séamus Mhac Óda et al. manuscript of verse, 19th c.
MS G 200: Peadar Ó Gaelacáin et al. manuscript of verse, 19th c.
MS G 203: Anonymous manuscript consisting of prayers for Mass, 19th c.
MS G 217: Mícheál Píocóid sermon manuscript for Jonathan Furlong, 19th c.
MS G 228: Rev. John Murray religious manuscript, 19th c.
MSS G 236–37: Charles Percy Bushe notebooks, 19th c.
MS G 320: Mícheál Óg Ó Longáin et al., miscellaneous secular writings, 19th c.
MS G 326: Séumus Ó Caoindealbháin manuscript of devotional material, 19th c.
MS G 327: Nioclás O hAe manuscript of religious material, 19th c.
MS G 335: Tomás Ó Iceadha et al., collection of miscellaneous sermons, 18th–19th c.
MS G 345: Anonymous collection of verse, 19th c.
MS G 349: Michael Hanrahan manuscript of oral tales and prose, 19th c.
MS G 368: Aindrias Ó Suilliobhain manuscript of devotional material and secular prose, 19th c.
MS G 389: John O'Daly correspondence, 19th c.
MS G 393: Daibhidh [Óg] do Barradh manuscript of poetry, 19th c.
MS G 403: Tomás Ó Iceadha et al. manuscript, verse, 19th c.
MS G 415: Tomás Ó Iceadha manuscript, devotional material, 19th c.
MS G 416: John O'Daly lecture script, 19th c.
MS G 435: Seaghan Ó Mullán manuscript, sermons, hagiography, instructional, 18th c.
MS G 467: S. Ó. F. of Kilkenny, devotional material, 18th c.
MS G 489: John Cal. O'Callaghan manuscript, Donlevy catechism, 19th c.
MS G 495: Miceal Brúnn manuscript, miscellaneous verse, 19th c.
MS G 634: Brian O'Looney manuscript of songs, oral tales, 19th c.
MS G 644: Michael Mhac Domhniel manuscript, devotional material, 19th c.
MSS G 732–34, 752–55, 769–70, 772–73: John Glynne notebooks, 19th c.
MS G 774: Brian O'Looney manuscript of lectures and poems, 19th c.
MS G 778: James Furlong notes on *Parrthas an Anma*, 19th c.

MS G 1002–1004: Reverend Maurice Power instructions on the Bible, 19th c.
MS G 1125: Father P. Meany collection of sermons, 19th c.
MS G 1252: William Smith O'Brien manuscript of oral tales, 19th c.

Photostat and Microfilm Copies of Gaelic Manuscripts Located at Other Archives

BL MS Add. 18948 (NLI p. 433): Seán and Diarmaid Ó Réagáin, etc., MS of prose and prayers, 19th c.
BL MS Add. 27946 (NLI p. 421): Eoghan Caomhánach, miscellaneous prose and poetry, 19th c.
BL MS Add. 29614 (NLI p. 422): Seán Ó Murchadha na Ráithíneach, religious verse, 18th c.
BL MS Add. 31875 (NLI p. 422): Anonymous copy of *Trí Bior-Ghaoithe an Bháis*, 18th c.
BL MS Egerton 113 (NLI p. 440): Composite items by Theophilius O'Flanagan, etc., political, 19th c.
BL MS Egerton 120 (NLI p. 441): Diarmuid Ó Mulchaoine, religious prose and prayers, 18th c.
BL MS Egerton 121 (NLI p. 441–442): Tomás Ó hIcheadha, *Vita Divina, Vie Devoté*, 19th c.
BL MS Egerton 126 (NLI p. 442): Finghin Ó Scannaill manuscript, prose on Irish language, 19th c.
BL MS Egerton 135 (NLI p. 442): Muirís Ó Gormáin et al., manuscript, misc. secular items, 18th c.
BL MS Egerton 155 (NLI p. 405): Fearghal Ó Raghallaigh manuscript, prose and secular verse, 18th c.
BL MS Egerton 193 (NLI p. 435): Edward Troy copy of *Eochair Phairthais*, 18th c.
BL MS Egerton 195 (NLI p. 435): Finghin Ó Scannail manuscript, prayer book, and poetry, 19th c.
BL MS Egerton 197 (NLI p. 435): Seán Ó Héidéin manuscript of religious prose and verse, 18th c.
CCG MS 3, NLI photostat: Father MacErlean, verse and miscellaneous, 18th–19th c.
CE MS 2 (NLI p. 4574): Tomás Ó Iceadha translation of de Sales, 19th c.
CE MS 7 (NLI p. 4653): Tomás Ó Iceadha translation of de Liguori, 19th c.
CF MS 1 (NLI p. 6037): Eadhmonn Ó Mathghamhna manuscript, religious prose, 19th c.
CF MS 5 (NLI p. 6038): Religious verse, scribe unknown, 19th c.
CF MS 24 (NLI p. 6042): Seán Ó Murchadha na Ráithíneach, religious and secular items, 18th c.
CF MS 26 (NLI p. 6043): Seán Ó Murchadha na Ráithíneach, catechism and prose, 18th c.
CF MS 27 (NLI p. 6043): Daniel Connellan manuscript, Donlevy catechism, 19th c.
FLK MS A 38 (NLI p. 8375): Tomás Ó Iceadha translation of Roman Missal, 19th c.
FLK MS A 39 (NLI p. 8377): Briain Ó Chathalán et al., religious verse and prose, 18th–19th c.

FLK MS A 40 (NLI p. 8377): Sylvester Gibney miscellaneous religious verse and prose, 19th c.

FLK MS A 41 (NLI p. 8377): Roland Swiney manuscript, mainly religious material, 18th c.

John Rylands Library Irish MS 56 (NLI p. 1713): James Mullaney autobiography, ca. 1856

ML MS 2 (NLI p. 6794): Uilliam Ó hOgan, religious and secular verse, 19th c.

ML MS 3 (NLI p. 6794): Diarmuid Ó Mulchaoine, secular and religious prose and verse, 18th c.

Microfilmed Papers of Cashel Diocesan Archives

NLI p. 5998–6000, Papers of Archbishop Thomas Bray
NLI p. 6000, Papers of Archbishop Patrick Everard
NLI p. 6000–6001, Papers of Archbishop Robert Laffan
NLI p. 6001–6004, Papers of Archbishop Michael Slattery
NLI p. 6005–6010, Papers of Archbishop Patrick Leahy
NLI p. 6010–6013, Papers of Thomas Croke

DUBLIN: ROYAL IRISH ACADEMY ARCHIVES

Main Collection

MS 4 B 1–20, MS 12 L 5: John Windele Papers and correspondence, ca. 1830–62
MS 24 K 4: Edward O'Reilly essay on the revival of the Irish language, 1823
Ordnance Survey Memoirs Box 49: Unpublished memoir records, Longford, Mayo, Meath, and Monaghan, ca. 1830–40

Gaelic Manuscripts Collection

MS 12 Q 13 (1126): Essays on the Irish language submitted to the Royal Irish Academy by John Fleming, Francis Keane, and Ulick Bourke, 1874–75
MS 23 A 1 (767): Daniel Malone manuscript of Carolan poems, 19th c.
MS 23 A 6 (219): Peadar Ó Longáin prayer book, 19th c.
MS 23 D 28 (243): Uilliam Ó Cleire tract on Christian doctrine, etc. 18th c.
MS 23 E 1 (522): James Hardiman manuscript, verse, and correspondence, 19th c.
MS 23 E 7 (534): Brian Ó Fearraghail religious verse, charms, prayers, prose, 18th c.
MS 23 E 21 (532): Michael Killeen et al., manuscript of poems by Carolan, 19th c.
MS 23 H 34 (718): Daniel Malone (?) et al., verses, correspondence, 18th–19th c.
MS 23 I 8 (768): Daniel Malone manuscript of songs, verse, 19th c.
MS 23 I 43 (427): Aodh Mac Ceagan prayer book, 19th c.
MS 23 O 35 (55): Brian Ó Fearraghail manuscript of secular and religious verse and prose, 18th c.
MS 23 O 45 (166): Pól Ó Longáin manuscript of poems by Carolan, 19th c.
MS 23 O 47 (569): Miscellaneous letters and correspondence to the *Nation*, etc., 19th c.
MS 24 B 6 (313): Timothy O'Regan-transcribed poems for William Smith O'Brien, 19th c.

MS 24 C 22 (318): William Smith O'Brien collected proverbs, miscellany, 19th c.
MS 24 C 26 (654): John Windele common-place book and miscellany, 19th c.
MS 24 M 5 (602): John O'Daly notebook of miscellaneous poetry, 19th c.

DUBLIN: TRINITY COLLEGE ARCHIVES

Congested Districts Board, Baseline reports, 1892–94
MS 4227: John Fleming, anthology of poems, ca. 1847
MS 5098: William Smith O'Brien, miscellaneous family papers, 19th c.
MSS 7644–47: Irish Society, proceedings of the committee, 1818–56
MS 7664: Islands and Coasts Society for Ireland, minute book, 1846–93

DUBLIN: UNIVERSITY COLLEGE, DUBLIN ARCHIVES

FLK MS A 48: Seaghan Ua Sgaunlane manuscript of miscellaneous secular and religious items, 19th c.
FLK MS A 54: Prayer book by scribe Tadhg Mha Cárrtha, 19th c.
FLK MS A 55: Anonymous manuscript of prayers and religious poems, 19th c.

GALWAY: GALWAY DIOCESAN ARCHIVES

Bishop Nicholas Archdeacon Papers
Warden Valentine Bodkin Papers

IRISH SCRIPT ON SCREEN: NEW NORCIA MONASTERY LIBRARY, AUSTRALIA

NN M75 985: John Howard prayer book, 18th c.

LONDON: BRITISH LIBRARY

BL MS Egerton 129: Composite MS including phonetic sermons and prose by Father Myles Gibbon, 18th c.

MELBOURNE, AUSTRALIA: STATE LIBRARY OF VICTORIA

SLV MS 10959: Dáibhí de Barra prayer book, 19th c.

NEWSPAPERS

MICROFILM/PRINT

An Claidheamh Soluis (Dublin)
Limerick Evening Post and Clare Sentinel (Limerick)
Limerick Reporter and Tipperary Vindicator (Limerick)
Londonderry Journal and Donegal and Tyrone Advertiser (Londonderry)
Mayo Constitution (Castlebar)

NINETEENTH-CENTURY BRITISH LIBRARY NEWSPAPERS (GALE.CENGAGE.CO.UK)

Belfast News-Letter (Belfast)
Bristol Mercury (Bristol)
Caledonian Mercury (Edinburgh)

Daily News (London)
Freeman's Journal (Dublin)
Glasgow Herald (Glasgow)
Hampshire Telegraph and Sussex Chronicle (Portsmouth)
Hull Packet and East Riding Times (Hull)
Leeds Mercury (Leeds)
Liverpool Mercury (Liverpool)
Manchester Times (Manchester)
Morning Chronicle (London)
Morning Post (London)
Pall Mall Gazette (London)
Royal Cornwall Gazette, Falmouth Packet & Plymouth Journal (Truro, Cornwall)
Standard (London)
Trewman's Exter Flying Post or Plymouth and Cornish Advertiser (Exeter)

PROQUEST HISTORICAL NEWSPAPERS (PROQUEST.COM)

Irish Times (Dublin)

THE TIMES DIGITAL ARCHIVE, 1785–2006 (GALE.CENGAGE.CO.UK)

Times (London)

Parliamentary Papers

Journals of the House of Commons. Vol. 63, 1st January 1808 to 16th January 1809.

CENSUS REPORTS

Abstract of the Census for Ireland, 1841 [459], H.C. 1843, li, 319.
Census of Ireland for the Year 1851. Part I: Area, Population, and Number of Houses, by Townlands and Electoral Divisions. Part IV: Report on Ages and Education [2053], H.C. 1856, xxix, 1.
Census of Ireland for the Year 1851. Part I: Area, Population, and Number of Houses, by Townlands and Electoral Divisions. Part VI, General Report [2134], H.C. 1856, xxxi, 1.
Census of Ireland for the Year 1861. Part I: Showing the Area, Population, and Number of Houses, by Townlands and Electoral Divisions, Vol. 1 [3204], H.C. 1863, liv, 1.
Census of Ireland for the Year 1861, Part II: Report and Tables on Ages and Education, Vol. 1 [3204-I], H.C. 1863, lvi, 1.
Census of Ireland for the Year 1861, Part II: Report and Tables on Ages and Education, Vol. 2 [3204-I], H.C. 1863, lvii, 1.
Census of Ireland for the Year 1861. Part V: General Report [3204-IV], H.C. 1863, lxi, 1.
Census of Ireland for the Year 1871. Part I: Area, Population, and Number of Houses; Also the Ages, Civil Condition, Occupations, Birthplaces, Religion, and Education of the People. Vol. I: Province of Leinster [C. 662], H.C. 1872, lxvii, 1.
Census of Ireland, 1871. Part I: Area, Houses, and Population; Also the Ages, Civil Condition, Occupations, Birthplaces, Religion, and Education of the People. Vol. II: Province of Munster [C.876], H.C. 1873, lxxii, pt. ii, 477.

Census of Ireland, 1871. Part I: Area, Houses, and Population; Also the Ages, Civil Condition, Occupations, Birthplaces, Religion, and Education of the People. Vol. III: Province of Ulster [C. 964], H.C. 1874, lxxii, pt. i, 1.

Census of Ireland, 1871. Part I: Area, Houses, and Population; Also the Ages, Civil Condition, Occupations, Birthplaces, Religion, and Education of the People. Vol. IV: Province of Connacht [C. 1106], H.C. 1874, lxxiv, pt. ii, 1.

Census of Ireland for the Year 1881. Part I: Area, House, and Populations; Also the Ages, Civil or Conjugal Condition, Occupations, Birthplaces, Religion, and Education of the People. Vol. I: Province of Leinster [C. 3042], H.C. 1881, xcvii, 1.

Census of Ireland for the Year 1891, Part I: Area, Houses, and Population: Also the Ages, Civil or Conjugal Condition, Occupations, Birthplaces, Religion, and Education of the People. Vol. I: Province of Leinster [C. 6515], H.C. 1890–91, xcv, 1.

Census of Ireland for the Year 1901. Part I: Area, Houses, and Population; Also the Ages, Civil or Conjugal Condition, Occupations, Birthplaces, Religion, and Education of the People. Vol. II, Province of Munster [Cd. 1058], H.C. 1902, cxxiv, 1.

Census of Ireland for the Year 1901. Part I: Area, Houses, and Population; Also the Ages, Civil or Conjugal Condition, Occupations, Birthplaces, Religion, and Education of the People. Vol. IV, Province of Connaught [Cd. 1059], H.C. 1902, cxxviii, 1.

EDUCATION REPORTS

Eighth Report of the Commissioners of Irish Education Inquiry. Dated London, 2d June 1827. Roman Catholic College of Maynooth, H.C. 1826–27 (509), xiii, 537.

Eighth Report of the Commissioners of National Education in Ireland, for the Year 1841 [398], H.C. 1842, xxiii, 339.

First Report of the Commissioners on Education in Ireland, H.C. 1825 (400), xii, 1.

Fourth Report of the Visitors of Maynooth College. 1849 [1080], H.C. 1849, xxiii, 87.

(Ireland) Eleventh Report from the Commissioners of the Board of Education in Ireland. Parish Schools, H.C. 1810–11 (107), vi, 927.

(Ireland) Fourteenth Report of the Commissioners of the Board of Education, in Ireland, H.C. 1812–13 (21), vi, 221.

Maynooth College. Report of a Visitation Held at the College of Maynooth on the 20th Day of June 1860, H.C. 1860 (413), liii, 649.

Maynooth College. Return of Number of Students Attending College of Maynooth, 1844–61, H.C. 1862 (450), xliii, 575.

Maynooth Commission. Report of Her Majesty's Commissioners Appointed to Inquire into the Management and Government of the College of Maynooth, Parts I–II [1896] [1896-I], H.C. 1854–55, xxii, 1, 355.

National Schools (Ireland) (Teaching of Irish). Copy of Correspondence Between the Irish Executive and the Commissioners of National Education in Ireland, with Respect to the Teaching of Irish in the Irish National Schools, H.C. 1884 (81), lxi, 617.

The Queen's Colleges Commission. Report of Her Majesty's Commissioners Appointed to Inquire into the Progress and Condition of the Queen's Colleges at Belfast, Cork, and Galway; with Minutes of Evidence, Documents, and Tables and Returns [2413], H.C. 1857–58, xxi, 53.

Report from the Select Committee of the House of Lords Appointed to Inquire into the Practical Working of the System of National Education in Ireland; and to Report Thereon to the House; Together with the Minutes of Evidence, Appendix, and Index. Session 1854, H.C. 1854 (525), xv, pt. i, 1, xv, pt. ii, 1.

Report of a Visitation Held at the College of Maynooth on the 20th Day of April, 1846 [731], H.C. 1846, xlii, 209.

Royal Commission of Inquiry into Primary Education (Ireland). Vol. III. Containing Evidence Taken Before the Commissioners from March 12th to October 30th, 1868. Questions and Answers 1 to 17608 [C.6-II], H.C. 1870, xxviii, pt. iii, 1.

Second Report of the Commissioners of Irish Education Inquiry. Dated Dublin, 16th September 1826, H.C. 1826–27 (12), xii, 1.

Second Report of the Visitors of Maynooth College. 1847 [890], H.C. 1847–48, xxix, 453.

Third Report of the Visitors of Maynooth College. 1847 [1072], H.C. 1849, xxiii, 85.

Twenty-Fifth Report of the Commissioners of National Education in Ireland, (for the Year 1858), with Appendices. Vol. I [2593] [2593-I], H.C. 1860, xxv, 1, 397.

Twenty-Fourth Report of the Commissioners of National Education in Ireland, (for the Year 1857), with Appendices. Vol. I [2456-I] [2456-II], H.C. 1859, vii, 1, 363.

Twenty-Second Report of the Commissioners of National Education in Ireland, (for the Year 1855), with Appendices [2142-I] [2142-II], H.C. 1856, xxvii, pt. i, 1, xxvii, pt. ii, 1.

Twenty-Third Report of the Commissioners of National Education in Ireland (for the year 1856), with Appendices, Vol. 1 [2304] [2304-I], H.C. 1857–58, xx, 213, 573.

ELECTION PETITIONS, ELECTION REPORTS, AND GRAND JURY EXPENSES

Clare Election. Minutes of Evidence Taken Before the Select Committee on the Clare Election Petition; with the Proceedings of the Committee, H.C. 1860 (178) (392), xi, 87, 153.

Election Expenses (Ireland). An Account of Expenses Incurred by the Returning Officer at Every Election for a County, or City, or Borough, in Ireland, During the Months of June and July 1841, H.C. 1843 (620), l, 235.

Election Expenses. Returns from Sheriffs and Other Returning Officers for Counties and Parliamentary Boroughs in Great Britain and Ireland, H.C. 1857 (331), xxxiv, 131.

First Report from the Select Committee on Fictitious Votes, Ireland; with the Minutes of Evidence, and Appendix, H.C. 1837–38 (259), xiii, pt. i, 1.

Grand Juries, Ireland. Returns of the Gross Sums Presented by the Several Grand Juries throughout Ireland, at the Spring and Summer Assizes 1830; Distinguishing the Amount of Such Presentments as Are Made Imperative by Law Upon Grand Juries, and over Which No Discretion Can be Exercised by Them, H.C. 1830–31 (324), xiv, 189.

Grand Juries, Sums Levied. Returns to an Order of the Honourable House of Commons, Dated the 10th February 1824; For an Account of All Sums of Money Levied in the Several Counties of Ireland, During the Two Years Last Past, by Authority of Grand Juries; Distinguishing the County from the Baronial Charge, and Specifying the Heads of Account to Which Those Separate Charges Were Applicable, H.C. 1824 (287), xxii, 357.

Grand Jury Presentments, Ireland. Account of Presentments Made by the Grand Juries of the County of the City of Limerick, in the Year 1821, H.C. 1822 (306), vii, 31.

(Ireland) Accounts, Presented to the House of Commons, of the Presentments Passed by the Grand Juries of Ireland, at the Spring and Summer Assizes, in the Year 1807, H.C. 1808 (205), xiii, 167.

(Ireland) A Bill For the Better Regulation of Elections of Members to Serve in Parliament for Places in Ireland, H.C. 1819–1820 (47), i, 473.

(Ireland) A Bill For the Better Regulation of Polls, and For Making Further Provisions Touching the Election of Members to Serve in Parliament for Ireland, H.C. 1819–1820 (60), i, 187.

(Ireland) A Bill to Regulate the Expenses of Elections of Members to Serve in Parliament for Ireland, H.C. 1821 (475), iii, 1675.

(Ireland) Sheriffs Charges and Expenses at Elections, 1818 and 1820. Returns to an Address of the House of Commons, of 13th June 1820; for an Account of All Sums of Money Paid to Sheriffs or Undersheriffs, at the General Election in 1818, and at the Last General Election, (1820) for Writs and Precepts, for Either Counties, Cities, or Boroughs, in Ireland . . . , H.C. 1820 (291), ix, 361.

Polls at Elections. (Ireland) A Bill to Regulate Polls at Elections in Ireland, H.C. 1839 (120), iii, 413.

Report from the Select Committee Appointed to Inquire into the Expenses of Sheriffs and Other Returning Officers, At Elections in Ireland; and Also into the Laws for Regulating Elections in Ireland, H.C. 1820 (226), iii, 269.

MISCELLANEOUS REPORTS

Courts of Law, &c. Return to an Address of the Honourable the House of Commons, Dated 7 August 1866; for, Return Showing in Detail, with a General Abstract, the Expenditure for the Year 1865-6, in Each of the Three Kingdoms, on Account of All Courts of Law and Justice and Legal Departments, Defrayed Wholly or in Part from Public Funds, H.C. 1867 (223) (223-I), lvii, 181, 379.

Fairs and Markets' Commission, Ireland. Report of the Commissioners Appointed to Inquire into the State of the Fairs and Markets in Ireland. Part II. Minutes of Evidence [1910], H.C. 1854–55, xix, 1.

First Report from His Majesty's Commissioners for Inquiring into the Condition of the Poorer Classes in Ireland, with Appendix (A) and Supplement, H.C. 1835 (369), xxxii, pt. i, 1, xxxii, pt. ii, 1.

First Report of the Commissioners of Inquiry into the State of Irish Fisheries; with the Minutes of Evidence, and Appendix [77], H.C. 1837, xxii, 1.

Land Acts (Ireland). Report of the Royal Commission on the Land Law (Ireland) Act, 1881, and the Purchase of Land (Ireland) Act, 1885 [C. 4969] [C.4969-I] [C.4969-II], H.C. 1887, xxvi, 1, 25, 1109.

Minutes of Evidence Taken Before the Select Committee of the House of Lords Appointed to Inquire into the Collection and Payment of Tithes in Ireland, and the State of the Laws Relating Thereto, and to Report their Observations Thereon to the House; and Who Had Leave Also to Report from Time to the House, H.C. 1831–32 (271), xxii, 1.

Minutes of Evidence Taken before the Select Committee of the House of Lords, Appointed to Inquire into the State of Ireland, More Particularly with Reference to the Circumstances which May Have Led to Disturbances in that Part of the United Kingdom. 24 March–22 June, 1825, H.C. 1825 (521), ix, 249.

Report From Her Majesty's Commissioners of Inquiry into the State of Law and Practice in Respect to the Occupation of Land in Ireland [605] [606], H.C. 1845, xix, 1, 57.

Report from the Select Committee of the House of Lords, Appointed to Enquire into the State of Ireland in Respect of Crime, and to Report Thereon to the House; with the Minutes of Evidence Taken Before the Committee, and an Appendix and Index, Part I. Report, and Evidence 22 April to 16 May 1839, H.C. 1839 (486), xi, 1, xii, 1.

Report from the Select Committee on Destitution (Gweedore and Cloughaneely); Together with the Proceedings of the Committee, Minutes of Evidence, Appendix, and Index, H.C. 1857–58 (412), xiii, 89.

Report from the Select Committee on Manor Courts, Ireland; Together with the Minutes of Evidence, Appendix and Index, H.C. 1837 (494), xv, 1.

Report from the Select Committee on Manor Courts, Ireland; Together with the Minutes of Evidence, Appendix, and Index, H.C. 1838 (648), xviii, 1.

Richmond Penitentiary, Dublin. Report of the Commissioners Directed by the Lord Lieutenant of Ireland, to Inquire into the State of the Richmond Penitentiary in Dublin; Together with the Evidence and Documents Connected Therewith, H.C. 1826–27 (335), xi, 567.

Royal Commission on Prisons in Ireland. Second Report [C. 4145], H.C. 1883, xlii, 671.

Royal Commission on Prisons in Ireland, Vol. 1. Reports, with Digest of Evidence, Appendices, &c. [C. 4233] [C. 4233-I], H.C. 1884–85, xxxviii, 1, 259.

State of Ireland. Minutes of Evidence Taken Before the Select Committee Appointed to Inquire into the Disturbances in Ireland, in the Last Session of Parliament, 13th May-18th June, 1824, H.C. 1825 (20), vii, 1.

Third Annual Report of the Directors of Convict Prisons in Ireland, for the Year Ended 31st December, 1856; with Appendix [2214], H.C. 1857, xxiii, 449.

Printed Primary Sources

Acta et Decreta Concilii Provinciae Casseliensis in Hibernia. Dublin: Jacob Duffy, 1854.

Alexander, James. *An Amusing Summer-Companion to Glanmire, near Cork: Being a Picturesque Delineation of That Beautiful Village, Together with Certain Prospects of the Surrounding Country; to Which Are Added Strong Sketches of the Manners of the Inhabitants and Some Useful Observations and Reflections.* Cork: H. Denmead, 1814.

Anderson, Christopher. *Ireland, but Still without the Ministry of the Word in Her Own Native Language.* Edinburgh: Oliver and Boyd, 1835.

———. *Memorial on Behalf of the Native Irish, with a View to Their Improvement in Moral and Religious Knowledge through the Medium of Their Own Language.* London: Gale, Curtis, & Fenner, 1815.

[Anon.]. *Leabhar Urnaighthe. Sagart Righalta do Ghleas.* Baile Átha Cliath: Comhlucht na Fírinne Catoilice, 1904.

[Anon.]. *Preaching the Gospel in Irish Not Contrary to Law; But Enjoyned Expressly by Several Statutes and Canons Now in Force in this Kingdom, As Well As By the Word of God*. Dublin: J. Carson, 1713.

An Soisgeal do Reir Lucais, agus Gniovarha na Neasbal. The Gospel According to St. Luke, and the Acts of the Apostles. Dublin: William Watson and Son, 1799.

An Teagasg Athchoimir Críostaighe, Tarruingthe as an Teagasg Críostaighe a tá Orduighthe le Cómhairle Thíorthamhail Mhagh-Núadhaith agus a tá Molta leis an g-Cairdinéal, na h-Árd-Easpogaibh, agus Easpogaibh na h-Eireann le Bheith in Úsáid Choitchionn tre Eaglais na h-Éireann. Aisdrighthe ón Sacs-Bheurla agus Clódhbhuailte le h-Ughdaras Ard-Easpoigh Thuama. Dublin: M. H. Gill and Son, 1886.

An Teagasg Críosdaidhe: The Catechism as Used in the Diocese of Cloyne, Republished with a Vocabulary. Edited by Peadar Ó Laoghaire. Dublin: Irish Book Company, 1906.

An Teagasg Críosdaighe. Do Réir Chomhairle Ard-Easboig Thuama, agus Easbog na Cúige Sin. Baile Átha Cliath: T. Coldamhell, 1839.

An Teagasg Criosdaighe. Do Réir Chomhairle Ard-Easboig Thuama, agus Easbog na Cúige Sin. Baile Átha Cliath: C. M. Mharrean, 1843.

An Teagasg Criosdaighe. Do Réir Chomhairle Ard-Easboig Thuama, agus Easbog na Cúige Sin. Dublin: C. M. Warren, 1869.

An Teagasg Criostaidhe; do Reir Cheiste agas Fhreagraidh, Athraidhthe go Gaodhailge, le Oideas Uilliam Coppinger, Easbog Chluana agas Rois, ua'n nGear-theagash. A Scriobodh Se Fein a mBeurla, Ath-leighte leis an Athair Domhnald O'Suilliobhain. Cork: Cormac Diolun, 1831.

An Teagasg Criostaidhe; do Reir Cheiste agas Fhreagraidh, Athraidhthe go Gaodhailge le Oideas Uilliam Coppiner, Easbog Chluana agas Rois, ua'n nGear-theagash a Sgriobodh Se Fein a mBeurla, Ath-leighte leis an Athair Domhnald O'Suilliobhain. Cork: Cormac Diolun, 1842.

An Teagasg Criostaidhe; do Reir Cheiste agas Fhreagraidh, Athraidhthe go Gaodhailge le Oideas Uilliam Coppiner, Easbog Chluana agas Rois, ua'n nGear-theagash a Sgriobhodh Se Fein a mBeurla, Ath-leighte leis an Athair Domhnald O'Suilliobhain. Cork: Daniel Mulcahy, 1849.

"Antiquarian and Literary Intelligence: Cork Cuvierian Society." *Gentleman's Magazine and Historical Review* 2 (Sept. 1865): 341–44.

Atkinson, A. *The Irish Tourist: In a Series of Picturesque Views, Travelling Incidents, and Observations Statistical, Political, and Moral, on the Character and Aspect of the Irish Nation*. Dublin: Thomas Courtney, 1815.

Barron, Philip. *Ancient Ireland. A Weekly Magazine* 1, nos. 1–5 (Jan.–May 1835).

———. *The Irish Catholic Prayer Book, with English Translation*. Dublin: J. S. Folds, n.d. [ca. 1835].

Battersby, T. C. F. *Carleton on Parliamentary Elections in Ireland: Together with the Practice in Election Petitions and an Appendix of Statutes and Forms*. 11th ed. Dublin: Hodges, Figgis & Co. 1892.

Bede, Cuthbert [Edward Bradley]. *The White Wife, with Other Stories, Supernatural, Romantic, and Legendary*. London: Sampson Low, Son, and Marston, 1865.

Best, W. M. *A Treatise on the Principles of the Law of Evidence; with Elementary Rules for Conducting the Examination and Cross-Examination of Witnesses.* 3rd ed. London: H. Sweet, 1860.

Bicheno, J. E. *Ireland and Its Economy, Being the Result of Observations Made in a Tour through the Country in the Autumn of 1829.* London: John Murray, 1830.

Binns, Jonathan. *The Miseries and Beauties of Ireland.* 2 vols. London: Longman, Orme, Brown and Co., 1837.

Blake, Henry, et al. *Letters from the Irish Highlands of Connemara.* London: John Murray, 1825. Repr., Clifden: Gibbons Publications, 1995.

Bolg an Tsolar: A Reprint of the Gaelic Magazine of the United Irishmen. Belfast: Northern Star Office, 1795. Repr., Belfast: Athol Books, 1999.

Borromeo, Charles. *The Contract and Testament of the Soule.* St. Omer: no printer, 1638.

Bourke, Ulick [Uileog de Búrca]. *The Aryan Origin of the Gaelic Race and Language.* London: Longmans, Green, and Co., 1875.

[Bray, Thomas, and William Coppinger]. *Oideas Athchoimir agus Urnaighthe do Dhaoine Eagcruadh agus Do'n Mhuintear Bhios ag Dul D'Eag, Maille re Gniomhartha Caoinduthrachta eile, a n-Gaoidheilg agus a m-Bearla, re Deagh Mholadh an Ollamahin, D.B. Ardeasbog Chaisil.* Cork: James Haly, 1807.

———. *Short Instructions and Prayers for Sick and Dying Persons, with Other Acts of Devotion, in English and Irish, Recommended by D.B. Abp. C.* Cork: James Haly, 1806.

Browne, Charles R. "The Ethnography of Ballycroy, County Mayo." *Proceedings of the Royal Irish Academy,* 3rd ser., vol. 4, no. 1 (1896): 74–111.

Browne, George Joseph. *An Authentic Account of the Trials at Large, of George Robert Fitzgerald, Esq.; Timothy Brecknock, James Fulton, and Others, for the Procurement of, and for the Murder of Patrick Randall M'Donnell and Charles Hipson.* London: John Stockdale, 1786.

Bullingbrooke, Edward. *An Abridgment of the Publick Statutes of Ireland, Now in Force and of General Use, and Also of Such English and British Statutes as Relate to and Bind Ireland, from Magna Charta to the Sixth Year of the Reign of His Present Majesty King George III, Inclusive.* 2 vols. Dublin: Boulter Grierson, 1768.

———. *An Abridgment of the Publick Statutes of Ireland, Now in Force and of General Use; and Also, of Such English and British Statutes as Relate to and Bind Ireland, from Magna Charta to the Twenty First and Twenty Second Years of the Reign of His Present Majesty King George the Third Inclusive.* 2nd ed. 2 vols. Dublin: George Grierson, 1786.

———. *An Abridgement of the Statutes of Ireland, from the First Session of Parliament in the Third Year of the Reign of King Edward the Second, to the End of the Twenty Fifth Year of the Reign of His Present Majesty King George the Second; and of All the English and British Statutes which Extend to and Bind Ireland; with Tables of the Statutes in their Chronological Order, Directing to the Heads Under which They are Abridged.* Dublin: George Abraham Grierson, 1754.

———. *The Duty and Authority of Justices of the Peace and Parish Officers for Ireland: Containing the Statutes which Give Jurisdiction to Such Magistrates; and Authorities from the Best and Latest Reports, Relative to the Exercise of their Office.* Rev. ed. Dublin: George Grierson, 1788.

Burgess, James. "Mapping and Place-Names of India." *Scottish Geographical Magazine* 7 (1891): 357–70.

Burke, Oliver. *Anecdotes of the Connaught Circuit from its Foundation in 1604 to Close Upon the Present Time.* Dublin: Hodges, Figgis, and Co., 1885.

Butler, Alban. *Lives of the Fathers, Martyrs, and Other Principal Saints: Compiled from Original Monuments, and Other Authentic Records: Illustrated with the Remarks of Judicious Modern Critics and Historians.* 3rd ed. 6 vols. Dublin: H. Fitzpatrick, 1802.

———. *The Lives of the Fathers, Martyrs, and Other Principal Saints, Compiled from Original Monuments and Other Authentic Records. Illustrated with the Remarks of Judicious Modern Critics and Historians by the Rev. Alban Butler.* 2 vols. Dublin: R. Coyne, 1836.

Butler, James. *Suim Athghar an Teagasg Criosduidhe.* Dublin: J. Boyce, 1784.

Butler, Mary E. L. *Gaelic League Pamphlets, No. 6: Irishwomen and the Home Language.* Dublin: Gaelic League, n.d.

Cameron, A. C. "On Gaelic and its Teaching in Highland Schools." *Celtic Magazine* 2 (1877): 181–240.

Carleton, William. *Traits and Stories of the Irish Peasantry.* 2 vols. Dublin: W. Curry, Jr., 1830–33. Repr., New York: Garland Publishing, 1979.

Carment, Samuel. *Glimpses of the Olden Time, Being Extracts Illustrative of the Social Life and Manners of the Olden Time.* Edinburgh: Macleod, 1893.

Carr, John. *The Stranger in Ireland, or, a Tour in the Southern and Western Parts of That Country, in the Year 1805.* London: Richard Phillips, 1806.

A Catechism, That is to Say, An Instruction to be Learned of Every Person, Before He be Brought to be Confirmed by the Bishop. To which are Prefixed Brief and Plain Rules for Reading Irish Language. London: E. Everingham, 1712.

Challoner, Richard. *Gairdín an Anama: Leabhar Urnaithe an Phobail.* Edited by Pádraig Ó Fiannachta. 1977. Repr., Má Nuad: An Sagart, 2002.

———. *Gairdín an Anma, Iar na Sgríobhadh, le Pol Ó Longáin chum Úsaide Speisialta Chaitillicidhe na hÉirionn.* Translated by Pól Ó Longáin. Corca: T. Ó Ceallacháin, 1844.

———. *The Garden of the Soul: or, a Manual of Spiritual Exercises and Instructions for Christians, Who (Living in the World) Aspire to Devotion.* Dublin: no printer, 1759.

———. *Machtnuig go Maih Air, no Leirsmuainte air Fhirine Mhor an Chreidiv Chriosduvuil do Gach La Anso Mioy.* Translated by Patrick Denn. Clonmel: John Hackett, 1819.

———. *Smuain go Maith Air: No Learsmuainteadh air Mhoirfhirinnidhe an Chreidimh Chriostaighe, do Gach Lá san Mi.* Translated by Eoghan Caomhánach. Baile Átha Cliath: Seon Coyne, 1820.

Chatterton, Henrietta. *Rambles in the South of Ireland During the Year 1838.* 2nd ed. 2 vols. London: Saunders and Otley, 1839.

[A Cistercian Monk]. *The Lives of the Irish Saints, Extracted from the Writings of the Rev. Alban Butler, and Now Placed in Order, with a Prefixed Callender; to which is*

Added, an Office and Litany in Their Honour, with a Defence of the Monastic Institute. By a Cistercian Monk. Dublin: J. Coyne, 1823.

Clarke, J. S., ed. *The Life of James the Second, King of England, &c., Collected Out of Memoirs Writ of His Own Hand, Together with the King's Advice to His Son, and His Majesty's Will.* 2 vols. London: Longman, Hurst, Orme, and Brown, 1816.

Clarke, Michael, trans. *Ireland's Dirge, an Historical Poem, Written in Irish.* Dublin: no printer, 1827.

Clarkson, John. *An Introduction to the Celebrated Devotion of the Most Holy Rosary, to which is Annexed a Method of Saying It, According to the Form Prescribed by His Holiness Pope Pius V.* London: Thomas Meighan, 1737.

Clayton, F. H. *Scenes and Incidents in Irish Life.* Montreal: John Lovell and Son, 1884.

A Collection of the Public General Statutes. 19 vols. London: George Eyre and Andrew Spottiswoode, 1833–66.

Connellan, Owen. *The Gospel According to St. John, in Irish, with an Interlined English Translation; and a Grammatical Praxis on the Gospel According to St. Matthew, in Irish.* Dublin: Richard Moore Tims, 1830.

Connellan, Thaddaeus, trans. *Reidh-Leighin air Ghnothuibh Cearba, Trachtail, Tuarasdal, Reic & Ceannach, &c &c. Chum Feidhme na ttAosóg, is do Gach Duine Lánaosda. Tairtheangtha Anois maille re Biseach le Tadhg O Coinniallain.* Dublin: R. Graisberridhe, 1835.

Coote, Charles. *General View of the Agriculture and Manufactures of the King's County, with Observations on the Means of their Improvement, Drawn Up in the Year 1801, for the Consideration, and Under the Direction of the Dublin Society.* Dublin: Graisberry and Campbell, 1801.

———. *General View of the Agriculture and Manufactures of the Queen's County, with Observations on the Means of their Improvement, Drawn Up in the Year 1801, for the Consideration, and Under the Direction of the Dublin Society.* Dublin: Graisberry and Campbell, 1801.

Coulter, Henry. *The West of Ireland: Its Existing Condition and Prospects.* Dublin: Hodges and Smith, 1862.

Coulter, John. *Curious Notions, Chiefly Concerning Alcoholic Liquors, Tobacco, and Those Who Consume Them: A Book for the People of the Period.* Belfast: John Reid and Co., 1890.

Cox, Edward W. *A Digest of All the Cases in All the Reports Decided by All the Courts Relating to Magistrates, Parochial, Ecclesiastical, Election, Municipal, and Criminal Law from 1856 to 1869.* London: Law Times Office, 1870.

Cox, Edward W., John Thompson, and R. Cunningham Glen, eds. *Reports of Cases in Criminal Law, Argued and Determined in All the Courts in England and Ireland.* 20 vols. London: John Crockford, 1846–1907.

Cox, Richard. *Hibernica Anglicana, or the History of Ireland from the Conquest Thereof by the English to the Present Time.* London: H. Clark, 1689.

Craig, Edward Thomas. *An Irish Commune: The History of Ralahine.* Dublin: William Curry, 1830. Repr., Dublin: Irish Academic Press, 1983.

Crashaw, William. *The Complaint or Dialogue, Betwixt the Soule and the Bodie of a Damned Man*. 2nd ed. London: G. E., 1622.
Croker, Thomas Crofton. *Researches in the South of Ireland, Illustrative of the Scenery, Architectural Remains, and the Manners and Superstitions of the Peasantry*. London: John Murray, 1824.
Cromwell, Thomas Kitson. *Excursions through Ireland: Comprising the Topographical and Historical Delineations of Each Province*. 2 vols. London: Longman, Hurst, Rees, Orme, and Brown, 1820.
Crowe, J. O'Beirne. *The Catholic University and the Irish Language*. Dublin: James Duffy, 1854.
Curwen, John Christian. *Observations on the State of Ireland, Principally Directed to Its Agriculture and Rural Population*. 2 vols. London: Baldwin, Cradock, and Joy, 1818.
Daunt, William J. O'Neill. *A Life Spent for Ireland. Being Selections from the Journals of the Late W. J. O'Neill Daunt Edited by His Daughter*. London: T. Fisher Unwin, 1896.
——. *Personal Recollections of the Late Daniel O'Connell, M.P.* 2 vols. London: Chapman and Hall, 1848.
Davies, John. *Historical Tracts: By Sir John Davies, Attorney General, and Speaker of the House of Commons in Ireland*. London: John Stockdale, 1786.
Dean, Joseph Joy. *Devotions to the Sacred Heart of Jesus; Exercises for the Holy Sacrifice of the Mass, Confession and Communion; Visits to the Blessed Sacrament; Feasts of the Sacred Heart, &c. with an Appendix of the Nature of Indulgences. Translated from the French*. Dublin: Chambers and Hallagan, 1820.
de Liguori, Alphonsus. *The Glories of Mary; from the Italian of St. Alphonsus Mary de Liguori*. Dublin: John Mullany, n.d.
Denn, Patrick. *Aighneas an Pheacaig Leis an mBás*. Edited by Patrick Power. Waterford: Harvey and Co., 1899.
——. *The Catholic Children's Religious Primer, Containing the Prayers, etc., Necessary for the Instruction of Youth & Even for the Adult, Also the Lord's Prayer, and the Principal Parts of the Mass Expounded, with the Rosaries and Litanies of Jesus, Mary, and Joseph, the Rosary for the Dead, and the Recommendation of a Soul Departing, &c., &c.* Cork: Daniel Mulcahy, 1858.
——. *Leavar Beag na Rosaries, mar aon leis na Liodain, agus le Toirvirt Suas an Anama aig dul Deag, &c. &c.* Clonmel: John Hackett, 1818.
——, ed. *A New Edition of Timothy O'Sullivan's, Commonly Called Taidhg Gaodhlach's Pious Miscellany*. 10th ed. Cork: John Connor, 1829.
——. *Stiúratheoir an Pheacuig*. Edited by Diarmuid Ó hEaluighthe. Cork: Daniel Mulcahy, 1860. Repr., Corcaigh: Cló Ollscoile Chorcaigh, 1945.
——. *Urnaighthe an Tighearna, nó, "An Paidir," an t-Aifreann Naomhtha Fós, agus Aitheanta Dé Mínighthe. Mar Aon le hUrnaighthibh le Rádh do Dhuine & É ag Dul chum Báis, & tar éis Bháis Dó*. Edited by Rev. Maurus Ó Faelan. Waterford: Gill, 1908.
Dewar, Daniel. *Observations on the Character, Customs, and Superstitions of the Irish; and Some of the Causes which have Retarded the Moral and Political Improvement of Ireland*. London: Gale and Curtis, 1812.

Donlevy, Andrew. *An Teagasg Críosduidhe do Réir Ceasda agus Freagartha, air na Tharruing go Bunudhasach as Bréithir Soilléir Dé, agus as Toibreachaibh Fíorghlana Oile*. Paris: Seumus Guerin, 1742.

Dutton, Hely. *A Statistical and Agricultural Survey of the County of Galway, with Observations on the Means of Improvement, Drawn up for the Consideration and by the Direction of the Royal Dublin Society*. Dublin: R. Graisberry, 1824.

——. *A Statistical Survey of the County of Clare, with Observations on the Means of Improvement, Drawn up for the Consideration and by Direction of the Dublin Society*. Dublin: Graisberry and Campbell, 1808.

Elizabeth, Charlotte. "Letters from Ireland, MDCCCXXXVII." In *The Works of Charlotte Elizabeth, with an Introduction by Mrs. H.B. Stowe*, vol. 1. New York: M. W. Dodd, 1844.

Faber, F. *The Lives of Father Paul Segneri, S.J., Father Peter Pinamonti, S.J., and the Ven. John de Britto, S.J*. New York: Edward Dunigan and Brother, 1851.

Fagan, William. *The Life and Times of Daniel O'Connell*. 2 vols. Cork: John O'Brien, 1847–48.

Fitzgerald, P., and J. J. McGregor. *The History, Topography, and Antiquities of the County and City of Limerick; with a Preliminary View of the History and Antiquities of Ireland*. 2 vols. Dublin: George MacKern, 1826–27.

Foley, Daniel. *An English-Irish Dictionary*. Dublin: William Curry and Company, 1855.

——. *A Missionary Tour through the South and West of Ireland, Undertaken for the Society*. Dublin: Edward Bull for the Irish Society, 1849.

Foot, Charles H. *The Grand Jury Laws of Ireland: Comprising All the Statutes Relating to the Powers and Duties of Grand Juries, Including Orders in Council*. 2nd ed. Dublin: Hodges, Figgis, and Co., 1884.

Foster, Thomas Campbell. *Letters on the Condition of the People of Ireland*. 2nd ed. London: Chapman and Hall, 1847.

The Four Gospels in the Irish Language. With Notes, Hymns, & Historical Facts. Adapted Principally for the Populous Province of Munster. London: Partridge & Oakey, n.d. [ca. 1849].

Full and Revised Report of the Eight Days' Trial in the Court of Queen's Bench on a Criminal Information Against John Sarsfield Casey at the Prosecution of Patten Smith Bridge; From November 27th to December 5th, 1877. Dublin: Central Tenants' Defence Committee, 1877.

Furlong, John Smith. *A Treatise on the Law of Landlord and Tenant, as Administered in Ireland*. 2 vols. Dublin: Hodges and Smith, 1845.

Furlong, Jonathan. *Aithghearughadh. An Teagaisg Críosdaighe Geinearáilte: Molta le hArdeasboig Eireann, Chum Usáide na Mionaosóige, aig nach bh-fuil Fós Intleacht Chum Níos Mó d'Fhoghluim. Aistrighthe a n-Gaoidhilig, le Jonathan Furlong, Sagart Cathoilice*. Dublin: T. Coldwell, 1839.

——. *Carad an Chríosdaigh; nó Leabharán iona bhfuil Urnuighthe Áirighthe Riachtanach chum Seirbhís Dhiadha do Chomhlíonadh*. Dublin: no printer, 1842.

——. *Compánach an Chríosdaigh; no Tiomsúgh D'Urnaíghibh Cráibhtheacha, Oireamhnach chum Gach Dualgais do Bhainas le Creideamh, do Chomhlíonadh*. Dublin: Tegg & Co., 1842.

———. *An Irish Primer, for the Use of Those Who are Already Acquainted with the Grammar of Any Language, and Who Can Speak the Modern Irish.* Dublin: T. Coldwell, 1839.

———. *The Irish Primer, for the Use of Those Who are Already Acquainted with the Grammar of Any Language, and Who Can Speak the Modern Irish.* 2nd ed. Dublin: John Mullany, 1842.

Gaelic League Pamphlets, No. 2: The Case for Bilingual Education in the Irish-Speaking Districts. Dublin: Gaelic League, n.d.

Gaelic League Pamphlets, No. 3: Irish in the Schools. Dublin: Gaelic League, 1900.

Gallagher, James. *Seventeen Irish Sermons, in an Easy and Familiar Stile, on Useful and Necessary Subjects, in English Characters; as Being the More Familiar to Generality of Our Irish Clergy, in which is Included, a Sermon on the Joys of Heaven.* Dublin: P. Wogan, 1795.

Gearnon, Antoin. *Parrthas an Anma.* Edited by Anselm Ó Fachtna. Louvain, 1645. Repr., Baile Átha Cliath: Institiúid Ard-Léinn Bhaile Átha Cliath, 1953.

George, Joseph Browne. *A Report of the Whole of the Proceedings Previous to, with a Note of the Evidence on the Trial of Robert Keon, Gent. for the Murder of George Nugent Reynolds, Esq. and Also of the Charges of the Judges thereon. Together with the Arguments and Replies of Counsel on the Motion in Arrest of Judgment; and the Decision of the Court Thereon.* Dublin: P. Byrne, 1788.

Gough, John. *A Tour in Ireland in 1813 and 1814.* Dublin: M. Gough, 1817.

Grant, James. *Impressions of Ireland and the Irish.* Philadelphia: G.B. Zieber and Co., 1845.

Gregg, John. *A Missionary Visit to Achill and Erris and Other Parts of the County of Mayo.* Dublin: William Curry and Co., 1850.

———. *A Missionary Visit to Connemara and Other Parts of the County of Galway.* 3rd ed. Dublin: William Curry and Co., 1850.

Hale, Matthew. *The History of the Common Law.* 4th ed. Dublin: James Moore, 1792.

Haliday, William. *Úraicecht na Gaedhilge, a Grammar of the Gaelic Language.* Dublin: John Barlow, 1808.

Hall, S. C., and A. M. Hall. *Ireland: Its Scenery, Character, &c.* 3 vols. London: How and Parsons, 1841–43.

Hands, William. *The Proceedings on Election Petitions, with Precedents.* London: William Walker, 1812.

Hardiman, James. *The History of the Town and County of Galway from the Earliest Period to the Present Time, Embellished with Several Engravings, to which is Added a Copious Appendix Containing the Principal Charters and Other Original Documents.* Dublin: W. Folds and Sons, 1820. Repr., Galway: Connacht Tribune Printing and Publishing Co., 1926.

———. *Irish Minstrelsy, or Bardic Remains of Ireland, with English Poetical Translations.* London: J. Robins, 1831. Repr., Shannon: Irish University Press, 1971.

Hardy, Philip Dixon. *The Holy Wells of Ireland, Containing an Authentic Account of Those Various Places of Pilgrimage and Penance which are Still Annually Visited by Thousands of the Roman Catholic Peasantry, with a Minute Description of the*

Patterns and Stations Periodically Held in Various Districts of Ireland. Dublin: P. D. Hardy, 1836.

Hastings, George Woodyatt, ed. *Transactions of the National Association for the Promotion of Social Science. Belfast Meeting, 1867.* London: Longmans, Green, Reader, and Dyer, 1868.

Historic Literature of Ireland: An Essay on the Publications of the Irish Archaeological Society, Founded A.D. 1840. Dublin: W. B. Kelly, 1851.

Hogan, John. "Patron Days and Holy Wells in Ossory." *Journal of the Royal Historical and Archaelogical Association of Ireland* 2, no. 2 (1873): 261–81.

Hughes, Thomas. *Doctor Kirwan's Irish Catechism.* Edited and translated by William J. Mahon. 8th ed. Dublin: C. M. Warren, ca. 1850. Repr., Cambridge, MA: Pangur Publications, 1991.

Hunt, F. Knight. *The Fourth Estate: Contributions towards a History of Newspapers, and of the Liberty of the Press.* 2 vols. London: David Bogue, 1850.

Huston, Robert. *Life and Labours of the Rev. Fossey Tackaberry, with Notices of Methodism in Ireland.* 2nd ed. London: John Mason, 1860.

[Hutchinson, Francis]. *An Irish Almanack for the Year of Christ, 1724/An Almanack an Gaoidheilg arson Uliana an Tighearna Croisda, 1724.* Dublin: no printer, 1724.

Hyde, Douglas. *Abhráin Diadha Chúige Connacht or the Religious Songs of Connacht. Being the Sixth and Seventh Chapters of the Songs of Connacht.* 2 vols. 1906. Repr., Shannon: Irish University Press, 1972.

———. *A Literary History of Ireland from Earliest Times to the Present Day.* London: T. Fisher Unwin, 1899.

Inglis, Henry D. *Ireland in 1834: A Journey throughout Ireland, During the Spring, Summer, and Autumn of 1834.* 3rd ed. London: Whittaker and Co., 1835.

Instructions for Gaining the Jubilee Granted by His Holiness Pope Clement XIV. Soon After His Election, which was on the 4th of June, 1769, Revised by Several Eminent Clergymen. Dublin: Bartholomew Corcoran, 1770.

An Irish and English Spelling Book for the Use of Schools and Persons in the Irish Parts of the Country. 12th ed. Dublin: M. Goodwin and Co., 1836.

An Irish and English Spelling Book for the Use of Schools and Persons in the Irish Parts of the Country. 23rd ed. Achill: Mission Press, for the Irish Society, 1852.

Irish Society. *Quarterly Extracts from the Correspondence of the Irish Society for Promoting the Education of the Native Irish through the Medium of Their Own Language.* Dublin: M. Goodwin, 1821–47.

———. *Reports of the Irish Society for Promoting the Education of the Native Irish through the Medium of Their Own Language.* Dublin: M. Goodwin, 1828–49, and Dublin: Irish Society, 1863–67.

Johnson, James. *Tour in Ireland, with Meditation and Reflections.* London: S. Highley, 1844.

Joyce, P. W. *The Origin and History of Irish Names of Places.* 4th ed. Dublin: McGlashan and Gill, 1874. Repr., Wakefield, UK: E. P. Publishing, 1972.

Kempis, Thomas à. *Searc-Leanmhain Chríost i g-Ceithre Leabhraibh.* Translated by Dónall Ó Súilleabháin. Dublin: Richard Coyne, 1822. Repr., Dublin: Dollard Printinghouse, 1886.

The Key of Paradise, Opening the Gate to Eternal Salvation. To this Edition is Added, a New Calendar. The Whole Revised and Corrected by the Reverend B[ernard] McM[ahon]. Dublin: Patrick Wogan, 1796.

Knight, Patrick. *Erris in the "Irish Highlands" and the "Atlantic Railway."* Dublin: Martin Keene and Son, 1836.

[Knill, Richard]. *Gaduighe a' Fághail Bháis, agus Slanathoir a' Fághail Bháis.* Limerick: R. P. Canter, n.d. [ca. 1836].

Knott, Mary John. *Two Months at Kilkee, a Watering Place in the County Clare, Near the Mouth of the Shannon, with an Account of a Voyage Down That River from Limerick to Kilrush.* Dublin: William Curry, Jr., and Co., 1836.

Kohl, Johann Georg. *Ireland: Dublin, the Shannon, Limerick, Cork, and the Kilkenny Races, the Round Towers, the Lakes of Killarney, the County of Wicklow, O'Connell and the Repeal Association, Belfast and the Giant's Causeway.* New York: Harper and Brothers, 1844.

———. *Travels in Ireland.* London: Bruce and Wyld, 1844.

Levinge, Edward. *The Justice of the Peace for Ireland: Comprising the Practice in Indictable Offences, and the Proceedings Preliminary and Subsequent to Convictions; with an Appendix of the Most Useful Statutes, and an Alphabetical Catalogue of Offences.* 2nd ed. Dublin: Hodges, Smith & Co., 1864.

Lynch, Patrick. *For-Oideas Ghnaith-Ghaoighilge na h-Eireand: An Introduction to the Knowledge of the Irish Language, as Now Spoken; Containing a Comprehensive Exemplification of the Alphabetic Sounds, and a Complete Analysis of the Accidents of the Declinable Parts; with the Pronunciation of Each Irish Word Employed in Illustration, So Far as Could Be Effected by the Substitution of English Characters; Systematically Arranged and Methodically Disposed, in Fourteen Short Synoptic Tables.* Dublin: Graisberry and Campbell, 1815.

———. *Hibernia Sancta; or, Lives of Irish Saints.* Dublin: Thomas Haydock, 1817.

Mac Aingil, Aodh. *Scáthán Shacramuinte na hAithridhe.* Edited by Cainneach Ó Maonaigh. Louvain, 1618. Repr., Baile Átha Cliath: Institiúid Ard-Léinn Bhaile Átha Cliath, 1952.

MacCurtin, Hugh [Aodh Mac Cruitín]. *A Brief Discourse in Vindication of the Antiquity of Ireland: Collected Out of Many Authentick Irish Histories and Chronicles, and Out of Foreign Learned Authors.* Dublin: S. Powell, 1717.

———. *The Elements of the Irish Language, Grammatically Explained in English.* Louvain: Martin Van Overbeke, 1728.

MacDonagh, Michael. *Irish Life and Character.* London: Hodder and Stoughton, 1898.

MacElligott, P. *Observations on the Gaelic Language.* Dublin: J. Barlow, 1808.

MacHale, John, trans. *An t'Íliad. Air Chogadh na Tróighe ro Chan Homear.* Baile Átha Cliath: Gudmhaín agus a Chómh-chuideacht, 1844.

———. *Craobh Urnaighe Cráibhthighte Tiomhsuigthe as an Sgriobhain Diadha, agus Rannta Toghtha na h-Eaglaise le Seaghan Mac Hale, Árdeaspog Thuama.* 2nd ed. Baile Átha Cliath: Seamus O Duibhthe, 1857.

———. *Toras na Croiche. Aistrighth le Seaghan Mac Hale, Ardeasbog Thuama*. Baile Átha Cliath: Seamus O Duibhthe, 1861.

———. *Toras na Croiche. Aistrighth le Seaghan Mac Hale, Ardeasbog Thuama*. Baile Átha Cliath: Seamus O Duibhthe, 1873.

MacParlan, James. *Statistical Survey of the County Leitrim, with Observations on the Means of Improvement, Drawn Up for the Consideration, and by Order of the Dublin Society*. Dublin: Graisberry and Campbell, 1802.

———. *A Statistical Survey of the County of Mayo, with Observations on the Means of Improvement, Drawn Up in the Year 1801 for the Consideration and Under the Direction of the Dublin Society*. Dublin: Graisberry and Campbell, 1802.

———. *A Statistical Survey of the County of Sligo, with Observations on the Means of Improvement, Drawn Up in the Year 1801 for the Consideration and Under the Direction of the Dublin Society*. Dublin: Graisberry and Campbell, 1802.

Madden, Samuel. *Reflections and Resolutions Proper for the Gentlemen of Ireland, as to their Conduct for the Service of their Country*. Dublin: R. Reilly, 1738.

Manni, Giovanni [aka John Baptistae, aka Eoin Baptista]. *Ceithre Soleirseadha de'n Eagnuidheacht Chriostuidhe, Tarraingthe o Cheithre Leur-Smuaintighthibh na Siorruidheachta. Air na Sgriobhadh go Bunnudhasach ann Iottailis le Eoin Baptista Manni, dhe Chomhluadar Iosa, agus Curtha a mBearla Sacsanach le W.V. agus Ionntoighthe o Shacs-bheulra, go Gaoidheilg le Seumas O'Scoireadh*. Translated by James Scurry [Séamus Ó Scoireadh].Portlairge: Eoin Bull, 1820.

———. *Four Maxims of Christian Philosophy, Drawn from Four Considerations of Eternity. Written in Italian by John Baptistae Manni, of the Society of Jesus, and Translated into English by W.V.* 12th ed. Dublin: The Catholic Book Society, 1833.

Marrable, William. *Sketch of the Origin and Operations of the Society for Irish Church Missions to the Roman-Catholics, Being a Record of Important Documents and Information to the Commencement of the Year 1852*. 2nd ed. London: Seeley, Hatchard, and Nisbet, 1852.

Mason, Henry Monck. *Reason and Authorities and Facts Afforded by the History of the Irish Society Respecting the Duty of Employing the Irish Language as a More General Medium for Conveying Scriptural Instruction to the Native Peasantry of Ireland*. Dublin: M. Goodwin and Co., 1835.

Mason, William Shaw. *A Statistical Account or Parochial Survey of Ireland, Drawn up from the Communications of the Clergy*. 3 vols. Dublin: Graisberry and Campbell, 1814–19.

Maurel, A. *The Christian Instructed in the Nature and Use of Indulgences*. Translated by Patrick Costelloe. 4th ed. Dublin: M. H. Gill and Son, 1885.

McCarthy, Daniel, ed. *Collections on Irish Church History. From the Mss. of the Late Very Rev. Laurence F. Renehan, D.D., President of Maynooth College*. 2 vols. Dublin: James Duffy and Sons, 1861–74.

McDonald, Walter. "Irish Ecclesiastical Colleges since the Reformation." *Irish Ecclesiastical Record*, new ser., vol. 10 (Feb. 1874): 203–7.

McEvoy, John. *Statistical Survey of the County of Tyrone, with Observations on the Means of Improvement; Drawn up in the Years 1801, and 1802, for the Consideration,* and under the Direction of the Dublin Society. Dublin: Graisberry and Campbell, 1802. Repr., Belfast: Friar's Bush Press, 1991.

McQuige, James. *The Importance of Schools for Teaching the Native Irish Language Demonstrated in a Letter from James McQuige to the Rev. Joseph Ivimey, Secretary to the Baptist Irish Society.* London: Button and Son, and Whittimore, 1818.

Meany, John. *Irish Sermons with Translations.* Dublin: John S. Folds, 1835.

Meditations and Prayers adapted to the Stations of the Holy Way of the Cross. Kilkenny: T. Shearman, n.d. [ca. 1840].

Molloy, Constantine. *The Justice of the Peace for Ireland: A Treatise on the Powers and Duties of Magistrates in Ireland in Cases of Summary Jurisdiction in the Prosecution of Indictable Offenses and in Other Matters.* Dublin: Hodges, Figgis, 1890.

Moore, H. Kingsmill. *An Unwritten Chapter in the History of Education. Being the History of the Society for the Education of the Poor in Ireland, Generally Known as the Kildare Place Society, 1811–1831.* London: Macmillan and Co., Limited, 1904.

Moran, Patrick Francis. *History of the Catholic Archbishops of Dublin, since the Reformation.* Dublin: James Duffy, 1864.

Morris, Henry [Énrí Ó Muirgheasa]. *Greann na Gaedhilge: An Chéad Chuid.* Baile Átha Cliath: Connradh na Gaedhilge, 1901.

———. "The Loss of the Irish Language and Its Influence on the Catholic Religion in Ireland." *Fáinne an Lae* 1, no. 13 (1898): 8–9.

The Most Rev. Dr. James Butler's Catechism, Revised, Enlarged, Approved, and Recommended by the Four R.C. Arch-Bishops of Ireland as a General Catechism for the Kingdom. 7th ed. Cork: Charles Dillon, 1814.

The Most Rev. Dr. James Butler's Catechism, Revised, Enlarged, Approved, and Recommended by the Four R.C. Bishops of Ireland, as a General Catechism for the Kingdom. 4th ed. Cork: James Haly, 1806.

Mullin, James. *The Story of a Toiler's Life.* Edited by Patrick Maume. Dublin: Maunsel and Roberts, 1921. Repr., Dublin: University College Dublin Press, 2000.

Neave, Richard Digby. *Four Days in Connemara.* London: Richard Bentley, 1852.

Neilson, William. *Cead Leabhar na Gaoidheilge, air na Chur a gClo, Chum Maitheas Puiblidhe na hEirin. Air Iartas agus Costas na Cuideachta Eirionaighe.* No place, 1810.

———. *An Introduction to the Irish Language in Three Parts.* Dublin: P. Wogan, 1808.

Newenham, Thomas. *A View of the Natural, Political, and Commercial Circumstances of Ireland.* London: T. Cadell and W. Davies, 1809.

Nicholson, Asenath. *Ireland's Welcome to the Stranger, or Excursions through Ireland in 1844 and 1845 for the Purpose of Personally Investigating the Condition of the Poor.* Edited by Maureen Murphy. 1847–51. Repr., Dublin: Lilliput Press, 2002.

———. *Lights and Shades of Ireland in Three Parts.* London: Charles Gilpin, 1850.

Nun, Richard, and John Edward Walsh. *The Powers and Duties of Justices of the Peace in Ireland, and of Constables as Connected Therewith; with an Appendix of Statutes and Forms.* Dublin: Hodges and Smith, 1841.

O Beaglaoich, Conchobhar, and Aodh Bhuidhe Mac Cuirtin. *The English Irish Dictionary. An Focloir Bearla Gaoidheilge.* Paris: Seamus Guerin, 1732.

O'Brennan, Martin. *Ancient Ireland: Her Milesian Chiefs, Her Kings and Princes, Her Great Men, Her Struggles for Liberty, Her Apostle St. Patrick, Her Religion*. Dublin: John Mullany, 1855.

———. *Irish Made Easy; or, A Practical Irish Grammar*. London: Catholic Publishing and Bookselling Company, Limited, 1859.

Ua Briain, S. G. "Sgéilíní ó Chill Choca." *Irisleabhar na Gaedhilge* 11, no. 130 (1901): 115–18.

O'Brien, John [Seán Ó Briain]. *Focalóir Gaoidhilge-Sax-Bhéarla or an Irish English Dictionary*. Paris: Nicolas-Francis Valleyre, 1768.

O'Daly, John. *The Poets and Poetry of Munster: A Selection of Irish Songs by the Poets of the Last Century*. 2nd ser. Dublin: John O'Daly, 1860.

O'Donovan, John. *A Grammar of the Irish Language, Published for the Use of the Senior Classes in the College of St. Columba*. Dublin: Hodges and Smith, 1845.

The Office of the Holy Week, According to the Roman Missal and Breviary. Containing the Morning and Evening Service from Palm-Sunday to Tuesday in Easter Week, with an Explanation of the Mysteries Represented in the Office and Ceremonies of the Holy Week. Embellished with Cuts. 9th ed. Dublin: Patrick Wogan, 1804.

O'Flaherty, Roderic. *Ogygia, or, a Chronological Account of Irish Events: Collected from Very Ancient Documents, Faithfully Compared with Each Other, and Supported by the Genealogical and Chronological Aid of the Sacred and Prophane Writings of the First Nations of the Globe*. Translated by James Hely. 2 vols. Dublin: W. McKenzie, 1793.

O'Grady, Standish Hayes. *Adventures of Donnchadh Ruadh Mac Con-Mara, a Slave of Adversity, Written by Himself, Now for the First Time Edited from an Original Irish Manuscript, with Metrical Translation, Notes, and a Biographical Sketch of the Author*. Dublin: John O'Daly, 1853.

Ó hEodhasa, Bonabhentura [Giolla Brighde]. *An Teagasg Críosdaidhe*. Edited by Fearghal Mac Raghnaill. Antwerp: Jacobus Mesius, 1611. Repr., Baile Átha Cliath: Institiúid Ard-Léinn Bhaile Átha Cliath, 1976.

O'Looney, Brian. *A Collection of Poems Written on Different Occasions by the Clare Bards, in Honor of the MacDonnells of Kilkee and Killone, in the County of Clare*. Dublin: John O'Daly, 1863.

Ó Maolchonaire, Flaithrí, *Desiderius. Otherwise Called Sgáthán an Chrábhaidh*. Edited by Thomas F. O'Rahilly. Louvain: 1616. Repr., Dublin: Stationery Office, 1941.

Ó Maolmhuaidh, Froinsias [Francisco O Molloy]. *Grammatica Latino-Hibernica Nunc Compendiata*. Rome: S. Cong. de Propag. Fide, 1677.

———. *Lucerna Fidelium*. Edited by Pádraig Ó Súilleabháin. Rome, 1676. Repr., Baile Átha Cliath: Institiúid Ard-Léinn Bhaile Átha Cliath, 1962.

Ua Nualáin, Eoin [Eoin Ó Nualláin; John Nolan]. *An Casán go Flaitheamhnas: Láimhleabhairín Urnuighe*. Dublin: M. H. Gill and Son, 1882.

———. *Leabhar-Urnuighe Naoimh Pádraic/St. Patrick's Prayer Book*. 5th ed. Dublin: James Duffy and Co., n.d. [ca. 1900]

Ordo Administrandi Sacramenta et Alia Quaedam Officia Ecclesiastica Rite Peragendi. Dublin: P. Wogan, 1812.

O'Reilly, Bernard. *John MacHale, Archbishop of Tuam: His Life, Times, and Correspondence.* 2 vols. New York: Fr. Pustet & Co., 1890.

O'Reilly, Michael. *An Teagask Creestye, agus Paidreacha na Mainne, agus an Tranona.* Dublin: Richard Grace, n.d.

———. *An Teagask Creestye, agus Paidreacha na Mainne, agus Tranona.* Dublin: C. M. Warren, n.d.

———. *An Teagask Creestye, agus Paidreagha na Mainne agus an Tranona.* Dundalk: Joseph Parks, 1793.

———. *An Teagask Creestye, agus Paidreagha na Mainne agus an Tranona.* Dublin: J. Dunn, 1800.

———. *A Catechism, or an Abridgment of the Christian Doctrine, Divided into Four Parts; to which are Added, a Catechism of the Sacrament of Confirmation, Morning and Evening Prayers; the Manner of Serving the Mass; Acts of Faith, Hope and Charity; Instructions and Prayers for Confession, Communion, Mass, etc.* Dublin: C. M. Warren, n.d.

Original Legends and Stories of Ireland. Dublin: C.M. Warren, n.d. [ca. 1830].

O'Sullivan, Tadhg Gaolach. *Pious Miscellany.* Dublin: John Daly, 1868.

Page, James. *Ireland: Its Evils Traced to Their Source.* London: R. B. Seeley and W. Burnside, 1836.

The Path to Paradise: Being a Choice Manual of Devout Prayers, to which are Added the Psalter of the Most Holy Name of Jesus, the Rosaries, Vespers, Hymns, and the Manner of Serving Mass. Kilkenny: T. Shearman, n.d. [ca. 1825].

Perceval, Arthur Philip, *The Amelioration of Ireland Contemplated in a Series of Papers. I: On the Use of the Irish Language in Religious Worship and Instruction.* 2nd ed. London: W. J. Cleaver, 1844.

Petersdorff, Charles. *A Concise, Practical Abridgment of the Common and Statute Law, as at Present Administered in the Common-Law, Probate, Divorce, and Admiralty Courts.* 2nd ed. 6 vols. London: Simpkin, Marshall, and Co., 1861–64.

Phipson, Sidney L. *The Law of Evidence.* London: Stevens and Haynes: 1892.

Pinamonti, John Peter. *True Wisdom; or Considerations for Every Day of the Week. Written in Italian, by the Pious and Learned Father John Peter Pinamonti, of the Society of Jesus. With an Appendix, of What is Necessary for a Good Confession and Communion.* Dublin: The Catholic Book Society, 1832

The Pocket Missal; or, Companion to the Altar, for All the Sundays, the Holydays, the Days of Devotion, &c. &c. Throughout the Year. Cork: James Haly, 1805.

The Poor Man's Manual of Devotions; or Devout Christian's Daily Companion, Containing Morning and Evening Prayer, Devotions for Sundays and Holydays, the Thirty Days' Prayer, Prayers at Mass, Prayers Before and After Confession and Communion, the Seven Penitential Psalms, the Psalter, Rosary and Litanies of Jesus; the Rosary and Litanies of the Blessed Virgin; Prayers of St. Bridget; Prayers and Litanies for the Sick; Prayers and Litanies for the Dead, with Several other Approved Devotions. To which are added, the Vespers in Latin and English. Belfast: Thomas Mairs and Co., 1818.

The Poor Man's Manual of Devotions; or the Devout Christian's Daily Companion Containing Morning and Evening Prayer, Devotions for Sundays and Holydays, Prayers at Mass, the Thirty Days' Prayer, Prayers Before and After Confession and Communion, the Seven Penitential Psalms, the Psalter, the Rosaries and Litanies; with Many other Approved Devotions. To which are added, the Vespers in Latin and English. Kilkenny: T. Shearman, n.d. [ca. 1839].

Ravenstein, E. G. "On the Celtic Languages in the British Isles: A Statistical Survey." *Journal of the Royal Statistical Society* 42, no. 3 (1879): 579–643.

R. D. *A Visit to the Wild West, or a Sketch of the Emerald Isles, Picturesque and Political, during the Past Autumn.* London: G. W. Nickisson, 1843.

Redpath, James. *Talks about Ireland.* New York: P. J. Kenedy, 1881.

Report of the Dingle and Ventry Mission Association, County of Kerry, Ireland, for the Year Ending First December 1848. Dublin: Purdon Brothers, 1849.

Richardson, John. *A Proposal for the Conversion of the Popish Natives of Ireland to the Established Religion, with the Reasons Upon which It is Grounded, and an Answer to the Objections Made to It.* 2nd ed. London: J. Downing, 1712.

———. *Seanmora ar na Priom Phoncibh na Chreideamh ar na Ttaruing go Gaidhlig, agus ar na Ccur a Ccló a Lunndain Tre Ebhlin Everingham.* London: Elinor Everingham, 1711.

———. *A Short History of the Attempts That Have Been Made to Convert the Popish Natives of Ireland, to the Established Religion: with a Proposal for their Conversion.* London: Joseph Downing, 1712.

Robbins, N. *An Exact Abridgment of All the Irish Statutes, from the First Session of Parliament in the Third Year of the Reign of King Edward II to the End of the Eighth Year of His Present Majesty King George II, Together with an Abridgment of All the English Statutes, in Force in Ireland, from Magna Charta to the End of the Eighth Year of His Present Majesty King George II.* Dublin: George Grierson, 1736.

Rochford, Robert. *The Life of the Glorious Bishop S. Patricke, Apostle and Primate of Ireland.* St. Omer's: John Heigham, 1625.

Rodenberg, Julius. *The Island of Saints: A Pilgrimage through Ireland.* Translated by Lascelles Wraxall. London: Chapman and Hall, 1861.

The Roman Missal for the Use of the Laity, Containing the Mass, with the Introit, Collect, Epistle, Gospel, &c. for Every Day Throughout the Year. Dublin: R. Coyne, 1832.

Rooper, George. *A Month in Mayo, Comprising Characteristic Sketches (Sporting and Social) of Irish Life, with Miscellaneous Papers.* London: Robert Hardwicke, 1876.

Rossa, Jeremiah O'Donovan. *Rossa's Recollections. 1838 to 1898. Childhood, Boyhood, Manhood. Customs, Habits, and Manners of the Irish People.* New York: Mariner's Harbor, 1898.

Runnington, Charles. *The History of the Common Law by Sir Matthew Hale, Knt.* 4th ed. Dublin: James Moore, 1792.

———. *The History of the Common Law of England; and, an Analysis of the Civil Part of the Law.* 6th ed. London: Henry Butterworth, 1820.

Sankey, W. S. *A Brief Sketch of Various Attempts which Have Been Made to Diffuse a Knowledge of the Holy Scriptures through the Medium of the Irish Language.* Dublin: Graisberry and Campbell, 1818.

Scurry, James [Séamus Ó Scoireadh]. *Remarks on the Irish Language, with a Review of Its Grammars, Glossaries, Vocabularies and Dictionaries. To which is Added, a Model of a Comprehensive Irish Dictionary*. Dublin: Graisberry, 1827.

Shand, Alexander Innes. *Letters from the West of Ireland, 1884*. London: William Blackwood and Sons, 1885.

Sheridan, Thomas. *British Education; or, the Source of the Disorders of Great Britain*. Dublin: George Faulkner, 1756.

Society for the Preservation of the Irish Language. *Annual Reports*. Dublin: Society for the Preservation of the Irish Language, 1879–1914.

———. *Report of the Proceedings of the Congress Held in Dublin, 15th–17th August 1882*. Dublin: Society for the Preservation of the Irish Language, 1884.

Spellissy, Michael Denis. *The Life of John Murphy, Priest and Patriot*. Dublin: M. H. Gill & Son, 1880.

Stapletonium, Theobaldum [Theobald Stapleton]. *Catechismus, Seu Doctrina Christiana, Latino-Hibernica, Per Modum Dialogi, Inter Magistrum et Discipulum*. Bruxelles: Huberti Anthonii, 1639.

Statuta Synodalia pro Unitis Dioecesibus Cassel et Imelac: Lecta, Approbata, Edita, et Promulgata in Synodo Dioecesana. 2 vols. Dublin: H. Fitzpatrick, 1813.

The Statutes at Large, Passed in the Parliaments Held in Ireland. 21 vols. Dublin: George Grierson, 1786–1804.

The Statutes of the United Kingdom of Great Britain and Ireland. 63 vols. London: Crown Statute and Law Printers and J. Butterworth, 1807–1869.

Stokes, Whitley, ed. *Lives of Saints from the Book of Lismore*. Oxford: Clarendon Press, 1890.

———. *Projects for Re-Establishing the Internal Peace and Tranquility of Ireland*. Dublin: James Moore, 1799.

———. *Seanraite Sholaim a Ghaoidheilge agus mBearla. The Proverbs of Solomon, in Irish and English*. Dublin: Graisberry and Cambell, 1815.

The Synodical Address of the Fathers of the National Council of Thurles to Their Beloved Flock, the Catholics of Ireland. Dublin: J. Q. Maguire, 1850.

"Taheitian and Irish Spelling Books." *The Eclectic Review* 6 (May 1810): 417–21.

Taylor, John Pitt. *A Treatise on the Law of Evidence, as Administered in England and Ireland, with Illustrations from Scotch, Indian, American, and Other Legal Systems*. 9th ed. 2 vols. London: Sweet and Maxwell, 1895.

———. *A Treatise on the Law of Evidence, as Administered in England and Ireland, with Illustrations from Scotch, Indian, American, and Other Legal Systems*. 10th ed. 2 vols. London: Sweet and Maxwell, 1906.

———. *A Treatise on the Law of Evidence, as Administered in England and Ireland; with Illustrations from the American and Other Foreign Laws*. 2nd ed. 2 vols. London: W. Maxwell, 1855.

Thompson, Robert. *Statistical Survey of the County of Meath, with Observations on the Means of Improvement, Drawn Up for the Consideration, and Under the Direction of the Dublin Society*. Dublin: Graisberry and Campbell, 1802.

Tighe, William. *Statistical Observations Relative to the County of Kilkenny, Made in the Years 1800 & 1801*. Dublin: Graisberry and Campbell, 1802.

Tomlins, Thomas Edlyne, et al., eds. *The Statutes of the United Kingdom of Great Britain and Ireland*. 29 vols. London: George Eyre, Andrew Strahan, and Andrew Spottiswoode, Printers to the King, 1804–69.

Townsend, Horatio. *Statistical Survey of the County of Cork, with Observations on the Means of Improvement; Drawn up for the Consideration, and by Direction of the Dublin Society*. Dublin: Graisberry and Campbell, 1810.

Transactions of the Gaelic Society of Dublin, Established for the Investigation and Revival of Ancient Irish Literature. Dublin: John Barlow, 1808.

Transactions of the Ossianic Society. 6 vols. Dublin: Printed by the Council, 1854–60.

Trench, W. Steuart. *Realities of Irish Life*. London: Longmans, Green, 1868.

Turas na Croiche agus an Chóroin Mhuire, Maille le Dántaibh Diadha, Faoi Chúram Phádraic Ui Dhomhnaill, Easboc Ratha-Bhoth. Baile Átha Cliath: M. H. Gill & a Mhac, 1902.

Twiss, Richard. *A Tour in Ireland in 1775. With a Map, and a View of the Salmon-Leap at Ballyshannon*. London: Richard Twiss and J. Robson, 1776.

[Uí / Ua—*see* Ó]

Vallancey, Charles. *A Grammar of the Iberno-Celtic, or Irish Language*. Dublin: R. Marchbank, 1773.

Wakefield, Edward. *An Account of Ireland, Statistical and Political*. 2 vols. London: Longman, Hurst, Rees, Orme, and Brown, 1812.

Weld, Charles Richard. *Vacations in Ireland*. London: Longman, Brown, Green, Longmans, and Robert, 1857.

Weld, Isaac. *Statistical Survey of the County of Roscommon, Drawn up under the Direction of the Royal Dublin Society*. Dublin: R. Graisberry, 1832.

Whately, Richard. *Easy Lessons on Money Matters, Commerce, Trade, Wages, etc. etc. for the Use of Young People, as Well as Adults, of All Classes. Further Enlarged by Thaddaeus Connellan, Author and Publisher of the Works Mentioned in Pages v, vi*. Dublin: R. Graisberry, 1835.

Wilde, William R. *Irish Popular Superstitions*. Dublin: James McGlashan, 1852. Repr., Totowa, NJ: Rowman and Littlefield, 1973.

Windele, John. *Hand Book to Killarney, through Bantry, Glengariff, and Kenmare*. 2nd ed. Cork: Messrs. Bolster, 1844.

———. "Present Extent of the Irish Language." *Ulster Journal of Archaeology* 5 (1857): 243–45.

Wood-Martin, W. G. *Traces of the Elder Faiths of Ireland: A Folklore Sketch*. London: Longmans, Green, 1902.

Wright, Thomas, ed. *The Latin Poems Commonly Attributed to Walter Mapes*. London: Camden Society, 1841.

———, ed. *A Selection of Latin Stories from Manuscripts of the Thirteenth and Fourteenth Centuries*. London: Percy Society, 1842.

[Young, Ursula]. *A Sketch of Irish History, Compiled by Way of Question & Answer, for the Use of Schools*. Cork: J. Geary, 1815.

Secondary Sources

Aalen, F. H. A. *Man and the Landscape in Ireland.* London: Academic Press, 1978.

Aarne, Antti, and Stith Thompson. *The Types of the Folktale: A Classification and Bibliography.* FF Communications No. 184. 2nd rev. ed. Helsinki: Suomalainen Tiedeakatemia, 1961.

Aarsleff, Hans. "The Rise and Decline of Adam and his *Ursprache* in Seventeenth-Century Thought." In *The Language of Adam/Die Sprache Adams: Proceedings of a Conference Held at the Herzon August Bibliothek, Wolfenbüttel, May 30–31, 1995,* edited by Allison P. Coudert, 277–95. Wiesbaden: Harrassowitz, 1999.

Abbott, T. K., and E. J. Gwynn. *Catalogue of the Irish Manuscripts in the Library of Trinity College, Dublin.* Dublin: Hodges, Figgis, & Co., 1921.

Adams, G. B. "Language Census Problems, 1851–1911." *Ulster Folklife* 21 (1975): 68–73.

———. "Language in Ulster, 1820–1850." *Ulster Folklife* 19 (1973): 50–55.

———. "The Validity of Language Census Figures in Ulster, 1851–1911." *Ulster Folklife* 25 (1979): 113–22.

Adams, J. R. R. "Swine-Tax and Eat-Him-All-Magee: The Hedge Schools and Popular Education in Ireland." In *Irish Popular Culture, 1650–1850,* edited by James S. Donnelly, Jr., and Kerby A. Miller, 97–117. Dublin: Irish Academic Press, 1999.

Agnew, John A. "Language Shift and the Politics of Language: The Case of the Celtic Languages in the British Isles." *Language Problems and Language Planning* 5, no. 1 (1981): 1–10.

Ahlqvist, Anders. *The Early Irish Linguist: An Edition of the Canonical Part of the Auraicept na nÉces, with Introduction, Commentary and Indices.* Helsinki: Societas Scientiarum Fennica, 1983.

Aiken, Riley. "Fifteen Mexican Tales." *Publications of the Texas Folklore Society* 32 (1964): 3–56.

Ainsworth, John. "Two Letters from the Eneas McDonnell Mss." *Archivium Hibernicum* 31 (1973): 95–101.

Akenson, Donald. *The Church of Ireland: Ecclesiastical Reform and Revolution, 1800–1885.* New Haven, CT: Yale University Press, 1971.

———. *The Irish Education Experiment: The National System of Education in the Nineteenth Century.* London: Routledge and Kegan Paul, 1970.

Allison, A. F., and D. M. Rogers. *A Catalogue of Catholic Books in English Printed Abroad or Secretly in England, 1558–1640.* 2 vols. 1956. Repr., London: Wm. Dawson & Sons, 1964.

Almqvist, Bo, and Roibeard Ó Cathasaigh. "'Sólás agus Leigheas ins Gach Aon Tri-oblóid': Paidreacha agus Orthaí ó Bhab Feiritéar." *Béaloideas* 73 (2005): 135–45.

Andrews, J. A., and L. G. Henshaw. "The Irish and Welsh Languages in the Courts: A Comparative Study." *The Irish Jurist* 18 (1983): 1–22.

Andrews, J. H. "More Suitable to the English Tongue: The Cartography of Celtic Placenames." *Ulster Local Studies* 14, no. 2 (1992): 7–21.

———. *A Paper Landscape: The Ordnance Survey in Nineteenth-Century Ireland.* Oxford: Clarendon Press, 1975.

[Anon.] "The Irish Language in Inishowen." *Donegal Annual* 45 (1993): 29–42.
Arensberg, Conrad M., and Solon T. Kimball. *Family and Community in Ireland*. Cambridge, MA: Harvard University Press, 1968.
Arrowood, Charles F. "There's a Geography of Humorous Anecdotes." *Texas Folk-Lore Studies Publication* 15 (1939): 75–84.
Asbjørnsen, Peter Christen, and Jørgen Moe. *Norwegian Folk Tales*. Translated by Pat Shaw and Carl Norman. Oslo: Dreyers Forlag, 1960.
Ashliman, D. L. *A Guide to Folktales in the English Language Based on the Aarne-Thompson Classification System*. New York: Greenwood Press, 1987.
Atkinson, Norman. *Irish Education: A History of Educational Institutions*. Dublin: Allen Figgis, 1969.
Auer, Peter. "A Postscript: Code-Switching and Social Identity." *Journal of Pragmatics* 37 (2005): 403–10.
Ayres, Alyssa. *Speaking Like a State: Language and Nationalism in Pakistan*. Cambridge: Cambridge University Press, 2009.
Baer, Friederike. *The Trial of Frederick Eberle: Language, Patriotism, and Citizenship in Philadelphia's German Community, 1790–1830*. New York: New York University Press, 2008.
Bailey, Richard W. "The Ideology of English in the Long Eighteenth Century." *Linguistic Insights—Studies in Language and Communication* 7 (2003): 21–44.
Bane, Liam. "Bishop John MacEvilly and the Catholic Church in Late Nineteenth Century Galway." In *Galway: History and Society; Interdisciplinary Essays on the History of an Irish County*, edited by Gerard Moran and Raymond Gillespie, 421–44. Dublin: Geography Publications, 1996.
Barber, Sarah. "Irish Migrant Agricultural Labourers in Nineteenth-Century Lincolnshire." *Saothar* 8 (1982): 10–23.
Barker, W. H., and Cecilia Sinclair. *West African Folk-Tales*. Northbrook, IL: Metro Books, 1972.
Barron, Milton L. "A Content Analysis of Intergroup Humor." *American Sociological Review* 15, no. 1 (1950): 88–94.
Barry, Kevin. "Critical Notes on Post-Colonial Aesthetics." *Irish Studies Review* 14 (1996): 2–11.
Bartlett, Thomas. *The Rise and Fall of the Irish Nation: The Catholic Question, 1690–1830*. Savage, MD: Barnes and Noble Books, 1992.
Baughman, Ernest. *Type and Motif-Index of the Folktales of England and North America*. Folklore Series Number 20. Bloomington: University of Indiana Press, 1966.
Bayly, C. A. *Empire and Information: Intelligence Gathering and Social Communication in India, 1780–1870*. Cambridge: Cambridge University Press, 1996.
Beames, Michael. *Peasants and Power: The Whiteboy Movements and Their Control in Pre-Famine Ireland*. New York: St. Martin's Press and Sussex: The Harvester Press, 1983.
Beecher, Seán. *An Ghaeilge in Cork City: An Historical Perspective to 1894*. Cork: Goldy Angel Press, 1993.
Bell, David. "Lingua Populi, Lingua Dei: Language, Religion, and the Origins of French Revolutionary Nationalism." *American Historical Review* 100, no. 5 (1995): 1403–37.

———. "The Unbearable Lightness of Being French: Law, Republicanism, and National Identity at the End of the Old Regime." *American Historical Review* 106, no. 4 (2001): 1215–35.

Ben-Amos, Dan. "The Myth of Jewish Humor." *Western Folklore* 32, no. 2 (Apr. 1973): 112–31.

Bergin, Osborn, ed. "Irish Grammatical Tracts." *Ériu* 8 (1916): i–60.

———. *Trí Bior-Ghaoithe an Bháis.* 2nd ed. Dublin: Hodges, Figgis, & Co., 1931.

Birch, Peter. *St. Kieran's College, Kilkenny.* Dublin: M. H. Gill and Son, 1951.

Black, Ronald. "Four O'Daly Manuscripts." *Éigse* 26 (1992): 43–79.

Blaney, Roger. *Presbyterians and the Irish Language.* Belfast: Ulster Historical Foundation and The Ultach Trust, 1996.

Blom, Franz, et al. *English Catholic Books 1701–1800: A Bibliography.* Aldershot, UK: Scolar Press, 1996.

Boltúin, Antoine. "Mac Héil agus an Ghaeilge: a Shaothar agus a Dhearcadh." PhD diss., National University of Ireland, Galway, 1992.

Bossy, John. *The English Catholic Community, 1570–1850.* Oxford: Oxford University Press, 1976.

Bossy, Michel-André. "Medieval Debates of Body and Soul." *Comparative Literature* 28, no. 2 (Spring 1976): 144–63.

Bourke, Angela. *The Burning of Bridget Cleary.* New York: Penguin, 1999.

Bourke, Joanna. *Husbandry to Housewifery: Women, Economic Change, and Housework in Ireland, 1890–1914.* Oxford: Clarendon Press, 1993.

Boyce, D. George, and Alan O'Day, eds. *The Making of Modern Irish History: Revisionism and the Revisionist Controversy.* London: Routledge, 1996.

Boyd, Elizabeth F. "James Joyce's Hell-Fire Sermons." *Modern Language Notes* 75, no. 7 (Nov. 1960): 561–71.

Boyne, Patricia. *John O'Donovan: A Biography.* Kilkenny: Boethius, 1987.

Bradshaw, Brendan, and Dáire Keogh, eds. *Christianity in Ireland: Revisiting the Story.* Dublin: Columba Press, 2002.

Brady, Ciaran, ed. *Interpreting Irish History: The Debate on Historical Revisionism.* Dublin: Irish Academic Press, 1994.

Brady, John. "Catholics and Catholicism in the Eighteenth-Century Press." *Archivium Hibernicum* 20 (1957): 273–304.

———. "The Irish Colleges in the Low Countries." *Archivium Hibernicum* 14 (1949): 66–91.

———. "Irish Interpreters at Meath Assizes." *Ríocht na Midhe. Records of the Meath Archaeological and Historical Society* 2, no. 1 (1959): 62–63.

———. "Prayers before Mass on Sundays and Holydays in Ireland." *Irish Ecclesiastical Record*, ser. 5, vol. 69 (1947): 657–67.

Breathnach, Ciara, and Catherine Lawless, eds. *Visual, Material and Print Culture in Nineteenth-Century Ireland.* Dublin: Four Courts Press, 2010.

Breathnach, Pól, ed. *Seanmóirí Muighe Nuadhadh.* 4 vols. Baile Átha Cliath: Muinntir Ghoill, 1906–11.

Breatnach, Pádraig A. "Meascra ar an Saol in Éirinn, 1841–44." *Éigse* 25 (1991): 105–12.

Breatnach, R. A. "Two Eighteenth-Century Irish Scholars: J.C. Walker and Charlotte Brooke." *Studia Hibernica* 5 (1965): 88–97.
Brenan, Martin. *The Confraternity of Christian Doctrine in Ireland: A.D. 1775–1835*. Dublin: Browne and Nolan, 1934.
Brewster, Paul. "Folk-Tales from Indiana and Missouri." *Folk-Lore* 50, no. 3 (1939): 294–310.
Briggs, Katharine. *A Dictionary of British Folk-Tales in the English Language*. 2 vols. London: Routledge and Kegan Paul, 1970.
Brihault, Jean, ed. *L'Irlande et ses langues: Actes du colloque 1992 de la Société Française d'Études Irlandaises*. Rennes: Presses Universitaires Rennes, 1992.
Brockliss, Laurence, and David Eastwood, eds. *A Union of Multiple Identities: The British Isles, c. 1750–c. 1850*. Manchester: Manchester University Press, 1997.
Brody, Hugh. *Inishkillane: Change and Decline in the West of Ireland*. London: Allen Lane, 1973.
Brown, Thomas N. "Nationalism and the Irish Peasant, 1800–1848." *Review of Politics* 15 (1953): 403–45.
Bruford, Alan. *Gaelic Folk-Tales and Mediaeval Romances*. Dublin: Folklore of Ireland Society, 1969.
Buckley, J. "Timothy O'Callaghan, A Cork Lithographer." *Journal of the Cork Historical and Archaeological Society* 41 (1936): 54.
Burke, Peter. "Introduction." In *The Social History of Language*, edited by Peter Burke and Roy Porter, 1–20. Cambridge: Cambridge University Press, 1987.
——. *Languages and Communities in Early Modern Europe*. Cambridge: Cambridge University Press, 2004.
Burke, Peter, and Roy Porter, eds. *The Social History of Language*. Cambridge: Cambridge University Press, 1987.
Burke, William P., ed. *The Irish Priests in the Penal Times (1660–1760)*. Shannon: Irish University Press, 1969.
Buttimer, Cornelius G. *Catalogue of Irish Manuscripts in the University of Wisconsin-Madison*. Dublin: Dublin Institute for Advanced Studies, 1989.
——. "Celtic and Irish in College, 1849–1944." *Journal of the Cork Historical and Archaeological Society* 94 (1989): 88–112.
——. "Cogadh Sagsana Nuadh Sonn: Reporting the American Revolution." *Studia Hibernica* 28 (1994): 63–101.
——. "A Cork Gaelic Text on a Napoleonic Campaign." *Journal of the Cork Historical and Archaeological Society* 95, no. 254 (1990): 107–19.
——. "The French Sources of Religious Teaching in Pre-Famine Gaelic Ireland." In *Transactions of the Eighth International Congress on the Enlightenment*, 620–24. Oxford: Voltaire Foundation, 1992.
——. "Gaelic Literature and Contemporary Life in Cork, 1700–1840." In *Cork: History and Society; Interdisciplinary Essays on the History of an Irish County*, edited by Cornelius Buttimer, Patrick O'Flanagan, and Gerard O'Brien, 585–653. Dublin: Geography Publications, 1993.

———. "A Gaelic Reaction to Robert Emmet's Rebellion." *Journal of the Cork Historical and Archaeological Society* 97 (1992): 36–53.

———. "An Irish Text on the 'War of Jenkins' Ear.'" *Celtica* 21 (1990): 75–98.

Cahill, Edward. "The Irish Language in the Penal Era." *Irish Ecclesiastical Record* 55 (1940): 591–617.

Calder, George, ed. *Auraicept na n-Éces. The Scholars' Primer*. Edinburgh: John Grant, 1917.

Cameron, Deborah. "Demythologizing Sociolinguistics: Why Language Does Not Reflect Society." In *Ideologies of Language*, edited by John E. Joseph and Talbot J. Taylor, 79–93. London: Routledge, 1990.

Canny, Nicholas. "Writing Early Modern History: Ireland, Britain, and the Wider World." *Historical Journal* 46, no. 3 (Sept. 2003): 723–47.

Caomhánach, Aodh P. "Na Bráithre Críostaí agus an Ghaeilge." In *Gníomhartha na mBráithre*, edited by Micheál Ó Cearúil, 123–56. Baile Átha Cliath: Coiscéim, 1996.

Carey, John. "Native Elements in Irish Pseudohistory." In *Cultural Identity and Cultural Integration: Ireland and Europe in the Early Middle Ages*, edited by Doris Edel, 45–60. Dublin: Four Courts Press, 1995.

———. *A New Introduction to Lebor Gabála Érenn: The Book of the Taking of Ireland*. 1993. Repr., Dublin: Irish Texts Society, 2006.

Carpenter, Andrew, ed. *Verse in English from Eighteenth-Century Ireland*. Cork: Cork University Press, 1998.

Carpenter, Inta Gale. *A Latvian Storyteller: The Repertoire of Jānis Pļavnieks*. New York: Arno Press, 1980.

Carroll, Clare. *Circe's Cup: Cultural Transformations in Early Modern Writing about Ireland*. Notre Dame, IN: University of Notre Dame Press, 2002.

Carroll, Clare, and Patricia King, eds. *Ireland and Postcolonial Theory*. Notre Dame, IN: University of Notre Dame Press, 2003.

Casey, Daniel, and Robert Rhodes, eds. *Views of the Irish Peasantry, 1800–1916*. Hamden, CT: Archon Books, 1977.

Cassell, Ronald D. *Medical Charities, Medical Politics: The Irish Dispensary System and the Poor Law, 1836–1872*. Suffolk, UK: The Boydell Press, 1997.

Cave, Terence C. *Devotional Poetry in France c. 1570–1613*. Cambridge: Cambridge University Press, 1969.

Chatterjee, Partha. *The Nation and Its Fragments: Colonial and Postcolonial Histories*. Princeton, NJ: Princeton University Press, 1993.

Chlopicki, Wladyslaw. "Review Article: *The Mirth of Nations*." *Humor* 16, no. 4 (2003): 415–24.

Clancy, Thomas H. *English Catholic Books, 1641–1700: A Bibliography*. Brookfield, VT: Ashgate, 1996.

Clark, Samuel, and James S. Donnelly, Jr., eds. *Irish Peasants: Violence and Political Unrest, 1780–1914*. Madison: University of Wisconsin Press, 1983.

Clark, William Smith. *The Irish Stage in the County Towns, 1720–1800*. Oxford: Clarendon Press, 1965.

Claude, M. *Calendar of the Papers of Dr. T. Bray, Archbishop of Cashel and Emly, 1792–1820*. Thurles: Diocesan Archives: 1966.
Cleary, Joe, and Claire Connolly, eds. *The Cambridge Companion to Modern Irish Culture*. Cambridge: Cambridge University Press, 2005.
Clifford, James. *The Predicament of Culture: Twentieth-Century Ethnography, Literature, and Art*. Cambridge, MA: Harvard University Press, 1988.
Cohn, Bernard S. *Colonialism and Its Forms of Knowledge: The British in India*. Princeton, NJ: Princeton University Press 1996.
Coleman, Michael. "'Eyes Big as Bowls with Fear and Wonder': Children's Responses to the Irish National Schools, 1850–1922." *Proceedings of the Royal Irish Academy*, Section C, 98 (1998): 177–202.
Collins, Kevin. *Catholic Churchmen and the Celtic Revival, 1848–1916*. Dublin: Four Courts Press, 2002.
Comerford, R. V. "Ireland, 1850–70: Post-Famine and Mid-Victorian." In *A New History of Ireland*, vol. 5, *Ireland under the Union, Part I, 1801–70*, edited by W. E. Vaughan, 372–95. Oxford: Clarendon Press, 1989.
Comyn, David, and Patrick S. Dinneen, eds. *Foras Feasa ar Éirinn le Seathrún Céitinn, D.D./The History of Ireland by Geoffrey Keating, D.D.* 4 vols. Irish Texts Society vols. 4, 8–9, 15. London: Irish Texts Society, 1902, 1908, 1914.
Condún, Treasa. "Purgadóir Phádraig Naomhtha." *Lia Fáil* 1 (1924): 1–48.
Conley, Carolyn A. *Melancholy Accidents: The Meaning of Violence in Post-Famine Ireland*. Langham, MD: Lexington Books, 1999.
Connell, K. H. *Irish Peasant Society: Four Historical Essays*. 1968. Repr., Dublin: Irish Academic Press, 1996.
Connell, Paul. *Parson, Priest, and Master: National Education in Co. Meath, 1824–41*. Maynooth Series in Local History 1. Dublin: Irish Academic Press, 1995.
Connolly, Sean. "Popular Culture: Patterns of Change and Adaptation." In *Conflict, Identity, and Economic Development: Ireland and Scotland, 1600–1939*, edited by Sean Connolly et al., 104–13. Preston, UK: Carnegie Publishing, 1995.
———. *Priests and People in Pre-Famine Ireland, 1780–1845*. 2nd ed. Dublin: Four Courts Press, 2001.
Connolly, Sean, R. A. Houston, and R. J. Morris, eds. *Conflict, Identity and Economic Development: Ireland and Scotland, 1600–1939*. Preston, UK: Carnegie Publishing, 1995.
Cook, S. B. *Imperial Affinities: Nineteenth-Century Analogies and Exchanges between India and Ireland*. New Delhi: Sage Publications, 1993.
Coolahan, John. "Education as Cultural Imperialism: The Denial of the Irish Language to Irish Speakers, 1831–1922." *Paedagogica Historica* 37, no. 1 (2001): 17–33.
Coolahan, John, with Patrick F. O'Donovan. *A History of Ireland's School Inspectorate, 1831–2008*. Dublin: Four Courts Press, 2009.
Corcoran, Timothy. "The Irish Language in the Irish Schools." *Studies* 14 (Sept. 1925): 377–88.
Corish, Patrick J. *The Catholic Community in the Seventeenth and Eighteenth Centuries*. Dublin: Helicon Limited, 1981.

---. *The Irish Catholic Experience: A Historical Survey.* Dublin: Gill and Macmillan, 1985.

---. *Maynooth College, 1795-1995.* Dublin: Gill and Macmillan, 1995.

Corkery, Daniel. *The Fortunes of the Irish Language.* 1954. Repr., Cork: Mercier Press, 1956.

---. *The Hidden Ireland: A Study of Gaelic Munster in the Eighteenth Century.* 1924. Repr., Dublin: Gill and Macmillan, 1967.

Cornips, Leonie. "Loosing Grammatical Gender in Dutch: The Result of Bilingual Acquisition and/or an Act of Identity?" *International Journal of Bilingualism* 12, nos. 1-2 (2008): 105-24.

Corrigan, Karen P. "'For God's Sake, Teach the Children English': Emigration and the Irish Language in the Nineteenth Century." In *The Irish World Wide: The Irish in the New Communities*, edited by Patrick O'Sullivan, 143-61. New York: St. Martin's Press, 1992.

Costello, Nuala. *John MacHale, Archbishop of Tuam.* Dublin: Talbot Press, 1939.

Costello, Peter. *Clongowes Wood: A History of Clongowes Wood College, 1814-1989.* Dublin: Gill and Macmillan, 1989.

Cousins, Mel. "Poor Law Politics and Elections in Post-Famine Ireland." *History Studies: University of Limerick History Society Journal* 6 (2005): 34-47.

Crawford, E. Margaret. *Counting the People: A Survey of Irish Censuses, 1813-1911.* Dublin: Four Courts Press, 2003.

Cronin, Anne. "The Sources of Keating's Forus Feasa ar Éirinn." *Éigse* 5 (1945-47): 122-35.

Cronin, Michael. "Brollach." In *Aistriú Éireann*, edited by Charles Dillon and Ríona Ní Fhrighil, ix-xi. Béal Feirste: Cló Ollscoil na Banríona, 2008.

---. "Rug-Headed Kerns Speaking Tongues: Shakespeare, Translation, and the Irish Language." In *Shakespeare and Ireland: History, Politics, Culture*, edited by Mark Thornton Burnett and Ramona Wray, 193-212. London: Macmillan Press, 1997.

---. *Translating Ireland: Translation, Languages, Cultures.* Cork: Cork University Press, 1996.

Cronin, Nessa, Seán Crosson, and John Eastlake, eds. *Anáil an Bhéil Bheo: Orality and Modern Irish Culture.* Newcastle, UK: Cambridge Scholars Publishing, 2009.

Cross, Tom Peete. *Motif-Index of Early Irish Literature.* Bloomington: University of Indiana Press, 1969.

Crossman, Virginia. *Local Government in Nineteenth-Century Ireland.* Belfast: The Institute of Irish Studies, The Queen's University of Belfast, for the Ulster Society of Irish Historical Studies, 1994.

---. "The New Ross Workhouse Riot of 1887: Nationalism, Class, and the Irish Poor Laws." *Past and Present* 179 (May 2003): 135-58.

Crowley, Tony. *Language in History: Theories and Texts.* London: Routledge, 1996.

---. *The Politics of Language in Ireland, 1366-1922: A Sourcebook.* London: Routledge, 2000.

---. *Standard English and the Politics of Language.* Urbana: University of Illinois Press, 1989.

———. *Wars of Words: The Politics of Language in Ireland, 1537–2004*. Oxford: Oxford University Press, 2005.

Crystal, David. *Language Death*. Cambridge: Cambridge University Press, 2000.

Cullen, Louis M. "Catholics Under the Penal Laws." *Eighteenth-Century Ireland/Iris an Dá Chultúr* 1 (1986): 23–36.

———. *The Emergence of Modern Ireland, 1600–1900*. New York: Holmes and Meier Publishers, 1981.

———. "The Hidden Ireland: Reassessment of a Concept." *Studia Hibernica* 9 (1969): 7–47.

———. *The Hidden Ireland: Reassessment of a Concept*. Mullingar: Lilliput Press, 1988.

———. "The Regions and Their Issues: Ireland." In *The Victorian Countryside*, vol. 1, edited by G. E. Mingay, 94–102. London: Routledge and Kegan Paul, 1981.

Cunningham, Bernadette. "Loss and Gain: Attitudes towards the English Language in Early Modern Ireland." In *Reshaping Ireland, 1550–1700: Colonization and Its Consequences; Essays Presented to Nicholas Canny*, ed. Brian Mac Cuarta, 163–86. Dublin: Four Courts Press, 2011.

———. *The World of Geoffrey Keating: History, Myth, and Religion in Seventeenth-Century Ireland*. Dublin: Four Courts Press, 2004.

Cunningham, Bernadette, and Raymond Gillespie. "'The Most Adaptable of Saints': The Cult of St. Patrick in the Seventeenth Century." *Archivium Hibernicum* 49 (1995): 82–104.

Cunningham, John. *St. Jarlath's College, Tuam, 1800–2000*. Tuam: SJC Publications, 1999.

Curtis, L. Perry, Jr. *Apes and Angels: The Irishman in Victorian Caricature*. Rev. ed. Washington, DC: Smithsonian Institution Press, 1997.

d'Alton, Ian. *Protestant Society and Politics in Cork, 1812–44*. Cork: Cork University Press, 1980.

Daly, Mary. "The Development of the National School System, 1831–40." In *Studies in Irish History Presented to R. Dudley Edwards*, edited by Art Cosgrove and Donal McCartney, 150–63. Dublin: University College Dublin, 1979.

———. *Dublin, the Deposed Capital: A Social and Economic History, 1860–1914*. Cork: Cork University Press, 1984.

———. "Literacy and Language Change in the Late Nineteenth and Early Twentieth Centuries." In *The Origins of Popular Literacy in Ireland: Language Change and Educational Development, 1700–1920*, edited by Mary Daly and David Dickson, 153–66. Dublin: Tony Moreau, 1990.

Daly, Mary, and David Dickson, eds. *The Origins of Popular Literacy in Ireland: Language Change and Educational Development, 1700–1920*. Dublin: Tony Moreau, 1990.

Davies, Christie. *Ethnic Humor around the World: A Comparative Analysis*. Bloomington: University of Indiana Press, 1990.

———. "European Ethnic Scripts and the Translation and Switching of Jokes." *Humor* 18, no. 2 (2005): 147–60.

———. "Exploring the Thesis of the Self-Deprecating Jewish Sense of Humor." *Humor* 4, no. 2 (1991): 189–209.

———. *The Mirth of Nations.* New Brunswick, NJ: Transaction Publishers, 2002.
Dawson, Ciarán. *Peadar Ó Gealacáin: Scríobhaí.* Baile Átha Cliath: An Clóchomhar Tta, 1992.
Day, Angélique, and Patrick McWilliams, eds. *Ordnance Survey Memoirs of Ireland.* Vol. 38, *Parishes of County Donegal I.* Belfast: Institute of Irish Studies, 1997.
———, eds. *Ordnance Survey Memoirs of Ireland.* Vol. 39, *Parishes of County Donegal II.* Belfast: Institute of Irish Studies, 1997.
Day, Lal Behari. *Folk-Tales of Bengal.* London: Macmillan and Co., 1912.
Deane, Seamus. *Strange Country: Modernity and the Nationhood in Irish Writing since 1790.* Oxford: Oxford University Press, 1997.
de Bhaldraithe, Tomás. "Nóta ar na Guthaí Roimh Chonsain Áithride i n-Oirthear na Gaillimhe." *Éigse* 5 (1945–47): 59–60.
de Blacam, Aodh. "The Other Hidden Ireland." *Studies* 23, no. 91 (Sept. 1934): 439–54.
de Brún, Fionntán, ed. *Belfast and the Irish Language.* Dublin: Four Courts Press, 2006.
———. "Expressing the Nineteenth Century in Irish: The Poetry of Aodh Mac Domhnaill (1802–67)." *New Hibernia Review* 15, no. 1 (Spring 2011): 81–106.
———. "The Fadgies: An 'Irish-Speaking Colony' in Nineteenth-Century Belfast." In *Belfast and the Irish Language,* edited by Fionntán de Brún, 101–13. Dublin: Four Courts Press, 2006.
de Brún, Pádraig. *Catalogue of Irish Manuscripts in King's Inns Library Dublin.* Dublin: Dublin Institute for Advanced Studies, 1972.
———. *Clár Lámhscríbhinní Gaeilge Choláiste Ollscoile Chorcaí: Cnuasach Thorna.* 2 iml. Baile Átha Cliath: Cló Bhréanainn, 1967.
———. "Forógra do Ghaelaibh 1824." *Studia Hibernica* 12 (1972): 142–66.
———. "An Irish Class of 1845." *Éigse* 17 (1977–78): 214.
———. "Irish in Prisons, 1822." *Éigse* 17 (1977–78): 392.
———. "The Irish Society's Bible Teachers, 1818–22." *Éigse* 19, no. 2 (1983): 281–332.
———. *Lámhscríbhinní Gaeilge: Treoirliosta.* Baile Átha Cliath: Institiúid Ard-Léinn Bhaile Átha Cliath, 1988.
———. "Scriptural Instruction in Irish: A Controversy of 1830–31." In *Folia Gadelica: Essays Presented to R.A. Breathnach,* edited by Pádraig de Brún, 134–59. Cork: Cork University Press, 1983.
———. *Scriptural Instruction in the Vernacular: The Irish Society and Its Teachers, 1818–1827.* Dublin: Dublin Institute for Advanced Studies, 2009.
de Brún, Pádraig, and Máire Herbert. *Catalogue of Irish Manuscripts in Cambridge Libraries.* Cambridge: Cambridge University Press, 1986.
DeCaro, Rosan Jordan. "Language Loyalty and Folklore Studies: The Mexican-American." *Western Folklore* 31, no. 2 (Apr. 1972): 77–86.
de Certeau, Michel. *The Practice of Everyday Life.* Translated by Steven Rendall. Berkeley: University of California Press, 1988.
de Certeau, Michel, Dominique Julia, and Jacques Revel. *Une politique de la langue: La Révolution français et les patois.* Paris: Gallimard, 1975.
de Fréine, Seán. "An Gorta agus an Ghaeilge." In *Gnéithe den Ghorta,* edited by Cathal Póirtéir, 55–68. Dublin: Coiscéim, 1995.

———. *The Great Silence*. Dublin: Foilseacháin Náisiúnta Teoranta, 1965.
Delabastita, Dirk. "Cross-Language Comedy in Shakespeare." *Humor* 18, no. 2 (2005): 161–84.
Delay, Cara. "The Devotional Revolution on the Local Level: Parish Life in Post-Famine Ireland." *U.S. Catholic Historian* 22, no. 3 (2004): 41–60.
———. "The Fire of Devotion: Catholicism, Conflict, and Community Life in Rural Ireland, 1850–1920." PhD diss., Brandeis University, 2002.
Demangeon, A. "La situation linguistique et l'état économique de l'ouest Irlandais." *Annales de Géographie* 36 (1927): 169–73.
de Nie, Michael. *The Eternal Paddy: Irish Identity and the British Press, 1798–1882*. Madison: University of Wisconsin Press, 2004.
des Périers, Bonaventure. *Nouvelles récréations et joyeux devis, I–XC*. Edited by Krystyna Kasprzyk. Paris: Librairie Honoré Champion, 1980.
Dickson, David. *Old World Colony: Cork and South Munster 1630–1830*. Madison: University of Wisconsin Press, 2005.
Dickson, David, and Breandán Mac Suibhne. "Introduction." In Hugh Dorian, *The Outer Edge of Ulster: A Memoir of Social Life in Nineteenth-Century Donegal*, edited by Breandán Mac Suibhne and David Dickson, 1–56. Notre Dame, IN: University of Notre Dame Press, 2001.
Dictionary of the Irish Language, Based Mainly on Old and Middle Irish Materials. Dublin: Royal Irish Academy, 1913–76.
Dillon, Charles. "An Beatha Chrábhaidh: A 'Popular' Translation." *Revue LISA/LISA E-Journal* [Online] 3, no. 1 (2005), par. 12. http://lisa.revues.org/2462.
———. "*An Ghaeilig Nua*: English, Irish and the South Ulster Poets and Scribes in the Late Seventeenth and Eighteenth Centuries." In *Irish and English: Essays on the Irish Linguistic and Cultural Frontier, 1600–1900*, edited by James Kelly and Ciarán Mac Murchaidh, 141–61. Dublin: Four Courts Press, 2012.
Dillon, Charlie, and Ríona Ní Fhrighil, eds. *Aistriú Éireann*. Béal Feirste: Cló Ollscoil na Banríona, 2008.
Dillon, Myles, Canice Mooney, and Pádraig de Brún. *Catalogue of Irish Manuscripts in the Franciscan Library Killiney*. Dublin: Dublin Institute for Advanced Studies, 1969.
Dinneen, Patrick, ed. *Amhráin Eoghain Ruaidh Uí Shúilleabháin*. 2nd ed. Baile Átha Cliath: Connradh na Gaedhilge, 1902.
———. *Foclóir Gaedhilge agus Béarla: An Irish-English Dictionary*. New ed. Dublin: Irish Texts Society, 1996.
Dinneen, Patrick, and Tadhg O'Donoghue, eds. *Dánta Aodhagáin Uí Rathaille: The Poems of Egan O'Rahilly*. 2nd ed. Irish Texts Society vol. 3. London: Irish Texts Society, 1965.
Dodson, Michael S. *Orientalism, Empire, and National Culture: India, 1770–1880*. Houndsmills, UK: Palgrave Macmillan, 2007.
Doherty, Gillian. *The Irish Ordnance Survey: History, Culture, and Memory*. Dublin: Four Courts Press, 2004.
Doherty, James. "Joyce and *Hell Opened to Christians*: The Edition He Used for His 'Hell Sermons.'" *Modern Philology* 61, no. 2 (Nov. 1863): 110–19.

Donnelly, James S., Jr. *The Land and the People of Nineteenth-Century Cork: The Rural Economy and the Land Question*. London: Routledge and Kegan Paul, 1975.

———. "Lough Derg: The Making of the Modern Pilgrimage." In *Donegal: History and Society: Interdisciplinary Essays on the History of an Irish County*, edited by William Nolan et al., 491–508. Dublin: Geography Publications, 1995.

———. "The Marian Shrine of Knock: The First Decade." *Éire-Ireland* 28, no. 2 (Summer 1993): 54–97.

Donnelly, James S., Jr., and Kerby A. Miller, eds. *Irish Popular Culture, 1650–1850*. Dublin: Irish Academic Press, 1999.

Dorian, Hugh. *The Outer Edge of Ulster: A Memoir of Social Life in Nineteenth-Century Donegal*. Edited by Breandán Mac Suibhne and David Dickson. Notre Dame, IN: University of Notre Dame Press, 2001.

Dorian, Nancy C., ed. *Investigating Obsolescence: Studies in Language Contraction and Death*. Cambridge: Cambridge University Press, 1989.

———. *Language Death: The Life Cycle of a Scottish Gaelic Dialect*. Philadelphia: University of Pennsylvania Press, 1981.

Dorson, Richard M. *Buying the Wind*. 5th ed. Chicago: University of Chicago Press, 1972.

———. *Negro Folktales in Michigan*. Cambridge, MA: Harvard University Press, 1956.

Dottin, Georges. "Le *Teanga Bithnua* du manuscrit de Rennes." *Revue Celtique* 24 (1903): 365–403.

———. "Une rédaction moderne du *Teanga Bithnua*." *Revue Celtique* 28 (1907): 277–307.

———. "Une version Irlandaise du *Dialogue du Corps et de l'Áme*, attribué à Robert Grosseteste." *Revue Celtique* 23 (1902): 1–39.

Douglas, Mary. *Implicit Meanings: Essays in Anthropology*. London: Routledge and Kegan Paul, 1975.

Dowling, Patrick John. *The Hedge Schools of Ireland*. Dublin: Talbot Press, 1935.

Dunleavy, Janet Egleson, and Gareth W. Dunleavy. *Douglas Hyde: A Maker of Modern Ireland*. Berkeley: University of California Press, 1991.

Dunleavy, John. "John Yates, a Traveller in Connemara, 1875." *Galway Archaeological and Historical Society Journal* 43 (1991): 128–38.

Dunne, Tom. "Voices of the Vanquished: Echoes of Language Loss in Gaelic Poetry from Kinsale to the Great Famine." *Journal of Irish and Scottish Studies* 1, no. 1 (Sept. 2007): 25–44.

Durkacz, V. E. *The Decline of the Celtic Languages: A Study of Linguistic and Cultural Conflict in Scotland, Wales, and Ireland from the Reformation to the Twentieth Century*. Edinburgh: J. Donald, 1983.

Edwards, John. "Did English Murder Irish?" *English Today* 6 (1986): 7–10.

———. *Language, Society, and Identity*. Oxford: Basil Blackwell, 1985.

———. *Multilingualism*. New York: Penguin Books, 1995.

Eiriksson, Andres. "Crime and Popular Protest in County Clare, 1815–1852." PhD diss., Trinity College Dublin, 1991.

Eliot, François. "L'emigration irlandaise et les prêtes irlandais en France." In *The Irish French Connection, 1578–1978*, edited by Liam Swords, 88–96. Paris: The Irish College, 1978.

El-Shamy, Hasan. *Types of the Folktale in the Arab World: A Demographically Oriented Tale-Type Index*. Bloomington: University of Indiana Press, 2004.

Elspaß, Stephan, Nils Langer, Joachim Scharloth, and Wim Vandenbushe, eds. *Germanic Language Histories "from Below" (1700–2000)*. Studia Linguistica Germanica Series, Vol. 86. Berlin: Walter de Gruyter, 2007.

Espinosa, Aurelio M., Jr. *Cuentos populares de Castilla y Leon*. 2 vols. Madrid: Consejo Superior de Investigaciones Cientificas, 1987–88.

Esposito, Mario. "On the Earliest Latin Life of St. Brigid of Kildare." *Proceedings of the Royal Irish Academy*. Section C, 30 (1912–13): 307–26.

Evans, E. Estyn. *Irish Folk Ways*. London: Routledge and Paul, 1957.

Evans, Robert J. W. "Language and State Building: The Case of the Habsburg Monarchy." *Austrian History Yearbook* 35 (2004): 1–24.

———. *The Language of History and the History of Language*. Oxford: Clarendon Press, 1998.

Fagan, Patrick. *Divided Loyalties: The Question of the Oath for Irish Catholics in the Eighteenth Century*. Dublin: Four Courts Press, 1997.

Fasold, Ralph. *The Sociolinguistics of Society*. Oxford: Basil Blackwell, 1984.

Fenning, Hugh. "Cork Imprints of Catholic Historical Interest, 1723–1804: A Provisional Checklist." *Journal of the Cork Historical and Archaeological Society* 100 (1995): 129–48.

———. "Cork Imprints of Catholic Historical Interest, 1805–1830: A Provisional Checklist (Part 2)." *Journal of the Cork Historical and Archaeological Society* 101 (1996): 115–42.

———. "Dublin Imprints of Catholic Interest: 1701–1739." *Collectanea Hibernica* 39/40 (1998): 106–54.

———. "Dublin Imprints of Catholic Interest: 1740–1759." *Collectanea Hibernica* 41 (1999): 65–116.

———. "Dublin Imprints of Catholic Interest: 1760–1769." *Collectanea Hibernica* 42 (2000): 85–119.

———. "Dublin Imprints of Catholic Interest: 1770–1782." *Collectanea Hibernica* 43 (2001): 161–208.

———. "Dublin Imprints of Catholic Interest: 1783–1789." *Collectanea Hibernica* 44/45 (2002–2003): 79–126.

———. "Dublin Imprints of Catholic Interest: 1790–1795." *Collectanea Hibernica* 46/47 (2004–2005): 72–141.

———. "Dublin Imprints of Catholic Interest: 1796–1799." *Collectanea Hibernica* 48 (2006): 67–108.

———. "The Library of the Augustinians of Galway in 1731." *Collectanea Hibernica* 31–32 (1989–1990): 162–95.

———. "Prayer-Books and Pamphlets, 1700–1829." *Seanchas Ard Macha* 16 (1994): 93–99.

Ferguson, Charles A. "Diglossa." *Word* 15, no. 2 (1959): 325–40.

Fiontar, DCU, and Brainse Logainmneacha. An Roinn Ealaíon, Oidhreachta agus Gaeltachta. *Bunachar Logainmneacha na hÉireann/Placenames Database of Ireland Online*. 2007–12. http://logainm.ie.

Fishman, Joshua. "Bilingualism with and without Diglossia; Diglossia with and without Bilingualism." *Journal of Social Issues* 23, no. 2 (1967): 29–38.

———, ed. *The Fergusonian Impact*. 2 vols. Berlin: Mouton de Gruyer, 1986.

———. *Language and Ethnicity in Minority Sociolinguistic Perspective*. Philadelphia: Multilingual Matters, 1989.

FitzGerald, Garret. "Estimates for Baronies of Minimum Level of Irish Speaking amongst Successive Decennial Cohorts: 1771–1781 to 1861–1871." *Proceedings of the Royal Irish Academy*, Section C, 84, no. 3 (1984; reprint, 2004): 117–55.

———. "Irish-Speaking in the Pre-Famine Period: A Study Based on the 1911 Census Data for People Born before 1851 and Still Alive in 1911." *Proceedings of the Royal Irish Academy*, Section C, 103, no. 5 (2003): 191–283.

Fitzpatrick, David. "Irish Farming Families before the First World War." *Comparative Studies in Society and History* 25, no. 2 (1983): 339–74.

Flaherty, Peter. "'Langue nationale/langue naturelle': The Politics of Linguistic Uniformity During the French Revolution." *Historical Reflections/Reflexions Historiques* 14, no. 2 (1987): 311–28.

Foley, Tadhg, and Seán Ryder, eds. *Ideology and Ireland in the Nineteenth Century*. Dublin: Four Courts Press, 1998.

Ford, Caroline. *Creating the Nation in Provincial France: Religion and Political Identity in Brittany*. Princeton, NJ: Princeton University Press, 1993.

Formigari, Lia. "Theories du langage et theories du pouvoir en France, 1800–1848." *Historiographia Linguistica* 12, nos. 1–2 (1985): 63–83.

Forsythe, John. "Clogher Diocesan Papers, Part 2." *Archivium Hibernicum* 44 (1989): 5–70.

Fox, Adam. *Oral and Literate Culture in England, 1500–1700*. Oxford: Clarendon Press, 2000.

Fox, J. R. "The Vanishing Gael." *New Society* 2 (1962): 17–19.

Friel, Bernadette. "Language Change in Urris." *Donegal Annual* 50 (1998): 66–75.

Furet, François, and Jacques Ozouf, eds. *Reading and Writing: Literacy in France from Calvin to Jules Ferry*. 2 vols. Cambridge: Cambridge University Press, 1982.

Gafaranga, Joseph. "Demythologising Language Alternation Studies: Conversational Structure vs. Social Structure in Bilingual Interaction." *Journal of Pragmatics* 37 (2005): 281–300.

Gaidoz, Henri. "Le Debat du Corps et de l'Áme en Irlande." *Revue Celtique* 10 (1889): 463–70.

Gailey, R. A. "Aspects of Change in a Rural Community." *Ulster Folklife* 5 (1959): 27–34.

Gal, Susan. *Language Shift: Social Determinants of Linguistic Change in Bilingual Austria*. New York: Academic Press, 1979.

Galbraith, V. H. "Nationality and Language in Medieval England." *Transactions of the Royal Historical Society*, ser. 4, vol. 23 (1941): 113–28.

Garnham, Neal. *The Courts, Crime and the Criminal Law in Ireland, 1692–1760.* Dublin: Irish Academic Press, 1996.
Garvin, Tom. *The Evolution of Irish Nationalist Politics.* New York: Holmes and Meier Publishers, 1981.
Gatrell, V. A. C. *The Hanging Tree: Execution and the English People, 1770–1868.* Oxford: Oxford University Press, 1994.
Geary, Laurence M., and Margaret Kelleher, eds. *Nineteenth-Century Ireland: A Guide to Recent Research.* Dublin: University College Dublin Press, 2005.
Gibbons, Luke. "Race against Time: Racial Discourse and Irish History." *Oxford Literary Review* 13 (1991): 95–117.
———. *Transformations in Irish Culture.* Cork: Cork University Press, 1996.
Gillespie, Raymond. "And Be Hanged by the Neck Until You Are Dead." In *Hanging Crimes,* edited by Frank Sweeney, 1–9. Cork: Mercier Press, 2005.
———. *Devoted People: Belief and Religion in Early Modern Ireland.* Manchester and New York: Manchester University Press, 1997.
———. "A Manor Court in Seventeenth-Century Ireland." *Irish Economic and Social History* 25 (1998): 81–87.
———, ed. *The Remaking of Modern Ireland, 1750–1950: Beckett Prize Essays in Irish History.* Dublin: Four Courts Press, 2004.
Giltrap, Risteárd. *An Ghaeilge in Eaglais na hÉireann.* Baile Átha Cliath: Cumann Gaelach na hEaglaise, 1990.
Glaeske, Keith. "The Children of Adam and Eve in Medieval Irish Literature." *Ériu* 56 (2006): 1–11.
Green, Ian. *The Christian's ABC: Catechisms and Catechizing in England c. 1530–1740.* Oxford: Clarendon Press, 1996.
Greene, David. *The Irish Language.* Dublin: Cultural Relations Committee of Ireland, 1966.
———. "Robert Atkinson and Irish Studies." *Hermathena* 102 (Spring 1966): 6–15.
Gregory, Lady [Isabella Augusta]. *Visions and Beliefs in the West of Ireland.* 2nd ed. Gerrards Cross: Colin Smyth, 1970.
Griffin, Sean. "The Catholic Book Society and Its Role in the Emerging System of National Education, 1824–1834." *Irish Educational Studies* 11 (1992): 82–98.
Grillo, R. D. *Dominant Languages: Language and Hierarchy in Britain and France.* Cambridge: Cambridge University Press, 1989.
Groeneboer, Kees. *Gateway to the West. The Dutch Language in Colonial Indonesia, 1600–1950.* Translated by Myra Scholz. Amsterdam: Amsterdam University Press, 1998.
Guinan, Joseph Canon. *The Soggarth Aroon.* 4th ed. Dublin: Talbot Press, 1944.
Guinnane, Timothy W. *The Vanishing Irish: Households, Migration, and the Rural Economy in Ireland, 1850–1914.* Princeton, NJ: Princeton University Press, 1997.
Gumperz, John J. *Discourse Strategies.* Cambridge: Cambridge University Press, 1982.
———. "Speech Variation and the Study of Indian Civilization." *American Anthropologist* 63, no. 5 (Oct. 1961): 976–88.
———. "Types of Linguistic Communities." *Anthropological Linguistics* 4, no. 1 (1962): 28–40.

Gumperz, John J., and Dell Hymes, eds. *Directions in Sociolinguistics: The Ethnography of Communication*. New York: Holt, Rinehart, Winston, 1972.

Gumperz, John J., and Stephen Levinson. "Rethinking Linguistic Relativity." *Current Anthropology* 32, no. 5 (1991): 613-23.

Haboucha, Reginetta. *Type and Motifs of the Judeo-Spanish Folktales*. New York: Garland Publishing, 1992.

Hall, Robert A. "The Significance of the Italian 'Questione Della Lingua.'" *Studies in Philology* 39, no. 1 (Jan. 1942): 1-10.

Hamell, Patrick. *Maynooth Students and Ordinations*. 2 vols. Maynooth: Cardinal Press, 1982 and 1984.

Hannan, Damian. "Kinship, Neighbourhood, and Social Change in Irish Rural Communities." *Economic and Social Review* 3 (1972): 163-88.

Hannigan, Ken. "An Analysis of County Wicklow's Irish Speakers in 1901." *Wicklow Historical Society Journal* 1, no. 7 (1994): 20-27.

Harford, Judith. "The Emergence of a National Policy on Teacher Education in Ireland." *Journal of Educational Administration and History* 41, no. 1 (Feb. 2009): 45-56.

Harmon, Maurice. "Aspects of the Peasantry in Anglo-Irish Literature from 1800 to 1916." *Studia Hibernica* 15 (1975): 105-27.

Harrison, Alan. *Ag Cruinniú Meala: Anthony Raymond (1675-1726), Ministéir Protastúnach, agus Léann na Gaeilge i mBaile Átha Cliath*. Baile Átha Cliath: An Clóchomhar Tta, 1988.

———. "Lucht na Simléirí." *Éigse* 15 (1973-74): 189-202.

Hartweg, Frederic. "'Langue esclave et langue de la liberté': La révolution et la langue allemande." *Documents: Revue des questions allemandes* 4 (1989): 75-84.

Hassell, James Woodrow. *Sources and Analogues of the Nouvelles Récreations et Joyeux Devis of Bonaventure des Périers*. Vol. 1. Chapel Hill: University of North Carolina Studies in Comparative Literature, 1957.

———. *Sources and Analogues of the Nouvelles Recreations et Joyeux Devis of Bonaventure des Périers*. Vol. 2. Athens: University of Georgia Press, 1969.

Hawkes, William. "Irish Forms of Preparation for Sunday Mass in the Eighteenth Century." *Reportorium Novum: Dublin Diocesan Historical Record* 1 (1955): 183-92.

Hayes, Richard J., ed. *Manuscript Sources for the History of Irish Civilisation, with First Supplement*. 14 vols. Boston: G. K. Hall & Co., 1965-79.

Hazen, Kirk. "Identity and Language Variation in a Rural Community." *Language* 78, no. 2 (2002): 240-57.

Hazlitt, W. Carew, ed. *Shakespeare Jest-Books: Reprints of the Early and Very Rare Jest-Books Supposed to Have Been Used by Shakespeare*. 3 vols. 1864. Repr., New York: Burt Franklin, 1964.

Hechter, Michael. *Internal Colonialism: The Celtic Fringe in British National Development, 1536-1966*. New ed. Brunswick, NJ: Transaction Publishers, 1999.

Hederman, Mark Patrick, and Richard Kearney, eds. *The Crane Bag Book of Irish Studies, 1977-1981*. Dublin: Blackwater Press, 1982.

Heimann, Mary. *Catholic Devotion in Victorian England*. Oxford: Clarendon Press, 1995.

———. "Catholic Revivalism in Worship and Devotion." In *The Cambridge History of Christianity*, vol. 8, *World Christianities c. 1815–c. 1914*, edited by Sheridan Gilley and Brian Stanley, 70–83. Cambridge: Cambridge University Press, 2006.
Hejaiej, Monia. *Behind Closed Doors: Women's Oral Narratives in Tunis*. London: Quartet Books, 1996.
Herbert, Máire. "Goddess and King: The Sacred Marriage in Early Ireland." In *Women and Sovereignty*, edited by Louise Fradenburg, 264–75. Edinburgh: Edinburgh University Press, 1992.
Herity, Michael, ed. *Ordnance Survey Letters, Donegal: Letters Containing Information Relative to the Antiquities of the County of Donegal, Collected during the Progress of the Ordnance Survey in 1835*. Dublin: Four Masters Press, 2000.
———, ed. *Ordnance Survey Letters, Dublin: Letters Containing Information Relative to the Antiquities of the County of Dublin, Collected during the Progress of the Ordnance Survey in 1837*. Dublin: Four Masters Press, 2001.
———, ed. *Ordnance Survey Letters, Kildare: Letters Containing Information Relative to the Antiquities of the County of Kildare, Collected during the Progress of the Ordnance Survey in 1837, 1838, and 1839*. Dublin: Four Masters Press, 2002.
———, ed. *Ordnance Survey Letters, Kilkenny: Letters Containing Information Relative to the Antiquities of the County of Kilkenny, Collected during the Progress of the Ordnance Survey in 1839*. Dublin: Four Masters Press, 2003.
———, ed. *Ordnance Survey Letters, Meath: Letters Containing Information Relative to the Antiquities of the County of Meath, Collected during the Progress of the Ordnance Survey in 1836*. Dublin: Four Masters Press, 2001.
Herzfeld, Anita. "Language and Identity: The Black Minority of Costa Rica." *Revista de Filologia y Linguistica* 20, no. 1 (1994): 113–42.
Hickey, Éanna. *Irish Law and Lawyers in Modern Folk Tradition*. Dublin: Four Courts Press in Association with the Irish Legal History Society, 1999.
Hickey, Raymond, ed. *Motives for Language Change*. Cambridge: Cambridge University Press, 2003.
Hidalgo, Margarita. "Sociolinguistic Stratification in New Spain." *International Journal of the Sociology of Language* 149 (2001): 55–78.
Higonnet, Patrice. "The Politics of Linguistic Terrorism and Grammatical Hegemony during the French Revolution." *Social History* 5, no. 1 (1980): 41–69.
Hill, Jacqueline. *From Patriots to Unionists: Dublin Civic Politics and Irish Protestant Patriotism, 1660–1840*. Oxford: Oxford University Press, 1997.
Hindley, Reg. *The Death of the Irish Language: A Qualified Obituary*. London: Routledge, 1990.
Hockett, Charles. *The View from Language*. Athens: University of Georgia Press, 1977.
Hodne, Ørnulf. *The Types of the Norwegian Folktale*. Oslo: Universitetsforlaget, 1984.
Hogan, Jeremiah J. *The English Language in Ireland*. Dublin: Educational Company of Ireland, 1927.
Hoppen, K. Theodore. *Elections, Politics, and Society in Ireland, 1832–1885*. Oxford: Clarendon Press, 1984.
———. *Ireland since 1800: Conflict and Conformity*. 2nd ed. Longman: New York, 1999.

Horstmann, Carl, ed. *Nova Legenda Anglie: As Collected by John of Tynemouth, John Capgrave, and Others, and First Printed, with New Lives, by Wynkyn de Worde A.D. MDXVI.* 2 vols. Oxford: Clarendon Press, 1901.

Houston, R. A. "'Minority' Languages and Cultural Change." In *Explaining Change in Cultural History*, Historical Studies XXIII, edited by Niall Ó Ciosáin, 13–36. Dublin: University College Dublin Press, 2005.

Howlin, Níamh. "Controlling Jury Composition in Nineteenth-Century Ireland." *Journal of Legal History* 30, no. 3 (Dec. 2009): 227–61.

Hurst, Michael. "Ireland and the Ballot Act of 1872." *Historical Journal* 8, no. 3 (1965): 326–52.

Hutchinson, John. *The Dynamics of Cultural Nationalism: The Gaelic Revival and the Creation of the Irish Nation State*. London: Allen and Unwin, 1987.

Hyde, Douglas. "Eachtra na gConnachta." *Lia Fail* 1 (1927): 153–60.

Hymes, Dell. "Models for the Interaction of Language and Social Life." In *Directions in Sociolinguistics: The Ethnography of Communication*, edited by John J. Gumperz and Dell Hymes, 35–71. New York: Holt, Rinehart, Winston, Inc., 1972.

Hynes, Eugene. "The Great Hunger and Irish Catholicism." *Societas* 8 (1978): 137–55.

——. *Knock: The Virgin's Apparition in Nineteenth-Century Ireland*. Cork: Cork University Press, 2009.

Imhoff, Brian. "Socio-Historic Network Ties and Medieval Navarro-Aragonese." *Neuphilologische Mitteilungen* 101, no. 3 (2000): 443–50.

Irvine, Judith T. "The Family Romance of Colonial Linguistics: Gender and Family in Nineteenth-Century Representations of African Languages." *Pragmatics* 5, no. 2 (1995): 139–53.

——. "Subjected Words: African Linguistics and the Colonial Encounter." *Language and Communication* 28 (2008): 323–43.

Irvine, Judith T., and Susan Gal. "Language Ideology and Linguistic Differentiation." In *Regimes of Language: Ideologies, Polities, and Identities*, edited by Paul V. Kroskity, 35–83. Santa Fe, NM: School of American Research Press and Oxford: James Currey, 2000.

Jansen, William Hugh. "The Esoteric-Exoteric Factor in Folklore." In *The Study of Folklore*, ed. Alan Dundes, 43–51. Englewood Cliffs, NJ: Prentice-Hall, 1965.

Jenkins, Geraint H. *A Concise History of Wales*. Cambridge: Cambridge University Press, 2007.

——. "The Cultural Uses of the Welsh Language, 1660–1800." In *The Welsh Language before the Industrial Revolution*, edited by Geraint H. Jenkins, 369–406. Cardiff: University of Wales Press, 1997.

——, ed. *The Welsh Language and Its Social Domains, 1801–1911*. Cardiff: University of Wales Press, 2000.

——, ed. *The Welsh Language before the Industrial Revolution*. Cardiff: University of Wales Press, 1997.

Jenkins, Geraint H., Richard Suggett, and Eryn M. White. "The Welsh Language in Early Modern Wales." In *The Welsh Language before the Industrial Revolution*, edited by Geraint H. Jenkins, 45–122. Cardiff: University of Wales Press, 1997.

Jenkins, Richard P. "Witches and Fairies: Supernatural Aggression and Deviance among the Irish Peasantry." *Ulster Folklife* 23 (1977): 33–56.

Jones, Charles. "Nationality and Standardisation: The English Language in Scotland in the Age of Improvement." *Sociolinguistica* 13 (1999): 112–28.

Jones, Dot. *Statistical Evidence Relating to the Welsh Language, 1801–1911/Tystiolaeth Ystadegol yn ymwneud â'r Iaith Gymraeg, 1801–1911.* Cardiff: University of Wales Press, 1998.

Jones, Frederick M. *Alphonsus de Liguori: The Saint of Bourbon Naples, 1696–1787.* Dublin: Gill and Macmillan, 1992.

Jones, Greta, and Elizabeth Malcolm. *Medicine, Disease, and the State in Ireland, 1650–1940.* Cork: Cork University Press, 1999.

Jones, J. Gwynfor. "The Welsh Language in Local Government: Justices of the Peace and the Courts of Quarter Sessions c. 1536–1800." In *The Welsh Language before the Industrial Revolution*, edited by Geraint H. Jenkins, 181–206. Cardiff: University of Wales Press, 1997.

Jones, Mari C. "Death of a Language, Birth of an Identity: Brittany and the Bretons." *Language Problems and Language Planning* 22, no. 2 (Summer 1998): 129–42.

Jones, Mark Ellis. "'An Invidious Attempt to Accelerate the Extinction of Our Language': The Abolition of the Court of Great Sessions and the Welsh Language." *The Welsh History Review. Cylchgrawn Hanes Cymru* 19, no. 2 (1998): 226–64.

Jordan, Donald. *Land and Popular Politics in Ireland: County Mayo from the Plantation to the Land War.* Cambridge: Cambridge University Press, 1994.

Jupp, Peter J. *British and Irish Elections, 1784–1831.* Newton Abbot, UK: David & Charles Holdings, 1973.

———. "Irish Parliamentary Elections and the Influence of the Catholic Vote, 1801–20." *Historical Journal* 10, no. 2 (1967): 183–96.

Jupp, Peter J., and Stephen Royle. "The Social Geography of Cork City Elections, 1801–1830." *Irish Historical Studies* 29 (1994): 13–43.

Kallen, Jeffrey. "The English Language in Ireland." *International Journal of the Sociology of Language* 70 (1988): 127–42.

———. "Language and Ethnic Identity: The Irish Language in the United States." In *Language Across Cultures: Proceedings of a Symposium Held at St. Patrick's College, Drumcondra, Dublin, 8–9 July 1983*, edited by Liam Mac Mathúna and David Singleton, 101–12. Dublin: Irish Association for Applied Linguistics, 1984.

Kavanagh, Robin J. "Pictures of Piety and Impropriety: Irish Religious Periodicals of the 1830s." In *Visual, Material and Print Culture in Nineteenth-Century Ireland*, edited by Ciara Breathnach and Catherine Lawless, 115–28. Dublin: Four Courts Press, 2010

Keating, John. "Saint John's College Waterford: Beginnings and History." *Capuchin Annual* (1959): 340–47.

Keenan, Desmond. *The Catholic Church in Nineteenth-Century Ireland: A Sociological Study.* Dublin: Gill and Macmillan, 1983.

Kelly, James. "Irish Protestants and the Irish Language in the Eighteenth Century." In *Irish and English: Essays on the Irish Linguistic and Cultural Frontier, 1600–1900*, edited by James Kelly and Ciarán Mac Murchaidh, 189–217. Dublin: Four Courts Press, 2012.

Kelly, James, and Ciarán Mac Murchaidh, eds. *Irish and English: Essays on the Irish Linguistic and Cultural Frontier, 1600–1900.* Dublin: Four Courts Press, 2012.

Kelly, James, and Dáire Keogh, eds. *History of the Catholic Diocese of Dublin.* Dublin: Four Courts Press, 2000.

Kennedy, John G. "Bonds of Laughter among the Tarahumara Indians: A Rethinking of Joking Relationship Theory." In *The Social Anthropology of Latin America: Essays in Honor of Ralph Leon Beals,* edited by Walter Goldschmidt and Harry Hoijer, 36–68. Los Angeles: University of California Press, 1970.

Kennedy, Liam. *Colonialism, Religion, and Nationalism in Ireland.* Belfast: Institute of Irish Studies, 1996.

———. "Profane Images in the Irish Popular Consciousness." *Oral History* 7 (1979): 42–47.

———. "Retail Markets in Rural Ireland at the End of the Nineteenth Century." *Irish Economic and Social History* 5 (1978): 46–63.

Kenny, Kevin. *The American Irish: A History.* New York: Longman, 2000.

Keogh, Dáire. "Christian Citizens: The Catholic Church and Radical Politics, 1790–1800." In *Protestant, Catholic, and Dissenter: The Clergy and 1798,* edited by Liam Swords, 9–19. Dublin: Columba Press, 1997.

———. *Edmund Rice and the First Christian Brothers.* 2nd ed. Dublin: Four Courts Press, 2009.

Kerr, Barbara. "Irish Seasonal Migration to Great Britain, 1800–38." *Irish Historical Studies* 3 (1942–43): 365–80.

Kerr, Donal. "The Early Nineteenth Century: Patterns of Change." In *Irish Spirituality,* edited by Michael Maher, 135–44. Dublin: Veritas Publications, 1981.

———. *Peel, Priests, and Politics: Sir Robert Peel's Administration and the Roman Catholic Church in Ireland, 1841–1846.* Oxford: Clarendon Press, 1982.

Kershwill, Paul. "Children, Adolescents, and Language Change." *Language Variation and Change* 8 (1996): 177–202.

Kiberd, Declan. "Irish Literature and Irish History." In *The Oxford Illustrated History of Ireland,* edited by Roy Foster, 275–337. Oxford: Oxford University Press, 2000.

Kidd, Colin. *British Identities before Nationalism: Ethnicity and Nationhood in the Atlantic World, 1600–1800.* Cambridge: Cambridge University Press, 1999.

Koestler, Arthur. *The Act of Creation.* New York: Macmillan Co., 1964.

Kroskrity, Paul V., ed. *Regimes of Language: Ideologies, Polities, and Identities.* Sante Fe, NM: School of American Research Press, 2000.

Kumar, Nootan, Pavel Trofimovich, and Elizabeth Gatbonton. "Investigating Heritage Language and Culture Links: An Indo-Canadian Hindu Perspective." *Journal of Multilingual and Multicultural Development* 29, no. 1 (2008): 49–65.

Labov, William. *Principles of Linguistic Change.* 2 vols. Oxford: Blackwell, 1994.

———. *The Social Stratification of English in New York City.* 2nd ed. Cambridge: Cambridge University Press, 2006.

Laheen, Kevin. *The Jesuits in Killaloe, 1850–1880*. Drumline, Newmarket-on-Fergus: O'Brien Book Publications, 1998.
Laird, Heather. *Subversive Law in Ireland, 1879–1920: From "Unwritten Law" to Dáil Courts*. Dublin: Four Courts Press, 2005.
Larkin, Emmet. "Before the Devotional Revolution." In *Evangelicals and Catholics in Nineteenth-Century Ireland*, ed. James H. Murphy, 15–24. Dublin: Four Courts Press, 2005.
———. "The Devotional Revolution in Ireland, 1850–1875." *American Historical Review* 77, no. 3 (1972): 625–52.
———. *The Making of the Roman Catholic Church in Ireland, 1850–1860*. Chapel Hill: University of North Carolina Press, 1980.
———. *The Pastoral Role of the Roman Catholic Church in Pre-Famine Ireland, 1750–1850*. Dublin: Four Courts Press, 2006.
———. "The Rise and Fall of Stations in Ireland, 1750–1850." In *Chocs et ruptures en histoire religieuse: Fin XVIIIe–XIXe siècles*, edited by Michel Lagrée, 19–32. Rennes: Presses Universitaires de Rennes, 1998.
Larson, Pier M. *Ocean of Letters: Language and Creolization in an Indian Ocean Diaspora*. Cambridge: Cambridge University Press, 2009.
Lawless, Catherine. "Devotion and Representation in Nineteenth-Century Ireland." In *Visual, Material and Print Culture in Nineteenth-Century Ireland*, Edited by Ciara Breathnach and Catherine Lawless, 85–97. Dublin: Four Courts Press, 2010.
Lee, J. Joseph. *Ireland, 1912–1985: Politics and Society*. Cambridge: Cambridge University Press, 1989.
———. *The Modernisation of Irish Society, 1848–1918*. Dublin: Gill and Macmillan, 1973.
Leerssen, Joep. *Mere Irish and Fíor-Ghael: Studies in the Idea of Irish Nationality, Its Development and Literary Expression prior to the Nineteenth Century*. Notre Dame, IN: University of Notre Dame Press, 1997.
———. *Remembrance and Imagination: Patterns in the Historical and Literary Representation of Ireland in the Nineteenth Century*. Notre Dame, IN: University of Notre Dame Press, 1997.
Lehning, James. *Peasant and French: Cultural Contact in Rural France during the Nineteenth Century*. Cambridge: Cambridge University Press, 1995.
Lennon, Joseph. *Irish Orientalism: A Literary and Intellectual History*. Syracuse, NY: Syracuse University Press, 2004.
Lew, Robert. "Exploitation of Linguistic Ambiguity in Polish and English Jokes." *Papers and Studies in Constructive Linguistics* 31 (1996): 127–33.
Limón, José. "Agringado Joking in Texas Mexican Society: Folklore and Differential Identity." *New Scholar* 6 (1977): 33–50.
Linebaugh, Peter. *The London Hanged: Crime and Civil Society in the Eighteenth Century*. Cambridge: Cambridge University Press, 1992.
Lloyd, David. *Anomalous States: Irish Writing and the Post-Colonial Moment*. Dublin: Lilliput Press, 1993.
Logan, John. "Book Learning: The Experience of Reading in the National School, 1831–1900." In *The Experience of Reading: Irish Historical Perspectives*, edited by

Bernadette Cunningham and Máire Kennedy, 173–95. Dublin: Rare Books Group of the Library Association of Ireland and Economic and Social History Society of Ireland, 1999.

Lucht, Felecia A. "Language Variation in a German-American Community: A Diachronic Study of the Spectrum of Language Use in Lebanon, Wisconsin." PhD diss., University of Wisconsin–Madison, 2007.

Lyne, Gerard J. "Daniel O'Connell, Intimidation, and the Kerry Elections of 1835." *Journal of the Kerry Archaeological and Historical Society* 4 (1971): 74–97.

Lyne, Gerard J., and M. E. Mitchell. "A Scientific Tour through Munster: The Travels of Joseph Woods, Architect and Botanist, in 1809." *North Munster Antiquarian Journal* 27 (1985): 15–61.

Lyons, Martin. "Politics and Patois: The Linguistic Policy of the French Revolution." *Australian Journal of French Studies* 18 (1981): 264–81.

Lysaght, Patricia. "Attitudes to the Rosary and Its Performance in Donegal in the Nineteenth and Twentieth Centuries." *Béaloideas* 66 (1998): 9–58.

Macalister, R. A. Stewart, ed. *Lebor Gabála Érenn: The Book of the Taking of Ireland*. 5 vols. Irish Texts Society vols. 34–35, 39, 41, 44. 1938–41, 1956. Repr., Dublin: Irish Texts Society, 1984–96.

———. "The Vision of Merlino." *Zeitschrift für Celtische Philologie* 4 (1903): 394–455.

Mac Aodha, Breandán S. "Aspects of the Linguistic Geography of Ireland in the Early Nineteenth Century." *Studia Celtica* 20–21 (1985–86): 205–20.

———. "Execution and Irish Placenames." *Nomina* 19 (1996): 51–60.

Mac Aogáin, Parthalán, ed. *Graiméir Ghaeilge na mBráthar Mionúr*. Baile Átha Cliath: Institiúid Ard-Léinn Bhaile Átha Cliath, 1968.

Mac Aonghusa, Proinsias. *Ar Son na Gaeilge: Conradh na Gaeilge 1893–1993, Stair Seanchais*. Baile Átha Cliath: Conradh na Gaeilge, 1993.

Macaulay, Ambrose. *William Crolly, Archbishop of Armagh, 1835–1849*. Dublin: Four Courts Press, 1994.

Mac Cana, Proinsias. *Collège des Irlandais, Paris and Irish Studies*. Dublin: Dublin Institute for Advanced Studies, 2001.

MacCulloch, Mary Julia. "Folklore of the Isle of Skye." *Folk-Lore* 33 (1922): 382–89.

Mac Domhnaill, Séamus, ed. *Dánta is Amhráin Sheáin Uí Ghadhra*. Baile Átha Cliath: Oifig an tSoláthair, 1955.

MacDonagh, Oliver. "Ideas and Institutions, 1830–1845." In *A New History of Ireland*, vol. 5, *Ireland under the Union, Part I, 1801–70*, edited by W. E. Vaughan, 193–217. Oxford: Clarendon Press, 1989.

———. *Ireland: The Union and Its Aftermath*. 1977. Repr., Dublin: University College Press, 2003.

MacDonagh, Oliver, W. F. Mandle, and Pauric Travers, eds. *Irish Culture and Nationalism, 1750–1950*. New York: St. Martin's Press, 1983.

Mac Erlean, John C., ed. [Eoin Mac Giolla Eáin]. *Dánta Amhráin is Caointe Sheathrúin Céitinn*. Baile Átha Cliath: Connradh na Gaedhilge, 1900.

———. *Duanaire Dháibhidh Uí Bhruadair: The Poems of David Ó Bruadair*. 3 vols. Irish Texts Society vols. 11, 13, 18. 1910–17. Repr., London: Irish Texts Society, 1986.

Mac Gabhann, Micheál [Micí]. *Rotha Mór an tSaoil*. Edited by Proinsias Ó Conluain. Transcribed by Seán Ó hEochaidh. Indreabhán: Cló Iar-Chonnachta, 1996.

Mac Giolla Chriost, Diarmait. *The Irish Language in Ireland: From Goídel to Globalization*. New York: Routledge, 2005.

MacKinnon, Kenneth. *Language, Education, and Social Processes in a Gaelic Community*. London: Routledge and Kegan Paul, 1977.

Mackridge, Peter. *Language and National Identity in Greece, 1766–1976*. Oxford: Oxford University Press, 2009.

MacLochlainn, Alf. "Broadside Ballads in Irish." *Éigse* 12 (1967): 115–22.

———. "The Irish Language in Clare and North Tipperary, 1820: Bishop Mant's Enquiry." *North Munster Antiquarian Journal* 17 (1975): 77–82.

———. "Social Life in County Clare, 1800–1850." *Irish University Review* 2, no. 1 (Spring 1972): 55–78.

Mac Mathúna, Liam. *Ár dTimpeallacht Logainmneacha Inniu agus Amárach*. Baile Átha Cliath: Coiscéim, 1990.

———. *Béarla sa Ghaeilge: Cabhair Choigríche; An Códmheascadh Gaeilge/Béarla i Litríocht na Gaeilge, 1600–1900*. Baile Átha Cliath: An Clóchomhar Tta, 2007.

———. *Dúchas agus Dóchas: Scéal na Gaeilge i mBaile Átha Cliath*. Baile Átha Cliath: Glór na nGael, 1991.

———. "Pobal Gaeilge Baile Átha Cliath: Oidhrí agus Ceannródaithe." In *An Ghaeilge i mBaile Átha Cliath*, edited by Ciarán Ó Coigligh, 29–47. Baile Átha Cliath: Saotharlann Staire Bhaile Átha Cliath, 1985.

Mac Murchaidh, Ciarán. "The Catholic Church, the Irish Mission and the Irish Language in the Eighteenth Century." In *Irish and English: Essays on the Irish Linguistic and Cultural Frontier, 1600–1900*, edited by James Kelly and Ciarán Mac Murchaidh, 162–88. Dublin: Four Courts Press, 2012.

MacNamee, James J. *History of the Diocese of Ardagh*. Dublin: Browne and Nolan, 1954.

MacNéill, Eóin. "Addendum on Charles Percy Bushe." *Béaloideas* 13 (1942): 277.

MacNeill, Máire. *The Festival of Lúghnasa: A Study of the Survival of the Celtic Festival of the Beginning of the Harvest*. 2nd ed. Dublin: Comhairle Bhéaloideas Éireann, 1982.

Mac Póilin, Aodán. "Language, Identity, and Politics in Northern Ireland." *Ulster Folklife* 45 (1999): 108–32.

Madec, Mary O'Malley. "English Discourse Markers in the Speech of Native Speakers of Irish." In *Béalra: Aistí an Theangeolaíocht na Gaeilge*, edited by Brian Ó Catháin and Ruairí Ó hUiginn, 260–73. Maynooth: An Sagart, 2001.

Maher, Michael, ed. "Correspondence of Dr. Bray, Archbishop of Cashel." *Archivium Hibernicum* 1 (1912): 222–47.

———, ed. *Irish Spirituality*. Dublin: Veritas Publications, 1981.

———. "Sunday in the Irish Church." *Irish Theological Quarterly* 60, no. 3 (1994): 161–84.

Mahon, William. "Scríobhaithe Lámhscríbhinní Gaeilge i nGaillimh, 1700–1900." In *Galway: History and Society; Interdisciplinary Essays on the History of an Irish*

County, edited by Gerard Moran and Raymond Gillespie, 623–50. Dublin: Geography Publications, 1996.

Máirtín, Caoimhe. *An Máistir: An Scoil agus an Scolaíocht i Litríocht na Gaeilge*. Baile Átha Cliath: Cois Life, 2003.

Malcolm, Ian. *Towards Inclusion: Protestants and the Irish Language*. Belfast: Blackstaff Press, 2009.

Mangione, Thomas. "The Establishment of the Model School System in Ireland, 1834–1854." *New Hibernia Review* 7, no. 4 (2003): 103–22.

Manning, H. Paul. "The Craft of Reference: The Welsh Language and the Division of Labor in Nineteenth Century Slate Quarries." *Language & Communication* 21 (2001): 209–23.

———. "English Money and Welsh Rocks: Divisions of Language and Divisions of Labor in Nineteenth-Century Welsh Slate Quarries." *Comparative Study of Society and History* 44, no. 3 (July 2002): 481–510.

Martin, F. X. "Provincial Rivalries in Eighteenth-Century Ireland." *Archivium Hibernicum* 30 (1972): 117–35.

Mason, Matthew E. "'The Hands Here Are Disposed to Be Turbulent': Unrest Among the Irish Trackmen of the Baltimore and Ohio Railroad, 1829–1851." *Labor History* 39, no. 3 (1998): 253–72.

Maurais, Jacques. "Petite histoire des législations linguistiques au Royaume-Uni." *L'Action Nationale* 80 (1990): 35–41.

McArdle, Joseph. *Irish Legal Anecdotes*. Dublin: Gill and Macmillan, 1995.

McAree, Noel. *Murderous Justice: A Study in Depth of the Infamous Connemara Murders*. Woodview Park, Limerick: Wildshaw Books, 1990.

McCabe, Desmond. "Law, Conflict and Social Order: County Mayo, 1820–1845." PhD diss., University College, Dublin, 1991.

———. "Magistrates, Peasants, and the Petty Session Courts: Mayo, 1823–50." *Cathair na Mart* 5 (1985): 45–53.

McDonald, Walter. *Reminiscences of a Maynooth Professor*. Edited by Denis Gwynn. Cork: Mercier Press, 1967.

McDowell, R. B. "The Irish Courts of Law, 1801–1914." *Irish Historical Studies* 10, no. 40 (Sept. 1957): 363–91.

McElligott, T. J. *Education in Ireland*. Dublin: Institute of Public Administration, 1966.

———. *Secondary Education in Ireland, 1870–1921*. Dublin: Irish Academic Press, 1981.

McEvoy, John. "Carlow College—Two Hundred Years of Education." *Carloviana* 40 (1992–93): 2–8.

McGrath, Michael, ed. *Cinnlae Amhlaoibh Uí Shúileabháin/The Diary of Humphrey O'Sullivan*. Parts 1–4. Irish Texts Society vols. 30–33. London and Dublin: Irish Texts Society, 1936–37.

McGrath, Thomas G. *The Pastoral and Education Letters of Bishop James Doyle of Kildare and Leighlin, 1786–1834*. Dublin: Four Courts Press, 2004.

———. *Politics, Interdenominational Relations and Education in the Public Ministry of Bishop James Doyle of Kildare and Leighlin, 1786–1834*. Dublin: Four Courts Press, 1999.

———. *Religious Renewal and Reform in the Pastoral Ministry of Bishop James Doyle of Kildare and Leighlin, 1786–1834*. Dublin: Four Courts Press, 1999.

———. "The Tridentine Evolution of Modern Irish Catholicism: A Re-Examination of the 'Devotional Revolution' Thesis." In *Irish Church History Today*, edited by Réamonn Ó Muirí, 84–99. Monaghan: Cumann Seanchais Ard Mhacha, 1991.

McGuinne, Dermot. *Irish Type Design: A History of Printing Types in the Irish Character*. Dublin: Irish Academic Press, 1992.

McGuire, James, and James Quinn, et al. *Dictionary of Irish Biography*. Cambridge: Cambridge University Press, 2009. http://dib.cambridge.org.

McKenna, Lambert, ed. *Dánta do Chum Aonghus Fionn Ó Dálaigh*. Dublin: Maunsel and Company, 1919.

McKenna, Malachy, ed. *The Spiritual Rose, or Method of Saying the Rosaries of the Most Holy Name of Jesus, and the Blessed Virgin, with Their Litanies*. Translated by Mathew Kennedy. Dublin: Dublin Institute for Advanced Studies, 2001.

———. "A Textual History of *The Spiritual Rose*." *Clogher Record* 14 (1991): 52–73.

McKenzie, Don F. "The Sociology of a Text: Oral Culture, Literacy, and Print in Early New Zealand." In *The Social History of Language*, edited by Peter Burke and Roy Porter, 161–97. Cambridge: Cambridge University Press, 1987.

McKibben, Sarah. *Endangered Masculinities in Irish Poetry, 1540–1780*. Dublin: University College Dublin Press, 2010.

McMahon, Richard. "The Court of Petty Sessions and Society in Pre-Famine Galway." In *The Remaking of Modern Ireland, 1750–1950: Beckett Prize Essays in Irish History*, edited by Raymond Gillespie, 101–37. Dublin: Four Courts Press, 2004.

———. "Homicide, the Courts, and Popular Culture in Pre-Famine and Famine Ireland." PhD diss., University College, Dublin, 2006.

———. "Manor Courts in the West of Ireland Before the Famine." In *Mysteries and Solutions in Irish Legal History*, edited by D. S. Greer and N. M. Dawson, 115–60. Dublin: Four Courts Press, 2001.

McMahon, Timothy G. *Grand Opportunity: The Gaelic Revival and Irish Society, 1893–1910*. Syracuse, NY: Syracuse University Press, 2008.

———. "Religion and Popular Culture in Nineteenth-Century Ireland." *History Compass* 5, no. 3 (2007): 845–64.

McManaway, James G. "John Shakespeare's 'Spiritual Testament.'" *Shakespeare Quarterly* 18, no. 3 (Summer 1967): 197–205.

McManus, Antonia. *The Irish Hedge School and Its Books, 1695–1831*. Dublin: Four Courts Press, 2002.

McPolin, Francis. "An Old Irish Catechism from Oriel." *Irish Ecclesiastical Record*, ser. 5, vol. 50 (1947): 509–17.

McQuillan, Peter. *Native and Natural: Aspects of the Concepts of "Right" and "Freedom" in Irish*. Cork: Cork University Press in Association with Field Day, 2004.

Mercier, Vivian. *The Irish Comic Tradition*. Oxford: Clarendon Press, 1962.

Messenger, John C. "Sex and Repression in an Irish Folk Community." In *Human Sexual Behavior: Variations in the Ethnographic Spectrum*, edited by Donald S. Marshall and Robert C. Suggs, 3–37. New York: Basic Books, 1971.

Metcalf, George J. "The Indo-European Hypothesis in the Sixteenth and Seventeenth Centuries." In *Studies in the History of Linguistics: Traditions and Paradigms*, edited by Dell Hymes, 233–57. Bloomington: Indiana University Press, 1974.

Mhág Craith, Cuthbert, ed. *Dán na mBráthar Mionúr*. Baile Átha Cliath: Institiúid Árd-Léinn Bhaile Átha Cliath, 1967.

Miller, David W. "Irish Catholicism and the Great Famine." *Journal of Social History* 9 (1975): 81–98.

———. "Landscape and Religious Practice: A Study of Mass Attendance in Pre-Famine Ireland." *Éire-Ireland* 40, nos. 1–2 (Spring/Summer 2005): 90–106.

Miller, David W., and Stewart Brown, eds. *Piety and Power in Ireland, 1760–1960: Essays in Honour of Emmet Larkin*. Belfast: Institute of Irish Studies, 2000.

Miller, Kerby A. *Emigrants and Exiles: Ireland and the Irish Exodus to North America*. New York and Oxford: Oxford University Press, 1985.

Milroy, James. "On the Role of the Speaker in Language Change." In *Motives for Language Change*, edited by Raymond Hickey, 143–58. Cambridge: Cambridge University Press, 2003.

Milroy, Leslie. *Language and Social Networks*. Oxford: Basil Blackwell, 1980.

Mingay, G. E. *The Victorian Countryside*. 2 vols. London: Routledge and Kegan Paul, 1981.

Mir, Farina. "Imperial Policy, Provincial Practices: Colonial Language Policy in Nineteenth-Century India." *Indian Economic and Social History Review* 43, no. 4 (2006): 395–427.

Mitchell, Lisa. *Language, Emotion, and Politics in South India: The Making of a Mother Tongue*. Bloomington: Indiana University Press, 2009.

Moloney, Maeve Mulryan. *Nineteenth-Century Elementary Education in the Archdiocese of Tuam*. Maynooth Studies in Irish Local History 36. Dublin: Irish Academic Press, 2001.

Moody, T. W., and W. E. Vaughan, eds. *A New History of Ireland*. Vol. 4, *Eighteenth-Century Ireland, 1691–1800*. Oxford: Clarendon Press, 1986.

Moody, T. W., F. X. Martin, and F. J. Byrne, eds. *A New History of Ireland*. Vol. 3, *Early Modern Ireland 1534–1691*. Oxford: Clarendon Press, 1976.

Mooney, Canice [Cainneach Ó Maonaigh], ed. "Manutiana: The Poems of Manus O'Rourke (c. 1658–1743)." *Celtica* 1 (1946–50): 1–63.

———. "Scríbhneoirí Gaeilge an Seachtú hAois Déag." *Studia Hibernica* 2 (1962): 182–208.

———, ed. *Seanmónta Chúige Uladh*. Baile Átha Cliath: Institiúid Ard-Léinn Bhaile Átha Cliath, 1965.

Mooney, Desmond. "Popular Religion and Clerical Influences in Pre-Famine Meath." In *Religion, Conflict, and Coexistence*, edited by R. V. Comerford, Mary Cullen, Jacqueline R. Hill, and Colm Lennon, 182–218. Dublin: Gill and Macmillan, 1990.

Mooney, Máirín. "Irish in the Liberties (1850–1911)." In *An Ghaeilge i mBaile Átha Cliath*, edited by Ciarán Ó Coigligh, 11–14. Baile Átha Cliath: Saotharlann Staire Bhaile Átha Cliath, 1985.

Moran, Gerard, and Raymond Gillespie, eds. *Galway: History and Society. Interdisciplinary Essays on the History of an Irish County*. Dublin: Geography Publications, 1996.

Morley, Vincent. *An Crann os Coill: Aodh Buí Mac Cruitín, c. 1680–1755*. Baile Átha Cliath: Coiscéim, 1995.

———. "The Continuity of Disaffection in Eighteenth-Century Ireland." *Eighteenth-Century Ireland/Iris an Dá Chultúr* 22 (2007): 189–205.

———. "The Idea of Britain in Eighteenth-Century Ireland and Scotland." *Studia Hibernica* 33 (2004–5): 101–24.

———. *Ó Chéitinn go Raiftearaí: Mar a Cumadh Stair na hÉireann*. Baile Átha Cliath: Coiscéim, 2011.

———. *Washington i gCeannas a Ríochta: Cogadh Mheiriceá i Litríocht na Gaeilge*. Baile Átha Cliath: Coiscéim, 2005.

Moyna, María Irene, and Magdalena Coll. "A Tale of Two Borders: 19th Century Language Contact in Southern California and Northern Uruguay." *Studies in Hispanic and Lusophone Linguistics* 1, no. 1 (Spring 2008): 105–38.

Mufwene, Salikoko S. *The Ecology of Language Evolution*. Cambridge: Cambridge University Press, 2001.

———. *Language Evolution: Contact, Competition, and Change*. London: Continuum International Publishing Group, 2008.

Mulchrone, Kathleen, ed. *Bethu Phátraic: The Tripartite Life of Patrick*. Dublin: Royal Irish Academy, 1939.

Murphy, Ignatius. *Before the Famine Struck: Life in West Clare, 1834–1845*. Dublin: Irish Academic Press, 1996.

———. *The Diocese of Killaloe, 1800–1850*. Dublin: Four Courts Press, 1992.

———. *The Diocese of Killaloe, 1850–1904*. Dublin: Four Courts Press, 1995.

Murphy, James H., ed. *Evangelicals and Catholics in Nineteenth-Century Ireland*. Dublin: Four Courts Press, 2005.

Murphy, Maura. "The Ballad Singer and the Role of the Seditious Ballad in Nineteenth-Century Ireland: Dublin Castle's View." *Ulster Folklife* 25 (1979): 79–102.

Murphy, P. J. "The Papers of Nicholas Archdeacon." *Archivium Hibernicum* 31 (1973): 124–31.

Naddeo, Barbara Ann. "Urban Arcadia: Representations of the 'Dialect' of Naples in Linguistic Theory and Comic Theater, 1696–1780." *Eighteenth-Century Studies* 35, no. 1 (Fall 2001): 41–65.

National Library of Ireland, and Richard J. Hayes. *Sources: A National Library of Ireland Database for Irish Research*. 2007–12. http://sources.nli.ie.

Neville, Grace. "God's Own Language? Attitudes to Irish, Then and Now." *Études irlandaises* 26, no. 2 (2001): 81–96.

———. "'He Spoke to Me in English, I Answered Him in Irish': Language Shift in the Folklore Archives." In *L'Irlande et ses langues: Actes du colloque 1992 de la Societé Française d'Études Irlandaises*, edited by Jean Brihault, 19–32. Rennes: Presses Universitaires Rennes, 1992.

New Catholic Encyclopedia. 15 vols. 2nd ed. Washington, DC: Catholic University of America in Association with Gale, 2003.

Nic Craith, Máiréad. *Malartú Teanga: An Ghaeilge i gCorcaigh sa Naoú hAois Déag.* Bremen: Cumman Eorpach Léann na hÉireann, 1994.

Nic Eoin, Máirín. *B'Ait leo Bean: Gnéithe den Idé-eolaíocht Inscne i dTraidisiún Liteartha na Gaeilge.* Baile Átha Cliath: An Clóchomhar Tta, 1998.

———. "Irish Language and Literature in County Kilkenny in the Nineteenth Century." In *Kilkenny: History and Society; Interdisciplinary Essays in the History of an Irish County,* edited by William Nolan and Kevin Whelan, 465–79. Dublin: Geography Publications, 1990.

Ní Chiosáin, Máire. "Meath na Gaeilge i gCléire." In *Aistí ar an Nua-Ghaeilge in Ómós do Bhreandán Ó Buachalla,* edited by Aidan Doyle and Siobhán Ní Laoire, 85–93. Baile Átha Cliath: Cois Life, 2006.

Nicholas, Stephen, and Peter R. Shergold. "Irish Intercounty Mobility Before 1840." *Irish Economic & Social History* 17 (1990): 22–43.

Nicolaisen, W. F. H. "Place-Name Legends: An Onomastic Mythology." *Folklore* 87, no. 2 (1976): 146–59.

Ní Dhonnachadha, Máire. "Irish Language Interpreting in the Courts since the 1850s." MA thesis, Dublin City University, 2000.

Ní Dhonnchadha, Máirín. "Neamhlitearthacht agus Gaeilge: Eagna na Staraithe?" *Comhar* 50 (1991): 22–25.

Nilsen, Kenneth E. "The Irish Language in New York, 1850–1900." In *The New York Irish,* edited by Ronald H. Bayor and Timothy J. Meagher, 252–74. Baltimore: Johns Hopkins University Press, 1996.

Ní Mhóráin, Brighid. *Thiar sa Mhainistir atá an Ghaolainn Bhreá: Meath na Gaeilge in Uíbh Ráthach.* An Daingean: An Sagart, 1997.

Ní Mhuirgheasa, Máire, ed. *Stair an Bhíobla. Ó Láimhsgríbhinn Do Sgríobh Uáitear Ua Ceallaigh Tuairim na Bliadhna MDCCXXVI.* Baile Átha Cliath: Oifig an tSoláthair, 1941.

Ní Mhuiríosa, Máirín. *Réamhchonraitheoirí. Nótaí ar Chuid de na Daoine a bhí Gníomhach i nGluiseacht na Gaeilge idir 1876 agus 1893.* Baile Átha Cliath: Clódhanna Teoranta, 1968.

Ní Mhunghaile, Lesa. "An Dearcadh a Léirítear ar Fheidhmiú an Dlí in Éirinn i bhFoinsí Gaeilge ón 18ú agus 19ú hAois." *Studia Hibernica* 36 (2011): 105–34.

———. "Bilingualism, Print Culture in Irish and the Public Sphere, 1700–c. 1830." In *Irish and English: Essays on the Irish Linguistic and Cultural Frontier, 1600–1900,* edited by James Kelly and Ciarán Mac Murchaidh, 218–42. Dublin: Four Courts Press, 2012.

———. "The Legal System in Ireland and the Irish Language, 1700–c. 1843." In *The Laws and Other Legalities of Ireland, 1689–1850,* edited by Michael Brown and Seán Patrick Donlan, 325–58. Farnham, Surrey, UK: Ashgate Publishing, 2011.

Ní Mhurchú, Máire, and Diarmuid Breathnach. *Beathaisnéis a Sé: 1782–1881.* 2nd ed. Baile Átha Cliath: An Clóchomhar Tta, 2008.

Ní Mhurchú, Máire, Diarmuid Breathnach, and Fiontar, DCU. *ainm.ie*. Dublin City University and Cló Iar-Chonnacht, 2011. http://ainm.ie.

Ní Shéaghdha, Nessa. *Collectors of Irish Manuscripts: Motives and Methods; Richard Irvine Best Lecture, 1984*. Dublin: Dublin Institute for Advanced Studies, 1985.

———. "Gairmeacha Beatha Roinnt Scríobhaithe ón 18ú agus ón 19ú Céad." *Celtica* 21 (1990): 567–75.

Ní Shéaghdha, Nessa, and Pádraig Ó Macháin. *Catalogue of Irish Manuscripts in the National Library of Ireland*. Fasciculi I–XIII. Dublin: Dublin Institute for Advanced Studies, 1967–96.

Ní Úrdail, Meidhbhín. "The Representations of the Feminine: Some Evidence from Irish-Language Sources." *Eighteenth-Century Ireland/Iris an Dá Chultúr* 22 (2007): 133–50.

———. *The Scribe in Eighteenth- and Nineteenth-Century Ireland: Motivations and Milieu*, Studien und Texte zur Keltologie 3. Münster: Nodus Publikationen, 2000.

Nolan, William, and Kevin Whelan, eds. *Kilkenny: History and Society; Interdisciplinary Essays in the History of an Irish County*. Dublin: Geography Publications, 1990.

Nolan, William, and Thomas P. Power, eds. *Waterford: History and Society; Interdisciplinary Essays on the History of an Irish County*. Dublin: Geography Publications, 1992.

Noonkester, Myron. "The Third British Empire: Transplanting the English Shire to Wales, Scotland, Ireland, and America." *Journal of British Studies* 36, no. 3 (1997): 251–84.

Norrick, Neal. *Conversational Joking: Humor in Everyday Talk*. Bloomington: University of Indiana Press, 1993.

Nowlan, Kevin. "Disestablishment: 1800–1869." In *Irish Anglicanism 1869–1969: Essays on the Role of Anglicanism in Irish Life Presented to the Church of Ireland on the Occasion of the Centenary of its Disestablishment By a Group of Methodist, Presbyterian, Quaker, and Roman Catholic Scholars*, edited by Micheal Hurley, 1–22. Dublin: A Figgis, 1970.

Noy, Dov, ed. *Folktales of Israel*. London: Routledge and Kegan Paul, 1963.

Ó Briain, Felim. "Irish Hagiography: Historiography and Method." In *Measgra i gCuimhne Mhichíl Uí Chléirigh. i. Miscellany of Historical and Linguistic Studies in Honour of Brother Michael Ó Cléirigh, O.F.M. Chief of the Four Masters 1643–1943*, edited by Sylvester O'Brien, 119–31. Dublin: Assisi Press, 1944.

O'Brien, Gerard. "The Establishment of Poor-Law Unions in Ireland, 1838–43." *Irish Historical Studies* 23, no. 90 (Nov. 1982): 97–120.

———, ed. *Parliament, Politics, and People: Essays in Eighteenth-Century Irish History*. Dublin: Irish Academic Press, 1989.

———. "State Intervention and the Medical Relief of the Irish Poor, 1787–1850." In *Medicine, Disease, and the State in Ireland, 1650–1940*, edited by Greta Jones and Elizabeth Malcolm, 195–207. Cork: Cork University Press, 1999.

O'Brien, Patrick, ed. *Eochair-Sgiath an Aifrinn, ar n-a Chnuasach agus ar n-a Sgríobhadh le Seathrún Céitinn, Sagart agus Doctúr Diadhachta*. Dublin: Patrick O'Brien, 1898.

Ó Buachalla, Breandán. *Aisling Ghéar: Na Stíobhartaigh agus an tAos Léinn, 1603–1788*. Baile Átha Cliath: An Clóchomhar Tta, 1996.

———. "From Jacobite to Jacobin." In *1798: A Bicentenary Perspective*, edited by Thomas Bartlett, David Dickson, Dáire Keogh, and Kevin Whelan, 75–96. Dublin: Four Courts Press, 2003.

———. *I mBéal Feirste Cois Cuain*. Baile Átha Cliath: An Clóchomhar Tta, 1968.

———. "Marbhchaoine an Athar Seán Ó Maonaigh." In *Saoi na hÉigse: Aistí in Ómós do Sheán Ó Tuama*, edited by Pádraigín Riggs, Breandán Ó Conchúir, and Seán Ó Coileáin, 197–208. Baile Átha Cliath: An Clóchomhar Tta, 2000.

———. "Nótaí ar Ghaeilge Dhoire agus Thír Eoghain." *Éigse* 13, no. 4 (1969–70): 249–78.

———. "A Speech in Irish on Repeal." *Studia Hibernica* 10 (1970): 84–94.

Ó Buachalla, Séamas. "Educational Policy and the Role of the Irish Language from 1831 to 1981." *European Journal of Education* 19, no. 1 (1984): 75–92.

Ó Cadhla, Stiofán. *Civilizing Ireland: Ordnance Survey, 1824–1842; Ethnography, Cartography, Translation*. Dublin: Irish Academic Press, 2007.

O'Carroll, Ciaran. "The Pastoral Politics of Paul Cullen." In *History of the Catholic Diocese of Dublin*, edited by James Kelly and Dáire Keogh, 294–312. Dublin: Four Courts Press, 2000.

Ó Casaide, Séamus. "Irish Versus Roman Characters." *Irish Book Lover* 20 (1932): 56–57.

Ó Casaide, Séamus, and E. R. McClintock Dix. *List of Books, Pamphlets, etc., Printed Wholly or Partly in Irish, from the Earliest Period to 1820*. Dublin: An Cló-Chumann Teoranta, 1905.

Ó Catháin, Séamas. "'Butter, Sir . . .'AT 1698 and 1699—a Typological Sandwich." *Béaloideas* 45–47 (1977–79): 84–117.

———. "Dáileadh Roinnt Scéalta de Chuid AT 1699: Misunderstanding Because of Ignorance of a Foreign Language." *Béaloideas* 42–44 (1974–76): 120–35.

Ó Catháin, Séamas, and Patrick O'Flanagan. *The Living Landscape: Kilgalligan, Erris, County Mayo*. Dublin: Comhairle Bhéaloideas Éireann, 1975.

Ó Ceallaigh, Aibhistín. "An Teagasc Críostaí in Éirinn, 1691–1800." *Galvia* 7 (1960): 50–62.

Ó Cearúil, Colm. *Aspail ar Son na Gaeilge: Timirí Chonradh na Gaeilge 1899–1923*. Baile Átha Cliath: Conradh na Gaeilge, 1995.

Ó Cearúil, Micheál, ed. *Gníomhartha na mBráithre*. Baile Átha Cliath: Coiscéim, 1996.

Uí Chatháin, Bláthnaid. *Éigse Chairbre: Filíocht ó Chairbreacha i gCo. Chorcaí agus ón gCeantar Máguaird, 1750–1850*. Baile Átha Cliath: An Clóchomhar Tta, 2006.

Ó Ciosáin, Éamon. *Buried Alive: A Reply to "The Death of the Irish Language."* Dublin: Dáil Uí Chadhain, 1991.

Ó Ciosáin, Niall. "Creating an Audience: Innovation and Reception in Irish Language Publishing, 1880–1920." In *The Irish Book in the Twentieth Century*, edited by Clare Hutton, 5–15. Dublin: Irish Academic Press, 2004.

———. "Gaelic Culture and Language Shift." In *Nineteenth-Century Ireland: A Guide to Recent Research*, edited by Laurence M. Geary and Margaret Kelleher, 136–52. Dublin: University College Dublin Press, 2005.

———. "Language, Print and the Catholic Church in Ireland, 1700–1900." In *Which Direction Ireland? Proceedings of the 2006 Mid-Atlantic Regional Conference*, edited by Donald McNamara, 125–36. Newcastle, UK: Cambridge Scholars Publishing, 2007.

———. *Print and Popular Culture in Ireland, 1750–1850*. New York: St. Martin's Press, 1997.

Ó Cléirigh, T. *Aodh Mac Aingil agus an Scoil Nua-Ghaedhilge i Lobháin*. Baile Átha Cliath: Oifig an tSoláthair, 1936. Repr., Baile Átha Cliath: An Gúm, 1985.

Ó Coigligh, Ciarán, ed. *An Ghaeilge i mBaile Átha Cliath*. Baile Átha Cliath: Saotharlann Staire Bhaile Átha Cliath, 1985.

Ó Coileáin, Seán. "The Irish Lament: An Oral Genre." *Studia Hibernica* 24 (1984–88): 97–117.

Ó Conaill, Tadhg, trans. *Trompa na bhFlaitheas*. Edited by Cecile O'Rahilly. Dublin: Dublin Institute for Advanced Studies, 1955.

Ó Conchubhair, Brian. *Fin de Siècle na Gaeilge: Darwin, an Athbheochan agus Smaointeoireacht na hEorpa*. Indreabhán: An Clóchomhar Tta, 2009.

Ó Conchúir, Breandán. *Clár Lámhscríbhinní Gaeilge Choláiste Ollscoile Chorcaí: Cnuasach Uí Mhurchú*. Baile Átha Cliath: Institiúid Ard-Léinn Bhaile Átha Cliath, 1991.

———. *Scríobhaithe Chorcaí 1700–1850*. Baile Átha Cliath: An Clóchomhar Tta, 1982.

———. "Teagasc Críostaí an Bhuitléaraigh." *Éigse* 17, no. 1 (1977): 69–87.

———. "Thomas Swanton, Réamhchonraitheoir in Iar Chairbre." *Journal of the Cork Historical and Archaeological Society* 98 (1993): 50–60.

O'Connell, Helen. "Improved English and the Silence of Irish." *Canadian Journal of Irish Studies* 30, no. 1 (2004): 13–20.

O'Connell, Patricia. *The Irish College at Alcalá De Henares, 1649–1785*. Dublin: Four Courts Press, 1997.

O'Connor, Anne V. "The Revolution in Girls' Secondary Education in Ireland, 1860–1910." In *Girls Don't Do Honours: Irish Women in Education in the 19th and 20th Centuries*, edited by Mary Cullen, 31–54. Dublin: Women's Education Bureau, 1987.

O'Connor, James. *History of Ireland, 1798–1924*. 2 vols. London: Edward Arnold & Co., 1925.

O'Connor, Thomas. "Towards the Invention of the Irish Catholic *Natio*: Thomas Messingham's *Florilegium* (1624)." *Irish Theological Quarterly* 64 (1999): 157–77.

O'Connor, Thomas, and Mary Ann Lyons, eds. *Irish Communities in Early-Modern Europe*. Dublin: Four Courts Press, 2006.

Ó Criomhthain, Tomás. *An tOileánach*. Edited by Seán Ó Coileáin. Baile Átha Cliath: Cló Talbóid, 2002.

———. *The Islandman*. Translated by Robin Flower. Dublin: Talbot Press, 1934.

Ó Crualaoich, Gearóid, and Diarmuid Ó Giolláin. "Folklore in Irish Studies." *Irish Review* 5 (1988): 68–74.

Ó Cuinn, Cosslett. *Scian a Caitheadh le Toinn: Scéalta agus Amhráin as Inis Eoghain agus Cuimhne ar Ghaeltacht Iorrais*. Edited by Aodh Ó Canainn and Seosamh Watson. Baile Átha Cliath: Coiscéim, 1990.

Ó Cuív, Brian. *Catalogue of Irish Language Manuscripts in the Bodleian Library at Oxford and Oxford College Libraries*. 2 vols. Dublin: Dublin Institute for Advanced Studies, 2001, 2003.

———. "*Dinnshenchas*—The Literary Exploitation of Irish Place-Names." *Ainm: Bulletin of the Ulster Place-Name Society* 4 (1989–90): 90–106.

———, ed. "Flaithrí Ó Maolchonaire's Catechism of Christian Doctrine." *Celtica* 1 (1946–50): 161–206.

———. *Irish Dialects and Irish-Speaking Districts: Three Lectures by Brian Ó Cuív*. Dublin: Dublin Institute for Advanced Studies, 1980.

———. "Irish Language and Literature, 1691–1845." In *A New History of Ireland*, vol. 4, *Eighteenth-Century Ireland, 1691–1800*, edited by T. W. Moody and W. E. Vaughan, 374–423. Oxford: Clarendon Press, 1986.

———. "The Irish Language in the Early Modern Period." In *A New History of Ireland*, vol. 3, *Early Modern Ireland, 1534–1691*, edited by T. W. Moody, F. X. Martin, and F. J. Byrne, 509–45. Oxford: Clarendon Press, 1976.

———. "Irish Translations of Thomas à Kempis's *De Imitatione Christi*." *Celtica* 2, no. 2 (1954): 252–74.

———, ed. "A Modern Irish Devotional Tract." *Celtica* 1 (1946–50): 207–37.

———. "The Penitential Psalms in Irish Verse." *Éigse* 8 (1955): 43–69.

———. "Some Developments in Irish Metrics." *Éigse* 12 (1967–1968): 273–90.

———. "The Stations of the Cross." *Celtica* 2, no. 1 (1952): 1–29.

———. "Two Items From Irish Apocryphal Tradition." *Celtica* 10 (1973): 87–113.

———, ed. *A View of the Irish Language*. Dublin: Stationery Office, 1969.

Ó Danachair, Caoimhín. "Dónall Ó Conaill i mBéalaibh na nDaoine." *Studia Hibernica* 14 (1974): 40–66.

———. "The Irish Language in County Clare in the Nineteenth Century." *North Munster Antiquarian Journal* 13 (1970): 40–52.

Ó Danachair, Liam. "Memories of My Youth." *Béaloideas* 17 (1947): 58–72.

Ó Domhnaill, Mághnus, ed. *An Bheatha Chrábhaidh*. Baile Átha Cliath: Oifig an tSoláthair, 1938.

Ó Dónaill, Niall, ed. *Foclóir Gaeilge-Béarla*. Baile Átha Cliath: An Gúm, 1992.

Ó Donnachadha, Rónán. *Mícheál Óg Ó Longáin, File*. Baile Átha Cliath: Coiscéim, 1994.

Ó Donnchadha, Diarmuid. *Castar an Taoide*. Baile Átha Cliath: Coiscéim, 1995.

O'Donoghue, Patrick. "Causes of the Opposition to Tithes, 1830–38." *Studia Hibernica* 5 (1965): 7–28

———. "Opposition to Tithe Payment in 1832–33." *Studia Hibernica* 12 (1972): 77–108.

———. "Opposition to Tithe Payments in 1830–31." *Studia Hibernica* 6 (1966): 69–98.

O'Donoghue, Thomas. "Bilingual Education in Ireland in the Late-Nineteenth and Early-Twentieth Centuries." *History of Education* 17, no. 3 (1988): 209–20.

———. *Bilingual Education in Pre-Independent Irish-Speaking Ireland, 1800–1922: A History*. Lewiston, NY: The Edwin Mellen Press, 2006.

Ó Dúghaill, Gréagóir. "Seanmóir ar an Troscadh." *Éigse* 15, no. 2 (1973): 131–39.

Ó Duibhir, Donnchadh. "Tomás Ó hÍcí, Scríobhaí Chill Náile." *Tipperary Historical Journal* 3 (1990): 97–102.

Ó Duibhir, P. "An Dies Irae." *Éigse* 2, no. 2 (Summer 1940): 137–45.

Ó Duilearga, Séamus. "Cnuasach Andeas: Scéalta agus Seanchas Sheáin Í Shé ó Íbh Ráthach; Sean-Scéalta." *Béaloideas* 29 (1961):1–153.

———. "Seana-Phaidreacha agus Orthaí ó Íbh Ráthach." *Béaloideas* 37–38 (1969–70): 107–22.

Ó Duinnshléibhe, Seán. "'Mar is fánach mac a' teacht go cruinn mar 'athair': Dáibhí de Barra's Surviving Translations." In *Visual, Material and Print Culture in Nineteenth-Century Ireland*, edited by Ciara Breathnach and Catherine Lawless, 257–70. Dublin: Four Courts Press, 2010.

Ó Dúshláine, Tadhg. *An Eoraip agus Litríocht na Gaeilge 1600–1650. Gnéithe den Bharócachas Eorpach i Litríocht na Gaeilge*. Baile Átha Cliath: An Clóchomhar Tta, 1987.

———. "*Fasciculus Morum*: Foinse Chomónta do Phrós Cráifeach na Gaeilge sa 17ú hAois?" *Studia Hibernica* 34 (2006–2007): 111–22.

———. "Gealán Dúluachra: Seanmóireacht na Gaeilge, c.1600–c.1850." In *Leann na Gaeilge: Súil Siar, Súil Chun Cinn*, Léachtaí Cholm Cille 26, ed. Ruairí Ó hUiginn, 83–122. Maigh Nuad: An Sagart, 1996.

———. "Seanmóirí Mhaigh Nuad." In *Maigh Nuad: Saothrú na Gaeilge, 1795–1995*, edited by Etaín Ó Siocháin, 63–78. Maigh Nuad: An Sagart, 1995.

O'Dwyer, Christopher. "Archbishop Butler's Visitation Book, Part 1." *Archivium Hibernicum* 33 (1975): 1–90.

———. "Archbishop Butler's Visitation Book, Part 2." *Archivium Hibernicum* 34 (1977): 1–49.

O'Dwyer, Peter. *Towards a History of Irish Spirituality*. Dublin: Columba Press, 1995.

Ó Fachtna, Anselm. "'An Bheatha Chrábhaidh' agus 'An Bheatha Dhiaga.'" *Éigse* 10, no. 2 (1962): 89–95.

———, ed. *An Bheatha Dhiadha nó an tSlighe Ríoghdha*. Baile Átha Cliath: Institiúid Ard-Léinn Bhaile Átha Cliath, 1967.

———. "Seanmóir ar Pháis Ár dTiarna Íosa Críost." *Éigse* 12 (1967–68): 177–98.

Ó Fearghail, Fearghus. "An Irish Instruction of 1775." *Ossory, Laois and Leinster* 3 (2008): 168–89

———. "An Ossory Instruction of 1773." *Archivium Hibernicum* 48 (1994): 25–36.

Ó Fiannachta, Pádraig. *Clár Lámhscríbhinní Gaeilge: Leabharlanna na Cléire agus Mionchnuasaigh*. Fascúl I–II. Baile Átha Cliath: Institiúid Ard-Léinn Bhaile Átha Cliath, 1978–80.

———. "Do Lochtuiv na Tangan." *Éigse* 12 (1967–68): 1–28.

———, ed. *Maigh Nuad agus an Ghaeilge*. Léachtaí Cholm Cille 23. Maigh Nuad: An Sagart, 1993.

———. *Milis an Teanga: Stair na Gaeilge ó Thús*. Corcaigh: Cló Mercier, 1974.

———. "Scéalta ón Magnum Speculum Exemplorum." *Irish Ecclesiastical Record* 99, no. 3 (1963): 177–84.

———. "Seanmóireacht Ghaeilge san Ochtú agus sa Naoú hAois Déag." *Irisleabhar Mhá Nuad* (1983): 141–49.

———. "Stíl na Seanmóireachta—Sampla." In *Léas ar Ár Litríocht*, edited by Pádraig Ó Fiannachta, 167–81. Maynooth: An Sagart, 1974.

O'Flanagan, Michael, ed. *Letters Containing Information Relative to the Antiquities of the County of Clare, Collected during the Progress of the Ordnance Survey in 1839.* 3 vols. Typescript, Royal Irish Academy, 1928.

———, ed. *Letters Containing Information Relative to the Antiquities of the County of Galway, Collected during the Progress of the Ordnance Survey in 1839.* 3 vols. Typescript, National Library of Ireland, 1928.

———, ed. *Letters Containing Information Relative to the Antiquities of the County of Kerry, Collected during the Progress of the Ordnance Survey in 1841.* Typescript, Royal Irish Academy, 1935.

———, ed. *Letters Containing Information Relative to the Antiquities of the County of Mayo, Collected during the Progress of the Ordnance Survey in 1838.* 2 vols. Typescript, National Library of Ireland, 1927.

———, ed. *Letters Containing Information Relative to the Antiquities of the County of Westmeath, Collected during the Progress of the Ordnance Survey in 1837.* 2 vols. Typescript, Royal Irish Academy, 1931.

Ó Flannghaile, Tomás, ed. *Duanaire na Macaomh. A Selection of Irish Poetry for Schools and Colleges.* Dublin: M. H. Gill and Son, 1910.

Ó Floinn, Donnchadh. "Magh Nuadhat agus an Athbheochaint." *Irish Ecclesiastical Record*, ser. 5, 66, no. 933 (1945): 201–7.

Ó Foghludha, Risteárd, ed. *Duanta Diadha Phádraig Denn, 1756–1828 cct.* Baile Átha Cliath: Oifig an tSoláthair, 1941.

Ó Giolláin, Diarmuid. "Folk Culture." In *The Cambridge Companion to Modern Irish Culture*, edited by Joe Cleary and Claire Connolly, 225–44. Cambridge: Cambridge University Press, 2005.

Ó Gliasáin, Mícheál. *Ceist na Teanga sa Daonaireamh/The Language Question in the Census of Population.* Dublin: Institiúid Tengeolaíochta Éireann, 1996.

Ó Gráda, Cormac. *Ireland: A New Economic History, 1780–1939.* Oxford: Clarendon Press, 1994.

———. "Seasonal Migration and Post-Famine Adjustment in the West of Ireland." *Studia Hibernica* 13 (1973): 48–76.

O'Grady, Standish H., Robin Flower, and Myles Dillon. *Catalogue of Irish Manuscripts in the British Museum* [now British Library]. 3 vols. London: British Museum, 1925–26, 1953.

Ó Háinle, Cathal. "Ar Bhás Sheáin Uí Neachtain." *Éigse* 19, no. 2 (1983): 384–94.

———. "The *Pater Noster* in Irish." *Celtica* 21 (1990): 470–88.

Ó hAodha, Mícheál. "Seanchas ós na Déisibh." *Béaloideas* 14 (1944): 53–112.

Ó hEarcáin, M. "Meath na Gaeilge i gCluain Maine agus in Iorras." *Donegal Annual* 47 (1995): 106–12.

Ó Héideáin, Eustás. *National School Inspection in Ireland: The Beginnings.* Dublin: Scepter Books, 1967.

Ó hÓgáin, Dáithí. *The Hero in Irish Folk History.* Dublin: Gill and Macmillan, 1985.

Ó Huallacháin, Colmán. *The Irish and Irish: A Sociolinguistic Analysis of the Relationship between a People and Their Language*. Dublin: Irish Franciscan Provincial Office, 1994.
Okulska, Urszula. "Historical Corpora and Their Applicability to Sociolinguistic, Discourse-Pragmatic, and Ethno-Linguistic Research." *Poznań Studies in Contemporary Linguistics* 41 (2006): 47–109.
Ó Labhraí, Seosamh. "Seanmóir ar Pháis Chríost." *Seanchas Ard Mhacha* 18, no. 1 (1999–2000): 100–16.
Ó Laoghaire, Diarmuid. *Ár bPaidreacha Dúchais: Cnuasach de Phaidreacha agus de Bheannachtaí Ár Sinsear*. Baile Átha Cliath: Foilseacháin Ábhair Spioradálta, 1982.
———. "Prayer and Hymns in the Vernacular." In *Introduction to Celtic Christianity*, edited by James P. Mackey, 268–304. Edinburgh: T. and T. Clark, 1989.
Ó Laoghaire, Peadar. *Mo Sgéal Féin*. Baile Átha Cliath: Brún agus Nuallán, 1915.
———. *My Story*. Translated by Cyril T. Ó Céirin. Cork: Mercier Press, 1970.
O'Leary, Paul. "Religion, Nationality and Politics: Disestablishment in Ireland and Wales, 1868–1914." In *Contrasts and Comparisons: Studies in Irish and Welsh Church History*, edited by John R. Guy and W. D. Neely, 89–112. Llandysul: Gomer Press, 1999.
O'Leary, Philip. *The Prose Literature of the Gaelic Revival, 1881–1921: Ideology and Innovation*. University Park: Pennsylvania State University Press, 1994.
Ó Loingsigh, Pádraig. "The Irish Language in the 19th Century." *Oideas* 14 (1974): 5–21.
Ó Macháin, Pádraig. *Catalogue of Irish Manuscripts in Mount Melleray Abbey, Co. Waterford*. Dublin: Dublin Institute for Advanced Studies, 1991.
———. "The Early Modern Irish Prosodic Tracts and the Editing of 'Bardic Verse.'" *Metrik und Medienwechsel/Metrics and Media* (1991): 273–87.
———. "Fr. Patrick Meany and the Dr. Keating Society, 1860–1865." *Studia Hibernica* 37 (2011): 165–94.
———. "Litir Ghaelach, 1848." *Decies: The Journal of the Waterford Archaeological and Historical Society* 57 (2001): 85–89.
———. "Tomás Ó Iceadha's Translation of the Roman Missal." *Celtica* 24 (2003): 264–69.
———. "Two Nugent Manuscripts: The Nugent Duanaire and Queen Elizabeth's Primer." *Ríocht na Midhe. Records of the Meath Archaeological and Historical Society* 23 (2012): 121–42.
Ó Macháin, Pádraig, Dublin Institute for Advanced Studies, and Dublin City University. *Irish Script on Screen/Meamram Páipéar Ríomhaire*. 1999. http://www.isos.dias.ie.
Ó Madagáin, Breandán. *An Ghaeilge i Luimneach 1700–1900*. Baile Átha Cliath: An Clóchomhar Tta, 1974.
———. "Ceol a Chanadh Eoghan Mór Ó Comhraí." *Béaloideas* 51 (1983): 71–86.
———. "Nótaí ar Chlaochlú Tosaigh an Ainmfhocail agus na hAidiachta i gCanúint de Chuid Cho. Chorcaí." *Éigse* 14 (1971): 81–86.
———, ed. *Teagasc ar an Sean-Tiomna*. Baile Átha Cliath: An Clóchomhar Tta: 1974.
Ó Maolalaigh, Roibeard, R. I. Best, and Rolf Baumgarten. *Bibliography of Irish Linguistics and Literature Online*. 2004. http://bill.celt.dias.ie.

Ó Maolfabhail, Art. "An tSuirbhéireacht Ordanáis agus Logainmneacha na hÉireann, 1824-1834." *Proceedings of the Royal Irish Academy*, Section C, 89, no. 3 (1989): 37-66.

[Bean] Uí Mhurchadha, Brighid. *Oideachas in Iar-Chonnacht sa Naoú Céad Déag.* Baile Átha Cliath: Oifig an tSoláthair, 1954.

Ó Mórdha, Séamus P., ed. "An Anti-Tithe Speech in Irish." *Éigse* 9, no. 4 (Winter 1960-61): 223-26.

———. "Údar *Tóruidheacht na bhFíreun air Lorg Chríosda.*" *Studia Hibernica* 3 (1963): 155-72.

Ó Muirgheasa, Énrí [Henry Morris], ed. *Dánta Diadha Uladh.* Baile Átha Cliath: Oifig Díolta Foillseacháin Rialtais, 1936.

Ó Muirithe, Diarmaid. *An tAmhrán Macarónach.* Baile Átha Cliath: An Clóchomhar Tta, 1980.

———. "An tAthair Pól Ó Briain." In *Maigh Nuad agus an Ghaeilge.* Léachtaí Cholm Cille 23. Edited by Pádraig Ó Fiannachta, 8-43. Maigh Nuad: An Sagart, 1993.

———, ed. *The English Language in Ireland.* 1977. Repr., Cork: Mercier Press, 1985.

———. "O'Connell in Irish Folk Tradition." In *Daniel O'Connell: Political Pioneer*, edited by Maurice R. O'Connell, 72-85. Dublin: Daniel O'Connell Association, 1991.

Ó Muraíle, Nollaig. "Staid na Gaeilge i gConnachta in Aimsir Sheáin Mhic Héil." In *Leon an Iarthair: Aistí ar Sheán Mac Héil, Ardeaspag Thuama, 1834-1881*, edited by Áine Ní Cheannain, 37-66. Baile Átha Cliath: An Clóchomhar Tta, 1983.

Ó Murchadha, Gearóid. "Amhráin Bheannuithe, agus Paidreacha ó Chorca Dhuibhne." *Éigse* 3 (1941-42): 79-100.

Ó Murchú, Máirtín. *The Irish Language.* Dublin: Department of Foreign Affairs and Bord na Gaeilge, 1985.

———. "Language and Society in Nineteenth-Century Ireland." In *Language and Community in the Nineteenth Century*, edited by Geraint Jenkins, 341-68. Cardiff: University of Wales Press, 1998.

———. "The Retreat from Irish: The Statistical Analysis and Other Aspects." In *Ireland in the Contemporary World: Essays in Honour of Garret FitzGerald*, edited by J. Dooge, 112-21. Dublin: Gill and Macmillan, 1986.

———. *Urlabhra agus Pobal/Language and Community.* Occasional Paper No. 1. Dublin: Stationery Office, 1970.

Ó Neachtain, Eoghan, ed. *Stair Éamuinn Uí Chléire, do Réir Sheáin Uí Neachtain.* Baile Átha Cliath: M. H. Mac an Ghuill & a Mhach, Teo., 1918.

Ó Néill, Eoghan. *Gleann an Óir: Ar Thóir na Staire agus na Litríochta in Oirthear Mumhan agus i nDeisceart Laighean.* Baile Átha Cliath: An Clóchomhar Tta, 1988.

Uí Ógáin, Ríonach. *Immortal Dan: Daniel O'Connell in Irish Folk Tradition.* Dublin: Geography Publications, 1995.

O'Rahilly, Cecile, ed. *Five Seventeenth-Century Political Poems.* Dublin: Institiúid Ard-Léinn Bhaile Átha Cliath, 1952.

O'Rahilly, Thomas F. *Irish Dialects Past and Present.* Dublin: Dublin Institute for Advanced Studies, 1976.

O'Rahilly, Thomas F., and Kathleen Mulchrone, et al. *Catalogue of Irish Manuscripts in the Royal Irish Academy.* Fasciculi I-XXVII. Dublin: Royal Irish Academy, 1926-70.

Ó Riagáin, Pádraig. *Language Policy and Social Reproduction: Ireland, 1893-1993.* Oxford: Clarendon Press, 1997.

Oring, Elliott. *Engaging Humor.* Urbana: University of Illinois Press, 2003.

Ortner, Sherry. "Theory in Anthropology since the Sixties." *Comparative Studies in Society and History* 26, no. 1 (Jan. 1984): 126-66.

Ó Saothraí, Séamus. *An Ministir Gaelach Uilliam Mac Néill, 1774-1821: Agus a Oidhreacht a dFhág Sé againn.* Baile Átha Cliath: Coiscéim, 1992.

O'Shea, James. *Priest, Politics, and Society in Post-Famine Ireland: A Study of County Tipperary, 1850-1891.* Dublin: Wolfhound Press, 1983.

Ó Síocháin, Etaín, ed. *Maigh Nuad: Saothrú na Gaeilge, 1795-1995.* Maigh Nuad: An Sagart, 1995.

Ó Snodaigh, Pádraig. *Hidden Ulster: Protestants and the Irish Language.* Belfast: Lagan Press, 1995.

Ó Súileabháin, Muiris [Maurice O'Sullivan]. *Fiche Blian ag Fás.* Baile Átha Cliath: Clólucht an Talbóidigh, Tta, 1933.

———. *Twenty Years A-Growing.* Translated by Moya Llewelyn Davies and George Thomson. London: Oxford University Press, 1953.

Ó Súilleabháin, Donncha. *Cath na Gaeilge sa Chóras Oideachais, 1893-1911.* Baile Átha Cliath: Conradh na Gaeilge, 1988.

———. *Na Timirí i Ré Tosaigh an Chonartha, 1893-1927.* Baile Átha Cliath: Conradh na Gaeilge 1990.

Ó Súilleabháin, Eoghan. "Scríobhaithe Phort Láirge 1700-1900." In *Waterford: History and Society; Interdisciplinary Essays on the History of an Irish County,* edited by William Nolan and Thomas P. Power, 265-308. Dublin: Geography Publications, 1992.

Ó Súilleabháin, Pádraig. "Agallamh na bhFíoraon." *Éigse* 10, no. 1 (1961): 26-34.

———. "An Dr. de Siún, Easpag Luimnigh (1796-1813), agus an Ghaeilge." *Studia Hibernica* 6 (1966): 155-57.

———, ed. *Buaidh na Naomhchroiche.* Baile Átha Cliath: Institiúid Ard-Léinn Bhaile Átha Cliath, 1972.

———. "Catholic Sermon Books Printed in Ireland, 1700-1850." *Irish Ecclesiastical Record* 99 (Jan.-June 1963): 31-36.

———. "Clódóireacht Chaitliceach in Éirinn san Ochtú hAois Déag." *Irisleabhar Mhá Nuad* (1964): 95-101.

———. "Leabhar Urnaithe an Ochtú hAois Déag." *Irish Ecclesiastical Record* 103 (1965): 299-302.

———. "Roinnt Caiticeasmaí Gaeilge." *Éigse* 11 (1965): 113-15.

———. "Seanmóir ar an mBás." *Éigse* 13, no. 1 (1969): 11-25.

———. "Seanmóir ar an Meisce." *Éigse* 15, no. 4 (1974): 314-17.

———. "Seanmóir ar Ghnáithchleachtadh an Pheacaidh." *Éigse* 13, no. 4 (1970): 279-90.

———. "Seanmóir ar Uimhir Bheag na bhFíréan." *Éigse* 14, no. 2 (1971): 107-20.

———. "Varia: Seanmóirí ón bhFrancis." *Éigse* 9 (1960-61): 233-42.

Ó Súilleabháin, Seán. *A Handbook of Irish Folklore.* Dublin: Educational Company of Ireland, 1942.

———. *Irish Folk Custom and Belief.* Dublin: Cultural Relations Committee of Ireland, 1967.

———. "Irish Oral Tradition." In *A View of the Irish Language,* edited by Brian Ó Cuív, 47–56. Dublin: Stationery Office, 1969.

———. *Irish Wake Amusements.* 1967. Repr., Cork: Mercier Press, 1969.

Ó Súilleabháin, Seán, and Reidar Th. Christiansen. *The Types of the Irish Folktale.* FF Communications No. 188. Helsinki: Suomalainen Tiedeakatemia, 1963.

O'Sullivan, Donal. "A Sermon for Good Friday by Father Michael Walsh of Sneem." *Éigse* 4 (1943–45): 157–72.

Ó Tuama, Seán, ed. *The Gaelic League Idea.* Dublin: Mercier Press, 1972.

Ó Tuama, Seán, and Thomas Kinsella, eds. *An Duanaire: An Irish Anthology, 1600–1900; Poems of the Dispossessed.* 1981. Repr., St. Paul: Irish Books and Media, 1985.

Ó Tuathaigh, Gearóid. "An Chléir Chaitliceach, an Léann Dúchais agus an Cultúr in Éirinn, c. 1750–c. 1850." In *Léann na Cléire,* Léachtaí Cholm Cille 16, edited by Pádraig Ó Fiannachta, 110–39. Maigh Nuad: An Sagart, 1986.

———. "Gaelic Ireland, Popular Politics and Daniel O'Connell." *Galway Archaeological and Historical Journal* 34 (1974–75): 21–34.

———. "Maigh Nuad agus Stair na Gaeilge." In *Maigh Nuad: Saothrú na Gaeilge, 1795–1995,* edited by Etaín Ó Siocháin, 13–35. Maigh Nuad: An Sagart, 1995.

Ua Tuathail, Domhnall, ed. *Tóraidheacht na bhFíreun air Lorg Chríosta, i gCeithre Leabhraibh. Tomás À Cempis a Sgríobh san Laidin. Aig so an Chéad Aistriughadh Gaedhilge. Sagart Éigin i n-aice le Dún Phádraig i gCo. an Dúin a d'Aistrigh, 1762.* Baile Átha Cliath: M. H. Mac Guill agus a Mhac, 1915.

Ó Tuathail, Éamonn. "Gleanings from Lough Ramor." *Béaloideas* 7, no. 2 (1937): 191–94.

———. "Meath Anecdotes." *Éigse* 4, no. 1 (1943–45): 9–14.

———, ed. *Rainn agus Amhráin: Cnuasacht Rann agus Amhrán ó Chonndae na Midhe, ó Chonndae Lughmhaidh agus ó Chonndae Árdmhacha.* Baile Átha Cliath: Brún agus Ó Nóláin, Teor., 1923.

Owens, Gary. "Nationalism without Words: Symbolism and Ritual Behaviour in the Repeal 'Monster Meetings' of 1843–5." In *Irish Popular Culture, 1650–1850,* edited by James S. Donnelly, Jr., and Kerby A. Miller, 242–69. Dublin: Irish Academic Press, 1999.

Page, Cornelius Albert, ed. *The Myrrour of Synneres.* Institute of Medieval & Renaissance Studies Monograph Series. Dobbs Ferry, NY: Mercy College, 1976.

Palmer, Patricia. "Interpreters and the Politics of Translation and Traduction in Sixteenth-Century Ireland." *Irish Historical Studies* 33, no. 131 (May 2003): 257–77.

———. *Language and Conquest in Early Modern Ireland: English Renaissance Literature and Elizabethan Imperial Expansion.* Cambridge: Cambridge University Press, 2001.

Parker, Henry. *Village Folk-Tales of Ceylon.* 3 vols. London: Luzac and Co., 1910–14.

Parry, Gwenfair, and Mari A. Williams. *The Welsh Language and the 1891 Census.* Cardiff: University of Wales Press, 1999.

Partridge, Angela. "Ortha an Triúr Bráithre: Traidisiún Meánaoiseach i mBéaloideas na Gaeilge." *Béaloideas* 48–49 (1980–81): 188–203.

Pašeta, Senia. *Before the Revolution: Nationalism, Social Change, and Ireland's Catholic Elite, 1879–1922.* Cork: Cork University Press, 1999.
Perry, Jay Martin. "Shillelaghs, Shovels, and Secrets: Irish Immigrant Societies and the Building of Indiana Internal Improvements." MA thesis, Indiana University Bloomington, 2009.
Pilkington, Lionel. "Language and Politics in Brien Friel's *Translations.*" *Irish University Review* 20, no. 2 (1990): 282–98.
Pino-Saavredra, Yolando, ed. *Folktales of Chile.* Translated by Rockwell Gray. New York: Routledge and Kegan Paul, 1967.
Plummer, Charles. *Irish Litanies: Text and Translation.* London: Harrison and Sons, 1925.
———. *Miscellanea Hagiographica Hibernica.* Bruxelles: Société des Bollandistes, 1925.
Powell, Fred. "The Irish Poor Law Controversy." *Social Policy & Administration* 15, no. 3 (Autumn 1981): 286–303.
Power, Canon Patrick. "The Gaelic Union: A Nonagenarian Perspective." *Studies* 38 (1949): 413–18.
Priestly, Tom. "Denial of Ethnic Identity: The Political Manipulation of Beliefs About Language in Slovene Minority Areas of Austria and Hungary." *Slavic Review* 55, no. 2 (Summer 1996): 364–98.
Printy, Michael. "The Intellectual Origins of Popular Catholicism: Catholic Moral Theology in the Age of Enlightenment." *Catholic Historical Review* 91, no. 3 (July 2005): 438–61.
Prior, Katherine, Lance Brennan, and Robin Haines. "Bad Language: The Role of English, Persian, and Other Esoteric Tongues in the Dismissal of Sir Edward Colebrooke as Resident of Delhi in 1829." *Modern Asian Studies* 35, no. 1 (2001): 75–112.
Proudfoot, Lindsay J., ed. *Down: History and Society; Interdisciplinary Essays on the History of an Irish County.* Dublin: Geography Publications, 1997.
Purcell, Mary. *The Story of the Vincentians.* Dublin: All Hallows College, 1973.
Radcliffe-Brown, A. R. "On Joking Relationships." *Africa* 13, no. 3 (1940): 195–210.
Rael, Juan. *Cuentos Españoles de Colorado y Nuevo Méjico.* 2 vols. Stanford, CA: Stanford University Press, 1957.
Raftery, Deirdre, and Susan M. Parkes. *Female Education in Ireland 1700–1900: Minerva or Madonna.* Dublin: Irish Academic Press, 2007.
Randolph, Vance. *Who Blew Up the Church House and Other Ozark Folk Tales.* 1952. Repr., Westport, CT: Greenwood Press, 1972.
Raskin, Victor. *Semantic Mechanisms of Humor.* Dordrecht: D. Reidel Publishing Co., 1985.
Resines, Luis. "El Catechismo de Diego de Ledesma." *Archivium Historicum Societatis Iesu* 66, no. 132 (1997): 249–74.
Risk, May H. "Charles Lynegar, Professor of Irish in 1712." *Hermathena* 102 (Spring 1966): 16–25.
———. "Seán Ó Neachtain: An Eighteenth-Century Irish Writer." *Studia Hibernica* 15 (1975): 47–60.

Robe, Stanley. *Index of Mexican Folktales, Including Narrative Texts from Mexico, Central America, and the Hispanic United States*. Berkeley: University of California Press, 1973.

Roberts, Peter R. "Tudor Legislation and the Political Status of 'the British Tongue.'" In *The Welsh Language before the Industrial Revolution*, edited by Geraint H. Jenkins, 123–52. Cardiff: University of Wales Press, 1997.

Robinson, Tim, ed. *Connemara after the Famine: Journal of a Survey of the Martin Estate, 1853, by Thomas Colville Scott*. Dublin: Lilliput Press, 1995.

Rouget, François. "La langue française: Obstacle ou atout de l'état-nation'?" *Renaissance and Reformation/Renaissance et Réforme* 29, no. 1 (2005): 7–23.

Ryan, David. "Catholic Preaching in Ireland, 1760–1840." In *The Remaking of Modern Ireland, 1750–1950: Beckett Prize Essays in Irish History*, edited by Raymond Gillespie, 72–100. Dublin: Four Courts Press, 2004.

Ryan, Salvador. "Bonaventura Ó hEoghusa's An Teagasg Críosdaidhe (1611/1614): A Reassessment of Its Audience and Use." *Archivium Hibernicum* 58 (2004): 259–67.

Ryan, Vincent. *The Shaping of Sunday: Sunday and Eucharist in the Irish Tradition*. Dublin: Veritas, 1997.

Schwarzbaum, Haim. *Studies in Jewish and World Folklore*. Berlin: Walter de Gruyter and Co., 1968.

Scott, James. *Weapons of the Weak: Everyday Forms of Peasant Resistance*. New Haven, CT: Yale University Press, 1985.

Sewell, William H. "The Concept(s) of Culture." In *Beyond the Cultural Turn: New Directions in the Study of Society and Culture*, edited by Victoria E. Bonnell and Lynn Hunt, 35–61. Berkeley: University of California Press, 1999.

Sharpe, Richard. *Medieval Irish Saints' Lives: An Introduction to Vitae Sanctorum Hiberniae*. Oxford: Clarendon Press, 1991.

Sheehy, Jeanne. *The Rediscovery of Ireland's Past: The Celtic Revival, 1830–1930*. London: Thames and Hudson, 1980.

Shields, Hugh. "Singing Traditions of a Bilingual Parish in North-West Ireland." *Yearbook of the International Folk Music Council* 3 (1971): 109–19.

Shimoda, Hiraku. "Tongues-Tied: The Making of a 'National Language' and the Discovery of Dialects in Meiji Japan." *American Historical Review* 115, no. 3 (June 2010): 714–31.

Shyama-Shankar, Pandit. *Wit and Wisdom of India: A Collection of Humorous Folk-Tales of the Court and Country-side Current in India*. London: George Routledge and Sons, 1924.

Simms, J. G. "Irish Catholics and the Parliamentary Franchise, 1692–1728." *Irish Historical Studies* 23, no. 45 (1960–61): 28–37.

Simms, Katherine. "Literacy and the Irish Bards." In *Literacy in Medieval Celtic Societies*, edited by Huw Pryce, 238–58. Cambridge: Cambridge University Press, 1998.

Sjoestedt-Jonval, Marie-Louise. *Description d'un parler Irlandais de Kerry*. Paris: Librairie Ancienne Honoré Champion, 1938.

———. "L'Influence de la langue anglaise sur un parler local irlandais." In *Étrennes de linguistique offertes par quelques amis a Émile Benveniste*, edited by A. Meillet, 81–122. Paris: Librairie Orientaliste Paul Geuthner, 1928.

Skowcroft, R. Mark. "Leabhar Gabhála, Part I: The Growth of the Text." *Ériu* 38 (1987): 81–142.

———. "Leabhar Gabhála, Part II: The Growth of the Tradition." *Ériu* 39 (1988): 1–66.

Smyth, William J., and Kevin Whelan, eds. *Common Ground: Essays on the Historical Geography of Ireland*. Cork: Cork University Press, 1988.

Sneddon, Andrew. "'Darkness Must be Expell'd by Letting in the Light': Bishop Francis Hutchinson and the Conversion of Irish Catholics by Means of the Irish Language, c. 1770–4." *Eighteenth-Century Ireland/Iris an Dá Chultúr* 19 (2004): 37–55.

Somerville-Woodward, Robert. "'Language without a Mouth': The Development of an Irish Language Consciousness, c. 1820–1878." PhD diss., University College Dublin, 1998.

Stenson, Nancy, ed. *An Haicléara Mánas: A Nineteenth-Century Text from Clifden, Co. Galway*. Dublin: Dublin Institute for Advanced Studies, 2003.

———, ed. "English Influence on Irish: The Last 100 Years." *Journal of Celtic Linguistics* 2 (1993): 107–28.

Stevens, Phillip, Jr. "Bachama Joking Categories: Toward New Perspectives in the Study of Joking Relationships." *Journal of Anthropological Research* 34 (1978): 47–71.

Stewart, James. "The Game of 'An Bhfuil Agat?—Tá,' or the Uses of Bilingualism." *Béaloideas* 45–47 (1977–79): 244–58.

Stokker, Kathleen. *Folklore Fights the Nazis: Humor in Occupied Norway, 1940–1945*. Madison, NJ: Farleigh Dickinson University Press, 1995.

Swords, Liam. "Collège des Lombards." In *The Irish-French Connection, 1578–1978*, edited by Liam Swords, 44–62. Paris: Irish College, 1978.

———. "History of the Irish College, Paris, 1578–1800." *Archivium Hibernicum* 35 (1980): 3–233.

———, ed. *The Irish-French Connection, 1578–1978*. Paris: Irish College, 1978.

Szultka, Zygmunt. "Le polonais comme langue écrite en Poméranie occidentale depuis le XVIe siècle jusqu'au XVIIIe." *Polish Western Affairs* 31, nos. 1–2 (1990): 81–95.

Taylor, Larry. *Occasions of Faith: An Anthropology of Irish Catholics*. Dublin: Lilliput Press, 1995.

Thomas, Brinley. "A Cauldron of Rebirth: Population and the Welsh Language in the Nineteenth Century." *Welsh Historical Review* 13 (1987): 418–37.

Thomason, Sarah. *Language Contact: An Introduction*. Edinburgh: Edinburgh University Press, 2001.

Thompson, Stith. *Motif Index of Folk-Literature*. 6 vols. Rev. ed. Bloomington: University of Indiana Press, 1955–58.

Thompson, Stith, and Jonas Balys. *The Oral Tales of India*. Bloomington: University of Indiana Press, 1958.

Thompson, Stith, and Warren E. Roberts. *Types of Indic Oral Tales: India, Pakistan, and Ceylon*. FF Communications No. 180. Helsinki: Suomalainen Tiedeakatemia, 1960.

Thrane, James R. "Joyce's Sermon on Hell: Its Source and Its Backgrounds." *Modern Philology* 57, no. 3 (Feb. 1960): 172–98.

Tierney, Mark. *Calendar of the Papers of Dr. Croke (1841–1902)*. Unpublished typescript, NLI, 1965.

———. *Calendar of the Papers of Dr. Leahy Archbishop of Cashel, 1857–1875.* Unpublished typescript, NLI, 1966.

———. *Calendar of the Papers of Dr. M. Slattery Archbishop of Cashel and Emly 1834–1857.* Unpublished typescript, NLI, 1965.

Timm, L. A. "Modernization and Language Shift: The Case of Brittany." *Anthropological Linguistics* 15 (1973): 281–98.

Ting, Nai-Tung. *A Type Index of Chinese Folktales in the Oral Tradition and Major Works of Non-Religious Classical Literature.* FF Communications No. 223. Helsinki: Suomalainen Tiedeakatemia, 1978.

Torna [Tadhg Ó Donnachadha]. "Congantóirí Sheáin Uí Dhálaigh." *Éigse* 1 (1939): 258–64.

———. "Congantóirí Sheáin Uí Dhálaigh." *Éigse* 2, no. 3 (Fall 1940): 213–23.

Trautmann, Thomas R. *Language and Nations: The Dravidian Proof in Colonial Madras.* Berkeley: University of California Press, 2006.

Travers, Pauric. "A Bloodless Revolution: The Democratisation of Irish Local Government 1898–9." In *County and Town: One Hundred Years of Local Government in Ireland; Lectures on the Occasion of the 100th Anniversary of the Local Government Ireland*, edited by Mary Daly, 12–23. Dublin: Institute of Public Administration, 2001.

Trudgill, Peter. "Colonial Dialect Contact in the History of European Languages: On the Irrelevance of Identity to New-Dialect Formation." *Language in Society* 37, no. 2 (2008): 241–80.

———. *On Dialect: Social and Geographical Perspectives.* New York: New York University Press, 1983.

Turner, Victor. *The Ritual Process: Structure and Anti-Structure.* Ithaca, NY: Cornell University Press Paperbacks, 1991.

Tuten, Donald N. "Identity Formation and Accommodation: Sequential and Simultaneous Relations." *Language in Society* 37, no. 2 (2008): 259–62.

———. *Koineization in Medieval Spanish.* Contributions to the Sociology of Language 88. Berlin and New York: Mouton de Gruyter, 2003.

Tynan, Michael. *Catholic Instruction in Ireland, 1720–1950: The O'Reilly/Donlevy Catechetical Tradition.* Dublin: Four Courts Press, 1985.

[Uí / Ua—*see* Ó.]

United Kingdom Parliament. *Hansard 1803–2005 Online.* Accessed August 5, 2011. http://hansard.millbanksystems.com.

Ureland, P. Sture, and George Broderick, eds. *Language Contact in the British Isles: Proceedings of the Eighth International Symposium on Language Contact in Europe, Douglas, Isle of Man, 1988.* Tübingen: Max Niemeyer Verlag, 1991.

Van Goethem, Herman. "La politique des langues en France, 1620–1804." *Revue du Nord* 71, no. 281 (1989): 437–60.

Vaughan, W. E., ed. *A New History of Ireland.* Vol. 5, *Ireland under the Union, Part I, 1801–70.* Oxford: Clarendon Press, 1989.

———, ed. *A New History of Ireland.* Vol. 6, *Ireland under the Union, Part II, 1870–1921.* Oxford: Clarendon Press, 1996.

Vendryes, Joseph. "Betha Iuiliana." *Revue Celtique* 33 (1912): 311–23.

———. "La Situation Linguistique en Irlande." *Études Celtiques* 4 (1940): 177–79.
Villiers-Tuthill, Kathleen. *A History of Clifden, 1810–1860*. Dublin: by the author, 1981.
———. *Patient Endurance: The Great Famine in Connemara*. Dublin: Connemara Girl Publications, 1997.
Wagner, Heinrich. *Linguistic Atlas and Survey of Irish Dialects*. 4 vols. Dublin: Dublin Institute for Advanced Studies, 1958–69.
Waldron, Jarlath. *Maamtrasna: The Murders and the Mystery*. Dublin: Edmund Burke Publisher, 1992.
Wall, Maureen. "The Decline of the Irish Language." In *A View of the Irish Language*, edited by Brian Ó Cuív, 81–90. Dublin: Stationery Office, 1969.
Wall, Thomas [Tomás de Bhál]. "Challoner's Contemporaries in Ireland." *Irish Ecclesiastical Record* 68 (1946): 289–98.
———. "Patterns of Prayers and Devotions, 1750–1850." In *Studies in Pastoral Liturgy*, vol. 3, edited by Placid Murray, 211–14. Dublin: Furrow Trust and Gill and Son, 1967.
———. *The Sign of Doctor Hay's Head, Being Some Account of the Hazards and Fortunes of Catholic Printers and Publishers in Dublin from the Later Penal Times to the Present Day*. Dublin: M. H. Gill and Son 1958.
Walsh, Aisling. "Michael Cardinal Logue, 1840–1924, Part I." *Seanchas Ard Mhacha* 17 (1997): 108–62.
Walsh, Paul. *Gleanings from Irish Manuscripts*. 2nd ed. Dublin: Sign of the Three Candles, Fleet Street, 1933.
Walsh, Paul, and Pádraig Ó Fiannachta. *Lámhscríbhinní Gaeilge Choláiste Phádraig Má Nuad*. Fascúl I–VIII. Má Nuad: An Sagart, 1943–80.
Walsh, T. J. "Compulsory Irish in France." *Journal of the Cork Historical and Archaeological Society* 58, no. 187 (1853): 1–6.
Ward, Robert, et al., eds. *Letters of Charles O'Conor of Belanagare: A Catholic Voice in Eighteenth-Century Ireland*. Washington, DC: Catholic University of America Press, 1988.
Watson, Seosamh. "Coimhlint an Dá Chultúr—Gaeil agus Gaill i bhFilíocht Chúige Uladh san Ochtú hAois Déag." *Eighteenth-Century Ireland/Iris an Dá Chultúr* 3 (1988): 85–104.
Way, Peter. "Shovel and Shamrock: Irish Workers and Labor Violence in the Digging of the Chesapeake and Ohio Canal." *Labor History* 30, no. 4 (1989): 489–517.
Weber, Eugen. *Peasants into Frenchmen*. Stanford, CA: Stanford University Press, 1976.
Weeks, Theodore R. "Religion and Russification: Russian Language in the Catholic Churches of the 'Northwest Provinces' after 1863." *Kritika: Explorations in Russian and Eurasiana History* 2, no. 1 (Winter 2001): 87–110.
Whelan, Bernadette, ed. *Women and Paid Work in Ireland, 1500–1930*. Dublin: Four Courts Press, 2000.
Whelan, Irene. *The Bible War in Ireland: The "Second Reformation" and the Polarization of Protestant-Catholic Relations, 1800–1840*. Madison: University of Wisconsin Press, 2005.
Whelan, Kevin. "The Regional Impact of Irish Catholicism, 1700–1850." In *Common Ground: Essays on the Historical Geography of Ireland*, edited by William J. Smyth and Kevin Whelan, 253–77. Cork: Cork University Press, 1988.

———. *The Tree of Liberty: Radicalism, Catholicism and the Construction of Irish Identity, 1760–1830*. Notre Dame, IN: University of Notre Dame Press, 1996.
White, Eryn M. "The Established Church, Dissent and the Welsh Language c. 1660–1811." In *The Welsh Language before the Industrial Revolution*, edited by Geraint H. Jenkins, 235–87. Cardiff: University of Wales Press, 1997.
———. "Popular Schooling and the Welsh Language 1650–1800." In *The Welsh Language before the Industrial Revolution*, edited by Geraint H. Jenkins, 317–41. Cardiff: University of Wales Press, 1997.
White, Helen C. *English Devotional Literature (Prose), 1600–1640*. Madison: University of Wisconsin Press, 1931.
Whyte, J. H. "Landlord Influence at Elections in Ireland, 1760–1885." *English Historical Review* 80, no. 317 (Oct. 1965): 740–60.
Wilkerson, Miranda E., and Joseph Salmons. "'Good Old Immigrants of Yesteryear' Who Didn't Learn English: Germans in Wisconsin." *American Speech* 83, no. 3 (Fall 2008): 259–83.
Williams, Nicholas, ed. "Eachtra Áodh Mhic Goireachtaidh." *Éigse* 13 (1969–70): 111–42.
———. *I bPrionta i Leabhar: Na Protastúin agus Prós na Gaeilge, 1567–1724*. Baile Átha Cliath: An Clóchomhar Tta, 1986.
———. "Na Canúintí a Theacht chun Solais." In *Stair na Gaeilge in Ómos do Pádraig Ó Fiannachta*, edited by Kim McCone, Damian McManus, Cathal Ó Háinle, Nicholas Williams, and Liam Breatnach, 447–78. Maigh Nuad: Roinn na Sean-Ghaeilge, 1994.
———, ed. *Pairlement Chloinne Tomáis*. Dublin: Dublin Institute for Advanced Studies, 1981.
Wilson, Ann. "Arts and Crafts and Revivalism in Catholic Church Decoration: A Brief Duration." *Éire-Ireland* 48, nos. 3–4 (Fall/Winter 2013): 5–48.
Wilson, Christopher. *Jokes: Form, Content, Use, and Function*. London: Academic Press, 1979.
Wilson, E. M. "Some Humorous English Folk Tales, Part One." *Folk-lore* 49, no. 2 (1938): 182–92.
Withers, Charles W. J. *Gaelic in Scotland, 1698–1981: The Geographical History of a Language*. Edinburgh: John Donald Publishers, 1984.
Wolf, Nicholas M. "Orthaí and Orthodoxy: Healing Charms in Nineteenth-Century Catholicism." In *Power and Popular Culture in Modern Ireland: Essays in Honour of James S. Donnelly, Jr.*, edited by Michael de Nie and Sean Farrell, 125–44. Dublin: Irish Academic Press, 2010.
Woodbine, George E. "The Language of English Law." *Speculum: A Journal of Mediaeval Studies* 18, no. 4 (Oct. 1943): 395–436.
Yates, Nigel. *The Religious Condition of Ireland, 1770–1850*. Oxford: Oxford University Press, 2006.
Zhivov, Victor. *Language and Culture in Eighteenth-Century Russia*. Translated by Marcus Levitt. Boston: Academic Studies Press, 2009.

Index

The letter "t" following a page number denotes a table.

2 Anne c. 7 (1703) (Ire.) (registration of Catholic clergy), 121

8 Anne c. 3 (1709) (Ire.) (registration of Catholic clergy), 121, 125, 130

2 Eliz. I c. 12 (1560) (Ire.) (Act of Uniformity), 117, 147

12 Eliz. I c. 1 (1570) (Ire.) (Act for the Erection of Free Schools), 119–20

8 Geo. I c. 12 (1721) (Ire.) (regulation of gifts in support of Protestant schools), 125

4 Geo. II c. 26 (1731) (Eng.) (prohibition on Latin and French in English and Scottish courts), 150

5 Geo. II c. 4 (1731) (Ire.) (regulation of gifts in support of Protestant schools), 125

6 Geo. II c. 14 (1753) (Eng.) (prohibition on Latin and French in Welsh courts), 150

7 Geo. II c. 14 (1733) (Ire.) (prohibition on filings for suits in Latin and French in Irish courts), 150

11 Geo. II c. 6 (1737) (Ire.) (all court proceedings in Ireland to be in English, not Latin or French), 150

17 Geo. II c. 8 (1743) (Ire.) (transactions of courts of exchequer must be in English), 150

31 Geo. II c. 9 (1757) (Ire.) (renewal of penal laws against clergy), 130

5 Geo. III c. 14 (1765) (Ire.) (regulation of grand jury presentments), 154

11 & 12 Geo. III c. 27 (1771–72) (Ire.) (renewal of penal laws against clergy), 130

13 & 14 Geo. III c. 32 (1773–74) (Ire.) (expenses for court interpreters), 15419 & 20 Geo. III c. 39 (1779–80) (Ire.) (renewal of penal laws against clergy), 130

19 & 20 Geo. III c. 39 (1779–80) (Ire.) (renewal of penal laws against clergy), 130

33 Geo. III c. 21 (1793) (Ire.) (Catholic relief act), 164–65, 170

35 Geo. III c. 29 (1795) (Ire.) (regulation of polls and election oaths in Ireland), 319n100

36 Geo. III c. 55 (1796) (Ire.) (expenses for court interpreters), 155

37 Geo. III c. 47 (1797) (Ire.) (regulation of polls and election oaths in Ireland), 319n100

Index

38 Geo. III c. 39 (1798) (Ire.) (prohibition on Latin in admiralty courts), 314n6

43 Geo. III c. 74 (1803) (Ire.) (regulation of polls and election oaths in Ireland), 319n100

51 Geo. III c. 77 (1811) (Ire.) (regulation of polls and election oaths in Ireland), 319n100

57 Geo. III c. 131 (1817) (Ire.) (election officers to provide interpreters to administer oaths), 166

1 Geo. IV c. 11 (1820) (Ire.) (election officers to provide interpreters to administer oaths), 166–67

1 & 2 Geo. IV c. 58 (1821) (Ire.) (election officers to provide interpreters to administer oaths), 167

4 Geo. IV c. 43 (1823) (Ire.) (Act to Regulate the Amount of Presentments of Grand Juries), 155, 157

4 Geo. IV c. 55 (1823) (Ire.) (election officers to provide interpreters to administer oaths), 167, 172

7 & 8 Geo. IV c. 67 (1827) (Ire.) (regulation of petty sessions), 316n41

10 Henry VII c. 8 (1495) (Ire.) (reaffirmation of Statues of Kilkenny), 114

28 Henry VIII c. 15 (1537) (Ire.) (Act for the English Order, Habit, and Language), 114–17, 122, 130

1 Vict. c. 43 (1837) (Ire.) (expenses for interpreters at quarter sessions), 155

7 & 8 Vict. c. 106 (1844) (Ire.) (expenses for interpreters at Dublin assizes), 155

13 & 14 Vict. c. 68 (1850) (Ire.) (regulation of polling booths at elections), 170

14 & 15 Vict. c. 57 (1851) (Ire.) (expenses for interpreters at quarter sessions), 155

14 & 15 Vict. c. 93 (1851) (Ire.) (regulation of petty sessions), 316n41

35 & 36 Vict. c. 33 (1872) (Ballot Act), 164, 167

7 Will. III c. 4 (1695) (Ire.) (Act to Restrain Foreign Education), 124–25

9 Will. III c. 38 (1697) (Ire.) (Irish courts of record permitted to use English), 150

6 & 7 Will. IV c. 116 (1836) (Ire.) (expenses for court interpreters), 155

Aarne-Thompson (AT) Type 1697, 86, 90, 92, 300n12

Aarne-Thompson (AT) Type 1698, 86, 94, 300n12, 302n35

Aarne-Thompson (AT) Type 1699, 84, 86, 88, 90, 92, 100, 102, 300n12, 300–301n17

Abhráin Diadha Chúige Connacht (1906), 182

"Abhránan Bhoicht-Aontadhóra" (song), 168

Abraham, Bishop William, 242, 259–60

Abridgement of the Christian Doctrine, An (1649), 198

Académie Française, 127, 129

academies of language, 127–28

Achill, Co. Mayo, 61, 187, 215

Act for the English Order, Habit, and Language (1537). *See* 28 Henry VIII c. 15

Act for the Settlement of Parochial Schools (1616), 120, 124

Act of Uniformity (1560). *See* 2 Eliz. I c. 2

Act of Union, Irish (1801), 50, 111, 113, 133, 149, 165, 179, 268, 273

Act to Restrain Foreign Education (1695). *See* 7 William III c. 4

Acta Sanctorum (1643), 199

Acta Sanctorum Hiberniae (1645), 199

Acts of Theological Virtues (prayers), 211, 212–14, 219, 232, 263

Index

Acts of the Three Theological Virtues (ca. 1780), 213
acts of union, Wales, 115, 150
Adam, 26; as speaker of Irish, 36–37
advertisements, commercial, 49; tendency of English language to dominate, 47
Africa, 137–38; linguistic classification of its peoples, 7
"Agallamh an Chuirp agus an Anam" (dialog), 192, 204–5
agents: general, 49; land, 176
"A Ghaoidhilge Mhilis" (poem), 35
"Aighneas an Pheacaigh leis an mBás" (poem), 204
Alcock, Reverend Edward Jones, 38
Alexander, James, 51
All Hallows College, Dublin, 250t, 344n125
alphabet: English, 142–43, 312n129; Irish, 139
altars, 212, 214, 217, 225–26
Ancient Ireland (1855), 28
Anderson, Christopher, 136–37, 277n6
Andrews, J. H., 80–81
Andrews, Thomas, 112
Angelus Domini, 214
Anne I, 121, 125, 241, 307n44
Annesley, Arthur, 121
Annesley, Francis, 121
Annesley, Hugh, 168
"An Paidrín Páirteach" (song), 203
anti-poor law meetings, 173
Antiquae Linguae Britannicae (1621), 29
antiquarians, 24, 35, 37, 40, 43, 80, 123, 130–31, 137, 189, 196,
anti-tithe meetings, 173, 175, 177, 179, 270, 323n159
Antrim (county), 3
Apostle's Creed, 211
Arabic language, 44, 132
Ár bPaidreacha Dúchais (1975), 182
Archdeacon, Bishop Nicholas, 232, 242, 341n45

Ardagh diocese (Catholic), 213, 220, 242
Armagh (county), 3, 33–34, 95, 157, 196, 205
Armagh archdiocese (Catholic), 241–42, 246
artisans, 42, 224
Ascendancy, Protestant, 11, 87, 111, 151
Asia, 27, 137–38; as site of creation of Irish, 26; south, 5, 301n23
assizes (county), 52–53, 125, 152–53, 161–62, 164, 178, 314n8; use of interpreters in, 154–59
Association, Catholic, 173
Association for Discountenancing Vice, 42
Atkins, Reverend Walter, 121
Atkinson, Robert, 131
attorneys, 152, 162, 270
Attwood, Mathias Wolverley, 171
"A Uaisle Éireann Áilne" (poem), 35
Auraicept na nÉces, 26–27, 29, 31
Austro-Hungarian Empire, 268, 273
Ave Maria (prayer), 211, 219–20

Ballinasloe, Co. Galway, 48, 67
Ballinasloe Fair, 294n162
Ballinrobe, Co. Mayo, 50, 159, 177, 229
Ballot Act (1872). *See* 35 & 36 Vict. c. 33
Ballyduff, Co. Kerry, 177–78
Ballyhale, Co. Kilkenny, 177–79
Banba, 30
bank notes, 152, 160
baptisms, 232
Baptist Society for Promoting the Gospel in Ireland, 135, 140, 147
barracks: military, 101; police, 47
Barracks, Mountjoy, 77
Barron, Philip, 231, 259, 327n38
Barry, Father John (of Melbourne), 211
Barry, John (of Cork), 253, 263
Battersby, William Joseph, 198
Becanus, Johannes Gropius, 30
Bedell, William, 118, 121, 307n34
Bedell Bible, 307n34

beggars, 4, 59, 101–2, 104, 294n162
Belfast (city), 4, 36, 112, 144–45
Belfast Agreement (1998), 314n7
Belfast News-letter, 139
Belgian language, 30
Benedict XIII, 213
Benedict XIV, 213
Bennis, Thomas, 156
Beresford, George Thomas, 178
Berkeley, Bishop George, 122
Bible, 38, 118–19, 121, 135, 137–39, 141, 145, 155, 182, 233, 239, 255–56, 260, 307n34
bilingualism, 83; advantage at fairs, 47–49; advantage over monolingualism, 102, 105–8; among Gaelic and Old English gentry, 117; growth among middle classes, 151; need for, to understand certain jokes, 104; networks as a determinant in, 46; of lawyers in Irish courts, 153; police ability, 50; preference for Irish after attaining, 57, 59–60; preference for shop boys possessing, 49; relation of diglossia to, 44–46; of Welsh courts, 150
Bilingual Program (1904), 148, 272–73
bination of mass, 233–34
Binn, Jonathan, 228
Blarney, Co. Cork, 99, 152
Blasket Islands, Co. Kerry, 99
Blennerhassett, Arthur, 168
blessed altars devotion, 184
boards of guardians, 50–51
Boer War, 85, 98
bogs and turf, 73–74, 86, 106
Bolland, Jean, 199
bookkeepers, 49
Book of Armagh, 79
Book of Common Order, 118
Book of Lismore, 200
booths, polling, 149, 166, 168, 170–71, 271
Borde, Andrew, 91

Borromeo, Charles, 206, 239, 333n114
Boulter, Archbishop Hugh, 126
Bourdaloue, Louis, 231
Bourke, Walter, 153
Bourne, John, 156
Boyle, George, 158
Boyle, Robert, 307n34
Boyounagh, Co. Galway, 76, 78
Bradie, Bishop Hugh, 118
Bray, Archbishop Thomas, 193, 210, 213, 231, 242, 252, 254, 328n53
Breastplate of the Virgin Mary, 211
Brenán, Saint, 200
Breton language, 187
breviaries, 216
Brew, Tomkins, 151
Brewer, John, 52
Bridget, Saint, 200, 330n82
Bridge v. Casey (1877), 159
Brief Discourse in Vindication of the Antiquity of Ireland, A (1717), 28
Brief Sketch of Various Attempts which Have Been Made to Diffuse a Knowledge of the Holy Scriptures through the Medium of the Irish Language, A (1818), 136
Bristol Mercury, 36
Britannia Sancta (1745), 199
British army, 90, 98; use of Irish by soldiers in, 11
British Education (1756), 129
British Empire, 132, 135, 137, 268–69, 273
Bromyard, John, 91
Brooke, Charlotte, 131, 310n83
Brooke, Henry, 165
Brown, Bishop George, 243
Browne, Father James (of Ballintober), 229
Browne, Father James (of Maynooth), 264
Browne, Reverend Nicholas, 121
Browne, William, 168
Brunot, Ferdinand, 6

Builléad, Seán, 195
Bull, John (printer), 207
Bullar, John, 136
Burke, Bishop Thomas, 210, 254
Burke, John, 158
Burke, Martin, 162
Burke, Oliver, 153
Burke, Peter, 5
Burrishoole, Co. Mayo, 176, 232
burses (for Irish continental colleges), 251–52, 257
Bushe, Charles Percy, 69–70
Butler, Alban, 198–99
Butler, Archbishop James, 210
Butler, Bishop George, 266
Butler catechism. *See* catechisms: Butler
Butt, Isaac, 159
Buttimer, Cornelius, 17

Caherciveen, Co. Kerry, 144, 334n125
Cahill, Edward, 125
cairns, 73, 76
Cais, Ruisdeard, 194
Calvin, John, 33
Campbell, Reverend Theophilius, 145
Campion, Edmund, 28, 116
Canny, Michael, 156
canons (Protestant), 118, 146–47
canticles, 185, 188
Cantwell, Bishop John, 215
Caomhánach, Eoghan, 50, 68, 208, 321n132, 334n125
Capgrave, John, 200
Cappoquin, Co. Waterford, 217, 265
card playing, 85, 87
Carleton, Lord Chief Justice Hugh, 153
Carleton, William, 226
Carlow (city), 230
Carlow (county), 78, 225, 300–301n17
Carlow, St. Patrick's College, 250t, 253, 259, 344n125
Carmelites, 208
Carpenter, Archbishop John, 193, 199, 206, 211, 213, 221, 230, 327–28n52

Carr, Father (of Ballinsmaula), 229
Carr, John, 151
Carrick-on-Suir, Co. Tipperary, 265, 326n27
Carsuel, Seon, 118
Casán go Flaitheamhnas, An (1882), 222
Cashel and Emly archdiocese (Catholic), 193, 213, 242, 246, 254
Cashel diocese (Protestant), 130, 144
Cassin, Reverend (of Limerick), 174
Castilian language, 29, 115
Castlebar, Co. Mayo, 53, 158–60, 162, 177, 238
Castleknock, St. Vincent's College, 250t, 344n125
catechisms, 71, 130, 209–10, 225, 230, 254, 260, 263, 270; as part of general education, 114; Butler, 188, 194, 198, 209–10, 213, 221, 239, 334n130; Catholic, 181, 184–88, 195, 199, 212, 219, 224; Coppinger, 188, 210, 213, 239; Donlevy, 130, 181, 188, 209, 213, 220, 346n159; Irish-language versions in homes of Catholics, 189; Kirwan, 188, 210, 213; Lloyd, 187, 209–10, 334n130; Loftus, 188–89, 213–14, 221, 255, 326n33, 328n53; Ó hEodhasa, 194, 202, 209, 212; O'Reilly, 140, 187–89, 193, 209–10, 213–14, 219, 334n130; Protestant, 119, 121, 126, 132–33; Pulleine, 187–88, 209, 221; Stapleton, 209; use of Irish language in, 236–40; Young, 188–89
Catholic Association, 174, 176
Catholic Book Society, 189, 198, 239
Catholic Children's Religious Primer, The (1825), 181, 217
Catholic Church: assignment of Irish-speaking priests to Irish-speaking parishes, 247–56; association of Irish language with, 33–34; bishops and hierarchy, 4, 112, 142, 161, 176, 206, 208, 213, 241, 251; bishops and

Catholic Church (*continued*)
  hierarchy proficiency in Irish, 241–43; blamed for language decline, 10; changes to congregation size and meeting locations, 227–28; depiction as feminine, 34; devotional reform of, 19, 208, 223; French and Italian developments in teaching-based missions and preaching, 205; historiography of church language policy, 225–27; initial acceptance of Irish-language Protestant missionary schools by members of, 141; plans to translate Roman Catholic version of Bible into Irish, 255; regional rivalries within, 66; target of eighteenth-century Irish government, 120
Catholic Society for Ireland, 239
Catholic Truth Society, 222
Caulfield, Patrick, 160
Cavan (county), 3, 157, 168, 205, 210, 316n47
Céitinn, Seathrún, 24, 27, 29, 32, 36, 95, 192, 194, 202, 204, 209, 215, 286n21
Celtic Society, 131
Census of Ireland: for 1851, 4, 83, 144, 147, 243t, 244, 244t, 244n(b); for 1861, 243t, 244, 244t, 244n(b); for 1871, 243t, 244, 244t, 244n(b); for 1881, 243t, 244, 244t, 244n(b); for 1891, 243t, 244, 244t; for 1901, 83; for 1911, 83
Cent nouvelles (1505–15), 91
Cessair, 29
Challoner, Richard, 191, 198, 204, 208, 216, 228, 332n99
chapels (Catholic), 158, 174–77, 212–13, 223, 254
Charles I, 78
charms, 219, 334n129
Charter Act (1813), 135
charter schools, Welsh, 125–26
Chatterjee, Partha, 53, 301n23
Chatterton, Henrietta, 48

Chesterfield, Lord, 128
chief secretary of Ireland, 121, 154, 158
Christ, 187, 202, 211–12, 214, 216–18, 220–21
Christian, Judge, 163–64
Christian Brothers, 197–98, 205–6, 208–9, 265, 329n72, 347n187
Chronicle of Eusebius (379 AD), 29
Ciarán of Clonmacnois, Saint, 200
Ciniféic, Father Muiris, 194, 328n57
circulating schools, Welsh, 126–27
Cistercians, 228
Claddagh, Co. Galway, 71
Claidheamh Soluis, An, 11, 39, 52, 56, 60, 86, 143–44
Claim of Millions of Our Fellow-Countrymen of Present and Future Generations, to Be Taught in Their Own and Only Language; the Irish, The (1821), 136
Clare (county), 3, 38, 43, 52, 55, 60, 63, 70–71, 75, 89, 139, 151–52, 154–55, 157, 168–69, 175–77, 189, 194–96, 200–201, 205, 208, 210, 230, 234, 239, 262, 300–301n17, 316n47, 336n150
Clarkson, John, 211
Clement XIV, 213
clerks, 49; chapel, 181; court, 153, 156, 158, 167
Clifden, Co. Galway, 51, 143, 229
Clifford, James, 88
clothing, 67, 74, 92, 99, 106, 114–15
Cloyne and Ross diocese (Catholic), 193, 215, 223, 231, 235, 240, 242–43, 247–50, 252–53, 260, 263, 344n122
Cloyne Cathedral, 121
Cloyne diocese (Catholic). *See* Cloyne and Ross diocese
Cnoc, Uilliam, 208
Coen, Bishop Thomas, 242
Cóir, Eoghan, 144
Colby, Thomas, 65, 76, 80
Colgan, John, 199
Collège de Lisieux, 257

Collège des Lombards, 257–58
Collège des Quatre Nations, 127
colleges, Irish clerical (continental), 66, 181, 196, 209, 226, 249, 251; curriculum for Irish language at, 257–58. *See also names of individual colleges*
colleges, Irish clerical (domestic), 225. *See also names of individual colleges*
Colley, Linda, 5
Collins, Bishop Michael, 215, 240, 243, 252
Collins, Jeremiah, 239
Collins, Kevin, 246, 249
Columba of Adomnán, Saint, 330n82
Columcille, Saint, 76, 192, 200, 226
Comarec, Frainsias Bizzarrini, 213
"Cómhnúadh na Gaeilge" (poem), 36
Commissioners of National Education, 56, 112, 133–34, 139–41, 147, 239, 272
Committee on Irish Language Attitudes Research, 290n89
communion (Catholic), 212, 215, 219, 254
Complete Manual of Catholic Piety, The (aka *The Christian's Guide to Heaven*, 1806), 198
Comyn, David, 85, 300n9
Concannon, Patrick, 51
concursus, 247–50, 253
confession (Catholic), 210, 212, 215, 218–19, 224, 228, 254, 270; use of Irish for, 235–36
confirmation (Catholic), 228, 237, 240
Confiteor, 212, 219
confraternities, 184, 197; catechetical, 240
Confraternity of the Christian Doctrine, 238–39
Congregatio de Propaganda Fide, 223, 257
Conlan, Mary, 160
Conmy, James, 162
Connacht (province), 3, 18, 48, 60–61, 64, 66–79, 85, 103, 142, 151, 153, 158, 164, 168–69, 177, 182, 188, 228, 232–34, 238–39, 255, 259, 306n7
Connellan, Owen, 57
Connellan, Thaddaeus, 131, 141
Connemara, Co. Galway, 54–55, 58, 66, 85, 89, 104, 158
Conner, Mary, 162
Connolly, Mary, 160
Connor, John, 206
constabulary. *See* police and constabulary
consumer goods, 98–99
Convocation of Protestant Established Church, 118, 122, 125, 145, 147 307n30; advocates of use of Irish language, 121
Conway, Bishop Denis, 241
Conway, Bishop Hugh, 242
Conway, Richard, 120
Coolahan, John, 141
Coote, Charles, 58
Coppinger, Bishop William, 193, 207, 242, 260, 328n53
Coppinger catechism. *See* catechisms: Coppinger
Corcoran, Bartholomew, 130, 213
Corcoran, Father Patrick, 230
Corcoran, Mark, 177
Corcoran, Michael, 160
Corish, Patrick, 214, 244n(a), 256, 261
Cork (city), 4, 48–49, 142, 170–71, 192, 206, 230, 265, 344n122
Cork (county), 3, 16–17, 23, 34–35, 38, 40–42, 48, 51, 55, 57, 59, 69, 72, 75, 84, 105, 142, 144, 152, 157, 160, 168, 170, 172, 175–77, 192–96, 200, 205, 208–9, 211–13, 225, 231–36, 239–40, 242, 247–50, 300–301n17, 316n47, 334n125, 338n174, 344n122
Cork diocese (Catholic), 215
Corkery, Daniel, 10–11, 17
Cork Examiner, 52
Cork Total Abstinence Society, 172–73
Cornish language, 123
Corofin, Co. Clare, 55, 153, 176, 228

Corrydon, John, 68
Coughlan, Daniel, 240
Council in the Marches, Wales, 150
Council of Trent, 209, 220
court, admiralty, 314n6
Courtney, J., 187
Court of Common Pleas, Dublin, 158
Court of Crown Cases Reserved, 162–64
Court of Queen's Bench, 159
courtrooms, 98, 101, 106, 271; English language in, 47
courts (system), 149; female Irish-speaking litigants at, 160; Latin and French as languages of, 150; prohibition of Latin and French in English and Scottish courts, 150; prohibition on Latin and French in Irish courts, 150; reach into lower class and informalism of, 151. *See also* assizes (county); petty sessions courts; quarter sessions courts
courts-leet, 314n9
cows, 63, 67, 75, 86, 98, 173, 178, 219, 222, 303n54
Cox, Richard, 69
Coy, Michael, 53
Coyne, Father Eugene, 229
Coyne, John, 199
Coyne, Reverend (of Annagh), 173
Coyne, Richard, 199
Crashaw, William, 332n105
"Creacht do Dháil Mé im Árthach Galair" (poem), 32
Credo, 219–20
Criostamhar, Uilliam, Jr., 201
Croagh Patrick, 79
Croker, Thomas Crofton, 204
Crolly, Bishop William, 261
Cromwell, Oliver, 179
Cromwell, Thomas, 115
Cromwell, Thomas Kitson, 134
Cross, Richard, 205, 334n126
Crotty, Bishop Bartholomew, 242, 252, 260, 264

Crowe, Michael, 171
Cruice, Daniel John, 151
Cullen, Archbishop Paul, 182, 184, 220, 252, 256, 266
Curran, Reverend (of Westport), 176
Currigan, Edward, 160
Curwen, J. C., 40

da Lucca, Pedro, 208
Daly, Reverend Robert, 139, 144–45
dánfhocail, 94
Danish language, 30
Daunt, William J. O'Neill, 141, 176, 215, 233, 322n143
Davies, John (d. 1644), 29
Davies, Sir John (d. 1626), 154
Davis, Thomas, 8
Davitt, Michael, 289n63
deafness, 93–94
Death of the Irish Language, The (1990), 244n(b)
de Barra, Dáibhí, 196, 211, 242, 325n20
De Besse, Pierre, 231
de Bhailis, Seán, 195
de Bhal, Pádraig, 191, 232
de Blacam, Aodh, 11
de Búrca, Uileog, 37, 48, 189, 233–34, 260, 345n141
de Certeau, Michel, 88
de Fréine, Seán, 13, 16, 87
de Granada, Louis, 202
de Guevara, Antonio, 208
De Imitatione Christi (ca. 1418), 327n51, 327–28n52
de Ledesma, Diego, 209
de Liguori, Alphonsus, 207, 221
Denn, Pádraig, 181, 189, 191, 201, 204, 208, 210, 217, 220–21, 232, 273, 332n102
Dent, John Dent, 146
De Regno Hiberniae Commentarius (1632), 69
Derry, Bishop John, 242
de Sales, Francis, 198, 208

de Siúnta, Earnán (An Buachaillín Buidhe), 60–61
des Périers, Bonaventure, 91
de Tillemont, Louis-Sébastien le Nain, 199
de Vigneulles, Phillippe, 91
devotional manuals, 184–86, 204–11
devotional revolution, 13, 182–84
Dewar, Daniel, 42, 58, 136–37
de Worde, Wynkyn, 200
dictionaries, 127–29
Dies Irae, 202, 226
diglossia, 44–46, 269
Dingle, Co. Kerry, 48–49, 158, 228, 230, 312n129
dinnseanchas, 295n2
Discovery of the True Causes Why Ireland Was Never Entirely Subdued, A (1619), 154
Disestablishment Act, Church of Ireland (1869), 145, 245
doctors, 4, 86, 96–97, 101–2
Doctrina Christiana (ca. 1720), 209
dogs, 39, 75, 87, 253
Doherty, Father John, 228
domains, linguistic, 44–46
Dominicans, 220
Donegal (county), 42, 48, 55, 60, 67–68, 79, 81, 98–100, 103, 106, 142, 151, 154, 156–59, 165, 210, 228, 237, 300–301n17, 316n47
Donelan, Father T., 232
Donlevy catechism. *See* catechisms: Donlevy
Donlevy, Andrew, 71, 130, 181, 188, 213, 346n159
Dorian, Hugh, 55–56
"Do Tharlaigh Inné Orm" (poem), 35
Dottrina del Ben Morire, 208
Dougan, Mary, 159
Douglas, Sylvester, 128
Doway Catechism in English and Irish (1738). *See* catechisms: Lloyd
Dowley, Father Philip, 245

Down (county), 3, 327–28n52
Down and Connor diocese (Catholic), 193, 242, 261
Down and Connor diocese (Protestant), 118, 122
Doyle, Bishop James Warren, 207, 233, 239, 242
"Duain Chroidhe Iosa" (song), 203
duanairí, 203
"Duan an Duine Dhosgaidh" (poem), 202
duanta diadha, 203. *See also* verse, religious
Dublin (city), 3–4, 50, 66, 77, 116, 118, 136–37, 154–55, 158, 174, 194–96, 199, 200, 205–6, 210–11, 213, 229–30, 252, 255, 265, 306n7, 317n59, 334n126
Dublin archdiocese (Catholic), 182, 184, 193, 213, 231, 241, 246, 254
Dublin Society, 57–58, 130
Duffy, James, 199, 206
Duggan, Bishop Patrick, 229, 242
Dunboyne School, Maynooth, 346n163
Dungarvan, Co. Waterford, 158, 171, 174, 265
Dunn, Darby, 75
Durcan, Bishop Patrick, 242
Durkacz, Victor, 5
Dutton, Hely, 58, 71
Dwyer, James, 158

Eachtra Áodh Mhic Goireachtaidh (ca. 1707–27), 95
Eagna Fhírinneach (*La Vera Sapienza*), 325n26
Éamuinn a' tSléibhe, 86–88
Easter, 97, 213
East India Company, 132, 135
Eathór, 26, 34
Edgar, Reverend (of Belfast), 145
Edgeworth, Maria, 129
Edward III, 150
Edward VI, 117

Edwards, Charles, 29
Egan, Bishop Cornelius, 242
Egan, Constable, 50
Egan, Thomas, 171
Egan, William, 162
Egypt, 27, 29, 179
Eibhear, 26
election laws, Ireland, 319n100
elections, 149; of 1818, 166–67, 171; of 1857, 168–69, 170–71; general, of 1835, 177
Elements of the Irish Language, Grammatically Explained in English, The (1728), 188
Elevation of the Soul, The (*L'âme élevée a Dieu*), 232
Elizabeth, Charlotte, 60
Elizabeth I, 117–18, 146, 178
Elphinston, James, 128
Emancipation, Catholic, 39, 54, 60, 149, 165, 172–73, 176, 178–79, 270
England, 65, 91, 94–95, 100–1, 115, 128–29, 136–37, 185–86
English language, 34, 205; associated with Protestantism, 38; believed lack of unorthodox payers in, 182; believed purveyor of Catholic reform, 183; believed tendency of Maynooth students to acquire, 256; blamed by speakers for decline of Irish language, 41; broken speech in, 86–87, 93–95, 97; Catholic texts in, 187; code switching, 59; concern about decline of, 128; correspondence and publications by Catholic Church in, 225; enables enemies to be identified, 39; encouraged use of, by penal law provisions on education, 124–25; enjoined on Tudor subjects in Ireland, 115; enjoined use in Pale under Statutes of Kilkenny, 114; fear of lack of gentility of Hiberno English, 128–29; as feminized victim of Irish speaker, 35; Hiberno English, 303n54; as high-prestige language, 44–46; inability to convey certain concepts, 88; increasing use in courts, 150; insistence by parents and teachers that student learn, 54; lack of, as sign of incivility, 116; as marker of Protestant version of Bible, 38; as masculine conqueror, 33; monoglots and monolinguals, 18, 33, 39, 48, 61, 63, 83, 97, 102, 105–8, 235, 249; Old and Middle English, 128; overly literal translations into, 86–88, 95; perceived insistence of use by Elizabethan administration, 146; predominance at urban classical schools, 264–65; prescribed in Welsh courts, 115, 150; presumed desire by Irish speakers to attain, 42; pride by Irish speakers in not knowing, 51; priests' lack of proficiency in, 240–41; Protestant liturgy in, 118; provisions to ease landlord support for schools to teach, 125; regarded as the language of outsiders and strangers, 59–60; Scots English, 92, 128; seen as inanimate object, 102; sermon books in, 231; speakers of, featured in Irish jokes, 101; spoken by New English, 33; struggle by schools in teaching, 55–56; survival after Normal conquest, 32; teaching of, as object of missionary societies, 138; tendency to dominate certain linguistic settings, 47; use in Elizabethan parish schools confirmed, 124; use in Incorporated Society charity schools, 125; use of Irish to teach, 142–44; use of terms Albanach and Sasanach to identify speakers of, 60–61
Enlightenment, 128–29, 132
Enna, Saint, 76
Enniskean, Co. Cork, 176, 194
Eochair Phairthais (*The Key of Paradise*), 211

Eochair-Sgiath an Aifrinn (ca. 1610), 194–95, 203–4, 209, 215, 332n99
erasure, 64
Ériu, 30
Errew Monastery, 265
Erris, Co. Mayo, 68, 71, 73, 143–44, 153
Esercizio della Via Crucis (1761), 207
Essay on the Antiquity of the Irish Language, An (1772), 130
European Charter for Regional or Minority Languages, 314n7
Eve, 36–37
Explanation of the Prayers and Ceremonies of the Holy Sacrifice of the Mass, An (1824), 198

faction fights, 59, 174
Fahy, John, 177
Fánaid, Co. Donegal, 55–56, 67
far downers, 67
farmers, 4, 48, 51–52, 55, 63, 72, 74, 86, 101, 106–7, 169–71, 173, 177, 183, 190, 192, 195, 234, 237
Farrel, John, 156
Féinius Farsaidh, 26–29, 31–32, 285n15, 286n21
Fenians, 10, 68
Ferguson, Charles, 44, 46
Fermanagh (county), 156, 158, 316n47
Ffrench, Edward, 252
Field, Charles, 265
Fifty Reasons, or Motives, Why the Roman Catholic, Apostolic Religion, Ought to be Preferred, 198
Fir Bolg, 29
fishermen, 74, 81, 84, 89, 158
Fishman, Joshua, 5, 44, 46
Fís Mherlino, 186
Fitzgerald, Father Patrick, 229
Fitzgerald, George Robert, 158
Fitzgerald, John, 239
Fitzgerald, Reverend E., 175
Fitzgerald, Reverend William, 174, 321n132

Fitzmaurice, Reverend (of Dromid), 175
Fitzpatrick, Father J., 263
Fitzpatrick, Hugh, 199
Fitzsimmon, Nicholas, 155
Flannagáin, Seán, 71
Flannelly, Father James, 229
Flemish language, 30
Fleury, Claude, 198
Florilegium Insulae Sanctorum (1624), 200
Flower, Robin, 201
Fódla, 30
Foirm na nUrrnuidheadh (1567), 118
Foley, Father (of Tulla), 63
Folklore Collection, Irish National, 25, 84, 87, 284n3, 299n4, 300–301n17
Folklore Commission, 25, 84–85, 87, 103, 185
Foras Feasa ar Éirinn (1634–35), 27, 29
Forhan, Patrick, 48
Fort St. George language college, 132
Fort William language college, 132
Forty Hours Adoration, 184, 230
forty-shilling voters, 165, 171; social class of Irish-speaking, 168–69. *See also* franchise and voting
Foster, Colonel (of Collon), 152
Four Maxims of Christian Philosophy (*Quattro Massime di Christiana Filosophia*), 198, 206
France, 115–16, 127, 226, 231, 242, 253; French Revolution (1789) and language policy, 6, 127–28; language standardization, 5–6; linguistic policies, eighteenth century, 127–28; linguistic policies, seventeenth century, 127
Franchise Act, Irish (1850), 165
franchise and voting, 113; attitude of Irish speakers toward, 168–69; borough, 165, 170–71; county, 165, 169; deference to landlords, qualifications and social class of Irish

franchise and voting (*continued*)
    speakers voting, 168; reinstatement of Catholic voting and changes to linguistic makeup of electorate, 164–66
Francis I, 115
Franciscans, 27, 181, 192, 200, 208
freeholders, 166, 170–71, 176–78
Freeman's Journal, 49, 71, 146, 190, 260
freemen, 170
French language, 34, 44, 54, 91, 127–29, 150, 163, 205, 225, 257–58, 265
Friel, Brian, 296n9
Furlong, Reverend Jonathan, 194, 210, 232, 328n55
Fursa, Saint, 78
Fynn, John, 50

Gaedhil, 26–27, 31–32, 34, 286n21
Gaedhil Glas, 27, 32
Gaelic League, 9–11, 39, 85, 143
Gaelic Society, 131
Gaelic Union, 8, 281n26
Gaels, 26–27, 32, 41, 178
Gaeltachtaí, 10–11, 25
Gahan, William, 198, 231–32
Gairdín an Anma (*Garden of the Soul*), 204
Gallagher, Denis, 61
Gallagher, Father Michael, 229
Gallagher, James, 140, 181, 188–89, 226, 230
Galway (city), 4, 49, 71, 79, 159–60, 170–71, 229
Galway (county), 3, 36–37, 40, 48, 51, 53, 58–59, 63, 68, 71, 75–76, 78–79, 85–86, 89, 100, 106–7, 142–43, 152, 155–60, 162, 167–69, 173, 175, 177, 205, 220, 229, 262, 300n7, 300–301n17
Galway Advertiser, 154
Garden of the Soul (1740), 204, 208, 216, 332n99, 334n126, 337n157
Gardiner's Act (1782), 263
Garnham, Neal, 152, 314n9

Garvey, Bishop Antonius, 193
Garvey, Patrick, 48
Gearnon, Antoin, 204, 210, 216
Gelasius, Saint, 200
gentry, 151, 173–74, 176
George II, 241
German language, 34, 91, 128; high and low varieties, 44
Germingham, Michael Blake, 173
Gibbons, Father Edward, 229
Gibbons, Father Myles, 232
Gibbons, Luke, 160
Gillespie (ad-hoc court interpreter), 158
Giraldus Cambrensis, 28, 199
Glorie di Maria, Le (1750), 207
Glover, Edward, 198
Gobinet, Charles, 198
Gorman, Father John, 194
Gorman, Sarah Anne, 162
Gospel, 216, 224, 233. *See also* John, Gospel of; Matthew, Gospel of
Gother, John, 198, 209
Grace, Richard, 206
Graham, Charles, 135
Graham, Robert, 155
Grammar of the Irish Language (1845), 28
grammars, 139; Irish, 259
grand juries, 51, 76, 167, 315n34; expenses for court interpreters, 154–59
Grant, James, 51
Grattan, Henry, 134
Great Famine, 4, 13, 100, 165, 182, 184, 266
Great Sessions court, Wales, 150
Greek language, 26, 34, 44, 54, 131, 258, 262–65
Grégoire, Abbé Henri-Baptiste, 128
Greine, Gil, 75
Griffith, Richard, 77
Griffith's Valuation, 77
Grimes, John, 160
Guerin, James, 130

Guiry, Patrick, 53
Gumperz, John, 5, 44

Hackett, John, 191
Hackett, William, 75, 80
hackler's tale, 85, 89–90, 103, 143
hagiographies (saints), 185–86, 192, 194, 199–201
Haitian Creole language, 44
Ham, 26
Hamilton, Lord Claude, 146
Hanley, Patrick, 177
Hanly, Charles, 239
Hardiman, James, 71, 131, 207, 310n83
Hardy, Philip Dixon, 229
Harney, Thomas, 178–79
Hart, George Vaughn, 165–66
harvesters, migratory, 67, 72, 102
hawkers, 126
Hay, Bishop George, 232
Hayes, Richard, 231
Hearne, John, 160
Hebraismorum Cambro-Britannicorum Specimen (1675), 29
Hebrew language, 26, 29, 34, 36, 95, 131, 258
Heely, John, 232
Heffernan, Father William, 191, 233, 252
"The Heights of Alma" (song), 162
Hell Opened to Christians (*L'Inferno Aperto al Cristiano*), 198, 206
Henilly, Denis, 177
Hennon v. Andrew Henry Lynch, MP (1839), 158–59
Henry VII, 114
Henry VIII, 114, 117
Heraghty, Martin, 160
Hibernia Anglicana (1689), 69
Hibernia Sancta; or, Lives of Irish Saints (1817), 329n73
Higgin, Father Paul, 241
Higgins, Anthony, 177
highland Scots, 92, 119–29, 124–26

highwaymen, 39
Hillas, James, 158
Hindi language, 132
Hindley, Reg, 244n(b), 247, 278n6, 284n57
Historical Memoirs of the Irish Bards (1786), 130–31
A Historie of Ireland (1571), 28
Hógáin, Uilliam, 209
holy days, 188, 210, 213–14, 254
holy wells, 79–80, 222
horses, 98, 114, 234
Hortus Pastorum (ca. 1626), 209
Hosty, Reverend (of Galway), 175
Humble, John Nugent, 171
Hume, Joseph, 134
humor: ambiguity of verbal versions of, 87; basis in incongruity and scripts, 95–96; Jewish, 105; predominance in folklore related to the Irish language, 84; Scottish, 105; wordplay in, 87
Huntington, Marquess (Spencer Compton Cavendish), 154
Hutchinson, Bishop Francis, 122–23
Hyde, Douglas, 11, 17, 47, 61, 85, 182, 185, 300n9
hymnals, 132
hymns, 185–86, 193, 202, 207, 211, 219

Iar, 26
Iberno-Celtic Society, 131
iconization, 64
Ignatius, Father (of Mount Melleray), 228
Iliad, 255
Imitation of Christ, The (*De Imitatione Christi*), 193, 195, 198–99, 228. See also *De Imitatione Christi*
Immaculate Conception, 221
imperialism, British, 4–5, 97. See also British Empire
In the Matter of an Application by Caoimhin MacGiolla Cathain for Judicial Review (2009), 314n7

432   Index

Incorporated Society for Promoting English Protestant Schools in Ireland, 125–27, 238
India, 65, 93, 132, 135–38
indulgences, 212–13
Inglis, Henry, 59, 155
Inglis, Liam, 35
inns, 58, 66
Instruction of Youth in Christian Piety (*Instruction de la jeunesse en la piété chréetienne*), 198
Instructions for Confession and Communion (1706), 198
Intermediate Education Board, 265, 347n187
interpreters, 51, 98, 106, 117, 150–53, 270, 272, 317n59; at 1807 county elections, 316n47; to collect agricultural estimates, 50; discretion in use of by court officers, 159; at elections, 166–72; expenses at elections, 167–68; 170–71; at fairs, 48; identities of, at elections, 171–72; in fifteenth-century courts, 315n32; non-provisions for, at petty sessions, 316n41; in quarter sessions and county assizes, 154–59; in shops, 49; types and identities at Irish courts, 156; use by bilinguals to forestall cross examination in court, 161; volunteers and ad-hoc, 158–59; volunteers at petty sessions, 155
Introduction à la Vie Dévote (1608), 208
Introduction to a Devout Life, An (*Introduction à la Vie Dévote*), 198
Introduction to the Celebrated Devotion of the Most Holy Rosary, An (1737), 211
Irish Catholic Penny Magazine, 198, 205, 208
Irish language: advocacy of circulating schools teaching in, 139; advocacy of non-religious printing in, 139; advocated use in Catholic Mass, 215; advocated use in national schools to combat Catholic superstition, 134; ambiguity in policies toward use of, in established Protestant church, 117–19; at anti–poor law meetings, 173; antiquarian view of, as non-living language, 130–31; at anti-tithe meetings, 173; associated with female in need of deliverance, 33; associated with masculine lineage, 30; association with aristocratic tories, 39; association with unorthodox religious practices, 182; awareness of poets of its decline, 41; beginnings of bilingual education program in, 147–48; believed foreign origins of, 29; believed irrelevant as marker of loyalty, 123; believed origins in east, 26–27, 118; believed purity and ancientness of, 29–30; believed to lack written corpus, 129; bill in Irish House of Commons requesting religious ministers competent in, 122; blame on Catholic Church for decline of, 41; blame on English language for decline of, 41; blame on national schools for decline of, 41; Catholic religious printing in, 187–89; claims that language could be understood by speakers of Asian and African languages, 137; claim that numbers of speakers underestimated, 136; code mixing, 86; code switching, 59; comparatively given less attention by imperial administrators, 132; concerns about Irish-speaking jurors addressed by parliamentary legislation, 153–54; concern with, at diocesan Cloyne concursus, 247–50; conflicting views on literacy in, as asset, 138; debates over use of Irish in education system, 133–44; denied diabolical nature of, 123;

discouragement of its use by English in Ireland, 114; as distinctly Catholic language, 33–34, 38; eighteenth-century decline in Protestant printing in, 309n75; enfranchisement of speakers of, 164–66, 170–71; enjoined use of, by Protestant ministers, 118; estimates of numbers of, 3–4, 278n6, 284n57; failure to recognize existence of, by outsiders, 58; gender of, 30, 286n21; as gift from God, 34; given great visibility by extension of state, 133–44; grammars, 28, 131; historiography of, 7–14; hope for its restoration, 35; inability of Devil to speak, 38; as an in-network form of communication, 57–59; insistence on use by bilinguals in courtroom, 160–64; insistence that election officers and poll administers prepare for Irish-speaking voters, 167; isoglosses of, 64; as language of conquest, 30; lectureship at Trinity College in, 121; localism and local dialects of, 64–65, 68–72; as low-prestige language, 44–46; at markets and fairs, 47–49; memorial (1710) urging use of, in Protestant outreach, printing, and religious services, 121–22; monoglots and monolinguals, 18, 48–49, 51, 58, 83, 97, 100, 102, 105–8, 117, 126, 130, 140–41, 151–54, 166, 169, 171; monoglot speakers on manor court juries, 152; negative attitudes toward, 40; newspapers translated orally into, 51–52; non-mention of, in proposal to create charity schools in Ireland, 125; non-recognition of, by eighteenth-century Irish authorities, 129–30; objections to use in education, 138; origin story of, 27–28; petition by Scottish Presbyterians to create education system using, 141; phonetic spelling of, 224, 232; plan to translate Roman Catholic Bible into, 255; poems in praise of its virtues, 35–36; policy of Incorporated Society charity schools toward, 126; portrayed as language of rebellion, 116; as preferred by God, 36; premature belief that it had disappeared, 130–31; prescribed use by synodal decree in pastoral duties, 254; pressed by speakers to use in courts, 159–64; proficiency of bishops in, 241–43; proficiency of priests in, 240–41, 243–50; Protestant liturgy in, 118; Protestant printing in, 130; as pure and holy, 34, 37; provisions for interpreters proficient in, 154–59; recommended use of, by lower house of Convocation, 1703, 121; recommended use of, in Protestant catechisms, 121; recommended use of, in Protestant liturgy, 121; recommended use of, in Protestant sermons, 121; recommended use of Protestant scripture readers proficient in, 121; required knowledge of, at continental colleges, 257; as scholarly language, 31; revival movement, 7–9, 53, 61, 222; seen as language of rebellion, 138; sermons in, 228–33; as sexual conqueror, 35; shock at finding higher numbers of, in 1851 census, 144–45; as sign of incivility, 116, 119–20, 129; speaker awareness of its health, 23–24; spoken by Protestants, 38; spoken in heaven and paradise, 36–37; stated need by Catholic Church to administer in, 223–24; stipulations that eighteenth-century clerical converts read liturgy or common prayer in, 121; superseded by Catholicism as target by Irish government in eighteenth century, 120; taught informally by tutors and teachers, 54; at temperance meetings,

Irish language (*continued*)
172–73; as threat to linguistic uniformity, 116; Ulster Presbyterian policies toward, 309n74; urban existence, 4; use at executions, 52–53; use at local board meetings, 50–51; use by children covertly at school, 54–55; use by magistrates and local law intermediaries, 150–51; use by police to understand accused, 49–50; use by Protestant ministers in pastoral care, 121; used to conceal speech, 39–40, 177; use during Mass, 233; use for catechetical teaching, 236–40; use for confessions, 235–36; use in court oaths, 162; use in manor courts, 151–52; use in post offices, 49; use in shops, 47, 49; use in schools, 53–56; use in temperance oaths, 173; use of Roman letters, 191; as world's original language, 37

Irish Minstrelsy, or Bardic Remains of Ireland (1831), 131

Irish National Teachers' Organization, 148

Irish Sermons with Translations (1835), 231

Irish Society for Promoting the Education of the Native Irish through the Medium of Their Own Language, 17, 37, 49, 54, 56, 59, 135–36, 139–41, 144–45, 147, 288n49

Irisleabhar na Gaeilge, 43

"Is Atuirseach Géar Mo Scéal" (poem), 32

Isidore of Seville, 29

"Is Olc an Ceart Fulang an Fhámuire" (poem), 32

Italian language, 34, 128, 163, 205, 225, 258

Italy, 226; as source for Irish devotional practices, 183–84; language standardization, 5–6

Iveragh, Co. Kerry, 14, 175

Jacobites, 16, 33, 126, 128
jailers, court, 156, 162
James I, 118
James II, 124
Japhet, 26, 29, 30, 36
jest-books, 91
Jesuits, 205–6, 209, 230, 257, 265, 339n25
Jocelin of Furness, 199
John, Gospel of, 262
Johnson, Samuel, 128
jokes: basis in incongruity and scripts, 95–96; conversational joking, 103; dependence on regional dialect for meaning, 305n81; prevalence in Irish National Folklore Collection, 84; reception of linguistic versions in nineteenth-century, 89–90; targets for linguistic ridicule, 87; tendency to feature local characters, 100–101; told by minority communities about self, 105; translatability of, 104–5, 305n82
Joli, Claude, 231
Jones, Griffith, 29, 126–27
Joyce, James, 206
Judas, 217
judges, 4, 68, 98, 101–2, 150, 152–53, 157, 159, 270; opposition to witness insistence on interpreters, 161–62
Juliana, Saint, 200
juries, 150, 153–54, 162, 270, 315n28; manor courts, 152
Juries (Ireland) Act (1833), 153–54
Juries (Ireland) Act (1871–72), 153–54
Juries (Procedure) Ireland Act (1876), 154
justices of the peace, 151, 155–56, 241

Keane, Bishop William, 235, 242, 253, 263
Kearns, John, 54
Keating Society, 189
Keenan, Patrick, 42, 54–56, 140, 142–44, 147, 189, 272

Kelly, Archbishop Oliver, 238
Kelly, Ignatius, 130
Kelly, James, 120, 124
Kelly, Patrick, 171
Kelly, Reverend (of Liverpool), 174
Kelly, Reverend James, 145
Kempe, Andreas, 30
Kempis, Thomas à, 193, 198, 202, 228
Kennedy, Matthew, 191, 210, 221
Keogh, John, 129
Kernan, Bishop Edward, 253
Kerr, Donal, 182–83
Kerry (county), 14, 27, 48, 56, 59–60, 68, 72, 91, 97, 99, 102, 106–7, 142, 144, 152, 156–57, 168–69, 175, 177–78, 205, 208, 228, 232, 234, 240, 252, 300–301n17, 334n125
Kerry diocese (Catholic), 242, 252–53
Key of Heaven, The. See *The Poor Man's Manual of Devotion*
Key of Paradise, The (ca. 1623), 211
Kiely, Father John, 42
Kildare (county), 243t, 244–45
Kildare and Leighlin diocese (Catholic), 207, 233, 239, 259
Kildare Place Society, 133, 140
Kilduff, Bishop John, 220
Kilfenora and Kilmacduagh diocese (Catholic), 232, 242
Kilgallian, Co. Mayo, 72–75
Kilkee, Co. Clare, 43, 54, 233
Kilkenny (city), 157
Kilkenny (county), 3, 36, 57, 74, 177–78, 194, 196, 225, 233, 259, 316n47, 323n162
Killala diocese (Catholic), 242, 253
Killaloe diocese (Catholic), 176, 251
Kilmacduagh diocese (Catholic). See Kilfenora and Kilmacduagh diocese
King, Reverend Robert, 69, 179
Kinneally, Michael, 55
Kinsale, Co. Cork, 48, 72, 171
Kinsella, Bishop William, 259
Kirkwood, James, 307n34

Kirwan, John, 153
Kirwan catechism. *See* catechisms: Kirwan
Knight, Patrick, 71
Knock, Co. Mayo, 173
Knott, Mary, 54
Kohl, Johann, 60, 193, 230, 255

laborers, 171, 222; agricultural, 4, 67, 72, 170, 192; canal, 67; farm, 48; railway, 67
Labov, William, 5, 15–16
Ladley, George, 156
Lagan River, 48, 68
Land League, 10, 289n63
landlords, 35, 38, 93, 101, 106, 118, 125–26, 138, 165, 168, 173
Lanesborough, Viscount (James Lane), 120
Lanigan, Bishop James, 231
Larcom, Thomas, 76–77, 80
Larkin, Emmet, 182–83, 251, 258
Larner, Constable (of Mayo), 50
Latin language, 26, 36, 54, 91, 115, 117–18, 124, 131, 145–46, 150, 200, 205, 214–15, 225–26, 241, 257–58, 262—66, 306n24
Lavelle, Father Mathias, 229
Lavelle, Patrick, 159
lawyers, 4, 126, 150, 153
Leabhar Urnaighthe (1904), 222
Leabhar-Urnuighe Naoimh Pádraic/St. Patrick's Prayer Book (ca. 1894), 222
Leader, Nicholas Philpott, 170
Lebor Gabála Érenn, 26–27, 29, 32
Lecky, William, 11
Lefroy, Judge, 163
Leinster (province), 3, 54, 60, 66–67, 69–70, 85, 142, 158, 173, 183, 189, 196, 204, 232, 259, 317n59
Leitrim (county), 58, 142, 156–57, 240
Lenihan, Maurice, 153, 151, 315n25
Lent, 229, 259
Letterkenny, Co. Donegal, 48, 60, 68

letters, immigrant, 97
Lew, Robert, 104, 305n82
Leyden, Father (Vincentian missionary), 230
Liberal Club, Clare, 139
libraries, lending, 239
Life of the Glorious Bishop S. Patricke, Apostle and Primate of Ireland, The (1625), 200
Lille, Irish College, 257
Limerick (city), 4, 49, 156–57, 168, 170, 175–76, 265
Limerick (county), 50, 59, 68, 75, 156–57, 167, 171, 174, 192, 194, 196, 201, 208, 210–11, 228, 233, 240
Limerick Chronicle, 157
Limerick diocese (Catholic), 189, 241–42, 266
L'Inferno Aperto al Cristiano (1688), 206
linguistics: historical sociolinguistics, 6; influence of paradigms of nation, 6–7; language ecology, 16; linguistic relativity, 15; sociolinguistics, 15
liquor sellers, 49
litanies, 210–12, 214, 217, 232
Litany of Jesus, 211, 219–20
Litany of Mary, 211, 219–20
literacy: English-language, 12, 47, 106, 125–28, 136, 138, 142–43, 147, 183; as goal of early modern governments, 127; Irish-language, 42, 53–54, 126–27, 135–36, 139; Scots Gaelic-language, 132; Welsh-language, 126–27
liturgy, Catholic, 215, 218
liturgy, Protestant, 118, 121, 145, 241
Lives of the Fathers, Martyrs, and Other Principal Saints (1756–59), 199
Lives of the Irish Saints (anon.), 198
Lives of the Irish Saints, Extracted from the Writings of the Rev. Alban Butler, The (1823), 329n73
Lives of the Saints (Butler, 1759), 198
Lloyd, Sylvester, 187

Lloyd catechism. *See* catechisms: Lloyd
localism, 66–68
Locke, John, 128
lodging houses, 95, 100–101, 106
Loftus catechism. *See* catechisms: Loftus
Loftus, Father Martin, 189, 255–56, 259–60, 326n33, 328n53
Logue, Cardinal Michael, 241, 259
Lombard, Peter, 69
London, 135, 206, 209
Londonderry (county), 37, 69, 76, 158, 161
London Hibernian Society, 135, 139–40, 176
Longfield, Robert, 170
Lord's Supper, 117, 214
Loreto shrine, 188, 214
Lough Derg, Co. Donegal, 229
Louth (county), 4, 36, 160, 179, 232, 256
Louvain, Irish College, 196, 250t
Lucerna Fidelium (1676), 194, 209
Lucht na Simléirí (ca. 1684), 95
Luther, Martin, 33–34, 38
Lyden, Mary, 53
Lyden, Patrick, 53, 300n7
Lynch, John, 50
Lynch, Patrick (of Clare), 70, 329n73
Lynch, Phil, 54
Lynegar, Charles, 121
Lyons, Dean John Patrick, 153, 172, 194, 253

Maam, Co. Galway, 59, 155
MacAdam, Robert, 40, 85, 144, 269, 300n9
Mac Aingil (Mac Caghwell), Aodh, 204
Mac an Bhaird, Fearghal Óg, 203
Mac Bionaid, Art, 196
Mac Cairteáin, Father Conchubhar, 209, 231
Mac Cairteáin, Uilliam, 41
Mac Cartan, Bishop Theophilus, 193, 242
Mac Cártha, Mícheál, 34

Index

Mac Cártha, Tadhg, 211, 221
MacCarthy, Owen, 239
MacCarthy, William, 178
Mac Ceagan, Aodh, 217
MacCloghan, Father (of Limerick), 59, 233
Mac Coitir, Uilliam, 208, 334n125
Mac Conmara, Donnchadh Rua, 85
Mac Craith, Eoghan, 203
Mac Cruitín, Aindrias, 195, 201
Mac Cruitín, Aodh Buí, 16, 28, 35, 139, 188, 196, 203
Mac Cuilionnán, Cormac, 203
Mac Cumhaigh, Art, 33
Mac Dáire, Dómhnall, 203
Mac Dáire, Tadhg, 203
Mac Domhnaill, Aodh, 16
MacDonnell, James, 8
MacEvilly, Archbishop John, 242, 260
Mac Gabhann, Micheál, 48, 67, 70, 143
Mac Gearailt, Seán, 222
Mac Gearruilt, Muiris, 203
MacHale, Archbishop John, 142, 161, 189, 193, 206–7, 210, 221, 228–29, 242, 253, 255, 326n33, 328n53
Machtnuig go Maih Air (*Think Well On't*), 191, 327n41
MacHugh, Father John, 229
MacMahon, Father Bernard, 199
MacManus, Father Patrick, 229
MacMullan, Bishop Patrick, 242
Macnamara, John, 139
Mac Óda, Séamus, 36
MacParlan, James, 58
Mac Raghnaill, Ríghrí, 41
Mac Reamoinn, Martan, 207
Madden, Samuel, 130
Mag Fhlainn, Seán, 143
magistrates, 4, 50, 60, 98, 151, 153, 158
Magrath, Timothy, 52
Maguidhir, Conchubhar, 143
managers, school, 143, 148
M'Ananey, Patrick, 160
Mangan, James Clarence, 77
Mangan, Michael, 158
Manni, Giovanni Battista, 198, 206
manor courts, 151–53, 161, 314n9
manuscripts, Irish-language: attachment of Irish speakers to, 43; cost to purchase, 190; devotional prose, 204–9; inclusion of hagiographies, 199–201; inclusion of religious verse, 201–4; practice of reading aloud from, 192; predominant religious genres in, 199; religious genres and, 185; survival rates of, 185–86; translations of English-language prayer books and devotional manuals, 210–11
Manx language, 4–5, 123, 278n6
Maori language, 132
Marchant, Jacques, 209
Marefoschi, Cardinal, 242
Margaret of Antioch, Saint, 200–201
Marian devotions, 214, 220–21
markets and fairs, 58, 60, 67, 84–87, 94, 101, 106, 116, 270, 294n162; use of Irish at, 47–49
marriage, 114, 254
Marsh's Library, 77
Martha's Vineyard (location of study by Labov), 15–16
Mary Magdelene, 217
Mason, Henry Monck, 58, 131, 136, 140, 155, 269
Mason, William Shaw, 57–58
Mass, 76, 176, 184, 193, 203–4, 210, 212–13, 222, 226–29, 231–33, 238, 241, 252, 254, 270; concern with Irish speakers' knowledge of content and meaning, 214–18
Mass houses, 212, 223
Massillon, Jean-Baptiste, 231
Mathew, Father Theobald, 172–73
mattens, 117
Matthew, Gospel of, 123
Maynooth, St. Patrick's College, 23, 139, 176, 209, 224–26, 233, 244–46, 249,

Maynooth, St. Patrick's College (*continued*)
  250t, 255–56, 258–62, 264, 266, 343n115, 344n125, 346n163
Mayo (county), 50, 60–61, 68, 71–75, 79, 85, 142–44, 152–53, 156–62, 172–73, 175–77, 194, 215, 228–29, 232, 262, 265, 300–301n17, 310n83, 316n47
McCarthy, Charles, 240
McCarthy, Daniel, 189
McCullagh, Pat, 236
McDonald, Father Walter, 256
McDonnell, Joseph Myles, 176
McEvoy, John, 130
McGeown, Father Peter, 236
McGettigan, Archbishop Daniel, 242
McGorke, Father Bernard, 241
McGuire, Francis, 171
McKenna, Bishop Matthew, 242
McLoughlin, Father John, 259
McQuige, James, 4, 48, 135, 138, 158, 161
Meany, Father John, 231, 260, 339n29, 340n40
Meany, James, 63
Meany, Patrick, 339n29
Meath (county), 3, 54, 57, 76, 78, 85, 118, 151, 155, 156, 205, 239, 259, 316n47
Meath diocese (Catholic), 213, 215, 254
Meehan, Father Michael, 230
Meenan, Mary, 236
meetings: monster, 174; temperance, 172–73
Meighan, Michael, 232
Mellet, James, 177
Memorial on Behalf of the Native Irish (1815), 136
merchants, 171, 183, 224
Messingham, Thomas, 200, 330n82
Methodists, 48, 119, 135
Mhac Anaosa, Eamonn Oig, 95
Mhac Domhniel, Michael, 221
Middle Ages, 115
Míl, 27, 29–30
Milesians, 27, 29, 32

"Milis an Teanga" (poem), 36
Milroy, James, 46
Milroy, Lesley, 46
ministers, Protestant, 69, 178
missals, 191
missions, parish (Catholic), 230, 329n72, 339n25
missions, Protestant, 4, 9, 42, 48, 130, 132–33, 135–37, 140, 145, 155, 188–89, 214
Misterios del Monte Calvario (1542), 208
Mochua of Balla, Saint, 200
"Moileamh na gCeithre Chúige" (poem), 66
"Mola na Gaodheilge" (poem), 36
Molloy, Sean Phátruic, 143
Monaghan (county), 3, 66, 202, 205
Monaghan, Judge, 163
Montgomery, Henry Conyngham, 165–66
Moore's Melodies (1808–34), 255
Moran, Archbishop Patrick Francis, 306n24
Moran, Father P. J., 262
Moriarty, Bishop David, 253, 264, 266, 345n141
Morley, John, 158
Morony, Joseph, 231–32
Morris, Reverend John, 50
Morris, Séamus, 162
Moses, 27, 179
Mount Melleray Abbey, 228
Moylan, Bishop Francis, 265
Mulkerrin, Father Michael, 229
Mullins, Father (of Ballindine), 229
Munchin's chapel, Saint, 176
Munster (province), 3, 11, 17–18, 47–48, 54, 57, 61, 64, 66, 68–72, 95, 103, 130, 142, 158, 169, 173, 177, 183, 188–89, 196, 201, 204, 206, 213, 228, 231–33, 239, 263, 334n126
Murphy, Barnaby, 231
Murphy, Bishop John, 193, 201, 206–7, 209–11, 215–16, 232, 242–43, 328n53

Murphy, Bishop Timothy, 242, 253
Murphy, Father John, 176–77, 228, 322n145, 322n147
Murphy, James, 160
Murphy, Michael, 25, 236, 284n3
Murphy, Reverend (of Kilrossanty), 174
Murray, Archbishop Daniel, 215, 238, 253
Murray, Father Thomas T., 235
Murray, Patrick, 233
Mylius, Abraham, 30

"Nach Ait an Nós" (poem), 41
Nagle, Nano, 207
Nation (newspaper), 37, 69
National Association for the Promotion of Social Science, 112
national schools, 40, 48, 53–56, 61, 112, 133, 140, 189, 240, 272–73, 305n2; beginnings of bilingual program, 147–48; blamed for language decline, 9–12; debates over use of Irish in education system, 134; slowness of growth in Irish-speaking regions, 141–42
Neave, Richard Digby, 138
"Ned M'Keown" (1830), 226
Needham, George, 50
Neilson, Reverend William, 137
Nél, 27, 29, 31
Nelson, Catherine, 162
Nemed, 29
Nenual, 31
Net for the Fishers of Men, A (1686), 198, 209
networks, linguistic, 46–47; Irish-language characteristics of, 57–60
New Testament, 118–19, 121, 132, 198, 216, 256
Newell, P. (schools inspector), 40
Newenham, Thomas, 59
newspapers, 49, 137, 143, 154, 150, 228; read aloud and interpreted to Irish speakers, 51–52; tendency of English language to dominate in, 47

Nicene Creed, 212
Nicholson, Asenath, 38, 66
Ní Conmara, Seabhán, 195
Nimrod's Tower, 26
Ní Shítheacháin, Peig, 55
Noah, 26, 29
Norreys, Sir Denham, 167
North Salt, Co. Kildare, 243t, 244–45
Nouvelles récréations et joyeux devis (1558), 91
Nova Legenda Angliae (1516), 200
Nuinseann, Chriostóir, 118

oaths: court, 156, 162; election, 149, 166, 171–72; temperance, 173
Oblates of Mary Immaculate, 339n25
O'Boyle (ad-hoc court interpreter), 158
Ó Briain, Bishop Seán, 223, 231, 242
Ó Briain, Father Seán Mac Diarmada, 206
O'Brien, Bishop Dominic, 191, 193, 207, 252, 260
O'Brien, Father Paul, 259–60
O'Brien, William Smith, 167, 175
Ó Bruadair, Dáibhídh, 32, 41, 332n99
Observations on the Character, Customs, and Superstitions of the Irish (1812), 136
Ó Caoindealbháin, Séamas (teacher), 321n132
Ó Caoindealbháin, Séamas Mac Donnchadha (weaver), 211, 221, 336n136
Ó Catháin, Donachadh, 334n125
Ó Catháin, Párthalán, 55–56
Ó Catháin, Proinsias, 40, 54, 155, 234–36
Ó Catháin, Séamas, 72–75, 86, 94, 103, 300n12
Ó Cathaláin, Father Brian (Bernard), 202
Ó Cathasaigh, Sémus, 50
Ó Ceallacháin, Donncha, 193
Ó Cearbhaill, Father Domhnall, 192

Ó Cearbhalláin, Toirdhealbhach, 131, 203
Ó Cearnaigh, Nioclás, 36, 256
Ó Céileachair, Father Eoin, 194, 217
Ó Cléirigh, Mícheál, 27
Ó Conáill, Father Seán, 206
Ó Conaill, Father Tadhg, 208
Ó Conaill, Seán, 27
Ó Conaill, Tadhg, 193, 195, 216
Ó Conaire, Reverend Seán, 231
Ó Concheanainn, Tomás, 11
Ó Conchubhair, Pádraig, 312n129
Ó Conchúbhair, Tadhg Ruadh, 203
Ó Conchúir, Muiris, 195, 329n65
Ó Conghaile, Father (of Galway), 234–35
O'Connell, Daniel, 9–10, 25, 37, 39–40, 60, 85, 87, 133, 141, 153, 170, 172, 175–79, 228, 289n64, 322n148
O'Connell, Morgan John, 168
O'Connor, Gerard, 178
O'Connor, Jeremiah, 178–79, 323n159
O'Conor, Charles, 37, 193, 199, 213
O'Conor, Thomas, 79, 81
Ó Criomhthain, Tomás, 99
Ó Cuív, Brian, 11–12, 117, 224, 244–46, 249
O'Curry, Eugene, 65, 77, 81, 201, 299n78
Ó Dálaigh, Aonghus Fionn, 201–3
Ó Dálaigh, Donnchadh Mór, 201, 203, 332n99
Ó Dálaigh, Gofradh Fionn, 203
Ó Dálaigh, Pilip, 200–201
O'Daly, John, 35, 43, 72, 131
Ó Danachair, Liam, 192
O'Doherty, Bishop John, 235
Ó Doirnín, Peadar, 35
Ó Domhnaill, Risteard, 191
Ó Domhnaill, Uilliam, 118–19
Ó Domhnald, Father Pattruig, 191
O'Donnell, Maurice, 175
O'Donovan, Father (of Cork), 176
O'Donovan, John, 28, 65, 69, 71, 74, 77–81, 236

Ó Dreada, Seán, 193–94, 217
Ó Dubhlaoich, Seán, 188, 209, 334n126
Ó Duinnín, Father Uilliam, 195
O'Dwyer, Father Austin, 229
Ó Faoláin, Risteard, 191
Ó Fearghail, Brian, 36
Ó Fheargusa, Sean, 195
officers, election, 166–67, 170
Ó Fiaich, Cardinal Tomas, 256
Ó Flaithbheartaigh, Ruaidhrí, 28, 285n15
O'Flanagan, Patrick, 72–75
Ó Flannagáin, Seán, 63
Ó Fúartháin, Labhrás, 194, 208
Ó Gadhra, Seán, 28
Ó Gealacáin, Peadar, 16, 195
Ó Gormáin, Muiris, 66, 195–96
O'Grady, Father (Vincentian missionary), 230
O'Grady, Standish Hayes, 85
Ó Gramhnaigh, Eoghan, 346n163
Ogygia (1685), 28
Ó hAnnracháin, Mícheál, 41, 190, 328n55
Ó hAodha, Uilliam, 212
O'Hea, Bishop Michael, 243
Ó Heidein, Seadhan, 211
Ó hEodhasa, Giolla Brighde, 188, 194, 201–4
Ó hEodhasa catechism. *See* catechisms: Ó hEodhasa
O'Higgins, Bishop William, 242
Ó Hóidh, Tomás, 187
Ó hUghbhair, Seán, 193
Ó Iceadha, Tomás, 191, 193, 201, 206–8, 210, 232, 260, 340n40
Oideas Athchoimir agus Urnaighthe (1807), 193
Oileánach, An t- (1929), 99
Ó Laochadh, Seadhan, 211
Ó Laoghaire, Peadar, 23, 72
Old English, 32–33, 35, 117, 119, 201, 241
Old Testament, 29, 121, 198, 216

Ó Longáin, Mícheál Óg, 16, 34, 41, 187, 192–95, 203–4, 206–7, 209, 269, 334n125
Ó Longáin, Peadar, 171, 193
Ó Longáin, Pól, 171, 193, 203–4, 209, 328n57
Ó Longáin, Seosamh, 131, 172
Ó Longáin family, 171–72, 201, 203, 205–6, 210
O'Mahony, Father (of Glenville), 236
O'Malley, Father Thomas, 230
Ó Maolchaoine, Dermod, 208
Ó Maolchonaire, Flathrí, 209
Ó Maoldomhnaigh, Diarmaid, 232
Ó Maolmhuaidh, Froinsias, 41, 194, 209
Ó Maolruanáigh, Éamonn, 195
Ó Maonadh, Gearóid, 260
Ó Mathúna, Éamann, 193–94
O'Meara, James, 191, 195
Ó Muirgheasa, Énrí, 9
Ó Muláin, Seán, 193, 208, 332n99
Ó Murchadha na Ráithíneach, Seán, 192, 195, 201, 206, 329n65
Ó Neachtain family, 205, 210
Ó Neachtain, Seán, 12, 95–96, 131, 206, 332n109
Ó Neachtain, Tadhg, 131, 196, 206, 211, 216, 332n109
O'Neill, Charles, 122
Ó Néill, Pádraig, 326n27
onomastic lore, 64, 73–77, 295n2
Ó Nualláin, Eoin, 222
Ó Raghallaigh, Pilib, 208, 333n121
Orange Order, 136–37, 151, 179
Ó Rathaille, Aogán, 32, 95–96
Order of Liberators, 176
Ordnance Survey of Ireland, 65–66, 76–78, 80–82
Ordo Administrandi Sacramenta (1785), 213, 255
Ordonnance de Villers-Cotterêts (1539), 115
O'Reilly, Archbishop Michael, 187, 193
O'Reilly, Bernard, 161

O'Reilly, Edward, 47, 65, 131, 153
O'Reilly catechism. *See* catechisms: O'Reilly
O'Riely, Hugh, 156
Orientalist scholars, 132, 135
O'Riordan, Father Robert, 253
Ó Riordann, Peadar, 195
Orpen, Charles, 136
Ó Scannail, Finghin, 221
Ó Scoireadh, Séamus, 8, 178, 206–7
O'Shaughnessy, Father Terence, 233
Ossianic Society, 131
Ossory diocese (Catholic), 194, 210, 231
Ossory diocese (Protestant), 241, 254, 259
Ó Súilleabháin, Amhlaoibh, 12, 40–41, 68–69, 179, 196, 323n162
Ó Súilleabháin, Eoghan Rua, 32
Ó Súilleabháin, Father Dónall, 193–95, 206, 209, 328n53
Ó Súilleabháin, Muiris, 99–100
Ó Súilleabháin, Tadhg Gaelach, 140, 181, 188–89, 193, 202
Ó Suilliobhain, Aindrias, 334n125
O'Sullivan, Father Eugene, 228
O'Sullivan, Michael, 43
O'Sullivan, Reverend Jeremiah, 175, 178
Ó Troih, Eadhbhart, 211
Oughterard, Co. Galway, 152, 220
Ouseley, Gideon, 135

paidrín. *See* rosary
Pairlement Chloinne Tomáis (ca. 1613), 32, 95
Pale, 114, 146, 306n7
Pall Mall Gazette, 268, 273
Paor, Father Matha, 194
Paor, Riocard, 210
Paris, 130, 242, 249, 258, 263
Paris, Irish College, 250t, 251, 253, 259
Paris, University of, 257
parliament, Dublin, 116–17, 120, 122, 126, 147, 178–79

parliament, Westminster, 47, 50, 54, 130, 132–33, 141, 146, 151–52, 154–56, 167, 223
Parnell, Charles Stewart, 52
parochial schools, Scottish, 125
Parrthas an Anma (1645), 204, 210, 216
Partholón, 29
Passionists, 339n25
Passion of Christ, 192, 201, 216, 218
Pastorini, 226
Pater Noster, 211, 219–20
The Path to Paradise, 211, 221
Patrick, Saint, 38, 76, 79, 200, 330n82
Patrick's Day, Saint, 141, 229
patrons, scribal, 191–96
pattern days, 254
Peel, Robert, 85, 179
penal laws, 33, 120, 122, 124–25, 178
Perceval, A. P., 307n30
Perrotin, Philipes Joseph, 258, 346n159
Persian language, 132
petitions, election, 165–66
petitions, parliamentary, 165
Petrie, George, 77, 81
petty constables, courts, 156
petty sessions courts, 49, 149, 153, 316n41; expansion of access for lower classes, 152–53; lack of authorization for interpreters' expenses for, 155
Pharaoh of Egypt, 27, 31, 179
Phipson, Sidney, 163
Phoenician language, 131
pigs, 48, 75, 84
Pinamonti, Giovanni Pietro, 188, 198, 205–6, 325n26
Píocóid, Mícheál, 194, 232
Pious Miscellany (1802), 140, 181, 188–90, 193–93, 202–3, 221, 332n102
place-names: mutability of, 74–75, 78–81; Ordnance Survey approach to, 65; quantity and types of, 73, 80–81; variations in pronunciation and meaning, 63
Pléimeann, Seán, 43, 144, 181, 190, 234

Plowden, Robert, 232
Plunket, Bishop George, 233
Plunkett, Bishop Patrick Joseph, 254
poets and patrons, 116; eighteenth century, 31, 33, 35; move to prophecy poems, 33; nineteenth century, 35; seventeenth century, 31; sixteenth century, 31
Poitiers, Irish College, 257
police and constabulary, 49–50, 60, 101, 162; peelers, 85, 107
Polish language, 115
Poll an Gharraigh national school, Co. Donegal, 237
Poor Law (1838), 172–73
Poor Law Inquiry (1835), 59
Poor Man's Manual of Devotion, The (aka *The Key of Heaven*), 184, 211, 221
poor scholars, 263–64
"The Poor Voter's Song," 168
Portrait of the Artist as a Young Man, A (1916), 206
post offices, 49
potatoes, 68, 92, 94, 104, 143, 219
Power, Maurice, 232
Powis Commission, 144, 148
Poynings's Parliament, 114
Practical Grammar of the Irish Language, A (1809), 259
Prague, Irish College, 208
prayer books, 118, 183–86, 190–91, 194, 199, 209–13, 221–22, 273, 325n20
prayers, 182–83, 185, 211–12, 215–17, 219, 223–24, 232, 270
Precursor Society, 175
Prendergast, Father P., 229
Presbyterian Missionary Society, 135
Presbyterians, 119, 135, 141, 145, 309n74
Presentation Sisters, 207, 265
priests, 50, 53–54, 59, 63, 68, 100, 125, 151, 158, 173, 184, 188, 190–94, 209, 213, 215–16, 218, 270–71; classical education of, 263–66; concern

with knowledge of Irish among seminarians, 251–53; delay in Maynooth-trained becoming majority of clergy, 226; evidence of use of Irish in pastoral duties by, 228–33; growth of English monoglots among, 235; involvement in scribal activity, 225; proficiency in Irish of, 240–41, 243–50; registration requirements, eighteenth century, 121; use of Irish for confession by and shortages of, 235–36; use of Irish to address crowds at meetings, 174–77, 322n147
Pringle, George, 140
prison warders, 50
prisons, 50–52
private chamber, legal settlement by, 151
Propaganda, Sacred Congregation of. See Congregatio de Propaganda Fide
proselytism, Protestant, 4, 9, 37–38, 42, 54, 126, 141, 176, 230
Protestant church, 113–14, 270; bishops and archbishops, 116, 118–19, 121, 126, 130, 132, 135, 138, 144–45, 263; blame of English government for discouraging use of Irish, 145–47; concerns about establishment in Ireland, 133, 145–47; concerns about linguistic heterogeneity in Ireland, 122; disestablishment of, 272; established church in Scotland, 119; established church in Wales, 119; linguistic policy in Ireland, 117, 119; ministers, 116, 118; missions to empire, 134–35; provisions to ease grants for school by, 125
psalms, 192, 216
psalters, 119
pubs, 101, 106
Pulleine, Reverend James, 187, 193
Pulleine catechism. See catechisms: Pulleine
puns, 96

Quaid, Reverend Patrick, 175–76
quarter sessions courts, 152–59, 161
Quattro Massime di Christiana Filosophia (1643), 206
Queen's County, 57, 166–67
Queen's University Belfast, 112
Queen's University Cork, 57
Quin, Father Peter, 253
Quinn, Father R., 229

rape, 53, 160, 162–63
Raphoe diocese (Catholic), 246
Rathcormuck National School, 144
Rathlin Island, 122
Ravenstein, Ernst Georg, 268–69
Reading Made Easy, 56
Reasons and Authorities and Facts Afforded by the History of the Irish Society (1829), 136
Reasons for Giving Moral Instruction of the Native Irish through the Medium of Their Vernacular Language (1817), 136
recusants, Catholic, 121
Redemptorists, 207, 339n25
Reeve, Joseph, 198
Reflections and Resolutions Proper for the Gentlemen of Ireland (1738), 130
Reform Act (1832), 165, 171–72
Reformation, 33, 113, 145–46, 178, 201, 205, 208, 214
Reformation, Second, 214
registrar of petty sessions clerk, 158
Reid, Nicholas, 187
Reilly, Bridget, 162
Reliques of Irish Poetry (1789), 131
Renehan, Laurence, 252
rent, Catholic, 173
Repeal, 51, 60, 172–73, 175–76, 179, 194
Repeal Association, 60, 175–76
Repeal reading rooms, 51
reporters, 40, 177, 322n148
Rice, Edmund, 265

Richardson, Reverend John, 57, 121–23, 125, 136, 327n51
Richmond General Penitentiary, 50
Rituale Romanorum (1776), 193, 230
Roche, Edmund Burke, 170
Roche, Father (of Macroom), 231
Roche, James, 192, 195
Roche, Reverend B. J., 173
Rochford, Robert, 200, 330n82
Rodenberg, Julius, 59, 233
Roman spelling (of Irish), 217
Rome, 209, 249, 257–58
Rome, Irish College, 250t
Rood, Patrick, 160
rosary, 184, 203, 217, 220, 222, 232
Rosary of Jesus, 218
Roscommon (county), 61, 142, 152, 205, 240, 316n47
Rossa, Jeremiah O'Donovan, 144
Ross diocese (Catholic). *See* Cloyne and Ross diocese
Royal Irish Academy, 8, 43, 57, 77, 131, 182, 187
Royal Statistical Society, 269
Rúindiamhair Chnuic Chealbhair (*Misterios del Monte Calvario*), 208
Russell, Thomas, 8
Russia, 91, 146, 313n148
R. v. Burke (1858), 162–64, 269, 272, 318n90
Ryan, Bishop John, 176
Ryan, Father William, 230
Ryan, Ned, 39

sacraments, 184, 212–13, 224, 230, 235; Protestant administration of, 117
Sacred Heart devotions, 184, 203, 210, 221, 338n174
Sainte Garde college, 242
salespersons, 49
Sall, Andrew, 307n34
Salve Regina, 207, 219
Sankey, W. S., 136, 138
Sanskrit language, 132

Sapir, Edward, 15
Sapir-Whorf theory, 15
Saunders's Newsletter, 36
Scáthan Shacramuinte na hAithridhe (1618), 204
schools and schooling, 53–56, 101–2, 112–13; charity schools (of eighteenth-century Incorporated Society), 122, 125–27, 134, 238; classical education in, 263–64; debates over use of Irish in education system, 133–44; inability of authorities to see Irish language as compatible with, 124; preference for teachers of English birth in Elizabethan diocesan schools, 119; Protestant missionary groups as part of educational debates, 133–38; restrictions placed on Catholic education by penal laws, 124; Royal free schools, 307n38; tendency of English language to dominate in, 47; Tudor diocesan schools, 119–20, 124, 307n38; Tudor parish schools, 116–17, 120, 124, 130, 307n38
Scoggin's Jests, 91
Scoitbhéarla, 29, 32, 285n15
Scot, Riphat, 285n15
Scota, 27
Scotland, 64, 65, 85, 100–101, 114, 116, 119–20, 123–29, 132, 139, 141, 277n6
Scots Gaelic language, 4–5, 42, 45–46, 85, 92, 119–20, 123–24, 126–27, 132, 187, 277–78n6, 307n34
Scottish Society for Promoting Christian Knowledge (SSPCK), 125–26, 132
scribes (Irish language), 12, 14, 16–17, 24, 27–28, 30, 34–35, 66, 68–69, 171–72, 181–82, 186–87, 190–92, 205, 218, 224–25, 231–32, 263, 283n49
Scupoli, Lorenzo, 198
Scythia, 26–27, 29, 31
"Seanchuimhne ar Aodhagán Ua Rathaille" (poem), 95

secret societies, 321n132
secretary, grand jury, 156, 158
Segneri, Father Paolo, 325n26
Senair, plain of, 26–27, 29, 34
Senán, Saint, 195, 200
seneschals, 151–53
sermons, 121, 188, 190, 192, 194, 225, 227–33, 270
Sermons and Exhortations for the Whole Year (1796), 232
Sermons and Moral Discourses for All the Sundays and Principal Festivals of the Year (1799), 232
Seven Dolours of the Virgin Mary, 222
Seymour, Reverend Joseph, 152
"Sgiathluithreach na Maighidine" (poetic prayer), 211
Shand, Alexander, 99
Shannon River, 60
Sharkey, B., 174
sheep, 67, 143
Shem, 26
Sheridan, John Edward, 144
Sheridan, Margaret, 162
Sheridan, Peter, 239
Sheridan, Thomas, 129
sheriffs, 156–57, 165, 167, 170
shopkeepers, 4, 49, 92, 99, 101, 158, 171
shops, 92, 99, 101; use of Irish at, 47, 49
Short Historical Catechism (*Petit Catéchisme Historique*), 198
Sidney, Sir Henry, 118
Sincere, Pious, and Devout Christian, The (1781), 232
"Siosma an Anma res an gColuin" (poem), 204
Sirr, Reverend Joseph D'Arcy, 136
Sisters of Mercy, 265
Sixteen Irish Sermons, in an Easy and Familiar Stile (aka *Seventeen Irish Sermons*, 1736), 140, 181, 188–89, 226, 230
Sketch of Irish History (1815), 28
Skibbereen, Co. Cork, 48, 239

Slattery, Archbishop Michael, 252
Sligo (county), 28, 54, 152, 156–58, 168–69, 171, 177, 240
Smith, Patrick, 157
Smith, William Cusack, 153
Sochar an Aifrinn, 212
Society for Promoting Christian Knowledge (SPCK), 125–26
Society for the Preservation of the Irish Language (SPIL), 8, 148, 265, 281n26
sodalities, 184
Sodality of the Living Rosary, 220
soldiers, 87, 95, 100–101
Southwell, Edward, 121
Spain, 27, 29, 94, 115, 226
Spanish Empire, 305n3
Spanish language, 34, 92, 128, 205–6, 209, 225, 258, 302n35, 305n3, 333n114
Spiddal, Co. Galway, 162, 229
Spike Island prison, 51
Spiritual Combat, The (*Il Combattimento Spirituale*), 198
Spiritual Rose, The (1800), 191, 202, 210, 213, 221
Spring-Rice, Thomas, 50, 65, 170
St. Colman's College, Fermoy, 250t, 344n125
St. Jarlath's College, Tuam, 37, 259–60
St. Jarlath's Gaelic Literary Institute, 173
St. John's College, Waterford, 191, 193, 207, 259, 340n40
St. Kieran's College, Kilkenny, 259, 265
St. Mary's College, Cork, 265
Stair Éamuinn Uí Chléire (ca. 1710), 95
Stanihurst, Richard, 28, 38, 69, 116
Stanley Letter, 140
Stapleton catechism. *See* catechisms: Stapleton
Stapleton, Theobald, 8
stations, 184, 212, 223, 227
stations of the cross, 184, 207
Statuta Synodalia pro Unitis Dioecesibus Cassel et Imelac (1813), 254

Statutes of Iona (1609), 116
Statutes of Kilkenny (1366), 114, 306n7
Steele, Thomas, 174, 176
Stewart, James, 86
Stiernhielm, Georg, 30
Stiúratheoir an Pheacuig (1824), 220-21
Stokes, Whitley, 130
Stuarts, 179; conquest of Ireland, 31-32; as kings of Ireland, 33; linguistic policy in Ireland, 111-12, 117, 122, 270-71
Stúndún, Pádraig, 157
Sughrue, Father Charles, 252
Suim Athchumuir an Chreideimh Chriostamuil (1775), 255
Suim Bhunudhasach an Teaguisg Chriosdaidhe (1663), 188, 209, 334n126
Sullivan, Daniel, 239
Sullivan, Father John, 253
Sullivan, James, 187
Sullivan, Reverend Andrew, 178
Sullivan, Sylvester, 50
Summa praedicantium (ca. 1348), 91
Summary of the Christian Religion, A (1773), 254-55
Sunday schools, 188, 209, 238, 270
Swanton, Thomas, 35, 40
Swedish language, 30
Swift, Edmund, 200
Swift, Jonathan, 128-29, 307n44
Synge, Edward, 176
synodal decrees, 225
Synod of Argyll, 124
Synod of Ayr, 141
Synod of Glasgow, 141
Synod of Thurles (1850), 19, 250, 339n25
synods, provincial, 251, 254

Tackaberry, Fossa, 48
"Tagra an Dá Theampall" (poem), 33-34
tailors, 101-2

"Tairngaireacht Dhuinn Fhírinne" (poem), 32
Taylor, J. S., 136
tea, 99-100, 107
teachers, 11, 16-17, 36-37, 40, 42-43, 48, 54-55, 89, 96, 101, 124-25, 127, 143, 147, 181, 194-95, 208-9, 212, 224, 272-73; as catechetical instructors, 238-40; use of Irish in classrooms, 142-44
Teagasg Criosdaidhe Angoidhleig, An (1748). See catechisms: Pulleine
Teagasg Críosduidhe do Réir Ceasda agus Freagartha, An. See catechisms: Donlevy
Teagasg Criostuidhe, agus na Gnáth-Úrnaighthe, An (ca. 1727). See catechisms: O'Reilly
temperance movement, 165, 172-73
tenants, 151-52, 165, 169-70, 173
Testamento o Ultima Voluntad del Anma (ca. 1576), 206
Therry, Mr. (of Limerick), 174
Think Well On't (1728), 191, 198, 208, 228
Thirty Days' Prayer, 221
Thirty Meditations (aka *Instructions and Advice to Catholicks*, 1750), 198
Thirty-Nine Articles of the Anglican Church, 118, 123, 308n50
Thomond, kingdom of, 306n7
Thornton, Martin, 162
Thurles College, St. Patrick's, 250t, 252, 344n125
Thurles, Co. Tipperary, 225, 265
Tighe, William, 57, 233
Times (London), 136-37
Tipperary (county), 72, 157, 167-69, 191, 194, 196, 201, 205, 210, 232-33, 300-301n17, 316n47, 323n162
tithe proctors, 173, 178
tithes, 39, 50, 149, 172, 178. See also anti-tithe meetings
Tobin, James, 187
Tóibín, Eoghan, 193

tories, 39
Tosach agus Aistriugha Míorbhuileach Theampoll Mhuire Loreto (1707), 188, 194
Tournai, Irish College, 257
Tower of Babel, 26, 36–37
Townsend, Horatio, 55
Transactions of the Gaelic Society of Dublin (1808), 28
Translations (1980), 296n9
translators. *See* interpreters
Treatise Containing a Plain and Perfect Description of Ireland (1577), 28
Trench, W. Steuart, 59
Trí Bior-Ghaoithe an Bháis (ca. 1631), 95, 187, 192, 194–95, 202, 204, 209
Tridentine reforms, 182, 197, 205, 208, 212
Trinity College, 58, 77, 118, 241, 263; Irish-language lectureship, 121
Tripartite Life of St. Patrick, 79, 200
Trompa na bhFlaitheas (*La Trompette du Ciel*), 208
Trompette du Ciel, La (1661), 208
Troy, Archbishop John, 213
"Truagh Daoine ar Dhith Litri" (poem), 41
True Piety (7th ed., 1808), 193
Tuam, Co. Galway, 48, 51, 143, 151, 225, 230, 234
Tuam archdiocese (Catholic), 189, 193, 228–29, 238, 242, 246, 255
tuatha, 30
Tuatha Dé Danann, 29
Tubal, 29
Tudors: conquest of Ireland, 31–32, 113; language policies in Ireland, 111–12, 114–20, 122, 270–71, 306n7, 306n24; language policies in Wales, 115
Tuibear, Risteard, 196, 211, 216
"Tuireadh na Gaedhilge agus Teastas na hÉireann" (poem), 28
"Tuireamh na hÉireann" (poem), 27
Tully, James, 256, 259

Turberville, Henry, 198
Tynemouth, John of, 200
Tyrone (county), 3, 25, 69, 156, 236, 284n3, 316n47

Ua Giobúin, Philib, 329n70
Ua Gnímh, Fearflatha, 179
Úa h-Úmhair, Seághan, 216
Ua Mohir, Dáibhí, 201
Ua Sganuill, Donochadh Mhurchoideadh, 195
Uí Chonaill, Michíl Pheaidí Dheann, 51–52
Uí Flathartha, Seánín, 37
Uí Riagáin, Seámus, 48, 234–35
Ulster (province), 3–4, 11, 40, 43, 60, 64, 66–67, 69–70, 103, 142, 155, 158, 165, 179, 234, 261
Ultan, Saint, 200
ultramontanism, 184
United Irishmen, 8, 34
Urdu language, 132
Ursuline Sisters, 207
Ussher, James, 199

Vallancey, Charles, 37, 130, 131
Vandeleur, Crofton Moore, 175
Vera Sapienza, La (1677), 188, 205–6, 325n26
Vereker, John Prendergast, 170
verse, religious, 186, 192, 194, 199, 201–4, 328n57
vespers, 184, 210, 217
vestments, 215, 232
Victoria, 85
Villiers-Stuart, Henry, 174, 178–79
Vincentians, 230, 339n25
Virgin Mary, 201–2, 207, 211, 214, 217, 219–22, 230
virtues, theological, 212–14
visitations, Catholic, 228, 237, 240, 245

Wakefield, Edward, 60, 151–52, 229, 254
wakes, 254

Wales, 29, 65, 114–15, 119, 123, 125–27, 129, 138–39, 150, 185, 277n6, 308n50
Walker, Joseph, 130
Wall, Maureen, 12–13, 16, 224
Walsh, Archbishop William, 241
Walsh, Bishop David, 242
Walsh, Father James, 228
Walsh, Father Stephen, 233
Walsh, Reverend John, 159
Walsh, Reverend R., 175
Warburton, George, 60
Ware, James, 199
Waterford (city), 4, 47, 49, 58, 156, 207, 230, 252
Waterford (county), 3, 36, 52–53, 144, 155, 157–58, 174, 178–79, 181, 189, 191, 194, 196, 201, 204–5, 208, 210, 217, 222, 231–32, 234, 252, 259, 316n47, 323n162
Waterford and Lismore diocese (Catholic), 193, 242
Waters, Matthew, 156
Watson, William Henry, 171
Way of the Cross, 212, 221
"We Three; For Money" (AT 1697), 86, 90–91
Welsh language, 4–5, 29, 42, 65, 91, 119, 123, 126–27, 150, 187, 277–78n6
West, Reverend John, 140
Westmeath (county), 3, 59, 79, 118, 156, 210, 316n47
Westport, Co. Mayo, 155, 160, 176, 238

Wexford (county), 3, 58, 156, 196, 205, 210, 225, 264, 316n47, 323n162, 329n70
Whiteboys, 241–42
Whorf, Benjamin Lee, 15
Wicklow (county), 3, 156, 316n47
Wigmore, John, 253
Wilberforce, William, 135
Wilde, William, 182
William III, 124
William the Conqueror, 32
Williamite war, 112, 120
Williams, William, 189
Windele, John, 40, 144, 236, 269
witnesses, court, 153, 156, 158–59; credibility based on linguistic capabilities when calling for interpreter, 162–64; insistence on interpreters to forestall cross examination, 161
Wogan, Patrick, 130
Woodward, Bishop Richard, 138
Wynne estates (Co. Sligo), 152
Wyse, Sir Thomas, 167

Yelverton, Judge Barry, 153
Y Ffydd Ddi-ffvant (1677), 29
Young, Bishop John, 242
Young, Ursula, 28
Young catechism. *See* catechisms: Young
Young Ireland movement, 8
Yvan, Antoine, 208

HISTORY *of* IRELAND
and the IRISH DIASPORA

Remembering the Year of the French: Irish Folk History and Social Memory
GUY BEINER

Ireland's New Worlds: Immigrants, Politics, and Society in the United States and Australia, 1815–1922
MALCOLM CAMPBELL

The Slow Failure: Population Decline and Independent Ireland, 1920–1973
MARY E. DALY

The Eternal Paddy: Irish Identity and the British Press, 1798–1882
MICHAEL DE NIE

Old World Colony: Cork and South Munster 1630–1830
DAVID DICKSON

Captain Rock: The Irish Agrarian Rebellion of 1821–1824
JAMES S. DONNELLY, JR.

Sinn Féin: A Hundred Turbulent Years
BRIAN FEENEY

The Shadow of a Year: The 1641 Rebellion in Irish History and Memory
JOHN GIBNEY

A Nation of Politicians: Gender, Patriotism, and Political Culture in Late Eighteenth-Century Ireland
PADHRAIG HIGGINS

Stakeknife: Britain's Secret Agents in Ireland
MARTIN INGRAM AND GREG HARKIN

New Directions in Irish-American History
EDITED BY KEVIN KENNY

Afterimage of the Revolution: Cumann na nGaedheal and Irish Politics, 1922–1932
JASON KNIRCK

The Same Age as the State
MÁIRE CRUISE O'BRIEN

The Bible War in Ireland: The "Second Reformation" and the Polarization of Protestant-Catholic Relations, 1800–1840
IRENE WHELAN

Tourism, Landscape, and the Irish Character: British Travel Writers in Pre-Famine Ireland
WILLIAM H. A. WILLIAMS

An Irish-Speaking Island: State, Religion, Community, and the Linguistic Landscape in Ireland, 1770–1870
NICHOLAS M. WOLF

www.ingramcontent.com/pod-product-compliance
Lightning Source LLC
Chambersburg PA
CBHW020632230426
43665CB00008B/135